*The Oxford History of the Archaic
Greek World*

**Oxford History of the Archaic Greek World**

This landmark series comprises seven volumes containing 22 in-depth studies of key city-states, sanctuaries, and regions during the Archaic period (c. 750 to c. 480 BCE). Ranging from Massalia in the west to Cyprus in the east and from Cyrene in the south to Lesbos in the north, and fully integrating the literary, epigraphic, and archaeological evidence, these studies present an authoritative and comprehensive portrait of a transformational era that witnessed the emergence of democracy, tragedy, temple architecture, and so many other features commonly associated with ancient Greece.

Volume I: Argos to Corcyra
Paul Christesen, Sylvian Fachard, Hans-Joachim Gehrke, Jonathan Hall, Giuseppe Lentini, Sarah Murray, Philip Sapirstein, Matt Simonton, and Samuel Verdan

Volume II: Athens and Attica
Robin Osborne

Volume III: Cumae to Cyprus
Erica Angliker, Grégory Bonnin, Paul Christesen, Matteo D'Acunto, Edward Henderson, Clayton Howard, Alex Karsten, Yannos Kourayos, Alexandra Sfyroera, and Anja Ulbrich

Volume IV: Cyrene to Metapontion
Zosia Archibald, Hélène Aurigny, Joseph Carter, Adolfo Domínguez, Gerry Schaus, and Michael Scott

Volume V: Miletus to Olympia
Cathy Morgan, Reinard Senff, and Anja Slawisch

Volume VI: Rhodes to Western Sicily
Franco De Angelis, Yannis Lolos, Valentina Mignosa, Thomas Heine Nielsen, Adam Schwartz, and Lone Wriedt Sørensen

Volume VII: Sparta
Paul Cartledge and Paul Christesen

# The Oxford History of the Archaic Greek World

*Volume I: Argos to Corcyra*

*Edited by*

PAUL CARTLEDGE AND
PAUL CHRISTESEN

OXFORD
UNIVERSITY PRESS

Oxford University Press is a department of the University of Oxford. It furthers
the University's objective of excellence in research, scholarship, and education
by publishing worldwide. Oxford is a registered trade mark of Oxford University
Press in the UK and certain other countries.

Published in the United States of America by Oxford University Press
198 Madison Avenue, New York, NY 10016, United States of America.

© Oxford University Press 2024

All rights reserved. No part of this publication may be reproduced, stored in
a retrieval system, or transmitted, in any form or by any means, without the
prior permission in writing of Oxford University Press, or as expressly permitted
by law, by license, or under terms agreed with the appropriate reproduction
rights organization. Inquiries concerning reproduction outside the scope of the
above should be sent to the Rights Department, Oxford University Press, at the
address above.

You must not circulate this work in any other form
and you must impose this same condition on any acquirer.

CIP data is on file at the Library of Congress

ISBN 978–0–19–938359–7

DOI: 10.1093/oso/9780199383597.001.0001

Printed by Integrated Books International, United States of America

# *Contents*

| | |
|---|---|
| *Series Editors' Preface* | xv |
| *Acknowledgments* | xxxi |
| *Contributors* | xxxiii |
| *Note to the Reader* | xxxvii |

CHAPTER 1.  Argos                                                        1

*Jonathan M. Hall*

    List of Illustrations   1

    List of Abbreviations   2

    1.1.  Introduction   2

    1.2.  Sources   8

        1.2.1.  Written Sources   8

        1.2.2.  Archaeological Evidence   8

    1.3.  Natural Setting   11

    1.4.  Material Culture   14

        1.4.1.  Settlement Pattern before the Archaic Period   14

        1.4.2.  Burial Practices   17

        1.4.3.  Ceramics   18

        1.4.4.  Settlement Organization of Argos Town   23

    1.5.  Political History   25

        1.5.1.  Early Colonies   25

        1.5.2.  Argive Hereditary Kings: The Temenids   25

        1.5.3.  Tyranny at Argos   29

        1.5.4.  Argive Political Offices   34

        1.5.5.  Divisions of the Citizen Body and Noncitizen Groups   36

vi           *Contents*

1.6. Legal History  38

1.7. Diplomatic History  39

    1.7.1. Argos and Asine  39

    1.7.2. Argive Plain  41

    1.7.3. Relationship of Argos with Mycenae and Tiryns  43

    1.7.4. Argos, Sparta, and Cynuria  45

    1.7.5. Military Organization at Argos  53

1.8. Economic History  54

1.9. Familial/Demographic History  56

1.10. Social Customs and Institutions  58

1.11. Religious Customs and Institutions  59

    1.11.1. Religious Sites within the City  59

        1.11.1.1. Cult Sites on the Acropolis 59

        1.11.1.2. Sanctuary of Apollo Lykeios 60

        1.11.1.3. Sanctuary of Aphrodite 62

        1.11.1.4. Other Cult Sites within the City 63

    1.11.2. Festivals  64

    1.11.3. Argive Heraion 65

1.12. Cultural History  72

    1.12.1. Sculpture and Music  72

    1.12.2. Argives in Athletic Competition  72

    1.12.3. Poetry  73

1.13. Conclusion  74

Guide to Further Reading  75

Gazetteer  75

Bibliography  80

CHAPTER 2. Chalcis and Eretria               95

*Sylvian Fachard and Samuel Verdan*

    List of Illustrations  95

    List of Abbreviations  97

2.1. Introduction  97

2.2. Sources  105

    2.2.1. Excavations and Surveys  105

    2.2.2. Textual Sources  106

2.3. Natural Setting  107

## Contents

2.3.1. Landforms and Geology  107

2.3.2. Paleoenvironment  111

2.3.3. Vegetational Landscape  112

2.4. Material Culture  112

    2.4.1. Settlement Organization and Settlement Patterns  113

        2.4.1.1. Settlement Organization of Chalcis 114

        2.4.1.2. Settlement Pattern of the Chalcidian *Chōra* 117

        2.4.1.3. Settlement Organization of Eretria 120

            2.4.1.3.1. Site 120

            2.4.1.3.2. Old Eretria 121

            2.4.1.3.3. Ninth and Eighth Centuries 122

            2.4.1.3.4. Seventh and First Half of Sixth Centuries 127

            2.4.1.3.5. Second Half of Sixth Century 130

        2.4.1.4. Settlement Pattern of the Eretrian *Chōra* 132

    2.4.2. Borders and Territoriality  139

        2.4.2.1. Chalcis 139

        2.4.2.2. Eretria 140

    2.4.3. Euboean Ceramics  141

    2.4.4. Euboean Funerary Practices  144

2.5. Political History  147

    2.5.1. Governance of Lefkandi  147

    2.5.2. Hippobotai and Hippeis  150

    2.5.3. Early Political Institutions  152

        2.5.3.1. Chalcis 153

        2.5.3.2. Eretria 155

2.6. Legal History  158

2.7. Diplomatic History  161

    2.7.1. "Lelantine War"  161

    2.7.2. Euboeans on the Move  167

        2.7.2.1. Early Euboean Navigation 169

            2.7.2.1.1. North Aegean 170

            2.7.2.1.2. Sicily–Southern Italy 172

            2.7.2.1.3. Corcyra 175

            2.7.2.1.4. North Africa 175

        2.7.2.2. Euboeans on the Move: Conclusions 175

viii *Contents*

2.7.3. Military Strength of Eretria and Chalcis in the Archaic Period 176

2.7.4. Euboea and Central Greece in the Sixth Century 177

    2.7.4.1. Eretria 177

    2.7.4.2. Chalcis 178

2.7.5. Persian Wars 180

2.8. Economic History 183

2.8.1. Natural Resources 183

2.8.2. Agriculture 184

2.8.3. Animal Husbandry 187

2.8.4. Maritime Trade 189

    2.8.4.1. Pottery 190

    2.8.4.2. Metals 191

2.8.5. Coinage 194

2.9. Familial/Demographic History 195

2.9.1. Demography 196

2.9.2. Onomastics, Prosopography, and Marriage 197

2.10. Social Customs and Institutions 198

2.10.1. Symposium 198

2.10.2. Pederasty 199

2.10.3. Festivals and Associations 199

2.11. Religious Customs and Institutions 200

2.11.1. Chalcis 200

2.11.2. Eretria 201

    2.11.2.1. Sanctuary of Apollo Daphnephoros 201

    2.11.2.2. Northern Sacrificial Area and Worship of Artemis 202

    2.11.2.3. Acropolis and Worship of Athena 203

    2.11.2.4. Heracles 203

    2.11.2.5. "Heroon" 204

    2.11.2.6. Great Rural Sanctuaries: Sanctuary of Artemis at Amarynthos and Sanctuary of Apollo at Tamynai 204

2.12. Cultural History 205

2.12.1. Alphabet 205

2.12.2. Language 206

2.12.3. Literature 206

2.12.4. Myths 207

## Contents

2.12.5. Sculpture and Pottery   207

2.13. Conclusion   210

Guide to Further Reading   212

Gazetteer   213

Bibliography   222

**CHAPTER 3. Chios–Lesbos–Samos**   245

*Paul Christesen, Giuseppe Lentini, Sarah Murray, and Matt Simonton*

List of Illustrations   245

List of Abbreviations   247

3.1. Introduction   248

Section A.  Chios   251

3.2A.  Sources for Archaic Chian History   251

3.3A.  Chian Natural Setting   260

3.4A.  Chian Material Culture   262

3.5A.  Chian Political History   273

3.6A.  Chian Legal History   278

3.7A.  Chian Diplomatic History   279

3.8A.  Chian Economic History   281

3.8A.1.  Agriculture and Animal Husbandry   282

3.8A.2.  Natural Resources and Craft Activity   282

3.8A.3.  Commerce   282

3.8A.4.  Coinage   285

3.9A.  Chian Familial/Demographic History   285

3.10A.  Chian Social Customs and Institutions   288

3.11A.  Chian Religious Customs and Institutions   293

3.11A.1. Athena   293

3.11A.2. Dionysus Omadios   293

3.11A.3. Cybele   294

3.12A.  Chian Cultural History   294

Section B.  Lesbos   298

3.2B.  Sources for Archaic Lesbian History   298

3.3B.  Lesbian Natural Setting   301

3.4B.  Lesbian Material Culture   303

3.4B.1.  Early History of the Island   303

3.4B.2.  Settlement Organization and *Chōra* of Mytilene   304

x  *Contents*

3.4B.3.  Settlement Organization and *Chōra* of Pyrrha  309

3.4B.4.  Settlement Organization and *Chōra* of Methymna  311

3.4B.5.  Settlement Organization and *Chōra* of Arisba (and the Sanctuary at Klopedi)  313

3.4B.6.  Settlement Organization and *Chōra* of Antissa  315

3.4B.7.  Settlement Organization and *Chōra* of Eresus  318

3.4B.8.  Settlement Patterns on Lesbos  320

3.4B.9.  Burial Customs on Lesbos  320

3.4B.10. Lesbian Ceramics  321

3.5B.  Lesbian Political History  322

3.6B.  Lesbian Legal History  330

3.7B.  Lesbian Diplomatic History  330

3.8B.  Lesbian Economic History  332

3.8B.1.  Agriculture and Animal Husbandry  332

3.8B.2.  Natural Resources and Craft Activity  333

3.8B.3.  Commerce  333

3.8B.4.  Coinage  335

3.9B.  Lesbian Familial/Demographic History  337

3.10B. Lesbian Social Customs and Institutions  338

3.11B. Lesbian Religious Customs and Institutions  338

3.12B. Lesbian Cultural History  341

3.12B.1.  Alcaeus  342

3.12B.2.  Sappho  344

3.12B.3.  Architecture and Sculpture  346

Section C.  Samos  349

3.2C.  Sources for Archaic Samian History  349

3.3C.  Samian Natural Setting  352

3.4C.  Samian Material Culture  354

3.4C.1.  Settlement Organization of Samos Town  355

3.4C.2.  Fortifications and Water Engineering  359

3.4C.3.  Sanctuaries and Cemeteries in Samos Town  362

3.4C.4.  The Heraion  364

3.4C.4.1.  Introduction 364

3.4C.4.2.  Early History of the Site to c. 675 365

3.4C.4.3.  Monumentalization of the Sanctuary in the First Half of the Seventh Century 367

*Contents*  xi

3.4C.4.4. Regularization and Further Monumentalization of the Sanctuary in the Second Half of the Seventh Century and the First Quarter of the Sixth Century 371

3.4C.4.5. Onset of Gigantism in the Second Quarter of the Sixth Century 373

3.4C.4.6. The Heraion in the Time of Polycrates 377

3.4C.5. Samian Burial Customs  380

3.4C.6. Samian Pottery  383

3.5C. Samian Political History  385

3.5C.1. Early History and Foundation  385

3.5C.2. The Sixth Century and Polycrates  388

3.5C.3. Overthrow of Polycrates  393

3.5C.4. Ionian Rebellion and the Fifth Century  394

3.6C. Samian Legal History  395

3.7C. Samian Diplomatic History  396

3.8C. Samian Economic History  409

3.8C.1. Agriculture and Animal Husbandry  409

3.8C.2. Natural Resources and Craft Activity  411

3.8C.3. Commerce  414

3.8C.4. Coinage  417

3.9C. Samian Familial/Demographic History  418

3.10C. Samian Social Customs and Institutions  421

3.11C. Samian Religious Customs and Institutions  422

3.11C.1. Cult of Hera and the Heraion  422

3.11C.2. Artemis  427

3.11C.3. Zeus Eleutherios  427

3.11C.4. Panionia  427

3.12C. Samian Cultural History  428

3.12C.1. Sculpture and Architecture  428

3.12C.2. Literature and Philosophy  429

3.13. Conclusion  434

Guide to Further Reading  435

Gazetteer  437

Bibliography  448

xii  *Contents*

CHAPTER 4.  Corcyra                                                    488

*Hans-Joachim Gehrke and Philip Sapirstein*

    List of Illustrations   488

    List of Abbreviations   490

    4.1. Introduction   490

    4.2. Sources   493

        4.2.1. Textual Sources   493

        4.2.2. Excavation and Surveys   494

    4.3. Natural Setting   497

    4.4. Material Culture   501

        4.4.1. Corfu up to the Arrival of the Greeks   501

        4.4.2. Settlement Organization   503

            4.4.2.1. Layout of the City 503

            4.4.2.2. Urban Development of Corcyra in the Archaic Period 505

            4.4.2.3. Fortifications 506

            4.4.2.4. Harbors and Port Facilities 507

            4.4.2.5. Agora 510

            4.4.2.6. Workshops 511

            4.4.2.7. Sanctuaries 512

                4.4.2.7.1. Artemision and Nearby Sanctuaries 513

                4.4.2.7.2. Temple at Mon Repos and Sanctuary of Apollo Corcyraios 517

                4.4.2.7.3. Kardaki Temple 519

                4.4.2.7.4. Sanctuary of Dionysus 520

                4.4.2.7.5. (Possible) Sanctuary of Apollo Agyieus and "Small Artemis Sanctuary" 520

                4.4.2.7.6. Other Cult Sites in Urban Corcyra 522

             4.4.2.8. Necropoleis 522

        4.4.3. Settlement Pattern   523

        4.4.4. *Peraia* of Corcyra   525

        4.4.5. Ceramic Assemblage   527

        4.4.6. Burial Customs   528

    4.5. Political History   534

        4.5.1. Overview   534

Contents                                                        xiii

4.5.2. Colonization of Corfu by Greeks   535

4.5.3. Corcyraean *Politeia* in the Archaic Period   539

4.5.4. Subdivisions of the Citizen Body   541

4.5.5. Corcyraean Whips and Their Social Connotations   542

4.6. Legal History   545

4.7. Diplomatic History   545

4.7.1. Relationship with Corinth at the Time of Foundation   545

4.7.2. Sea Battle with Corinth and Its Ramifications   548

4.7.3. Detente with Corinth under the Cypselid Tyranny   549

4.7.4. Establishment and Disintegration of Corinthian Rule   553

4.7.5. An Independent Corcyra   554

4.8. Economic History   557

4.8.1. Natural Resources   558

4.8.2. Agriculture and Animal Husbandry   559

4.8.3. Craft Production   562

4.8.4. Trade and Other Mercantile Activity   564

4.8.5. Coinage   566

4.8.6. Summary   566

4.9. Familial/Demographic History   567

4.10. Social Customs and Institutions   568

4.11. Religious Customs and Institutions   569

4.11.1. Sanctuaries of Artemis and Apollo   569

4.11.2. Sanctuary of Hera   572

4.11.3. Other Deities at Corcyra   574

4.12. Cultural History   575

4.12.1. Corcyraean *Technai* and Innovation   575

4.12.2. Material Culture and Identity   582

4.13. Conclusion   585

Guide to Further Reading   586

Gazetteer   587

Bibliography   593

*Index*   609

# Series Editors' Preface

THIS VOLUME FORMS part of a larger project, the *Oxford History of the Archaic Greek World* (*OHAGW*), that consists of 22 in-depth studies of city-states, sanctuaries, and regions, ranging from Massalia in the west to Cyprus in the east and from Cyrene in the south to Lesbos in the north. All those studies, written by more than 30 eminent scholars with deep expertise in their sites, focus on the period from c. 750 to c. 480 and are aimed at a scholarly audience.

*OHAGW* is available in both print and digital versions (the latter on the website of Oxford University Press). The 22 studies in *OHAGW* are collected in seven volumes and presented in alphabetic order by site name.

**Contents of and Contributors to the *Oxford History of the Archaic Greek World***

| Site | Author(s) | Placement in OHAGW |
|------|-----------|--------------------|
| Argos | Jonathan Hall | Volume 1 |
| Athens | Robin Osborne | Volume 2 |
| Chalcis and Eretria | Sylvian Fachard<br>Samuel Verdan | Volume 1 |
| Chios, Lesbos, Samos | Paul Christesen<br>Giuseppe Lentini<br>Sarah Murray<br>Matt Simonton | Volume 1 |
| Corcyra | Hans-Joachim Gehrke<br>Philip Sapirstein | Volume 1 |
| Cumae and Pithecusae | Matteo D'Acunto | Volume 3 |

| Site | Author(s) | Placement in OHAGW |
|---|---|---|
| The Cyclades | Erica Angliker<br>Grégory Bonnin<br>Paul Christesen<br>Edward Henderson<br>Clayton Howard<br>Alex Karsten<br>Yannos Kourayos<br>Alexandra Sfyroera | Volume 3 |
| Cyprus | Anja Ulbrich | Volume 3 |
| Cyrene | Gerry Schaus | Volume 4 |
| Delphi | Hélène Aurigny<br>Michael Scott | Volume 4 |
| Macedonia | Zosia Archibald | Volume 4 |
| Massalia | Adolfo Domínguez | Volume 4 |
| Metapontion | Joseph Carter | Volume 4 |
| Miletus | Anja Slawisch | Volume 5 |
| Northwestern Greece | Catherine Morgan | Volume 5 |
| Olympia | Reinhard Senff | Volume 5 |
| Rhodes | Thomas Heine Nielsen<br>Adam Schwartz<br>Lone Wriedt Sørensen | Volume 6 |
| Sicyon | Yannis Lolos | Volume 6 |
| Sparta | Paul Cartledge<br>Paul Christesen | Volume 7 |
| Syracuse | Franco De Angelis<br>Valentina Mignosa | Volume 6 |
| Thebes | Hans Beck | Volume 6 |
| Western Sicily | Clemente Marconi<br>Andrew Ward | Volume 6 |

## Project Design

The primary goal of *OHAGW* is to facilitate study of a broad array of Greek communities during the Archaic period. In pursuit of that goal, the editors of and contributors to *OHAGW* have made a concerted effort to ensure that the studies in *OHAGW* are—individually and collectively—comprehensive, commensurable, and convenient.

There are numerous pre-existing publications that offer comprehensive coverage of the ancient Greek world. One might note in particular the *Cambridge Ancient History*, in its second, revised edition and, more recently, the *Inventory of Archaic and Classical Greek Poleis*, edited by Mogens Herman Hansen and Thomas Heine Nielsen (Hansen and Nielsen 2004). Those and similar works remain valuable resources, not least because they are expansive in their spatial and temporal coverage. Yet that sort of breadth comes inevitably at the expense of depth.

In designing *OHAGW* we sought to find a compromise between breadth and depth that leaned toward the latter. The decision to pursue depth even at the expense of breadth reflects our belief that there is a pressing need for fine-grained studies of specific sites that consolidate large, disparate, and complex arrays of evidence. Scholars studying the ancient Greek world are increasingly adrift on a continually expanding sea of information that is far beyond the capacity of any individual to manage. The bibliographic database provided by *L'année philologique* increases by approximately 12,000 items each year; given that the *L'année philologique* is by no means exhaustive, one might venture the suggestion, as a rough approximation, that on an average day 40 new scholarly books, theses, and articles on ancient Greece are published and take their place in an already luxuriant landscape of secondary literature. Someone interested in, for instance, developing a thorough knowledge of Cyrene would need to put in months, if not years, of work in order to identify, collect, and read the relevant scholarly literature, which includes, but is by no means limited to, reports from dozens of excavations conducted by various teams of American, British, French, Italian, and Libyan archaeologists starting in 1884 (for further discussion, see the *OHAGW* essay on Cyrene by Gerry Schaus). To make matters worse, the bibliography is highly site-specific. An examination of the bibliography for the *OHAGW* studies of the neighboring *poleis* of Samos and Miletus shows that only about 20 percent overlap (i.e., 20 percent of the sources cited in those studies are identical).

With that in mind, we gave contributors the room to explore their sites in depth, with the length of any given study varying from a little under 30,000 words to well over 100,000 words. At the same time, we made certain that *OHAGW* included studies of a sufficiently large and diverse array of cities, sanctuaries, and regions to achieve reasonably broad coverage of the Archaic Greek world as a whole.

Inevitably, trade-offs had to be made to keep the project to a manageable size. Many Greek sites that merit detailed exploration are not treated in *OHAGW*, and the project focuses solely on the Archaic period (see below for discussion of the criteria used to select sites and of the decision to focus on the Archaic period as we conceive it). Even with those limitations, the project attained a scale—in the neighborhood of 1.5 million words—that was, at times, daunting.

We also sought from the outset to make *OHAGW* comprehensive in the sense that each study takes into consideration both textual and material evidence. To that end, all contributors were asked to employ an approach that we have chosen to call "archaeohistory." Despite the laudable emphasis on interdisciplinarity in recent decades, there remains a divide between scholars who study ancient Greece largely on the basis of texts and scholars who study ancient Greece largely on the basis of material evidence. That divide is driven, to some extent, by a previously touched upon issue—the sheer volume of the relevant information and the impossibility of familiarizing oneself with even a small fraction of it. Nevertheless, the textual evidence and the material evidence for ancient Greece each has its own particular lacunae and limitations, and their full value is realized only when they are brought into dialog with each other. Much of the best scholarship on the Archaic period produced in the past 30 years is notable for combining successfully literary and inscriptional texts with material evidence such as pottery, coins, and statuary. The term "archaeohistory" reflects our desire to fuse together seamlessly the emphasis on material evidence associated with archaeology and the emphasis on textual evidence associated with history. The commitment to archaeohistory will, we believe, be evident in every study in *OHAGW*.

A second major concern in designing and producing *OHAGW* was to create a collection of studies with a high degree of commensurability to facilitate comparison and contrast across the Greek world. Before discussing that facet of *OHAGW*, it is necessary to raise the question of whether "ancient Greece" is anything more than a modern construct. As the inhabitants of the southern end of the Balkan peninsula, what might be called the Greek homeland, dispersed throughout much of the Mediterranean and Black Sea basins, the different environmental and human ecosystems they encountered led almost inevitably to important differences among the settlements in which they lived. Furthermore, each of those settlements developed its own unique set of sociopolitical institutions and practices, and even communities that were situated relatively close to one another frequently responded in very different ways to similar demographic, political, social, and economic challenges.

The absence of anything resembling a single territorial state embracing a significant fraction of what is typically described as "the Greek (or Hellenic) world" means that "Greek" needs to be construed culturally, not politically, along the lines of a perceived common ethnicity or shared cultural traits. The work of Jonathan Hall (author of the *OHAGW* essay on Argos) in the late 1990s and early 2000s created an awareness that Hellenic ethnic identity was a relatively late arrival—Hall suggested that it emerged in the seventh and sixth centuries BCE (Hall 1997; Hall 2002).

As indicated by its title, this project is based in part on the assumption that there was a sufficiently high degree of shared ethnic identity and cultural traits among certain communities in the Mediterranean to speak meaningfully of the "Greek world" in the Archaic period. Those communities were bound together by a loosely structured but highly active network of commercial, cultural, diplomatic, and military ties. In addition, certain places and events—most notably Olympia and the Olympic Games—attracted participants from Greek communities throughout the Mediterranean and beyond and became sites for the production and inculcation of a deeply embedded sense of belonging to a distinct group (for further discussion see the *OHAGW* essay on Olympia by Reinhard Senff).

Other terminology has also proved awkward. Recent scholarship has emphasized that the term "colonization" is a problematic label for the complex process of long-term, multidirectional cultural exchange and ongoing mobility of individuals and small groups that led to the movement of people outward from the southern end of the Balkan peninsula (see, for example, Mac Sweeney 2017). While communities such as Pithecusae have long been recognized as multiethnic (see the *OHAGW* essay on Cumae and Pithecusae by Matteo D'Acunto for further discussion), it now seems evident that ethnic diversity was a feature of many, if not most, communities typically described as Greek.

Our concern with commensurability was motivated by a keen awareness that the study of ancient Greece in the Archaic period entails exploration of simultaneous difference and sameness—we see the complex interplay of diversity and uniformity as one of the most fundamental and fascinating traits of the ancient Greek world. In constructing *OHAGW* we wanted to ensure that the project would greatly simplify the process of comparison and contrast. In doing so we were particularly alert to the fact that, even though there were pre-existing scholarly monographs on sites such as Miletus and Syracuse that are included in *OHAGW* (see, for example, Gorman 2001; Evans 2016), those works took widely varying approaches with respect to the periods of time covered, types of evidence considered, and methodologies used, which in turn makes it difficult to explore divergences and convergences across communities.

To ensure a high degree of commensurability within *OHAGW*, all of its component studies are built around the same 11 rubrics (framed by an introduction and a conclusion): (1) sources of evidence, (2) natural setting, (3) material culture, (4) political history, (5) legal history, (6) diplomatic history (including warfare), (7) economic history, (8) familial/ demographic history, (9) social customs and institutions, (10) religious customs and institutions, (11) cultural history. All those rubrics are covered in every study (although not necessarily in precisely the order given above), so that there is a high level of commonality in the structure and general contents among the various components of *OHAGW*. We have pursued commensurability at a level below that of the rubrics by placing specific types of subject matter that could conceivably fall under more than one rubric under the same rubric in every study. For example, pottery, which might be placed under "material culture" or "cultural history," is consistently placed under the rubric of "material culture."

Both the rubrics themselves and the division of material among rubrics are to a certain extent arbitrary, and we experimented with various arrangements before arriving at the one employed in *OHAGW*. Different arrangements had different advantages and disadvantages, and none was, in our view, perfect. We nonetheless persisted in the use of a consistent set of rubrics primarily because that feature of the project will make it possible to explore diversity and uniformity across the Greek world with much greater ease and in greater depth than ever before. Moreover, the material within each study would perforce need to be subdivided in some fashion, and the absence of a single, shared set of rubrics would have, in effect, resulted in the creation of a different set of rubrics for each of the 22 studies in *OHAGW*. The arbitrary element in the selection and division of material would still be present, but the benefits of a shared organizational template would be lost.

A third key trait we had in mind when designing *OHAGW* was convenience. The scale of *OHAGW* is such that most readers will want to examine specific parts of the project rather than the project as a whole, and we wanted to make it easy for readers to access the material of particular interest to them. The high degree of structural and methodological commensurability among the component studies in *OHAGW* makes it possible to read either vertically (reading a complete study of a single site) or horizontally (reading, for example, the rubric of political history of a number of different sites). Reading vertically will enable scholars to familiarize themselves relatively quickly with a number of different Archaic Greek sites. Reading horizontally will enable scholars to familiarize themselves relatively quickly with how specific institutions and practices manifested themselves from place to place across the Greek world.

Reading horizontally, however, does present certain difficulties: the section on the political history of, say, Metapontion inevitably assumes that the reader is aware of particular items of information such as places, names, and dates that are discussed in earlier sections of that study. (The alternative would have been to construct each rubric as a stand-alone piece, which would have entailed a massive amount of repetition.) To minimize that difficulty, the Introduction to each study discusses essential places, names, and dates that feature in other parts of the study. Readers who wish to work through *OHAGW* horizontally are strongly encouraged to take the time to read the Introduction to a study before they look at the text under any of the aforementioned 11 rubrics. We have also supplied a generous amount of cross-references throughout each study so that readers working horizontally can easily find more information about a subject treated elsewhere in the study. Each study, moreover, is prefaced by a detailed table of contents.

*OHAGW*, by its very nature, discusses literally hundreds of places, many of which will not be immediately familiar, even to many specialists in ancient Greece: examples are Parauaia and Tymphaia, which feature in Zosia Archibald's study of Macedonia. Every study in *OHAGW* thus includes a set of maps and site plans that shows the location of sites and buildings featured in the essay, as well as a gazetteer (located at the end of each study) that lists every site and building shown on a map or site plan and gives the relevant map number(s) and grid-square(s).

Finally, we asked all contributors to make their work readily accessible to an audience consisting largely of scholars who have some substantial grounding and serious interest in the ancient Greek world. While, given that audience, there was no need for them to explain the plot of the Homeric poems or the nature of Thucydides' work, we did want to make certain that every part of every study could be understood and appreciated regardless of whether a reader was trained as an archaeologist, historian, philologist, epigrapher, art historian, etc. Our hope is that each study is a self-contained, self-sufficient piece of scholarship that a reader who knows little or nothing about the site in question beforehand can comprehend fully without immediate reference to any other scholarship.

## *Site Selection*

In selecting places to include in *OHAGW* we began by looking for sites that were in some fashion and by some criterion significant in the Archaic period, that had notable physical remains (which had been excavated and published), and for which there was considerable textual evidence, either epigraphic or literary. From among the many places that fulfilled those criteria we assembled a group of approximately 30 places that included various geographies and site types. We make no claim that the sites treated in *OHAGW* constitute a representative sample, in the sense that careful study of the *OHAGW* sites would reveal all the major features of Archaic Greek communities broadly speaking, but we would say that the *OHAGW* sites collectively give some substantial sense of the diversity of the Greek world in the Archaic period.

xxii *Series Editors' Preface*

The exigencies involved in carrying out a large-scale project over multiple years and the manifold hardships created by the COVID-19 pandemic produced a certain degree of attrition, and the roster of sites covered in *OHAGW* is not identical to that which we originally outlined. At a certain point we decided that it was more important to publish the very considerable collection of valuable material that the contributors had produced than to delay publication to add more sites. Our feeling was that adding five or even ten more sites would not bring us across some crucial threshold, and that *OHAGW* could not possibly become an encyclopedic treatment of the Archaic Greek world in any sort of reasonable timespan.

That said, certain sites (such as Aegina) are perhaps conspicuous by their absence. Our hope is that the 22 studies that currently constitute *OHAGW* will find an enthusiastic audience and that in short order it will be desirable and possible to commission additional studies that extend the template that has already been established.

## *Periodization*

The choice to focus on the Archaic period reflects our conviction that it was a critical, formative era in Greek history. As Anthony Snodgrass eloquently argued in his foundational *Archaic Greece: The Age of Experiment* (1980), the institutions and practices that took shape in Greek communities during the Archaic period differed from what came before, and remained influential, even definitive, among Greek communities for centuries thereafter. Indeed, much of what is now seen as distinctive about Greek culture—democracy, stone temples, and nude athletics, to name but a few—first developed within the boundaries of the Archaic period. The history of this period thus merits careful study by anyone interested in the ancient Greek world and its legacy.

The decision to concentrate on the Archaic period raised *ab initio* the question of how to define its temporal boundaries.[1] The traditional periodization of Greek history is a *post eventum* and fluctuating construct, and the Archaic period (which is typically understood as stretching from some point in the eighth century to c. 479 BCE) as a construct has a long history. The perception of events corresponding in time roughly to the beginning and end of the Archaic period as key

---

1. It is not possible here to offer a complete conspectus of the scholarship on the Archaic period as an historical construct. We are not aware of a single publication that covers the full range of possible considerations, but there are several relevant, stimulating books, theses, and articles, among which we would highlight Heuss 1946; Golden and Toohey 1997 (esp. the article by Ian Morris in that volume); Davies 2009; Lange 2015; and Étienne 2017.

epochs can be traced all the way back to ancient Greece. According to the Roman grammarian Censorinus (active in the third century CE), Varro (active in the first century BCE) divided the history of the world into three parts: the "obscure" period (stretching from Creation to the Flood), the mythical period (from the Flood to the first Olympiad), and the historical period (everything after the first Olympiad) (*De die natali* 21.1–3). For Varro, the first Olympiad marked the point at which it was possible to separate fact from legend in accounts of past events.

It is probable that Varro derived his three divisions from a Greek chronographer, possibly Eratosthenes or Castor of Rhodes (see Frances Pownall's commentary on Eratosthenes F1c in the second edition of *Brill's New Jacoby*). Both Eratosthenes and Castor dated the first numbered Olympiad to 776 (Christesen 2007: 173–8, 311–20), and that date has repeatedly featured in modern scholarship on ancient Greece as an important epoch. George Grote, in his 12-volume *History of Greece* (1846–1856), claimed that "the history of Greece falls most naturally into six compartments," the first of which starts in 776. He notes that "I begin the real history of Greece with the first recorded Olympiad, or 776 B.C." (Grote 1846–1856: vol. 1: x–xi, vii). Anne Jeffery set the upper boundary of the Archaic period at 776, in her monograph entitled *Archaic Greece* (Jeffery 1976: 24–8).

The lower boundary of the Archaic period has traditionally been tied to the (second) Persian invasion of the Greek homeland in 480–479. The stature of that event as marking a key historical epoch can be traced to the enduring influence of the *Histories* of Herodotus, for whom any event post-479 BCE was after "ta Mēdika." Diodorus Siculus, for example, so arranged his *Library of History* that Book 11 begins with Xerxes' crossing into Europe in 480. Here again, modern historians have generally followed suit. For example, Grote's second historical "compartment" ends with the defeat of Xerxes' invasion of Greece.

Starting in the eighteenth century, the timespan between roughly the first Olympiad on one hand and the Persian Wars on the other became identified as a distinct period of art history, and it was expositions of art history that provided the currently prevailing terminology. In his *Geschichte der Kunst des Alterthums* (first edition 1764) Johann Winckelmann, working primarily with reference to sculpture, divided Greek art into four chronological phases that formed part of a pattern of growth and decay: der ältere Stil, der hohe Stil, der schöne Stil, and der Stil der Nachahmer; the "ältere Stil" encompassed art from the earliest times up to the work of Phidias (see, for example, Winckelmann 1764: 39, 214, 433–62; Dittmann 1991; Potts 2000: 67–112). The conversion of Winckelmann's "ältere Stil" to "Archaic period" was due primarily to anglophone authors.

Of particular note in that regard are Charles Cockerell and Edward Dodwell, who were familiar with Winckelmann's work and who in 1811 were among a group that discovered several pedimental sculptures at the Temple of Aphaea on Aegina that were seen as the embodiment of the "ältere Stil." Cockerell and Dodwell wrote about what they called the "archaic style" in Greek art (see, for example, Cockerell 1819: 340; Dodwell 1819: vol. 1: 571, vol. 2: 199, 201; Lange 2015: 154–8 and *passim*). By 1833, Henry Ellis, in a guide to sculptures in the British Museum, could write about "the archaic period, as it is called, of Grecian art" that "extended through eight almost unknown centuries, nearly to the time of Phidias" (Ellis 1833: 100). As archaeological explorations began to produce large quantities of material from what would now be called the Bronze and Early Iron Ages, chronologies were adjusted accordingly, and the starting point of the Archaic period was pushed downward. In Leonard Whibley's *Companion to Greek Studies* from 1905, the sculpture of the Archaic period is placed between 750 and 500 BCE (Whibley 1905: 234).

While there is a long tradition of identifying epochs in the eighth century and in the early fifth century, and thus at the beginning and end of the Archaic period as typically defined, and while the intervening centuries have long been read as a distinct era in the history of Greek art, there is no compelling necessity to identify the time period between the eighth and the early fifth century as a distinct phase of Greek history broadly construed. This is immediately evident from Grote's work: he recognized 776 and 479 as significant dates, but he divided what we call the Archaic period into two distinct "compartments," one running from 776 to c. 560 (the accession of Pisistratus and Croesus) and another running from c. 560 to the defeat of Xerxes in 479. Closer to home, two contributors to *OHAGW*, Jonathan Hall and Robin Osborne, have written surveys of the Archaic period in ancient Greece that begin c. 1200 (Osborne 2009; Hall 2014). This is because, for them, the events of the end of the Bronze Age set in motion a series of changes that played themselves out without any major breaks until the early fifth century.

Scholars who identify the Archaic period as a distinct historical phase and who place its boundaries at the eighth and early fifth centuries have given varying reasons for doing so. For example, Anthony Snodgrass started his account of Archaic Greece in the eighth century because he placed in that time period a "structural revolution" that established the basic economic, social, and political framework within which the multiplicity of Greek communities operated for centuries thereafter (Snodgrass 1980: 13).

We firmly subscribe to the idea that the Archaic period can be reasonably characterized as a distinct historical phase that extended from roughly the middle of the eighth century to roughly the end of the sixth century, and we agree that it was, as Snodgrass put it, "a complete episode in its own right" (Snodgrass 1980: 13). From our perspective, there are two determinant factors: politics and sources. The beginning of the Archaic period is marked by the re-emergence of formal political institutions in the Greek world, including the widespread creation of *poleis*. The end of our Archaic period is marked by the emergence of democracy as a fully developed form of governing a *polis*, completing the set of six forms of governance (monarchy, tyranny, aristocracy, oligarchy, *politeia*, and democracy) identified by Plato and Aristotle (see, for example, *Eth. Nic.* 1160a31–b12; *Pol.* 1279a22–b8). While significant developments in the political life of Greece communities certainly took place in the centuries after the Persian invasions, the basic repertoire of possibilities was established within the timeframe we call the Archaic period.

The Archaic period is also arguably a "complete episode" with respect to the textual sources. The wealth of extant literary and epigraphic texts written in Greek represent a remarkable and—globally speaking—highly unusual resource for the study of the history of a group of people in the pre-modern period. The reappearance of literacy in Greek communities occurred in the eighth century: that and its gradual dissemination, due to the invention of an alphabet, to a much broader segment of the population than had been literate in the Late Bronze Age constitute an epoch in its own right. The Homeric poems, not coincidentally transcribed within a framework of alphabetic literacy, make it possible to explore the Greek world of the eighth century in ways that are simply not feasible for the Early Iron Age.

Moreover, the literary texts of the Archaic period are sufficiently different from those that follow as to form a distinct group: A. R. Burn thus wrote a history of the Archaic period under the title *The Lyric Age of Greece* (Burn 1960), which captures one particular new source of poetic and cultural sensibility. As for the qualitative difference between the Archaic period and what follows, an important variable is the degree to which the literary texts of the former were produced against the background of a society that remained strongly oral in its orientation and social memory (see the discussion and cautionary comments in Thomas 1992). With the appearance of properly historical texts in the early part of the Classical period, the Greeks' approach to their past changed in fundamental ways.

In parenthesis, however, it is important to note that putting political institutions and textual sources front and center is a choice that necessarily excludes other possibilities. As Kostas Vlassopoulos has pointed out, variant perspectives on ancient Greek history, for example, those that emphasize the agency of subaltern populations, entail variant periodizations, each of which is, by definition, partial (Vlassopoulos 2018: 215).

A further consideration that materially shaped our approach to the Archaic period was a desire to give contributors a certain degree of flexibility to adjust the temporal parameters of their studies to fit the contours of their particular xxvi *Series Editors' Preface*

site. This was most obviously necessary in the case of sites such as Cyrene and Metapontion, which did not receive any substantial number of Greek migrants until the second half of the seventh century. At the other end of the temporal scale, for many Greek communities within the broader cultural horizon of Hellas, the Persian invasion of the Aegean Greek homeland in 480–479 was an event of at best minor significance. Far more important for most Sicilian Greek communities, for example, was the invasion of their island from Carthage, though as it happens the contemporaneous Battle of Himera in 480 could be considered epoch-making too. Contributors were therefore asked to define the Archaic period in a way that suited their site, while staying roughly within the boundaries of the eighth century and the fifth century. To give but one example, in their study of Syracuse, Franco De Angelis and Valentina Mignosa set the upper limit at the time of the arrival of substantial numbers of Greek migrants, the third quarter of the eighth century, and the lower limit at 461, at which point the last of the Deinomenid tyrants was overthrown and a democratic government established that endured, in one form or another, to the end of the fifth century.

## Transliteration and the Spelling of Names, Places, and Titles of Literary Works

We have taken the *Oxford English Dictionary* (*OED*) as our guide in deciding what Greek words (other than names, places, and titles of literary works) to anglicize and what words to transliterate. Ancient Greek words that have a direct equivalent in the *OED* are given as they are in the *OED*, without italics. For example, ἀκρωτήριον has a direct equivalent in the *OED*, "acroterion," that is used throughout *OHAGW*, without italics. On the other hand, χώρα has no direct equivalent in the *OED* and hence is given in transliterated form, italicized and with the long vowels marked with macrons (e.g., "The *chōra* of Metapontion consisted of a series of relatively flat, well-watered natural terraces rising from a coastal plain to a hilly and dissected interior"). Names, places, and titles of literary works presented special challenges and were treated differently.

*OHAGW* will be available in both print and digital form. Insofar as we view *OHAGW* as a collectivity, we wanted to simplify as much as possible the process of searching across the entirety of the digital version of *OHAGW*, and, to that end, we wanted to be both consistent and predictable in the spelling of Greek names, places, and titles of literary works. The complication of course is trying to find a balance between transliterating in such a way as to be as faithful as possible to original spellings while taking into account established usages (e.g., Korinthos or Corinth?).

*Series Editors' Preface*      xxvii

We considered producing a complete list of all the Greek names, places, and literary works mentioned in *OHAGW* to serve as a guide for searches, but we decided that the list would be sufficiently cumbersome to locate and use that most readers would not refer to it. Instead, we have implemented the following practices throughout *OHAGW*, a general awareness of which should make it possible to carry out searches without any great difficulty:

(1) Greek names and places that have their own lemma in the *Oxford Classical Dictionary* (*OCD*) are spelled as they are in the *OCD*. Our rationale was that the provision of a lemma in the *OCD* was a reasonably good measure of the prominence of a person or place and hence the likelihood that there was an established usage for the spelling of the person or place in question. In addition, our assumption is that most scholars interested in the ancient Greek world, the intended audience of *OHAGW*, would have easy access to the *OCD*.

(2) Greek names and places that do not have their own lemma in the *OCD* were transliterated into English. We did not, however, provide long marks to distinguish *epsilon* from *eta* and *omicron* from *omega* because that would have produced a rather strange orthographic mixture such as Sappho for Σαπφώ (as per the *OCD*) and Phrynōn for Φρύνων (who does not have a lemma in the *OCD*).

(3) References in the main text to the titles of well-known Greek literary works are typically given in the most common and obvious English translation; for example, the *OHAGW* essays refer to Aristotle's *Politics* rather than Πολιτικά or *Politika* or *Politica*. In parenthetical citations of Greek literary works, the title is given in accordance with the list of abbreviations provided in the *OCD*; for example: "The practices explored by Aristotle in the *Politics* extend beyond the bounds of the Greek world; Aristotle, for instance, claims that political offices are distributed on the basis of height in Ethiopia (*Pol.* 1290b4–5)," to keep the text in parenthetical citations as brief and therefore legible as possible. For literary works not included in the *OCD*'s list of abbreviations, the title used in the main text is also used in parenthetical citations.

(4) We maintained established usages for Greek literary works that are habitually known by titles in Greek transliteration or in Latin translation. For example, Athenaeus' Δειπνοσοφισταί is in the main text of *OHAGW* studies referred to as the *Deipnosophistai* (whereas, in accordance with the *OCD*, it is in parenthetical citations referenced, for example, as Ath. 145b), and the (pseudo-) Aristotelian Οἰκονομικά is referred to as the *Oeconomica* in the main text (and *Oec.* in parenthetical citations).

xxviii

*Series Editors' Preface*

(5) For more obscure Greek literary works, we have used the title given in the *Canon of Greek Authors and Works* produced by the Thesaurus Linguae Graecae (TLG), both in the main text and in parenthetical citations. For example, the work on prosody produced by Aelianus Herodianus in the second century CE, ἡ καθ' ὅλου προσῳδία, is referred to under the title assigned by the TLG: *De prosodia catholica*. We are less than entirely enthusiastic about the TLG's practice of latinizing Greek titles, but the TLG does provide a convenient reference point without which all sorts of difficulties would arise. Aelianus Herodianus' work on prosody, for instance, is referenced in ancient sources by three different titles.

In implementing these practices, we found it necessary to make a number of judgment calls, a handful of which are worth specific mention here:

| Author | Title in Greek | Title in main text of OHAGW |
|---|---|---|
| ? | Ἐτυμολογικὸν Μέγα | *Etymologicum Magnum* |
| Aristophanes | Most of the titles of Aristophanes' plays have been translated into English, with the exception of the *Ecclesiazusae* and the *Thesmophoriazusae*. | |
| [Aristotle] | All of the titles of the 158 Aristotelian *politeiai* are referred to as the "*Constitution of the . . .*" with the city ethnic in the plural; e.g., *Constitution of the Athenians*. | |
| Herodotus | Ἱστορίαι | *Histories* |
| Marmor Parium | n/a | Marmor Parium (rather than Parian Marble or Parian Chronicle) |
| Pausanias | Ἑλλάδος Περιήγησις | *Guide to Greece* |
| Polyaenus | Στρατηγήματα | *Strategemata* |
| pseudo-Scylax | Περίπλους | *Periplous* |
| pseudo-Scymnus | Περίοδος πρὸς Νικομήδη | *Periplous* |
| Stephanus of Byzantium | Ἐθνικά | *Ethnica* |

The same basic practices were used for the titles of Latin literary works: the titles of more frequently cited texts (e.g., Cicero, *On the Laws*) are given in English translation, whereas less frequently cited Latin works are referred to in the Latin original.

## Bibliography

Burn, A. R. 1960. *The Lyric Age of Greece*. New York: St. Martin's Press. 2nd edition, 1978.

Christesen, P. 2007. *Olympic Victor Lists and Ancient Greek History*. Cambridge: Cambridge University Press.

Cockerell, C. R. 1819. "On the Aegina Marbles." *The Journal of the Science and the Arts* 6: 327–41.

Davies, J. K. 2009. "The Historiography of Archaic Greece." In *A Companion to Archaic Greece*, edited by K. Raaflaub and H. van Wees, 3–21. Malden, MA: Wiley-Blackwell.

Dittmann, L. 1991. "Zur Entwicklung des Stilbegriffs bis Winckelmann." In *Kunst and Kunsttheorie 1400–1900. Vorträge gehalten anläßlich des 22. Wolfenbütteler Symposions "Kunstgeschichte von Vasari bis Winckelmann" vom 1.–5.12.1987 und des 24. Wolfenbütteler Symposions "Kunstgeschichte seit Winckelmann" vom 27.11.–1.12.1988*, edited by P. Ganz and M. Gosebruch, 189–218. Wiesbaden: Harrassowitz.

Dodwell, E. 1819. *A Classical and Topographical Tour through Greece during the Years 1801, 1805, and 1806*. 2 vols. London: Rodwell and Martin.

Ellis, H. 1833. *The British Museum. Elgin and Phigaleian Marbles. Volume 1*. London: Charles Knight.

Étienne, R. 2017. "Introduction: Can One Speak of the Seventh Century BC?" In *Interpreting the Seventh Century BC: Tradition and Innovation. Proceedings of the International Colloquium Conference Held at the British School at Athens, 9th–11th December 2011*, edited by X. Charalambidou and C. A. Morgan, 9–14. Oxford: Archaeopress.

Evans, R. J. 2016. *Ancient Syracuse, from Foundation to Fourth Century Collapse*. London: Routledge.

Golden, M., and P. Toohey, eds. 1997. *Inventing Ancient Culture: Historicism, Periodization and the Ancient World*. London: Routledge.

Gorman, V. B. 2001. *Miletos, the Ornament of Ionia: A History of the City to 400 B.C.E.* Ann Arbor: University of Michigan Press.

Grote, G. 1846–1856. *History of Greece*. 12 vols. London: John Murray.

Hall, J. M. 1997. *Ethnic Identity in Greek Antiquity*. Cambridge: Cambridge University Press.

Hall, J. M. 2002. *Hellenicity: Between Ethnicity and Culture*. Chicago: University of Chicago Press.

Hall, J. M. 2014. *A History of the Archaic Greek World, ca. 1200–479 BCE*. 2nd ed. Chichester: Wiley-Blackwell.

Hansen, M. H., and T. H. Nielsen, eds. 2004. *An Inventory of Archaic and Classical Poleis*. Oxford: Oxford University Press.

Heuss, A. 1946. "Die archaische Zeit Griechenlands als geschichtliche Epoche." *Antike und Abendland* 2: 26–62. Now in *id.* 1995. *Gesammelte Schriften in 3 Bänden*. Stuttgart: Franz Steiner, vol. 1: 2–38.

Jeffery, L. H. 1976. *Archaic Greece: The City-States c. 700–500 B.C.* New York: St. Martin's Press.

Lange, A. 2015. "Die Entdeckung der Archaik—Ein ungeschriebenes Kapitel Wissenschaftsgeschichte. Die Etablierung des Terminus technicus "archaisch" in der Klassischen Archäologie in Deutschland." PhD diss., Humboldt-Universität zu Berlin.

Mac Sweeney, N. 2017. "Separating Fact from Fiction in the Ionian Migration." *Hesperia* 86: 379–421.

Osborne, R. 2009. *Greece in the Making, 1200–479 BC.* 2nd ed. London: Routledge.

Potts, A. 2000. *Flesh and the Ideal: Winckelmann and the Origins of Art History.* New Haven: Yale University Press.

Snodgrass, A. M. 1980. *Archaic Greece: The Age of Experiment.* Berkeley: University of California Press.

Thomas, R. 1992. *Literacy and Orality in Ancient Greece.* Cambridge: Cambridge University Press.

Vlassopoulos, K. 2018. "Marxism and Ancient History." In *How to Do Things with History: New Approaches to Ancient Greece*, edited by D. Allen, P. Christesen, and P. Millett, 209–35. New York: Oxford University Press.

Whibley, L., ed. 1905. *A Companion to Greek Studies.* Cambridge: Cambridge University Press.

Winckelmann, J. J. 1764. *Geschichte der Kunst des Alterthums.* Dresden: Waltherischen Hof-Buchhandlung.

# *Acknowledgments*

OVER THE COURSE of the decade that we have worked on this project in one form or another, we have benefited greatly from the assistance of many individuals, institutions, and organizations. First and foremost, we would like to express our profound gratitude to the contributors to *OHAGW*. The need to cover a broad sweep of subject matter, without the possibility of skipping over areas about which one might, initially at least, be less than fully informed, and to synthesize the textual and material evidence, means, as we have all discovered, that writing a study for *OHAGW* is a Herculean labor. The willingness of *OHAGW*'s contributors to put in the requisite hard work and to persist in the face of manifold difficulties and delays is a testimony to their professionalism and dedication. We have learned an immense amount from reading the studies in *OHAGW*, and we are certain that *OHAGW*'s readers will, like its co-editors, be thankful to the contributors for sharing their remarkable expertise.

This project would not have been possible without support from the Trustees of the A. G. Leventis Foundation. Their generosity made it possible for Paul Christesen to spend the better part of two years in Cambridge working solely on *OHAGW* and for Paul Cartledge, as an A. G. Leventis Senior Research Fellow (of Clare College, Cambridge), to dedicate much of his time to the project for the past near-decade. The Leventis Foundation also provided funding for two post-doctoral research associates—Drs. Estelle Strazdins and Carol Atack—who made enormous contributions to the almost inconceivable amount of editorial work necessary to bring this project to completion. Paul Christesen's time at Cambridge was also supported by a stipend from Clare Hall, which additionally provided pleasant living quarters and workspace along with a highly congenial intellectual community.

The deans of Dartmouth College's Arts and Sciences faculty have offered invaluable support on a continuing basis. That support made it possible to bring *OHAGW*'s contributors together in Hanover, New Hampshire, for a very productive conference in the spring of 2018 and helped fund leave time for Paul

Christesen. Dartmouth also provided a grant that made it possible to hire a copy editor and project manager, Aurora McClain, who handled much of the logistical heavy lifting of the final stage of the project, and to hire two graduate students, Adlai Everett Lang and Evelyn Rick, who helped with editorial work. Another graduate student, Evan Levine, lent us his expertise in establishing the basic design used in virtually all of the maps in *OHAGW*. Dartmouth also defrayed the cost of hiring undergraduate students who have been invaluable in moving *OHAGW* along. In addition to Duncan Antich, Ben Bonner, Albert Chen, Gray Christie, Ryan Fraser, Gracie Goodwin, Elizabeth Hadley, Shania Kee, Nathaniel Kramer, Anshul Lalan, Naomi Meron, Brian Morrison, Anindu Rentala, and Thomas Rover, we would like to single out for special mention Tim Hannan, who did most of the organizational work for the aforementioned conference, and Katie Goyette, who did a final round of editing on all of the *OHAGW* essays before they went to Oxford University Press.

Speaking of Oxford University Press, we cannot fail to mention Stefan Vranka, the commissioning editor. Stefan had the vision and patience to move *OHAGW* from concept to reality, and his enthusiastic support proved to be invaluable at every stage. The many colleagues who have offered assistance along the way are too numerous to name here, but we hope that they are aware of our appreciation of everything that they have done and continue to do for us. Last but by no means least, we would like to express our gratitude to our families. Editorial and authorial work take a special toll of their own, and our families have supported us in good times and bad.

# Contributors

**PAUL CHRISTESEN** is William R. Kenan Professor of Ancient Greek History at Dartmouth College. He is the author of three books, including most recently *A New Reading of the Damonon Stele* (2019).

**SYLVIAN FACHARD** is Professor of Classical Archaeology at the University of Lausanne and Director of the Swiss School of Archaeology in Greece. He previously taught at the universities of Geneva and Brown and the American School of Classical Studies at Athens, where he held the position of A. W. Mellon Professor (2017–2020). A specialist in the fortifications and territories of Greek city-states, he has directed excavations and surveys in Eretria, Amarynthos, Argos, and Attica.

**HANS-JOACHIM GEHRKE** is Professor Emeritus at the University of Freiburg (Breisgau) and Director of Outreach of University College Freiburg. He was Professor of Ancient History at the Universities of Würzburg, FU Berlin, and Freiburg (1982–2008) and President of the German Archaeological Institute (2008–2011). He is a member of the Academia Europaea, the Leopoldina–Nationale Akademie der Wissenschaften, the Heidelberger Akademie der Wissenschaften, and the Academy of Athens. His research and publications range widely, from Archaic, Classical, and Hellenistic Greece to the Roman Republic and Empire, from social and political history to the history of political concepts and theories. His main publications include *Stasis: Untersuchungen zu den inneren Kriegen in den griechischen Staaten des 5. Und 4. Jahrhunderts v. Chr.* (1985); *Geschichte des Hellenismus* (4th ed., 2008); *Alexander der Grosse* (6th ed., 2013, translated into many languages); *Geschichte der Antike: Ein Studienbuch* (4th ed,. 2013); and *Geschichte als Element antiker Kultur* (2014).

**JONATHAN M. HALL** is the Phyllis Fay Horton Distinguished Service Professor in the Humanities and Professor of History and Classics at the University of Chicago, where he has taught since 1996, receiving the Llewellyn John and Harriet Manchester Quantrell Award for Excellence in Undergraduate Teaching in 2009. He has written a series of books, articles, and chapters in edited volumes concerning the political, social, and cultural history of Greece, ancient ethnicities, historical methodologies, and the relationship between material cultural and textual documentation. He currently works on issues of archaeological heritage in modern Greece.

**GIUSEPPE LENTINI** is Associate Professor of Greek Language and Literature at the Sapienza University in Rome. He holds a PhD from the Scuola Normale Superiore in Pisa; he was Arnaldo Momigliano Scholar at University College London and Junior Fellow at the Center for Hellenic Studies in Washington, DC. He held positions at the University of Siena and at the Université de Fribourg. He is the author of *Il "padre di Telemaco": Odisseo tra Iliade e Odissea* (Pisa, 2006) and of several articles on ancient Greek literature, especially Homer, lyric poetry, and drama.

**SARAH MURRAY** is Associate Professor of Classics at the University of Toronto. She is the author of *The Collapse of the Mycenaean Economy: Trade, Imports, and Institutions, 1300–700 BCE* (2017). Her research focuses on assessing economic, demographic, and social change using archaeological evidence from early Greece.

**PHILIP SAPIRSTEIN** has been an Assistant Professor of Art History at the University of Toronto since 2018. Having received his doctorate in Art History and Archaeology from Cornell University (2008), he was an Assistant Professor from 2013–2019 in the School of Art, Art History & Design at the University of Nebraska–Lincoln. His primary interests are the history of art and architecture of the Mediterranean, in particular that of ancient Greece, Rome, and the Near East. Digital techniques for the 3D recording and analysis of ancient art and architecture, including photogrammetry, are another important area of research. Dr. Sapirstein has held numerous prestigious fellowships (e.g., from the NEH, the ACLS, Mellon, the Fulbright Foundation, and the American School of Classical Studies in Athens) and has published widely on both the history and technology of Greek architecture and digital methodologies.

**MATT SIMONTON** is Associate Professor of History at Arizona State University. His first book, *Classical Greek Oligarchy: History, Institutions, Political Conflict*, was published in 2017 by the Princeton University Press and was joint winner of the Runciman Award of the Anglo-Hellenic Society (London). His research interests include Archaic and Classical Greek political history, the

*Contributors*     xxxv

history of institutions, Greek constitutional thought and practice, and the study of authoritarianism.

**SAMUEL VERDAN** IS Senior Researcher at the Swiss School of Archaeology. He has directed excavations in Eretria and taught at the University of Lausanne. He studies Geometric and Early Archaic pottery and is collaborating in the exploration of the Sanctuary of Artemis at Amarynthos.

# *Note to the Reader*

This volume represents one component of The *Oxford History of the Archaic Greek World* (*OHAGW*). All of the 22 studies in *OHAGW* are organized around an identical set of 11 rubrics: (1) sources, (2) natural setting, (3) material culture, (4) political history, (5) legal history, (6) diplomatic history (including warfare), (7) economic history, (8) familial/demographic history (including education), (9) social customs and institutions, (10) religious customs and institutions, (11) cultural history. Each study begins with an introduction and ends with a conclusion.

If you wish to read a specific part of a given study, rather than the entire study from start to finish, we would strongly advise that you first read the introduction to the study in question—the introductions in *OHAGW* are designed to provide basic background information that sets the stage for the discussion that follows.

The Series Editors' Preface that appears at the beginning of each volume of *OHAGW* offers an overview of the project as a whole and information on transliteration and the spelling of names, places, and titles of literary works. The latter is likely to be helpful if you are accessing *OHAGW* in digital form and wish to search across one or more studies.

# *I*

# *Argos*

*Jonathan M. Hall*

## *List of Illustrations*

| | | |
|---|---|---|
| Map 1.1: | Some key sites in the Argive plain mentioned in this essay. @ Paul Christesen 2024. | 4 |
| Map 1.2: | Some key sites in the northeastern Peloponnese mentioned in this essay. @ Paul Christesen 2024. | 5 |
| Map 1.3: | Some key sites in the Peloponnese mentioned in this essay. @ Paul Christesen 2024. | 6 |
| Map 1.4: | Some key sites in the wider Mediterranean mentioned in this essay. @ Paul Christesen 2024. | 7 |
| Map 1.5: | Topography of the city of Argos. @ Paul Christesen 2024. | 9 |
| Map 1.6: | Some key sites in the city of Argos mentioned in this essay. @ Paul Christesen 2024. | 10 |
| Figure 1.1: | Coastline of the Argive plain c. 2500 BCE, showing Lake Lerna. After Zangger 1991: fig. 5. © Paul Christesen 2024. | 13 |
| Figure 1.2: | Bronze cuirass and helmet; last quarter of the eighth century; height: 47.4 cm (cuirass), 46 cm (helmet); from Tomb 45. Argos Archaeological Museum B. 26, 27. Image from École française d'Athènes (EFA) Photothèque X555, armure d'Argos. EFA/ Ph. Collet. © EFA/ Ph. Collet. Reproduced with permission. | 19 |
| Figure 1.3: | Monumental pyxis; 750–730; height: 1 m; from Tomb 23 in the Bakaloiannis Plot at Argos; the pyxis was reused about 25 years after its manufacture to contain the inhumed remains of a woman, approximately 35 years old. Argos Archaeological Museum C. 209. © Album / Art Resource, NY. | 20 |

Jonathan M. Hall, *Argos* In: *The Oxford History of the Archaic Greek World*. Edited by: Paul Cartledge and Paul Christesen, Oxford University Press. © Oxford University Press 2024. DOI: 10.1093/oso/9780199383597.003.0001

2 THE OXFORD HISTORY OF THE ARCHAIC GREEK WORLD

Figure 1.4:   Fragment of a Protoargive kratēr showing the blinding of the
Cyclops Polyphemus by the companions of Odysseus; second
quarter of the seventh century; height: 24.5 cm, width: 31 cm;
from excavations south of the South Cemetery at Argos. Argos
Archaeological Museum C. 149. Image from École française
d'Athènes (EFA) Photothèque X747, fragment de cratère avec
le Cyclope Polyphème aveuglé par Ulysse et ses compagnons.
EFA/ Ph. Collet. © EFA/ Ph. Collet. Reproduced with
permission.                                                                             22
Figure 1.5:   Plan of the agora of Argos. © Paul Christesen 2024.              23
Figure 1.6:   Polygonal terrace wall on the east flank of Larisa.
© Jonathan Hall 2024.                                                          24
Figure 1.7:   Plan of Asine. © Paul Christesen 2024.                             40
Figure 1.8:   Foundations of the temple of Athena Polias on the Larisa.
© Jonathan Hall 2024                                                          60
Figure 1.9:   Flight of stairs in the Sanctuary of Apollo Pythaeus on Deiras
ridge. © Jonathan Hall 2024.                                               62
Figure 1.10:  Plan of the Argive Heraion in the early fifth century.
© Paul Christesen 2024.                                                       66
Figure 1.11:  "Cyclopean" terrace wall at the Argive Heraion.
© Jonathan Hall 2024.                                                          67
Figure 1.12:  Remains of the fifth-century temple at the Argive Heraion.
The Larisa acropolis at Argos can be seen across the plain in
the center of the photograph. © Jonathan Hall 2024.               71

## List of Abbreviations

FGrH     Jacoby, F. 1923–1958. *Die Fragmente der griechischen Historiker.* 3v. in
14 vols. Berlin: Weidmann.

IC       Guarducci, M. 1935–1950. *Inscriptiones creticae, opera et consilio Friderici
Halbherr collectae.* 4 vols. Rome: Libreria dello Stato.

IG       *Inscriptiones Graecae.* 1873–. Berlin: Walter de Gruyter.

SEG      *Supplementum Epigraphicum Graecum.* 1923–. Leiden: Brill.

## 1.1. Introduction

The fundamental principle that underlies what might be called an archaeo-
historical methodology is that the documentary record, constituted by literary texts and inscriptions, and the material record, generated by archaeological
investigation, are two mutually implicated facets of antiquity and that both

have to be explored fully in any reconstruction of the past. At the same time, the entire enterprise is fraught with challenges. For one thing, the textual and the material are entirely different discourses, each of which requires its own distinctive methods and approaches (Hall 2014a: 207–12). For another, we are at the mercy of the capricious survival of evidence, which is seldom distributed equally or evenly across the two types of testimony. This is especially true with regard to the archaeohistory of Archaic Argos. The archaeological record, for example, is far fuller and more illuminating for Argos in the eighth century than it is in the seventh or even the sixth. By contrast, with one or two dubious exceptions, our literary sources are ignorant of any "events" prior to the seventh century. Worse still, many of those "events" are related to us by authors who were writing anytime up to eight centuries later. This, of course, is a problem that is common to all historians of the Archaic Greek world, though in this case, it is exacerbated by a tendency that may be peculiar to the Argives—namely, a propensity to employ mythical discourse to overvalue the past and blur the distinction between myth and history (Adshead 1986: 23). Ancient psychologizing is always a risky venture, though it is hard to avoid the suspicion that the Argives took refuge in nostalgia to compensate for the lack of status they believed was their due.

The issue of periodization is inevitably a vexed one for Archaic Greece (Hall 2014b: 320–2). Most histories of the period conclude with the Persian War of 480–479,[1] but the upper terminus may fluctuate between c. 1200 and c. 700. In what follows, I concentrate primarily on the period between c. 750 and c. 450. The upper limit is determined by the aforementioned wealth of archaeological material for eighth-century Argos, which cannot be ignored, even if it encounters little illumination from literary sources. The lower limit has been set in the recognition that the Persian War hardly constituted a chronological watershed for Argos, which maintained a position of strict neutrality throughout the conflict. A far more traumatic episode was the annihilation of the Argive army by the Spartan king Cleomenes I, probably about 15 years earlier, though the consequences of that massacre would be felt throughout the 470s. The most important transformation at Argos, however, occurred shortly before the middle of the fifth century, with the destruction of neighboring cities, the incorporation of their inhabitants within the Argive citizen body, and the introduction of democracy. (See Maps 1.1–1.4.)

---

1. All dates are BCE unless otherwise indicated.

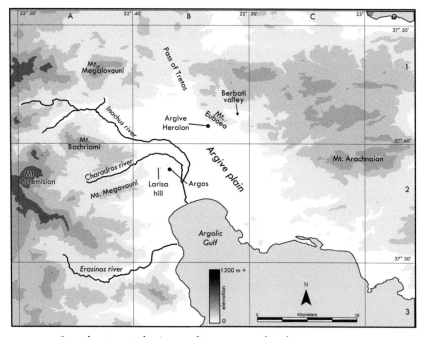

MAP 1.1. Some key sites in the Argive plain mentioned in this essay.

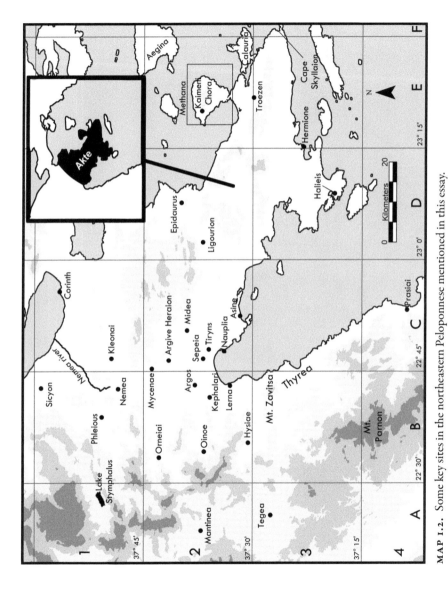

MAP 1.2. Some key sites in the northeastern Peloponnese mentioned in this essay.

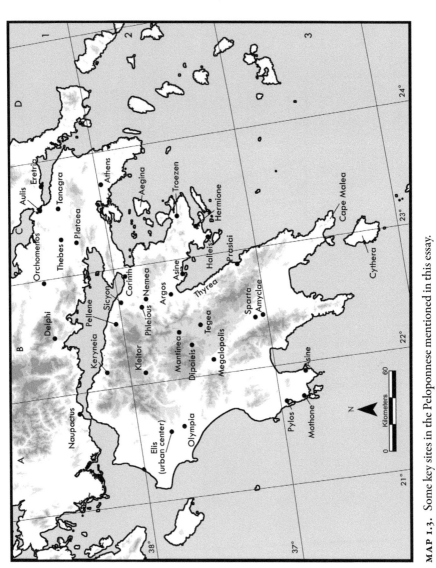

MAP 1.3. Some key sites in the Peloponnese mentioned in this essay.

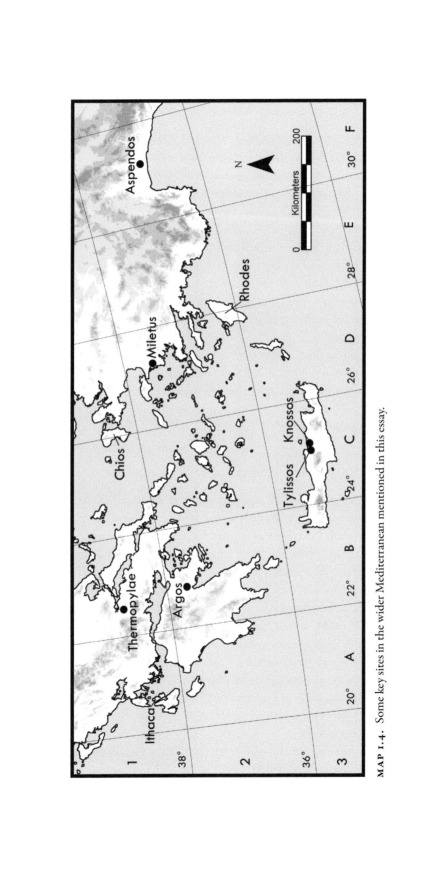

MAP 1.4. Some key sites in the wider Mediterranean mentioned in this essay.

## *1.2. Sources*
### 1.2.1. Written Sources

As with many other ancient cities in mainland Greece, Pausanias' account of his visit to Argos is invaluable for topographical considerations in his own day, though he provides very little information for the Archaic period. Herodotus recounts events of varying credibility, especially in the context of Argos' apparently perennial hostility with Sparta, while scholars have sometimes retrojected into the Archaic period some of the features that Thucydides observes at Argos at the time of the Peloponnesian War. Some isolated notices in Plutarch also purport to relate to Archaic Argos. There is a substantial amount of epigraphic material from the sixth and fifth centuries, including more than a hundred inscriptions on bronze sheets and around a dozen inscriptions on stone, that offer testimony for political, religious, and economic arrangements at Argos in the Archaic period.

In more modern times, Argos does not seem to have attracted much outside interest until 1668, when it was described by the Turkish traveler Evliyâ Çelebi. The following year, André de Monceaux was dispatched to Argos by Louis XIV's finance minister, Jean-Baptiste Colbert, in order to buy coins and manuscripts (Sève 1993: 9–10).

### 1.2.2. Archaeological Evidence

Limited excavations, largely in search of works of art, were conducted in 1729 by Michel Fourmont, professor of Syriac at the Collège Royal, and in the early 19th century by Veli Pasha, the governor of the Morea (Peloponnese) and son of the infamous Ali Pasha, the "Lion of Ioannina." In 1891, the local historian Ioannis Kofiniotis excavated in the theater at Argos (Kofiniotis 1892: 86–9; Mandis 2013: 19; Piérart 2013: 33). The first systematic excavations of the town were conducted between 1902 and 1912 by Carl Wilhelm Vollgraff, a Dutch scholar enrolled in the *section étrangère* of the École Française d'Athènes. Vollgraff focused much of his attention on the summit of Prophetes Elias and the Deiras ridge, as well as a polygonal terrace on the eastern flank of the Larisa that supports a Roman nymphaeum and the area around the Hellenistic theater and Roman baths to the south of the town (see Figure 1.6 in Section 1.4.4). In 1928, he returned to Argos to investigate further the Larisa and the agora (Dorovinis 2013: 44–5; Piérart 2013).

A renewed phase of French archaeological activity at Argos was initiated in the 1950s: a new archaeological museum was built while investigations continued to the north and south of the town. In coordination with the Greek Archaeological

*Argos*

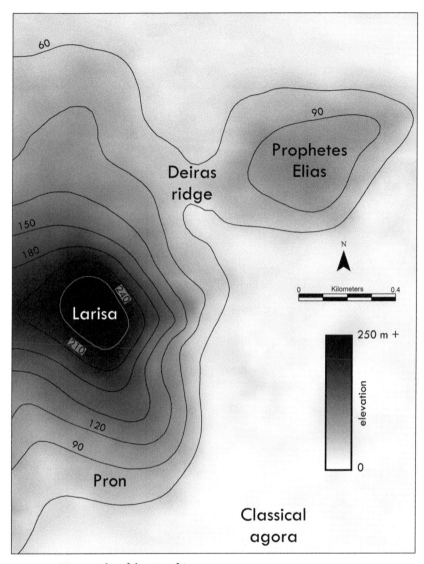

MAP 1.5. Topography of the city of Argos.

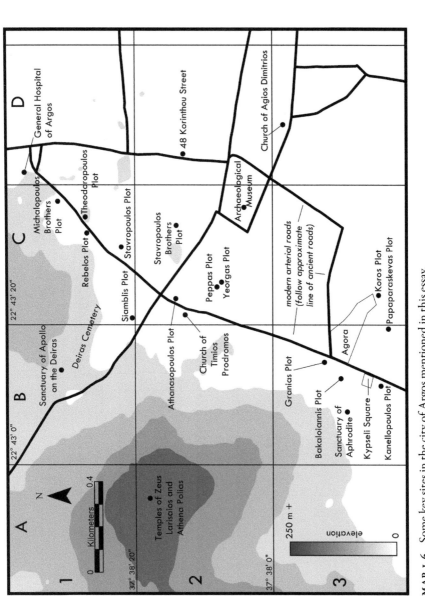

MAP 1.6. Some key sites in the city of Argos mentioned in this essay.

Service, the French were also invited to conduct several rescue excavations in the center and south of the town. These were occasioned by the arrival of newcomers from Arcadia and Crete and the consequent uncontrolled development of the town; the population of Argos rose 12.7% in the decade 1961–1971, becoming double what it had been in 1923 (Reynal and Rio 1980: 21, 51; Croissant 2013; Dorovinis 2013: 43–5). (See Map 1.5.)

Indeed, save for the hill of Prophetes Elias and the Deiras as well as the zone around the theater and the Roman baths, which are all relatively free from later building activity, much of the ancient city lies directly beneath the modern town and can therefore be investigated only by means of rescue excavations, undertaken by the Argolid Ephorate of the Greek Archaeological Service. Although such rescue excavations, which have recently averaged around 18 per year (Kolokotsas 1998: 442), are dictated by modern exigencies such as redevelopment and infrastructural improvement rather than scholarly agendas, they do at least constitute a "random" sample and have been conducted with sufficient frequency to form a rough idea of how the ancient city developed. (See Map 1.6.)

## 1.3. *Natural Setting*

The Argolid region, in the northeast Peloponnese, comprises the Argive plain (Argeia) to the west and the eastern Argolic peninsula (Akte) to the east. The triangular-shaped plain (see Maps 1.1 and 1.2) is approximately 21 km from north to south, 14 km wide at the coast, and has a surface area of 243 sq km. It consists largely of alluvium that was deposited in the Early Bronze Age, perhaps as a consequence of an intensification of agricultural practices (Tomlinson 1972: 8; Kelly 1976: 3; Zangger 1993: 1, 52–3). Much of this alluvium was deposited by the Inachus river, which floods on average once every 15 years, as well as by its tributary, the Charadros (the modern Xerias). Today both rivers are effectively torrent beds: as General Thomas Gordon (Gordon 1832: vol. 1: 425) observed of the Inachus, "[t]here is seldom a drop of water in its channel; but after heavy rains, or the melting of snow, it rolls a fearful torrent, sweeping every thing before it." Pausanias (2.15.5) had observed the same phenomenon some 16 centuries earlier. Only the Erasinos river, which originates in Lake Stymphalus in Arcadia and enters the Argolic Gulf approximately 6 km south of Argos, is perennial (Zangger 1993: 18).

Recent geomorphological analysis has shown that around 18,000 BP (uncalibrated), the sea level was 100–200 m lower than present, so the coastline ran approximately 10 km to the south of the current shore. Around the middle of the third millennium, by contrast, the sea level was at its highest and the coast approximately 1 km north of its present location. For much of antiquity, a large freshwater lagoon occupied the coastal part of the plain, directly south of Argos (see Figure 1.1). The lagoon was separated from the sea by a beach barrier formed by sediment transported by the Inachus and redeposited by the westward longshore current. Subsequently, major episodes of alluviation caused the regression of the coast, so that the shoreline already resembled its current shape by the Late Bronze Age (Zangger 1993: 62–5). The freshwater lagoon, known in historical times as Lake Lerna, actually increased in size during the Hellenistic and Roman periods before becoming marshy. Indeed, prior to its drainage in the 19th century CE, much of the shoreline was marshy, especially in the area surrounding Tiryns (Zangger 1993: 19–21, 64–5; Piérart 1997: 323; Piérart 2006: 6–7).

The Argive plain is enclosed by mountains, save for its southern access to the Argolic Gulf. To the west, where the peaks are formed from Upper Cretaceous limestone, Mt. Artemision rises to a height of 1,771 m, preceded by the lower peaks of Megalo, Bachriami, and Megavouni. Three passes, situated near Orneiai, Oinoe, and Kaimeni Chora, lead into Arcadia (Lehmann 1937: 3; Tomlinson 1972: 8; Foley 1988: 22; Zangger 1993: 8). At the foot of the easternmost extension of Mt. Artemision lies Argos, which was the most important city of the Argolid from the Early Iron Age through to Late Antiquity. In part, it owed its preeminence to its location on an important route linking Corinth with Tegea and Sparta (Piérart 1997: 322). Approximately 10 km to the south and near the coast was Lerna, which was one of the most important sites of the plain during the Early Bronze Age. South of Lerna, Mt. Parnon (1,035 m) separates the Argolid from the coastal region of Thyrea,[2] which was frequently an object of dispute between Argos and Sparta. To the north, the narrow pass of Tretos (known today as Dervenaki, the site of a resounding Greek victory over Ottoman forces in July 1822) offers access to the Sanctuary of Zeus at Nemea, the *poleis* of Kleonai and Phleious, and Corinthia; an alternative route into Corinthia leads from the Berbati valley on the eastern side of the plain (Tomlinson 1972: 13; Foley 1988: 22).

The plain's eastern extent is bounded by Mt. Arachnaion (1,199 m), which consists largely of Paleocene-Maastrichtian flysch and Upper Cretaceous limestone (Zangger 1993: 8; Piérart 1997: 321). The most important ancient sites on this eastern side were Mycenae, Midea, Tiryns, Nauplia, and the Sanctuary of

---

2. The name Thyrea can be applied to a town and to a wider region that is also referred to as Thyreatis (Shipley 2004: 594–5). The latter is sometimes used interchangeably with Cynuria. However, some scholars argue that the Thyreatis was the northern part of the larger region of Cynuria (Phaklaris 1990: 18–20, 88).

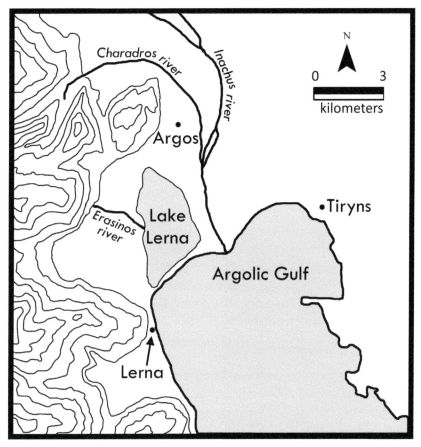

**FIGURE 1.1.** Coastline of the Argive plain c. 2500 BCE, showing Lake Lerna.

Hera Argeia at Prosymna (the "Argive Heraion"). Asine occupies its own microplain to the southeast of Nauplia. Beyond Mt. Arachnaion, Akte is bisected, from west to east, by the Adheres mountain range (1,113 m), which terminates in Cape Skyllaion. A pass via Ligourion leads from the Argive plain into the territory of Epidaurus. To the east of Epidaurus were the *poleis* of Troezen and Methana and the offshore island of Calauria (modern Poros), while the *poleis* of Hermione and Halieis (modern Porto Cheli) were located on the southern coast of Akte.

The city of Argos itself is dominated by two hills (see Map 1.5). The Larisa (c. 290 m), which forms the western limit of the settlement, served as the acropolis of the city in the historical period. To the northeast of the Larisa rises a lower, conical hill of c. 80 m, which is today known as either the Aspis or Prophetes

Elias, after the chapel that stands on its summit. Unfortunately, there is considerable disagreement about the ancient toponyms of Argos. Many of the early 19th-century CE travelers to the city (e.g., Gell 1817: 166) identified the hill of Prophetes Elias with the Aspis mentioned by Plutarch (*Pyrrh.* 32; *Cleom.* 17, 21). This was largely due to its resemblance to the round hoplite shield (ἀσπίς), whose invention Pausanias (2.25.7) credits to Argos (Vollgraff 1907: 165–9). But Plutarch's description of the Aspis does not fit well with the hill of Prophetes Elias, and it has been suggested that it is better understood as referring to a pronounced foothill, known in antiquity as the Pron, which lies on the southeast flank of the Larisa, overlooking the Sanctuary of Aphrodite (Lambrinoudakis 1969–1970). This was where, according to the scholiast to Euripides' *Orestes* (871–2), the Argives convened in assembly and held judicial proceedings. Alternatively, Croissant (1972) has proposed that Aspis was an alternative name for the entire Larisa but had gone out of use by the time of Pausanias, who fails to mention it. In this case, the hill of Prophetes Elias may have been known as the Deiras—the name given today to the col that connects it to the Larisa (Piérart 1990: 327–8; Piérart 1997: 322; Piérart 2006: 5). To the north and east, the Charadros river flows around Prophetes Elias and, in antiquity though not today, met the Inachus to the north of the town (Piteros 1998: 179–85; Marchetti 2000: 279).

The region sees warm summers, largely because southerly winds predominate between March and October, with average maximum temperatures in August of around 29 degrees Celsius. Winters are generally mild, though minimum temperatures as low as -6 degrees Celsius have been recorded (Lehmann 1937: 34, 39). The average annual rainfall is 80–100 cm, with virtually no precipitation during the summer months (Reynal and Rio 1980: 5). Although there is no reason to suppose that the climate was drastically different in antiquity, the evidence of radiocarbon dates and analysis of ice cores in Greenland suggest that conditions were somewhat cooler and wetter in the period 850–600 (Thommen 2012: 25).

## *1.4. Material Culture*
### 1.4.1. Settlement Pattern before the Archaic Period

While the earliest traces of settlement in the Argolid date to c. 50,000 years ago and were found at Kephalari, about 5 km southwest of Argos, signs of human occupation at Argos itself date back to the Late Neolithic period. Evidence for a more substantial settlement appears starting in the Middle Helladic period (c. 2000–1600). At that time, houses and tombs seem to have extended over an area of about 30 ha, though focused primarily on the area at the foot of the Larisa and the hill of Prophetes Elias, where a substantial settlement has been brought to light (Piérart and Touchais 1996: 13–20; Piérart 2004a: 599). In the Late Helladic period (c. 1600–1100), the center of gravity shifts to the eastern side of the Argive plain, where the sites of Mycenae, Midea, and Tiryns were clearly of more importance than Argos itself. To date, no evidence has come to light at Argos of a Late Bronze Age palace, tholos tomb, or Linear B tablets. Vollgraff did, however, discover "cyclopean" fortifications inside the inner enceinte of the medieval castle on the summit of the Larisa, as well as a massive lintel block, weighing approximately 6 tons, which was built into the south gate of the castle and which is of similar dimensions to the lintel over the Lion Gate at Mycenae (Vollgraff 1928: 320). In addition, the discovery of a Syrohittite or Cyprominoan cylinder seal might lead us to suspect that some palatial-like structure may originally have crowned the Larisa hill (Viret-Bernal 1992: 66–8; Piteros 2013: 337–9).

Argos was not abandoned at the end of the Late Helladic IIIB period (c. 1200), when virtually all of the Late Bronze Age palaces in the Greek mainland collapsed or were destroyed. Six of the 36 chamber tombs in the Deiras cemetery continued to be used into the succeeding Late Helladic IIIC, Submycenaean, and Protogeometric periods (twelfth to tenth centuries), indicating continued occupation of the area, albeit at a reduced level (Foley 1988: 24; Siriopoulos 1989: 323; Touchais and Divari-Valakou 1998: 12). Sites on the eastern side of the plain such as Mycenae and Tiryns were also eventually occupied or reoccupied, but it is now Argos that becomes the most important settlement in the region. The Protogeometric (tenth-century) settlement lies a little farther south than its Bronze Age predecessor and may occupy an area as large as approximately 2.5 sq km, though it is dispersed in nature; a metallurgical furnace, probably for silver cupellation, was discovered in the area of the modern archaeological museum (Hågg 1982: 298–300; Siriopoulos 1989: 324; Touchais and Divari-Valakou 1998: 13–14). The reconstruction of the settlement pattern in the tenth and ninth centuries is largely based on the distribution of graves rather than the much scantier remains of residences. These seem to indicate three or four separate clusters of village-like communities—a situation comparable to that of Athens, Corinth, and Eretria in this period or to Thucydides' description (1.10.2) of Sparta in his own day (Aupert 1982: 2; Hågg 1982: 300; Hall 1997a: 93–9; Touchais and Divari-Valakou 1998: 14–16; Vink 2002: 56; Hall 2014b: 76–8).

The eighth-century settlement pattern is also largely predicated on the distribution of graves, though a couple of apsidal houses have been unearthed

## 16   THE OXFORD HISTORY OF THE ARCHAIC GREEK WORLD

in the south of the town, and what has tentatively been identified as a Late Geometric textile-dyeing plant has been excavated at the foot of the Larisa (see Section 1.8). By the end of the eighth century, there is evidence for worship on the summit of the Larisa and in the Sanctuary of Apollo Pythaeus on the Deiras, while votive material has also been discovered at six other locations throughout the town (see Section 1.11.1.4). It is still possible to recognize separate village-like clusters, dispersed over a large area, though the gaps that separate them become less distinct (Touchais and Divari-Valakou 1998: 16; Vink 2002: 56). From c. 750, there is a steep increase in the number of known burials at Argos; in fact, it has been calculated that the number of recovered burials per 30-year generation in the Late Geometric phase is three times what it had been in the preceding Middle Geometric phase (Foley 1988: 35).[3] A similar phenomenon is known from Athens and Attica (Snodgrass 1980: 22–4), and it may be that a greater percentage of the Argive population was now being granted more formal—and hence archaeologically visible—burial (Morris 1987). Since, however, three times as many settled archaeological sites are attested in the Argolid during the ninth and eighth centuries compared with the tenth century (Foley 1988: 23), it is highly likely that there was also an increase in the population at this time, which would account for the seemingly denser settlement pattern at Argos as well.

Around 700, the settlement area at Argos seems to contract when compared with the more dispersed pattern of the eighth century, being now largely restricted to the zone in the southwest where the agora would later develop (Marchetti 2013: 324). Although some burials continue to be found throughout the area occupied by the modern town, the majority are concentrated to the south and increasingly to the north, in the zone around the modern General Hospital of Argos and the Charadros river bed. Furthermore, there is a precipitous decline in the number of recorded seventh-century burials, which tend to be much poorer with regard to grave goods. Burial in cist graves is largely abandoned, and a new cylindrical type of pithos becomes the favored mode of inhumation (Foley 1988: 47–52). Foley wonders whether the Argolid at this time experienced a crippling drought, which has been hypothesized for Attica, where a similar pattern of apparent decline is witnessed (Camp 1979). Yet if both Attica and the Argolid were victims of a drought in the closing years of the eighth century, it is difficult to explain how Corinth escaped the same fate. As has been suggested for Attica

---

3. Courbin (1966: 557–62) dates the subphases of the Argive Geometric period as follows: Early Geometric, 900–820; Middle Geometric, 820–740; Late Geometric, 740–c. 710. Coldstream's (1968: 330) dates are only slightly different: Early Geometric, 900–830/825; Middle Geometric, 830/825–750; Late Geometric, 750–690.

and other areas of Greece in the seventh century (Osborne 1989; Vink 1997; Hall 2014b: 190–4), the explanation might lie in changed modes of behavior—especially with regard to how seventh-century Argives related to their past—or in our own misidentification or misinterpretation of the material evidence or in a combination of both. For example, since fewer grave goods are now found in pithos burials, they are consequently harder to date, so their numbers may have been underestimated. But it is also possible that many residents of Argos now decided to live outside the main nucleus of the settlement and farm land in the plain (Marchetti 2013: 325).

There are two finds, in fact, which make the prospect of an impoverished Argos rather unlikely. The first is a large orthogonal complex, dating to the first third of the seventh century, which was excavated in the square framed by Tripoli, Praxitelous, Archeas Olimbias, and Fidiou Streets (formerly known as Kypseli Square), in the southwest of the modern town. A socle of large, well-cut blocks probably supported walls of mud-brick (Bommelaer and Grandjean 1971: 740). A second complex of rooms was discovered somewhat to the east of the first in the area of the later Argive agora, on a natural mound beneath the foundations of the fifth-century Building P. Finds of votive material, inscribed and uninscribed lead plaques, and weights strongly suggest a public or administrative function for this complex, although there is little to indicate that the surrounding zone, which was marshy, served as a civic center for the city at this early date (Pariente, Piérart, and Thalmann 1998: 212–13; Piérart 2004a: 606; Marchetti 2013: 324). Furthermore, at least six new sanctuaries are indicated by finds of seventh-century votive deposits in the center of the modern town as well as to its north and south (Hall 1997a: 102–3).

## 1.4.2. Burial Practices

There are four types of graves in eighth-century Argos (Courbin 1974; Hägg 1974; Foley 1988: 34–40). The first is a simple rectangular pit. The second is a cist grave—a pit lined and roofed with stone slabs, often with a pebble floor. The standard of workmanship can vary, and their length ranges from around 1 m to more than 3 m. The third type is a pithos burial, whereby the body was inserted into a large ovoid pithos, which was then buried in the ground at a 45° angle. The mouth of the pithos was usually covered by a stone slab. The choice of burial type does not seem to be dictated by gender. Children are commonly buried in a fourth type of grave—a smaller ceramic vessel such as an amphora or a hydria. Cremation is virtually unknown. The body usually lies supine or on its side with its legs contracted, and the head tends to be oriented toward the west, though this is not a fixed rule. Typical grave goods include wheel-made and handmade ceramics and, in some cases, bronze vessels. In the case of female graves, bronze jewellery such as pins, rings, hair spirals, and fibulas are common, though bronze rings and pins are also found in male burials. A few male burials are accompanied by weapons and armor, as well as by iron spits (*oboloi*), often in multiples of six. The number of grave goods tends to increase in the later eighth century, and although cist graves are wealthier on average than pit or pithos burials, many cist graves contained no grave goods at all, while an infant pithos burial (grave 48) in the Theodoropoulos Plot in northern Argos was accompanied by 14 pots (Protonotariou-Deïlaki 1980: 63). The general rule is for single inhumation, though some pithoi and about one-third of cist graves were reused for subsequent inhumations. In the Papaparaskevas Plot, southeast of the agora, four especially large cist graves (graves 263, 265, 266, and 278) contained 25 burials and more than 200 pots among them (Hågg 1974: 40–2; Foley 1988: 36–9, 209). The burial practices at Argos are largely replicated in the other settlements of the Argive plain, though there are some slight variations, which are more pronounced at Asine (Hågg 1998).

An especially impressive grave was excavated in 1953 next to the fifth-century "Theater with Square Steps" (Courbin 1957). Tomb 45—sometimes known as the "Panoply" Tomb—was a cist grave, more than 3 m in length and about 1 m wide, which had been accidentally disturbed during the construction of a Roman wall. Its occupant, a male between 25 and 45 years old (Charlier 2013: 213), was accompanied by costly grave goods, including bronze and gold rings, two iron axes, 12 iron spits, and a cuirass and helmet (see Figure 1.2). The bell-shaped cuirass, which weighs about 3.4 kg, was formed from two sheets of bronze. The front was engraved in a highly stylized representation of musculature. Coldstream (2003: 148) has suggested that its form is influenced by corselets known from the Urnfield culture of Central Europe. The conical helmet was fashioned from four sheets of bronze riveted together, with a bronze stem supporting the horseshoe-shaped crest. One of the more unusual items in the grave was a pair of iron firedogs, 1.6 m long, that mimic the shape of a ship's prow and helm; parallels with Cyprus or Etruscan Italy have sometimes been suggested (Viret-Bernal 1992: 76; Coldstream 2003: 146). On the basis of the largely fragmentary ceramic materials found in the tomb—an amphora, two skyphoi, five cups, and a kratēr—Courbin dated the tomb to the last quarter of the eighth century.

### 1.4.3. Ceramics

Argos was home to a thriving pottery industry (Courbin 1966; Coldstream 2008: 112–47, 461–2; Foley 1988: 56–9). From the beginning of the Protogeometric

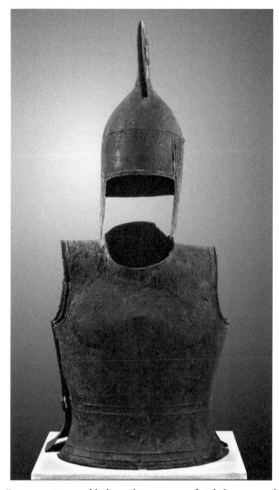

**FIGURE 1.2.** Bronze cuirass and helmet; last quarter of eighth century; height: 47.4 cm (cuirass), 46 cm (helmet); from Tomb 45. Argos Archaeological Museum B. 26, 27.

style in the late eleventh century to the Early Geometric style of the ninth century, Argive potters seem to have been influenced by their counterparts in Attica (Lemos 2002: 13–14, 17, 21–2; Dickinson 2006: 16–17). By the eighth century, however, a certain conservatism and resistance to outside influences set in (Piérart and Touchais 1996: 29–30). Figured scenes become more common, starting with rows of birds in profile on Middle Geometric II skyphoi. In the second half of the eighth century, popular figured representations include horses—especially the motif of a male standing between two horses—and files of women holding branches. An especially fine example is C. 209, a monumental pyxis, standing 1 m tall, which was found in the Bakaloiannis Plot (Tomb 23) in the southwest sector of Argos (see Figure 1.3). The entirety of the pyxis' surface is covered with bands of wavy lines, key patterns, and stepped meanders (an Argive innovation), while metopes frame representations of birds, fish, snakes, and horses; under the handles is a panel on which two men wrestle. The

FIGURE 1.3. Monumental pyxis; 750–730; height: 1 m; from Tomb 23 in the Bakaloiannis Plot at Argos. The pyxis was reused about 25 years after its manufacture to contain the inhumed remains of a woman approximately 35 years old. Argos Archaeological Museum C. 209.

vessel as a whole gives the appearance of an elaborately woven textile that, when compared with contemporary Attic Late Geometric pottery, fails to offer the viewer a single focal point. A broadly "Argive" style of Geometric pottery can be found throughout the other settlements of the Argive plain, though there are slight differences of fabric and motif, especially at Asine (Foley 1988: 59–61; Morgan and Whitelaw 1991).

Argive potters and their products do not seem to have ventured much beyond the Argolid (see Section 1.8). The same is not true of Argive metalworkers. Many of the bronze pins and fibulas deposited in graves or dedicated in sanctuaries were of local manufacture (Rolley 1992: 38–9). The helmet found in Tomb 45 has a number of parallels at Olympia, where a significant number of bronze figurines of horses, bulls, and warriors, as well as a type of cast bronze tripod with zigzag and chevron relief decoration, have been identified as being of Argive manufacture. That tradition of Argive bronze working stretches back into the ninth, if not the tenth, century. Miscast figurines suggest that itinerant Argive craftsmen traveled to Olympia (Heilmeyer 1979: 54–9; Foley 1988: 80–96; Morgan 1990: 85–9; Rolley 1992: 40, 44; Piérart 2006: 14–15). In the previous one to two centuries, craftsmen had tended to alloy copper with lead to make bronze. With the re-establishment, however, of long-distance contacts with the Near East c. 750, Athenian and Corinthian bronze workers began to use tin instead of lead, resulting in higher-quality products. Their Argive counterparts followed suit but added tin in much smaller quantities (around 2%) than was the practice elsewhere—another sign, perhaps, of Argive resistance to outside influences (Rolley 1992: 47).

Argive potters continued to produce a restricted range of "Subgeometric" vessels for the first two decades of the seventh century. Especially characteristic are the "Fusco Kraters," named after the cemetery at Syracuse where local copies of the style were first identified (Rizza and De Miro 1985: 141–2; Foley 1988: 69–70; De Angelis 2016: 243). These were deep-bodied kratēres with stirrup handles and a low foot, decorated with vertical and horizontal bands of zigzags, wavy lines, chevrons, and checkerboard patterns; often a central metope framed a horse or a file of dancing women. Although Argive workshops did not adopt "orientalizing" motifs with as much enthusiasm as their Corinthian counterparts, dotted rosettes do make their appearance. At least one workshop experimented with an orientalizing figured style known as Protoargive, of which the best-known example is a polychrome fragment (see Figure 1.4) in the Argos Museum, dated c. 660, which depicts Odysseus and his companions blinding the Cyclops Polyphemus (Courbin 1955b). Such examples are, however, rare, and Argives increasingly came to rely on imports of ceramic fine ware—first from Corinth and then, toward the end of the seventh century, from Attica—as well as locally made monochrome wares (Foley 1988: 69–72). Craftsmen seem instead to have turned their attention to terracotta figurines, a tradition that begins in the eighth century and becomes more prevalent in the seventh and sixth. The figurines may be hand-made or manufactured using a mold. Among the rather crude, handmade class of figurines, the most common types are a standing female figure with upraised arms, perhaps representing an adorant; a female seated on a throne; and mounted male warriors with tall helmets and a shield. Figurine groups, such as seated women holding hands, are also attested (Foley 1988: 102–11).

FIGURE 1.4. Fragment of a Protoargive kratēr showing the blinding of the Cyclops Polyphemus by the companions of Odysseus; second quarter of the seventh century; height: 24.5 cm, width: 31 cm; from excavations south of the South Cemetery at Argos. Argos Archaeological Museum C. 149.

## 1.4.4. Settlement Organization of Argos Town

In the sixth century, the Larisa was fortified with a polygonal terrace wall, from which a trapezoidal extension eastward of the north wall was added in the middle of the fifth century (Piteros 2013: 339–40; see Figures 1.5 and 1.6). Prior to this, there is no indication that the entire city was surrounded by a circuit of fortifications; indeed, Herodotus (6.77.1) recounts that when the Spartan king Cleomenes I launched an invasion of the Argolid, probably in the early fifth century (see Section 1.7.4), the Argives sent an army to the coast, which might suggest that there was no fortified city to defend (Marchetti 2013: 323). Presumably, a city wall existed by 417, when the Argives constructed long walls to the sea to protect themselves—unsuccessfully—against a Spartan invasion (Thuc. 5.82.5; Diod. *Sic.* 12.81.1; Plut. *Alc.* 15.2). Pithos and pit burials remain the norm, although a cluster of graves, discovered in the Stavropoulos Brothers Plot in 2006–2007, included

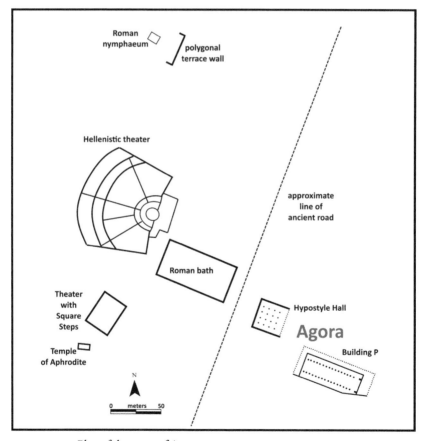

**FIGURE 1.5.** Plan of the agora of Argos.

FIGURE 1.6. Polygonal terrace wall on the east flank of Larisa.

three cist graves. One of them, dated by pottery to the second quarter of the sixth century, was of monumental proportions and accommodated the burial of a hoplite, accompanied by greaves and a Corinthian helmet (Sarri 2018).

At least five ancient arterial roads in the city have been identified, most of which follow the course of the modern streets of the town (see Map 1.6). The most important of these was the road that linked Corinth and Nemea to Mantinea via the hill of Prophetes Elias and the agora. At least one of these roads—that connecting the agora to the Theater—dates back to the sixth century (Barakari-Gleni and Pariente 1998; Marchetti 2013: 328). An impressive polygonal terrace wall on the eastern flank of the Larisa is probably to be dated to the Late Archaic period, though its original identification as the Kritērion—the law court where the legendary king Danaus supposedly prosecuted his daughter Hypermestra for not assassinating her husband (Paus. 2.20.7)—is unconfirmed by any archaeological or epigraphic evidence (Marchetti and Rizakis 1995: 439–40).

The earliest public building to be constructed in the agora is known as the Hypostyle Hall, a large square building with sides of 32.75 m and a roof supported by 16 internal Ionic columns, with a Doric colonnade on its east side. It has been interpreted as the *bouleutērion* of the city, and its construction c. 460 may coincide with the establishment of democracy at Argos (see Section 1.5.4). The decision, however, to create a designated open space at the foot of the Larisa in a formerly marshy part of the city seems to have been taken at the beginning of the fifth century, to judge from the construction of a massive drain in the eastern part of the agora. Shortly after the middle of the fifth century, Building P, a large pi-shaped Doric structure, was built on the natural hillock above the remains of the seventh-century administrative buildings. At about the same time, the "Theater with Square Steps" was constructed on the Pron; with a capacity of 2,300–2,500 persons, it is identified as the Aliaia (Ἁλιαία), which was the site of meetings of the popular assembly (Ginouvès 1972; Piérart and Touchais 1996: 47–52).

## *1.5. Political History*
### 1.5.1. Early Colonies

According to tradition, the Argives had already established colonies on Rhodes (Thuc. 7.57.6; Pind. *Ol.* 7.19), Cyprus (Hdt. 5.113.1; Strabo 14.6.3), Crete (Ephorus *FGrH* 70 F146; Diod. *Sic.* 5.80.3; Strabo 14.2.6), and at Aspendos in Pamphylia (Strabo 14.4.2) by the Late Bronze Age, although our literary evidence for these foundations does not predate the fifth century. By contrast, and unlike neighboring Corinth, Argos is not credited with having established colonies in the eighth or seventh century. There was, however, a tradition known to the early-fifth-century historian Hippys of Rhegium (*FGrH* 554 F4) that a certain Pollis of Argos became the "king" (*basileus*) of Syracuse. The historicity of this notice is difficult to establish (De Angelis 2016: 147), though the "Fusco kraters" found in burials at Syracuse certainly suggest Argive influence (see Section 1.4.3).

### 1.5.2. Argive Hereditary Kings: The Temenids

Ancient authors believed that early Argos was ruled by hereditary kings, who traced their dynasty back to Temenos, one of Heracles' descendants (the Heraclidae), who ostensibly led the Dorians into the Peloponnese during what we would call the Early Iron Age (Pind. *Pyth.* 5.70; Paus. 4.3.3; Apollod. *Bibl.* 2.8.4–5). Indeed, Aristotle (*Pol.* 1297b) evidently took it for granted that kingship had preceded warrior aristocracies throughout much of Greece. Elsewhere in the *Politics* (1310b), he observes that Pheidon established himself as tyrant of Argos when he was already serving as king. Pausanias offers only fragmentary information about the kings of Argos; he notes, for example, that at around the time of the First Messenian War, the Argives attacked the city of Asine under their king Eratos (2.36.4), whereas toward the end of the Second Messenian War, Nauplia was attacked by the Argives under a king named Damokratidas (4.35.2; cf. 4.24.4; Tomlinson 1972: 68; Drews 1983: 61–2; see Section 1.7.2).

26    THE OXFORD HISTORY OF THE ARCHAIC GREEK WORLD

It is, however, the end of kingship at Argos that attracted the most interest among later authors. According to Pausanias (2.19.2), "the Argives, just as they loved equality and independence right from the earliest times, reduced to the minimum the scope of the kings' power so that to Medon, son of Keisos, and his successors, only the name of kingship was left; but the people convicted Meltas, son of Lakedas and tenth in line from Medon, and deprived him completely of power" (see Drews 1983: 65).[4] It is often assumed that Meltas is the unnamed king mentioned in a fragment of Diodorus (7.13.2) and that both Diodorus' and Pausanias' accounts derive ultimately from Ephorus (Tomlinson 1972: 84; Carlier 1984: 385). What Diodorus says is that the Argives were faring badly in a war against the Spartans but managed to restore the Arcadians to their ancestral lands.[5] Afterward, the Argive people, indignant that land was being given to exiles rather than divided into lots and shared among themselves, blamed their king, who was forced into exile at Tegea. In another fragment (7.14), Diodorus explains that the kingship at Argos lasted 549 years. Ephorus seems to have dated the return of the Heraclidae and the establishment of Temenos' rule at Argos to 1069, which would mean that the Argive kingship was abolished in 520. However, Carlier (1984: 386) justly cautioned that Diodorus may have been referring to the legendary dynasty of Argive kings from Inachus to Triopas rather than the Temenids. Forrest (1960: 225–6) suggests that Meltas was expelled c. 600, while Kelly (1976: 133) dates the event to the second quarter of the sixth century.

The problem is that kings continue to be attested after Meltas. Plutarch (*Mor.* 340c) recounts how after the Heraclid (Temenid) line had been extinguished, the Argives, prompted by an omen, chose Aigon as their king. Huxley (1958: 598) argued that Meltas was simply the last Temenid king of Argos rather than the last king tout court, though that is not what Pausanias implies. Carlier (1984: 394; cf. Tuci 2006: 216) has hypothesized that with the expulsion of Meltas, the Argives switched from a hereditary to an elective monarchy. Herodotus (7.149) also suggests the existence of an Argive king c. 480. When requested by an embassy of Greek cities to join in the defense of Greece against the Persians, the Argives replied that they would be willing to contribute forces if they could secure a 30-year peace with Sparta and be granted joint command of the coalition. In response, the Spartan delegates pointed out that the best the Argives could hope for was a one-third share in the command, "because they themselves had two kings whereas the Argives had only one." The fact that Herodotus has "forgotten"

---

4. All translations are my own.

5. It is unclear whether the Arcadians are thought of as allies of the Argives or—as Kelly (1976: 136) argues—of the Spartans.

that ever since 506, the Spartans had sent only one of their kings out on campaign (5.75) hardly detracts from the assumption that his audience was presumably familiar with the existence of a king at Argos (Carlier 1984: 381). Finally, a treaty between Argos, Knossos, and Tylissos (Meiggs and Lewis 1988: #42), dated to c. 450, was concluded "when Melantas was king." Kelly (1976: 138) has attempted to resolve these difficulties by supposing that the kingship, suspended shortly before 550, had been reintroduced by the fifth century, but perhaps too much credence has been given to the literary sources for Argive kingship.

It is not simply that much of the testimony for the Argive kingship derives from late authors. The fact of the matter is that there is no independent confirmation either from epigraphy (save for the single example from c. 450) or from archaeology. There are certainly relatively wealthy graves at Argos, at least in the eighth century (see Section 1.4.2), but none that is truly exceptional (Foley 1988: 37); no royal burials, let alone dynastic cemeteries, have been identified to date. The key to the conundrum may reside in terminology.

By the Classical period, the Greeks regularly used the word *basileus* to denote a hereditary monarch, especially the ruler of a non-Greek people. But a linguistic ancestor of the word, *pa-si-re-u* or *qa-si-re-u*, already appears in the Linear B tablets of the Mycenaean palaces, where it describes a relatively low-ranking local official. When it makes its next appearance, in the Homeric epics, *basileus* clearly has a meaning rather different from our modern understanding of kingship. First, there were relative gradations to the authority of *basileis*: in the *Iliad* (9.69), Nestor describes Agamemnon as βασιλεύτατος ("the most *basileus*"), while Agamemnon himself notes that he is βασιλεύτερος ("more of a *basileus*") than Achilles (9.160). Second, there appears to be a plurality of *basileis*: the suitor Antinous remarks that there are "many other *basileis* of the Achaeans in sea-girt Ithaca, both young and old" (*Od.* 1.394–5), and Alcinous notes that the Phaeacians have "twelve distinguished *basileis* who bear sway as leaders in the region, and I myself am the thirteenth;" (*Od.* 8.390–1). Hesiod, too, talks about *basileis* in the plural (*Op.* 88, 429–30). Third, while there may be an expectation of filial succession, there is no guarantee—as Telemachus discovers. Homeric *basileis*, then, are not so much kings as something between a "big man" and a chieftain—leaders whose authority is "achieved" by means of charisma, military prowess, generosity, and the ability to persuade, rather than "ascribed" through the office they hold (Qviller 1981; Donlan 1985; Whitley 1991; Hall 2014b: 127–34).

This situation matches well with the archaeological record of eighth-century Argos. Contrary to what is sometimes written (e.g., Whitley 2001: 96), warrior graves are not especially common: the "Panoply" Tomb 45 (see Section 1.4.2) continues to be unparalleled in this period. A second bronze helmet, perhaps manufactured by the same workshop that was responsible for the helmet in

Tomb 45, was found in a grave in the Stavropoulos Plot (Protonotariou-Deïlaki 1971: 81–2), but the Stavropoulos Plot is more than 1 km away and almost certainly belongs to a separate village-like community. Not far from this second grave, in the Theodoropoulos Plot, a third grave yielded evidence for another helmet as well as two spearheads and six *obeloi* (Deïlaki 1973: 99), but this grave probably dates to approximately one generation before the burial in the Stavropoulos Plot. Beyond these, a handful of graves with spearheads, swords, or daggers constitute largely isolated occurrences. It is, then, tempting to regard eighth-century Argive *basileis* more as chieftains or warlords, exercising an "achieved" authority over small, village-like communities (Tomlinson 1972: 68). Whether one of these was named Eratos and whether he launched a raid against Asine is, of course, impossible to know with any certainty.

At some point, however, the memory of these chieftain-like *basileis* seems to have become confused with the establishment of a fixed, "ascribed" magistracy carrying the same name. Similar magistracies with the name *basileus* are attested on Chios by at least the mid-sixth century (Meiggs and Lewis 1988: #8) and at Athens by c. 620, if the late-fifth-century republication of Draco's homicide law (Meiggs and Lewis 1988: #86) faithfully follows the original. By the Classical period, the Athenian *basileus* was the second-highest-ranking of the nine archons, charged with administering "all the traditional sacrifices" (Arist. [*Ath. Pol.*] 57.1). The assumption that the magistracy represents the vestiges of an abolished hereditary monarchy is quite unnecessary, given that there is no more evidence for this at Athens than there is at Argos.[6] Melantas, who is named as *basileus* in the mid-fifth-century treaty between Argos, Knossos, and Tylissos, was almost certainly an official similar to the archon *basileus* at Athens, probably with religious responsibilities (Tomlinson 1972: 196; Jeffery 1990: 157 n. 1). Whether he also had military responsibilities (Drews 1983: 62; Carlier 1984: 392) or whether this is an assumption derived from the traditions related to earlier, warlike chieftains is difficult to know. Since military actions were always accompanied by ritual, perhaps the distinction is artificial. Carlier (1984: 382) notes that Melantas is not identified by his tribe (as is Lykotadas, the president of the assembly) or by his phratry (as is Archistratos, the president of the council) and takes this to indicate that the magistracy of *basileus* did not rotate among the tribes and might therefore be of long duration or even for life. On the other hand, identification practices do not at this period seem to have followed any set formula, so it is perhaps inadvisable to push the evidence too far. The *basileus* who is invoked in

---

6. Similarly, at Rome, the existence of the Rex Sacrorum is often—though possibly quite erroneously—taken as evidence for the fundamental trustworthiness of the traditions relating to the seven kings. (Hall 2014a: 150–4).

Herodotus' account of the embassy to Argos (7.149) denotes, I would suggest, the same office that Melantas would later hold. In fact, since it is scarcely credible that the Spartans would have entertained for even one moment the prospect of yielding one-third of their command to the Argives, their retort is probably best understood as an example of proverbial Spartan humor.

Melantas is the last individual to be named as *basileus*. No *basileus* is named by Thucydides (5.47) in connection with the 100-year treaty that the Argives contracted with the Athenians, Eleians, and Mantineians in 420. In an inscribed casualty list dating to the end of the fifth century (Kritzas 1980), we find, alongside an ἱαρεύς (priest), a στρατηγός (general), and a μάντις (prophet), not a βασιλεύς but a προβασιλεύς (i.e., someone who acts "on behalf of" or perhaps "instead of" the *basileus*). The fact that the προβασιλεύς seems to have religious competences, even outranking the στρατηγός (Carlier 1984: 383–4), might lend support to the religious nature of the earlier office of *basileus*. But the change in name is intriguing. Had the office of *basileus* been suspended or abolished? Had it been so discredited that it was deemed necessary to avoid using the name? Was Melantas blamed for this, and is Pausanias' story about Meltas, whether or not he is to be equated with Diodorus' king who fled to Tegea, simply a "badly distorted recollection" of Melantas (Drews 1983: 66)? Either way, the literary tradition concerning Argive kingship is, I would suggest, fundamentally unreliable. Pausanias' account about Medon and Meltas is framed within a story about the primeval disposition of the Argives toward equality and independence and, as such, can only have arisen after the introduction of democracy in the mid-fifth century (Carlier 1984: 385).

## 1.5.3. Tyranny at Argos

Mention has already been made of the tyrant Pheidon. Although our sources offer a wealth of information about him, they are utterly irreconcilable when it comes to determining when he ruled or what he achieved (Foley 1995: 84–5). Our earliest source, Herodotus (6.127.3), says that he "introduced measures for the Peloponnesians" and was "by far the most arrogant of all the Greeks, because he dismissed the Eleian umpires and administered the contest in Olympia himself." The occasion for this notice is Herodotus' account of the competition for the hand of Agariste, daughter of the Sicyonian tyrant Cleisthenes; among the suitors was Pheidon's son Leokedes. Since the wedding of Agariste is conventionally placed c. 570, this testimony would suggest that Pheidon ruled at Argos in the late seventh or early sixth century. Ephorus (*FGrH* 70 F176) notes that Pheidon struck the first silver coins on the island of Aegina—a detail that is repeated by the *Etymologicum Magnum* (s.v. ὀβελίσκος), which goes on to say that, after issuing the coinage, he dedicated to Argive Hera the bronze or copper spits (*obeliskoi*) that had previously been used as a type of monetary currency. The "turtles" of Aegina represent one of the earliest coinages of Greece. If one accepts a high date of c. 580–570 for their emission, then this would not be incompatible with Herodotus' date for Pheidon. But they could be several decades later, and it is not, in any case, clear why Pheidon should be minting on Aegina rather than at Argos, where coinage does not appear until the early fifth century (Kagan 1960: 136; Kelly 1976: 104). Nor is it at all certain that the large number of spits discovered at the Argive Heraion should be associated with Pheidon's removal from circulation of an earlier currency, as Carlier (Carlier 1984: 387–8) suggests, since these are of iron, not copper or bronze (see Section 1.8).

Elsewhere, Ephorus (*FGrH* 70 F115) refers to Pheidon introducing measures, as well as new weight standards and silver coins. He also goes into more detail about Pheidon's usurpation of the Olympic Games, describing it as a pattern of violence whereby the tyrant attacked *poleis* that he claimed had originally been captured by his ancestor Heracles. Furthermore, he is said to have deprived the Spartans of the hegemony they had formerly exercised over the Peloponnesians. But Ephorus also claims that Pheidon was "tenth in line from Temenos," which would date him to around the middle of the eighth century (Carlier 1984: 386 n. 67). This earlier date aligns with that of Pausanias (6.22.2), who says that the people of Pisa (the region surrounding Olympia) invited Pheidon of Argos, "the most violent of the tyrants of Greece," to help them celebrate the eighth Olympiad of 748. Huxley (1958: 588; cf. Koiv 2003: 239–97) defended an eighth-century date for Pheidon because he argued that this was when Argos was at its most prosperous, at least to judge from the archaeological record. We have, however, already had reason to note that the apparent impoverishment of Argos in the seventh century may be an archaeological mirage (see Section 1.4.1).

Carlier (1984: 389) has sought to reconcile the two dates by appealing to an older theory put forward by Lenschau (1936), according to which the Olympic Games were celebrated annually from 632 to 584 and then every four years thereafter. On this reckoning, Pausanias' eighth Olympiad would actually fall in 625, somewhat closer in time to Herodotus' date for Pheidon. But not only do such ingenious calculations ignore the possibly dubious historicity of the earlier entries in the Olympic victors' lists (Christesen 2007: 45–160), they also fail to address the testimony of Ephorus and several other authors, who posit a much earlier date for Pheidon. Plutarch (*Mor.* 772d–773b), for example, dates Pheidon to two generations before the foundation of Syracuse in 733, which is reconcilable with Eusebius' date of 1,220 years after Abraham (= 796 BCE). The mid-third-century Marmor Parium (*FGrH* 239 F30), on the other hand, dates Pheidon to 895/4, perhaps influenced in part by Theopompus' claim (*FGrH* 115 F393) that Pheidon was not tenth but fifth in line from Temenos—though this genealogy was probably coined for the benefit of the ruling Argead family of Macedonia, which, from at least the early fifth century, claimed descent from Temenos (Drews 1983: 67–8).

To make matters worse, some scholars have suggested an entirely different date for Pheidon's activities (e.g., Andrewes 1956: 36–41; Kagan 1960: 127; Tomlinson 1972: 81–2). As we have seen, Pausanias mentions collusion between Pheidon and the Pisatans, and Eusebius says that the Pisatans celebrated the 28th Olympiad of 668. Since Strabo (8.3.30) says that the games were celebrated without interruption by the Eleians down to 672, it has been suggested that Pausanias' "eighth" Olympiad is actually an error of transmission and that the text should instead be emended to read "28th." Furthermore, it has been hypothesized that Pheidon's intervention at Olympia was made possible by his victory over the Spartans at Hysiae, a battle noted only by Pausanias (2.24.7), who dates it to the fourth year of the 27th Olympiad—that is, to 669. The chief stumbling block here, though, is that not a single author connects Pheidon with a victory over the Spartans. Although a date for Pheidon in the late seventh or early sixth century is probably the most likely (Kelly 1976: 111; Carlier 1984: 387–8; Billot 1989–1990: 65; Robinson 1997: 83; Ragone 2006: 30–5), it should be admitted that acceptance of any one of the dates offered for the tyrant automatically excludes some of the activities that tradition associates with his name (Hall 2014b: 154–64).

As noted earlier, Aristotle (*Pol.* 1310b) implies that Pheidon already had "royal power" (βασιλεία) when he seized power, and this may be one of the reasons he lists him among the earlier tyrants. But the idea that tyranny was an "unconstitutional" form of autocracy is almost certainly a creation of fourth-century political theory (Anderson 2003), meaning that it is difficult to understand what benefit tyranny would offer over monarchy in the Archaic period. In fact, it is entirely possible that Aristotle's source meant that Pheidon held the magistracy of the *basileus* when he aspired to greater power—especially if we are to date this to the early sixth century. In this respect, Pheidon resembles more the Ionian tyrants or Phalaris, tyrant of Acragas, who are said to have seized power after being chosen for the chief magistracies (ἐπὶ τὰς κυρίας ἀρχάς). His first order of business would have been to establish legitimacy, and it is not unreasonable to suppose that it was he who invented a lineage stretching back to Temenos, thereby retroactively establishing a dynastic succession that may never have existed hitherto. Interesting in this respect is Ephorus' statement (*FGrH* 70 F115) that Pheidon "recovered the entire lot (λῆξιν) of Temenos, which had been dispersed into a number of parts (εἰς πλείω μέρη)." This has usually been interpreted as meaning that Pheidon (re)captured neighboring cities in the Argive plain and possibly the eastern Argolid that were thought to have originally been assigned to Temenos when the Peloponnese was divided up among the Heraclidae (Tomlinson 1972: 82; Billot

32    THE OXFORD HISTORY OF THE ARCHAIC GREEK WORLD

1989–1990: 65). But if this was his aspiration, it is far from clear that it was ever realized (see Section 1.7.2). Furthermore, in the earliest version that we have of the partition of the Peloponnese (Pind. *Pyth.* 5.70), it is not the territories of the Argolid, Laconia, and Messenia that are assigned to the Heraclidae but the cities of Argos, Lacedaemon, and Pylos. There are, then, reasons to suppose that λῆξις here does not mean "that which is won by lot"—a meaning that would eventually win out in stories that told of Kresphontes' deceit in winning Messenia (Paus. 4.3.4–6; Apollod. *Bibl.* 2.8.4)—but has its more specialized meaning of "that which is apportioned by inheritance," especially since the word μέρος can also mean "inheritance" (Hall 1995: 586–7). In other words, the "lot of Temenos" is really about establishing sole claims to legitimacy.

Little is known of Pheidon's end. The late-first-century historian Nicolaus of Damascus (*FGrH* 90 F35) says that "a" Pheidon—it is unclear whether the Argive tyrant is intended—was killed while assisting some Corinthians in a revolt. Plutarch (*Mor.* 772d) relates how Pheidon interfered in Corinthian affairs but does not say that this resulted in his death. Elsewhere, he mentions an Argive *basileus* named Lacydes, who was accused of effeminacy because of his hairstyle and the way he walked (*Mor.* 89e). If this Lacydes is the same as Herodotus' Leokedes, son of Pheidon, then the story might represent an a posteriori justification for the suppression of one-man rule (Carlier 1984: 393), but that is mere conjecture. Thanks to two inscriptions, however, we do at least have some idea as to how Argos was governed in the middle decades of the sixth century.

The first (*IG* IV.614; Jeffery 1990: 168 #7; van Effenterre and Ruzé 1994–1995: vol. 1: #87), built into the southern wall of the Larisa fortress, had been visible to travelers since at least the 18th century CE; Gell (1817: 166), for example, discusses an inscription "in very ancient characters" under a circular tower. The heading, in boustrophedon, reads: ἐνν[έϝα δ]αμιοργοὶ ἐϝ | [αν]άσσαντο ("nine *damiorgoi* ruled"). There then follows a list of nine names: Potamos; Sthenelas, son of Echedamidas; Hipomedon; Charon, son of Archesilas; Adrastus; Orthagoras; Ktetos, son of Minton; Aristomachos; and Ichonidas. The inscription is dated by Jeffery to c. 575–550. Vollgraff (1928: 321–3; 1931–1932: 377–92) was struck by the fact that at least four of the names recall legendary Argive kings: Sthenelas (which might be a variation of Sthenelus), who was the leader, along with Diomedes and Euryalos, of the Argive contingent in the Catalog of Ships (Hom. *Il.* 2.563–5); Hippomedon, who was a king of Lerna (Eur. *Phoen.* 126); Adrastus, the leader of the doomed expedition against Thebes, whose cult Cleisthenes of Sicyon is said to have expelled at about the same time as this inscription was commissioned (Hdt. 5.67); and Aristomachos, son of Kleodaios and father of Temenos (Paus. 2.7.6). Vollgraff concluded that the inscription listed earlier legendary rulers of Argos, with Potamos ("the river") standing in for Inachus, the first king of the

Argives (Acusilaus *FGrH* 2 F23c), and that it might even have been Pheidon himself who set up the inscription in order to justify his ancestral right to rule (cf. Carlier 1984: 394).

There are, however, difficulties with this interpretation. First, three individuals named Sthenelus or Sthenelas are attested in Argive myth: apart from Diomedes' co-ruler, who is described as the son of Capaneus, there is Sthenelas, son of Krotopos, and Sthenelus, son of Perseus (Hall 1997b: 84–5 figs. 9–10). No Sthenelas, son of Echedamidas, is known (Hammond 1960: 34). Second, the order in which the names appear in *IG* IV.614 does not match the Argive genealogies at all. Even if we take Sthenelas to be the son of Krotopos, seven generations intervene between him and Inachus. If, on the other hand, we associate him with the more famous leader of Argos at the time of the Trojan War, then his name should appear after, not before, that of Adrastus. Third, it is difficult to account for why three of the names should have patronymics if this is a list of well-known legendary rulers of Argos. That leading men of the sixth century might have been named after heroic figures is not unimaginable, given the known propensity of the Argives for overvaluing their past and blurring the distinction between myth and history. It is, then, preferable to see this as a list of contemporary *damiorgoi*— a name that the *Etymologicum Magnum* (s.v. δημιουργός) says was given to "those who exercise office among the Argives and the Thessalians." The fact that they are described as "ruling" (ἐϝανάσσαντο) would indicate that they are the most important magistrates at Argos. To judge from a seventh-century law from Dreros (Meiggs and Lewis 1988: #2) or a sixth-century law from Gortyn (*IC* 4.14), the office was probably held for one year with some limitations on iteration. The question is whether *IG* IV.614 lists the names of single *damiorgoi* ruling over a span of nine consecutive years or a board of nine *damiorgoi* ruling jointly in a single year. Jeffery (1990: 156–7) preferred the former, largely because ἐϝανάσσαντο is in the aorist, rather than the imperfect tense, though her suggestion that the list is of former *damiorgoi* who were elected *basileus* in nine consecutive years is perhaps a little forced. Most scholars, however, prefer to see the inscription as evidence for a board of nine co-ruling *damiorgoi*, akin to the nine archons of Athens (Hammond 1960; Wörrle 1964: 61–70; Kelly 1976: 69, 131–2; Drews 1983: 58–9; van Effenterre and Ruzé 1994–1995: vol. 1: #87–8; Tuci 2006: 213).

The latter interpretation finds some confirmation in another inscription (*SEG* 11.314; Vollgraff 1929; Jeffery 1990: 168 #8; van Effenterre and Ruzé 1994–1995: vol. 1: #88), also dated to c. 575–550, which was discovered in 1928 built into the west wall of the Larisa fortress. The text, which is written in boustrophedon, relates to the consecration of objects to Athena Polias (see Sections 1.6 and 1.11.1.1), and begins by stating ἐπὶ τονδεονὲν δαμιοργόντον ("when these were *damiorgoi*"). A list of six names, running down the left side of the block, is appended: Syleus, Eratuios, Polyktor, Exakesto[s], Hagi[-], and Eryko[iros]. Here there can be no question that we are dealing with a plurality of *damiorgoi*, though it is troubling that they are six, rather than nine, in number (Jeffery 1990: 158). Perhaps the number of *damiorgoi* had been revised at some point within the second quarter of the sixth century (Carlier 1984: 394; van Effenterre and Ruzé 1994–1995: vol. 1: #87–9), or this reflects a period of instability in the wake of the tyranny (Kelly 1976: 133–4). Alternatively, it could be that there was a distinction at Argos between three senior and six junior magistrates, just as at Athens the eponymous archon, the archon *basileus*, and the *polemarchos* were considered more senior than the six θεσμοθέται. At Athens, the archon *basileus* was the second-highest-ranking official, but unless the office of *basileus* was suspended and then reintroduced by the time of the Persian War (see Section 1.5.2), it is entirely possible that at Argos, it denoted the paramount *damiorgos*. Either way, the fact that the chief magistrates at Argos were known by a name derived from *damos* ("people") may not be insignificant. Huxley (1958: 600) interpreted it as a democratic reaction to Temenid rule in the mid-seventh century, but that seems rather anachronistic. More likely, it was simply intended to signify a break from the autocracy of a single individual—perhaps Pheidon himself.

### 1.5.4. Argive Political Offices

We are remarkably well informed about Argive administration in the Classical period, thanks to a chance find made in 2000–2001 in the basement of a structure at 48 Korinthou Street. In an area that had been used for both burial and settlement in the Middle Geometric period, a structure was built in the sixth or fifth century that has been interpreted as belonging to a sanctuary. More specifically, the excavated part of the building served as storage for public documents that had been inscribed on 134 thin bronze plaques and deposited in a bronze kratēr, a terracotta kratēr, and a stone chest (Papadimitriou 2013). The plaques, most of which date to the second half or the end of the fifth century, concern the transactions of what is effectively a state treasury under the patronage of Pallas Athena and testify to a number of magistracies and institutions. Some are known from slightly earlier sources: for instance, the *stratēgoi* (generals) or the Council of 80 that, according to Thucydides (5.47.9), swore to the terms of the alliance with Athens, Elis, and Mantinea in 420 and that the new inscriptions tell us was divided into eight groups and assisted by two secretaries. Similarly, the four *hiaromnamones* of Hera are first attested in a mid-fifth-century decree found in the agora at Argos (van Effenterre and Ruzé 1994–1995: vol. 1: #110); from the treasury records, we learn that they were the supreme authority for religious affairs and that they were also responsible for consecrating silver arising from confiscations or sale of land belonging to those who were exiled or executed. A number of offices are, however, attested for the first time. These include the ἐπιγνώμονες, financial officials of whom there were eight; four haϝεθλοθέται, responsible for financing the Hekatombaia Games in honor of Hera; and various relatively obscure titles such as the ἀνελατῆρες, the ὁδωτῆρες, or the κριθοχύται. Interestingly, most of the magistracies, with the notable exception of the *hiaromnamones*, are semestral rather than annual (Kritzas 2006; Kritzas 2013).

We are not yet in a position to know how many of these offices and institutions date back to the Archaic period. The Council of 80 is not attested before 420, although many have suspected that it originated as an aristocratic council akin to the Areopagus at Athens, in which case it may have played a part in the governance of the city in the sixth century, alongside the *damiorgoi* and, presumably, the *aliaia* or assembly (Tomlinson 1972: 196; Piérart 2004c: 168). But if, as many believe, it was constituted by 20 representatives from each of the four tribes and if there was a tribal reform in the 460s (Piérart 1997: 333; Piérart 2000: 307; see Section 1.5.5), then the fifth-century Council of 80 would have to be a reconstituted version of any Archaic predecessor. Piérart (2000: 304–5) suggests that it was a body that existed independently of the popular council (βωλά) rather than constituting a section of it (i.e., the equivalent of the Athenian prytany).

In his account of events in 481, immediately prior to the Persian War, Herodotus (7.148–9) refers to an Argive βουλή. The Doric form for this word is βωλά (Tuci 2006: 219–20). The earliest epigraphic reference to a βωλά is on a bronze plaque of much-discussed provenance (*IG* IV.554; van Effenterre and Ruzé 1994–1995: vol. 1: #107), dated to 480–470, that deals with the procedures to be adopted if the treasury of Athena is used for the city's needs. Unreliable reports said that the inscription had been found at Hermione, but on the basis of its letter forms, Jeffery (1990: 161) preferred to assign it to Argos. Jameson's (1974) attempt to reassign it to Halieis was not universally accepted (Brandt 1992; Billot 1997–1998: 23), and the archaeological confirmation of a treasury to Pallas Athena within the city of Argos now makes it highly probable that this is the treasury to which *IG* IV.554 refers (Kritzas 2013: 282). Although the inscription makes no mention of the *damiorgoi*, there is a reference to officials named the *sunartunai* (συναρτύοντες, l.2). In his description of the peace of 420, Thucydides (5.47.9) recounts that the oath was taken by the Council of 80 alongside the *aliaia* and the *artynai*, which suggested to Tomlinson (1972: 198) that the office of *damiorgos* was replaced by that of the *(sun)artunai*—though *damiorgoi* are later attested at Hellenistic Mycenae (*IG* IV.497), which was by then a dependency of Argos (Piérart 2000: 301–2). That the *damiorgia* at Argos had been abolished by the middle of the fifth century is almost certainly correct—it does not appear in the treaty between Argos, Knossos, and Tylissos (Meiggs and Lewis 1988: #42)

36 THE OXFORD HISTORY OF THE ARCHAIC GREEK WORLD

or in the new treasury inscriptions—but these inscriptions also make it clear that the term ἀρτῦναι did not designate specific officials but was a generic term for all political offices, akin to the Athenian *archai* (Kritzas 2013: 284; cf. Piérart 2000: 305).

At some point in the fifth century, there seems to have been a change of political regime at Argos. Gehrke (1985: 361–3) believes that democratic reforms were introduced at Argos shortly after 490, perhaps as a consequence of the crushing defeat at Sepeia (see Section 1.7.4). Piérart (1997: 333), on the other hand, partly by analogy with the reforms of Cleisthenes at Athens, connects the introduction of democracy to a repartition of land and reorganization of the tribal structure that he dates to 470–460. If *IG* IV.554, with its attestation of the βωλά and omission of the *damiorgoi*, is correctly assigned to Argos, then this might suggest that the process of democratization extended over a period of time but commenced rather earlier than Piérart believes (Wörrle 1964: 70–2). It was clearly well under way by the time of publication of an inscribed bronze plaque (*SEG* 13.239; Jeffery 1990: 169 #22; van Effenterre and Ruzé 1994–1995: vol. 1: #35), found in the agora of Argos and possibly dating to the 470s (Forrest 1960: 226 n. 8). The inscription not only refers to the Argive *aliaia* but also records that it was the authority that took the decision to award a grant of *proxenia* to Gnosstas of Laconian Oinous.[7]

## 1.5.5. Divisions of the Citizen Body and Noncitizen Groups

By the Classical period, Argive citizens were distributed among four *phylai* or "tribes"—the three "Dorian" *phylai* of the Hylleis, Pamphyloi, and Dymanes together with the Hyrnathioi. It is normally assumed that the three Dorian *phylai*, which match those attested at Sparta in the seventh century (Tyrtaeus F19 West), were in existence from an early date, while the Hyrnathioi were added either at the time of Pheidon (Tomlinson 1972: 189) or after the defeat at Sepeia (Hammond 1960: 33–6; Tuci 2006: 229; see Section 1.7.4). In fact, the evidence is far more equivocal. Herodotus' statement (5.68.1) that Cleisthenes of Sicyon "gave other names to the Dorian tribes so that those at Sicyon should not be the same as those at Argos" ought to imply the existence at Argos of the three Dorian *phylai* in the early sixth century, but there is no contemporary confirmation in the epigraphic record of Argos, and Herodotus' account of Cleisthenes can hardly be taken at face value (Hall 2014b: 211–13). The attestation of nine (*IG* IV.614) and then six (*SEG* 11.314) *damiorgoi* in sixth-century Argos *might* be taken as evidence for the existence of three *phylai* (Wörrle 1964: 61–70; Lotze 1971: 104;

---

7. The exact location of Oinous remains unknown.

Tuci 2006: 214), but contemporary Athens had nine archons for four *phylai* (Koiv 2003: 221), and none of the names listed on the Argive documents is assigned to a *phylē*. The earliest inscribed document to mention the Hylleis is a bronze plaque dated to 575–550 and found at the Argive Heraion (*IG* IV.506; Jeffery 1990: 169 #25; van Effenterre and Ruzé 1994–1995: vol. 1: #100). Nevertheless, there are some doubts that the Heraion was under exclusive Argive control at this time (see Section 1.11.3), so the inscription may not tell us about social organization at Argos itself. Indeed, it may be telling that a later inscription (*IG* IV.517; van Effenterre and Ruzé 1994–1995: vol. 1: #86) found at the Heraion and dating to c. 460–450 lists the *phylai* in a completely different order (Dymanes–Hylleis–Hyrnathioi–Pamphyloi) from that in which they are normally recorded in inscriptions from Argos (Hylleis–Pamphyloi–Hyrnathioi–Dymanes; see Piérart 2000: 298). In this case, the observation that four *hiaromnamones*—perhaps, but not necessarily, indicating the existence of four *phylai*—are attested at the Heraion in the first quarter of the fifth century (Jeffery 1990: #16777; Piérart 2004c: 167–8) need not be entirely relevant to the situation at Argos.

At Argos itself, the earliest reference to a named *phylē* is the proxeny decree for Gnosstas of Laconian Oinous (*SEG* 13.239; Jeffery 1990: 169 #22; van Effenterre and Ruzé 1994–1995: vol. 1: #35), dated to c. 475–450, which notes that the president of the *aliaia* was Epicrates, son of Rinon, of the Pamphyloi. At about the same time, it is clear that each of the four *phylai* was subdivided into twelve phratries, from which time Argive citizens tended to be designated by their name, patronymic, and phratronym but not phyletic (Kritzas 1980; Kritzas 1992; Piérart 1983; Charneux 1984; Piérart 1985; Piérart 1997: 332–4; Piérart 2000: 298–9; Piérart 2004c: 168; Piérart 2004b: 25). The institutional reform by which the phratries were created is normally attributed to the synoecism of the plain (see Section 1.7.2), though parallels from Sicyon, Cyrene, and perhaps even Athens suggest that tribal reform is itself often triggered by the acquisition of new territory (Anderson 2003: 13–42; Hall 2014b: 249). It is entirely possible that the Argive citizen body was divided among the three Dorian *phylai* in the sixth century and that the fourth *phylē* of the Hyrnathioi was added c. 460–450, along with the subdivisions into phratries. But given the lack of evidence, we cannot rule out the possibility that all four *phylai* resulted from a wide-ranging tribal reform shortly before the middle of the fifth century.

Finally, the second-century CE scholar Pollux (*Onom.* 3.83) describes a group named the γυμνῆτες as possessing a status "between free men and slaves," akin to the Laconian Helots or the Thessalian penestae. Some (e.g., Lotze 1959; Willetts 1959; Tomlinson 1972: 97–9; van Compernolle 1975: 360–1; Piérart 2004c: 177–8) have supposed that the γυμνῆτες were agricultural serfs, perhaps to be equated with Herodotus' δοῦλοι (6.83). However, Stephanus of Byzantium (s.v. Χίος), who names them γυμνήσιοι, implies that they were attendants, and other occurrences of the term seem to suggest that they served as light-armed soldiers. No other author mentions them in connection with Argos.

## 1.6. Legal History

No tradition of lawgivers or codifications of law is associated with Argos. For the Archaic period, the only attested laws are inscribed religious ordinances and prohibitions. The earliest, dated to c. 600, comes not from Argos but from Tiryns and was carved in a serpentine manner on the covering slabs of two pipes that had been constructed to provision the citadel with water during the final phase of the Mycenaean palace (*SEG* 30.380; Verdelis, Jameson, and Papachristodoulou 1975; Koerner 1985; Jeffery 1990: 444; van Effenterre and Ruzé 1994–1995: vol. 1: #78). The law, which has been reconstructed from 23 fragments, resembles early laws from other parts of Greece in that it defines the jurisdiction and competences of officials named *platiwoinarchoi* (πλατιϝοινάρχοι) as well as the fines to be levied on them if they fail in their duties. As is often the case, the law is concerned primarily with procedural matters. Reference is made to a ἱαρομνάμων, charged with administering finances, and an ἐπιγνώμων, who issues judgments, as well as to a *damos* and an *aliaia*—both terms that indicate the existence of a popular assembly. Since the *damos* could choose where it met, it is likely that it was also empowered to take other decisions.

The earliest-known sacred law to originate from Argos was discovered built into the medieval fortifications on the Larisa (*SEG* 11.314; Jeffery 1990: 168 #8; van Effenterre and Ruzé 1994–1995: vol. 1: #88). Dating to c. 575–550, the law regulates the use of objects consecrated to Athena Polias, stipulating that an individual cannot use the inventoried material outside the temenos of Athena. Six *damiorgoi* are mentioned as enforcers of the law (see Section 1.5), as well as a temple official known as the ἀμφίπολος, who is "to attend to the matter." Of approximately the same date is a fragmentary bronze plaque, inscribed with a sacred law (*IG* IV.506; Jeffery 1990: 169 #25; van Effenterre and Ruzé 1994–1995: vol. 1: #100), that appears to prescribe exile and the confiscation of property as well as invoking the curses of Hera for anybody who ignores or alters the law written on the inscription. An official named the *progrophos* (πρόγροφος) is mentioned, and provision is taken for the possibility that there may not be a *damiorgos* (Gagarin 2008: 62–3; see Section 1.11.3). A similar situation is envisaged in a law from Mycenae (*IG* IV.493; Jeffery 1990: 174 #1; van Effenterre and Ruzé 1994–1995: vol 1: #101), dated to c. 525, which stipulates that, in the absence of the *damiorgos*, the *hiaromnamones* of the heroon (or fountain house?) of Perseus are to serve as judges. Finally, the bronze plaque (*IG* IV.554; van Effenterre and Ruzé 1994–1995: vol. 1: #107), whose provenance has been contested but which probably originates from Argos and dates to c. 480–470 (see Section 1.5.5), carries a law that requires the approval of the *aliaia* and the guarantee of immunity for anybody who uses the treasure of Athena for the needs of the city.

## *1.7. Diplomatic History*
### 1.7.1. Argos and Asine

The first recorded act of hostility involving Argos concerns the destruction of Asine. Pausanias, who is our principal source for the attack, says that the people of Asine lent aid to the Spartan king Nicander, son of Charillos, in an invasion of the Argolid; in retribution, the Argives under Eratos attacked Asine. Although the inhabitants of Asine resisted for a time and slew the Argive nobleman Lysistratus, their fortifications were eventually breached. The Asinaioi embarked their wives and children on boats and abandoned their territory while the Argives razed the city to the ground and annexed its territory to their own, sparing only the Sanctuary of Apollo Pythaeus, where they buried Lysistratus (2.36.4–5; cf. 3.7.4). Pausanias offers no precise date, though elsewhere (4.4.4; cf. Tyrtaeus F5 West) he says that Nicander's successor Theopompus was reigning when the First Messenian War broke out— an event that he dates to 743 (4.5.10). Later, in his description of Messenia, Pausanias recounts how a generation after being expelled from their homeland by the Argives, the Dryopes of Asine participated, under duress, in the First Messenian War (4.8.3). Afterward, the Spartans gave them the coastal part of Messenia, "which even now the Asinaioi inhabit" (4.14.3). Pausanias also tells us (4.34.9) that the Dryopes had originally lived beneath Mt. Parnassos near Delphi but were defeated by Heracles and taken to Delphi as offerings to Apollo, who ordered them to be settled at Argolic Asine. Elements of this story were perhaps already known in the fifth century. A hymn by Bacchylides (F4) in honor of Apollo Pythaeus talks about the Delphic oracle that ordered Heracles to settle the Dryopes at Asine, and when Herodotus (8.73) describes Argolic Hermione and "the Asine in front of Kardamyle in Laconia" as Dryopean cities, he presumably imagines that Argolic Asine was also originally inhabited by Dryopes (cf. Diod. *Sic.* 4.37.2; Strabo 8.6.13).

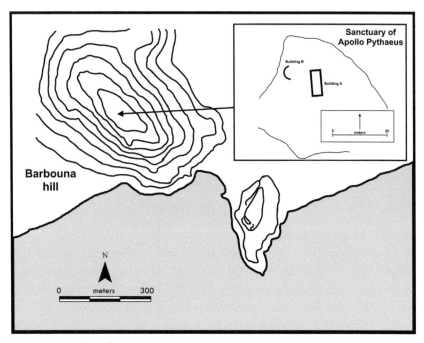

FIGURE 1.7. Plan of Asine.

What has deterred most scholars from simply dismissing the account is the fact that archaeology seems to offer at least partial confirmation of it. Swedish excavations on the Barbouna hill (see Figure 1.7) at Asine have found evidence that the walls that surrounded the summit collapsed as part of a violent destruction before the end of the Late Geometric phase. An apsidal building (Building B) on the summit of the hill, which is normally identified as the Temple of Apollo Pythaeus, was—contrary to Pausanias—also destroyed in Late Geometric IIB(c. 720–710), though it was replaced within a decade or two by the rectangular Building A, which continued in use until the beginning of the fifth century (Frödin and Persson 1938: 148; Wells 1987–1988: 349–52; Billot 1989–1990: 41; Wells 1990). Archaeology cannot, of course, reveal the identity of the aggressor, but it is highly suggestive that at about the time Asine was attacked, a sanctuary to Apollo Pythaeus was established on the southwest slope of the Prophetes Elias hill at Argos (Vollgraff 1956). From then on, the cult carried a markedly Argive character. In Bacchylides' hymn, it was originally introduced by the Argive seer Melampous; according to Pausanias (2.35.2), the fifth-century Argive poet Telesilla had told how the cult had been introduced directly to Argos by Pythaeus, son of Apollo; and Thucydides (5.53) recounts how by 419, the Argives controlled a cult of Apollo Pythaeus in which the Epidaurians—and perhaps the Troezenians (Diod. *Sic.* 12.78)—shared (Barrett 1954; Billot 1989–1990: 37–57; Tausend 1992: 9–12; Kowalzig 2007: 144–5).

Ratinaud-Lachkar (2004) has, it is true, cast doubt on the entire story, suggesting that it was Theopompus (cf. *FGrH* 115 F383) who first connected Argolic and Messenian Asine and that it was only the latter that was properly Dryopean. In her view, Bacchylides' reference (F4.47) to ἀσινεῖς does not refer to the inhabitants of Argolic Asine—who were more properly named Ἀσιναῖοι—but means that the Dryopes were rendered "harmless" by Heracles. In other words, there is nothing to connect the hymn to Argolic Asine as opposed to, say, Hermione, which is described as a Dryopean settlement in the fifth century (Hdt. 8.73). Although she accepts that Argos did annex the territory of Asine and usurp the cult of Apollo Pythaeus, she dates this not to the late eighth century but to the 460s. Most scholars, however, are less skeptical, even if they doubt Pausanias' explanation that the attack was provoked by Asine's participation in a Spartan invasion (see Section 1.7.4). For some, the dispute arose from ethnic differences (Billot 1989–1990: 37; Kowalzig 2007: 133–42); others view it within the context of Argive claims over the entire Argive plain, whether the attack on Asine was a warning shot (Kelly 1967; Kelly 1976: 64–6) or took place after communities such as Mycenae and Tiryns had already been conquered (Tomlinson 1972: 75).

## 1.7.2. Argive Plain

There is little scholarly consensus regarding the status of Argos' neighbors within the plain during the Archaic period. Matters are not helped by the fact that the toponym Argos could be used to describe the city, the Argive plain, the Peloponnese, or even Greece as a whole (Wathelet 1992). It is not always easy to distinguish when Argos is used to define the city and when it designates the plain (Brillante 2004: 37–8). One might suppose that this simply means that the Argive plain was coterminous with the extent of Argive territory, but matters are not so simple. Thus, while "Argos" is named as the domain of Diomedes in the Homeric epics (*Il.* 6.224, 14.119; *Od.* 3.180), it is also described as the kingdom of Agamemnon, based at Mycenae (*Il.* 1.30; 2.108, 115; 4.171; 9.141). Similarly, "Argos" normally denotes the city in the pseudo-Hesiodic *Catalog of Women*, but when the toponym is associated with the legendary king Proetus, who ruled at Tiryns (F37.10 Merkelbach-West), the entire Argive plain must be intended (Cingano 2004: 59). This ambiguity is why caution should be exercised in assuming too readily that Argos controlled Tiryns in the early sixth century simply because a number of authors (e.g., Apollod. *Bibl.* 2.3; Hyg. *Fab.* 124, 145.2; schol.

Eur. *Or.* 932; Paus. 2.16.1) made the Tirynthian hero Peiren/Peiras(os) the son of the eponymous hero Argos (Koiv 2003: 313–15).

It cannot be disputed that from the Early Iron Age onward, Argos was the largest and most important settlement in the plain, but whether this extended to absolute dominion over its neighbors is another matter. Pausanias (4.24.4; cf. Strabo 8.6.11) states that after the conclusion of the Second Messenian War, which he dates to 668 (4.23.4), the Spartans gave the territory of Messenian Mothone to the inhabitants of Nauplia, "who had recently been expelled from Nauplia by the Argives." Later (4.35.2) he adds that the Naupliotes had been expelled because of their pro-Spartan sympathies at a time when Damokratidas was *basileus* at Argos. Further support for the destruction of Nauplia has been sought in Strabo's description (8.6.14) of the Calaurian Amphictiony. According to the geographer, the amphictiony, based around the Sanctuary of Poseidon on Calauria, was a sacred league of seven cities: Hermione, Epidaurus, Aegina, Athens, Prasiai (in Cynuria), Nauplia, and Minyan Orchomenus (in Boeotia). He then adds that the Argives contributed on behalf of the inhabitants of Nauplia and the Spartans on behalf of the inhabitants of Prasiai, which might suggest that Argos acceded to membership following the destruction of Nauplia.

There has been considerable debate about the Calaurian Amphictiony. Müller (1817: 30–6) and Farnell (1896–1909: vol. 4: 10) thought that it was a Mycenaean trading league, partly because of the inclusion of Minyan Orchomenus. Kelly (1966; cf. Billot 1989–1990: 63–4), on the other hand, considered it a seventh-century defensive league against Argive expansionism— though his substitution of Arcadian Orchomenus for its Boeotian homonym creates as many problems as it solves. But the real problem regards whether this solitary literary notice deserves to be taken so seriously. Renewed Swedish excavations in the Sanctuary of Poseidon at Calauria have now revealed extensive cultic activity in the eighth century (Evely, Hall, Morgan, et al. 2008: 13) but no concrete evidence that would support the details of Strabo's notice. We know from an inscription (*IG* IV.842) that an amphictiony based on Calauria existed in the second century, but whereas it no doubt claimed an illustrious and deep pedigree, there is no independent evidence to support an Archaic predecessor (Hall 1995: 584–5; Piérart 1997: 347 n. 25). Furthermore, the similarity between the accounts about the destruction of Nauplia and the attack on Asine cannot but arouse suspicion. Both Asine and Nauplia occupied fortified promontories controlling the entrances to the Argolic Gulf, and the inhabitants of both were supposedly expelled by the Argives for their pro-Spartan tendencies and resettled a mere 40 km from one another, at Mothone and Asine in Messenia. In this case, archaeology offers no assistance, since overbuilding means that Archaic Nauplia is very poorly known (Foley 1995: 81). It was undoubtedly a casualty of the Argives at some point but not, perhaps, before the middle of the fifth century (Hall 1995: 583–4; Piérart 1997: 347 n. 28; Piérart 2006: 20–1).

### 1.7.3. Relationship of Argos with Mycenae and Tiryns

There are indications that Mycenae and Tiryns preserved some degree of independence for at least part, if not all, of the Archaic period. The appearance of an *aliaia* in the sacred law from Tiryns suggests strongly the existence of a sovereign popular assembly c. 600, which might, in turn, suggest political independence on the part of Tiryns (see Section 1.6). Furthermore, the inscription also attests to the presence at Tiryns of an official named an ἐπιγνώμων—a title not attested at Argos until the second half of the fifth century. Some support for that conclusion is offered by what purports to be a Delphic oracular response that is preserved in the *Greek Anthology* (14.73). The consultors—here the Megarians, though other versions concern the people of Aigion—have asked Apollo whom he deems to be the greatest of the Greeks, to which he responds: "Best of the whole earth is Pelasgian Argos, the horses of Thessaly, the women of Sparta, and the men who drink the water of fair Arethousa (the Chalcidians). But better still than these are those who dwell between Tiryns and Arcadia, rich in sheep—the Argives with their linen corselets, goads of war." The oracle is first cited by Ion of Chios in the fifth century but is clearly derived from an earlier, composite tradition. Suárez de la Torre (2004: 250–1) supposes that the first part belongs to a post-Homeric Chalcidian stratum, while the verses concerning Argos date to the seventh or sixth century. What is important here is that describing the Argives as living *between* Tiryns and Arcadia makes no sense if Tiryns was subordinate to Argos at the time (Kelly 1976: 129; Hall 1995: 587–8). Finally, an inscription found built into the Hellenistic Perseia Fountain House at Mycenae and dated to c. 525 stipulates that if there is no *damiorgos*, the *hiaromnamones* of Perseus are to serve as judges (*IG* IV.493; Jeffery 1990: 174 #1; van Effenterre and Ruzé 1994–1995: vol. 1: #101). Since Argos was governed by a board of either nine or six *damiorgoi* (see Sections 1.5.3 and 1.5.5), the reference to a single *damiorgos* seems to suggest that Mycenae had its own administration in this period.

Notwithstanding this, Piérart (1997: 334–6) prefers to imagine a hierarchized organization of the Argive plain whereby settlements such as Mycenae and Tiryns had some internal autonomy but were ultimately in a situation of dependency upon Argos similar to the relationship between the perioikic cities of Laconia and Sparta. He notes, for example, an inscribed lead plaque, found beneath the fifth-century Building P in the agora of Argos, which bears the name of "Gnathis, son of Aristoboulos; beautiful; Lyrkeieus" (i.e., from the town of Lyrkeion)—though why a citizen of an independent neighboring community would have any less reason than a *perioikos* to conduct business at Argos is not explained. Ultimately, however, Piérart's conclusion is based on what he sees as a cultural unity throughout the plain by c. 600, signaled through written scripts and myths (cf. Foley 1988: 127; Antonaccio 1992: 104). While there is a certain cultural uniformity throughout the plain in terms of scripts and, we might add, material culture (see Section 1.4.3)—which could, after all, be the consequence of itinerant craftsmen—there are also slight variations. So, for example, the sacred law from Tiryns reveals that the Tirynthian alphabet is practically identical to that employed at Argos (Verdelis, Jameson, and Papachristodoulou 1975: 187–8), but there are subtle distinctions between the script of Mycenae and that of Argos, including the fact that Mycenae had adopted the letter sigma at a time when Argos was still using san (Hall 1997b: 147–53). Furthermore, there are slight differences in dialect between Argos and Mycenae (Hall 1995: 610–1), with Argos preserving –ns– consonantal clusters (*IG* V.1.231: χρονσθο) and Mycenae simplifying them (*IG* IV.493: χροσ[θο]). There may also be slight variations in dedicatory behavior between the western and eastern sides of the plain, particularly relating to the deposition of pins and fibulas in graves and sanctuaries (Hall 1995: 606–7), though it has to be admitted that the sample is small (Boehringer 2001: 219–21). A similar argument has been made for early sixth-century kratēriskoi with female protomes, which are typical of communities on the eastern side of the plain but are thus far absent from Argos (Ekroth 2013).

It is, however, more difficult to maintain that both sides of the plain were integrated within a single mythographical system. Eastern communities such as Mycenae, Midea, and Tiryns promoted heroes belonging to the lineage of Perseus, which included Heracles. As we have seen, there were cultic officials (*hiaromnamones*) for Perseus at Mycenae by c. 525 (*IG* IV.493), and the sacred law from Tiryns attests either a sanctuary or a festival of Heracles by c. 600 (Verdelis, Jameson, and Papachristodoulou 1975: 182–3). At Argos, by contrast, it is the lineage of Proetus that is emphasized, especially the heroes who were said to have marched on Thebes under the Argive king Adrastus. That the Perseid and Proitid stemmata were competing, rather than complementary, genealogical traditions is suggested by the fact that both are said to have ruled over the entire plain (Hom. *Il.* 6.157–9; 19.122–4; Pind. *Nem.* 10.77). It was an attempt to rationalize and harmonize these two competing traditions that led later mythographers to posit that Perseus' father, Acrisius, and Acrisius' brother,

Proetus, had initially divided the Argive plain between themselves but that, in the succeeding generation, Perseus and Proetus' son Megapenthes swapped their kingdoms (Hall 1995: 608–9; Hall 1997a: 93–9). Kowalzig (2007: 161–80) has further pointed out that with their promotion of the lineage of Heracles, the communities of the eastern plain were employing myths that intermeshed with those of Argos' archenemy Sparta (cf. Hdt. 7.22.4 with Vannicelli 2004: 287)—a connection that is already sketched out at the beginning of the fifth century by Acusilaus of Argos (*FGrH* 2 F24), who makes the eponymous Mykeneus the son of Sparton.

## 1.7.4. Argos, Sparta, and Cynuria

This possible relationship between the eastern communities of the plain and Sparta resonates with the traditions that told of a long-lasting conflict between the Argives and the Spartans for the possession of the Thyreatis (ancient Cynuria), a mountainous stretch of "no man's land" on the eastern seaboard of the Peloponnese between Laconia and the Argolid. According to Pausanias (3.2.3), the Spartans first made war on the Argives when they charged them with having annexed Cynuria and with attempting to induce the perioikic cities to revolt. This event is dated to the reign of the Spartan king Labotas, whom the periegete dates four generations prior to the Argive assault on Asine—that is, the early ninth century. This information has sometimes been read alongside Herodotus' claim (1.82) that the entire eastern seaboard of the Peloponnese down to Cape Malea and including the island of Cythera and other islands had once belonged to the Argives. Modern scholars have, however, expressed skepticism. Kelly points out that Herodotus' testimony probably derives from the Homeric statement (*Il.* 2.108) that Agamemnon "ruled over many islands and the whole of Argos [here understood as the Peloponnese]" and goes on to argue that the first hostilities between Argos and Sparta over the Thyreatis are unlikely to predate the mid-sixth century. In his view, the entire notion of an age-old enmity between the two was an invention of Ephorus (Kelly 1970b: 985–7; Kelly 1976: 73–4; cf. Beloch 1912–1927: vol. 1.1: 204 n. 1; Robertson 1992: 188–9; Ratinaud-Lachkar 2004: 74–5). Kelly also casts doubt on the historicity of the Battle of Hysiae, dated by Pausanias (2.24.7) to 669, arguing that the Spartans could not have reached Cynuria until Arcadian Tegea was pacified in the mid-sixth century, and wonders whether Pausanias' source has confused a fictitious seventh-century battle with a Spartan attack on Hysiae in 417 that is reported by Thucydides (5.83.1–2; Kelly 1970a; Kelly 1970b: 980–1; Kelly 1976: 86–7; Robertson 1992: 209–12; Bershadsky 2013: 172–5). Whether this skepticism needs to be reconsidered in the light of a fragment of Tyrtaeus (F23a

West), which mentions Ἀργείων (Cartledge 2002: 109; cf. Piérart 2006: 20), depends on whether the lines refer to a historical, rather than mythical, conflict (Tausend 1993).

Herodotus (1.82) is our earliest source for the mid-sixth-century conflict over the region of Thyrea. He tells us that the Argives and the Spartans agreed to field an army of 300 men each to decide the issue, while the remainder of the respective armies should retire from the area. After an evenly matched battle, only two Argives and one Spartan remained. The Argives, assuming that they had won the contest, returned to Argos, but the sole Spartan survivor, Othryades, remained on the battlefield, stripping the arms off the Argive dead and conveying their weapons to his camp. The next day, after a heated discussion as to who had been victorious, both sides engaged with their whole armies, and after many deaths, the Spartans were victorious.[8] Herodotus adds two further details: first, that from that day on, the Argives swore that no man would grow his hair long nor would any woman wear golden jewellery until they had recovered the Thyreatis, whereas the Spartans decreed that they would wear their hair long; and second, that Othryades, out of shame at having survived the battle, took his own life on the battlefield.

The "Battle of the Champions," as it is called in modern scholarship, figures in the accounts of several later authors. Thucydides (5.41.2–3) records that in 420, after the expiration of their truce with Sparta, the Argives proposed a rerun of the battle to decide possession of Cynuria. Plutarch (*Mor.* 231e; cf. Paus. 3.7.5) cites a speech of the Spartan king Polydorus, made "after the Argives had again been completely defeated in combat after the battle of the 300." Elsewhere (*Mor.* 306a–b), he says that the Spartan survivor Othryades erected a trophy inscribed with his own blood but differs from Herodotus in claiming that the final result was determined not by a second battle but by a vote of the Delphic Amphictiony. An epigram in the *Greek Anthology* (7.431), attributed—perhaps wrongly—to Simonides, implies that Othryades died of his wounds rather than committing suicide. Pausanias (10.9.12), on the other hand, presents what is evidently an Argive version of the contest, noting that in the theater of Argos, he had seen a statue group of the Argive Perilaos killing Othryades (Robertson 1992: 201–2).

Kelly (1970b: 983–4; 1976: 139) regards the Battle of the Champions as historical; in fact, he suggests that it may have been provoked in part by Spartan

---

8. Bearzot (2006: 110) suggests that this defeat may have prompted the Argives to extend their influence toward the isthmus region, pointing to the dedication at Olympia, between c. 530 and 490, of eight shields, five helmets, and a greave captured "from the Corinthians"—an event that is perhaps alluded to by Pausanias (6.19.12–14).

concerns about a closer relationship between Argos and Athens, signaled by the dispatch of Argive mercenaries to support Pisistratus (Hdt 1.61) and the fact that Pisistratus is said to have had an illegitimate son by an Argive woman named Timonassa (Hdt. 5.94; Arist. *Ath. Pol.* 17.3–4; 19.4). Other scholars are more skeptical. Brelich (1961: 80–4) noted the ritual elements of the story, especially Herodotus' reference to hairstyles, and conjectured that Herodotus' story arose from a ritual battle, performed as part of a male coming-of-age rite. In fact, boys' choruses commemorating the Battle of the Champions were performed at the Spartan festival of the Gymnopaidiai in honor of Apollo Pythaeus (Sosibius *FGrH* 595 F5; *Suda* s.v. γυμνοπαιδεία); the battle is also supposed to have been celebrated at the festival of the Parparonia, probably held in the Thyreatis on or near Mt. Zavitsa (Robertson 1992: 179–80), and perhaps also at the Argive festival of the Endymatia (Robertson 1992: 207; Bershadsky 2013: 211–12). Dillery (1996) has noted that Herodotus' account in many ways prefigures the telling of the Battle of Thermopylae: in both cases, the Spartans number 300; in both cases, there is a focus on the long hair of the Spartans (Hdt. 7.208.3); and the story of Othryades committing suicide in some sense foreshadows the fate of one of the Thermopylae survivors, Aristodemus, who, after being humiliated at Sparta for his cowardice, carried out a suicidal sally at the Battle of Plataea (Hdt. 7.229–31).

Building on both Brelich and Dillery, Bershadsky (2013: 176–223) argues that we need to separate Herodotus' story of the Battle of the Champions from a genuine historical annexation of Cynuria by the Spartans in the mid-sixth century. In her view, Herodotus attempts to historicize and anchor to the time of the Lydian king Croesus a legendary tradition that was repeatedly performed by means of a series of adolescent ritual battles that predate the actual conquest of Cynuria. Robertson (1992), on the other hand, denies a mid-sixth-century annexation of Cynuria tout court. First, he argues, Herodotus' synchronism of the battle with Croesus' appeal for Spartan aid c. 546 does not match with Plutarch's belief (*Mor.* 231e) that it took place during the reign of the Spartan kings Theodorus and Polydorus, traditionally dated to the late eighth or early seventh century, or Eusebius' date of 720/719. Second, he argues that the plain of Thyrea is hardly suitable for a pitched hoplite battle. In his view, the Spartans did not gain possession of the Thyreatis until their invasion of the Argive plain under King Cleomenes I.

For that event, Herodotus (6.76–82) is again our earliest source. Cleomenes, after being told by the Delphic oracle that he would capture Argos, advanced with an army as far as the Erasinos river but failed to obtain favorable omens to cross it. He then pulled back to Thyrea, newly conquered according to Robertson (1992: 191), and shipped his troops over to the other side of the Argolic Gulf, where they disembarked ἔς τε τὴν Τιρυνθίην χώρην καὶ Ναυπλίην ("in the territory of Tiryns and Nauplia")—which might suggest not only that Tiryns was still independent at the time (Hall 1995: 589) but also that Nauplia had not, in fact, been exterminated a century earlier.[9] The Argives marched to Sepeia, near Tiryns, where a large number of them fell in battle. The survivors fled to a sacred grove, dedicated to the eponymous hero Argos, where around 50 of them were lured out with the promise of ransom, only to be promptly killed on Cleomenes' orders. Cleomenes then had his slaves burn down the grove—an act of impiety which Herodotus lists as one of four explanations given for why Cleomenes eventually went mad and committed suicide in a horrific manner (Hdt. 6.75). Later (7.148.2) we are told that the Argive losses amounted to 6,000. Upon learning that the grove was dedicated to Argos, Cleomenes realized that the oracle had been fulfilled and, after offering sacrifice—against the wishes of the temple personnel—at the Argive Heraion, returned to Sparta, where he was charged with having accepted a bribe not to attack Argos. Cleomenes explained that a flame shooting from the breast (as opposed to the head) of the cult statue in the Heraion indicated that he was not destined to take the city of Argos and was subsequently acquitted. Herodotus (cf. 6.19, 77) synchronizes this episode with the fall of Miletus, which would place it c. 494. Pausanias (3.4.1), on the other hand, places it early in Cleomenes' career, shortly after 520 (Tomlinson 1972: 93; Vannicelli 2004: 285–6).

Herodotus is probably drawing on a pro-Argive source, which stressed Cleomenes' impiety, as well as a Spartan version that sought to justify his failure to attack the city (Franchi 2012: 209). An entirely different, pro-Argive account is relayed by Plutarch (*Mor.* 245c–f), apparently following the Hellenistic historian Socrates of Argos (*FGrH* 310 F6) and perhaps also other historians such as Derkyllos, Demetrius, and Deinias (Franchi 2012: 211). According to Plutarch, Cleomenes did attack Argos. In the absence of the men who had been killed at Sepeia, the poet Telesilla armed and organized the young women in defense of the city, driving back not only Cleomenes but also his co-ruler Demaratus. The women then founded a Sanctuary of Enyalius. According to the *Suda* (s.v. Τελέσιλλα), the Spartans refused to attack the city because it would have been dishonorable to fight women (cf. Paus. 2.20.9).

Pausanias (2.20.8–10) seeks to reconcile Herodotus' version with that of Socrates. The occasion for his digression is a relief *stēlē* in the Sanctuary of

---

9. Later, Herodotus (6.92) tells us that Aegina and Sicyon had provided the ships for Cleomenes' campaign, for which Argos fined each 500 *talanta*; the Sicyonians paid, but the Aeginetans refused. Kelly's (1976: 67–8) suggestion that this indicates the existence of an "Argive Amphictiony," perhaps centered on the Heraion, is dismissed by Tausend (1992: 8–9).

Aphrodite, near the Theater with Square Steps, that depicted Telesilla throwing down her books and about to don a helmet. He then recounts the Battle of Sepeia, the burning of the grove, and Telesilla's organization of resistance—adding, for good measure, that the poet also marshaled house slaves (οἰκέτας) and those who were weak because of youth or old age—and then cites part of the oracle that Herodotus reports was given to the Argives sometime before the event. According to Herodotus (6.19, 77), a "common" (ἐπίκοινον) oracle was given to both the Milesians and the Argives. The part of the oracle concerning the Argives ran: "But when the female has defeated and driven out the male and reaped glory for the Argives, then it will cause many Argive women to tear their cheeks. So that one day, it will be said by the men that are to come, 'the terrible thrice-coiled (τριέλικτος) serpent perished, subdued by the spear.'"

It is easy to understand why Pausanias' sources should have wanted to associate this oracle with the narrative related to Telesilla, but that does not explain why the female victory should *precede* the bereavement of Argive widows. In fact, the two versions about Cleomenes' invasion are utterly incompatible: much of the thrust of Herodotus' account focuses on why Cleomenes did *not* attack Argos (Forrest 1960: 221). Furthermore, Eusebius dated Telesilla's floruit to 451, more than four decades after the events Herodotus describes. Even if Herodotus had been aware of the poet, he gives no indication that he knows of a tradition that related her to Cleomenes' invasion (Graf 1984: 247–8; Piérart 2004c: 175; Franchi 2012: 215–16). It is, then, entirely possible that an older "stock" tradition about a warrior poet was later grafted onto the story of Cleomenes' invasion and the real-life Telesilla, perhaps in the context of the Argive festival of the Hybristika. In fact, Plutarch (*Mor.* 245e) goes on to recount how the Battle of Sepeia took place in the month of Hermaios, during which were celebrated the Hybristika, "when they drape the women in men's tunics and cloaks and the men in women's robes and veils" (Graf 1984: 249–50; Franchi 2012: 217; see Section 1.11.2). As for the oracle, the victory of the female over the male could be understood in terms of a carnivalesque inversion of the normative social order, mirrored by the rule of slaves over their masters (Vidal-Naquet 1981). Sauzeau (1999), on the other hand, sees it as reflecting a series of specifically Argive myths, including Hera's victory over Poseidon for patronage of the Argolid (Paus. 2.15.5) and the murder of their husbands by the daughters of Danaus. It was only later that the Argives rewrote their history and employed the oracle to create the myth of the female defense of the city (cf. Piérart 2003).

That Mycenae and Tiryns were independent in 480–479 is virtually assured by the fact that they contributed troops to the Battles of Thermopylae and Plataea (Meiggs and Lewis 1988: #27; Hdt. 7.202; 9.28.4; Diod. *Sic.* 11.65.2; Moggi

1974: 1252–4). Tomlinson (1972: 239), who believes that Argos unified the plain in the eighth century, concedes that there may have been a brief period in which Mycenae was independent, but it is easier to assume that it retained some degree of autonomy all along. The Argives, on the other hand, abstained from the Persian War. Herodotus (7.150–2) notes that there was a widespread suspicion throughout Greece that they had been bribed by the Persians to remain neutral, but he is presumably drawing on an Argive source when he remarks that they were reluctant to participate because "6,000 of their own had recently been killed by the Spartans and Cleomenes, son of Anaxandridas" (7.148.2; cf. 7.149.2). Certainly, the deaths of 6,000 male adults would have constituted a devastating loss—perhaps as much as half the entire citizen body (see Section 1.9). But, as Plutarch (*Mor.* 245d) guessed, the figure is almost certainly an exaggeration. First, we hear elsewhere (Hdt. 6.92.2–3) that 1,000 Argive volunteers, under the command of Eurybates, fought with considerable losses in support of the Aeginetans in their war against Athens at some point not long after Sepeia (Forrest 1960: 221). Second, as we have seen (see Section 1.5.2), the Argives may have offered to join the coalition if they could secure a 30-year peace with Sparta and share in the command of the forces (Hdt. 7.148.4)—notwithstanding a Delphic oracle that had apparently urged neutrality (7.148.3; Vannicelli 2004: 286). There is, however, good reason to suppose that the Argives also had other troubles with which they had to contend.

Herodotus (6.83.1) relates how after the loss of men at Sepeia, "Argos was so bereft of men that their slaves (δοῦλοι) took hold of all business, both ruling and managing everything until the sons of those who had perished came of age." He goes on to say that the latter seized power back and expelled the δοῦλοι, who captured Tiryns in battle. For a while, there was harmony between the two factions, but an Arcadian seer named Kleandros persuaded the δοῦλοι to attack their masters, and after a long-drawn-out war, the Argives were victorious. Bourke (2011) suggests that an allusion to the expulsion of the δοῦλοι from Argos is to be found in the 11th ode of Bacchylides, which he dates to 478 and which describes the rivalry between the legendary kings Acrisius and Proetus and the departure of the latter for Tiryns. Although Moggi (1974: 1263) takes Herodotus at his word, most commentators exclude the possibility that the men who briefly seized power at Argos really were δοῦλοι, in the sense of "chattel slaves." Indeed, Forrest (1960: 222–3) may have been right in suggesting that the term was a derogatory one, used by the ruling elites to describe their political opponents and inferiors. The episode seems to bear all the hallmarks of a phenomenon that was to dog the Greek city-states throughout the fifth century: *stasis.*

Matters are, however, complicated by the rather conflicting information given by later authors. Aristotle (*Pol.* 1303a8), in a passage in which he is discussing how *stasis* can occur when the relationship between the rich and the poor is thrown out of balance, writes, "in Argos, when the men had been destroyed by the Spartan Cleomenes on the seventh day [?], they were compelled to accept some of the people who dwelled around (τῶν περιοίκων τινάς)." A fragment of Diodorus (10.26), typically supposed to refer to Argos (although the text is not explicit), states, "The hatred that the citizens harbored for the many, though concealed previously, broke out in full force as soon as it recognized the opportunity; out of ambition, they freed the slaves (δούλους), preferring to give a share of freedom to their house slaves (οἰκέταις) rather than citizenship to the free." Finally, Plutarch (*Mor.* 245f) notes that the Argives, "in order to correct the shortage of manpower, gave citizenship not to the slaves (δούλοις), as Herodotus says, but to the best among those who dwelled around (τῶν περιοίκων . . . τοὺς ἀρίστους) and married them to their women."

Scholars have gone to quite extraordinary lengths to attempt to reconcile these four accounts. Some (Willetts 1959; Lotze 1971; Tomlinson 1972: 97–9; van Compernolle 1975: 360–1; Piérart 2004c: 177–8) argue that Herodotus' δοῦλοι were serfs, noting that Pollux (*Onom.* 3.83) compares the γυμνῆτες of Argos to other serf-like populations such as the Helots of Laconia or the Penestae of Thessaly (Lotze 1959). On this view, the term *perioikos* (περίοικος) is a synonym for δοῦλος and simply means a "bonded tiller of the soil." Others (Forrest 1960: 222–4; Bearzot 2006: 113; Bourke 2011: 142–4) maintain that the *perioikoi* are equivalent to the *perioikoi* of Laconia, that is, the free populations of the communities in the plain who owed certain obligations to Argos; if Herodotus describes them as δοῦλοι, then he simply means that they were subject to someone else's authority. Bershadsky (2013: 316–24), on the other hand, posits two traditions: an Argive "democratic" account involving the *perioikoi*, which she believes developed in the 460s, and an Argive "oligarchic" account that told of the illegal seizure of power by the δοῦλοι and which she dates to a period shortly after 450.

There is, of course, always the possibility that later authors confused two separate events of which Herodotus mentioned only the first (cf. Kritzas 1992: 232–3). This first was the usurpation of power by the δοῦλοι—probably members of the Argive δᾶμος who had formerly been excluded from officeholding. It is impossible to determine whether this event had anything to do with the refusal of Argos to aid Aegina c. 490 (Hdt. 6.92; Forrest 1960: 225) or with an inscription (*SEG* 26.449; van Effenterre and Ruzé 1994–1995: vol. 2: #28; Piérart 2004c: 177–8), dated to 475–450 and found at Epidaurus, which records how a certain Kallipos of Argos together with his slaves (ϝοικιάται) sought asylum in the Sanctuary of Apollo Maleatas at Epidaurus. This would represent an obvious context in which the first steps were taken to establish a more democratic constitution—including, perhaps, the establishment of the popular βωλά (Forrest 1960: 222; Gehrke 1985: 361–3; see Section 1.5.4). It is possible that a more oligarchic constitution was established with the expulsion of the δοῦλοι—as Forrest (1960: 225), who dates this event to c. 467, suggests—but this would require the unlikely and unsupported supposition that democracy was established anew just a few years after it was suppressed (Tuci 2006: 223–4). Perhaps the sons of those who fell at Sepeia exacted their revenge on the perpetrators of democracy without dismantling it.

The second event is the decisive—though not, perhaps, entirely planned (Sansone di Campobianco 2008)—unification of the plain and the reorganization of the citizen body in the 460s (see Section 1.5.5). In recounting the foundation of Megalopolis a century later, Pausanias (8.27.1) notes that the unification combated the threat of Spartan aggression: the Argives, "when they increased Argos with a multitude of men, after destroying Tiryns, Hysiae, Orneiai, Mycenae, Midea, and various other insignificant towns in the Argolid, had less to fear from the Spartans and also strength against those who dwelled around (τοὺς περιοίκους)." Diodorus (11.65) relates that Argos attacked Mycenae in 468, razing the city and selling its inhabitants into slavery (cf. Paus. 2.15.4). Strabo (8.6.19) adds that the cities of Kleonai and Tegea assisted the Argives with the attack, while Pausanias (7.25.5–6) notes that some of the survivors found refuge in Achaean Keryneia, Macedonia, and—oddly enough—Kleonai. Tiryns and Midea were also destroyed, with Tirynthians escaping to Epidaurus and Halieis (Hdt. 7.137; Ephorus *FGrH* 70 F56; Strabo 8.6.11; Paus. 2.17.5). According to Pausanias (2.25.8), the Argive motivation was "to take fellow settlers (συνοίκους) and enlarge Argos." The language of synoecism is explicit here and, although Moggi (1974) argues that Mycenae, Tiryns, and Midea were destroyed rather than incorporated, he does believe that the populations of smaller communities such as Orneiai and Hysiae were enrolled in the citizenry of Argos, albeit at a slightly later date (cf. Piérart 1997: 336–7). The destruction of Mycenae, Tiryns, and Midea made land available for redistribution, but an increased Argive citizen population had to be recruited from somewhere.

To summarize the tentative reconstruction of events suggested here, Herodotus records the memory of an event, shortly after the massacre at Sepeia c. 494, in which power was wrested away from the elites by the people—or δοῦλοι, as Herodotus rather ungenerously terms them. This was the opening salvo in a civil war (*stasis*) that would continue, two to three decades later, with the counterinsurgency of the sons of the aristocrats who fell at Sepeia, the retreat of the democrats to Tiryns, and the renewed hostilities provoked by Kleandros.

Aristotle is aware of the initial democratic revolt that lies behind Herodotus' version of events, but he has confused it with a slightly later enrollment within the Argive citizen body of "some of the *perioikoi*"—meaning the free inhabitants of some of the surrounding cities in the plain but not Mycenae, Tiryns, or Midea. Here "*perioikoi*" should be understood in a general geographic sense ("those who live around") rather than the more technical political sense in which it is applied in Laconia (cf. Shipley 1997: 196). Plutarch is guilty of the same error. Diodorus, on the other hand, has misunderstood Herodotus in taking his usage of the term δοῦλοι literally but may betray an awareness that this event was distinct from the later synoecism, in the 460s, when citizenship was given "to the free."

Somewhere in all this, we need to place the Battle of Tegea, in which the Argives allied with the Arcadians against the Spartans—a strategy that has sometimes been attributed to the machinations of Themistocles, who is said to have spent part of his exile in Argos (Thuc. 2.135.3; Bearzot 2006: 115–16). The battle is mentioned by Herodotus (9.35), who tells how the Eleian seer Teisamenos correctly foretold Spartan victory in five successive contests: Plataea, Tegea, Dipaieis, the Isthmus (perhaps Ithome is meant), and Tanagra. No date is given for any of these battles, though Forrest (1960: 232; cf. Tomlinson 1972: 102–6) suggests that since the Tegeates are supposed to have assisted Argos in its attack on Mycenae in 468, the battle should date to around that time. In 461, the Argives contracted a ten-year alliance with Athens—an event that seems to be commemorated in Aeschylus' *Suppliant Women*. Along with their new allies, they were defeated by the Spartans at the Battle of Tanagra in 458/7 (Thuc. 1.107–8) but were apparently able, with Athenian help, to repel a Spartan attack on Argolic Oinoe in the same decade (Paus. 10.10.3; Tomlinson 1972: 111–12). Finally, in 451, the Argives secured the 30-year peace with Sparta that they had requested at the time of the Persian War (Thuc. 5.14.4). This is approximately the period to which the treaty with Knossos and Tylissos (Meiggs and Lewis 1988: #42) dates and may be the context in which there arose a tradition, recorded by Diodorus (5.80.3), that the Argives and the Spartans had founded several cities on Crete following the return of the Heraclidae (Graham 1964: 154–65).

## 1.7.5. Military Organization at Argos

We have no explicit information as to how the Argive army was organized prior to the late fifth century. During the Peloponnesian War, the army was divided into five regiments—one for each of the four tribes and one for an elite regiment of 1,000 soldiers (Piérart 2004c: 169; Kritzas 2013: 286). Diodorus (12.75.7) says this last regiment was recruited from those who were young, athletically fit, and wealthy and that they were maintained at public expense in order to free them for continuous practice and exercise. Thucydides (5.67.2) also mentions this elite unit as fighting at the Battle of Mantinea in 418. It is, however, unknown whether the 1,000 men who fought at Tanagra in 458/7 (Thuc. 1.107) were all members of this regiment. Those who died were given full funerary honors at Athens, as we know from a casualty list that has been reconstructed from fifteen fragments found in scattered locations throughout Athens (*IG* I³.1149; Meiggs and Lewis 1988: #35; Meritt 1945). The names, which may have numbered as many as 400, seem to have been listed by tribe, though this offers little help in deciding whether the dead belonged to an elite regiment that recruited from all tribes or whether they were part of a levy drawn from the four tribal regiments (Papazarkadas and Sourlas 2012: 599). Interestingly, we never hear of any organized navy in Archaic Argos (Kelly 1970b: 978).

## *1.8. Economic History*

As in most parts of Greece, the economy of Archaic Argos must have been based predominantly on agricultural production. According to Zangger (1993: 85; *contra* Bintliff 1977: vol. 2: 271–369), save for the coastal strip near Tiryns, there has been little geological change in the soils of the Argive plain since the Early Bronze Age. The citrus cultivation that is today ubiquitous dates back only to the 1960s CE. In the 19th century CE, the plain was given over to the cultivation of grain, vine, rice, cotton, and tobacco (Kofiniotis 1892: 68; Dorovinis 2013: 43). In antiquity, Argos was described as πολυδίψιον ("very thirsty") in both the *Iliad* (4.171) and the first line of the now lost epic poem the *Thebaid*. This description might mean that the Argolid was thought of as dry but is more likely to be a reference to the fact that it was well watered; elsewhere in the *Iliad* (9.141), it is described as οὖθαρ ἀρούρης (literally, "the udder of the farmland," which would seem to connote fertility), and Strabo (8.6.8) says that although Argos itself was located in a waterless place, there were many wells that were ascribed to the daughters of the legendary king Danaus. Strabo goes on to cite a fragment of Hesiod (F128 Merkelbach-West), which reads, "the daughters of Danaus made waterless Argos well watered." Two other epithets are attached to the name of Argos in the *Iliad*. The first is πολύπυρος ("rich in wheat," *Il.* 15.372), which would suggest that cereals were an important staple within the agricultural regime of the area. Indeed, Lehmann (1937: 77–8) has calculated that the plain could have produced around 320,000 hl of grain each year. The second is ἱππόβοτος ("horse-rearing," *Il.* 2.287), which would account for why horses are so prominent in figured decoration on Middle and Late Geometric vessels or as bronze figurines.

Craft production was also clearly of importance, although its representation in the archaeological record may have inflated its original contribution to the overall economy of the region. At the foot of the Larisa, near the Panagitsa chapel, a Late Geometric establishment with three clay basins, a standing pithos, and an irregularly plastered floor has been tentatively identified as a textile-dyeing plant (Daux 1959: 755 fig. 3; Hägg 1982: 304; Foley 1988: 27). Traces of a potter's workshop, dated to the Protogeometric period, have been discovered in the area of the Archaeological Museum (Daux 1959: 768), and, as we have seen (see Section 1.4.3), Argos was home to a thriving ceramic industry. But despite its quality, Argive Geometric pottery was not widely exported beyond the region, nor are there many ceramic imports in the Argolid during that period (Courbin 1966: 549–55; Tomlinson 1972: 72–3; Billot 1989–1990: 36). This marks a stark contrast with the seventh and sixth centuries, when imported ceramic fine wares were widely used at Argos. Argive metalworkers, on the other hand, were a little more ambitious. In his account of the foundation of Cyrene, Herodotus (4.152.4) notes that the Samians spent six *talanta* on producing a "bronze vessel, in the fashion of an Argive kratēr, with griffins' heads all around the rim projecting outward." This is a type of vessel well known at Olympia, where large numbers of tripods, bronze animal figurines, and bronze shield bands have been identified as the products of Argive craftsmen (Kelly 1976: 57–8; Jeffery 1990: 158–9; Rolley 1992). At the same time, the prominence of Argive metalworkers should not be exaggerated; Rolley (1992: 39) notes that only 15 examples of a particular type of bronze pin (Kilian-Dirlmeier 1D) manufactured at Argos are found outside the region.

The first series of silver *drachmai*, minted on the Aeginetan standard and depicting the wolf of Apollo Lykeios in profile on the obverse and two small square punch marks and the letter alpha on the reverse, probably dates to c. 500 or a little later (Kelly 1976: 104; Flament 2009: 83; Flament 2012: 162–3). A series of similarly decorated *triōboloi* likely belongs to the same period (Flament 2012: 163–4). It is, however, often supposed that Argos had employed a proto-currency prior to this (Courbin 1983). According to the *Etymologicum Magnum* (s.v. ὀβελίσκοι), "Pheidon of Argos was the first to mint coins on Aegina, and as he distributed the coins, he collected the spits (ὀβελίσκους) and dedicated them to Hera in Argos." It just so happens that somewhere between 96 and 120 iron spits, together with what has been interpreted as a weight standard, have been discovered at the Heraion (Ragone 2006: 69–70). Furthermore, spits have been excavated in several wealthier eighth-century burials in Argos, where they are often found in multiples of six, which calls to mind Plutarch's description (*Lys.* 17.3; cf. *Lyc.* 9.1) of the bulky iron currency of Classical Sparta and his observation that "even now coins are called *oboloi* (ὀβολοὺς), and six *oboloi* make up a drachmē, for this is the number that can be grasped with a hand." Whether or not the equation of ὀβελοί ("spits") with ὀβολοί is a false etymology, it was clearly one that had already been proposed by ancient authors (Guzzo 1995–1996). Needless to say, the notice in the *Etymologicum Magnum* should not be taken at face value, at least in its entirety. Even the latest date that ancient authors offer for Pheidon (see Section 1.5.3) may predate the earliest coinage in Greece, let alone Argos, and it may be that the story was invented to explain the visible presence of so many spits at the Heraion (Schaps 2004: 103). On the other hand, Ragone (2006), who cautiously accepts that it was Pheidon who dedicated the spits at the Heraion, suggests that the tyrant replaced these spits not with coined silver but with smaller, weighed bars of silver. If so, and it should be noted that there is no archaeological confirmation of the hypothesis, it might be these that are included among the χρήματα ("objects" but also "money") discussed in the sacred law (*SEG* 11.314) from the Sanctuary of Athena Polias on the Larisa. That there were, however, also other forms of financial reckoning is indicated by the sacred law from Tiryns (see Section 1.6), where fines are assessed in *medimnoi*—that is, measures of grain.

## *1.9. Familial/Demographic History*

Virtually nothing is known about family life at Argos. The existence of multiple burials and the non-segregation of infant burials suggest that, at least in the eighth century, burial practices were structured according to kinship (Langdon 2001: 585), and there is no special reason to doubt that the nuclear family was the norm in Archaic Argos. Of particular interest is a female burial (Tomb 23) in the Bakaloiannis Plot, near the agora. As Langdon (2001: 587–92) points out, the 35-year-old deceased was buried in a large decorated Late Geometric I pyxis (see Figure 1.3) that had been manufactured about 25 years earlier—a date established by the fact that the mouth of the pyxis had been closed by a kratēr that dates to the Late Geometric IIB phase. Langdon tentatively suggests that the pyxis had been a trousseau given to the woman when she first came of age. The kratēr, on the other hand, evokes the more masculine ambit of the symposium, and Langdon notes that such "male" gendered items accompany only the burials of older women—women, that is, who had attained a new "social" age characterized by gender ambiguity and increased authority within the household. The tradition related to Telesilla (see Section 1.7.4) is not inconsistent with this picture. Certainly, as elsewhere in Greece, wives frequently outlived their husbands. An inscribed Doric capital, found near the Heraion, carries an elegiac epitaph telling how a woman named Kossina buried Hyssematas—assumed to be her husband—near the hippodrome (*SEG* 11.305); we are told that he had died in war at a young age. Daly (1939), who dated the inscription to the early fifth century, suggested that Hyssematas had been a casualty of the defeat at Sepeia (see Section 1.7.4), though Jeffery (1990: 168 #15) dated the epitaph to the last quarter of the sixth century.

In terms of population, Tomlinson (1972: 18) has estimated that the area available for habitation within the Classical walls of Argos amounts to about 80 ha; if we take a density of 125 people per hectare, then the total population of Argos would have been about 10,000—a figure that is comparable to the population of the town throughout much of the 19th and early 20th centuries CE (Lehmann 1937: 85). However, Tomlinson may have overestimated the area enclosed by the Classical fortifications, while a sizable number of Argive inhabitants are likely to have lived outside the urban center, farming land in the plain, which may have been able to support around 585 inhabitants per square kilometer (Kelly 1976: 4 n. 10). Hansen (1985: 11–21) starts from Xenophon's description (*Hell.* 4.2.17) of the Battle of the Nemea River in 394, where the Argives contributed 7,000 troops, and estimates a total adult male population of about 12,000. On a rough estimate, this would yield a total population in the region of 60,000–75,000 for the Classical period, although the level was almost certainly lower for the Archaic period—especially if Argos did not exercise total control over the entirety of the plain (see Section 1.7.2).

In 1963, Charles published an anthropological analysis of 139 skeletons, dating from the Early Helladic period through to the Middle Ages, that were excavated by the École Française d'Athènes in Argos during the 1950s (Charles 1963). The analysis—not atypically for its time—relied heavily on craniometric considerations in order to identify "racial" (Cromagnoid, Grimaldoid, Atlantic-Nordic, and Mixed) groups. However, a reanalysis (Charlier 2013) of the osteological material from Argos, carried out in 2003, has challenged some of Charles' interpretations. For example, Charles (1963: 49) believed that the severely disabled male occupant of an Early Geometric burial (Tomb 16) had been subjected to trepanation, whereas the perforation to the skull may, in fact, be due to a taphonomic anomaly during the excavation of the grave (Charlier 2013: 208). Similarly, the new analysis failed to find any evidence for postmortem cranial perforations that Charles claimed for the Middle Geometric burial in Tomb 176–1 (Charles 1963: 68; Charlier 2013: 208). Forty-two skeletons dating from Early Geometric through to the end of the sixth century have been reanalyzed. Of the 15 for which sex can be determined, eight are male and seven are female. In terms of age structure, three individuals were older than 45, 29 (69% of the sample) were between 25 and 45, two between 20 and 25, one between 15 and 20, one between five and ten, four between one and six months, and one in utero. The average height for men was 166.8 cm, for women 151.3 cm (Charlier 2013: 213–14). Among the pathologies observed are inflammation of the ear canal, osteoarthritis and necrosis of the hip, rickets, spinal tuberculosis, hydrocephalus, acoustic neuroma, and exostosis, along with multiple fractures, hematomas, and rampant tooth decay (Charlier 2013: 204–8).

## *1.10. Social Customs and Institutions*

By the fifth century, the Argives appear to have believed that they were Dorian Greeks, whose ancestors had arrived in the Peloponnese at the end of the Heroic Age, under the leadership of the Heraclidae. Sophocles (*OC* 1301)—anachronistically, since he is referring to mythical events prior to the return of the Heraclidae—refers to Argos as "Dorian"; Pindar (*Pyth.* 5.70) narrates how the offspring of Heracles ruled over Sparta, Argos, and Pylos; and Thucydides (1.12.3) dates the Dorian and Heraclid capture of the Peloponnese to 80 years after the capture of Troy. Attempts have sometimes been made to trace the Dorians in the archaeological record of Argos. Tomlinson (1972: 205), for example, has suggested that Apollo Lykeios may have been a god introduced by the Dorians, whereas Apollo Pythaeus was a pre-Dorian deity, and Foley (1988: 38–40; 1998) has argued that cist graves represent Dorian burials because they not only are the dominant mode of burial within the city during the ninth and eighth centuries but are also richer and more centrally clustered than other forms of burial. It is true that instances of tomb cult at Late Bronze Age chamber tombs in the vicinity of the Sanctuary of Apollo Pythaeus may represent "ancestralizing strategies" that are closer to practices in the eastern plain than in the rest of Argos (Hall 1997b: 138–40), but for the most part, there is no evidence for "ethnic zoning" in the city. While cist graves tend to contain, on average, more grave goods than pithoi or pit burials, the differential is not huge, and if eighth-century Argos was not a single compact conurbation (see Section 1.4.1), then cist graves do not appear to be particularly centralized. In fact, different modes of burial were employed even within the same cemetery, such as the Theodoropoulos Plot, where there is a variety of cist, pithos, and pit graves with a uniform orientation (Deïlaki 1973: 98–9). This is an unusual situation, if distinct grave types are diacritically linked to different ethnic groups—unless ethnicity was not a salient dimension of local identity, in which case any direct relationship between a particular grave type and an ethnic group is irrelevant. Furthermore, the theory fails to explain why c. 700, the cist grave abruptly falls out of favor as the predominant mode of burial (Hall 1997b: 122–8).

The Argives certainly spoke a West Greek dialect, related to the "Doric" dialects of the Peloponnese, Crete, and the Dodecanese, though some linguists believe that the similarities were not inherited from a protodialect but evolved through contact with both Doric and non-Doric dialects (López Eire 1978;

Fernández Alvarez 1981; see Hall 1997b: 161–2). Furthermore, the tradition that Argos was captured by the Dorians and their Heraclid leaders toward the end of the Heroic Age is almost certainly a later elaboration and rationalization of a far more complicated and haphazard pattern of migration and mobility at the transition from the Late Bronze to the Early Iron Age. While Dorian Sparta does seem to be a new foundation of c. 950 after a couple of centuries in which Laconia was significantly underpopulated (Cartledge 2002: 81; Cavanagh, Mee, and James 2005: 6–7), there is no marked discontinuity in settlement at Argos, nor are there especially close material links between the Argolid and Laconia, whose Dark Age pottery belongs rather to a West Greek *koinē* that includes Messenia, Achaea, Aetolia, and Ithaca but not the Argolid or Corinthia (Coulson 1985: 55, 71). There are some grounds for supposing that the myth of the Heraclidae returning to their ancestral lands in the Peloponnese may have been coined in the Argolid. For one thing, the lineage of Heracles was more deeply rooted in the genealogical and topographical traditions of the Argolid than in Laconia or Messenia. For another, it was, properly speaking, only the Argolid to which the descendants of Heracles had hereditary birthrights; both Laconia and Messenia had instead been granted to Heracles by virtue of conquest (Hall 2007: 81). Nevertheless, the earliest explicit literary association of Dorians with the city of Argos is not found before the sixth-century *Catalog of Women* (F10a.3–4, 6–7 Merkelbach-West), where Doros' son Aegimius is linked with Argos. West (1985: 59) suggested that the poem told of Doros' marriage to the daughter of the Argive *Urvater* Phoroneus.

## *1.11. Religious Customs and Institutions*
### 1.11.1. Religious Sites within the City
#### *1.11.1.1. Cult Sites on the Acropolis*

A large votive deposit, consisting mainly of ceramics but also some bronze figurines and jewellery, was found within the enceinte of the medieval castle on the Larisa, testifying to cult on the acropolis of Argos since at least the middle of the eighth century. Although the material included a few Protogeometric sherds, it is not certain that they originated in a cultic context, nor is there a continuous sequence of material between the Protogeometric and Late Geometric periods (Béquignon 1930: 480; Roes 1953; Courbin 1955a: 314; Hägg 1992: 11; Billot 1997–1998: 23). On the basis of Pausanias' description (2.24.3) of the Larisa, Vollgraff (1928) identified two sets of foundations as the temples of Zeus Larisaios and Athena. The identification of the Athena temple (see Figure 1.8), which probably dates to either the late sixth or early fifth century, is virtually assured because of

**FIGURE 1.8.** Foundations of the Temple of Athena Polias on the Larisa.

an inscription (*SEG* 11.314; Vollgraff 1929; Jeffery 1990: 168 #8; van Effenterre and Ruzé 1994–1995: vol. 1: #88), found built into the west wall of the Larisa fortress and dating to c. 575–550, which regulates the property of Athena Polias (see Section 1.6). Billot (1997–1998: 23) has argued that Athena Polias was the principal deity of Argos until the establishment of democracy in the mid-fifth century, when Apollo Lykeios assumed that role. However, the earliest coinage of Argos, which dates to the early fifth century, already carries the image of the wolf, the symbol of Apollo Lykeios (Kelly 1976: 104; Flament 2009: 83), which should suggest that his cult was preeminent before the end of the Archaic period.

### 1.11.1.2. Sanctuary of Apollo Lykeios

The importance of the Sanctuary of Apollo Lykeios to the civic life of Argos is indicated by the fact that a copy of the 100-year treaty, sworn between Athens, Argos, Mantinea, and Elis in the summer of 420, was set up "in the agora, in the Sanctuary of Apollo" (Thuc. 5.47.11). Pausanias (2.19.3) describes it as the "most distinguished" (ἐπιφανέστατον) sanctuary of Argos and says that it was founded by the legendary king Danaus. Although it has not yet been identified archaeologically, literary sources are unanimous that it was located in the agora. It was probably not far from the Hypostyle Hall (see Section 1.4.4), since a Late

Antique overbuilding reused blocks of a triglyph altar and perhaps even of a temple, to which were attached proxeny decrees specifying that they were to be set up in the Sanctuary of Apollo Lykeios (des Courtils 1981). In describing the dedications that stood inside the Temple of Apollo, Pausanias (2.19.7) mentions a statue of Hermes, "who has taken the shell of a tortoise in order to make a lyre of it." It is, then, interesting that a short distance away, in the Granias Plot near the Hellenistic Theater, the French excavated a small square structure that overlay what may have been a *bothros* and a small tumulus in which, among ceramics, figurines, fragments of bones, and ashes, were found two tortoise shells. One of the shells was perforated, apparently to form the sounding board of a lyre. The associated material dates to the end of the sixth century (Daux 1957: 674; Courbin 1980). A little further to the south, in the Kanellopoulos Plot at 26 Tripolis Street, a Late Archaic underground chamber was discovered, constructed directly above a Geometric grave that contained two skeletons. The chamber contained the bone fragments of a secondary burial and a large quantity of vases, together with a clay figurine of a young man making a lyre out of a tortoise shell (Pariente 1992: 205). If these two finds have any connection with the Sanctuary of Apollo Lykeios, then its existence can be traced back to at least the late sixth century, while the sanctuary itself was probably situated where an artificial terrace has been identified at an important junction, a little to the north of the currently excavated part of the agora (Courbin 1998; Marchetti 2000: 274–6).

Pausanias (2.24.1–2) describes two sanctuaries on the Deiras ridge—one to Apollo Deiradiotis and one to Athena Oxyderkes. The location of the latter is not known with certainty, though Roux (1957: 484; cf. Tomlinson 1972: 207) proposed identifying it with a round "tholos" structure on the Deiras ridge. Most of the other remains that Vollgraff excavated on the Deiras are assigned to the Sanctuary of Apollo. Apollo was worshipped under various names at the Deiras over the course of time.

The votives here begin toward the end of the eighth century (Vollgraff 1956: 11), which has suggested to several scholars that the Argives installed the cult on the Deiras after destroying the Sanctuary of Apollo Pythaeus at Asine (Barrett 1954: 439; Billot 1989–1990: 35; see Section 1.7.1), though the Argive poet Telesilla apparently claimed that the sanctuary at Argos, founded by Apollo's son Pythaeus, was the first to be instituted in Greece after Delphi (Paus. 2.35.2; cf. 2.24.1). Certainly, the cult title "Pythaeus" is attested in later inscriptions from the site, alongside "Chresterios" and "Deiradiotis" (Vollgraff 1956: 27). Architectural fragments might suggest that the sanctuary received a temple before the end of the sixth century, though it is unclear whether it stood at the head of a flight of stairs, east of the Hellenistic altar (see Figure 1.9) and under the remains of a sixth-century CE Byzantine basilica (Vollgraff 1956: 24), or in its more normal position,

FIGURE 1.9. Flight of stairs in the Sanctuary of Apollo Pythaeus on Deiras ridge.

west of the altar on the now-denuded slope of the ridge (Roux 1957: 484). By Pausanias' day, the sanctuary housed an oracle where a virgin woman prophesied once a month after drinking the blood of a female lamb (2.24.1).

### 1.11.1.3. Sanctuary of Aphrodite

The Sanctuary of Aphrodite was identified by the École Française d'Athènes in 1967 a short distance to the south of the Theater with Square Steps, or Aliaia (see Section 1.4.4). The first simple structure and earliest votives, which include miniature vases, terracotta figurines, and plaques, date to the end of the seventh century. A small Doric temple was built in the fifth century. The identification of the sanctuary is assured by an inscription on a sixth-century Attic red-figure stamnos, which is incised [ἀνέ]θεκε τἀφρ[ο]δ[ί]ται (Daux 1968; Daux 1969; Foley 1988: 141; Croissant 2009: 181–3). The proximity of the sanctuary to the Aliaia, which was itself identified by an inscribed statue base set up in the Sanctuary of Aphrodite to Timanthis, priestess of Aphrodite, suggests that the cult of Argive Aphrodite was closely linked to the political life of the city (Croissant 2009: 184, 191). Pausanias (2.20.8) describes a sculpted *stēlē* that stood in front of the temple and depicted Telesilla throwing down her books and about to put on a helmet.

### 1.11.1.4. *Other Cult Sites within the City*

Three other cults are securely attested for the Archaic period. The first is that of Pallas Athena, whose financial records were discovered at 48 Korinthou Street (see Section 1.5.4). Papadimitriou (2013: 267–8) has tentatively hypothesized that the structure with which the archive is associated was the Sanctuary of Athena and that it dates to the late sixth century. If this is correct, then either the urban habitat extended farther to the east than is currently assumed or the sanctuary was a suburban precinct.

The second is a cult to the war god Enyalius. This is known from an inscribed bronze plaque found with votive objects on the Larisa, although it is not certain that this is where the sanctuary was located (Vollgraff 1934). On one side of the plaque is represented a naked horseman wearing a crested Corinthian helmet and holding reins in his right hand and a whip in his left. On the other side is the depiction of a nude, beardless man with long hair, holding a spear in his right hand, together with an inscription that reads τὸνυϝαλίο ιαρά ("sacred to Enyalius"). The letter forms would date the plaque to the late seventh or early sixth century (Jeffery 1990: 168 #2). If this is the same cult that Plutarch (*Mor.* 245c–f) mentions, then it clearly was not founded after Telesilla's successful defense of Argos in the wake of the Battle of Sepeia (see Section 1.7.4).

The third cult is a hero cult to the "Seven against Thebes." This is known from an inscription, dated c. 550 and reading Ἐρόον τον ἐν Θέβαις ("of the heroes in Thebes"), which was incised onto one of nine stone posts found in the Karmoiannis Plot in the northern part of the excavated agora. The posts surrounded a pit filled with ash, calcinated logs, and fragmentary ceramics and lamps. The enclosure has been interpreted as a hearth that dates to the first half of the fourth century CE—perhaps a revival, under the emperor Julian, of the "Fire of Phoroneus" that Pausanias (2.19.5) had seen two centuries earlier—but the posts had clearly been reused from an earlier, Archaic monument (Pariente 1992). The original heroon is the material reflex of Argive mythical discourse, which emphasized the Proitid over the Perseid dynasty (see Section 1.7.3); it should almost certainly be viewed within the context of contemporary Spartan claims to the legacy of Agamemnon and his heirs, as witnessed in the cult to Zeus Agamemnon and Alexandra/Cassandra near Amyclae (Stesichorus *apud* schol. Eur. *Or.* 46; Pind. *Pyth.* 11.32; Paus. 3.19.6; Clem. Al. *Protr.* 32; schol. Lycoph. *Alex.* 1123, 1369; Hooker 1980: 60-2; Jeffery 1990: 447) and the "repatriation" of the bones of Orestes (Hdt. 1.67–8) and of Teisamenos (Paus. 7.1.8). While the Argives employed the myth of the Seven against Thebes as a charter for their own claims to hegemony over the Peloponnesians, on the grounds that the original expedition had been commanded by the Argive king Adrastus, the Spartans appealed to the more expansive and Panhellenic coalition that Agamemnon assembled against Troy (Hall 1999: 52–9; Hall 2007: 333–8).

Votive deposits indicate the existence of several other Archaic cults in Argos: in the Bonoris, Pilios, Koros, and Maniates/Tsoukrianis Plots and "Sondage 73," all in the area of the later agora (Daux 1959: 761; Deïlaki 1973: 108–9; Kritzas 1973–1974: 212, 28, 30–42; Consolaki and Hackens 1980; Touchais 1980: 599; Foley 1988: 141–2); in the Yeorgas, Siamblis, and Athanasopoulos Plots and around the church of Timios Prodromos on the eastern flank of the Larisa (Kritzas 1972: 198; Kritzas 1973: 130–2; Deïlaki 1973–1974: 208; Protonotariou-Deïlaki 1980: 191; Protonotariou-Deïlaki 1982: 39; Foley 1988: 142); in the Peppas Plot, which was probably a suburban sanctuary to the east of the city (Kritzas 1972: 203); in the Michalopoulos Brothers Plot (Protonotariou-Deïlaki 1980: 191); and on the slopes of Prophetes Elias (Vollgraff 1907: 155–61; Touchais 1980: 698; Foley 1988: 142). The identification of these sanctuaries with cults known from literary or epigraphic sources is next to impossible, although the nature of the votives in the Bonoris Plot and on the southern slope of Prophetes Elias—terracotta wreaths, fruits, and figurines—might suggest Hera cults, perhaps to Hera Antheia (Paus. 2.22.1) and Hera Akraia (2.24.1), respectively (Hall 1995: 604–5), although some believe that a Classical temple in the Koros Plot, east of the agora excavations, might be that of Hera Antheia (Marchetti 2000: 275 n. 12). Finally, a rescue excavation conducted between 1998 and 2000 in the Rebelos Plot, a little more than 1 km east of the agora, brought to light an additional cult location. A number of dedications—primarily figurines of humans, horses, rams, and oxen, as well as vases, lamps, loom weights, and clay spools—were found in association with burials dating back to the eighth century. These included three child burials, the burial of an adult with a dog, and an equine burial that should all be assigned to the Archaic period. The finds seem to suggest a tomb cult or hero cult, though the excavator also noted that some of the material is similar to assemblages typically found in Hera sanctuaries (Barakari-Gleni 2013).

## 1.11.2. Festivals

Much of the evidence for festivals comes from later sources, and we do not know how early they were instituted. So, for example, Plutarch (*Mor.* 1134c) is our only source for the existence of an Argive festival named the Endymatia (the "festival of the garments"), which he likens to the Spartan festival of the Gymnopaidiai, supposedly commemorating the battle for Thyrea (Robertson 1992: 207; see

Section 1.7.4). Again, it is Plutarch (*Mor.* 245e) who is our principal source for the festival of the Hybristika, "when they drape the women in men's tunics and cloaks and the men in women's robes and veils." Plutarch associates the festival with the female defense of Argos against Cleomenes and with the union between Argive women and "the best of the *perioikoi*" due to "the shortage of manpower" after Sepeia (see Section 1.7.4). Plutarch adds that the women showed little respect to their new husbands, whom they regarded as their social inferiors, "which is why they [the Argives] enacted a law bidding that married women must wear a beard when sleeping with their husbands" (*Mor.* 245e). Although Plutarch does not explicitly link the beard-wearing brides with the transvestite festival of the Hybristika, Bershadsky (2013: 260–5) believes that the "law" is a mythical *aition* for the festival, generated in the context of the establishment of democracy at Argos. Another festival attested at Argos is the Agrania, which Hesychius (s.v. Ἀγράνια) associates with one of the daughters of Proetus—the so-called Proitidai who were driven mad by either Dionysus (Hes. F131 Merkelbach-West) or Hera (Acusilaus *FGrH* 2 F28; Casadio 1994: 51–122). Finally, although Pausanias makes no mention of the typically Dorian cult of Apollo Karneios at Argos, and while Theopompus (*FGrH* 115 F357) claims that the Argives worshipped Apollo Karneios under the names Zeus and Hegetor ("leader"), a month named Karneios is attested in a third-century proxeny decree for Theainetos of Mantinea (*SEG* 17.143; Charneux 1958: 7). Thucydides' account (5.54.2–4) of how in the winter of 420/419, the Argives kept postponing the antepenultimate day of the month before Karneia in order to ravage Epidaurus with impunity may suggest a familiarity with—if not a profound respect for—the festival.

## 1.11.3. Argive Heraion

The most important sanctuary of the Argive plain was located not at Argos but 8 km to the northeast of the city at Prosymna, on the slopes of Mt. Euboea. The earliest ceramic evidence for cultic activity at the Sanctuary of Argive Heraia—more commonly known as the Heraion—is provided by Middle Geometric II sherds, dating to around the middle of the eighth century (Courbin 1966: 177); whether some pins and fibulas dating back to the Protogeometric period are indications for earlier cult or are instead heirlooms that were dedicated sometime after their manufacture is more difficult to assess (Snodgrass 1980: 52–3; Strøm 1988: 176; Hägg 1992: 14–15). The earliest architectural structure at the site is a monumental terrace wall (see Figures 1.10 and 1.11), whose large "Cyclopean" blocks have sometimes been taken to indicate a prehistoric date (Waldstein 1902–1905: vol.

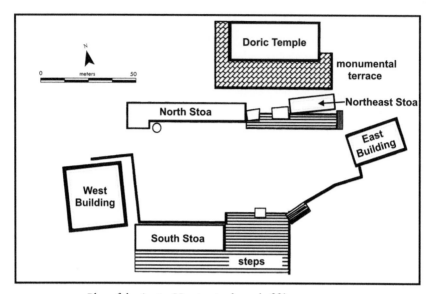

FIGURE 1.10. Plan of the Argive Heraion in the early fifth century.

1: 28; Plommer 1984). Most scholars now generally assign the terrace to the end of the eighth century (Blegen 1939: 427–8; Wright 1982: 186–92; Foley 1988: 135–6; Strøm 2009: 74), though it has also been argued that it may not predate the mid-seventh century (Drerup 1969: 57–89; Antonaccio 1992: 95–8). The earliest identifiable—though poorly preserved—Doric temple on this terrace has been dated variously to c. 700–650 (Amandry 1952: 225, 73; Strøm 1988: 191; Strøm 2009: 74, 139), to 650–625 (Mallwitz 1981: 610–21; Wright 1982: 190–1; Foley 1988: 136; Morgan and Whitelaw 1991: 85; Antonaccio 1992: 98), or even as late as the mid-sixth century (Bergquist 1967: 19–20).

It is now increasingly doubted that the Subgeometric terracotta model excavated at the Heraion and now in the National Archaeological Museum is a representation of an eighth-century temple as opposed to a secular structure (Fagerström 1988: 155–6; Antonaccio 1992: 97; Pfaff 2003: 1; Strøm 2009: 141). From the mid-seventh through to the early fifth century, a sequence of buildings was constructed on the slopes below, including the North and Northeast Stoas, the East Building, and a peristyle court (the West Building), which probably housed dining facilities (Amandry 1952: 240, 73; Strøm 2009: 77, 94).

There exists considerable disagreement as to who administered the sanctuary throughout the Archaic period. Part of the difficulty arises from the fact that Hera's epithet, "Argeia," can mean both "Hera of Argos" and "Hera of the

FIGURE 1.11. "Cyclopean" terrace wall at the Argive Heraion.

plain." A number of scholars have maintained that the Heraion was under the authority of Argos from at least the eighth century (Kelly 1976: 62–4; Wright 1982: 199; Foley 1988: 154; Morgan and Whitelaw 1991: 82–5; Antonaccio 1992: 105; Boehringer 2001: 219–21). Especially influential in this respect has been the thesis of de Polignac (1984: 41–92), according to which the Heraion constitutes an archetypal example of the "extra-urban" sanctuary, established in the second half of the eighth century to mark out for the first time the limits of the *chōra* of the *polis*. The emplacement of this extra-urban sanctuary, which was often more impressive than any contemporary urban sanctuaries, forges a "cultic axis" between the urban core and the rural periphery, which is physically marked by the solemn procession (*pompē*) that leaves the town for the extra-urban sanctuary on the occasion of the deity's festival. De Polignac would later modify his position, conceding that the Heraion might have originally served as a common meeting place for elites from Argos and other towns of the Argive plain, where they might compete among themselves for status, although he still maintained that "the rearrangement of the sanctuary and of its cults at the end of the eighth century carries a clear imprint of Argos and establishes the fundamental town-sanctuary axis of the Archaic and Classical city, without other

68    THE OXFORD HISTORY OF THE ARCHAIC GREEK WORLD

cities being excluded thereby from the cult" (de Polignac 1994: 13; cf. de Polignac 1995: 52–3).

Just as with the discussion of the independent status of Argolic settlements throughout the Archaic period (see Sections 1.7.1, 1.7.2, and 1.7.3), there are grounds for doubting whether Argos exerted direct control over the Heraion from the eighth century. To begin with, descriptions of the procession of armed youths, maidens, and cattle, which left Argos for the Heraion on the occasion of the goddess' festival, tend to derive from late authors (Dion. Hal. *Ant. Rom.* 1.21; Hesychius, s.v. ἀγὼν χάλκειος; Aen. Tact. 17.1; Palaephatus 51; schol. Pind. *Ol.* 7.83). Ostensibly, an earlier procession might be inferred from a story that Herodotus puts into the mouth of Solon, in which the youths Cleobis and Biton yoked themselves to the cart that was meant to convey their mother, the priestess of Hera, from Argos to the Heraion because the oxen had not returned from the fields in time for the festival. Upon arrival, their mother asked the goddess to grant her sons the greatest mortal blessing, which turned out to be everlasting sleep, and the Argives "made statues of them, as men who turned out best, and dedicated them at Delphi" (1.31.5). If we could identify these statues with the two *kouroi* that were excavated by the French at Delphi in 1893–1894, then we might have indirect evidence that the sacred procession from Argos to the Heraion already existed by c. 600, the date ascribed to the *kouroi*. Unfortunately, the identification of the twin *kouroi* is not secure, since it has been suggested that they represent instead the Dioscuri (Vatin 1982; Faure 1985; Hall 1995: 594–6). There is, then, the strong possibility that the story was no more than a generation old when Herodotus first heard it— assuming, of course, that it was not an outright invention on the historian's part. This means that the earliest reference to the procession from Argos to the Heraion occurs in Pindar's Tenth Nemean Ode, normally dated to c. 464 (Bowra 1964: 11).

Strøm (2009) has argued that in terms of the archaeological record, there is little that connects the Heraion to Argos in the eighth and early seventh centuries. For one thing, the sort of monumental architecture attested at the Heraion is not replicated at Argos. For another, the types of metal objects found at the Heraion seem to indicate an entirely different procurement network from that which brought items to Argos. So, for example, the Heraion shows links with Corinthia, northern Greece, and, beyond that, Phrygia and North Syria, whereas Argos has greater material connections with Attica, the Cyclades, and Cyprus (Strøm 2009: 76, 86, 91). In Strøm's view, many of the metal finds at the Heraion may not be dedications as much as ritual paraphernalia that were procured by an administrative body of officials that was independent from Argos. Along similar lines, Rolley (1992: 46) has noted that more of the tripods at the Heraion seem to be of Corinthian rather than Argive manufacture.

Billot (1989–1990: 57, 65–6) regards the Heraion as an originally common sanctuary, shared by the various communities of the plain, but suggests that it came under Argive hegemony during the reign of Pheidon in the late seventh or early sixth century. Strøm (2009: 76–7) also believes that the sanctuary came under Argive control in the second half of the seventh century but certainly prior to 575–550, when the divergences between the material culture of the Heraion and that of Argos seem to decrease. She also notes (Strøm 2009: 100; cf. Koiv 2003: 302) that this is the date assigned to an inscribed bronze plaque (*IG* IV.506; Jeffery 1990: 169 #25; van Effenterre and Ruzé 1994–1995: vol. 1: #100), found at the Heraion, in which there is mention of a *damiorgos*—a magistracy that is attested at Argos in this period. Yet, as we have seen (see Sections 1.5.3 and 1.5.5), it is now generally agreed that Argos was governed by a college of nine—or six—*damiorgoi* at any one time. The Sacred Law from the Heraion, on the other hand, makes contingencies "in case there is no *damiorgos*" (cf. *IG* IV.493; Jeffery 1990: 174 #1; van Effenterre and Ruzé 1994–1995: vol. 1: #101 from Mycenae), which argues rather for an administrative structure that is independent of Argos (Kelly 1976: 132; Hall 1995: 610). As for the archaeological evidence, although the divergences between the Heraion and Argos in the procurement of metal objects in the eighth century offer a strong indication for administrative independence, the narrowing of material differences in the seventh and sixth centuries need not be a direct reflection of a change in administration, especially given the well-attested mobility of craftsmen.

In fact, there are some hints that the Heraion continued to remain free of direct Argive control and to maintain connections with the other communities of the eastern plain throughout the sixth century. *IG* IV.506 is extremely fragmentary, with much of its left and right edges missing, making it especially difficult to read. One word that can be read on the second line, however, is τὰς ἀρὰς—a word that can mean "prayer," "vow," or "curse." Jeffery (1990: 15) and Boehringer (2001: 220–2) have argued that τὰς ἀρὰς is genitive singular, but if it is, instead, accusative plural (Gagarin 2008: 62–3; Rigsby 2009: 73–5), then this would represent a simplification of the intervocalic –ns– consonantal cluster, a linguistic phenomenon that is attested at Mycenae but not Argos (Hall 1995: 610–11; see Section 1.7.3). In earlier mythical discourse, the Heraion was also tied to the communities of the eastern plain. According to the tradition recorded in the *Catalog of Women* (Hes. F124 Merkelbach-West) and Acusilaus (*FGrH* 2 F26), Io, the legendary first priestess at the Heraion, was the daughter of Peiren, whom West (1985: 77) identifies with the Peiras, Peiranthos, or Peirasos of other sources. According to Plutarch (F10 Bernardakis), Peirasos had founded the cult of Hera at the Heraion, while Pausanias (2.17.5) notes that he dedicated the ancient pearwood statue of Hera at Tiryns. Finally, an inscription from the Heraion (*SEG* 13.246; Jeffery 1990: 169 #25), dated to c. 475, names its dedicator as Βᾶλος Ἀργεῖος ("Balos of Argos")—a designation that makes little sense if the Heraion was exclusively, or even predominantly, an Argive sanctuary at this date (Forrest 1960: 230). Indeed, Diodorus' notice (11.65.2–5), probably derived from Ephorus, that Argos waged war on Mycenae in the 460s (see Section 1.7.3) because of a dispute concerning "the rites of Hera" assumes that Mycenae had some sort of vested stake in the Heraion.

Palaiologou (2013: 396) supposes that the Heraion came under Argive control in the late sixth century and then reverted briefly back to Mycenaean control after the Argive defeat at Sepeia, but the far more economic hypothesis would be that the sanctuary was never exclusively Argive until Argos destroyed Mycenae, Tiryns, and Midea—not least because it is from this date that we see the most profound transformations at the sanctuary. Almost immediately after Argos had consolidated its control over the plain, Pindar was commissioned to write an ode honoring the Nemean victor Theaios, in which Argos is described as "befitting the goddess Hera" (*Nem.* 10.2). In the poem, the Perseid dynasty of the eastern plain is now accommodated alongside the Proitid stemma of Argos (4–17; cf. Kowalzig 2007: 168–77), while a clear allusion is made to the Argive festival of the Hekatombaia at the Heraion (21–3)—an athletic festival. Victories won at Argos, presumably at the Hekatombaia, are mentioned in three of Pindar's other victory odes (*Ol.* 7.83, 9.88, 13.107) and one composed by Bacchylides (10.32). Five inscribed bronzes (three hydriai, one lebēs, and one tripod) dating to the fifth century seem to have been given as prizes at the Hekatombaia (Forrest 1960: 228–9; Amandry 1980: 212–16; Hall 1995: 611–12; Nielsen 2018: 41–2). Indeed, a bronze tripod, dated to c. 460–450 and inscribed παρ' ἡέρας Ἀργείας ἐμὶ τὸν ἀϝέθλον ("I am from the games of Hera Argeia"), was deposited more than a century later as an heirloom in the "royal" Tomb 2 at Vergina (*SEG* 29.652; Andronikos 1984: 164–6).

Although a new temple (see Figure 1.12) was not begun until the old temple burned down in 423 (Thuc. 4.133), a close analysis of the South Stoa and the steps that are associated with it demonstrates that the terrace on which the new temple would stand was begun earlier, around the middle of the fifth century (Amandry 1952: 256, 73; Amandry 1980: 236; des Courtils 1992: 246; Pfaff 2003: 6–7). The contemporary appearance of the Heraieis among the new phratries that resulted

**FIGURE 1.12.** Remains of the fifth-century temple at the Argive Heraion. The Larisa acropolis at Argos can be seen across the plain in the center of the photograph.

from the reorganization of the Argive tribes may also speak to a recent territorial acquisition (Piérart 1983: 207; see Section 1.5.5). In the near aftermath of the takeover, the ancient pearwood statue that Peirasos had supposedly dedicated at Tiryns was transferred to the Heraion (Paus. 2.17.5), and the renowned mythographer Hellanicus of Mytilene, who was the first to compile a list of the priestesses of the sanctuary, detached Io from her Tirynthian ancestry and made her the daughter of Iasos, son of the Argive hero Triopas (Hellanicus *FGrH* 4 F36; cf. Paus. 2.16.1; Schol. Eur. *Or.* 6). In 421, the head of Hera appears for the first time on Argive *statēres*, minted to commemorate the alliance with Elis (Head 1911: 438; Jeffery 1990: 151; though see Flament 2012: 161), and before the end of the century, the Heraion was connected—for the first time, as far as we can tell— to Argos by a processional route (Hall 1995: 612; Marchetti 2000: 286; Marchetti 2013: 328; Palaiologou 2013). Indeed, McAuley (2019) has recently suggested that this is the period from which it is possible to recognize the emergence of a pan-Argolic ethnic solidarity that would, from the late fifth century, serve as the basis for an Argive theoric network.

# 1.12. Cultural History
## 1.12.1. Sculpture and Music

Argive sculptors came to the fore in the early sixth century. The earliest, and best-known, example is the twin *kouroi*, discovered at Delphi in 1893–1894 and traditionally associated with Herodotus' account (1.31) of Cleobis and Biton. Dated to c. 580, the two statues were the work of two separate Argive artists—perhaps Polymedes and Aristogeiton (Faure 1985). Distinctive regional characteristics include the short torsos, which display a musculature similar to that engraved on the cuirass in Tomb 45 (see Section 1.4.2); fleshy thighs and forearms; and what appear to be farmer's boots. The works of Ageladas, reputed to be the instructor of Phidias, Myron, and Polyclitus, are known only from literary references, which suggest a career that spanned from c. 520 to c. 460, when, according to Pausanias (4.33.2), he created the statue of Zeus Ithomatas for the Messenians of Naupactus (Kofiniotis 1892: 255–7; Tomlinson 1972: 254–6; Jeffery 1990: 161).

In his discussion of how the physician Democedes of Croton came to work for the sixth-century Samian tyrant Polycrates, Herodotus (3.131.3) notes that the Crotoniates were renowned for their medical skill, closely followed by the Cyreneans. An odd comment, which might be the insertion of a later commentator, follows: "at this same time, also the Argives were spoken of as the foremost of the Greeks with regard to music." One star performer was a certain Sacadas, who won the prize for flute playing at the Pythian Games of 586, 582, and 578 (Paus. 10.7.4; Piérart 2004a: 605). Another was the kitharist Aristonicus, whom Menaechmus of Sicyon (*FGrH* 131 F5) dates to the time of Archilochus. In addition, Cleisthenes of Sicyon's supposed ban on rhapsodic contests because they glorified Argos and the Argives (Hdt. 5.67.1) might be taken to indicate a lively musical scene at Argos in the sixth century (Kowalzig 2007: 129).

## 1.12.2. Argives in Athletic Competition

Argos also enjoyed modest success in athletic contests (Kofiniotis 1892: 277–81). An inscribed capital (*IG* IV.510), set up by a certain Timocles at the Heraion between 525 and 500, refers to victories at Nemea, the Arcadian cities of Tegea and Kleitor, and Pellene in Achaea. A *stēlē*, dated to 500–480 and found built into the church of Agios Dimitrios at Argos (*IG* IV.61; Jeffery 1990: 169 #17), commemorates an athlete named Aischyllos, who scored four victories in the *stadion* (c. 200 m dash) and three in the *hoplitodromos* (foot race in armor). At some point in the late sixth or early fifth century, Eurybates, who led 1,000 Argive volunteers in support of Aegina (see Section 1.7.4), is said to have been a pentathlon victor at the Nemean Games (Hdt. 6.92; Paus. 1.29.5). In 472, the Argive athlete

Dandes won the *stadion* at the Olympic Games (Diod. *Sic.* 11.53.1). An epigram, supposedly written by Simonides (*Greek Anthology* 13.14), lauds him for two victories at Olympia, three at the Pythian Games of Delphi, two at Isthmia, and no fewer than 15 at Nemea. Finally, in his epinician in honor of Theaios' victory in the wrestling competition at the Nemean Games (see Section 1.11.3), Pindar (*Pyth.* 10) refers to two further victories at Nemea, alongside one victory at the Pythian Games, three at Isthmia, two at the Argive Hekatombaia, and two at the Great Panathenaea.

### 1.12.3. Poetry

Assuming that the poet Telesilla was active in the middle, rather than the early part, of the fifth century (see Section 1.7.4), the only Argive author of note during the Archaic period was the mythographer and historian Acusilaus. Dionysius of Halicarnassus (*Thuc.* 6.1.2) describes him as a συγγραφεύς—that is, a type of compiler akin to an epic poet, which might explain some of the more pseudo-biographical details attached to him (Calame 2004: 229). For example, the *Suda* (s.v. Ἀκουσίλαος) says that he came from Kerkas, near Aulis in Boeotia, and that he based his *Genealogies* on inscribed bronze tablets that his father Kabas discovered while digging on his property. Calame (2004: 232–3) considers this notice to be reminiscent of the tradition that told of how a copy of Hesiod's *Works and Days* was inscribed on a lead tablet and deposited at the Hippokrene fountain in Boeotia (Paus. 9.31.3–5). Hesiod, of course, claims to have visited Aulis (*Op.* 650–3), and it may be this that accounts for the tradition concerning Acusilaus' birthplace, despite the fact that epigraphic evidence (e.g., *IG* IV.530; Vollgraff 1909: 183–4; Piérart 1983: 273; Charneux 1984: 217) makes it abundantly clear that Kerkas was actually a village in the vicinity of Argos. Clement of Alexandria (*Strom.* 6.2.26.7) goes so far as to accuse Acusilaus of copying Hesiod into prose and passing it off as his own work. Josephus (*Ap.* 1.15–16), on the other hand, states that Acusilaus often "corrects" Hesiod and dates him shortly before the Persian War of 480–479. From the scattered fragments that exist of the *Genealogies*, it seems that the work began with a theogony that derived the divinities Gaia and Eros from Chaos (Pl. *Symp.* 178a–b) before turning to the lineages of mortals, beginning with Phoroneus, the first king of Argos (Calame 2004: 236).

Acusilaus' oeuvre points to characteristics that, as we have seen, served to distinguish Argos from its Peloponnesian neighbors—namely, tendencies to engage in a prodigious amount of mythopoiesis and to overvalue the past (Adshead 1986: 23). Curiously, notwithstanding Cleisthenes' alleged accusations of pro-Argive bias in the Homeric epics, the Argives seem to have exploited the *Thebaid*

74    THE OXFORD HISTORY OF THE ARCHAIC GREEK WORLD

(a now-lost epic poem composed in the seventh century by an unknown author about the conflict between Eteocles and Polynices) far more than the Trojan epic cycle, as indicated by the sixth-century heroon to the Seven against Thebes (see Section 1.11.4). Indeed, Agamemnon and his Atreid lineage were grafted onto an earlier genealogical tradition in which they were never to fit entirely comfortably (Wathelet 1992: 115; Hall 1997b: 89–99; Cingano 2004).

## *1.13.  Conclusion*

Did Archaic Argos follow more in the tradition of Athens or of Sparta? Or is it more representative of what Hans-Joachim Gehrke (1986) has termed "the Third Greece"? The answer depends, in part, on the approach that one adopts toward the written sources. In contrast to some other studies (e.g., Tomlinson 1972), the reconstruction offered here paints a rather more modest picture of Argos in the period 750–450. Doubt has been cast on the existence of a hereditary kingship, on the degree to which Argos exercised complete hegemony over the entire Argive plain, and on the expansionist aspirations of the tyrant Pheidon, as well as on the duration and extent of hostilities with Sparta and the possibility of a servile insurrection in the early fifth century. The reason for skepticism extends beyond the lack of confirmation from archaeological evidence, since some of these episodes cannot reasonably be expected to be reflected or paralleled in the material record. It is rather the Argive tendency to glorify the past that dictates an especially critical approach to the literary documentation.

Such mythopoetical glorification might remind us of the "Spartan mirage," and in fact, excessive credulity when dealing with the textual sources could lead us to suppose that, as "Dorian" cities, Argos and Sparta developed in similar ways. For those who attribute far-flung territorial claims to Pheidon, Argos and Sparta are the natural rivals for the hegemony of the Peloponnese. Further parallels have been implied by those who view the γυμνῆτες as Argive equivalents to the Helots of Laconia and Messenia or by those for whom the *perioikoi* who were enrolled in the Argive citizen body are the functional counterparts of their Laconian namesakes. But a more critically aware approach to the literary sources, one that seeks to pierce through *le mirage argien*, reveals a rather different picture.

In terms of urban development, especially in the late eighth and seventh centuries, Argos resembles Athens more than Sparta, in terms of the pace of monumentalization and the relatively late date at which a formal agora was laid out (Papadopoulos 1996; Piérart and Touchais 1996: 47–52). Unlike at Sparta, the evidence for hereditary kingship is tenuous in both Athens and Argos. Both cities seem to have introduced ascribed offices in the course of the seventh century, including a magistrate named *basileus*, and both were governed by an annually appointed college of nine officials. Again, unlike Sparta, which prided itself on the stability of its constitution, both Athens and Argos witnessed a complete overhaul of both the citizen body and the tribal system within little more than a generation of each other, and both developed democratic systems of government that probably took some time to evolve but were essentially complete before the middle of the fifth century. This last feature may not be entirely coincidental, especially if any credence is given to the view that Themistocles imported democratic currents of thought during his exile in Argos (Forrest 1960). What is perhaps more significant is that Argos evidently considered itself sufficiently "in step" with Athens to contemplate the reforms in the first place.

## Guide to Further Reading

Tomlinson (1972) and Kelly (1976) offer general historical accounts of Argos, though the archaeological evidence in both is now rather outdated; Foley (1988) is a more recent archaeological survey of the region for the period 800–600. Piérart and Touchais (1996) synthesize, though not in a great deal of depth, the results of recent excavations in their survey of Argos from prehistory to the present day. For the geoarchaeology of the Argolid, Lehmann (1937) is now largely replaced by Zangger (1993), though their aims are rather different. For Argive political institutions, the fundamental work of Wörrle (1964) has been updated by various publications by Piérart (e.g., 2000). Finally, a selection of useful papers can be found in the edited proceedings of conferences organized jointly by the École Française d'Athènes and the Greek Archaeological Service (notably, Piérart 1992; Pariente and Touchais 1998; and Mulliez and Banaka-Dimaki 2013).

## Gazetteer

| Name | Figure/Map# | Grid Designation |
| --- | --- | --- |
| 48 Korinthou Street, Argos | Map 1.6 | D2 |
| Aegina | Map 1.2 | E2 |
| | Map 1.3 | C2 |
| Agora | Map 1.6 | B/C3 |
| Akte | Map 1.2 | insert |
| Amyclae | Map 1.3 | B2 |
| Archaeological Museum, Argos | Map 1.6 | C2 |

# 76 THE OXFORD HISTORY OF THE ARCHAIC GREEK WORLD

| Name | Figure/Map# | Grid Designation |
|---|---|---|
| Argive Heraion | Map 1.1 | B1 |
| | Map 1.2 | C2 |
| Argive plain | Map 1.1 | B2 |
| Argolic Gulf | Map 1.1 | B2 |
| | Figure 1.1 | |
| Argos | Map 1.1 | B2 |
| | Map 1.2 | B2 |
| | Map 1.3 | B2 |
| | Map 1.4 | B2 |
| | Figure 1.1 | |
| Asine (near Argos) | Map 1.2 | C2 |
| | Map 1.3 | B2 |
| Asine (near Pylos) | Map 1.3 | A3 |
| Aspendos | Map 1.4 | F2 |
| Athanasopoulos Plot, Argos | Map 1.6 | C2 |
| Athens | Map 1.3 | C2 |
| Aulis | Map 1.3 | C1 |
| Bakaloiannis Plot, Argos | Map 1.6 | B3 |
| Barbouna hill, Asine | Figure 1.7 | |
| Berbati valley | Map 1.1 | B1 |
| Building A, Sanctuary of Apollo Pythaeus, Asine | Figure 1.7 | |
| Building B, Sanctuary of Apollo Pythaeus, Asine | Figure 1.7 | |
| Building P, agora, Argos | Figure 1.5 | |
| Calauria | Map 1.2 | E/F2 |
| Cape Malea | Map 1.3 | C3 |
| Cape Skyllaion | Map 1.2 | F3 |
| Charandros river | Map 1.1 | A/B2 |
| | Figure 1.1 | |
| Chios | Map 1.4 | C/D1 |
| Church of Agios Dimitrios, Argos | Map 1.6 | D3 |
| Church of Timios Prodromos, Argos | Map 1.6 | C2 |
| Classical agora, Argos | Map 1.5 | |

| Name | Figure/Map# | Grid Designation |
|---|---|---|
| Corinth | Map 1.2 | C1 |
| | Map 1.3 | B2 |
| Cythera | Map 1.3 | B/C3 |
| Deiras cemetery, Argos | Map 1.6 | B1 |
| Deiras ridge, Argos | Map 1.5 | |
| Delphi | Map 1.3 | B1 |
| Dipaieis | Map 1.3 | B2 |
| Doric temple, Argive Heraion | Figure 1.10 | |
| East Building, Argive Heraion | Figure 1.10 | |
| Elis | Map 1.3 | A2 |
| Epidaurus | Map 1.2 | D2 |
| Erasinos river | Map 1.1 | A2/B2/A3/B3 |
| | Figure 1.1 | |
| Eretria | Map 1.3 | C1 |
| General Hospital of Argos, Argos | Map 1.6 | D1 |
| Granias Plot, Argos | Map 1.6 | B3 |
| Halieis | Map 1.2 | D3 |
| | Map 1.3 | C2 |
| Hellenistic theater, agora, Argos | Figure 1.5 | |
| Hermione | Map 1.2 | E3 |
| | Map 1.3 | C2 |
| Hypostyle Hall, agora, Argos | Figure 1.5 | |
| Hysiae | Map 1.2 | B2 |
| Inachus river | Map 1.1 | A1/B1/B2 |
| | Figure 1.1 | |
| Ithaca | Map 1.4 | A1 |
| Kaimeni Chora | Map 1.2 | E2 |
| Kanellopoulos Plot, Argos | Map 1.6 | B3 |
| Kephalari | Map 1.2 | B2 |
| Keryneia | Map 1.3 | B1 |
| Kleitor | Map 1.3 | B2 |
| Kleonai | Map 1.2 | C1 |
| Knossos, Crete | Map 1.4 | C3 |

| Name | Figure/Map# | Grid Designation |
| --- | --- | --- |
| Koros Plot, Argos | Map 1.6 | C3 |
| Kypseli Square, Argos | Map 1.6 | B3 |
| Lake Lerna | Figure 1.1 | |
| Lake Stymphalus | Map 1.2 | A1 |
| Larisa hill, Argos | Map 1.1 | B2 |
| | Map 1.5 | |
| Lerna | Map 1.2 | B2 |
| | Figure 1.1 | |
| Ligourion | Map 1.2 | D2 |
| Mantinea | Map 1.2 | A2 |
| | Map 1.3 | B2 |
| Megalopolis | Map 1.3 | B2 |
| Methana | Map 1.2 | E2 |
| Michalopoulos Brothers Plot, Argos | Map 1.6 | C1 |
| Midea | Map 1.2 | C2 |
| Miletus | Map 1.4 | D2 |
| Monumental terrace, Argive Heraion | Figure 1.10 | |
| Mothone | Map 1.3 | A3 |
| Mt. Arachnaion | Map 1.1 | B2 |
| Mt. Artemision | Map 1.1 | A2 |
| Mt. Bachriami | Map 1.1 | A1/2 |
| Mt. Euboea | Map 1.1 | B1 |
| Mt. Megalovouni | Map 1.1 | A1 |
| Mt. Megavouni | Map 1.1 | A2 |
| Mt. Parnon | Map 1.2 | B4 |
| Mt. Zavitsa | Map 1.2 | B3 |
| Mycenae | Map 1.2 | C2 |
| Naupactus | Map 1.3 | A1 |
| Nauplia | Map 1.2 | C2 |
| Nemea | Map 1.2 | B1 |
| | Map 1.3 | B2 |
| Nemea river | Map 1.2 | B/C1 |
| North Stoa, Argive Heraion | Figure 1.10 | |

| Name | Figure/Map# | Grid Designation |
| --- | --- | --- |
| Northeast Stoa, Argive Heraion | Figure 1.10 | |
| Oinoe | Map 1.2 | B2 |
| Olympia | Map 1.3 | A2 |
| Orchomenos | Map 1.3 | B1 |
| Orneiai | Map 1.2 | B2 |
| Papaparaskevas Plot, Argos | Map 1.6 | B3 |
| Pass of Tretos | Map 1.1 | B1 |
| Pellene | Map 1.3 | B1 |
| Peppas Plot, Argos | Map 1.6 | C2 |
| Phleious | Map 1.2 | B1 |
| | Map 1.3 | B2 |
| Platea | Map 1.3 | C1 |
| Polygonal terrace wall, agora, Argos | Figure 1.5 | |
| Prasiai | Map 1.2 | C4 |
| | Map 1.3 | B2 |
| Pron, Argos | 1.5 | |
| Prophetes Elias, Argos | 1.5 | |
| Pylos | Map 1.3 | A3 |
| Rebelos Plot, Argos | Map 1.6 | C1 |
| Rhodes | Map 1.4 | D2/E2/D3 |
| Roman bath, agora, Argos | Figure 1.5 | |
| Roman Nymphaeum, agora, Argos | Figure 1.5 | |
| Sanctuary of Aphrodite, Argos | Map 1.6 | B3 |
| Sanctuary of Apollo of the Deiras, Argos | Map 1.6 | B1 |
| Sanctuary of Apollo Pythaeus, Asine | Figure 1.7 | |
| Sepeia | Map 1.2 | C2 |
| Siamblis Plot, Argos | Map 1.6 | C1 |
| Sicyon | Map 1.2 | B1 |
| | Map 1.3 | B2 |
| South Stoa, Argive Heraion | Figure 1.10 | |
| Sparta | Map 1.3 | B2 |
| Stavropoulos Brothers Plot, Argos | Map 1.6 | C2 |

| Name | Figure/Map# | Grid Designation |
| --- | --- | --- |
| Stavropoulos Plot, Argos | Map 1.6 | C1 |
| Tanagra | Map 1.3 | C1 |
| Tegea | Map 1.2 | A3 |
| | Map 1.3 | B2 |
| Temple of Aphrodite, agora, Argos | Figure 1.5 | |
| Temples of Zeus Larisaios and Athena Polias, Argos | Map 1.6 | A2 |
| Theater with Square Steps, agora, Argos | Figure 1.5 | |
| Thebes | Map 1.3 | C1 |
| Theodoropoulos Plot, Argos | Map 1.6 | C1 |
| Thermopylae | Map 1.4 | B1 |
| Thyrea | Map 1.2 | B/C3 |
| | Map 1.3 | B2 |
| Tiryns | Map 1.2 | C2 |
| | Figure 1.1 | |
| Troezen | Map 1.2 | E2/3 |
| | Map 1.3 | C2 |
| Tylissos, Crete | Map 1.4 | C3 |
| West Building, Argive Heraion | Figure 1.10 | |
| Yeorgas Plot, Argos | Map 1.6 | C2 |

## BIBLIOGRAPHY

Adshead, K. 1986. *Politics of the Archaic Peloponnese: The Transition from Archaic to Classical Politics.* Amersham, UK: Avebury.

Amandry, P. 1952. "Observations sur les monuments de l'Héraion d'Argos." *Hesperia* 21: 222–74.

Amandry, P. 1980. "Sur les concours argiens." *Études argiennes, Bulletin de correspondance hellénique* Supplément 6: 211–53. Paris: De Boccard.

Anderson, G. 2003. *The Athenian Experiment: Building an Imagined Political Community in Ancient Attica, 508–490 B.C.* Ann Arbor: University of Michigan Press.

Andrewes, A. 1956. *The Greek Tyrants.* London: Hutchinson.

Andronikos, M. 1984. *Vergina: The Royal Tombs and the Ancient City.* Athens: Εκδοτική Αθηνών.

Antonaccio, C. M. 1992. "Terraces, Tombs, and the Early Argive Heraion." *Hesperia* 61: 85–105.

Aupert, P. 1982. "Argos aux VIIIe–VIIe siècles: Bourgade ou métropole?" *Annuario della Scuola Archeologica di Atene e delle Missioni Italiane in Oriente* 44: 21–32.

Barakari-Gleni, K. 2013. "Ἕνας νέος χώρος λατρείας στο Ἄργος." In *Στα βήματα του Wilhelm Vollgraff: Εκατό χρόνια αρχαιολογικής δραστηριότητας στο Ἄργος*, edited by D. Mulliez and A. Banaka-Dimaki, 373–92. Athens: École Française d'Athènes.

Barakari-Gleni, K., and A. Pariente. 1998. "Argos du VIIe au IIe siècle av. J.-C: Synthèse des données archéologiques." In *Argos et l'Argolide: Topographie et urbanisme*, edited by A. Pariente and G. Touchais, 165–75. Paris: De Boccard.

Barrett, W. S. 1954. "Bacchylides, Asine and Apollo Pythaeus." *Hermes* 82: 421–44.

Bearzot, C. 2006. "Argo nel V secolo: Ambizioni egemoniche, crisi interne, condizionamenti esterni." In *Argo: Una democrazia diversa*, edited by C. Bearzot and F. Landucci, 105–46. Milan: Vita e Pensiero.

Beloch, J. 1912–1927. *Griechische Geschichte*. 2nd ed. 4 vols. Berlin: Walter de Gruyter.

Béquignon, Y. 1930. "Chronique des fouilles et découvertes archéologiques dans l'orient hellénique." *Bulletin de correspondance hellénique* 54: 452–528.

Bergquist, B. 1967. *The Archaic Greek Temenos: A Study of Structure and Function*. Skrifter utgivna av Svenska institutet i Athen 4° 13. Uppsala: Akademisk Avhandling.

Bershadsky, N. 2013. "Pushing the Boundaries of Myth: Transformations of Ancient Border Wars in Archaic and Classical Greece." Ph.D. diss., University of Chicago.

Billot, M.-F. 1989–1990. "Apollon pythéen et l'Argolide archaïque: histoire et mythes." *Archaiognosia* 6: 35–100.

Billot, M.-F. 1997–1998. "Sanctuaires et cultes d'Athéna à Argos." *Opuscula Atheniensia* 22–23: 7–52.

Bintliff, J. L. 1977. *Natural Environment and Human Settlement in Prehistoric Greece*. 2 vols. Oxford: British Archaeological Reports.

Blegen, C. 1939. "Prosymna: Remains of Post-Mycenaean Date." *American Journal of Archaeology* 43: 410–44.

Boehringer, D. 2001. *Heroenkulte in Griechenland von der geometrischen bis zur klassischen Zeit: Attika, Argolis, Messenien. Klio* Beihefte Neue Folge 3. Berlin: Akademie Verlag.

Bommelaer, J.-F., and Y. Grandjean. 1971. "Argos. I: Secteur δ, A; Place de Kypséli." *Bulletin de correspondance hellénique* 95: 736–45.

Bourke, G. 2011. "Bakkhylides 11 and the Rule of the 'Slaves' at Argos." *Chiron* 41: 125–48.

Bowra, C. M. 1964. *Pindar*. Oxford: Clarendon Press.

Brandt, H. 1992. "*IG* IV 554: Aus Argos oder Halieis?" *Chiron* 22: 83–90.

Brelich, A. 1961. *Guerre, agoni e culti nella Grecia arcaica*. Bonn: Rudolf Habelt.

Brillante, C. 2004. "Genealogie argive: dall' 'asty Phoronikon' alla città di Perseus." In *La città di Argo: Mito, storia, tradizioni poetiche*, edited by P. A. Bernardini, 35–56. Rome: Edizioni dell'Ateneo.

Calame, C. 2004. "Le funzioni di un racconto genealogico: Acusilao di Argo e la nascita della storiografia." In *La città di Argo: mito, storia, tradizioni poetiche*, edited by P. A. Bernardini, 229–43. Rome: Edizioni dell'Ateneo.

Camp, J. M. II. 1979. "A Drought in the Late Eighth Century B.C." *Hesperia* 48: 397–411.

Carlier, P. 1984. *La royauté en Grèce avant Alexandre*. Strasbourg: AECR.

Cartledge, P. 2002. *Sparta and Lakonia: A Regional History 1300–362 BC*. 2nd ed. London: Routledge.

Casadio, G. 1994. *Storia del culto di Dioniso in Argolide*. Rome: Gruppo Editoriale Internazionale.

Cavanagh, W. G., C. B. Mee, and P. A. James. 2005. *The Laconia Rural Sites Project*. British School at Athens Supplementary Volume 36. London: British School at Athens.

Charles, R. P. 1963. *Étude anthropologique des nécropoles d'Argos: Contribution á l'étude des populations de la Grèce antique*. Paris: J. Vrin.

Charlier, P. 2013. "Réexamen des squelettes d'Argos (nécropole Sud): Rapport de la paléopathologie à l'évaluation de l'état de santé des populations." In *Στα βήματα του Wilhelm Vollgraff: Εκατό χρόνια αρχαιολογικής δραστηριότητας στο Άργος*, edited by D. Mulliez and A. Banaka-Dimaki, 201–17. Athens: École Française d'Athènes.

Charneux, P. 1958. "Inscriptions d'Argos." *Bulletin de correspondance hellénique* 82: 1–15.

Charneux, P. 1984. "Phratries et kômai d'Argos." *Bulletin de correspondance hellénique* 108: 207–27.

Christesen, P. 2007. *Olympic Victor Lists and Ancient Greek History*. Cambridge: Cambridge University Press.

Cingano, E. 2004. "Tradizioni epiche intorno ad Argo da Omero al 6° sec. a.C." In *La città di Argo: Mito, storia, tradizioni poetiche*, edited by P. A. Bernardini, 59–78. Rome: Edizioni dell'Ateneo.

Coldstream, J. N. 2008. *Greek Geometric Pottery: A Survey of Ten Local Styles*. 2nd ed. London: Methuen.

Consolaki, H., and T. Hackens. 1980. "Un atelier monétaire dans un temple argien?" *Études argiennes*, *Bulletin de correspondance hellénique* Supplément 6: 279–94. Paris: De Boccard.

Coldstream, J. N. 2003. *Geometric Greece: 900–700 BC*. 2nd ed. London: Routledge.

Coulson, W. D. E. 1985. "The Dark Age Pottery of Sparta." *Annual of the British School at Athens* 80: 29–84.

Courbin, P. 1955a. "Argos: Quartier sud." *Bulletin de correspondance hellénique* 79: 312–14.

Courbin, P. 1955b. "Un fragment de cratère protoargien." *Bulletin de correspondance hellénique* 79: 1–49.

Courbin, P. 1957. "Une tombe géométrique d'Argos." *Bulletin de correspondance hellénique* 81: 322–86.

Courbin, P. 1966. *La céramique géométrique de l'Argolide.* Paris: De Boccard.

Courbin, P. 1974. *Tombes géométriques d'Argos.* Paris: J. Vrin.

Courbin, P. 1980. "Lyres d'Argos." *Études argiennes, Bulletin de correspondance hellénique* Supplément 6: 93–114. Paris: De Boccard.

Courbin, P. 1983. "Obéloi d'Argolide et d'ailleurs." In *The Greek Renaissance of the Eighth Century B.C.: Tradition and Innovation, Proceedings of the Second International Symposium at the Swedish Institute in Athens, 1–5 June, 1981,* edited by R. Hägg, 149–56. Skrifter utgivna av Svenska institutet i Athen 4° 30. Stockholm: Paul Åströms Förlag.

Courbin, P. 1998. "Le temple d'Apollon Lycien à Argos: Quelques suggestions." In *Argos et l'Argolide: Topographie et urbanisme,* edited by A. Pariente and G. Touchais, 261–6. Paris: De Boccard.

Croissant, F. 1972. "Note de topographie argienne (à propos d'une inscription de l'Aphrodision)." *Bulletin de correspondance hellénique* 96: 137–54.

Croissant, F. 2009. "Identification d'une déesse: Questions sur l'Aphrodite argienne." In *Le donateur, l'offrande et la déesse: Systèmes votifs dans les sanctuaires de déesses du monde grec, Actes du 31e colloque international organisé par l'UMR Halma-Ipel (Université Charles-de-Gaulle/Lille 3, 13–15 décembre 2007),* edited by C. Prêtre, 181–202. *Kernos* Supplément 23. Liège: Centre International d'Étude de la Religion Grecque Antique.

Croissant, F. 2013. "Cinquante ans de recherche de l'École Française d'Athènes (1952–2002)." In *Στα βήματα του Wilhelm Vollgraff: Εκατό χρόνια αρχαιολογικής δραστηριότητας στο Άργος,* edited by D. Mulliez and A. Banaka-Dimaki, 59–74. Athens: École Française d'Athènes.

Daly, L. 1939. "An Inscribed Doric Capital from the Argive Heraion." *Hesperia* 8: 165–9.

Daux, G. 1957. "Chronique des fouilles et découvertes archéologiques en Grèce en 1956." *Bulletin de correspondance hellénique* 81: 496–713.

Daux, G. 1959. "Chronique des fouilles et découvertes archéologiques en Grèce en 1958." *Bulletin de correspondance hellénique* 83: 567–793.

Daux, G. 1968. "Argos: Secteur δ." *Bulletin de correspondance hellénique* 92: 1021–39.

Daux, G. 1969. "Argos: Secteur δ." *Bulletin de correspondance hellénique* 93: 986–1013.

De Angelis, F. 2016. *Archaic and Classical Greek Sicily: A Social and Economic History.* Oxford: Oxford University Press.

Deïlaki, E. 1973. "Ἀρχαιότητες καὶ μνημεῖα Ἀργολιδο-Κορινθίας." *Ἀρχαιολογικόν Δελτίον* 28 Β1: 80–122.

Deïlaki, E. 1973–1974. "Ἀνασκαφικαὶ ἐργασίες." *Ἀρχαιολογικόν Δελτίον* 29 Β2: 200–10.

De Polignac, F. 1984. *La naissance de la cité grecque: Cultes, espace et société VIIIe–VIIe siècles avant J.-C.* Paris: Éditions La Découverte.

84 THE OXFORD HISTORY OF THE ARCHAIC GREEK WORLD

De Polignac, F. 1994. "Mediation, Competition and Sovereignty: The Evolution of Rural Sanctuaries in Geometric Greece." In *Placing the Gods: Sanctuaries and Sacred Space in Ancient Greece*, edited by S. E. Alcock and R. Osborne, 3–18. Oxford: Oxford University Press.

De Polignac, F. 1995. *Cults, Territory, and the Origins of the Greek City-State*. Translated by J. Lloyd. Chicago: University of Chicago Press.

Des Courtils, J. 1981. "Note de topographie argienne." *Bulletin de correspondance hellénique* 10: 607–10.

Des Courtils, J. 1992. "L'architecture et l'histoire d'Argos dans la première moitié du Ve siècle avant J.-C." In *Polydipsion Argos: Argos de la fin des palais mycéniens à la constitution de l'état classique*, edited by M. Piérart, 241–51. Paris: De Boccard.

Dickinson, O. T. P. K. 2006. *The Aegean from Bronze Age to Iron Age: Continuity and Change between the Twelfth and Eighth Centuries B.C.* London: Routledge.

Dillery, J. 1996. "Reconfiguring the Past: Thyrea, Thermopylae, and Narrative Patterns in Herodotus." *American Journal of Philology* 117: 217–54.

Donlan, W. 1985. "The Social Groups of Dark Age Greece." *Classical Philology* 80: 293–308.

Dorovinis, V. K. 2013. "Γαλλικές ανασκαφές στο Άργος και η αντίδραση του κοινού: Η περίπτωση του Wilhelm Vollgraff." In *Στα βήματα του Wilhelm Vollgraff: Εκατό χρόνια αρχαιολογικής δραστηριότητας στο Άργος*, edited by D. Mulliez and A. Banaka-Dimaki, 41–57. Athens: École Française d'Athènes.

Drerup, H. 1969. *Griechische Baukunst in geometrischer Zeit.* Archaeologia Homerica Vol. 2. Göttingen: Vandenhoeck & Ruprecht.

Drews, R. 1983. *Basileus: The Evidence for Kingship in Geometric Greece.* New Haven, CT: Yale University Press.

Ekroth, G. 2013. "Between Bronze and Clay: The Origin of an Argive, Archaic Votive Shape." In *Forgerons, élites et voyageurs d'Homère à nos jours: Hommages en mémoire d'Isabelle Ratinaud-Lachkar*, edited by M.-C. Ferriès, M. P. Castiglioni, and F. Létoublon, 63–77. Grenoble: Presses Universitaires de Grenoble.

Evely, D., H. Hall, C. A. Morgan, et al. 2008. "Archaeology in Greece 2007–2008." *Archaeological Reports* 54: 1–113.

Fagerström, K. 1988. *Greek Iron Age Architecture: Developments through Changing Times.* Studies in Mediterranean Archaeology 81. Gothenburg: Paul Åströms Förlag.

Farnell, L. R. 1896–1909. *The Cults of the Greek States.* 5 vols. Oxford: Clarendon Press.

Faure, P. 1985. "Les Dioscures à Delphes." *L'Antiquité classique* 54: 56–65.

Fernández Alvarez, M. P. 1981. *El argólico occidental y oriental en las inscripciones de los siglos VII, VI y V a. C.* Salamanca: Universidad de Salamanca.

Flament, C. 2009. "Classement stylistique et essai de périodisation des monnaies au loup d'Argos." *Revue numismatique* 165: 81–105.

Flament, C. 2012. "Classement stylistique et essai de périodisation des monnaies au loup d'Argos, II: Les émissions du Ve siècle." *Revue numismatique* 168–9: 159–78.

Foley, A. 1988. *The Argolid, 800–600 B.C.: An Archaeological Survey*. Gothenburg: Paul Åströms Förlag.

Foley, A. 1995. "Idle Speculation about Argos? Some Thoughts on the Present State of Eighth and Seventh Century Argive Studies." In *Klados: Essays in Honour of J. N. Coldstream*, edited by C. Morris, 79–86. London: Institute of Classical Studies.

Foley, A. 1998. "Ethnicity and the Topography of Burial Practices in the Geometric Period." In *Argos et l'Argolide: Topographie et urbanisme*, edited by A. Pariente and G. Touchais, 137–43. Paris: De Boccard.

Forrest, W. G. 1960. "Themistokles and Argos." *Classical Quarterly* 10: 221–41.

Franchi, E. 2012. "Conflitto e memoria ad Argo arcaica: Le tradizioni cittadine intorno a Telesilla." In *Forme della memoria e dinamiche identitarie nell'antichità greco-romana*, edited by E. Franchi and G. Proietti, 207–28. Trento: Università degli Studi di Trento.

Frödin, O., and A. Persson. 1938. *Asine: Results of the Swedish Excavations, 1922–1930*. Stockholm: Generalstabens Litografiska Anstalts Förlag.

Gagarin, M. 2008. *Writing Greek Law*. Cambridge: Cambridge University Press.

Gehrke, H.-J. 1985. *Stasis: Untersuchungen zu den inneren Kriegen in den griechischen Staaten des 5. und 4. Jahrhunderts v. Chr.* Vestigia 35. Munich: C. H. Beck.

Gehrke, H.-J. 1986. *Jenseits von Athen und Sparta: Das Dritte Griechenland und seine Staatenwelt*. Munich: C. H. Beck.

Gell, W. 1817. *Itinerary of the Morea, Being a Description of the Routes of That Peninsula*. London: Rodwell and Martin.

Ginouvès, R. 1972. *Le théatron à gradins droits et l'Odéon d'Argos*. Paris: J. Vrin.

Gordon, T. 1832. *History of the Greek Revolution*. 2 vols. Edinburgh: William Blackwood.

Graf, F. 1984. "Women, War, and Warlike Divinities." *Zeitschrift für Papyrologie und Epigraphik* 55: 245–54.

Graham, A. J. 1964. *Colony and Mother City in Ancient Greece*. Manchester: Manchester University Press.

Guzzo, P. G. 1995–1996. "Gli spiedi di Fidone." In *L'incidenza dell'antico: Studi in memoria di Ettore Lepore*, edited by A. Storchi Marino, L. Breglia Pulci Doria, and C. Montepaone, 2: 307–11. 3 vols. Naples: Luciano.

Hägg, R. 1974. *Die Gräber der Argolis in submykenischer, protogeometrischer und geometrischer Zeit: 1: Lage und Form der Gräber*. Uppsala Studies in Ancient Mediterranean and Near Eastern Civilizations 7.1. Stockholm: Almqvist & Wiksell.

Hägg, R. 1982. "Zur Stadtwerdung des dorischen Argos." In *Palast und Hütte: Beiträge zum Bauen und Wohnen im Altertum von Archäologen, Vor- und Frühgeschichtlern*, edited by D. Papenfuß and V. M. Strocka, 297–307. Mainz: Philipp von Zabern.

Hägg, R. 1992. "Geometric Sanctuaries in the Argolid." In *Polydipsion Argos: Argos de la fin des palais mycéniens à la constitution de l'état classique*, edited by M. Piérart, 9–35. Paris: De Boccard.

Hägg, R. 1998. "Argos and Its Neighbours: Regional Variations in the Burial Practices in the Protogeometric and Geometric Periods." In *Argos et l'Argolide: Topographie et urbanisme*, edited by A. Pariente and G. Touchais, 131–4. Paris: De Boccard.

Hall, J. M. 1995. "How Argive Was the 'Argive' Heraion? The Political and Cultic Geography of the Argive Plain, 900–400 B.C." *American Journal of Archaeology* 99: 577–613.

Hall, J. M. 1997a. "Alternative Responses within *Polis* Formation: Argos, Mykenai and Tiryns." In *Urbanization in the Mediterranean in the 9th to 6th Centuries BC*, edited by H. Damgard Andersen, H. Horsnaes, S. Houby-Nielsen, et al., 89–109. *Acta Hyperborea* 7. Copenhagen: Museum Tusculanum Press.

Hall, J. M. 1997b. *Ethnic Identity in Greek Antiquity*. Cambridge: Cambridge University Press.

Hall, J. M. 1999. "Beyond the *Polis*: The Multilocality of Heroes." In *Ancient Greek Hero Cult: Proceedings of the Fifth International Seminar on Ancient Greek Cult, Organized by the Department of Classical Archaeology and Ancient History, Göteborg University, 21–23 April 1995*, edited by R. Hägg, 49–59. Skrifter utgivna av Svenska institutet i Athen 8° 16. Stockholm: Swedish Institute at Athens.

Hall, J. M. 2007. "Politics and Greek Myth." In *The Cambridge Companion to Greek Mythology*, edited by R. D. Woodard, 331–54. Cambridge: Cambridge University Press.

Hall, J. M. 2014a. *Artifact and Artifice: Classical Archaeology and the Ancient Historian*. Chicago: University of Chicago Press.

Hall, J. M. 2014b. *A History of the Archaic Greek World, ca. 1200–479 BCE*. 2nd ed. Chichester, UK: Wiley-Blackwell.

Hammond, N. G. L. 1960. "An Early Inscription at Argos." *Classical Quarterly* 10: 33–6.

Hansen, M. H. 1985. *Demography and Democracy: The Number of Athenian Citizens in the Fourth Century B.C.* Herning, Denmark: Systime.

Head, B. V. 1911. *Historia Numorum: A Manual of Greek Numismatics*. 2nd ed. Oxford: Clarendon Press.

Heilmeyer, W.-D. 1979. *Frühe olympische Bronzefiguren: Die Tiervotive*. Olympische Forschungen 12. Berlin: Walter de Gruyter.

Hooker, J. T. 1980. *The Ancient Spartans*. London: J. M. Dent.

Huxley, G. L. 1958. "Argos et les derniers Téménides." *Bulletin de correspondance hellénique* 82: 588–601.

Jameson, M. H. 1974. "A Treasury of Athena in the Argolid (*IG* IV 554)." In *Φόρος: Tribute to Benjamin Dean Meritt*, edited by D. W. Bradeen and M. F. McGregor, 67–75. Locust Valley, NY: J. J. Augustin.

Jeffery, L. H. 1990. *The Local Scripts of Archaic Greece: A Study of the Origin of the Greek Alphabet and Its Development from the Eighth to the Fifth Centuries B.C.* Rev. ed. with a supplement by Alan Johnston. Oxford: Oxford University Press.

Kagan, D. 1960. "Pheidon's Aeginetan Coinage." *Transactions of the American Philological Association* 91: 121–36.

Kelly, T. 1966. "The Calaurian Amphictiony." *American Journal of Archaeology* 70: 113–21.

Kelly, T. 1967. "The Argive Destruction of Asine." *Historia* 16: 422–31.

Kelly, T. 1970a. "Did the Argives Defeat the Spartans at Hysiae in 669 B.C.?" *American Journal of Philology* 91: 31–42.

Kelly, T. 1970b. "The Traditional Enmity between Sparta and Argos: The Birth and Development of a Myth." *American Historical Review* 75: 971–1003.

Kelly, T. 1976. *A History of Argos to 500 B.C.* 9. Minneapolis: University of Minnesota Press.

Koerner, R. 1985. "Tiryns als Beispiel einer frühen dorischen Polis." *Klio* 67: 452–7.

Kofiniotis, I. 1892. *Ιστορία του Άργους από των αρχαιοτάτων χρόνων μέχρις ημών.* Athens: Palamedes.

Koiv, M. 2003. *Ancient Tradition and Early Greek History: The Origins of States in Early-Archaic Sparta, Argos and Corinth.* Tallinn: Avita.

Kolokotsas, K. 1998. "Η ανάπτυξη του Άργους μετά την ανεξαρτησία και τα προβλήματά της σε σχέση με το αρχαιολογικό υπόστρωμα." In *Argos et l'Argolide: Topographie et urbanisme*, edited by A. Pariente and G. Touchais, 439–51. Paris: De Boccard.

Kowalzig, B. 2007. *Singing for the Gods: Performances of Myth and Ritual in Archaic and Classical Greece.* Oxford: Oxford University Press.

Kritzas, C. 1972. "Ἀρχαιότητες καὶ μνημεῖα Ἀργολιδοκορινθίας." *Ἀρχαιολογικὸν Δελτίον* 27 Β1: 192–219.

Kritzas, C. 1973. "Ἄργος." *Ἀρχαιολογικὸν Δελτίον* 28 Β1: 122–35.

Kritzas, C. 1973–1974. "Ἀνασκαφικαὶ ἐργασίαι." *Ἀρχαιολογικὸν Δελτίον* 29 Β2: 212–49.

Kritzas, C. 1980. "Κατάλογος πεσόντων ἀπὸ τὸ Ἄργος." In *Στήλη, τόμος εἰς μνήμην Νικολάου Κοντολέοντος*, edited by K. Schefold and J. Pouilloux, 497–510. Athens: Σωματεῖο φίλων του Νικολάου Κοντολέοντος.

Kritzas, C. 1992. "Aspects de la vie politique et économique d'Argos au Ve siècle avant J.-C." In *Polydipsion Argos: Argos de la fin des palais mycéniens à la constitution de l'état classique*, edited by M. Piérart, 231–40. Paris: De Boccard.

Kritzas, C. 2006. "Nouvelles inscriptions d'Argos: Les archives des comptes du trésor sacré (IVe s. av. J.-C.)." *Comptes rendus des séances de l'Académie des Inscriptions et Belles-Lettres* 5: 397–434.

Kritzas, C. 2013. "Οι νέοι χαλκοί ενεπίγραφοι πίνακες από το Άργος ΙΙ. Πρόδρομη ανακοίνωση." In *Στα βήματα του Wilhelm Vollgraff: Εκατό χρόνια αρχαιολογικής δραστηριότητας στο Άργος*, edited by D. Mulliez and A. Banaka-Dimaki, 275–301. Athens: École Française d'Athènes.

Lambrinoudakis, V. K. 1969–1970. "Προβλήματα περὶ τὴν ἀρχαίαν τοπογραφίαν τοῦ Ἄργους." *Athena* 71: 47–84.

Langdon, S. 2001. "Beyond the Grave: Biographies from Early Greece." *American Journal of Archaeology* 105: 579–606.

Lehmann, H. 1937. *Argolis I: Landeskunde der Ebene von Argos und ihr Randgebiete.* Athens: Deutsches Archäologisches Institut.

Lemos, I. S. 2002. *The Protogeometric Aegean: The Archaeology of the Late Eleventh and Tenth Centuries BC.* Oxford: Oxford University Press.

Lenschau, T. 1936. "Forschungen zur griechischen Geschichte im VII. und VI. Jahrhundert v. Chr." *Philologus* 91: 278–307, 85–411.

López Eire, A. 1978. "El retorno de los Heraclidas." *Zephyrus* 28–9: 287–97.

Lotze, D. 1959. *Μεταξύ ἐλευθερῶν καὶ δουλῶν: Studien zur Rechtsstellung unfreier Landbevölkerungen in Griechenland bis zum 4. Jahrhundert v. Chr.* Berlin: Akademie Verlag.

Lotze, D. 1971. "Zur Verfassung von Argos nach der Schlacht bei Sepeia (Aristoteles, *Politik* 5, 1303a6–8)." *Chiron* 1: 95–109.

Mallwitz, A. 1981. "Kritisches zur Architektur Griechenlands im 8. und 7. Jahrhundert." *Archäologischer Anzeiger*: 599–642.

Mandis, A. 2013. "Η μέριμνα για τις αρχαιότητες του Άργους κατά το δεύτερο μισό του 19ου αιώνα." In *Στα βήματα του Wilhelm Vollgraff: Εκατό χρόνια αρχαιολογικής δραστηριότητας στο Άργος*, edited by D. Mulliez and A. Banaka-Dimaki, 17–30. Athens: École Française d'Athènes.

Marchetti, P. 2000. "Recherches sur les mythes et la topographie d'Argos, V, Quelques mises au point sur les rues d'Argos: À propos de deux ouvrages récents." *Bulletin de correspondance hellénique* 124: 273–89.

Marchetti, P. 2013. "Argos: La ville en ses remparts." In *Στα βήματα του Wilhelm Vollgraff: Εκατό χρόνια αρχαιολογικής δραστηριότητας στο Άργος*, edited by D. Mulliez and A. Banaka-Dimaki, 315–34. Athens: École Française d'Athènes.

Marchetti, P., and Y. Rizakis. 1995. "Recherches sur les mythes et la topographie d'Argos, IV, L'agora revisitée." *Bulletin de correspondance hellénique* 119: 437–72.

McAuley, A. 2019. "*Sans la lettre*: Ethnicity, Politics, and Religion in the Argive *Theôria*." In *Ethnos and Koinon: Studies in Ancient Greek Ethnicity and Federalism*, edited by H. Beck, K. Buraselis, and A. McAuley, 131–48. Stuttgart: Franz Steiner Verlag.

Meiggs, R., and D. M. Lewis. 1988. *A Selection of Greek Historical Inscriptions to the End of the Fifth Century B.C.* 2nd ed. Oxford: Clarendon Press.

Meritt, B. D. 1945. "The Argives at Tanagra." *Hesperia* 14: 134–47.

Moggi, M. 1974. "I sinecismi e le annessioni territoriali di Argo nel v secolo a. C." *Annali della Scuola Normale Superiore di Pisa* 4: 1249–63.

Morgan, C. A. 1990. *Athletes and Oracles: The Transformation of Olympia and Delphi in the Eighth Century BC.* Cambridge: Cambridge University Press.

Morgan, C. A. and T. M. Whitelaw. 1991. "Pots and Politics: Ceramic Evidence for the Rise of the Argive State." *American Journal of Archaeology* 95: 79–108.

Morris, I. 1987. *Burial and Ancient Society: The Rise of the Greek City-State.* Cambridge: Cambridge University Press.

Müller, K. O. 1817. *Aegineticorum liber.* Berlin: Libraria Reimeriana.

Mulliez, D., and A. Banaka-Dimaki, eds. 2013. *Στα βήματα του Wilhelm Vollgraff: Εκατό χρόνια αρχαιολογικής δραστηριότητας στο Άργος.* Athens: École Française d'Athènes.

Nielsen, T. H. 2018. *Two Studies in the History of Ancient Greek Athletics.* Scientia Danica, Series H, Humanistica, 8, Vol. 16. Copenhagen: Kongelige Danske Videnskabernes Selskab.

Osborne, R. 1989. "A Crisis in Archaeological History? The Seventh Century in Attica." *Annual of the British School at Athens* 84: 297–322.

Palaiologou, E. 2013. "Ένας δρόμος προς το Ηραίο του Άργους." In *Στα βήματα του Wilhelm Vollgraff: Εκατό χρόνια αρχαιολογικής δραστηριότητας στο Άργος,* edited by D. Mulliez and A. Banaka-Dimaki, 393–403. Athens: École Française d'Athènes.

Papadimitriou, A. 2013. "Οι νέοι χαλκοί ενεπίγραφοι πίνακες από το Άργος I. Ανάλυση των ανασκαφικών δεδομένων από το οικόπεδο Εθ. Σμυρναίου στην οδό Κόρινθου 48." In *Στα βήματα του Wilhelm Vollgraff: Εκατό χρόνια αρχαιολογικής δραστηριότητας στο Άργος,* edited by D. Mulliez and A. Banaka-Dimaki, 261–74. Athens: École Française d'Athènes.

Papadopoulos, J. K. 1996. "The Original Kerameikos of Athens and the Siting of the Classical Agora." *Greek, Roman, and Byzantine Studies* 37: 107–28.

Papazarkadas, N., and D. Sourlas. 2012. "The Funerary Monument for the Argives Who Fell at Tanagra (*IG* I.3 1149): A New Fragment." *Hesperia* 81: 585–617.

Pariente, A. 1992. "Le monument argien des 'Sept contre Thèbes.'" In *Polydipsion Argos: Argos de la fin des palais mycéniens à la constitution de l'état classique,* edited by M. Piérart, 195–229. Paris: De Boccard.

Pariente, A., M. Piérart, and J.-P. Thalmann. 1998. "Les recherches sur l'Agora d'Argos: Résultats et perspectives." In *Argos et l'Argolide: Topographie et urbanisme,* edited by A. Pariente and G. Touchais, 211–24. Paris: De Boccard.

Pariente, A., and G. Touchais, eds. 1998. *Argos et l'Argolide: Topographie et urbanisme.* Paris: De Boccard.

Pfaff, C. A. 2003. *The Argive Heraion I: The Architecture of the Classical Temple of Hera.* Princeton, NJ: American School of Classical Studies at Athens.

Phaklaris, P. B. 1990. *Αρχαία Κυνουρία: Ανθρώπινη δραστηριότητα και περιβάλλον.* Athens: Υπουργειο Πολιτισμου, Ταμειου Αρχαιολογικων Πορων και Απαλλοτριωσεων.

Piérart, M. 1983. "Phratries et Kômai d'Argos." *Bulletin de correspondance hellénique* 107: 207–27.

Piérart, M. 1985. "À propos des subdivisions de la population argienne." *Bulletin de correspondance hellénique* 109: 345–56.

Piérart, M. 1990. "Un oracle d'Apollon à Argos." *Kernos* 3: 319–33.

Piérart, M., ed. 1992. *Polydipsion Argos: Argos de la fin des palais mycéniens à la constitution de l'état classique*. Paris: De Boccard.

Piérart, M. 1997. "L' attitude d'Argos à l'égard des autres cités d'Argolide." In *The Polis as an Urban Centre and as a Political Community, Symposium, August 29–31, 1996*, edited by M. H. Hansen, 321–51. Copenhagen: Munksgaard.

Piérart, M. 2000. "Argos: Une autre démocratie." In *Polis and Politics: Studies in Ancient Greek History Presented to Mogens Herman Hansen on His Sixtieth Birthday*, edited by P. Flensted-Jensen, L. Rubinstein, and T. Heine Nielsen, 297–314. Copenhagen: Museum Tusculanum Press.

Piérart, M. 2003. "The Common Oracle of the Milesians and the Argives (Hdt. 6. 19 and 77)." In *Herodotus and His World: Essays from a Conference in Memory of George Forrest*, edited by R. Parker and P. Derow, 275–96. Oxford: Oxford University Press.

Piérart, M. 2004a. "Argolis." In *An Inventory of Archaic and Classical Poleis*, edited by M. H. Hansen and T. H. Nielsen, 599–619. Oxford: Oxford University Press.

Piérart, M. 2004b. "Deux voisins: Argos et Épidaure." In *La città di Argo: Mito, storia, tradizioni poetiche*, edited by P. A. Bernardini, 19–34. Rome: Edizioni dell'Ateneo.

Piérart, M. 2004c. "Qu'est ce qu'être Argien? Identité civique et régime démocratique à Argos au Ve s. avant J.-C." In *Poleis e politeiai: Esperienze politiche, tradizioni letterarie, progetti costituzionali, Atti del convegno internazionale di storia greca, Torino, 29–31 maggio 2002*, edited by S. Cataldi, 167–85. Fonti e studi di storia antica 13. Alessandria: Edizioni dell'Orso.

Piérart, M. 2006. "Argos des origines au synœcisme du VIIIe siècle avant J.-C." In *Argo: Una democrazia diversa*, edited by C. Bearzot and F. Landucci, 3–26. Milan: Vita e Pensiero.

Piérart, M. 2013. "'Arrivé au train d'une heure': Les fouilles de Wilhelm Vollgraff à Argos." In *Στα βήματα του Wilhelm Vollgraff: Εκατό χρόνια αρχαιολογικής δραστηριότητας στο Άργος*, edited by D. Mulliez and A. Banaka-Dimaki, 31–9. Athens: École Française d'Athènes.

Piérart, M., and G. Touchais. 1996. *Argos: Une ville grecque de 6000 ans*. Paris: CNRS Éditions.

Piteros, C. 1998. "Συμβολή στην αργειακή τοπογραφία: Χώρος, οχυρώσεις, τοπογραφία και προβλήματα." In *Argos et l'Argolide: Topographie et urbanisme*, edited by A. Pariente and G. Touchais, 179–210. Paris: De Boccard.

Piteros, C. 2013. "Η ακρόπολη της Λάρισας και τα τείχη της πόλης του Άργους." In *Στα βήματα του Wilhelm Vollgraff: Εκατό χρόνια αρχαιολογικής δραστηριότητας στο Άργος*, edited by D. Mulliez and A. Banaka-Dimaki, 335–52. Athens: École Française d'Athènes.

Plommer, W. H. 1984. "The Old Platform in the Argive Heraeum." *Journal of Hellenic Studies* 104: 183–4.

Protonotariou-Deïlaki, E. 1971. "Ἀρχαιότητες καὶ μνημεῖα Ἀργολιδο-Κορινθίας." *Ἀρχαιολογικόν Δελτίον* 26 B1: 64–84.

Protonotariou-Deïlaki, E. 1980. "Οἱ τύμβοι τοῦ Ἄργους." PhD diss., University of Athens.

Protonotariou-Deïlaki, E. 1982. "Ἀπὸ το Ἄργος τοῦ 8ου και 7ου αἰώνα." *Annuario della Scuola Archeologica di Atene e delle Missioni Italiane in Oriente* 60: 33–48.

Qviller, B. 1981. "The Dynamics of the Homeric Society." *Symbolae Osloenses* 56: 109–55.

Ragone, G. 2006. "Riflessioni sulla documentazione storica su Fidone di Argo." In *Argo: Una democrazia diversa*, edited by C. Bearzot and F. Landucci, 27–103. Milan: Vita e Pensiero.

Ratinaud-Lachkar, I. 2004. "Insoumise Asiné? Pour une mise en perspective des sources littéraires et archéologiques relatives à la destruction d'Asiné par Argos en 715 avant notre ère." *Opuscula Atheniensia* 29: 73–88.

Reynal, G., and H. Rio. 1980. "Argos: Urbanisme et patrimoine." Unpublished report (ARGOS 3-A-2a2). Athens: École Française d'Athènes.

Rigsby, K. 2009. "Notes on Sacred Law." *Zeitschrift für Papyrologie und Epigraphik* 170: 73–80.

Rizza, G., and E. De Miro. 1985. "Le arti figurative dalle origini al v secolo a.C." In *Sikanie: Storia e civiltà della Sicilia greca*, edited by G. Pugliese Carratelli, 125–42. Milan: Istituto Veneto di Arti Grafiche.

Robertson, N. 1992. *Festivals and Legends: The Formation of Greek Cities in the Light of Public Ritual.* Toronto: University of Toronto Press.

Robinson, E. W. 1997. *The First Democracies: Early Popular Government outside Athens. Historia* Einzelschriften 107. Stuttgart: Franz Steiner Verlag.

Roes, A. 1953. "Fragments de poterie géométrique trouvés sur les citadelles d'Argos." *Bulletin de correspondance hellénique* 77: 90–104.

Rolley, C. 1992. "Argos, Corinthe, Athènes: Identité culturelle et modes de développement (IXe–VIIIe s.)." In *Polydipsion Argos: Argos de la fin des palais mycéniens à la constitution de l'état classique*, edited by M. Piérart, 37–54. *Bulletin de correspondance hellénique* Supplément 22. Paris: De Boccard.

Roux, G. 1957. "Le sanctuaire argien d'Apollon pythéen." *Revue des Études Grecques* 70: 474–87.

Sansone di Campobianco, L. 2008. "Argo in lotta, frammenti di storia argiva fra il 475 e il 460 a.C." *Rivista Storica dell'Antichità* 38: 17–43.

Sarri, E. 2018. "Πρόσφατα ευρήματα των αρχαϊκών χρόνων από το Ἄργος." In *Τὸ Αρχαιολογικό Έργο στην Πελοπόννησο· Πρακτικά του Διεθνούς Συνεδρίου Τρίπολη, 7–11 Νοεμβρίου 2012 (ΑΕΠΕΛ1)*, edited by E. Zumi, A. B. Karapanagiotou, and M. Xanthopoulou, 271–84. Kalamata: University of the Peloponnese.

Sauzeau, P. 1999. "'Quand la femelle victorieuse . . .': Interprétations contextuelles d'un oracle énigmatique (Hérodote, VI, 77)." *Revue de l'Histoire des Religions* 216: 135–65.

Schaps, D. M. 2004. *The Invention of Coinage and the Monetization of Ancient Greece.* Ann Arbor: University of Michigan Press.

Sève, M. 1993. *Les voyageurs français à Argos.* Paris: De Boccard.

Shipley, D. G. J. 1997. "'The Other Lakedaimonians': The Dependent Perioikic *Poleis* of Laconia and Messenia." In *The Polis as an Urban Centre and as a Political Community, Symposium, August 29–31, 1996*, edited by M. H. Hansen, 189–281. Copenhagen: Munksgaard.

Shipley, D. G. J. 2004. "Lakedaimon." In *An Inventory of Archaic and Classical Poleis*, edited by M. H. Hansen and T. H. Nielsen, 569–98. Oxford: Oxford University Press.

Siriopoulos, K. 1989. "Τὸ Ἄργος κατὰ τους υστερομυκηναϊκούς και μεταμυκηναϊκούς χρονούς και η εγκατάστασις των Δωριέων εις αυτό." *Πελοποννησιακά* 14: 321–38.

Snodgrass, A. M. 1980. *Archaic Greece: The Age of Experiment*. Berkeley: University of California Press.

Strøm, I. 1988. "The Early Sanctuary of the Argive Heraion and Its External Relations (8th–Early 6th Cent. B.C.): The Monumental Architecture." *Acta Archaeologica* 59: 173–203.

Strøm, I. 2009. "The Early Sanctuary of the Argive Heraion and Its External Relations (8th–Early 6th Cent. B.C.): Conclusions." *Proceedings of the Danish Institute at Athens* 6: 73–159.

Suárez de la Torre, E. 2004. "Los oráculos sobre Argos." In *La città di Argo: Mito, storia, tradizioni poetiche*, edited by P. A. Bernardini, 245–62. Rome: Edizioni dell'Ateneo.

Tausend, K. 1992. *Amphiktyonie und Symmachie: Formen zwischenstaatlicher Beziehungen im archaischen Griechenland*. Stuttgart: Franz Steiner Verlag.

Tausend, K. 1993. "Argos und der Tyrtaiospapyrus P. Oxy. XLVII 3316." *Tyche* 8: 197–201.

Thommen, L. 2012. *An Environmental History of Ancient Greece and Rome*. Translated by P. Hill. Cambridge: Cambridge University Press.

Tomlinson, R. A. 1972. *Argos and the Argolid from the End of the Bronze Age to the Roman Occupation*. Ithaca, NY: Cornell University Press.

Touchais, G. 1980. "Chronique des fouilles et découvertes archéologiques en Grèce en 1979." *Bulletin de correspondance hellénique* 104: 581–688.

Touchais, G., and N. Divari-Valakou. 1998. "Argos du néolithique à l'époque géométrique: Synthèse des données archéologiques." In *Argos et l'Argolide: Topographie et urbanisme*, edited by A. Pariente and G. Touchais, 9–18. Paris: De Boccard.

Tuci, P. A. 2006. "Il regime politico di Argo e le sue istituzioni tra fine VI e fine V secolo a.C.: Verso un'instabile democrazia." In *Argo: Una democrazia diversa*, edited by C. Bearzot and F. Landucci, 209–71. Milan: Vita e Pensiero.

Van Compernolle, R. 1975. "Le mythe de la gynécocratie-doulocratie argienne." In *Le monde grec: Pensée, littérature, histoire, documents, Hommages à Claire Préaux*, edited by G. Nachtergael, J. Bingen, and G. Cambier, 355–64. Brussels: Éditions de l'Université de Bruxelles.

Van Effenterre, H., and F. Ruzé. 1994–1995. *Nomima: Recueil d'inscriptions politiques et juridiques de l'archaïsme grec*. 2 vols. Rome: École Française de Rome.

Vannicelli, P. 2004. "Eraclide e Perseidi: Aspetti del conflitto tra Sparta e Argo nel V sec. a.C." In *La città di Argo: Mito, storia, tradizioni poetiche*, edited by P. A. Bernardini, 279–94. Rome: Edizioni dell'Ateneo.

Vatin, C. 1982. "Monuments votifs de Delphes, V: Les couroi d'Argos." *Bulletin de correspondance hellénique* 106: 509–25.

Verdelis, N., M. H. Jameson, and I. Papachristodoulou. 1975. "Ἀρχαϊκαὶ ἐπιγραφαὶ ἐκ Τίρυνθος." *Ἀρχαιολογικὴ Ἐφημερίς*: 150–205.

Vidal-Naquet, P. 1981. "Slavery and the Rule of Women in Tradition, Myth and Utopia." In *Myth, Religion and Society*, edited by R. Gordon, 187–200. Cambridge: Cambridge University Press.

Vink, M. C. 1997. "The Archaic Period in Greece: Another Dark Age?" In *Debating Dark Ages: Papers on Mediterranean Archaeology*, edited by M. Maaskant-Kleibrink and M. C. Vink, 1–18. Groningen: Archaeological Institute, Groningen University.

Vink, M. C. 2002. "Sanctuaries and Cults in an Early Urban Context: Argos c. 900–500 BC." In *Peloponnesian Sanctuaries and Cults: Proceedings of the Ninth International Symposium at the Swedish Institute at Athens, 11–13 June 1994*, edited by R. Hägg, 53–61. Skrifter utgivna av Svenska institutet i Athen 4° 48. Stockholm: Swedish Institute at Athens.

Viret-Bernal, F. 1992. "Argos: Du palais à l'agora." *Dialogues d'histoire ancienne* 18: 61–88.

Vollgraff, W. 1907. "Fouilles d'Argos." *Bulletin de correspondance hellénique* 31: 139–84.

Vollgraff, W. 1909. "Inscriptions d'Argos." *Bulletin de correspondance hellénique* 33: 171–200.

Vollgraff, W. 1928. "Arx Argorum." *Mnemosyne* 56: 315–28.

Vollgraff, W. 1929. "Inscriptio in arce Argorum reperta." *Mnemosyne* 57: 208–34.

Vollgraff, W. 1931–1932. "De titulo argivo antiquissimo anno MCMXXVIII recuperato." *Mnemosyne* 59: 369–93.

Vollgraff, W. 1934. "Une offrande à Enyalios." *Bulletin de correspondance hellénique* 58: 138–56.

Vollgraff, W. 1956. *Le sanctuaire d'Apollon Pythéen à Argos*. Paris: J. Vrin.

Waldstein, C., ed. 1902–1905. *The Argive Heraeum*. 2 vols. Boston: Houghton Mifflin.

Wathelet, P. 1992. "Argos et l'Argolide dans l'épopée, spécialement dans le *Catalogue des Vaisseaux*." In *Polydipsion Argos: Argos de la fin des palais mycéniens à la constitution de l'état classique*, edited by M. Piérart, 99–116. Paris: De Boccard.

Wells, B. 1987–1988. "Apollo at Asine." *Πελοποννησιακά* 13: 349–52.

Wells, B. 1990. "The Asine Sima." *Hesperia* 59: 157–61.

West, M. L. 1985. *The Hesiodic Catalogue of Women: Its Nature, Structure, and Origins*. Oxford: Clarendon Press.

Whitley, J. 1991. "Social Diversity in Dark Age Greece." *Annual of the British School at Athens* 86: 341–65.

Whitley, J. 2001. *The Archaeology of Ancient Greece*. Cambridge: Cambridge University Press.

# 94 THE OXFORD HISTORY OF THE ARCHAIC GREEK WORLD

Willetts, R. F. 1959. "The Servile Interregnum at Argos." *Hermes* 87: 495–506.

Wörrle, M. 1964. "Untersuchungen zur Verfassungsgeschichte von Argos im 5. Jahrhundert v.C." Ph.D. diss., University of Erlangen-Nuremberg.

Wright, J. 1982. "The Old Temple Terrace at the Argive Heraeum and the Early Cult of Hera in the Argolid." *Journal of Hellenic Studies* 102: 186–201.

Zangger, E. 1991. "Prehistoric Coastal Environments in Greece: The Vanished Lanscapes of Dimini Bay and Lake Lerna." *Journal of Field Archaeology* 18: 1–15.

Zangger, E. 1993. *Argolis II: The Geoarchaeology of the Argolid*. Berlin: Mann Verlag.

# 2

## Chalcis and Eretria

### Sylvian Fachard and Samuel Verdan

### List of Illustrations

Map 2.1:  Euboea and surrounding regions. © Paul Christesen 2024.           98

Map 2.2:  Some key sites in Euboea, Boeotia, and Attica mentioned in
this essay. © Paul Christesen 2024.                                        99

Map 2.3:  Some key sites in mainland Greece mentioned in this essay.
© Paul Christesen 2024.                                                   102

Map 2.4:  Some key sites in the Aegean mentioned in this essay.
© Paul Christesen 2024.                                                   103

Map 2.5:  Some key sites in the eastern Mediterranean mentioned
in this essay. © Paul Christesen 2024.                                    104

Map 2.6:  Mountain ranges and plains regions in central Euboea.
© Paul Christesen 2024.                                                   108

Map 2.7:  Topographic map of Euboea. © Paul Christesen 2024.              109

Map 2.8:  Some key sites in the *chōra* of Chalcis mentioned in this essay. ©
Paul Christesen 2024.                                                     118

Map 2.9:  Some key sites in the *chōra* of Eretria mentioned in this essay. ©
Paul Christesen 2024.                                                     134

Map 2.10: Some key sites in the north Aegean mentioned in this essay.
© Paul Christesen 2024.                                                   171

Map 2.11: Some key sites in the central Mediterranean mentioned in this
essay. © Paul Christesen 2024.                                            174

Map 2.12: Some key sites on and near Euboea mentioned in Section 2.8. ©
Paul Christesen 2024.                                                     185

---

Sylvian Fachard and Samuel Verdan, *Chalcis and Eretria* In: *The Oxford History of the Archaic Greek World*.
Edited by: Paul Cartledge and Paul Christesen, Oxford University Press. © Oxford University Press 2024.
DOI: 10.1093/oso/9780199383597.003.0002

| Table 2.1: | Main characteristics of the tombs in the Heroon burial plot in Eretria. | 147 |

Table 2.1: Main characteristics of the tombs in the Heroon burial plot in Eretria. 147

Table 2.2: Main Chalcidian and Eretrian colonies in the Mediterranean according to written sources (after Tsetskhladze 2006–2008: lxvii–lxxiii; Mercuri 2004: 206). 168

Figure 2.1: Plan of Chalcis. © Sylvian Fachard 2024. 115

Figure 2.2: Plan of Eretria at the end of the Geometric period. © École Suisse d'Archéologie en Grèce 2024. 123

Figure 2.3: Plan of the Sanctuary of Apollo Daphnephoros in the Geometric period. © École Suisse d'Archéologie en Grèce 2024. 125

Figure 2.4: Walls built to control flooding in Eretria; c. 700. © École Suisse d'Archéologie en Grèce 2024. 126

Figure 2.5: Plans and sections of temples to Apollo in the Sanctuary of Apollo Daphnephoros in the seventh and sixth centuries. © École Suisse d'Archéologie en Grèce 2024. 128

Figure 2.6: Plan of Eretria at the end of the Archaic period. © École Suisse d'Archéologie en Grèce 2024. 129

Figure 2.7: Model showing the Doric Temple of Apollo Daphnephoros under construction, c. 530. © École Suisse d'Archéologie en Grèce 2024. 132

Figure 2.8: Plan of the Sanctuary of Artemis Amarysia, Geometric and Archaic phases. © École Suisse d'Archéologie en Grèce 2024. 136

Figure 2.9: Offering deposit (figurines, Attic black-figure vases, local ritual vessels, and various small objects) from a temple at the Sanctuary of Artemis Amarysia; late sixth century. © École Suisse d'Archéologie en Grèce 2024. 137

Figure 2.10: Pendant semicircle skyphos; first half of eighth century; height: 8.6 cm. Produced in Euboea and found on Cyprus. Metropolitan Museum New York 74.51.589. Image in public domain. 142

Figure 2.11: Kratēr attributed to a Euboean workshop (the Cesnola Painter); c. 750; height with lid: 181.6 cm. Found at Curium in Cyprus. Metropolitan Museum New York 74.51.965. Image in public domain. 143

Figure 2.12: Phase plan of the Heroon at Eretria. © École Suisse d'Archéologie en Grèce 2024. 148

Figure 2.13: *Poros* blocks with inscriptions (IG XII.9.1273–4) from Eretria; last quarter of sixth century; length: c. 60 cm, height: c. 54 cm. Archaeological Museum of Eretria 1206. © École Suisse d'Archéologie en Grèce 2024. 158

Figure 2.14: Black-figure plate showing horseman in center and frieze of cattle around edge; attributed to an Eretrian workshop; c. 540; diameter: 31.2 cm. Unknown provenance. Antikenmuseum der Universität Heidelberg 68-2. Photo by Einsame Schütze. Reproduced under Creative Commons Attribution-Share Alike 4.0 International license; https://commons.wikimedia.org/wiki/File:Antikenmuseum_der_Universit%C3%A4t_Heidelberg_68-2.jpg.                                          188

Figure 2.15: Marble sculpture showing Theseus and Antiope, originally part of an Amazonomachy, from the west pediment of the Temple of Apollo Daphnephoros; last quarter of the sixth century; height in present form: 1.10 m. © Ecole Suisse d'Archeologie en Grece 2024.                                          209

# List of Abbreviations

FGrH      Jacoby, F. 1923–1958. *Die Fragmente der griechischen Historiker.* 3v. in 14 vols. Berlin: Weidmann.

FHG      Müller, K. 1878–1885. *Fragmenta historicorum graecorum.* 5 vols. Paris: Didot. https://www.dfhg-project.org.

ICGH      *Inventory of Greek Coin Hoards* (http://coinhoards.org)

IG      *Inscriptiones Graecae.* 1873–. Berlin: Walter de Gruyter.

SEG      *Supplementum Epigraphicum Graecum.* 1923–. Leiden: Brill.

## 2.1. Introduction

The island of Euboea is a thin strip of land that runs in a roughly NW–SE direction for 175 km along the eastern coast of the central Greek mainland.[1] Its coastline is 7,900 km long, twice the length of the entire Mediterranean east to west. No other Greek island shares maritime borders with so many ethnically and culturally diverse regions, from the Cyclades to Attica, Boeotia, Locris, Phthiotis, Thessaly, and the Sporades (see Map 2.1). And no other island enjoys such easy access to the continent; the Euripos (the 8-km-long strait, with Chalcis at its northern end, that separates Euboea from the mainland; see Map 2.2) is a mere 50–80 m wide at its narrowest point. The minimal distance between Euboea and

---

1. The authors would like to thank Edward Harris for his help in revising this chapter for publication. Our thanks also go to Pierre Ducrey, Thierry Theurillat, Karl Reber, and Sarah C. Murray for carefully reading the first draft of this paper.

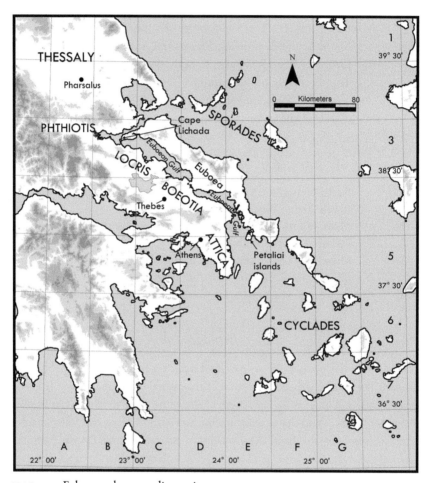

MAP 2.1. Euboea and surrounding regions.

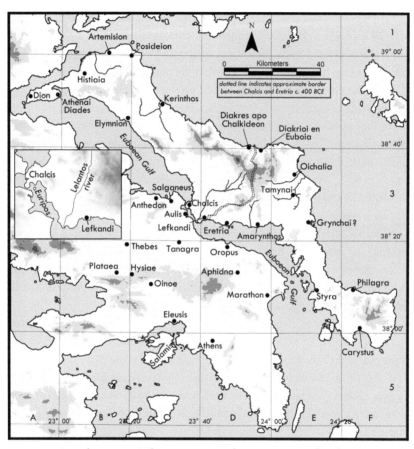

MAP 2.2. Some key sites in Euboea, Boeotia, and Attica mentioned in this essay.

100    THE OXFORD HISTORY OF THE ARCHAIC GREEK WORLD

the mainland and the existence of numerous convenient bases for ferries on both sides of the Euboean Gulf (the c. 165-km-long body of water separating Euboea from the mainland) helped create a web of maritime contacts and exchange opportunities penetrating well beyond the respective coastlines.[2] So, for example, Hesiod claims to have traveled from the Boeotian heartland to Aulis, from where he was ferried to Chalcis (*Op.* 650–5).

Euboea's shape and position thus encouraged maritime activity, and throughout the Archaic period, Euboea could only be reached by boat (the bridge at Chalcis was a Classical construction). Indeed, the Euboeans who built and sailed ships are the first of the island's inhabitants to appear on the Mediterranean stage. In the Mycenaean period, the island was never the seat of a palatial center, but it was well exploited, and the inhabitants of its central and southern districts were in the sphere of influence of the palace at Thebes, perhaps assuming an ever-growing role as the base of sailors operating on the sea routes connecting Thebes with the wider Mediterranean. This knowledge of maritime routes might have survived the demise of the palatial system and persisted throughout the Early Iron Age. Such a view would provide a partial explanation for the prosperity of Lefkandi in the 11th to 9th centuries and the later ascendancy of Chalcis and Eretria on some of the busiest and most lucrative sea routes of the Mediterranean in the eighth to sixth centuries.[3]

The traditional narrative focuses on the "big" sites (Lefkandi, Chalcis, and Eretria) and passes over the others in silence. Yet it is important to remember that at least 16 polities existed in Euboea in the Archaic and early Classical periods; from north to south, they are Histiaia, Dion, Elymnion, Kerinthos, Athenai Diades, Posideion, Diakres apo Chalkideon, Chalcis, Eretria, Amarynthos, Tamynai, Oichalia, Diakrioi en Euboia, Grynchai, Styra, and Carystus.[4] Among the communities situated in central Euboea, Chalcis, Lefkandi, Eretria, Amarnythos, Tamynai, and Oichalia seem initially to have been the most prominent. By the end of the fifth century, there were only four *poleis* on Euboea: Histiaia, Chalcis, Eretria, and Carystus (pseudo-Scylax 58), with the site of Lefkandi (where habitation ended c. 700) having been absorbed into the territory controlled by Chalcis and with Amarynthos, Tamynai, and Oichalia having been absorbed into the

---

2. The Euboean Gulf is typically understood as having two halves, north and south. The northern half stretches from the northern end of the Euripos to Cape Lichada (ancient Kenaion); the southern half stretches from the southern end of the Euripos to the Petaliai islands (located to the west of Carystus).

3. All dates are BCE unless otherwise indicated.

4. Diakres apo Chalkideon and the Diakrioi en Euboea appear as independent polities in the Athenian assessment of 425/4 (*IG* I³ 71.i.83–4 and 93–4). See Reber, Hansen, and Ducrey 2004: 649–50; Fachard 2012: 69–70. The Homeric Catalog of Ships (*Il.* 536–9) lists seven cities on Euboea: Carystus, Chalcis, Dion, Eretria, Histiaia, Kerinthos, and Styra.

territory controlled by Eretria. The tendency of larger communities to absorb the smaller ones is first evident in the Archaic period and had important consequences.

By the end of the Archaic period, both Chalcis and Eretria controlled large territories (each *polis* had a *chōra* of c. 1,000 sq km at that point in time); by the end of the fifth century, Chalcis and Eretria had emerged as the leading powers of the island, occupying 80% of its surface and exploiting its richest land and natural resources. The present study focuses on these two cities, but we will try to do justice to the others as well when information is available. Because this chapter is structured around Chalcis and Eretria, in each section, we will present the existing evidence for each *polis* separately, but in some cases, we opt for a common narrative. This dual approach, due to the limitations of the evidence, will produce data-related disparities between the cities, but it will allow the reader to examine the data for each city separately.

The relationship between Chalcis and Eretria was frequently hostile in the Archaic period, and Eretria seems to have emerged as the stronger of the two *poleis* in the sixth century. Moreover, despite their propinquity, there were significant divergences between the two *poleis*. For example, whereas Chalcis seems to have had strong links to Boeotia, Eretria had a close relationship with Athens. Indeed, there is good reason to believe that shortly after the establishment of democracy at Athens in 508, Eretria adopted a democratic form of government and carried out a tribal reform that had striking similarities to the Cleisthenic system.

On the other hand, both cities often appear as "Euboeans" in our literary sources, mainly in relation to their participation in the colonization movement, to the point where it is often impossible to distinguish Chalcidians from Eretrians. Perhaps the farther Chalcidians and Eretrians were from home, the more they identified themselves as Euboeans in markets and in myth. The same could be said of their pottery, widely distributed throughout the Mediterranean but quite difficult to attribute specifically to Chalcidian or Eretrian workshops.

Easy access to the sea, which created so many important opportunities, also created risks (Arist. *Pol.* 1327a15–29). The Euboean Gulf was too narrow to keep the emerging powers of mainland Greece—Athens and Boeotia—at a respectful distance. The transition between the sixth and fifth centuries marks the beginning of their constant intrusion into Euboean affairs. From that point on, the history of the island was increasingly linked to developments on the mainland. A key turning point came in 506, when Athenians defeated the Chalcidians in battle and settled cleruchs on land confiscated from rich Chalcidian landowners. In 490, the sea brought Eretria's doom when a Persian fleet landed on its coast and sacked the city.

We have in this introduction touched on the "highlights" of the history of Archaic Euboea, but we will see in the course of this essay that some of them need to be nuanced or even deconstructed, while others must be placed in a broader

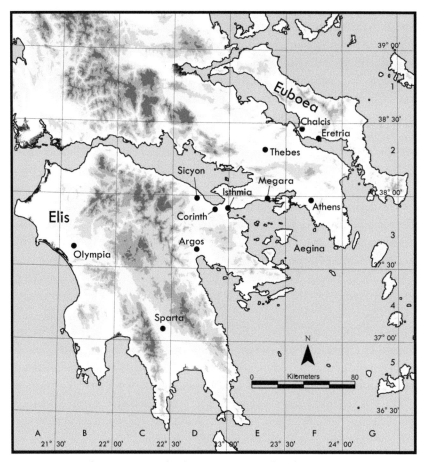

MAP 2.3. Some key sites in mainland Greece mentioned in this essay.

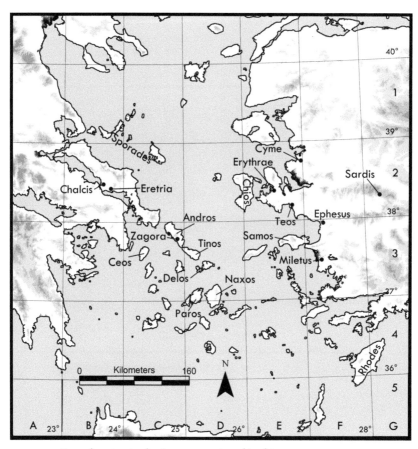

MAP 2.4. Some key sites in the Aegean mentioned in this essay.

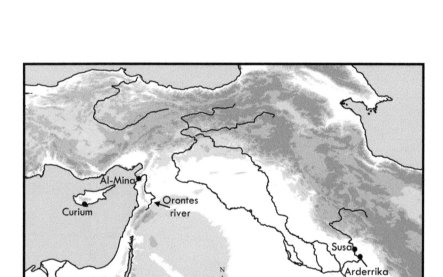

MAP 2.5. Some key sites in the eastern Mediterranean mentioned in this essay.

Mediterranean perspective. Our goals throughout are to summarize the latest archaeological evidence, to assess the textual sources critically, and to present the main issues related to the archaeohistory of Archaic Euboea.

A final note on chronology is warranted before turning to the issue of sources. Although 700 is often considered to be the "beginning" of the Archaic period in Euboea, we have opted for a start date in the Early Iron Age (tenth to ninth centuries), because many issues and developments originate then. At the other end, the fall of Eretria to the Persians in 490 provides a convenient terminus, but the decades down to 446 (when Pericles led an invasion force into Euboea that successfully put down a revolt from the Delian League) form an epilogue for both cities.

## 2.2. Sources
### 2.2.1. Excavations and Surveys

With respect to material evidence, there is a dramatic imbalance between Chalcis and Eretria, which will not be rectified anytime soon. Chalcis has never been systematically investigated from an archaeological point of view, while Eretria is among the most thoroughly excavated sites in Greece. The former became the seat of Negroponte, one of the largest medieval and Byzantine towns in Hellas, and many remains were despoiled during these centuries. In the modern period, the town expanded indiscriminately over the ancient city. As a result, our knowledge of Chalcis depends on piecemeal rescue excavations (with results available in the *Archaiologikon Deltion*). While archaeological overviews have been published (Sampson 1976; Bakhuizen 1985; Kalamara 2015; Kalamara, Kosma, Boukaras, et al. 2015), a systematic and exhaustive study of the ancient city is much needed.

The situation at Eretria has been more favorable. Unlike Chalcis, Eretria was abandoned after the late Roman period. Although it was refounded by King Otto in 1834, the long gap in habitation preserved the ancient remains in an exceptional fashion. The first excavations were carried out in 1885, under the authority of the Archaeological Society at Athens, closely followed by the American School of Classical Studies (1891–1895). Konstantinos Kourouniotis conducted the first excavations at the Sanctuary of Apollo Daphnephoros in 1899, followed by systematic work in other areas of the ancient city at the beginning of the 20th century. A new impetus made itself felt in 1964, when a Greco-Swiss mission was invited to join the excavations. Large areas of the ancient city have been excavated and preserved ever since. There have been published so far 25 monographs in the *Eretria* series, two guidebooks (Schefold and Auberson 1972; Ducrey, Fachard, Knoepfler, et al. 2004), one exhibition catalog (Martin Pruvot, Reber, and

Theurillat 2010; Kaltsas, Fachard, Psalti, et al. 2010 [in Greek]), and hundreds of scholarly articles.

The first survey of an extensive nature on the island was conducted by a British team in the 1960s (Sackett, Howell, Jacobsen, et al. 1966). This pioneering work, which revealed many important prehistoric sites (Lefkandi and Amarynthos, among others), still serves as a reference today. In the 1980s and 1990s, survey work was conducted in the area around Carystus under the auspices of the Canadian Institute (see Keller 1985; Cullen, Talalay, Keller, et al. 2013; Wickens, Rotroff, Cullen, et al. 2018). In the 2000s, an intensive survey (18 sq km) was conducted outside Eretria (Simon 2000; Simon 2001; Simon 2002; Simon 2007). It was followed by a larger project, extensive in nature and covering the central and southern parts of the island, roughly from Chalcis to Philagra (Fachard 2012). Additional survey work on the island has been conducted in the area around Carystus, under the lead of the Norwegian Institute and the Euboea Ephorate (Tankosić and Chidiroglou 2010; Tankosić 2017). Last, an intensive survey between Eretria and Amarynthos was initiated in 2021 by the Swiss School of Archaeology in Greece and the Euboea Ephorate (Fachard 2022).

## 2.2.2. Textual Sources

The epigraphic evidence (collected in *IG* XII.9 and Supplement) is richer for Eretria than for Chalcis, due to the systematic character of the excavations there, especially in and around the Sanctuary of Apollo Daphnephoros. The leading figure in Euboean epigraphy is Denis Knoepfler, whose tireless labor is responsible for much of our knowledge of Eretrian and Chalcidian institutions (Knoepfler 1997; Knoepfler 2008). Overall, Archaic inscriptions are scarce, but Eretria is well known for its early legal texts (see Section 2.6). Also noteworthy is the collection of c. 500 lead tablets found in the territory of Styra and dating to c. 475; those tablets are inscribed with names, mostly in the nominative to which is sometimes appended another name (possibly a patronymic) and/or an abbreviation that seems to represent a civic subdivision. The tablets seem to have served as identifiers for citizens of Styra (*IG* XII.9.56 #1–464; Jeffery 1990: 86; Masson 1992), which was originally an autonomous *polis* but became part of the Eretrian *polis* in the later fifth century.[5]

The literary sources for Euboea were first collected by Erich Ziebarth in 1915 (in *IG* XII.9). A new volume of testimonia, currently being prepared by Knoepfler, includes texts referring to Euboea more generally and those focusing

---

5. A new, full edition of the tables will be published by Francesca Dell'Oro in the *Eretria* series.

on Eretria. For the Archaic period proper, texts dealing with Euboea and its inhabitants are few and consist primarily of passages in Homer's Catalog of Ships (*Il.* 2.536–45), the *Homeric Hymn to Apollo* (218–23), Archilochus (F3 West), Theognis (1.891–4), Hesiod (*Op.* 650–1, 654–9), and Herodotus (1.61–3; 5.31, 99; 6.43–4, 74, 77, 94, 98–102, 105–7, 115, 127; 7.183, 189, 192; 8.4–7, 13–5, 19–20, 22, 23–5, 46, 66, 69, 86, 112, 121; 9.28, 31). Regarding the "Lelantine War," the main sources are Herodotus (5.99.1) and Thucydides (1.15.3). References to Archaic institutions and political leaders are found in Aristotle (*Pol.* 1289b, 1306a, 1316a; [*Ath. Pol.*] 15.2). The 158 *politeiai* compiled by Aristotle and his students included treatises on Chalcis and Eretria, but only a handful of fragments survives (Rose FF603, 611.40, 611.63). References to relevant passages from the work of other, later authors (such as Strabo and Plutarch) are found throughout the essay.

## 2.3. *Natural Setting*
### 2.3.1. Landforms and Geology

The island of Euboea, with a surface area of some 3,700 sq km, is the sixth-largest island of the Mediterranean (see Maps 2.3-2.4). It is mostly mountainous (80%). The central part of Euboea is dominated by the chain of Mt. Dirphys, which runs from Mt. Kandili (1,236 m, c. 30 km northwest of Chalcis) to Steni Dirphys (1,746 m, c. 20 km northeast of Chalcis) to Mt. Servouni (773 m, c. 10 km east of Eretria) (see Map 2.6). The limestone masses of Mt. Dirphys form a natural limestone amphitheater, opening to the west, which encloses the largest alluvial areas: the Psachna plain, the basin of the Lelantos (modern Lilas) river (i.e., the famous Lelantine plain), the plain of Eretria, and the valley of the Sarandapotamos river north of Amarynthos. This is the part of the island originally dominated by Chalcis and Eretria, but both eventually extended their influence beyond these geographical limits (see Sections 2.4.1–2).

Mountainous barriers separate the central part of the island from the rest of Euboea (see Map 2.7). Mt. Kandili, the western end of which terminates in precipices that border the Euboean Gulf and creates an inhospitable coast up to Limni (c. 40 km northwest of Chalcis, site of the ancient settlement of Elymnion), forms, together with Mt. Pixaria (1,352 m), a steep barrier between central and northern Euboea. One of the few viable land routes between central and northern Euboea is the pass of Derveni. Another mountainous barrier farther north is formed by the mass of Mt. Telethrion (969 m; Strabo 10.1.3–5; Theophr. *Hist. pl.* 9.15.4; Plin. *HN* 25.94), which marks the southern limits of the territory surrounding Oreos and Histiaia to the north and Aidepsos to the west.

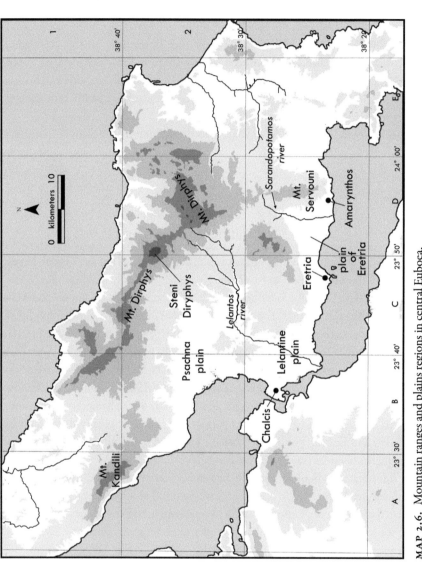

MAP 2.6. Mountain ranges and plains regions in central Euboea.

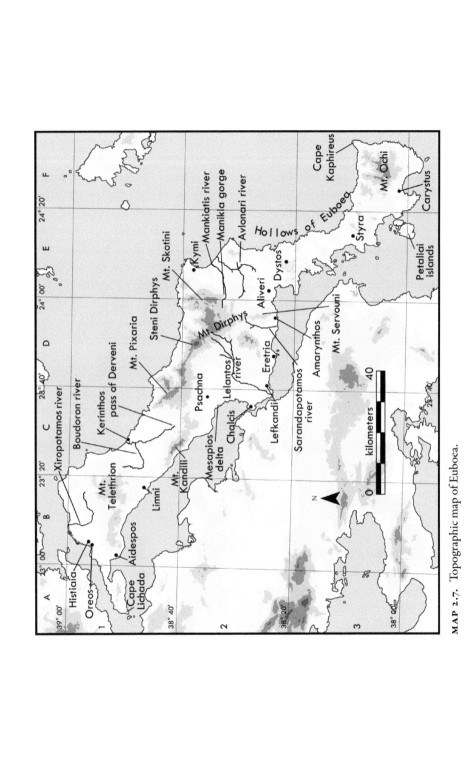

MAP 2.7. Topographic map of Euboea.

East of Eretria, Mt. Servouni joins with Mt. Skotini to form a continuous barrier, oriented N–S and running some 34 km from the Euboean Gulf to the Aegean (see Map 2.7). There are few natural land routes through this barrier: a coastal route between Amarynthos and Aliveri and a mountain route through the Manikia gorge, linking the upper Lelantos river valley with southern Euboea. The latter is the easiest route between central Euboea and the Aegean.

To the east of the Mt. Servouni–Mt. Skotini barrier lies a roughly rectangular area, with its long sides oriented generally N–S, running from Aliveri near the Euboean Gulf to the modern site of Kymi on the Aegean (see Map 2.7). This area is composed of several river basins and represents one of the most agriculturally productive districts of Greece. East of Aliveri, the landscape changes dramatically, and the southern part of the island, dominated by marble and schists, is part of the Attico-Cycladic metamorphic belt. This section of the island is also the narrowest (6 km), before widening again around the southernmost part of Mt. Ochi (1,399 m). That mountain overlooks Carystus and the stormy Cape Kaphireus (Kavo Doros), to the north of which lie the famous Hollows of Euboea.

The main rivers of Euboea emerge from Mt. Dirphys and are located in the central part of the island. Alluviation from these rivers created large plains that represented the most important stretches of farmland on Euboea, as well as marshy deltas whose coastlines have greatly evolved since antiquity. The Lelantos, the largest and the longest, forms the Lelantine plain and its vast delta near the site of Lefkandi (Ghilardi, Kinnaird, Kouli, et al. 2022). Several streams from Mt. Dirphys converge at Psachna (7 km north of Chalcis), forming the large Mesapios delta. The Sarandapotamos river runs south from Mt. Dirphys and forms a verdant valley whose large delta defined the site of Amarynthos.

To the north of Mt. Kandili are the Nileus and Kireus rivers (see Map 2.7), constituting the ancient Boudoron river (Strabo 10.1.4–5) and associated with the site of Kerinthos (on the Aegean coast about 45 km northwest of Chalcis). At the northern extremity of the island lies the large Xiropotamos river delta, occupied by the sites of Histiaia and Oreos.[6] To the east of the Mt. Servouni–Mt. Skotini barrier, the largest watercourses are the Avlonari and Manikiatis rivers, which debouch into the Aegean. These rivers were described in the 19th century as having water throughout the year. They constitute the most fertile and verdant valleys of the entire island and have sustained a multitude of settlements since antiquity (e.g., Tamynai, Oichalia).

---

6. Histiaia and Oreos were located close to each other; both settlements belonged to the same *polis*, which was referred to as either Histiaia or Oreos (with the latter name predominating after the mid-fifth century, when Oreos became the primary urban center) (Reber, Hansen, and Ducrey 2004: 656–8).

## 2.3.2. Paleoenvironment

In the present day, the dramatic topography of Euboea creates multiple micro-regions with varied environments. Current annual precipitation is normally low at Chalcis and Eretria (432.3 mm) but exceeds 800 mm at Kymi (on the Aegean coast, c. 50 km east of Chalcis) and on the mass of Mt. Dirphys. For the entire month of July, most of the island gets less than 10 mm of rain, while the Kymi area enjoys 10–25 mm, the equivalent of northwestern Greece. The climate in the Archaic period might have been, broadly speaking, comparable to nowadays, although slightly cooler and more humid (Finné, Holmgren, Sundqvist, et al. 2011; Bresson 2014).

More dramatic and marked changes have affected coastlines on the Euboean Gulf. In the Chalcis area, sediment accumulation, in the form of fine-grained deposits, accelerated between c. 1050 and 400. This may correspond to periods of increased human activity in combination with changes in local tectonics (uplift) and sediment supply from the Lelantos river (Ghilardi, Colleu, Pavlopoulos, et al. 2013). At Amarynthos, a general incidence of deltaic progradation and gradual extension of the shoreline toward the south from the Middle Helladic period onward has been noted. But around 750, a transition took place that resulted in the transformation of a small lagoon into coastal swamps by 700.

Major changes also took place at Eretria. Following a marine intrusion (the penetration of salt water into coastal freshwater aquifers) in the second millennium, a new deltaic sedimentation is recorded in the early stages of the tenth century. The latter is characterized by an increase in fluvial sediments, entailing deltaic progradation and the formation of coastal marshes and lagoons and pushing the shore toward the south. The settlement was subject to frequent and sudden flooding in the eighth century until the deltaic plain was artificially drained, starting around 700. This project was very successful, and by 550, there are no traces of alluviation inside the settlement, resulting in the modern landscape we see today (Ghilardi, Müller Celka, Theurillat, et al. 2016).

Several conclusions can be drawn about changes in the environment of Euboea since the Archaic period. First, sea levels in the Euboean Gulf were, generally speaking, about 1–1.5 m lower than today. Second, coastal swamps should be tentatively restored at the mouths of the largest rivers flowing into the Euboean Gulf. Due to deltaic progradation since antiquity, it is extremely difficult to trace the Archaic coastline for these deltas, but in the case of the Lelantos, the coastline might have been some 500–700 m further inland than it is nowadays. Third, several elements suggest an acceleration of erosion in the second half of the eighth century. Various complex factors were responsible for this change, but faster sedimentation might have been partly triggered by population growth and the clearing of forest areas in the upper Lelantos river valley and in the mountain chains surrounding Eretria.

### 2.3.3. Vegetational Landscape

Given the scarcity of pollen cores from central Euboea, it is currently impossible to trace the evolution of the vegetational landscape during the Pleistocene.[7] As elsewhere in Greece, strong variations are often evident in neighboring micro-regions. Maquis (shrubs) and garrigue (undershrubs) are found on the exposed limestone slopes of south-central Euboea (from Dystos to Styra), while vegetation (including laurels, sycamores, willows, elms, poplars, and blackberry bushes) can become luxuriant along the Avlonari and Manikiatis rivers. The slopes of hills and low mountains, when not laid out for olive cultivation, are dominated by a mosaic of maquis and garrigue, which covered up to one-third of Euboea in 1905 and has increased ever since. On a larger scale, cereals were concentrated in the plains, along with olive, almond, walnut, fig, and vine.

The dense forests found on the upper slopes of the mountains forming the Dirphys range are assumed to have existed in antiquity (see Map 2.6). They are mostly composed of Greek fir (*Abies cephalonica*), pine (*Pinus nigra*), juniper, and chestnut (Theophr. *Hist. pl.* 4.5.4). Forest penetration toward the plains is harder to estimate. At Amarynthos, new cores have shown that arboreal taxa represent 42% to 60% of the pollen spectra, with pines and oaks being the most abundant species. On the whole, neither ancient sources nor 19th-century CE travelers allow us to imagine a dramatically more wooded landscape than the one seen today. Diachronically, it can be presumed, also based on parallels from Attica and Boeotia (Kramer-Hajós 2008: 30–1; Kouli 2012), that pronounced arboreal clearing did occur in the Late Bronze Age, while an increased erosional phase, perhaps partly triggered by forest clearing, took place in central Euboea in the eighth century (Ghilardi, Kinnaird, Kouli, et al. 2022). By the end of the Archaic period, the vegetational landscape probably shared more similitudes with the 19th and early 20th centuries CE than it did with its Early Bronze Age counterpart.

## *2.4. Material Culture*

The sites of Chalcis, Lefkandi, Eretria, and Amarynthos all had notable advantages, including locations on the main sea and land routes running N–S and nearby fertile farmland. However, Chalcis and Eretria ended up controlling 50% to 60% of Euboea's arable land by the end of the fifth century, including its most

---

7. At Amarynthos, cereal pollens were found in small numbers, and the presence of *olea* pollen is attested only for later periods (K. Kouli, personal communication).

fertile regions and the vast majority of its forests. Those two *poleis* occupied the best natural harbors and the only two limestone acropoleis available on a 52-km-long coastal strip stretching from Mt. Kantili to Mt. Servouni. Chalcis and Eretria were thus better sited than Lefkandi and Amarynthos, in that they had larger, deeper harbors capable of accommodating more ships and maritime traffic and acropoleis that could be used for defense and visual control.

Lefkandi represents a particularly interesting case in that it flourished in the Late Bronze Age and Early Iron Age only to be abandoned c. 700. The cessation of habitation at Lefkandi has been connected to the so-called Lelantine War (see Section 2.7.1) but can more probably be attributed to an ongoing process of concentration of population at Chalcis and Eretria.

To judge from the archaeological record, the sites of Chalcis and Eretria were occupied in the Late Helladic IIIC period but sparsely inhabited thereafter until the tenth and ninth centuries, respectively.[8] Around 800, Chalcis, Amarynthos, and, perhaps to a lesser degree, Eretria and Manika, all show signs of permanent occupation. Chalcis and Eretria appear to have equaled Lefkandi and Amarynthos in size by c. 750 and to have superseded them by c. 700.

Population movements in Euboea during this period are impossible to trace, and it is perhaps a mistake to limit them to one or two distinct patterns of emigration/immigration. Much has been said about the "sudden" foundation of Eretria and its supposed relationship with Lefkandi, but this scenario does not take into account the wider population dynamics of the region. Instead, it is reasonable to assume that after 750, substantial numbers of people moved to Chalcis and Eretria from other sites in central Euboea and perhaps from neighboring areas such as Attica (Knoepfler 2008: 597).[9] It is plausible, yet in no way demonstrable, that many people chose to leave Amarynthos for Eretria and Lefkandi for Chalcis (Knoepfler 2008: 600).

## 2.4.1. Settlement Organization and Settlement Patterns

Despite the progress achieved since the 1960s, archaeological evidence from central Euboea for the tenth to sixth centuries remains patchy overall and completely absent in many cases. The data are still inadequate for reconstructing reliable, archaeologically grounded, comprehensive accounts of the foundations of both cities. Until systematic work is done at Chalcis (nearly a total archaeological blank spot for these periods) and Amarynthos, Eretria and Lefkandi will

---

8. On the Protogeometric finds at Chalcis, see Bakhuizen 1985: 94 fig. 60; Sampson 1976: 12. For those at Eretria, see Verdan 2015a.

9. See also Knoepfler in *Bulletin Épigraphique* 2008 #267.

remain in the spotlight, and the drama will unfold without two of the key players. Moreover, many other poorly documented sites played important supporting roles. In this regard, the scarcity of a large-scale, intensive field survey is regrettable (see Section 2.2.1), especially since the landscape has been dramatically altered by modern construction from the 1950s onward.

In the following sections, we will describe the sites of Chalcis and Eretria, offer some remarks about the extra-urban settlement patterns, tackle the question of borders and territoriality, and offer an overview of central Euboean material culture for the Archaic period.

### 2.4.1.1. Settlement Organization of Chalcis

Chalcis might hold the distinction of being the only major Greek city that has never been systematically excavated and whose architectural remains continue to elude us. This situation is particularly striking when one compares our fragmentary knowledge of the city with the lively account of Heraclides Criticus, who visited the town in the third century:

> From Anthedon to Chalcis is seventy *stadia*. . . . Chalcis is [ . . . ] *stadia* in circumference, longer than the road that leads to it from Anthedon. It is all hilly and shady. Most of the springs are salty, but there is one called Arethusa of which the water, though brackish, is wholesome, cool, and so abundant that it suffices for the whole city. Public buildings are a remarkable feature in the city: gymnasiums, stoas, sanctuaries, theaters, paintings, statues, while the location of the agora was unsurpassed as regards the requirements for economic activities. For the currents that come from the direction of Salganeus in Boeotia and from the direction of the Euboean Gulf [to the south] converge in the Euripos and flow past the very walls of the harbor, exactly where the Emporion Gate happens to be, and the agora, which is spacious and surrounded by three stoas, lies next to this gate. The proximity of the market-place to the harbor, and the speed with which cargoes can be unloaded, attract many ships to the port. Indeed, the Euripos itself, which can be sailed into from two sides, draws merchants to the city. (1.26–9; translated by Bakhuizen 1985: 16, modified)

None of this can be currently spotted on the ground, for the reasons outlined above (see Section 2.2.1). Local topography has also been dramatically transformed in modern times, with the silting up of old bays and the quarrying of the acropolis. Restoring the ancient city plan from the disparate rescue excavations is

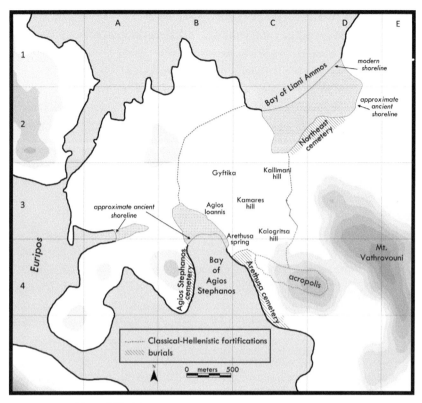

FIGURE 2.1. Plan of Chalcis.

difficult and leads to an incomplete sketch (Sampson 1976; Calligas 1990; Kosma 2015; Charalambidou 2020). The Archaic phase of the city is almost a blank space dotted with a few pits and wells. In order to delineate the likeliest position of the Archaic *asty*, there is no other solution than to map the meager remains and the Classical and Hellenistic city grid (see Figure 2.1).

Chalcis was situated on a roughly oval peninsula (c. 2.5 km E–W and c. 2 km N–S at its maximum extent) that was bordered on the north, west, and south by the sea and was naturally protected on its eastern and southeastern side by the limestone mass of Mt. Vathrovouni (189 m; Bakhuizen 1985). The acropolis was located on the southeastern side of the city, on a spur of Mt. Vathrovouni. Two major bays to the north (Liani Ammos) and south (Agios Stephanos) penetrated inland, thus providing natural harbors on both sides of the peninsula. The terrain between the two harbors was marked by a succession of low hills enclosing fertile ground (thus, the adjective γεώλοφος, "hilly," used by Heraclides at 1.27).

According to Heraclides, the site lacked fresh water, but the spring of Arethusa produced copious amounts of slightly brackish water. From Geometric times, the city developed between the two harbors and the acropolis hill. As at Eretria, the site's main assets were the harbors and a strong acropolis.

No Archaic architectural remains have been found to date, and the archaeological evidence from the site for this period is limited to ceramics. Geometric and Archaic pottery (including terracotta horse figurines) from wells or shafts was excavated at Gyftika and Agios Ioannis (Andreiomenou 1960: 150 pl. 32; Andreiomenou 1972: 170–2). Archaic pottery is known from the Kamares hill (Boardman 1957: 1–2), while sherds from the same period were picked up on Kallimani hill (Sampson 1976: 15).

Regarding the extent of the Archaic town, we can rely only on the fragmentary plan of the Classical fortifications (Kosma and Chairetakis 2017). The acropolis hill was fortified by a 2-km-long polygonal enceinte. To the south, a wall descended toward the sea and enclosed the Arethusa spring. This is where the road to Eretria exited, and a long string of graves (the Arethusa cemetery) was discovered along this route. From the acropolis, a fortification wall descended toward the north, taking in the hills of Kalogritsa and Kallimani and reaching the northern bay of Liani Ammos, where a gate communicated with the main road to northern Euboea. No wall has been found on the west side (the closest to the Byzantine town), but the limits of the city can be traced thanks to the position of Classical and Hellenistic graves. A west gate connected the city with the Euripos, which was bridged for the first time in 411. Excavations have shown that the first phase of the city walls dates back to the fifth century (Kosma 2015; Kosma and Chairetakis 2017). On the acropolis hill, however, some stretches of the polygonal wall could be older, so the presence of a late-sixth-century stronghold should not be ruled out.

Beyond this general outline, the existence of a few monuments can be inferred from later testimonies. First, it seems plausible to situate the Archaic agora under the Hellenistic one, which has not been precisely located but, as indicated by Heraclides, lay close to the harbor (probably the harbor in the bay of Agios Stephanos). Plutarch records the existence in the agora of a funerary column (μέγας κίων, *Mor.* 761a) marking the grave of Kleomachos of Pharsalus, a hero warrior who perished during the Lelantine War (on which see Section 2.7.1) while aiding the Chalcidians in a battle against the Eretrians (*Mor.* 760e–1b). Yet in the same passage, Plutarch reports another tradition, recorded by Aristotle, according to which Kleomachos was a Chalcidian from Thrace. Several cults attested for later periods (see Section 2.11.1) likely had an Archaic origin, but no physical remains of sanctuaries from that period have been found. The existence of a large Doric temple dating to the years 500–470 can be inferred from five large conglomerate capitals reused in later buildings (Georgopoulou Melanidi and Papadakis 1974), but its original location is unknown. The shrine of Apollo Delphinios was perhaps located at Agios Ioannis (Themelis 1969: 159), where Archaic pottery is attested. Overall, the evidence is meager, and the extent of the Archaic town cannot be accurately estimated.

### 2.4.1.2. *Settlement Pattern of the Chalcidian* Chōra

The *chōra* of Chalcis expanded significantly over the course of the Archaic period and beyond, but it is impossible, given the information currently at our disposal, to trace that process in any detail or to establish precise boundaries. By the end of the Archaic period, the *polis* of Chalcis seems to have controlled a territory of c. 1,100–1,200 sq km (see Section 2.4.2.1 for further discussion).

A ring of necropoleis, strung out along the main roads exiting Chalcis, surrounded the town. The most important were the Arethusa and Northeast cemeteries (Bakhuizen 1985: 58–70). Protogeometric and possibly Archaic graves were excavated at Nea Lampsakos along the ancient road leading to Eretria (Andreiomenou 1960: 150). It is unclear whether this site was a settlement or just an extension of the Chalcidian necropolis, but it has been identified with ancient Harpagion (Ath. 13.77; Themelis 1969; Knoepfler 1981: 306). Another road might have followed the course of the Lelantos river, securing access to its fertile upper river valley (see Map 2.8).

Some parts of the Lelantine plain, the breadbasket of Chalcis, were close enough to be exploited by people residing in the town. The scarce archaeological remains—the surface of the plain has been continuously covered by silt, and the exploitation of clay for modern tile factories has done much damage—are mostly known on the edges of the plain (Bakhuizen 1985: 135; Coulton 2002: 99–110; Kosma 2015: 218). On the west bank of the Lelantos, a Geometric to Archaic sanctuary with votive offerings, including 12 bronze bull figurines, was discovered at Pei Dokou.[10] After the abandonment of Lefkandi, the only known Archaic site on the left bank of the Lelantos is the short-lived fort at Vrachos, perhaps a site linked to the Athenian cleruchy that exploited the plain in the late sixth century (see Section 2.7.4.2). The area around the villages of Vassiliko and Vourlaki yielded abundant finds from the Geometric, Classical, Hellenistic, and Roman periods (Fachard 2012: 299–300), and so the absence of Archaic material might just be due to an accident of preservation.

---

10. Papavasileiou 1910: 43–5; Sackett, Howell, Jacobsen, et al. 1966: 57. A photograph of the bronze animal figurines, which apparently date to the end of the eighth century, is found on the front cover of Tankosić, Mavridis, and Kosma 2017.

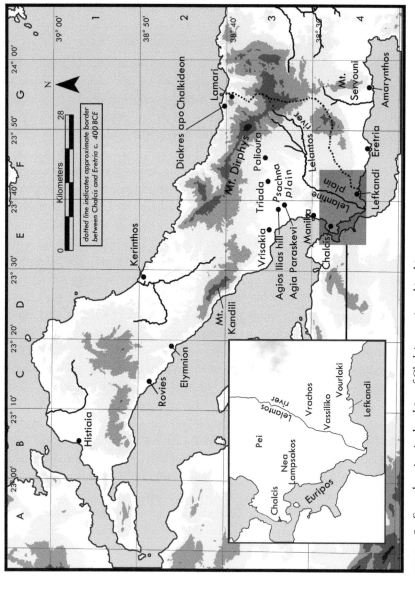

MAP 2.8. Some key sites in the *chōra* of Chalcis mentioned in this essay.

The site of Lefkandi, which was occupied from the Early Bronze Age through the early seventh century, was ultimately encompassed within the *chōra* of Chalcis. Just what Lefkandi was called in Greek antiquity remains a burning question of Euboean topography and toponymy. Claims made for Euboea, Old Eretria, and Oichalia should be rejected (Knoepfler 1981: 309–12). Instead, following Knoepfler's proposal, the most likely possibility is Argoussa/Argoura, from the root ἀργ- ("white," "bright"), perhaps referring to the white cliffs that every mariner would see from afar when approaching the site. This enduring landmark made its way into the 18th-century toponym for the site, Leucadia (from λευκό = white), and into the simplified form, Lefkandi (Knoepfler 1981). In the Classical period, Argoura was probably the seat of a sanctuary of Hera, situated close to the border with Eretria (Knoepfler 1981).

From Chalcis, an ancient road left the northern part of town and ran north, skirting the marshy coast near Manika, toward the broad and fertile Psachna plain. This was the main route connecting Chalcis with the northern parts of its *chōra*, and the *poleis* of northern Euboea. Graves of the sixth century and an ancient temple of unknown date were found at Agia Paraskevi (Papavasileiou 1900: 64–5; Sackett, Howell, Jacobsen, et al. 1966: 56). The main settlement of the Psachna plain, located on the hill of Agios Ilias, was occupied in the Geometric period and, in the Classical period, was a deme of the *polis* of Chalcis whose name is unknown. A possible Archaic site is to be found farther north, east of Vrisakia (Sackett, Howell, Jacobsen, et al. 1966: 53). The northern part of the Psachna plain, in the area of the modern villages of Triada and Palioura, remains terra incognita, but beyond doubt, this rich land was farmed in the Archaic period.

Evidence shows that in the Archaic period, Chalcidian territory extended well beyond Mt. Kandili and shared borders with Histiaia. Kerinthos, located on the east coast of the northern part of the island, is mentioned in the Catalog of Ships (*Il.* 2.538) and might have been an independent polity in the eighth and early seventh centuries. However, later in the Archaic period, it became part of the *polis* of Chalcis (Gehrke 1994: 338; Knoepfler 1997: 353; see also Thgn. 1.891–4). Elymnion, located on the west coast of the northern part of the island, also belonged to Chalcis in the Archaic period, as suggested by the fact that the founders of Kleonai on the Acte (modern Athos) peninsula were "Chalcidians from Elymnion" (Heraclides Lembus, *Excerpta politiarum* 62a; Gehrke 1994: 339-41). It later became a deme of Histiaia/Oreos (Reber, Hansen, and Ducrey 2004: 656–8). Beyond Mt. Dirphys, along the rugged east coast of Euboea but still within the bounds of Chalcidian territory, Archaic pottery was spotted at Lamari (Fachard

2012: 330; Sackett, Howell, Jacobsen, et al. 1966: 52). A possible site in this area, which still needs to be verified, could be connected with the community of the Diakres apo Chalkideon, a member of the Delian League and perhaps a small *polis* in the Archaic period (see Section 2.1).

This rapid survey of the Chalcidian *chōra* emphasizes the gaps in our documentation more than it provides a basis for reconstructing settlement patterns. We assume that the half dozen known Archaic rural sites do not represent a complete roster of actual settlements. The model of a central *asty* surrounded by a series of villages distributed throughout the most fertile regions of the *chōra* seems likely, yet such a conclusion hardly satisfies our curiosity, as the settlement patterns, the forms of rural settlements (nucleated, isolated), as well as the evolution and density of human occupation in the seventh to sixth centuries remain unknown.

### 2.4.1.3. *Settlement Organization of Eretria*

#### 2.4.1.3.1. SITE

Like Chalcis, the site of Eretria enjoyed a combination of four topographical assets: first, a deep bay protected from the NE–SW winds and offering a sheltered anchorage; second, an easily defensible seaside acropolis that provided an excellent viewpoint as well as a landmark to guide sailors; third, a plain with sufficient fertile farmland to support the development of a large urban center; and finally, the main road connecting northern and southern Euboea running E–W through the site. Eretria's position along the Euboean Strait was not as well placed as that of Chalcis, but this disadvantage was offset by the development of unique ferrying opportunities with Oropus and Attica.

The settlement extended from an acropolis (modern Kastelli), a limestone outcrop 123 m in height, south to the shoreline. The area from the foot of the acropolis to the shore was a deltaic plain measuring roughly 800 m N–S and 1,000 m E–W. That plain was formed by alluviation from a seasonal stream that ran along the west side of the acropolis and then, prior to its canalization, split into two main branches, one of which ran south to the sea and the other of which ran east along the foot of the acropolis and into a marsh on the east side of the plain. A number of smaller watercourses connected to the aforementioned seasonal stream and ran roughly N–S through the deltaic plain, segmenting it. The coastline on the south side of the plain was divided into three bays, the largest of which was well protected by the small island of Pezonisi ("the island one can walk to") and served as the main harbor throughout the centuries.

The intensive program of excavation carried out in Eretria means that, unlike that of Chalcis, the evolution of the settlement organization here can be traced diachronically. Indeed, Eretria provides a unique opportunity for observing the evolution of a settlement in an open area during the Geometric and Archaic periods.

### 2.4.1.3.2. OLD ERETRIA

Before proceeding, it is worth pausing briefly to discuss "Old Eretria," which is mentioned only by Strabo:

> Next in order I must make a circuit of the country, beginning at that part of the coastline opposite Euboea which joins Attica. The beginning is Oropus and the Sacred Harbor, which is called Delphinion,[11] opposite this harbor is Old Eretria in Euboea, the distance across being sixty *stadia*. Next after Delphinion, at a distance of twenty *stadia*, is Oropus; and opposite Oropus is the present Eretria, and to it the passage across the strait is forty *stadia*. (9.2.6, translated by H. L. Jones, modified)

> Now the old city was razed to the ground by the Persians, who "netted" the people, as Herodotus says, by means of their great numbers, the barbarians being spread about the walls (the foundations are still to be seen, and the place is called Old Eretria), but the Eretria of today was founded on it. (10.1.10, translated by H. L. Jones)

These passages have generated a considerable amount of scholarly debate, and some have interpreted them as referring to an Ur-Eretria, variously located at Lefkandi, Magoula, or Amarynthos.[12] Strabo never visited Eretria; in this part of his work, he relied on Artemidorus of Ephesus, author of a *Periplous*, a treatise for seafarers mentioning a series of coastal landmarks. Following Knoepfler (1981: 310 n. 79), we believe that Old Eretria is the acropolis of Eretria, easily visible from the Sacred Harbor (the Delphinion) and matching exactly the distance given by Strabo (Baladié 1996: 253–4). According to Knoepfler's inspired proposal, Old Eretria would be another reference to the παλαιον ἄστυ, the old city, designating the acropolis (= Ἀστυπάλαια). In the fourth century, an urban deme was probably called Astypalaia (Knoepfler 1997: 363; Fachard 2012: 52).

---

11. Strabo's Sacred Harbor (the Delphinion) has been plausibly associated with the remains at Kamaraki, c. 4 km southeast of Oropus (Roller 2018: 515–16).

12. For Lefkandi: Sackett, Howell, Jacobsen et al. 1966: 68; Schefold and Auberson 1972: 18–19; Auberson 1975a; Coldstream 2003: 197; Bérard 1978: 93 n. 25. For Magoula (2 km east of Eretria): Boardman 1957: 22–4. For Amarynthos: Bakhuizen 1976a: 78–82.

### 2.4.1.3.3. NINTH AND EIGHTH CENTURIES

As mentioned above, the site of Eretria was occupied in the Late Helladic IIIC period but was thereafter sparsely inhabited or perhaps abandoned until the ninth century, when a scatter of tombs and pottery suggests small-scale occupation.[13] Architectural remains appear in the first half of the eighth century, a prelude to a rapid and steady growth of the settlement (see Figure 2.2). It is worth noting that the settlement did not develop from a primary core, as the eighth-century remains are disseminated over a wide area of some 40–50 ha. During that period, there were a number of separate settlement clusters consisting of residences (some surrounded by periboloi; Mazarakis Ainian 2007). The positions of settlement clusters were dictated primarily by topographical factors: the aforementioned array of seasonal stream beds and a changing coastline created a patchwork of solid, sandy soils alternating with marshy or lagoon areas (Ghilardi, Müller Celka, Theurillat, et al. 2016). This geomorphological footprint remained visible in the plan of the city for the rest of its history and impeded the development of anything resembling an orthogonal street grid. The resulting loose and unorganized aspect of the first settlement does not match the idea one might have of a nascent *polis* (and less so of one participating in "colonial" enterprises overseas; Stissi 2016). However, this pattern of habitation proves that such preconceptions need to be reconsidered.

The first half of the eighth century was also the period when cult activity began at what would become a key center for religious activity in the urban center of Eretria, the Sanctuary of Apollo Daphnephoros ("the laurel-bearer"). The sanctuary was located in the geographic center of the site of the city and was situated along one of the small watercourses that ran roughly N–S through the deltaic plain. In its earliest form, the sanctuary contained a circular altar as well as four small, apsidal or oval buildings (see Figure 2.3). Only the rubble foundations of those buildings survive, and their function remains unclear, though pits located close to these buildings contained pottery intended for consumption of liquids, probably wine, and remains of bronze working (Verdan 2013: 204–7; see Section 2.11.2.1 for discussion of ritual activities at this site).

One of the apsidal buildings (Ed1), measuring 9.75 m x 6.50 m and sometimes called the Daphnephoreion, was identified by its excavators as the first temple at the site. Claude Bérard suggested that this building reproduced a mythical temple

---

13. Note that the plain and the acropolis had been occupied in the prehistoric period, but the settlement in the plain was abandoned at the beginning of the Early Helladic period, following a sea-level rise (Ghilardi, Colleu, Pavlopoulos, et al. 2013).

*Chalcis and Eretria* 123

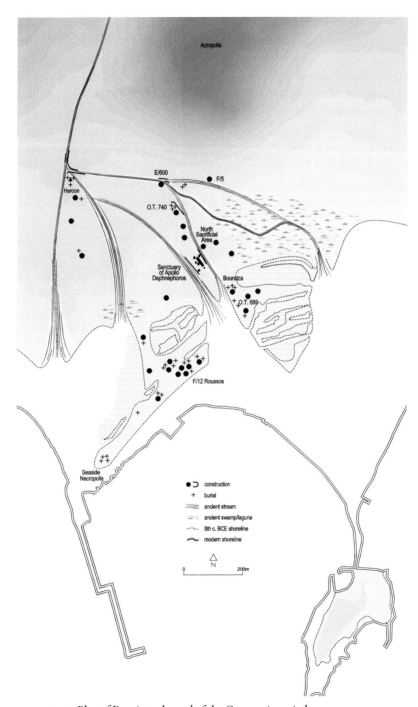

FIGURE 2.2. Plan of Eretria at the end of the Geometric period.

at Delphi that Apollo built from laurel branches (Paus. 10.5.9), since its walls were made from this material (Bérard 1971; see also Auberson 1974). Further textual evidence is to be found in the *Homeric Hymn to Apollo* (l.219–21), which claims that Apollo, while looking for a place to found an oracle, visited the Lelantine plain, among other places, prior to settling on Delphi. Bérard's suggestion has over the years met with increasing skepticism (see, for example, Mazarakis Ainian 1997: 59–60).

Alexander Mazarakis Ainian (1997: 58–63; 2016: 15–22) argued that the buildings belonging to the earliest phase of activity at the site constituted the residence of a powerful Eretrian (the ruler of the community or a member of the aristocracy) in charge of the cult. According to this interpretive approach, known as the "from ruler's dwelling to temple theory," it is only later that the sanctuary developed, when the cult came under the control of the *polis*. This is a seductive interpretation, but it cannot be definitively proven. Moreover, it implies a connection between the cult's development and assumed political changes for which we have no conclusive evidence in the eighth century.

An alternative explanation can be provided: a full-fledged sanctuary was in existence at the very beginning. That sanctuary centered around an altar and included buildings serving as banquet halls and possibly as places for the deposition of offerings (Verdan 2013: 179–98); the development of the sacred space coincides with Eretria's growth and reflects the prominence of Apollo in the *asty*.

In the last third of the eighth century, two of the four older buildings at the Apollo sanctuary disappeared, and two new structures were built, one of which is among the earliest-known monumental religious buildings in post-Mycenaean Greece. That structure (Ed2 in Figure 2.3; see Verdan 2013: 57–8, 201–2), oriented toward a preexisting altar, was 35 m long and 8 m wide. Its apsidal plan and building techniques (mud-brick walls and thatched roof) were directly inherited from Geometric domestic architecture. Apart from possible decorations (of which nothing has survived), its monumental character derives from its large dimensions in comparison with normal houses. Since it apparently reached the symbolic length of 100 feet (on the basis of the Ionic foot of 0.349 m), it can be called *hekatompedon*. The finds from inside that building include hearths, bones, and pottery.

The construction of this building has been interpreted as an important instance of a collective initiative and, as a result, a manifestation of the transformation of the Eretrian community into a *polis*. This view requires qualification. First, religious activities involving a large part of the population predate the appearance of this building. For local identity, the foundation of a communal

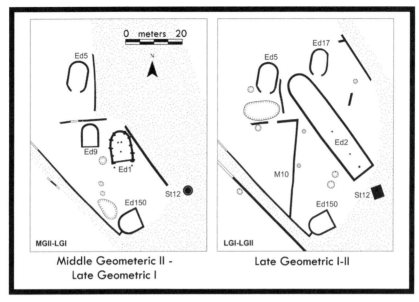

FIGURE 2.3. Plan of the Sanctuary of Apollo Daphnephoros in the Geometric period.

cult may be more important—though less visible in the material record—than temple building. Second, the collective nature of such building programs is unclear, because the construction of a monumental temple could result from the initiative of a powerful individual (or a group of leading men) capable of mobilizing labor and resources (Hall 2014b: 88). In any case, the outcome remains the same: the monument is a substantial addition to the sanctuary as a topographical focal point, a landmark contributing to the Eretrian sense of place.

A more clear-cut instance of a communal enterprise is the channeling of the seasonal stream west of the settlement. Around 700–680, massive walls running E–W were built for a length of several hundred meters at the foot of the acropolis (see Figure 2.4). This building project was so large that it was first interpreted as a fortification wall. However, this hypothesis should be rejected on historical, topographical, and archaeological grounds (Fachard 2004). The deltaic plain did not offer a suitable environment for the building of a continuous defensive perimeter, as the various nuclei of habitation would have necessitated a continuous wall defending an area of some 40–50 ha, something unparalleled in mainland Greece at that time. If needed, a strong defensive position was available on the acropolis, which had been used as a natural stronghold since the Bronze Age. Rather, the construction of embankment walls, often running in parallel lines, served to canalize the seasonal stream that ran through the deltaic plain and directed it into the marsh located on the east side of the site, perhaps partially draining it, thereby protecting the settlement from flooding (Fachard, Theurillat, Psalti, et al. 2017: 141–60). Such a communal undertaking implied collective risk assessment and advanced spatial planning. It resulted in a vast improvement in urban development and the community's standard of living. It is hard to find a parallel for a cooperative building program of such amplitude in seventh-century Greece (Verdan, Theurillat, Fachard et al., 2020). In the course of the century, Eretria achieved a pronounced urban character, joining a global trend in the Mediterranean (Broodbank 2013: 537).

Before moving on to discuss later periods, it is worth pointing out that there is evidence for cult activity at a site, the so-called North Sacrificial Area, located to the northeast of the Sanctuary of Apollo Daphnephoros, starting in the second half of the eighth century (Huber 2003). It is likely that the cult here was dedicated to Artemis (see Section 2.11.2.2).

In the second half of the eighth century, a series of elaborate burials were made in the northwestern part of the site (see Section 2.4.4). The main road connecting northern and southern Euboea later entered the city at this point, and it is likely that the same was true at this time. Not long after the last burial, the position of the graves was signaled on the ground by a large triangle made of massive

FIGURE 2.4. Walls built to control flooding in Eretria; c. 700.

stone slabs. Small buildings were erected nearby, defining a space that remained in continuous use throughout the Archaic period. This area has been interpreted as a heroon, a place dedicated to the cult of a local hero (see Section 2.11.2.5), though doubts remain.

### 2.4.1.3.4. SEVENTH AND FIRST HALF OF SIXTH CENTURIES

A new temple was constructed in the Apollo Daphnephoros sanctuary (Ed3 on Figure 2.5; see Auberson 1968: 11–15) at some point in the seventh century (the edifice is poorly preserved, and its chronology is uncertain). It was built on top of and had the same proportions as its eighth-century predecessor and may have been conceived as a new *hekatompedon*. The ground plan, however, was now quadrangular, and the orientation was slightly altered (perhaps because the location of the altar had changed). Ed3 had larger and stronger foundations than Ed2, allowing us to reconstruct a heavier superstructure: its roof must have been covered with clay tiles; the walls, however, may still have been made of mud-brick, probably consolidated by elements in wood and stone (no element of the superstructure is preserved). To get an idea of this Early Archaic temple, we must look at better-known buildings of the same period, such as the Old Temple of Apollo in Corinth (Rhodes 2003).

Whereas in the ninth and eighth centuries, small burials were situated on the margins of the settlement (along the shore and the stream), in the seventh century, they seem to have been concentrated in denser necropoleis (following demographic rise?) situated at the eastern and western edges of the site. Of particular note is the "Seaside Necropolis," located in the southwestern part of the city, which was in use from the eighth through the fifth centuries (see Figure 2.6).

Although archaeological discoveries indicate a continuous urban development during the seventh and sixth centuries, traces of Archaic dwellings are barely known on the site (Charalambidou 2006). Such low visibility should not necessarily be interpreted as the result of a decline following defeat in the Lelantine War (as has been suggested by Themelis 1979: 50; Themelis 1983: 157–8; see also Section 2.7.1). On the contrary, Eretria was in a position to dedicate two monumental temples to its tutelary god during this period (the aforementioned temple dating to the seventh century and a second one dating to the latter part of the sixth century; see Section 2.4.1.3.5 for further discussion of the sixth-century temple). The absence of settlement remains could be explained by heavy erosion, by the burying and reuse of building materials in later periods, and by the lack of systematic excavation of the relevant parts of the site. The difficulty of dating remains based on sparse and poorly studied pottery also plays a role.

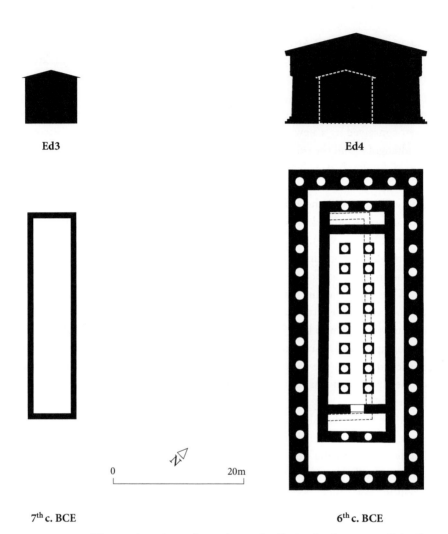

FIGURE 2.5. Plans and sections of temples to Apollo in the Sanctuary of Apollo Daphnephoros in the seventh and sixth centuries.

## Chalcis and Eretria

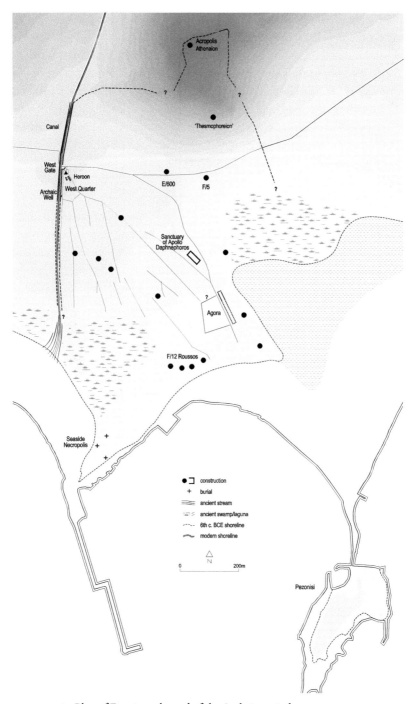

FIGURE 2.6. Plan of Eretria at the end of the Archaic period.

On the summit of the acropolis, a sanctuary dedicated to Athena was in use at least from the end of the seventh century onward (Huber 2012). The origins of the cult are dated on the basis of the oldest votive objects found at the spot, but the cult could have a history that stretches back farther in time. Sixth-century architectural terracottas depicting armed riders and charioteers decorated a sacred building of some kind (Huber 2007; Huber and Maillard 2015). Overall, the scarcity of seventh- and sixth-century architectural remains must rather be explained by the impact of later building activities on the Archaic levels (whereas lower Geometric layers are better preserved).

#### 2.4.1.3.5. SECOND HALF OF SIXTH CENTURY

The urban fabric of Eretria was transformed over the course of the second half of the sixth century by a series of ambitious communal building projects. Among the earliest and most important of those projects was the construction of a new set of walls that canalized the seasonal stream so that it ran from the acropolis directly south to the sea. For the first time, the entire deltaic plain was permanently dry.

That, in turn, made it possible to use the old riverbeds as streets. Although there was not an orthogonal street grid, the road connecting northern and southern Euboea ran E–W across the northern end of the city and formed a major urban thoroughfare. In addition, a major road ran south from that thoroughfare and led past the Sanctuary of Apollo Daphnephoros to the harbor.

Alongside that road and just to the south of the Daphnephoros sanctuary, an agora was laid out (see Figure 2.6). It was marked out to the east by a stoa that was built in the second half of the sixth century. The area might have been used as a meeting place at an earlier date, but excavations have not been conducted extensively there, and nothing is more elusive than an agora prior to its monumentalization. The sector, however, was probably reclaimed from the sea from the beginning of the seventh century onward (Ghilardi, Müller Celka, Theurillat, et al. 2016: 156 fig. 6C), which could give a terminus post quem for the existence of an agora in that specific location.

Nearby, a fountain, which would have delivered fresh drinking water to the community, was constructed. In other parts of the settlement, the Eretrians had to rely on wells, which provided access to the typically brackish groundwater. Such wells could display a monumental public character, as did, for instance, the Archaic well of the West Quarter (Auberson 1975b). This well's coping was made of fine-grained conglomerate blocks, some of them inscribed with graffiti (e.g., Ἐπιχάρης καλός). The improvement of water-supply facilities in the late sixth century echoes the impressive projects completed in the same period on Samos (the Eupalinos tunnel; Christesen, Lentini, Murray, et al. in this volume: section 3.4C.2) and in Athens by the Pisistratids (Camp 1986: 42–3).

Eretria's most ambitious collective project at that time was undoubtedly its city walls. In his account of the Persian attack on Eretria in 490, Herodotus (6.101.2) notes that Eretria's fortifications were strong enough to resist the Persians' assault for six days and that the city was ultimately taken by betrayal rather than military action. Although material remains are still elusive, Eretria offers indisputable proofs for the presence of an urban fortification in the second half of the sixth century (Fachard 2004; Frederiksen 2011: 138–41). Traces of a fortification wall, consisting of a double-faced foundation wall in stone supporting a mud-brick superstructure, were excavated on the acropolis. Further segments certainly remain to be found, but a significant percentage of these Archaic remains was destroyed and recycled in the course of constructing the Classical city walls. Because of the low visibility of the Archaic city wall, claims have been made for a "broken" circuit, consisting of discontinuous fortified gates and strongpoints along the canal. This position goes against the most fundamental rules of siege warfare and should be dismissed.

An important element of the sixth-century fortification walls was a fortified gate on the west side of the city (the West Gate), close to the aforementioned collection of elaborate late-eighth-century burials and the so-called heroon and at the place where the main road connecting northern and southern Euboea entered the city. This was an axial-type gate with a tower that was constructed with a stone socle supporting a partially preserved mud-brick superstructure. Curtain walls extended north and south from the gate, behind the dike walls that channeled the river toward the sea. The riverbed thus both protected the settlement from flooding and served as a defensive ditch in front of the fortification wall. It is likely that foot and wheeled traffic entering the city crossed the dike channel by means of a wooden bridge. As part of the construction of the West Gate, the extant buildings connected to the so-called heroon were abandoned, and new ones were constructed farther east. In the late sixth or early fifth century, the West Gate was reconstructed with two square towers on stone bases with mud-brick superstructure. At the same time, a more substantial bridge, 6.9 m long, seems to have been built. Nine pillars, arranged in a 3 x 3 configuration, have been excavated.

The Daphnephoros sanctuary also received attention in the same general time frame. In the last quarter of the sixth century, the construction of a new temple to Apollo was initiated (Ed4, see Figure 2.7). With its Doric character, this temple was very different from its two predecessors (Auberson 1968). Still, it had the same orientation as Ed3 and partially rests on its foundation; there is thus continuity between the two buildings. The new temple measured 47.8 × 20.55 m; its plan was hexastyle, that is, with six columns across the facade and 14 along the sides (still not the 6 × 13 formula that will become the rule later on). Much of the architectural detail is unknown, the building having been reduced to its foundations already in ancient times. A fragment of an acroterion found in the sanctuary suggests that the temple was roofed, at least in part, with marble tiles (Touloupa and Korres 2002). The most famous ornament of the temple is a group of statues coming from the west pediment, including the figures of Athena, Theseus, and Antiope, queen of the Amazons, which formed part of an Amazonomachy (see Section 2.12.5).

One of Eretria's most prominent features was its harbor, which hosted both commercial ships and the city's navy (on which see Section 2.7.3). Unfortunately, the plan of the Archaic harbor remains unknown. In the Classical period, a long mole was built to the west, which, along with the Pezonisi island and reef, formed the harbor proper. It is possible, yet still impossible to demonstrate, that a section of the west mole was built in the Archaic period, along with the first building phase of the city walls. Such a construction would have dramatically improved the harbor, the innermost tip of which appears to be conveniently close to the Archaic agora.

### 2.4.1.4. *Settlement Pattern of the Eretrian* Chōra

In this section, we discuss what is known about settlement patterns in areas that certainly or possibly formed part of the Eretrian *chōra* in the Archaic period; in

**FIGURE 2.7.** Model showing the Doric Temple of Apollo Daphnephoros under construction, c. 530.

the following section, we discuss what is known about the extent and boundaries of the Eretrian *chōra* in the Archaic period. To anticipate conclusions reached below, at the end of the Archaic period, Eretria seems to have controlled a territory of c. 1,000 sq km (see Map 2.9).

The steady growth of Eretria in the seventh and sixth centuries certainly favored urbanization, but the rest of the territory must have been occupied by villages in order to be properly exploited. Evidence from literary sources is scarce but could suggest a wider distribution of settlements than the image projected by the archaeological record. Herodotus reports that prior to the siege of 490, the Persian army and cavalry were deployed east of Eretria, at the localities of Temenos, Choireai, and Aigilia (Hdt. 6.101.1).[14] All three sites, called χωρία by Herodotus, are later attested as demes in the Eretrian system of demes, districts, and tribes. By the end of the fifth century at the latest (but perhaps earlier; see Section 2.5.3.2), Eretria had a territorial organization based on some 50 to 60 demes, distributed among five geographical districts called *chōroi* (χῶροι), as well as among six geographically based tribes or *phylai*. Each tribe was named after an eponymous hero.[15]

The demes were in existence by the end of the fifth century at the latest, but it is possible that they were instituted by 506–490 (Fachard 2019; see Section 2.5.3.2 for further discussion). Thanks to the work of Knoepfler (1997), most of the demes are now securely positioned within a district, and many are identified with an archaeological site or a region of the *chōra*. Although it is perilous to build upon the later evidence for demes as proof of settlement in the Archaic period, that evidence is at minimum suggestive of the situation in the late Archaic period. We can also partly rely on the evidence from the reformed version of the Eretrian tribal system.

Amarynthos, the homeland of the eponymous hero Narkittos (Narkittis tribe), was a substantial settlement and religious center located c. 11 km east of the city of Eretria. The most important Eretrian religious site was undoubtedly the Sanctuary of Artemis Amarysia at Amarynthos (see Figure 2.8). The precise location of the shrine was definitively established only recently: 2 km east of the modern town of Amarynthos, at the foot of Paleoekklisies hill; in the Archaic period, the sanctuary was delimited to the west by marshes (Ghilardi, Fachard, Pavlopoulos, et al. 2012). Excavations have for the first time started to bring to light its remains (Fachard, Knoepfler, Reber, et al.

---

14. These three sites have not been definitively located; see Scott 2005: 354–5.

15. On the Eretrian demes and the organization of the *chōra*, see Knoepfler 1997; Fachard 2012: 47–76; Fachard 2019.

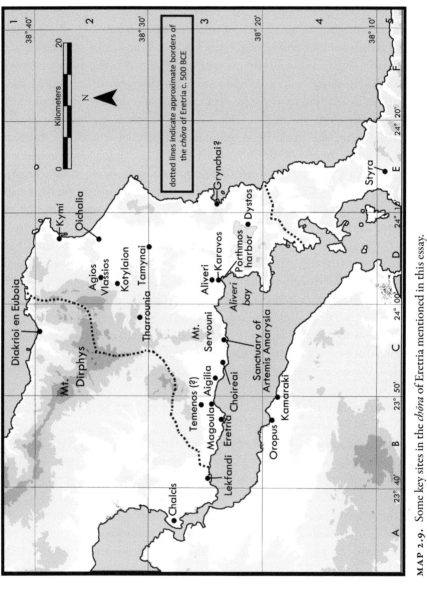

MAP 2.9. Some key sites in the *chōra* of Eretria mentioned in this essay.

2017; Verdan, Theurillat, Krapf, et al. 2020; Fachard, Simossi, Krapf, et al. 2022), and, although a great deal of work remains to be done, some preliminary observations can already be made. (See Section 2.11.2.6 for discussion of religious activities at the sanctuary.)

First, Amarynthos was a site of local importance in the Bronze Age (Early Helladic II–Late Helladic IIIC), and the toponym is mentioned in Linear B tablets from Mycenaean Thebes (Knoepfler 1988; Krapf 2011). It also displays continuity of occupation, stretching from the Bronze Age to the Iron Age, that Eretria in contrast seemingly lacks. Second, Geometric and Archaic buildings have been located under the remains of a large, late Classical stoa (Reber, Knoepfler, Ackermann, et al. 2013: 103), suggesting continuity of cult from the Geometric period onward. But the sanctuary's core in the Archaic period was the area of the temples. To date, three superimposed buildings have been discovered: a Geometric building of unsecure date and function; a late eight-/seventh-century temple with an apsidal plan, housing a massive horseshoe-shaped altar; a late-sixth-century temple preserved to the level of its foundations . In the latter, a succession of large bases roughly aligned on the central axis attests to the existence of a central colonnade; the eastern facade is oriented toward an altar, and the rear part to the west features an inner room (Fachard, Simossi, Krapf, et al. 2022). This temple can be dated to the end of the sixth century thanks to the discovery of a large deposit under its floor level (see Figure 2.9). It contains more than 700 objects, including dozens of complete vases, terracotta female figurines, seals and small jewels (in gold, silver, bronze, glass, faience, and bone), bronze phialai, and several pieces of armour.

It is interesting to note that the Sanctuary of Artemis Amarysia at Amarynthos developed outside the *asty*, in a community that became subordinate to Eretria in the Archaic period, a phenomenon observed elsewhere in Archaic Greece (de Polignac 1995). Thus, what started as a local shrine (focused on the worship of Artemis and of the hero Narkittos, son of Amarynthos) progressively became a meeting point for the local population of the Eretrian plain and finally emerged as the greatest sanctuary of the Eretrian state. This trajectory, in our opinion, strongly suggests that the community of Amarynthos played a decisive role in the formation of the Eretrian *polis* in the Archaic period.

East of Mt. Servouni was the deep bay of Aliveri and the excellent natural harbor of ancient Porthmos. The modern town of Karavos is situated on the edge of Porthmos harbor; the modern town of Aliveri is situated just to the north of Karavos. Protogeometric and early Classical pottery is known from this area,

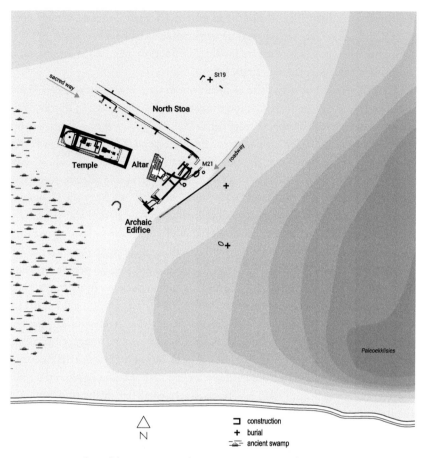

FIGURE 2.8. Plan of the Sanctuary of Artemis Amarysia in the Geometric and Archaic phases.

but recent excavations have unearthed traces of an Archaic cemetery (Kalamara 2015: 158). Given the advantages of its position, the presence of an Archaic settlement is very likely.

Farther north, in the long corridor stretching between Aliveri and Kymi (see Section 2.3.1), traces of Archaic settlements are unfortunately scarce. An important site in this area was Tamynai, the homeland of the eponymous hero Admetus (Admetis tribe, on which see Section 2.5.3.2) and the location of a sanctuary to Apollo. The sanctuary, which has not been found yet, hosted a festival (the Tamyneia) that played a prominent role in Eretrian religious life (on which see Section 2.11.2.6). Tamynai became an Eretrian deme, but Geometric and Archaic occupation in the area are clearly attested, raising the issue of its earliest political

**FIGURE 2.9.** Offering deposit (figurines, Attic black-figure vases, local ritual vessels, and various small objects) from a temple at the Sanctuary of Artemis Amarysia; late sixth century.

identity. Limited excavations have unearthed sherds from the Geometric and Archaic periods. The origin of the cult of Apollo could go back to the Geometric period, and the sanctuary of Apollo might have played an important political and religious role in the unification of the Eretriad (Fachard 2012). Isolated discoveries are worth further study: the discovery of late-sixth-century lekythoi at Paramerites, near Tharrounia, shows that settlements and exploitation of the land were not limited to the plains.

North of Tamynai, another important settlement was partially excavated at Viglatouri. It should be identified with Oichalia, a town described by Hecataeus of Miletus, writing around 500, as located in an area called Skios that formed part (μοίρα) of Eretria (*FGrH* 1 F28). Besides a Bronze Age occupation, most excavated remains (houses, pottery workshops, graves) date to the Geometric period, but Archaic pottery was found as well. The town had a mythical past—it was allegedly stormed by Heracles (Strabo 10.1.10)—and might have been the seat of the Iphitis tribe (Knoepfler 2010: 120–2).

In the hilly district to the west of Oichalia, isolated finds include an Archaic coin hoard buried between 500 and 480 at Agios Vlassios, and some reported Archaic sherds at the deme site of Kotylaion. Farther north, isolated in a mountainous canton opening toward the Aegean, was the site of Metochi, where the discovery of a *kouros* testifies to the existence of a settlement. Metochi is probably the site of the ancient community of the "Diakrioi en Euboia," which formed an independent *polis* (Fachard 2012: 69–70, 199–202).

A survey of the *chōra* of Archaic Eretria would be incomplete without mentioning the site of Dystos (Reber, Hansen, and Ducrey 2004: 650), located southeast of Aliveri. Except for House K, tentatively dated to the sixth century, signs of Archaic occupation are exiguous (Fachard 2012: 207). Dystos was a Classical Eretrian deme, but its status in the Archaic period is unclear. Unlike its neighbors Grynchai and Styra—former *poleis* that were integrated into the Eretriad at the end of the fifth century—Dystos never appears as an independent polity in the Athenian tribute list (or in other documents). This fact leads to two hypotheses: either Dystos was part of the Eretriad before 450, or it was part of the *polis* of Styra. Given the fact that its population was not distributed among the six Eretrian tribes in the Classical period, the first possibility seems preferable. As a hypothesis, Dystos could have been already part of the Eretriad in the later sixth century, and the sixth tribe—probably called Dystos (Knoepfler 1997: 399–400)—might have been rooted in this region.

Styra was an independent *polis* in the Archaic and early Classical periods, before being integrated into the Eretriad at the end of the fifth century (Knoepfler 1971). A *sympoliteia* treaty between Eretria and Styra from the late fifth century, arguably the earliest to be known in the Greek world, was discovered in 2017 in the Sanctuary of Artemis Amarysia at Amarynthos (see, provisionally, Knoepfler, Reber, Karapaschalidou, et al. 2018: 135–6), thus confirming that Styra became a deme of the Eretriad. For the early fifth century, close to 500 lead tablets record the names of citizens from Styra (*IG* XII.9.56 #1–464; Jeffery 1990: 86; Masson 1992), some of which reappear in later inscriptions (Knoepfler 2014: 61).

Overall, due to the scarcity of remains, the low visibility of Archaic sites, and the lack of systematic research, our knowledge of the occupation of the Eretrian *chōra* in the Archaic period remains patchy. In fact, the inadequate data preclude the reconstruction of settlement patterns for the seventh and sixth centuries. However, thanks to the tribal system, it can be inferred that by the end of the sixth century at the latest, Eretria displayed the territorial characteristics of a *polis*, dominated by a powerful *asty* whose authority extended over a wider *chōra* stretching beyond the Eretrian plain. The process of unification remains unclear, but Amarynthos, Tamynai, and Oichalia were secondary centers whose religious and political roles seem to have been decisive in the formation of the Eretrian state. Beyond these hubs, the existence of smaller villages and hamlets can be inferred from isolated finds, and we believe that the density of occupation was greater than the current archaeological data suggest.

## 2.4.2. Borders and Territoriality

Given that Chalcis and Eretria shared a border and had at least at some points in time a rivalrous relationship, the question of the borders of their respective *chōrai* in the Archaic period is best discussed in conjunction with each other. Although incomplete, the archaeological record addresses a series of issues related to the formation of the *poleis* of Chalcis and Eretria. How much territory was controlled and exploited by the two *poleis*, and what borders separated them? This is a fundamental question, yet it has never been thoroughly addressed. Border conflicts are well attested in Greece from the late sixth century onward, and the literary landscape resonates with earlier "mythical" conflicts involving emerging *poleis* fighting over borderlands; the Lelantine War (see Section 2.7.1) is the paradigmatic example. The identification of relevant sites and toponyms between as well as around Chalcis and Eretria is, therefore, crucial for studying issues of territoriality in Archaic Euboea.

### 2.4.2.1. Chalcis

By locating Argoussa at Lefkandi and Old Eretria on the Eretrian acropolis, we can remove obstacles to progress in the study of Euboean topography. Lefkandi/Argoussa was the entry point to the Lelantine plain from the east, and Eretria could have repeatedly tried to overrun it in order to grab the left bank of the Lelantos. Border unrest and skirmishing over more than a century eventually became the stuff of legend (see Section 2.7.1). However, this territorial conflict became irrelevant when the Athenians confiscated the Lelantine plain in 506 and established a short-lived garrison at the Vrachos fort (see Section 2.7.4.2). The promontory of Lefkandi/Argoussa was abandoned by then, but the toponym persisted (in a rhotacized form) well into the Classical period, when the small bay east of the promontory, the seat of a sanctuary of Hera in Chalcidian territory, was called Argoura (Knoepfler 1981).

This reconstruction of events leads us to situate by the end of the sixth century the Chalcidian-Eretrian borderlands c. 2 km east of Lefkandi, leaving the site of Lefkandi to Chalcis (Fachard 2012). Both polities could only extend their territorial base to the north and south, respectively, which they eventually did.

The northwestern borders of Chalcidian territory can be set in the hills between the modern town of Rovies and the ancient settlement of Elymnion (modern Limni). Northeast of Chalcis, beyond Mt. Dirphys, were the borders with the Diakres apo Chalkideon, an independent polity occupying a mountainous and isolated district facing the Aegean. As such, the Chalcidian *chōra* covered a surface area of c. 1,100–1,200 sq km in the Archaic period. It should, therefore, be added to the small group of "super *poleis*" (i.e., those that had a territory of more than 1,000 sq km). However, the current evidence suggests that Chalcidian territory might have slightly decreased in the Classical period, as a result of the loss of Elymnion (partially compensated for by the integration of Diakres apo Chalkideon after 411).

### 2.4.2.2. *Eretria*

The reformed tribal system (see Section 2.5.3.2) that seems to have been put in place c. 500 is particularly important for our understanding of the development of the Eretrian *chōra*. The names of three of the six tribes—each taking its appellation from an eponymous hero—in that system are securely attested: Narkittis, Admetis, and Mekistis. Another tribal name, Iphitis, can be inferred with a high degree of probability (Knoepfler 2010: 120–2). It is essential to emphasize that the eponymous heroes of the six tribes were rooted in different regions of central Euboea. Narkittos was connected with Amarynthos and its Sanctuary of Artemis Amarysia (Knoepfler 2010); Admetus was connected to Tamynai (Strabo 10.1.10). The tribe probably called Iphitis had close links with Oichalia (Knoepfler and Ackermann 2012: 948–9). Given the local roots of these eponymous heroes, it appears that the Eretrians decided to name their tribes after heroes who represented various regions of the territory, quite possibly to bolster unity within the polity. This process is echoed in other *poleis*, where the incorporation of new land within the *polis* was accompanied by tribal reform (Hall 2014b: 249–51).

If our interpretation is correct, it could establish that the fertile canton of Tamynai (and its northern neighbor of Oichalia) was part of the Eretriad around 500 at the latest and, with it, the entire corridor linking the Euboean Strait with the Aegean. The region of Tamynai was among the richest of Euboea and ideally suited for horse breeding (hippotrophy); it was known for its Sanctuary of Apollo, who served Admetus as a groom or farmhand according to myth (Strabo 10.1.10; Knoepfler and Ackermann 2012: 937–8), and later for its hippodrome (Aeschin. *In Ctes.* 87; Fachard 2012: 260–1). Admetus was the mythical prototype of a wealthy landowner and a horse breeder (Knoepfler and Ackermann 2012: 938). One might thus conclude that Tamynai was involved in hippotrophy from an early stage, that it shared common values with the Eretrian Hippeis (on whom see Section 2.5.2), and that the two groups gradually merged. An alliance based on ties of friendship that eventually resulted in military cooperation might have existed in the seventh century, thus gradually facilitating the final and "official" integration of Tamynai within the Eretrian state in the course of the sixth. Because of the nature and composition of the tribal system, it now seems certain that by c. 500, a citizen of Tamynai enjoyed the same civic rights as a citizen living in the *asty* and considered himself an Eretrian. By then, the synoecism of the Eretrian *polis*, which was an ongoing process, marked a new milestone.

The evidence thus suggests that Eretrian territory progressively expanded toward the east and the south. The integration of Tamynai, Oichalia, and possibly Dystos might have been the result of a gradual process that began in the early seventh century. By the end of the sixth century, these important villages were part of the Eretriad, as the tribal system seems to indicate. In the sixth century, Eretria shared a border with the community of the Diakrioi en Euboia (Fachard 2012: 69–70) and with the independent *polis* of Styra to the south. By the end of the Archaic period, the *polis* of Eretria controlled a territory of 850–1,000 sq km (1,000–1,100 sq km if Dystos was part of it).

### 2.4.3. Euboean Ceramics

Chalcidian and Eretrian material assemblages can be analyzed together, even though the numbers and types of artifacts vary greatly from one site to the other. Whether it be pottery, sculpture, or other types of material production, scholars have been unable to identify convincingly distinctive features that would differentiate Chalcidian from Eretrian artifacts.

Euboean pottery is very well known, especially for the Geometric period, when it was widely exported (Coldstream 2008: 189–95; Verdan, Kenzelmann-Pfyffer, and Léderrey 2008). It bears a distinctive style but shares close similarities with the ceramics of neighboring areas as well. In the tenth to ninth centuries, the beginning of the period covered in this essay, the local pottery (best illustrated by the finds from the necropoleis of Lefkandi; Popham, Sackett, and Themelis 1980: 281–350) shows clear signs of conservatism: whereas Attic workshops have developed a new "geometric" style from around 900, soon to be copied in other regions, Euboean potters continued to employ Protogeometric designs (hence a style called Subprotogeometric). Most emblematic are skyphoi and plates decorated with concentric pendant semicircles, which have been found in many Mediterranean sites, from the Levantine coast to southwestern Spain (see Figure 2.10; Kourou 2020).

Significant changes occur after 800, when elements of Attic Middle Geometric pottery gradually find their way into the local repertoire. From that time on, Attic innovations are quickly adopted by Euboean potters (as Corinthian shapes and motifs will be during the Late Geometric). This trend is not (or not only) a matter of aesthetic taste. Imports to Lefkandi and Eretria reveal the interest of local elites in prestigious Attic vases (some possibly acquired through gift exchanges) and related social practices (for instance, the display of monumental grave markers; Blandin 2007, vol.

1: 65–74). Soon after the emergence of the Late Geometric style in Athens (Dipylon workshop), Euboean potters introduced figured scenes into their repertoire. However, the funerary iconography that flourished in Athens at that time was not imported, and other themes, predominantly horse breeding, were favored. The interchange of artistic influences is best illustrated by the monumental vase, dated to c. 750, that was found in Curium on Cyprus and is now in the Metropolitan Museum in New York (see Figure 2.11 and Map 2.5). This vase, painted in the style associated with the Athenian Dipylon workshop, has been plausibly attributed to the Euboean artist known as the Cesnola Painter (Coldstream 2008: 172–4). Horses, at the manger or grazing, are likely emblematic of the chief concerns of the Euboean horse breeders. The same motifs also make their appearance on Boeotian and Cycladic vases, a phenomenon that suggests affiliations among these three regional pottery productions. The vases decorated with figured scenes are mainly

FIGURE 2.10. Pendant semicircle skyphos; first half of eighth century; height: 8.6 cm; produced in Euboea and found on Cyprus. Metropolitan Museum New York 74.51.589.

kratēres, jugs, and cups (kantharoi and skyphoi), forming the typical drinking equipment used in elite banquets.

Around the end of the Late Geometric (c. 700–680), the quality of Euboean pottery seems to decline (Verdan, Kenzelmann-Pfyffer, and Léderrey 2008: 110). During the Archaic period, Euboean ceramics become primarily a local product, in that the only site outside of Euboea where they

FIGURE 2.11. Kratēr, attributed to a Euboean workshop (the Cesnola Painter); c. 750; height with lid: 181.6 cm; found at Curium in Cyprus. Metropolitan Museum New York 74.51.965.

are found in any quantity seems to be Delos.[16] There is no equivalent in the Eretrian or Chalcidian workshops of the rich Protoattic, Protocorinthian, or East Greek styles. Instead, Eretrian and Chalcidian workshops kept on producing vessels decorated with simple geometric motifs; this Subgeometric style was produced locally through the entire Archaic period (Charalambidou 2017a: 123–6). There are exceptions, however, which include a series of pedestaled amphoras found in an Eretrian necropolis and adorned with groups of female figures and orientalizing beasts (lions and sphinxes; Boardman 1952). Less conspicuous, yet composing a coherent group, are high-neck jugs, which are mainly found in Eretrian religious contexts (see Section 2.11.2.2) but also in Oropus and Boeotia (Huber 2013). Apparently, the focus was not on banquet vessels anymore but on vases used in cultic, funerary, or nuptial contexts.

The production of amphoras with pedestals continued into the sixth century. The last examples of this series, dated to the middle of the century, were decorated in the black-figure technique and are close in both shape and iconography to early lebētes gamikoi from Attica. In fact, there is a whole range of black-figured vases produced by Euboean workshops in the sixth century (Boardman 1998: 216; Paspalas 2012: 74–5). Their identification is problematic because they are very similar to their Attic models in design if not in quality. It is possible that potters from Athens (or at least trained there) were working in Chalcis and Eretria. Few of these vases have been found in Chalcis and Eretria, because the Archaic cemeteries at those sites have not been systematically excavated. Many examples come from nearby Boeotia. Without competing with Attic production, Euboean black-figured pottery was nonetheless suitable for limited export.

### 2.4.4. Euboean Funerary Practices

For our knowledge of Euboean funerary customs, the richness of Lefkandi's Protogeometric/Subprotogeometric burial plots (see Popham, Sackett, and Themelis 1980) stands in stark contrast with the situation during subsequent periods. Neither in Chalcis nor in Eretria are there Geometric/Archaic necropoleis well known enough to permit an extensive analysis of funerary customs. In Chalcis in particular, only scattered graves have been discovered, so we will mainly dwell on the case of Eretria.

---

16. For a distribution map of Euboean pottery exported during the seventh century, see Descoeudres 2006–2007.

## Chalcis and Eretria

Several groups of Geometric tombs have been found at Eretria, generally located near the shore or along the main stream. The largest of them is the "Seaside Necropolis," southwest of the city. In use from the eighth century down to the middle of the fifth century, it could have been an important source of knowledge, but the main excavations took place a long time ago, and only a very small portion of the finds have been published (Blandin 2007, vol. 2: 59–71). For the Geometric period, another group of tombs stands out: the rich burial plot of the "Heroon" (described in more detail below). Its location is "atypical," since it is not close to the shore but at the foot of the acropolis in the sector of the future West Gate, along an important communication axis.

For the Archaic period, a few graves are known on the western margin of the city (including the Seaside Necropolis" mentioned in Section 2.4.1.3.4). At that time, the necropoleis probably started to expand westward from the city, along the main road connecting northern and southern Euboea; that situation is well attested for the Classical to Hellenistic periods, but the relevant evidence for the Archaic period is still missing. A few late Archaic tombs have also been discovered on that same road where it exited the east side of the city.[17]

The predominant burial customs for adults were primary cremation and inhumation.[18] Secondary cremation, where the remains of the deceased are collected from the funeral pyre and buried in a vessel, seems to have been for people of rather high status; the best examples, the Geometric graves of the Heroon, involve the use of bronze cauldrons as cinerary urns and are richly furnished (see below). As a rule, pre-adults were inhumed, while the bodies of very young (perinatal) children were buried in large vases (*enchytrismos*). In Eretria, this form of burial is attested with remarkable continuity from the second half of the eighth century to the middle of the sixth (Blandin 2007, vol. 1: 58–63). More than the practice of *enchytrismos*, it is the quality of the vases that deserves to be underlined here. Indeed, in addition to several coarse-ware pithoi decorated with incisions, we find a series of large pedestaled pithoid amphoras that are lavishly ornate (Boardman 1952: 13–39). The use of this type of vase for graves underlines the investment undertaken for the burial of young children and, therefore, an increased importance attached to this age group in this period. These pedestaled amphoras, commonly labeled "funerary," were certainly not produced for the grave alone. They could have served as nuptial vases, comparable to the later Attic lebēs gamikos (Verdan 2015b), and thus provide a trace of wedding customs,

---

17. For a list of the necropoleis and their period of use, see Gex 1993: 13–14.

18. A thorough description of the burial types for the Geometric period can be found in Blandin 2007, vol. 1: 39–65; vol. 2: pl. 116–23.

146 THE OXFORD HISTORY OF THE ARCHAIC GREEK WORLD

which are otherwise poorly known for the Archaic period. That the best pottery from Euboean workshops was produced for this practice could indicate the increased importance of wedding rituals.

Apart from the vases used for *enchytrismos*, a fair amount of pottery was deposited in tombs, forming more or less rich assemblages. This practice is characteristic of Greek necropoleis and thus does not deserve special attention here. Important to note, however, is the deposition of miniature vases and "feeding bottles" in the tombs of children (Blandin 2007, vol. 1: 88–9) and, from the late Archaic onward, the almost ubiquitous presence of lekythoi (Martin Pruvot, Reber, and Theurillat 2010: 301–3). As for non-ceramic offerings, a distinctive group of golden diadems comes from the Eretrian necropoleis of the Geometric period, allowing one to speak of a local workshop (Blandin 2007, vol. 1: 92–8).

Evidence for grave markers is elusive. For the Geometric period, fragments of monumental vases (both imported and locally made) have been retrieved in the area south of the Heroon burial plot (Blandin 2007, vol. 1: 69–70). They might have once stood above the tombs of Eretrian aristocrats. For Archaic Chalcis, it has been suggested that *kouroi* fragments of uncertain provenance might come from a funerary context (Kalamara, Kosma, Boukaras, et al. 2015: 37). One case stands out: the triangular monument placed upon the Geometric graves of the Heroon in Eretria.

Located northwest of the city, close to the place of the future monumental West Gate, the burials of the Heroon date from broadly the second half of the eighth century to the very beginning of the seventh century (Bérard 1970; Blandin 2007, vol. 2: 35–58 and pl. 55–115).[19] In total, 19 tombs have been identified (see Table 2.1), some of them heavily disturbed. Seven adults, males and females alike, were cremated and their ashes deposited in bronze cauldrons. Except for one case, the male graves contain weapons (swords and spearheads), sometimes in great number (especially in Tomb 6); swords were ritually destroyed so as to accompany their owner in the afterlife. Children are inhumed in pits; offerings in their tombs include pieces of jewellery and small vases. The location of the graves was marked by a large triangle (about 9 m on each side) made of stone slabs, a very unusual marker for this period in Greece (see Figure 2.12). The building of this *sēma* also foreshadows the transition to a new phase in the use of the area: in the Archaic period, cultic activities may have been conducted here, possibly honoring a hero (or heroes) of the Eretrian *polis* (for this heroic cult, see Section 2.11.2.5).

---

19. The traditional date is 720–690, but on ongoing study suggests that several graves go back to the middle of the eighth century.

**Table 2.1.** Main characteristics of the tombs in the Heroon burial plot in Eretria.

| Number | Type | Age, sex | Weapons | Jewellery | Pottery |
|---|---|---|---|---|---|
| 5 | Cremation | Adult, male | 2 spears | | |
| 6 | Cremation | Adult, male | 4 swords, 6 spears | x | |
| 7 | Cremation | Adult, male | | | |
| 8 | Cremation | Adult, male | 1 spear | | |
| 9 | Cremation | Adult, male | 2 swords, 4 spears | x | x |
| 10 | Cremation | Adult, female | | x | |
| 11 | Inhumation | Child ±2 | | x | x |
| 12 | Inhumation | Child ±3 | 1 knife | | x |
| 13 | Cremation | Adult, female? | | | |
| 14 | Inhumation | Child ±1 | | x | x |
| 15 | Inhumation | Child ±15 | | | |
| 16 | Inhumation | Child 5–6 | | | x |
| 17 | Inhumation | ? | | | |
| 18 | Inhumation | ? | | | x |
| 19 | Inhumation | ? | | | x |
| 20 | Inhumation | ? | | | |
| 22 | ? | ? | 1 sword, 1 spear | | |
| 23 | Inhumation | Child ±15 | | | x |
| 24 | Inhumation | Adult, male | | | |

The Heroon graves—where the deposit of the deceased's ashes in bronze cauldrons echoes the heroic funerals described in the Homeric epics—are of exceptional character, but they were also the acts of a small group of elites over a limited time period. Other members of the Eretrian elite were buried in a different manner, without necessarily establishing a hierarchy between these funerary customs (Crielaard 1998; Crielaard 2007).

## 2.5. *Political History*
### 2.5.1. Governance of Lefkandi

The Greek *polis* did not emerge fully formed at a single instant in time. Instead, the *polis* as a socio-political institution took shape by means of a long-term and gradual process that developed throughout the Archaic period and whose origins can be traced much earlier (Hall 2007: 59). Central Euboea offers an excellent

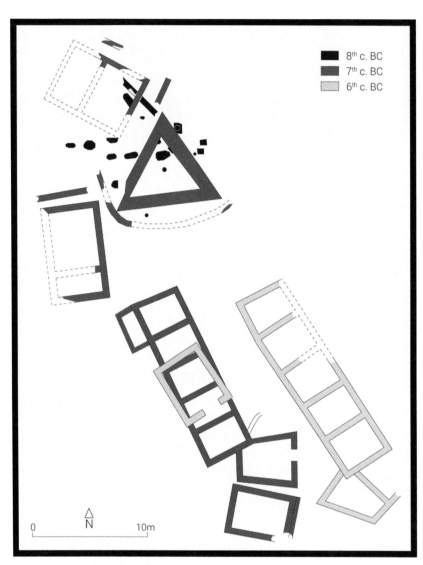

FIGURE 2.12. Phase plan of the Heroon at Eretria.

*Chalcis and Eretria* 149

case study for understanding the development of the *polis*, mainly because the development of polities starting in the Early Iron Age can be traced on the basis of archaeological evidence.

The spotlight should first be turned on Lefkandi, since Protogeometric Chalcis is barely known, and Eretria becomes archaeologically visible only in the eighth century (see Section 2.4.1). Lefkandi offers an example of a community living on the fringe of palatial control. Not only did it survive after the collapse of the palatial system, but it even took advantage of it, mainly by preserving and adapting some forms of socio-political structures and territorial organization set in place by the former system and by preserving knowledge of sea routes and overseas connections. Already in the Late Helladic IIIC period, Lefkandi was a large settlement (Lemos 2014: 173–6; Lemos 2020). At a later date, one can detect social stratification in the funerary sphere, while a high level of social organization is evident in the management of the burial plots. Some individuals, like the ones buried in the monumental building at Toumba, controlled large amounts of wealth and must have wielded significant power in the community. But collective interests were also at stake. The Toumba building (middle of the tenth century)—erected, destroyed, and buried thanks to a communal effort (Crielaard 2011: 99)—might have briefly served as a gathering place, and its large storage capacity evokes the intention of accumulating, exchanging, and possibly redistributing agricultural products. Additionally, once the building was destroyed and covered by a mound, more than one single elite group seem to have benefited from the prestige of association with a powerful ancestor (Lemos and Mitchell 2011).

The example of Lefkandi raises several regional questions, among which the nature and importance of Protogeometric Chalcis are paramount. Given their proximity, they were undeniably in close contact, although one can only wonder about the relationship between the two communities. But two sites in such close proximity and relying on the same agricultural land were on an inevitable collision course. With the development of new forms of settlement, the need for better harbors, and population growth both at Chalcis and Eretria in the Late Geometric period, Lefkandi appears to have found itself in a disadvantageous position. Its gradual abandonment at the very end of the eighth century has often been contrasted with Eretria's growth, but Chalcis could have played an even more decisive role in this process.

In the ninth and eighth centuries, the nature of the ruling power in these communities is a matter of debate. Was it concentrated in the hands of a single individual or shared among a restricted group of the elite? Literary tradition is of no help. There is not much to get out of mentions of mythical kings said to have ruled over Euboea, except that their names provided convenient origins for ethnonyms and toponyms (Abas/Abantes, Lelantos/Lelantine plain, Chalkodon/Chalcis; see Section 2.12.4). During the Early Iron Age, the possibility that a single monarch could have reigned over the entire island (or even a significant portion of it) is remote. Instead, it seems more likely that Lefkandi, Chalcis, and Eretria were autonomous polities. But who held power in each of them?

For Lefkandi, the "big man" buried inside the Toumba building has been portrayed as the leader of his community. But it might be erroneous to view the community as having been dominated by a single man. The funerary evidence from Lefkandi from this period is characterized by the permanence of distinct burial plots and the use of exotic imported items as grave goods, and status seems to have been based at least in part upon engagement in maritime trade and links with regional (Attica, north Aegean) and distant (Cyprus, Levant) partners. All of that suggests the existence of a complex and dynamic elite group (Lemos and Mitchell 2011).

### 2.5.2. Hippobotai and Hippeis

It is interesting to note that the political situation in Lefkandi looks much like that in other Greek communities during the Late Geometric and Early Archaic periods, when aristocracy was predominant. In fact, throughout the Early Iron Age, aristocracy seems to have been the dominant form of governance (Duplouy 2006: 264–71). In the late eighth century, there are signs that Eretrian aristocratic families competed in the funerary sphere (Crielaard 1998; Crielaard 2007). In the "Heroon" necropolis (see Section 2.4.4), the wealthiest grave (Tomb 6) unquestionably belonged to a powerful individual, possibly a warrior remembered and honored long after his death. But it appears increasingly unlikely that this adult male was the "prince" of Eretria, as was initially claimed, or that his funeral signposts the transition from a monarchic to an oligarchic system.[20] The same can be said of Amphidamas, who is mentioned by Hesiod (*Op.* 650–7). Although he

---

20. Bérard 1982. This view is mainly based on the presence of a bronze spearhead, interpreted by Bérard as an heirloom dating back to Mycenaean times and handed over as a symbol of power, the "scepter of the ruler." However, it has been shown that the weapon in question is of Italic origin and might be more correctly interpreted as war booty (Verdan 2015a: 186–7). We also believe that the Heroon should be set in the wider context of aristocratic practices in the form of competition between kin groups by way of wealth and status display on public occasions, in particular funerary ceremonies and religious festivals (Crielaard 1998; Crielaard 2007).

Chalcis and Eretria

received full (military?) honors in a widely attended funeral, he is by no means characterized as sole ruler of Chalcis.

Written sources consistently indicate that both Chalcis and Eretria were governed by aristocracies for most of the Archaic period. The ruling aristocrats were called the Hippobotai, "the feeders of horses," in Chalcis (Hdt. 5.77, 6.100; Arist. F603 Rose; Plut. *Per.* 23.3–4) and the Hippeis, "the horse riders," in Eretria (Arist. [*Ath. Pol.*] 15.2–3, *Pol.* 1306a35–7). As indicated by their names, both groups may have initially built their power on horse breeding and on the use of the horse in warfare. A section of the Chalcidian *chōra*, perhaps the Lelantine plain, was also known as horse-breeding land (ἱππόβοτον χώραν; Ael. *VH* 6.1 and Hdt 5.77). This definition of status was deeply rooted in the two communities' past, as suggested by the importance given to the horse already in Lefkandi.[21] The ubiquity of the horse in the iconography of Late Geometric Euboean pottery provides an additional sign that Euboean aristocrats used the horse as a status symbol (see Sections 2.4.3, 2.8.3, 2.9.2).[22]

Apart from this dominant aspect of their identity, we know very little about the two aristocratic groups. A passage of Aristotle cited by Strabo (10.1.8; Arist. F603 Rose, but note Sprawski 2008) mentions that Chalcidian "colonies" in Sicily, Italy, and Thrace (Psoma 2017) were founded under the regime of the Hippobotai. According to Aristotle, the Hippobotai formed a property class that provided the magistrates of the city's aristocratic government. Two traditions (one about property classes and another about magistracies) have probably been combined here, but this passage leads us to believe that the Hippobotai were already in existence in the second half of the eighth century, while the existence of a property class might relate to a sixth-century situation, comparable to that of Athens predating or following the Solonian reforms. One might speculate that this class owned most of the land and eventually accumulated a surplus that could be exchanged and invested, for example, in maritime trade. Indeed, some of the Hippobotai, willing to diversify their assets, might have been interested in sponsoring overseas trade, which would explain why they were involved with *apoikiai* in Sicily and southern Italy.

---

21. There are many relevant pieces of evidence: the horses buried beside the "hero" in the Toumba building (Popham, Calligas, Sackett, et al. 1993: 21 pl. 12 and 22), the taming scene incised on a fibula (Popham, Sackett, and Themelis 1980: 132, fig. 5), and a centaur figurine (Popham, Sackett, and Themelis 1980: 169–70, 215, 344–5 pl. 251–2).

22. In a recent article, Duplouy (2022: 152–3) has argued that the Eretrian *hippeis* represented not an elite group but "all the members of the Geometric and Archaic polis." We disagree with this view and believe instead, mostly on economic grounds, that horse breeding and horse riding were available only for a wealthy minority of the citizen body who could afford such activities.

In Eretria, various pieces of evidence indicate the strength of the Hippeis throughout the Archaic period. First, it is worth noting the existence of a month called Hippion in the Eretrian calendar (Knoepfler 2000: 75 n. 302, 61). Second, the Hippeis offered a safe haven to Pisistratus during his first exile and probably contributed to his exploitation of the Pangaion gold mines during his second exile; later they seemed to have enjoyed close ties with the mighty Athenian Alcmeonids (see Section 2.7.4.1). Finally, the Hippeis displayed their wealth and power annually during the Artemisia, the highlight of which was the parading of 600 horsemen and 60 chariots along the sacred road linking Eretria to Amarynthos (see Sections 2.7.1, 2.10.3, 2.11.2.6). It seems very likely that this procession, which was repeatedly reorganized over time, had an Archaic origin. If that is true, a contingent of 600 cavalrymen was a singular force for the time (though military numbers in ancient sources tend to be hyperbolic). An echo of this power is found in Aristotle: when referring to oligarchic regimes relying on strong cavalries, he specifically cites Chalcis and Eretria as examples (*Pol.* 1289b36–41).

The Hippobotai's aristocratic-oligarchic regime came to an end in 506, when the young Athenian democracy defeated the Chalcidians and settled cleruchs on the lands of the rich landowners (see Section 2.7.4.2). During roughly the same period, the Eretrian Hippeis were dispossessed of their political predominance by Diagoras (Arist. *Pol.* 1306a35–7 [5.5.10] and below, Section 2.5.3.2), who was most likely one of their own ranks. But even if they lost their monopoly in the political sphere, the Euboean aristocrats did not lose political influence entirely. In the middle of the fourth century, Eretria still had an "active and powerful" oligarchy, whose defenders were no doubt included among its impressive corps of 500 attested *hippeis* (Knoepfler 1985: 256–7).

### 2.5.3. Early Political Institutions

Judging from the impact that the discovery of the Aristotelian *Constitution of the Athenians* in the sands of Egypt has had on our knowledge of Athenian political institutions, one can only imagine the effect that the recovery of the *Constitution of the Eretrians* and the *Constitution of the Chalcidians* (even in a partial form) would have on our understanding of Euboean *poleis* and their Archaic political history. Instead, we are left with secondary references and scraps of information from later sources, often coming down to a lone surviving name.

The case of Tynnondas provides a good example. This early "tyrant of the Euboeans" is mentioned by Plutarch in the *Life of Solon* (14.7). Plutarch cites

Aristotle as a source, perhaps drawing the information from a passage of one of the lost Aristotelian *politeiai*. No other mention of Tynnondas has come down to us, and when Plutarch uses the term "Euboeans," we do not know if he means the entire island, Chalcis and Eretria together, or only one of the two cities. As a result, not much can be said beyond the fact that Tynnondas was perhaps an early Euboean tyrant, possibly active before 600. Of course, one can speculate. If one accepts that Tynnondas was in fact a tyrant in Euboea in the Archaic period, then it seems likely that he ruled over a single city, as it is extremely unlikely that there was any form of political unification of the island during the Archaic period. A possible Boeotian origin of the name (Jeffery 1976: 68) could suggest that he was from neighboring Boeotia, perhaps from the regions closest to the Euripos; given Chalcis' ties with Boeotia, culminating in the anti-Athenian alliance of 506, identifying Tynnondas as an early tyrant of Chalcis is a possibility yet nothing more than an educated guess.

This example highlights the great scarcity of sources for the Archaic period and their limitations. As a result, the political institutions of Chalcis and Eretria in the Archaic period can only be sketched with a very broad brush. In this section, we will nevertheless review the evidence for each *polis* individually and try to complement that evidence, where possible and appropriate, with early Classical elements whose origin can be traced back to the Archaic period.

### 2.5.3.1. Chalcis

The suggestion has been made above that the Hippobotai of Chalcis represented an aristocratic ruling class in the eighth century. In the seventh century, such political dominance might have evolved into an oligarchic form of government. The Hippobotai certainly formed the wealthiest class(es), arguably comparable, mutatis mutandis, to the Athenian *pentakosiomedimnoi* and *hippeis*, who together perhaps amounted to 10% of the population (van Wees 2006: 361–2). Producing 500 *medimnoi* of barley—sufficient to feed more than 50 people for a year—would have required a considerable amount of arable land, somewhere in the vicinity of 42 ha. That amount of land was enough to breed the horses of which the Hippobotai were so fond and upon which they relied so much.

Herodotus, in his account of the events of 506, clearly states that the Hippobotai were the "fat" (i.e., rich) Chalcidians (5.74, 77). Ownership of much of the best land in Chalcis must have empowered this class both economically and politically. Evidently, they dominated the early magistracies. Perhaps their most prominent representatives formed a college of archons. The existence of the latter (also attested at Eretria; see Section 2.5.3.2) is suggested by a fragment of Polyzelus of Rhodes (who seems to have been active in the Hellenistic period) that mentions an archon called Tynes in relation to Hesiod's visit to Chalcis (*FGrH* 521 F9). Like the Bacchiads at Corinth (Hall 2014b: 143), the Hippobotai could have ruled Chalcis in common, selecting magistrates from among their ranks. However, this might not have lasted, as it is reasonable to assume that Chalcis was not immune to the social and political tensions that shook similar forms of government in the sixth century. If true, they might increasingly have been forced to share some of their political advantages with a wider group of less wealthy but still notably affluent individuals.

The names of several tyrants have been associated with Chalcis. We have already raised the possibility that Tynnondas might have been one of them. Aristotle (*Pol.* 1316a31–2) states that Antileon was a tyrant of Chalcis who was overthrown and replaced by an oligarchy. This passage might suggest that Antileon (briefly?) interrupted an aristocratic regime in place in Chalcis in the sixth century (Robinson 1997: 89; Knoepfler forthcoming). Aristotle names another tyrant of Chalcis, Phoxos, whom he claims was killed by the *dēmos* with the help of the γνώριμοι, the "notables" (*Pol.* 1304a29–30). The γνώριμοι were certainly elites, perhaps chosen from among the Hippobotai (Robinson 1997: 89–90), or they might have been a slightly inferior property class. This event, which marked a change in *politeia*, should not necessarily be understood as a "democratic revolution." It could have been a temporary alliance in which the γνώριμοι relied on popular support to take down Phoxos, perhaps with the promise of certain concessions. This episode, otherwise unknown, cannot be dated. It has been assigned to the sixth century (Robinson 1997: 89–90), but a regime change involving the participation of the *dēmos* (even short-lived) is not easy to fit in before the Athenian intervention of 506.

In summary, it is probable that the political institutions of Chalcis in the Archaic period were dominated by the Hippobotai. That group formed an aristocratic-oligarchic regime that remained in power until 506, perhaps interrupted by brief periods of tyranny. The existence of a tribal system (one of the tribes of which was named Abantis) is first attested in an inscription from the Roman period (*IG* XII.9.946; Knoepfler 2000: 75), but its origin might go back to the sixth century (see Section 2.5.3.2). After 506, it is likely that a change of regime was imposed by the democratic Athenians, although the political consequences of the Athenian expedition are unclear. The confiscation of land for the cleruchs (Hdt. 5.77) appears to have taken place to the detriment of the Hippobotai, thus perhaps limiting opposition to the Athenians among the most disadvantaged sections of the population. In any case, this event marks an abrupt

Chalcis and Eretria

break in Chalcis' history, perhaps giving the opportunity for Eretria to rise to unprecedented levels.

### 2.5.3.2. Eretria

In eighth-century Eretria, the ruling class was probably formed by the Hippeis. The high profile of this aristocratic elite is perhaps best illustrated by the burials at the West Gate, which might have belonged to one of the *polis*' most powerful families (see Section 2.4.4). The Hippeis were certainly an elite group, perhaps amounting to 10% of the population[23] and owning the best lands in amounts sufficient for intensive horse-breeding. In the seventh century, the Hippeis probably formed an oligarchic government, whose officials were exclusively selected from this class, in rotation.

In the sixth century, the chief governing official was the ἀρχός, who appears in an inscription dated to c. 525 (*IG* XII.9.1273–4; Vanderpool and Wallace 1964; see Section 2.6). However, this magistracy might have been in existence much earlier, perhaps even in the seventh century (as in Athens). His area(s) of jurisdiction and the nature of his power are not known, but he appears to have been involved with the legal system. As in other oligarchic regimes of the time, the Hippeis probably controlled the supreme office, yet they might have gradually been forced to agree to compromise with emerging elites and other groups. By 550, the population had perhaps doubled since 700 (based on a 1% annual rise, see Section 2.9.1). Demographics would suggest that the Eretrian *chōra* extended beyond the Eretrian plain at that time and that other regional groups were now part of the *polis*. Those groups may have pressed the oligarchic regime to select governing officials representing a broader geographical area. In any case, in the middle of the sixth century, the oligarchic regime was still dominated by the Hippeis, who welcomed Pisistratus to Eretria during his second exile (Hdt. 5.99; Arist. [*Ath. Pol.*] 15.2).

However, by the end of the sixth century, the days of the Hippeis were numbered. Aristotle tells us that a man called Diagoras dissolved the regime, following an injustice regarding marriage (*Pol.* 1306a35–6). This event can be most plausibly dated to the period between 540 and 510 (Knoepfler 2008: 602). Marriage agreements among aristocratic elites could be a source of conflict,

---

23. Based on the numbers recorded for the procession to Amarynthos (see Section 2.7.1), the ratio between the *hippeis*, hoplites, and *psiloi* suggests that the *hippeis* represented about 10% of the force; in terms of population representation, it corresponds to what has been estimated at Athens for the first two census classes, namely the *pentakosiomedimnoi* and the *hippeis* (van Wees 2006: 361–2).

although the exact causes are here unknown. It has been observed that Diagoras might have been a "good tyrant," comparable to Pisistratus (Walker 2004), or a "sort of Eretrian Solon, preserving a balance between the prerogatives of the ancient oligarchs and the new popular aspirations" (Knoepfler 2008: 602). Knoepfler has persuasively argued that Diagoras was able to overthrow an obsolete regime, first with the help of a faction of dissatisfied aristocrats, later with popular support, at a time when, in Athens, Pisistratus' sons were encountering their first setbacks (Knoepfler 2008: 602–3). Interestingly, Diagoras left his city (like Solon) and died at Corinth on his way to Sparta. He was apparently celebrated by the Eretrians with an εἰκών, a statue portrait (Heraclides Lembus *FHG* II 217).

What followed the fall of the Hippeis is unclear. Given the neighboring example of Cleisthenes' reforms at Athens and the ties that connected both *poleis*, it is tempting to hypothesize that a democratic regime came into existence in Eretria sometime around 500, or perhaps even 506, when the Athenians defeated the Chalcidians. However, the first secure evidence for the existence of a democratic regime is a proxeny decree dated by Jeffery to the first quarter of the fifth century and by Knoepfler to before the 440s (*IG* XII Supp. 549; Jeffery 1990: 88 #15; Knoepfler 2000: #I; Knoepfler 2008: 603). The decree (unfortunately a *pierre errante*, most likely attributable to Eretria, although Chalcis cannot be entirely excluded) refers in the opening lines to "the *dēmos* being in regular session," while text attesting to the presence of a council (*boulē*) should be restored. The opening formula ([ἔδοχσεν : τῆι βο]- | [λῆ]ι : καὶ τῶι [δέμōι]) leaves little doubt that Eretria had a democratic regime in the middle decades of the fifth century.

The decree also sheds light on the tribal system, stating that the tribe Mekistis holds the ἐπιμήνια, or monthly presidency (Knoepfler 2000: 74–6). The evidence for the Eretrian tribal system consists primarily of inscriptions, including but not limited to *SEG* 45.1141, *IG* XII.9 245, and *IG* IX Supp. 555. By the end of the fifth century, the citizenry of Eretria was divided into six geographically based tribes, and the Eretrian *chōra* was divided into 50–60 demes that were distributed among five geographical districts called *chōroi* (Knoepfler 1997; Fachard 2012: 47–76). Some of the demes (e.g., Styra) were formerly autonomous *poleis* that had been integrated into the polity of the Eretrians. Each tribe consisted of all of the residents of 10 to 12 demes (with demes from all five *chōroi* in each tribe) and, in addition, some citizens from certain demes (e.g., Grynchai and Styra) whose residents were divided among all six tribes.

The names of three of the six tribes are currently known: Mekistis, from the hero Mekistos (displaying links with Elis; see Strabo 10.1.10); Narkittis, from the famous Narkittos (Narcissus; see Knoepfler 2010), and Admetis, from the hero Admetus (Knoepfler and Ackermann 2012). A fourth tribal name, Iphitis, can be plausibly reconstructed (Knoepfler 2010: 120–2). The name of just one *chōros* is attested, Mesochoros (*IG* XII.9.241.37; Knoepfler 2010: 375–7).

The systems of the tribes, demes, and *chōroi* overlapped, but the deme was the basis of the entire civic, political, and territorial organization. As in Attica, the Eretrian deme represented a community controlling a micro-territory delimited in some cases by boundaries (Fachard 2016). The deme was represented by a *dēmarchos*, attested in the last quarter of the fifth century at the latest (*IG* XII.9.189.23–4). Demes provided a number of councilors to the Eretrian *boulē*, as well as ephebes. The number of original demes is unknown (40–50?), but at the end of the fifth century, it amounted to 50–60. Because each tribe was composed of demes from different regions of the Eretrian *chōra*, the entire civic population was mingled, as in Attica.

The fact that by the time the aforementioned decree had been enacted, the old Ionian tribes had been replaced by a new tribal system, in which the tribes were named after local heroes, suggests that the Eretrians were influenced by the Cleisthenic reforms. But a wider agenda might lie behind this tribal change. An increase in the number of tribes could be justified by civic reorganization, an extension of the participation of citizens, including a probable enlargement of the citizen body. By way of hypothesis, an ambitious territorial reorganization, accompanied by the implementation of the deme system, could have been put in place at that time, as in Athens. Therefore, it is tempting to believe that the entire territorial organization of the Eretriad, with its association of demes and tribes as attested for the last quarter of the fifth century, might have been implemented sometime between 506 and 490 (Fachard 2019).

Another issue regarding the early territorial and civic system concerns the existence and number of *chōroi* (districts). In the later system, the Eretriad was divided into five geographical entities, which were somehow comparable to the three regional entities of Attica: *asty, paralia, mesogeios*. There are still many issues regarding the date and extent of an earlier deme system at Eretria. However, if the early date is confirmed in the future, the existence of such a system adopted in the wake the Cleisthenic reforms in Athens would provide another case of social and political propinquity between the two *poleis*.

Political emulation, the fast transmission of political and civic ideals, and an increase in complexity are part of Renfrew's (1986) concept of "peer polity interaction." The structural homologies between Athens and Eretria provide a good case for the use of this notion and attest to the many points of convergence between the two *poleis* in the late Archaic period.[24]

## 2.6. Legal History

The first-known Euboean legal documents are inscriptions from Eretria and date to the last quarter of the sixth century. The texts are, however, fragmentary and difficult to interpret. The texts provided below are those given in *SEG* 41.725.[25] Like other legal documents of this period, very little is known about their original context (Harris 2006: 4).

The inscriptions consist of four texts on two adjoining blocks (*IG* XII.9.1273–4) that were prominently displayed at the corner of a building of unknown identity, perhaps located near the harbor (see Figure 2.13). The blocks were later broken and reused in the Classical city walls.[26] Two of the texts concern public procedure and were meant to regulate the formal and peaceful settlement of disputes, one deals with wages at sea, and one is too fragmentary to permit meaningful interpretation.

**FIGURE 2.13.** *Poros* blocks with inscriptions (*IG* XII.9.1273–4) from Eretria; last quarter of sixth century; length: c. 60 cm, height: c. 54 cm. Archaeological Museum of Eretria 1206.

---

24. We are grateful to P. Cartledge for suggesting this parallel.

25. The English translations of A, B, and C are those provided in Cairns 1991: 313; the English translation of D is that provided in van Wees 2010: 205.

26. Papavasileiou 1913: 210–11; Vanderpool and Wallace 1964; Cairns 1984; Cairns 1991; van Effenterre and Ruzé 1994–1995: 330–3; van Wees 2010.

| | |
|---|---|
| 1273/4 A | The judge (or arbiter) shall award the penalty after he has taken an oath. The defendant will pay on the third day goods that are acceptable and sound. If he does not pay, the plaintiff shall seize (or remove?) him.<br><br>δίκεν ⋮ ἐπεὰν ⋮ κατομόσει ⋮ τίν[υ]- boustrophedon<br>σθα(ι) ⋮ τρίτει ἡεμέ[ρ]ει ⋮ χρέματα<br>δόκιμα ⋮ κα[ί ἡ]υγιᾶ ἰὰν· μὲ τείσ-<br>ει [[⋮ ἡέρα̣ι]] |
| 1273/4 B | In the archonship of Golos in the city . . .<br><br>v v v ἐπὶ Γόλο· ἄρχ[ο]ντος· ἐν πόλε̣[ι] ι̣[- - -] |
| 1273/4 C | [(?) If he does not pay (?), he shall] owe on the second day two [statēres, on the third day] ten statēres. If he does not pay, the magistrates are to act in accordance with the regulations. Any magistrate who does not do so shall himself be liable to pay.<br><br>[- - - 17-25 - - -]ιν· τε̃ι ἡυστέρει· δύϝε<br>[στατε̃ρε· τ]ε̃ι [τρίτ]ει· δέκ[α· σ]τατε̃ρας· ὀφέλεν [⋮]<br>ἰὰν μὲ τείσει· ἀρχὸς· ἀπὸ ρετὸν· ποιε̃σα[ι]<br>v v? ἡόστις ἂν· μὲ ποιε̃ι αὐτὸν· ὀφέλεν |
| 1273/4 D | Those who sail are to receive a wage if they go beyond the Petalai or Kenaion. Everyone must contribute. Those who are in the country Anyone who took . . . will not be open to dispute.<br><br>τὸς πλέοντας· ἀρ[έσ]θαι μισθὸν<br>ἡοίτινες ἂν Π[ε]ταλὰς· ἒ Κέναιον<br>ἀ]μείπσονται· φέ[ρ]εν δὲ πάντας<br>v v v v v v τος ἐπιδ[έ]μος ἐόν[τας - c. 3 -]<br>[- c. 6 -]ονγνον̣ [. c. 2 .]νασεν vacat<br>vacat (8-10) ἡός [ἄ]ν ἡελοι [- c. 7 -]<br>[- 7 or 8 -]ιαρφιν[. c. 2.] v ἀναφισβετεει |

The first law refers to the existence of a judge or an arbiter responsible for supervising the payment of a penalty. There is a *rasura* at the end of line 4, but if the

## 160 THE OXFORD HISTORY OF THE ARCHAIC GREEK WORLD

suggestion hέραι is accurate, it means that the defendant would be seized if he failed to pay. In the third text, which was carved later, the law states that in case of nonpayment, the archons are to act in accordance with the ῥητά (regulations), a procedure also found in the Gortyn Code (Cairns 1984: 306–7). The chief magistrate, or ἀρχός, is liable to pay if he fails to respect the procedure in collecting fines (Harris 2006: 20). The swearing of an oath before trial, the payment of fines at a particular time, and a penalty for nonpayment are "basic procedural rules applying presumably to all trials at Eretria" (Gagarin 1986: 92).

A particular clause of the first text has attracted considerable attention: the fine is payable in χρέματα | δόκιμα κα[ὶ h]υγιᾶ. This is not necessarily a reference to coined money but should instead be understood as "valid precious metals that have to be tested," perhaps silver bullion.[27] Another suggestion has been made by Dubois (2015: 55), reading [ζ]ύγια, which is attested for later periods with the meaning "tested and weighted value." Interestingly, the third text also refers to a case of default on payment, but the penalties are this time payable in *statēres*. The word "στατήρ" could designate official weights or even coinage (Cairns 1984: 154). Here it is tempting to link the *statēres* with the abundant coinage issue (bearing octopus/cow) dated to the last decade of the sixth century (see Section 2.8.5). Both laws might provide evidence for a transitional phase when a currency system encompassing bullion, official weights, and coinage was employed.

The meaning of the fourth text on the stone, carved after the others, has long remained poorly understood (Cairns 1991: 310–2). However, a new interpretation by van Wees (2010; 2013b: 27–8) suggests it dealt with the payment of a wage (μισθός) to the crews serving in the Eretrian navy when operating beyond the Euboean Gulf. The two landmarks mentioned here are well known. The Petaliai islets constitute a southern limit, while Kenaion (modern Cape Lichada) is situated near the northwest tip of Euboea. These points do not define Eretria's "territorial waters" but rather represent two geographical markers to be used by the crews operating the ships, as well as the naval administration and the *polis*. When the navy sails beyond these markers, the crews receive a wage, and all taxpayers contribute to the effort. Such operations evidently refer not to routine journeys or daily missions of surveillance but to costly overseas expeditions. The existence of a law regulating several aspects of such expeditions might reflect earlier disputes regarding pay and the funding source(s). Early Archaic warships perhaps

---

27. Cairns (1984; 1991: 298–9) suggests that this phrase refers to precious objects, such as *obeloi* and tripods. However, this seems anachronistic, since silver bullion was used for public purposes in communities such as Athens starting in the sixth century at the latest. See Kroll 1998 and Kroll 2012, who does not mention the Eretrian law.

belonged to individual citizens (de Souza 1998: 272), but this law definitely situates the Eretrian navy in the public sphere (van Wees 2010). Eretria's navy enjoyed a high degree of prestige in the Aegean during the late sixth century (see Section 2.7.3). Eretria's sizeable navy required a strong organization, financial planning, and a legal framework, all of which seem to be referenced in this law. This regulation of state naval funding precedes the Athenian evidence by some 40 years (van Wees 2010).

To conclude, the Eretrian laws show that a degree of state regulation and financial organization was in place in the Archaic period, as well as procedural rules applying to trials. Unfortunately, these procedures do not tell us which disputes they were supposed to settle.

## 2.7. *Diplomatic History*
### 2.7.1. "Lelantine War"

This conflict appears to be the earliest and most famous confrontation opposing Chalcis and Eretria. It is also a most vexed issue for historians, mainly due to complications with the relevant textual sources and concomitant chronological uncertainties. In terms of scholarship, there are two basically opposed schools of thought: some have attempted to reconstruct an entire sequence of events (e.g., Parker 1997; Walker 2004: 152–65), while others have doubted its existence (e.g., Fehling 1979: 199–210; Hall 2014b: 4–8). In this section, we review the evidence and the divergent interpretations, then attempt to collect the elements worth retaining.

It is best to start with Thucydides, who mentions an old war between the two cities. The context is key. First, Thucydides states that the Peloponnesian War was a war like no other because of its "global" character. In comparison, previous wars had a more "local" character, being essentially conflicts between neighbors. The only previous war that involved two belligerents backed by large alliances of Greek cities was the war between Chalcis and Eretria: "But it was chiefly in the war that arose a long time ago between the Chalcidians and the Eretrians, that all the rest of Hellas took sides in alliance with the one side or the other" (1.15.3, trans. C. F. Smith).[28] Were Thucydides' testimony our only source, this war would have gone down as a border conflict in which each side was backed by a coalition of numerous yet unnamed *poleis*.

---

28. μάλιστα δὲ ἐς τὸν πάλαι ποτὲ γενόμενον πόλεμον Χαλκιδέων καὶ Ἐρετριῶν καὶ τὸ ἄλλο Ἑλληνικὸν ἐς ξυμμαχίαν ἑκατέρων διέστη.

162 THE OXFORD HISTORY OF THE ARCHAIC GREEK WORLD

However, other texts have been associated—rightly or wrongly—with this war. Among the sources predating Thucydides, the most specific probable reference to the conflict is found in Herodotus, who, in his account of the Ionian Rebellion, reports that Miletus once helped Eretria against the Chalcidians, who were allied with Samos (5.99.1); the only chronological indication Herodotus supplies for the Milesian aid is πρότερον, so this passage may well but does not unquestionably refer to the supposed Lelantine War.

Scholars have identified what they believe to be allusions to the Lelantine War in various Archaic poems, supposedly contemporary with the war itself. Archilochus, in the middle of the seventh century, refers to the fierce fighting qualities of Euboean lords (F3 West):

> Not many bows will be stretched nor will there be
> numerous slings, whenever Ares brings together the
> press of battle on the plain; it will be the woeful
> work of swords. This is the warfare in which those
> spear-famed lords of Euboea are skilled. (trans. D. Gerber)

Although this passage does not mention a war between Chalcis and Eretria, Hesiod famously won a tripod at the funerary games held in honor of Amphidamas of Chalcis, but the poet never indicates the circumstances of his death (*Op.* 654–7). One of the poems ascribed to Theognis (885–94) describes fighting and laments the destruction of Kerinthos and the ravaging of vineyards along the Lelantos river, though the damage done to the vineyards could have taken place during the Athenian campaign of 506 (Bershadsky 2018a).

Whereas none of the sources discussed above makes explicit mention of a conflict over control of the Lelantine plain, this aspect of the war is more prominent in later testimonies. Some eight centuries after Hesiod's journey to Chalcis, Plutarch places a speech in the mouth of Periander of Corinth, in which the latter characterizes Amphidamas as having caused much trouble to the Eretrians and having fallen in a battle for control of the Lelantine plain (*Mor.* 153f). Elsewhere he mentions an episode in which Thessalian horsemen helped the Chalcidians gain a victory over the Eretrian cavalry "when the Lelantine War . . . was at its height" (*Mor.* 760e–1b).

Two passages from Strabo, recording two *stēlai* whose contents have typically been associated with the Archaic period, deserve special mention here. In his description of Eretria, Strabo stresses the power that the Eretrians had once exercised and cites as evidence a *stēlē* "which once stood in the Sanctuary of Artemis Amarysia." According to Strabo, the inscription on that *stēlē* recorded that Eretrian processions on public occasions included 3,000 hoplites, 600 cavalry, and 60 chariots (10.1.10). Strabo goes on to say that Chalcis and Eretria generally enjoyed an amicable relationship and that even when they went to war with each other over the Lelantine plain, they agreed on certain conditions on the basis of which fighting would be conducted. Here again, he cites as evidence a (different) *stēlē* from the Sanctuary of Artemis Amarynthia. According to Strabo, the inscription on that *stēlē* recorded a prohibition on the use of long-range missiles (μὴ χρῆσθαι τηλεβόλοις, 10.1.12). It is important to remember that Strabo never visited Euboea. In both passages, therefore, he must have relied on other authors, among whom was Artemidorus of Ephesus (see Section 2.4.1.3.2).

In addition to these sources—or one might say *because* of them—various pieces of archaeological evidence have been correlated with the "Lelantine War." Signs of decline (and destruction?) evident at Lefkandi around 825 have been interpreted as the result of an initial attack by Chalcis (Walker 2004: 82–3, 89–90). The "warriors" cremated and buried during the last quarter of the eighth century in Eretria's West Quarter (see Sections 2.4.4, 2.11.2.5) have been seen as Lelantine War heroes (Bérard 1970: 31–2, 68–70; Mazarakis Ainian 1997: 20; Coldstream 2003: 182). The final abandonment of the settlement of Lefkandi, some alleged signs of destruction in Eretria, the abandonment of Zagora (claimed by some to have been a "Euboean" settlement on Andros), and the general decline in the visibility of Euboeans in the Mediterranean, east and west alike, have all been interpreted as proof that Chalcis and Eretria had been "exhausted" by the war.[29]

None of this evidence, whether textual or archaeological, is unambiguous. Before turning our attention to the varied scholarly views about the Lelantine War, it will be helpful to state our views on the *stēlai* mentioned by Strabo, which present particularly complicated interpretive challenges. In the first *stēlē*, the presence of chariots—irrelevant in combat after 700—has been used to suggest a historical link with the Lelantine War. However, this is implausible. Strabo had precise numbers at his disposal regarding Amarynthos, so he might have copied them from a fourth-century source that had access to a "sacred law." The *stēlē*, if it ever existed, appears to be later than the sixth century, because the numbers seem to relate to a period when Eretria had six tribes instead of four, which happened only after c. 506–500 (Knoepfler 1997: 392; Fachard 2012: 112; see Section 2.5.3.2). It is likely that the person(s) responsible for the erection of the *stēlē* provided an

---

29. Lefkandi: Popham, Sackett, and Themelis 1980: 369; Parker 1997: 38; Walker 2004: 85, 90, 161. Eretria: see Section 2.4.1.3.4 and discussion in Walker 2004: 89–92. Zagora: Cambitoglou, Birchall, Coulton et al. 1988: 241–2; Coldstream 2003: 193; Walker 2004: 92, 96. For the general decline in Euboean activities in the Aegean and beyond, see Boardman 1980: 48; Coldstream 2003: 182; Walker 2004: 161–2. A summary of the archaeological arguments can be found in Parker 1997: 91–2.

archaizing trait (chariots) to inflate the antiquity of Eretria's strength and prestige. The numbers of hoplites and cavalrymen, however, appear to be plausible, as each tribe would have been able to provide 500 hoplites and a cavalry 100 strong for the procession from the fifth century onward.

The second *stēlē* is more problematic. Strabo directly connects the ban on long-range missiles with the conflict for the Lelantine plain. There are two issues here: (1) Is it reasonable to assume that such a ban was implemented? (2) Could there have been such a text inscribed on a *stēlē* in the seventh century, the most probable date for the Lelantine War (see below)? Some form of Euboean disdain for bows and slings is evident in a mid-seventh-century passage from Archilochus, celebrating the fierce fighting qualities of Euboean lords (F3 West), but there is no mention of a ban on projectile weapons. Peter Krentz (2002: 23–39) has highlighted the fact that Archaic battles included many projectile weapons. A ban on long-range projectile weapons is mentioned only in the later sources of Polybius and the aforementioned passage from Strabo. Polybius denounces the perfidy of his own time and recalls an age when "the ancients" (οἱ ἀρχαῖοι) banned the use of long-range missiles—though without mentioning Eretria or Chalcis (13.3.1–5). Both authors perhaps rely on the same source, Ephorus, who might have invented the passage (Wheeler 1987; Parker 1997).

From the point of view of Greek warfare, it is highly improbable that such a formal ban ever existed. But what about the *stēlē*? According to Jeffery (1976: 66), such a "written pact would be epigraphically possible in the seventh century." This might be true, but the erection of such a *stēlē* in the seventh century in Amarynthos nevertheless seems far-fetched. According to Everett Wheeler (1987), Strabo's source, Ephorus, invented the Amarynthos *stēlē* and used it as a literary topos denouncing the development of artillery in the fourth century. According to Victor Parker (1997: 100–7), a *stēlē* did exist and was read by Ephorus in the Sanctuary of Artemis Amarysia at Amarynthos, but the text was written subsequent to the Lelantine War. Doubts regarding the early date of the *stēlē* were also expressed by Ducrey and Brélaz (2007). We believe that such a *stēlē* was not erected in the seventh century. However, it is probable that the Eretrians (or Euboeans) inscribed such a text in the Classical or Hellenistic period in order to bring fame to their ancestors and to illustrate their noble behavior in war.

As one might expect, given the nature of the relevant evidence, virtually every aspect of the Lelantine War has been the subject of extended and lively discussion. The main subjects of debate are the date and duration of the war, the cities involved, and causes and results. Scholars have advocated both a high date (end of the eighth to the beginning of the seventh century), based on various interpretations of the archaeological evidence and Hesiod's testimony, and a low date (end of the seventh to the beginning of the sixth), arguing that large alliances between cities are unlikely to have been established before this period (for an extensive discussion with further bibliography, see Parker 1997: 59–93).

It has also been suggested that the Lelantine War was initially a local conflict, that the "Panhellenic" phase of the war only ran for a couple of decades in the early seventh century, and that the war ended by the time of the conquest of Ionia by the Persians in the middle of the sixth century (Knoepfler 2008: 600–1). For some, the conflict lasted a few years or decades, while others have suggested a "Hundred Years War," which is also a convenient way of accommodating all the possible evidence.

Regarding the belligerents, minimalist accounts include only Chalcis and Eretria, but many historians add Miletus and Samos (relying on Herodotus), as well as Thessaly (based on Plutarch). The respective alliances can be extended to Corinth and Megara, Chios and Erythrae, as later epigraphic documents and literary sources seem to refer to such coalitions: a Hellenistic epigram inscribed around 200 on a polyandrion at Miletus records a "great war" (μεγάλου . . . πο[λέ]μου, 732.6) and mentions Megarians opposed to Milesians (Herrmann 1998, vol. VI 2: 732; Knoepfler 2008: 600).[30]

As for the casus belli, two main causes have been alleged: a dispute over fertile land on the one hand and competition over maritime trade on the other (Parker 1997: 153–60). Most scholars believe that Chalcis prevailed in the conflict, while there is general agreement that both cities were weakened by the struggle, resulting in a dramatic decline of Euboean activities overseas from c. 700 onward (see the sources cited in note 28).

More recently, modern narratives about the Lelantine War have been deconstructed. Natasha Bershadsky has argued that during the Archaic period, young aristocrats from Eretria and Chalcis confronted each other in iterated, highly ritualized battles that were understood as re-enactments of battles fought over the Lelantine plain by the legendary Curetes. According to Bershadsky, the ritualized battles took place in sacred space that changed hands depending on the outcome of any given battle and that provided grazing for the horses of the winning side (until the next battle). From this perspective, the chariots mentioned by Strabo were included in the ritual battles in order to provide a suitably archaizing tone (Bershadsky 2018b).

Others have gone farther and called the entire tradition of the Lelantine War into question (Hall 2014b: 4–8). A major reason for doubting the existence or importance of the conflict is the wide variations in how it is described in the ancient sources. Not only are some testimonies very late compared with the alleged date of the war, but even the authors who might have lived at the time

---

30. On the involvement of these four cities in the war, see also Parker 1997: 128–44 (who includes Corinth and Megara but excludes Chios and Erythrae from the list).

of the conflict are spread from the late eighth to the sixth centuries (Hesiod, Archilochus, Theognis). The texts deal with two aspects of the war that are not easily reconciled: a border conflict of local significance and a large system of alliances. Other inconsistencies are found in the various combat operations mentioned: fighting according to a "code" banning long-range weapons, cavalry charges, and even a naval battle.[31] In sum, the sources, when they are not pure inventions, seem to refer to very different realities, and it is best to abandon the attempt to integrate all elements into a single coherent picture.

On the other hand, when taken individually, each element of the narration can be linked with part of the history of Euboean communities during the Archaic period. Border conflicts were a common cause of disputes between neighboring Greek cities. In central Euboea, the proximity of Lefkandi and Chalcis, separated by the Lelantine plain, offers all the ingredients for a strained relationship. A struggle for this area is more likely to have occurred at an early period, before Lefkandi was abandoned.[32] With Eretria, the geopolitical situation is rather different. Eretria is situated 10 km from the edges of the Lelantine plain, and the hilly terrain along the shore of the Euboean Gulf makes it difficult to access the Lelantine plain from the east. Eretria's natural center of gravity lies east, toward Amarynthos and the fertile region of Tamynai. In the long term, this is where the Eretrian *chōra* expanded. It is also important to emphasize that not a single border dispute is recorded between Chalcis and Eretria from the beginning of the Classical period onward, unlike most long-standing and often mythical border conflicts such as those opposing Sparta to Argos or Athens to Boeotia, which span several centuries. In other words, if a border war took place, it was finished by 506 and had no consequence for later periods (Fachard 2012: 80–1).

We are thus inclined to hypothesize the existence of a series of early conflicts that fueled the construction of a long-lasting tradition that became increasingly elaborate with the passage of time. Such conflicts, in their original form and phase, would not have been a war between two *poleis* but, instead, strife between small aristocratic parties, most likely competing for access to good pastures for horses (Howe 2008: 82–4).

Moreover, it is difficult to believe that distant Aegean communities would have been involved in a border conflict of local significance. One solution is to consider these alliances as later fabrications, aimed at legitimating and strengthening

---

31. According to a tradition transmitted by Plutarch (F 84 Sandbach), Amphidamas died in a naval battle against the Eretrians (see discussions in Parker 1997: 90–1; Walker 2004: 160–1).

32. This is not to say that Lefkandi's abandonment was necessarily the result of this conflict. There are many other explanations. The topography of the site might have prevented the settlement from developing into a major center, like Chalcis and Eretria, and the site might have lost its suitability for maritime activities, due to the silting up of its harbors.

diplomatic relationships between cities by boasting old ties. If, however, there is some degree of reality behind them, it should be sought in the many links fostered by the Euboeans along sea routes.

One point deserves special comment here. A dramatic decline of Chalcis and Eretria after 700 has been widely assumed and attributed to the Lelantine War. This picture, however, relies too much on the distribution of pottery and requires revision. The seeming disappearance of their pottery in the Mediterranean at that time does not mean that Euboeans stopped sailing and trading. They still had more valuable commodities to deal in, such as metals, wool, leather, agricultural products, and perhaps wood. The decrease in their colonial activities is also not necessarily a sign of decay. On the contrary, it might suggest that the two cities had reached some level of stability. After the creation of new sea routes, other Greeks either caught up with or went beyond the Euboeans, who had enjoyed a leading position in overseas activities during the Early Iron Age (Broodbank 2013: 550).

## 2.7.2. Euboeans on the Move

A large part of Chalcis' and Eretria's "diplomatic" history for the Early Archaic period is intertwined with their overseas activities. The latter should not be understood as a homogeneous phenomenon; instead, Euboeans were engaged in a broad range of enterprises whose patterns varied over time and space but whose main incentives were maritime trade and settlement abroad. As the economic aspects will be discussed later (Section 2.8.4), we start by looking at the nature of these "colonial" activities, although it is evident that both spheres are closely interconnected. Commercial contacts preceded, most of the time, a lasting settlement, without necessarily being part of a "trade before flag" process.

Euboea enjoyed a strategic importance in the wider Mediterranean, and the Euboean Gulf encouraged coastal mobility early on (Knodell 2017; see Section 2.3.1). According to the literary evidence, Chalcidians and Eretrians were among the first people from Central Greece to settle in the north Aegean, southern Italy, and Sicily in the second half of the eighth century.[33] But besides a list of names and dates (see Table 2.2), texts do not provide much information regarding the phenomenon. We must, therefore, rely upon the archaeological evidence in order to follow the movement of Euboean people and/or goods overseas. But

---

33. For collections and discussions of the relevant literary sources, see Graham 1982 (general); Tiverios 2006–2008 (esp. 4–6, north Aegean); Mercuri 2004: 205–10; Domínguez 2006–2008: 253–69 (southern Italy and Sicily).

**Table 2.2. Main Chalcidian and Eretrian colonies in the Mediterranean according to written sources (after Tsetskhladze 2006–2008: lxvii–lxxiii; Mercuri 2004: 206).**

| Region | Colony | Mother city/cities | Sources | Literary foundation dates |
|---|---|---|---|---|
| Adriatic | Corcyra | Eretria | Plut. *Mor.* 293a | before 732 |
| Gulf of Naples | Pithecusae | Chalcis | Livy 8.22.5–6 | before Cumae |
| | | Chalcis + Eretria | Strabo 5.4.9 | |
| | Cumae | Chalcis | Thuc. 6.4.5 | eighth century |
| | | Chalcis + Cyme (?) | Strabo 5.4.4 | (1050 Euseb.) |
| | | Eretria + Chalcis | Dion. Hal. 7.3.1 | |
| Strait of Messina | Zancle | Cumae + Chalcis | Thuc. 6.4.5–6 | eighth century |
| | | Naxos (Sicily) | Strabo 6.2.3 | |
| | Rhegium | Chalcis | Thuc. 6.44.3, 6.79.2 | eighth century |
| | | Zancle + Chalcis + Messenians | Strabo 6.1.6 | |
| Sicily | Naxos | Chalcis + Naxos (Cycl.) | Hellanicus F 82 | shortly before 733 (Thuc.) |
| | | Chalcis | Thuc. 6.3.1 | (737 Euseb.) |
| | | | Paus. 6.13.8 | |
| | Leontini | Chalcis + Naxos (Sicily) | Thuc. 6.3.3, 6.44.3, 6.79.2 | shortly before 728 (Thuc.) |
| | Catana | Chalcis + Naxos (Sicily) | Thuc. 6.3.3 | c. 728 (Thuc.) |
| | | | Strab. 6.2.3 | (737/6 Euseb.) |
| North Aegean | Mende | Eretria | Thuc. 4.123.1 | |
| | Methone | Eretria | Plut. *Mor.* 293b | c. 733 |
| | Dikaia | Eretria | *ATL* I 266–7 | |
| | Torone | Chalcis | Diod. 12.68.6 | before c. 650 |

the interpretation of archaeological data is far from straightforward, and many aspects of Euboean colonization are still debated.[34]

A critical assessment of founding narratives related to Archaic colonization (Hall 2006–2008) highlights the customary character of the chronology provided by ancient authors. In the case of Euboean colonies, however, the archaeological record matches the textual evidence in situating the peak of activity in the second half of the eighth century. Interestingly, source criticism forces us to consider carefully the actual contribution of Chalcis and Eretria to all the foundations that have been attributed to them. It is indeed puzzling, if not implausible, to assign to two rising cities of the eighth century responsibility for founding so many new communities overseas.

However, it seems that large contingents of colonists were unnecessary; a small group (accompanied or joined by other Greeks) would suffice to establish the Euboean character of a new community (Malkin 2009). Sources provide examples of heterogeneous populations of colonists, grouped around a Euboean core (Naxos: Strabo 6.2.2; Zancle: Paus. 4.23.7), and a majority of Euboean colonies were probably defined by this character from the start. This view better explains the actual role that Euboeans could have played in this process. Navigators, like the Euboeans, with a sound knowledge of sea routes and trading posts were in the best position to take the lead, and the Euboeans likely provided many οἰκισταί, several of whose names have come down to us.

Regarding the archaeological evidence, there has been a debate about the interpretation of the broad diffusion of Late Geometric Euboean material overseas. A key issue is the "marketing" of Euboean pottery (see Section 2.8.4.1) but also the permanent presence of Euboeans on several sites. There is no need to revisit the "pots = people" debate. It is evident that there is no automatic link between the production site of a vase and the identities of its carrier and consumer. Pottery is only one factor in a complex equation, and others deserve to be taken into account. For example, traces of the Euboean alphabet in the north Aegean and in Sicily and southern Italy (see Section 2.12.1) provide a stronger signature than the presence of vases.

### 2.7.2.1. Early Euboean Navigation

Euboean contacts with the north Aegean and eastern Mediterranean before the eighth century and its wave of colonial enterprises are well attested, in particular by the funerary material from Lefkandi and by the distribution of Euboean pottery (Lemos 2001; Lemos 2005; Luke 2003: 31–44; Descoeudres 2006–2007; Kourou 2020). The origins of these profitable connections must be sought in

---

34. For a recent discussion on this topic, see Kotsonas 2020.

the Late Bronze Age, when harbors along the Euboean Gulf played a significant role in maritime trade, notably with respect to supplying Boeotian palaces (Papadopoulos 2011: 125–7). Lying on the margins of the palatial system, it seems that the Euboean communities did not suffer too much from its collapse. In comparison with other regions, they were able to recover quickly, essentially by maintaining some seafaring activities and by preserving their knowledge of sea routes and contacts overseas (Crielaard 2006; Knodell 2021: 240–3).

From the tenth century onward, Euboean communities seem to have progressively multiplied their contacts, securing access to exchange networks and increasing their maritime activities for commercial purposes. This eventually generated favorable conditions for the creation of permanent settlements overseas. Only from a modern point of view can this phase be described as pre- or proto-colonial. There was by no means an agenda involving an evolution from maritime trade to colonization, and even if the latter can be seen as a logical consequence of the former, it depended on many other factors (Esposito 2012).

### 2.7.2.1.1. NORTH AEGEAN

Early on, Euboean sailors were primarily active in the north Aegean in general and on the shores of the Thermaic Gulf and Chalcidice peninsula in particular (see Map 2.10). Geographical proximity is the first explanatory factor: with good wind conditions, the journey to the north Aegean (along the Thessalian coast or the Sporades) was short enough (around five days)[35] and could be made more than once during the same sailing season. The Euboeans had many reasons for heading north. The availability of metals (gold, in particular) was a key incentive (Graham 1982: 115; Tiverios 2006–2008: 21); the places they visited or settled were close to ores and were involved in the production of metals. This is especially true of the sites located in the vicinity of gold-bearing rivers (Gallikos, Axios, and Haliakmon), such as Methone (Verdan 2023), and of mining areas, such as Torone (Papadopoulos 2005: 588–90). Timber might have been another incentive.

Concerning Eretrian and Chalcidian colonization in the north Aegean (see Table 2.2), the only date given by a textual source (Plut. *Mor.* 293b, for the foundation of Methone) falls in the second half of the eighth century. This matches the archaeological record from the area around Methone, which reveals a strong Euboean footprint during this period (on Methone, see Besios, Tzifopoulos, and Kotsonas 2012; Clay, Malkin, and Tzifopoulos 2017; Morris and Papadopoulos 2023). The archaeological signature attests to the circulation of goods, both

---

35. Estimation calculated via *Orbis: The Stanford Geospatial Network Model of the Roman World*, http://orbis.stanford.edu/.

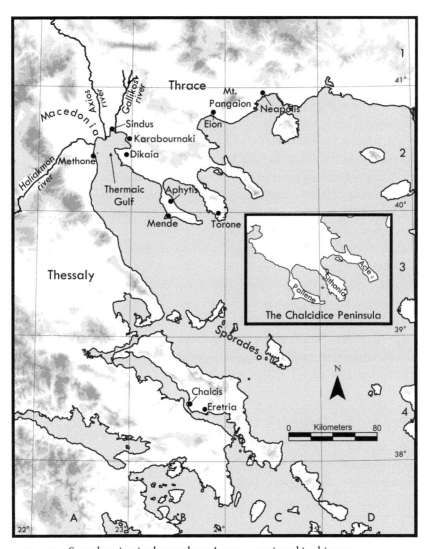

MAP 2.10. Some key sites in the northern Aegean mentioned in this essay.

northward and southward (Leone 2015). People originating from other places in the Aegean and the eastern Mediterranean were linked to Methone's networks.

There is no doubt that contacts existed during the Mycenaean period as well. Tiverios (2006–2008: 10–51) has argued that Euboeans first settled in the north Aegean toward the end of the 11th century, as part of the Ionian migration, and that there was a second wave of settlement in the eighth century. This multiphase model neatly combines ancient traditions and material evidence for periods of increased mobility. But subtler processes over the long term need to be added to the picture. The commercial networks linking Euboea, central Macedonia, and Chalcidice permitted individuals to move and settle abroad (temporarily or permanently) long before the appearance of polities that eventually entered the historical record as Eretrian or Chalcidian foundations. There were a number of different paths that led to the foundation of a colony.[36]

Whereas Eretrians concentrated their activities in the Thermaic Gulf and on the peninsula of Pallene in the Chalcidice, Chalcis is supposed to have founded colonies on the peninsula of Sithonia in the Chalcidice (Strabo 10.1.8).[37] Evidence for the latter is still elusive. This seems to be in apparent contradiction to the link, already established in antiquity, between the name of the Chalcidice and Chalcis in Euboea, and to the mention by Strabo (Book 7, F 11) of some 30 Chalcidian colonies in the area. It must be emphasized, however, that the origin of the name Chalcidice and the way it was understood by ancient people are far from certain (Papadopoulos 1996: 166–74; Hornblower 1997), and the figure given by Strabo is highly unrealistic. Even Torone, a good candidate for the status of Chalcidian colony according to written sources, remains a disputed case (Papadopoulos 2005: 583–92; Tiverios 2006–2008: 45–7). However, there are undeniable relationships between Chalcis and the Chalcidians of Thrace, who shared a common dialect, alphabet, calendar, and acrophonic system, as well as onomastics (Psoma 2017).

### 2.7.2.1.2. SICILY–SOUTHERN ITALY

As is the case for the north Aegean, it would be a mistake to impose a rigid interpretive framework on Euboean "colonial" activities in the western Mediterranean.

---

36. There are also sites closely connected to Euboea that did not eventually welcome a population of colonists (Sindus, Karabournaki: Tiverios 2006–2008: 21–4, 27–31; Kotsonas 2012: 249; Charalambidou 2017b: 152).

37. To the colonies attributed to Euboeans in written sources (Eretrians: Methone and Dikaia in the Thermaic Gulf, Mende on Pallene; Chalcidians: Torone on Sithonia; see Table 2.2), the following names can be added (after Tiverios 2006–2008: 17–44): Neapolis (founded by Mende: *Athenian Tribute List* I 354–5, 464, 526), Eion and Aphytis on Pallene. Many other sites might have been founded by Chalcis on Sithonia or Eretria on the Acte (see Tiverios 2006–2008: 45–51), but identifications and "attributions" remain strongly hypothetical.

Each case is different, depending on its geographical position, the nature of the site, the composition of the group of colonists (as well as their intentions), the types of contact with the local population, and the subsequent development of each community (long-term settlement of a *polis* or not).

Euboeans in the Early Iron Age possibly inherited Late Bronze Age knowledge of the western Mediterranean, even though there is no trace of continuity in this area. In the eighth century, the foundation of colonies was preceded by a period of contacts between Euboeans and indigenous communities, particularly well attested at the site of Pontecagnano in Campania (D'Agostino 2006–2008; D'Agostino 2014). The situation evolves at a different pace from one region and site to another. The creation of a colony does not signify that trade contacts without permanent installation break off elsewhere (Esposito 2012).

In the west, Euboean colonization primarily focused on two regions: the Gulf of Naples and the Strait of Messina (see Map 2.11). In the former, the Euboeans found a promising location for their commercial activities (Malkin 2002; D'Agostino 2006–2008). Several local population groups were already interacting with each other, as well as with the Phoenicians. The proximity of metal sources (Etruscan hinterland and Elba) provided a steady supply of ore, while keeping a distance from the large Etruscan centers might have prevented conflicts between neighbors. Pithecusae and Cumae exemplify two foundations that emerge within a brief time span and in close proximity to each other in this area but whose destiny is quite divergent (see D'Acunto Forthcoming for further discussion).

In the Strait of Messina, a vital passage on the route linking Greece with the coastal regions of southern Italy, the settlement of Euboeans aimed to take advantage of sea lanes. Here again, two colonies were founded close to each other on both sides of the strait: Zancle in Sicily and Rhegium on the continent. Less than 50 km south of the strait, on the Sicilian coast, a third colony, Naxos, was founded by Euboeans. The written sources indicate that the three sites were linked from the outset, as people from Naxos took part in the foundation of Zancle, which, in turn, sent a contingent to Rhegium (Strabo 6.1.6, 6.2.3). These early colonies likely represented the endeavors of small groups of individuals who collaborated and remained connected with one another and with their mother city.

According to the literary evidence, Chalcis held a more dominant role in southern Italy and Sicily compared with Eretria, whose participation is recorded only at Pithecusae and subsequently Cumae, always in association with Chalcis (Strabo 5.4.9; Dion. Hal. 7.3.1). Explaining this imbalance by a decline at Eretria, supposedly the big loser of the Lelantine War, is implausible. Each city possibly enjoyed a privileged area of activity, and Eretria appears more active than Chalcis in the north Aegean. It is equally possible that the apparent Chalcidian

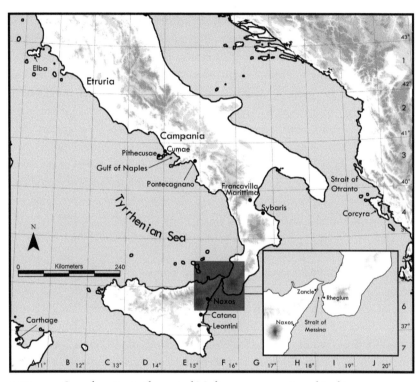

MAP 2.11. Some key sites in the central Mediterranean mentioned in this essay.

prominence in the west amounted to a rewriting of history aimed at valorizing Chalcis (Mercuri 2004: 206–9). In any case, what is certain is that material evidence, mainly pottery and alphabetical inscriptions, provides no help for distinguishing a Chalcidian from an Eretrian contribution in this colonial context.

Finally, mention should be made of the Euboean presence in the area of Sybaris, especially at Francavilla Marittima. That site offers an example of Greeks and indigenous people living side by side, which did not develop into a real colony, perhaps due to the importance of Sybaris, a Peloponnesian foundation (Jacobsen 2013).

### 2.7.2.1.3. CORCYRA

Plutarch (*Mor.* 293a) tells the story of how Eretrians settled in Corycra were expelled by the Corinthians and how, after seeing their right of return being rejected by their mother city, went on to found Methone in the north Aegean. Scholars are divided over the Euboean presence in Corcyra. While some find an element of truth in Plutarch's account (Malkin 1998a), others stress the absence of archaeological remains that can be connected to Euboeans and the prominence of Corinthian material in this area (Morgan 1998). Overall, the presence of Eretrians in Corcyra is more plausible if we think in terms of maritime traffic rather than colonization. Euboean navigators circumnavigating the Peloponnese in order to make the crossing to Italy would have perceived the advantage of continuing up to Corcyra before crossing the Strait of Otranto. They could have benefited from this stopping-off point for some time, without leaving many traces. Plutarch's account should perhaps be read as a story of merchants competing for the control of a harbor next to a vital sea lane (see Gehrke and Sapirstein in this volume: Sections 4.4.1, 4.5.2, for further discussion).

### 2.7.2.1.4. NORTH AFRICA

Several hints suggest a Euboean presence on the coast of North Africa. The Euboean Geometric pottery found at Carthage does not obviously provide definitive evidence, as it could have reached this destination in the cargo of non-Euboean ships (Kourou 2002). Firmer hints are found in toponyms such as Pithecusae and Euboea, recorded in pseudo-Scylax (Boardman 2006). The geography of the *Periplous* does not imply the foundation of colonies, of course, but the presence of such toponyms suggests that a Euboean core could have been significant enough to ensure a toponymic continuity.

### 2.7.2.2. *Euboeans on the Move: Conclusions*

In the Early Archaic period, the "colonial" ventures of Chalcis and Eretria constituted an important part of their overseas activities. It would be valuable to learn

176  THE OXFORD HISTORY OF THE ARCHAIC GREEK WORLD

more about the "rebound effect" of colonization on the mother cities, and yet this topic is virtually unexplored. As much as we can decode the "genetic inheritance" of the colonies, the benefits to the mother cities continue to elude us. In any case, it is clear that any colonial enterprise implies bilateral relationships.

In theory, we can assume benefits in several domains. When it comes to trade, enjoying safe landing places in exchange zones guaranteed that merchants enjoyed better access to resources, as well as more possibilities to sell their products. From a socio-political point of view, the departure of groups of colonists (undesirable or not) necessarily constituted a political event for the city, with potential benefits for its development (Malkin 1994). Moreover, the experience acquired in the "colonial world" could serve as an example for changes in the organization of mother cities. In the cases of Chalcis and Eretria, however, these ideas are speculative. It is difficult to identify the effects that the Euboean colonies had on their mother cities.

### 2.7.3. Military Strength of Eretria and Chalcis in the Archaic Period

In the last quarter of the sixth century, the Eretrians appear to have had a strong navy. The city enjoyed a long tradition of maritime activity and might well have been among the first to build a fleet of triremes. An important legal document of the last quarter of the sixth century discussed above (see Section 2.6) mentions the payment of wages to sailors operating beyond the Euboean Gulf. This "law" seems to set the Eretrian navy within a legal and public frame. According to a passage in Strabo (10.1.10), the Eretrians "ruled over the peoples of Andros, Tinos, Ceos, and other islands," which, if true, would have required a significant number of ships. According to Pausanias (9.22.2), the Eretrian navy led an attack on Tanagra, which ended with the defeat of the Eretrian forces, supposedly before c. 520 (Walker 2004: 192). Later lists of thalassocracies place Eretria as the leading maritime power in the Aegean, succeeding the Naxians (Diod. 7.11 = Euseb., *Chron* I 225; van Wees 2010: 216–18). According to Herodotus (5.99), the Eretrians sent five triremes during the Ionian Rebellion (a force of 1,000 sailors), which is the "earliest force of triremes" recorded outside the Persian sphere of influence (van Wees 2010: 218). Eretria probably had a fleet of at least 20 triremes by the end of the sixth century (Knoepfler 2008: 604), which constituted a considerable force of 4,000 sailors. Eretria contributed only seven ships to the Greek fleet at Artemision and Salamis (Hdt. 8.1, 8.46), but those battles were fought only a decade after the devastating Persian attack on Eretria in 490 (see Section 2.7.5), which must surely have significantly reduced the size of the naval forces it could deploy.

Less can be said about Eretria's land forces. The inscription on the *stēlē* referenced by Strabo (10.1.10) describes an Eretrian procession with 3,000 hoplites and 600 cavalry, but it is impossible to achieve any certainty about the reliability of Strabo's description or about the period to which it refers (see Section 2.7.1), and in any case, there is no reason to believe that the procession represented a full military levy. That said, given the size and productivity of the *chōra* of Eretria (see Sections 2.4.1.4 and 2.4.2.2), it is reasonable to believe that Eretria could have put a force of at least 3,000 hoplites into the field in the sixth century. Demographic projections (see Section 2.9.1) suggest that there were perhaps 4,000–5,000 males of military age in Eretria in c. 500. Herodotus states that 600 Eretrians and Styraeans fought at Plataea (9.28), but here again, the aftereffects of the Persian sack of 490 need to be taken into account. The importance of the elite groups known as the Hippeis at Eretria and the Hippobotai at Chalcis (see Section 2.5.2) may perhaps suggest that cavalrymen played a particularly significant role in the armies of those *poleis* in the Archaic period.

Less evidence is available about the military of Chalcis during the Archaic period. We have no evidence suggesting the naval strength of Eretria was counterbalanced by Chalcis, and as we have seen, it seems that the Eretrians enjoyed some sort of local hegemonic status at sea. Nonetheless, at Artemision and Salamis, the Chalcidians manned 20 hulls provided by the Athenians (Hdt. 8.1, 8.46), which suggests a contingent of 4,000 sailors. The army of Chalcis in 506 has been estimated—on the basis of analogy with Eretria—as consisting of 3,000 hoplites (Krentz 2010: 41), and the *chōra* of Chalcis, like its Eretrian counterpart, would presumably have been capable of supporting a force of that size or larger. The Greek army at Plataea included 400 Chalcidians (Hdt. 9.28), a relatively small contingent.

## 2.7.4. Euboea and Central Greece in the Sixth Century

### *2.7.4.1. Eretria*

Eretria appears to have been a favorite place for prominent Athenians from various and often opposed political sides. An epitaph from c. 525 for Chairion of Athens, whom the text of the epitaph identifies as one of the Eupatrids, was found in Eretria (*IG* I³.1516; Duplouy 2003: 4–5; Knoepfler 2008). Connections with the Alcmeonids seem to have been particularly close. The Alcmeonid Hippocrates married Koisyra, a seemingly extravagant woman from a wealthy Eretrian family. Six *ostraka* for the banishment of their son Megacles in 487/6 bear Koisyra's name, and Eretria might even be mentioned on another one: "Megacles, son of Hippocrates, out again (?) . . . but don't go to Eretria" (Brenne 2002: 106–12). Based on scholia to Aristophanes' comedies, some scholars have postulated the existence of at least two other women called Koisyra, married to Alcmaeon and Pisistratus, respectively (Shear 1963), but the historicity of these two figures is hypothetical. In any case, the name, originally belonging to an Eretrian lady, remained synonymous with a luxurious lifestyle in democratic Athens throughout the fifth century (Ar. *Nub.* 48, 800; *Ach.* 614).

A mention of Pisistratus' marriage with an Eretrian woman may be a scholiast's misunderstanding (Schol. Ar. *Nub.* 48), but the link between the Athenian tyrant and Eretria is well documented. According to Herodotus (1.61–2), Pisistratus took refuge in Eretria when exiled for the second time around 555, and from there he returned to Athens ten years later. Euboea's proximity to Athens was a strategic advantage for a landing in Attica. Pisistratus certainly had strong connections in Eretria (and maybe even properties in its territory). He eventually received military support from Eretrian Hippeis when regaining his power (Arist. [*Ath. Pol.*] 15.2). Last but not least, he benefited from the Eretrian presence in the north Aegean and access to sources of metal (see Section 2.8.4.2) to settle first in the Thermaic Gulf and then operate silver mines at Mt. Pangaion (Viviers 1987), which provided him with resources vital to his military and political ambitions.

### 2.7.4.2. *Chalcis*

At the end of the sixth century, Chalcis enjoyed close political and military ties with Boeotia, an area with which it was naturally connected from a geographical point of view. However, this brought Chalcis into direct confrontation with Athens.

Shortly after the Cleisthenic reforms, the Boeotians joined forces with the Peloponnesians and Chalcidians in order to invade Attica (see Osborne 2023: Section 2.7.1.2 for detailed discussion). King Cleomenes of Sparta, at the head of a Peloponnesian army, invaded Eleusis; the Boeotians attacked Hysiae and Oinoe; and the Chalcidians plundered other areas of Attica (Hdt. 5.74). The discovery of an inscribed *kioniskos* in Thebes confirms and supplements Herodotus' account (Aravantinos 2006; Beck Forthcoming: section 2.7.4). However, the Peloponnesian army dissolved at Eleusis, freeing the Athenians from their biggest threat, and they took advantage of the opportunity to march against Chalcis. The Boeotians sent some help, but the Boeotian forces were defeated, and 700 of them were taken prisoner. The Athenians then crossed to Euboea the same day and crushed the Chalcidians (Hdt. 5.77).

These victories established Athens as a major military power in central Greece. However, Athenian propaganda may have exaggerated many of the details. It is indeed hard to believe that an Athenian army would have been able to fight two full hoplite battles on the same day, not to mention crossing to Euboea. Since there was no bridge, crossing the Euripos would have been impossible without a fleet. It has been suggested that Athenian ships followed the army along the coast (van Wees 2010: 224); alternatively or additionally, the Eretrians may have, willingly or unwillingly, provided assistance to the Athenians.

In any case, the consequences for Chalcis were devastating. First, after the crushing defeat, Chalcidian prisoners were taken and later ransomed for two *mnai* each (Hdt. 5.77). With the ransom of the prisoners, the Athenians set up a bronze τέθριππον ("four-horse chariot") at the entrance to the acropolis (Meiggs and Lewis 1988: #15; Krentz 2010: 188 n. 38, 203–4). Second, according to Herodotus (5.77), 4,000 cleruchs were settled in Chalcis' territory, on the lands of the Hippobotai. This was a considerable occupying force, probably the equivalent of the Chalcidian army in number. However, this figure could be corrupt (Manfredini 1968). Aelian, writing in the second century CE, records that the Athenians divided the region called Hippoboton into 2,000 κλῆροι, dedicated τεμένη to Athena at the place called Lelantos (most probably a locality within the Lelantine plain), and rented out the remaining lands (*VH* 6.1). Confirmation of the information found in Aelian has been provided by the discovery of a *horos* marking the borders of a temenos of Athena in the northwestern part of the Lelantine plain (*IG* XII.9.934; *SEG* 10.304.3), as well as the presence of Athenian properties at a place named Lelantos in the late fifth century (*IG* I³.422). However, Aelian's passage could also refer to Pericles' intervention of 446 (Brunt 1966: 87–9).

One discovery might very well provide us with an archaeological signature of the presence of this cleruchy in the Lelantine plain: the Vrachos fort. This fortified camp of 1.4 ha encloses a long building of 112 m x 7 m divided into 20 identical rectangular rooms that could accommodate a force of some 200 men (Coulton 2002: 42–3). The camp occupies an ideal place on a rocky outcrop at the eastern entrance of the Lelantine plain, dominating the entire plain and guarding the main roads connecting Chalcis and Eretria. The camp was built at the end of the sixth century and abandoned at the beginning of the fifth; it is best interpreted as a fort linked to the Athenian cleruchy (Coulton 2002: 113–14). The exploitation and control of 2,000 to 4,000 lots of land confiscated at the expense of the most powerful Chalcidians could not be easily perpetuated in absentia. By comparison, the cleruchs sent to Salamis had to remain on the island and were not allowed to rent their allotted land (*IG* I³.1; Meiggs and Lewis 1988: #14). Under those circumstances, a military presence is very likely. The cleruchs were not all necessarily concentrated in the Lelantine plain but might also have controlled areas in the Psachna plain and the upper Lelantos river valley. In 490, 4,000 cleruchs were summoned to offer their help to the Eretrians and subsequently left the island. It is unclear whether they ever came back.

The events of 506 mark a dramatic break in the history of Chalcis. The *polis* of Chalcis was not destroyed, but it was greatly weakened. This is evident from the fact that the Chalcidians were able to take part in the battles of Artemision and Salamis only because the Athenians lent them 20 trireme hulls (Hdt. 8.1.2, 8.46.2). Chalcis' defeat left a clear field for Eretria, which found itself in an unmatched position of power in Euboea.

## 2.7.5. Persian Wars

In the late sixth century, Eretria became one of the major players on the Aegean scene. It enjoyed a strong reputation as a naval power (see Section 2.7.3), as suggested by Eusebius' thalassocracy list (*Chron* I 225), and it was among the first *poleis* to have a state-funded fleet (van Wees 2010; van Wees 2013b: 27–8, 57). This navy maintained a grip on the Euboean Gulf, from Kenaion to Petaliai, and intervened beyond these points, although very few traces of such expeditions are recorded. One such expedition had fateful consequences.

In 499, Aristagoras of Miletus initiated a rebellion against Darius and appealed for help (Hdt. 5.99; Slawisch Forthcoming: Section 1.2.5.6). Athens answered the call with 20 ships, probably penteconters with 50 to 80 men each (Krentz 2010: 66), while Eretria sent five triremes, the best warship of the time. The Eretrian navy was perhaps three or four times larger, but this expeditionary force was nevertheless 1,000 men strong and hence by no means negligible. The Eretrians were led by an Olympic victor, Eualkidas, whose triumph was commemorated by Simonides (Hdt. 5.102). The Greek forces raided and burned Sardis in 498 but retreated to Ephesus, where they were crushed, and Eualkidas died in the battle. The role of the Eretrians is confirmed by Plutarch (*Mor.* 861a–c) and Lysanias of Mallus (*FGrH* 426), author of a *History of Eretria* that was written in the first or second century CE. Although this latter source should be viewed critically and possibly amended, there is no strong reason to dismiss the Eretrian participation in the Sardis raid. The Eretrians also seem to have contributed ships to the Greek fleet that sailed out of Cyprus two years later and won a victory over the Persians (Knoepfler 2008: 604–5; Hurter 2007). Plutarch criticizes Herodotus for mentioning the Eretrians "quite casually and passing over their great epic achievement in silence" (*De Herodoti Malignitate, Mor.* 861b). Miletus fell in 494, and a year later, the Ionian Rebellion was quelled. Darius could now plan an invasion of Greece.

Preparations began in 493, and Mardonius was put in charge. In 492, a Persian armada left the Hellespont intending to sail to Eretria and Athens, which were "the pretexts for the expedition," and to subdue many Greek cities on the way

(Hdt. 6.43–4). According to Aristotle, the main aim was to take revenge for the Athenian and Eretrian raid on Sardis (*An. post.* 94a–b). The Persian fleet encountered a disastrous storm while sailing around the Acte peninsula while the army pushed no farther south than Macedonia and Thessaly. The next expedition, commanded by Artaphernes and Datis, sailed for Euboea through the Cyclades in 490, with probably 300 triremes and 300 transport ships (Krentz 2010: 91). After several stops along the way, the fleet arrived at Carystus, laid waste to the countryside, and took the city.

At this point, the Eretrians were on full alert, but they had few options. A naval battle was not among them, since a fleet of 20 or even 30 triremes could hardly oppose a fleet of 300. Athenian reinforcements were out of the question, since the entire army was needed in Attica, the next objective; nevertheless, the Athenians sent the 4,000 cleruchs stationed in Chalcis. This would have been a considerable force for the Eretrians, who could already count on their own 4,000–5,000 men. However, according to Herodotus (6.100–1), the cleruchs, after arriving at Eretria and seeing the population highly divided over which defensive strategy to adopt, were "gallantly" advised by Aeschines son of Nothon, a prominent figure among the Eretrians, to leave the city to its fate. This is perhaps Herodotus' way of exculpating the behavior of the cleruchy, which ended up crossing to Oropus just before the Persian landing. The Eretrians decided to attempt to withstand the siege; from the top of their acropolis, the Eretrians would have seen with awe the formidable spectacle of a Persian armada of 600 ships landing on their beaches.[38]

Herodotus records the locations where the Persian landings took place: Temenos, Choireai, and Aigilia, all Eretrian demes known in the Classical period and located between Eretria and Amarynthos. This was the best terrain for the Persian cavalry and the establishment of their camp. The first frontal attack must have come from the east. The assault, Herodotus says, was very violent, and many men fell on both sides. The Eretrians resisted for six days. But on the seventh, two leading Eretrians betrayed the city to the Persians: "These entered the city and plundered and burnt the temples, in revenge for the temples that were burnt at Sardis; moreover, they enslaved the townspeople, according to Darius' command" (Hdt. 6.101, trans. A. D. Godley). After a few days' rest, the Persians sailed to Marathon.

---

38. For the size of the Persian army, we must rely on the (considerably inflated) numbers supplied by the ancient sources for the subsequent Battle of Marathon. For a recent estimate, see Krentz 2010: 91–3, 209.

## 182 THE OXFORD HISTORY OF THE ARCHAIC GREEK WORLD

What were the consequences of the fall of Eretria? This question has given rise to considerable discussion (Knoepfler 2008: 606–8; Hall 2014a: 35–53; Fachard and Harris 2021: 11-13). While destruction layers were initially identified and associated with a *Perserschutt*, most recent studies tend to suggest that whatever destruction took place, it left few and indirect archaeological traces. In the agora, the East Stoa was destroyed but quickly repaired (Saggini Forthcoming). The Temple of Apollo, built 525–500 (see Section 2.4.1.3.5), was certainly burned, but the extant sculptures from the pediment show no fire damage. Elsewhere in the city, traces of destruction are few and of indirect nature.[39] Herodotus says that the population was enslaved, and there is little doubt that some Eretrians were sent to Asia, where the Great King spared their lives and settled them at Arderrika, near Susa, where they could still be found in Herodotus' day (6.119–20).

The idea of the entire Eretrian population, however, being caught by the "net" created by the Persian soldiers joining hands to form an encircling line from one sea to the other (Hdt. 6.31) is as much an exaggeration as it is a later literary topos (Pl. *Menex.* 240a–c; *Leg.* 698c–d; Strabo 10.1.10). Philostratus, citing a local tradition, claims that 780 Eretrians were deported (*VA* 1.24). A deportation of the entire population was obviously impossible on logistical grounds. It is more reasonable to conclude that some Eretrians died during or immediately after the siege, some escaped, and some were deported.

In due course, the city recovered. In 480, Eretria contributed to the Greek war effort by sending seven triremes, as well as a contingent of 600 hoplites who fought at Plataea (Hdt. 8.1.2, 8.46.2; Meiggs and Lewis 1988: #7). The Eretrians dedicated a bronze bull at Olympia at roughly this time (Paus. 5.27.9; Dittenberger and Purgold 1896: #248). A limited revival of coinage has been suggested after 480 (Kraay 1976: 91), and in c. 475–440, the *polis* issued proxeny decrees, a sign that its political institutions were functioning (see Section 2.5.3.2; Knoepfler 2000: # I). New coin issues from the middle of the fifth century suggest that the city might have enjoyed some degree of prosperity (Ducrey, Fachard, Knoepfler, et al. 2004: 31; see Section 2.8.5 for further discussion). The best sign of Eretria's vitality is found in 446, when it was confident enough to join forces with Chalcis and to revolt, unsuccessfully, against the Athenians.

Nonetheless, the events of 506 and 490 brought devastating defeats for Chalcis and Eretria. Their steady rise and in particular Eretria's hegemonic status in Euboea were undone. Both Chalcis and Eretria entered the Classical Age greatly diminished and as vassals of Athens.

---

39. On the destruction layers associated with the Persian siege , see Saggini Forthcoming.

## 2.8. Economic History
### 2.8.1. Natural Resources

Broadly speaking, some 40% of Euboea could be exploited for agriculture (see 2.8.2).[40] The island has substantial but unequally distributed agricultural potential: arable land is concentrated in the central part of the island and was therefore exploited primarily by Chalcis and Eretria. However, other than the proverbially fertile Lelantine plain, Euboea's agricultural potential lags far behind the richest grain-growing regions of Greece. Although it is true that grain shortages are rarely attested in our sources for later periods and that the island provided supplies to Athens in the fifth century, it must be underlined that Euboea's overall agricultural potential, with the exception of some fertile niches, should be placed among Central Greece's average (see Section 2.8.2).

More remarkable seems to have been Euboea's grazing potential. Judging from its very name (*Eu-boia*, "the island favorable to oxen" or "famed for its oxen") and its early coinage (see Section 2.8.5), the island apparently offered an excellent setting for bovine breeding. The breeding of horses, which require the same kind of pastures as cattle, was also an important activity. The importance and influence of horse breeding are mostly felt in the early political system of Chalcis and Eretria (see Section 2.5.2), vase painting (Section 2.4.3), and onomastics (Section 2.9.2). Moreover, Euboea's landscape provided abundant grazing resources for sheep and goats, and Euboean pastures were occasionally used by Attic flocks in the fifth to third centuries (see, for example, Thuc. 2.14.1).

Apart from agriculture and animal husbandry, the island enjoyed easy and widespread access to aquatic resources. Euboean sole, porgy, and tuna are well attested in our sources. Octopus and cuttlefish were also abundant in Eretrian waters, to the point of becoming both the emblem of the *polis* on its coinage and the object of some mockery (Plut. *Them.* 11.6; Flacelière 1948; Seyrig 1950). The remains of fish, cuttlefish, crabs, oysters, mussels, murex, and other marine mollusks are all well represented in Late Geometric and Archaic strata at Eretria and Oropus (Theodoropoulou 2007; Verdan 2013).

With respect to mineral resources, limestone and marble were widely available. The clay beds of the Lelantine plain, today several meters deep, were extensively used by central Euboean workshops (Kerschner and Lemos 2014). Iron ores were present in the territories of Chalcis and Eretria, but no archaeological traces of their exploitation in the Archaic period have been found to date.

---

40. According to the EU Corinne Land Cover census, 36% of Euboea is currently under cultivation (1,316.84 sq km). For the application of the census to ancient Euboea and the reasons the modern estimate of 36% serves as a valid proxy for antiquity, see Fachard 2012: 110–23.

Despite Chalcis' reputation among later authors for the manufacture of iron blades (Plut. *Mor.* 434a; Bakhuizen 1976a: 43–4; Snodgrass 1999a: 70–1; see Section 2.8.4.2), its territory does not seem to have been an important source of iron ore. Strabo refers, probably mistakenly, to an exhausted iron and copper mine in the Lelantine plain. Iron ores have been located in the vicinity of the sites of Psachna and Metochi, though without any sign of ancient slags (Strabo 10.1.9; Bakhuizen 1976a: 43–69; Knodell 2021: 174–5) (see Map 2.12). These lateritic ores contained enough iron to make them exploitable. However, the only currently known archaeological evidence for the exploitation of iron ores in Euboea comes from the Archampolis valley in southern Euboea (Classical period, possibly Early Iron Age; see Keller 1984; Domergue 2008: 91–2) and above Eretria (Hellenistic period; see Kampouroglou 1986; Fachard 2012: 306, 14).

Euboea's timber resources have been perhaps overlooked and understudied. Theophrastus (*Hist. pl.* 5.2.1) has nothing good to say about Euboean building timber, but this still attests that it was used, perhaps widely, in minor to medium-scale constructions. When one contemplates the vast forests situated on the Dirphys range, it is very hard indeed to think that the chestnut trees (*Castanea vulgaris*), firs (*Abies cephalonica*), walnuts (*Juglans regia*), and tall pines (*Pinus nigra*) found there were not exploited in antiquity for shipbuilding (Boardman 1982: 754), domestic architecture, and furniture. Top-quality timber was not always in demand, and Euboean forests offered quantity over quality, as well as quick delivery to Attica (Meiggs 1982: 194). Yet the main forests remained fairly remote from the centers of Eretria and Chalcis and were perhaps best exploited in the Archaic period from small harbor sites such as Metochi, situated on the island's rugged eastern coast.

## 2.8.2. Agriculture

Agriculture was the main source of wealth in the ancient world (Bresson 2016: 118). Calculating figures for ancient agricultural production, however, is fraught with difficulty. In Eretria, roughly 30% of the territory (in 500, without Dystos and Styra; see Section 2.4.1.4) was arable land that could have been exploited for agriculture (including grain, olives, grapes, pulses, and legumes).[41] Of the approximately 26,000 ha of arable land, the best land for grain amounted to 10,800 ha, enough to feed more than 17,000 people.[42] In theory, this would provide enough

---

41. C. 260 sq km of mixed agricultural land was available for a territory whose size is estimated at 874 sq km. On the agricultural resources of Eretria, see Fachard 2012: 110–23.

42. These figures are purposefully low and cautious. Half the land is assumed to have been left fallow. On our method, see Fachard 2012: 110 fig. 57 and 13–18.

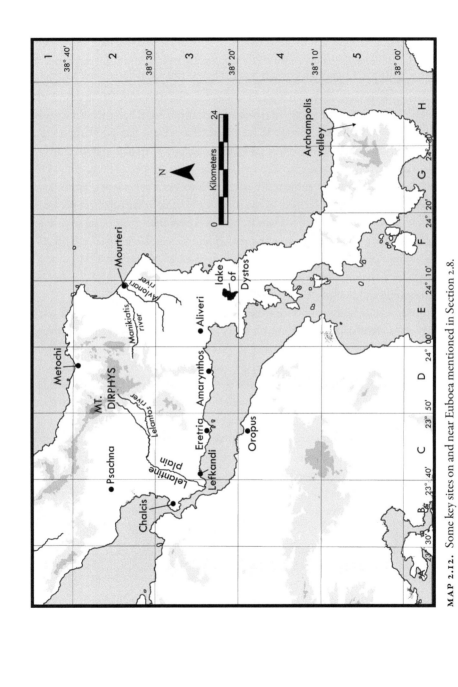

MAP 2.12. Some key sites on and near Euboea mentioned in Section 2.8.

186    THE OXFORD HISTORY OF THE ARCHAIC GREEK WORLD

agricultural land for 5,400 properties composed of 2 ha of prime land for grain cultivation (each one providing 640 kg annually, after deduction for seed). Every property would also have 2.75 ha of secondary land (for olives, grapes, barley, and pulses). Additional marginal land was available, but it required more work and investment. This approach suggests that the Eretrian *chōra* could have supported 5,400 households living on a plot of some 5 ha, arguably the minimum property level to serve as a hoplite (van Wees 2013a: 224).

For Chalcis, 21% of its territory in 500—27,900 ha in all—was arable land. We do not have a precise survey of land categorization, but if half this surface was dedicated to grain, it was enough to feed more than 22,000 people.[43] Therefore, there were 5,000 theoretical lots of 2.8 ha or 6,000 lots of 2.3 ha for grain cultivation. This still leaves the same amount of land for olives, grapes, or more grain. On the Lelantine plain alone, some 2,260 ha could have been cultivated according to our estimates. Given the fertility of the soil, a yield of 1,000 kg of wheat per ha is feasible, producing 1,130 tons of wheat, perhaps more than 170,000 *drachmai* at market value (5 *drachmai* per *medimnos* of 33 kg; see van Wees 2013a: 230), a sizable amount of money. In sum, this minimal assessment suggests that agricultural land at Chalcis could have supported a population of 5,000–6,000 households, each owning a plot of some 5 ha.

It is fundamentally important to remember that in Chalcis and Eretria, horses likely ate a significant proportion of the grain harvest. A horse relying entirely on grain would consume an amount sufficient to feed a family of four to five people.[44] But horses also needed fresh grass and fodder, which could be found on cultivated land left fallow. Herds devoted to reproduction could graze on pasture, while horses kept for a frequent use (warfare, racing) were fed on grain (Simon and Verdan 2014). On average, we estimate that 1,000 horses would consume 500–1,000 tons of grain annually, the quantity required to feed 2,500–5,000 people. To some degree (and mostly during difficult times), horses were in competition with the human population.

Based on an interpretation of a passage of Thucydides (7.28.1), it has often been asserted that Euboea was some sort of granary for Athens.[45] However, the numbers

---

43. 27,900 ha/2 = 13,950 ha for grain cultivation. With biennial fallow 6,975 ha (13,950/2) x 640 kg/ha = 4,464 tons. Since a family of 4.5 consumes 900 kg per year, 22,320 people could be fed.

44. Grain consumption per horse has been estimated at 30 *medimnoi* of barley per year (van Wees 2006: 358 n. 37; but see also Spence 1993: 272–86). At 27.4 kg per *medimnos*, this would amount to 822 kg per year and per horse as a minimal threshold. A family of four to five people would consume annually 900 kg of grain (see Fachard 2012: 14 and n. 24 for references).

45. Osborne 1987: 101; Moreno 2007: 71–143. For an opposite view, see Picard 1979: 335–9; Fachard 2012: 115. See also Westlake 1948.

above seem to contradict this view.[46] Chalcis and Eretria were mostly self-sufficient in grain, they are never portrayed as Aegean exporters, and Euboean surplus and exports were negligible compared to Athens' enormous needs (Fachard 2012: 115). The two cities enjoyed high-quality land but in relatively limited quantity in proportion to their respective populations. Consequently, agricultural production might have been more famous for its quality than for its quantity.[47]

## 2.8.3. Animal Husbandry

Little is known about horse breeding on Euboea in the Archaic period, except that the local aristocracy partly relied on it for its wealth, prestige, and perhaps success in early warfare (see Section 2.5.2). Ancient sources are silent about how and where the herds were kept. Horses painted on local pottery (see Section 2.4.3) echo the importance of the animal but are of little help in understanding the practical aspects of breeding (Simon and Verdan 2014). Osteological data remain scarce. Thus, we are left with general considerations about possible pasture areas in Chalcis' and Eretria's territories.

Except when left fallow, arable lands were almost certainly not "sacrificed" for feeding any animal. The best zones to put horses out to pasture were wetlands, which are abundant in the deltaic landscapes around Eretria, Amarynthos, Aliveri, and Mourteri, as well as inland, around the lake of Dystos, and in the valleys of the Avlonari and Lelantos rivers (Fachard 2012: 119–20; Simon and Verdan 2014: 17).[48] It is no coincidence that Tamynai, situated on the Avlonari river, is the place where Apollo guarded Admetus' horses, according to a version of the hero's myth (Strabo 10.1.10). The god had a sanctuary there, with a hippodrome, where hippic competitions were most likely held in honor of both Admetus and Apollo (Knoepfler and Ackermann 2012: 935–46). Hippobotai and Hippeis used their horses to go to war, but the noble animal might also have been a source of profit if exported to other regions.[49]

As noted above (see Section 2.8.1), based on its name (*Eu-boia*, "the island favorable to oxen" or "famed for its oxen") and its early coinage (see Section 2.8.5), the island seems to have offered an ideal setting for cattle breeding. The

---

46. On the low volume of Euboean export containers, see Section 2.8.4.1.

47. See Fachard 2012: 115. Territorial expansion and agricultural intensification could change the parameters of this situation, and it is indeed what seemed to have happened in the Classical period, when Chalcis and Eretria ended up controlling 55% of Euboean agriculture, including its most fertile lands, and the vast majority of its forests.

48. On horse-breeding regions in the Greek world more generally, see Blaineau 2015: 68–113.

49. Euboean horses traveling on merchant ships has been suggested by Lane Fox (2008: 113).

pastures required for horses and cattle are largely identical. The decoration of black-figure plate, dated to the mid-sixth century and attributed to an Eretrian workshop (Ure 1973: 25–6), nicely illustrates the complementarity, and hierarchy, of the two animals in the Euboean pastoral (and political) economy (see Figure 2.14).

Finally, sheep and goats were no doubt the most common animals seen in Euboea, and there was enough pastureland to support large herds. They are the most visible in the sacrificial economy of the Eretrian sanctuaries (Sanctuary of Apollo and Sacrifical Area, Artemision in Amarynthos). Sacrificed animals might have represented a proxy of the animal population in terms of bovine, sheep, and caprine proportions. Interestingly, before the Peloponnesian War, Athenian cattle were transported to the island for security (Thuc. 2.14.1). Beyond the proximity

FIGURE 2.14. Black-figure plate showing horseman in center and frieze of cattle around edge, attributed to an Eretrian workshop; c. 540; diameter: 31.2 cm; unknown provenance. Antikenmuseum der Universität Heidelberg 68-2.

## 2.8.4. Maritime Trade

In ναυσικλειτή ("famed for shipping"; *Hom. Hymn Apollo* 219) Euboea, the early history of its communities is shaped by their active involvement in maritime trade. However, whereas Euboeans' overseas networks in the Geometric period can be mapped thanks to abundant imports and exports, we are left with only a handful of indirect literary testimonies for the Archaic period, mostly concerning Eretrian maritime power (see Section 2.7.3, with relevant sources). This does not necessarily point to radical shifts regarding Euboea's economic position, because various factors could explain such a heterogeneous data set.

For the Geometric period, the archaeological evidence has been interpreted in different ways. Given the fact that other groups of merchants, especially Cypriots and Phoenicians, were active at the same time and in many of the places where Euboean pottery has been found (Crielaard 1996; Coldstream 1998; Niemeyer 2004; Papadopoulos 1997; Papadopoulos 2011), the main issue revolves around the extent of the Euboeans' initiative and their actual presence along sea routes. Regarding imports found in Lefkandi and Eretria, as well as Euboean pottery found scattered all over the Mediterranean, the same question always arises: who transported these artifacts? Unless they bear clear "ethnic markers" (a debatable notion), such as alphabetic inscriptions, the objects cannot answer by themselves. The general context must be taken into account and various modes of dissemination considered. It is undeniable that not all Euboean vases were brought to their final destination by Euboeans. However, each export or import does imply a contact between a Euboean and another partner, whether in the motherland, in the Levant, in the west, or somewhere in between. In this respect, Euboea may have been less active on the sea than one usually deduces from the diffusion of its pottery but still very well connected to trade networks.

A model proposed by Kourou (2017; 2020) draws a distinction between three phases for the development of Euboean commercial contacts during the Protogeometric and Geometric periods. In the first phase (tenth-early ninth century), ports on the Euboean Gulf such as Lefkandi become a destination for Eastern ships, first Cypriot and then Phoenician, attracted by various resources (metals, agricultural products, wood, etc.). The second phase (ninth–early eighth century) sees an increase in exchanges, and the Euboeans gradually become involved in seafaring, either by joining Eastern crews or on their own ships. This leads them to visit ports in the Levant (Al-Mina; see below), as well as maritime routes traced by the Phoenicians in North Africa and to the Far West (Iberia).

It is not until the third phase (from the second quarter of the eighth century onward) that a proper Euboean "expansion" toward the west took place, first marked by commercial exchanges, then by the installation of permanent settlements in southern Italy and Sicily (see Section 2.7.2.1.2).

An interesting issue is the debate regarding Al-Mina, a site at the mouth of the Orontes river on the Syrian coast. Whereas Greek pottery reached other sites in the region already in the ninth and perhaps in the tenth century (Boardman 1990; Luke 2003: 31–7), it is found in Al-Mina from the eighth onward. In the earliest levels, imports from Euboea are predominant. First identified as a Greek colony by the excavator, the site has been considered by some scholars as an *emporion* (or a "port of trade") founded by Greeks, and Euboeans in particular, while others favor the view that it was a non-Greek settlement with the permanent or temporary presence of Greek merchants; others even doubt that the site welcomed any Greeks (Boardman 1990; Descoeudres 2002; Luke 2003; Niemeyer 2004; Niemeyer 2006; Vacek 2017).[50] Arguments for a settlement founded and occupied by Levantine people are based on the local character of architecture, house furniture, and domestic ware (Luke 2003: 12–13). Taking into account all the material evidence on site, but also the supposed nature of maritime trade at that time, the most plausible interpretation is to consider Al-Mina as a port of trade visited by merchants of various origins: Greeks, Easterners, and Cypriots alike. That being said, it must be emphasized that our understanding of trade flows relies mainly on the interpretation of pottery, only used here "by default," that is, in the absence of other preserved traded goods.

### 2.8.4.1. Pottery

(For an overview of Euboean ceramics in the Early Iron Age and Archaic period, see Section 2.4.3.) Although Euboean pottery reached many sites of the Mediterranean during the Geometric period (Descoeudres 2006–2007: 9–24), it should be viewed only as a subsidiary commodity in merchant ships. Given the extent to which potters in the north Aegean, southern Italy, and Sicily seem to have produced local imitations of Euboean wares, Eretria and Chalcis may have exported more potters and stylistic trends than vases.[51] Consequently, the dramatic drop in Euboean exports after 700 implies not necessarily an actual setback

---

50. The bibliography on the subject is huge. See Descoeudres 2002: 61–9 for a synthetic view of the main interpretations given between 1936 and 2001.

51. For examples of local "Euboeanizing" productions in the north Aegean, see Besios, Tzifopoulos, and Kotsonas 2012: 128–34, 236. For Pithecusae, see Ridgway 2007: 148–9. For Francavilla Marittima, see Jacobsen 2013. For southern Italy and Sicily, see Mercuri 2004; Denoyelle and Iozzo 2009: 33–45.

*Chalcis and Eretria* 191

for the two cities but changing modes of interactions with local people as well as new trends in the marketing of Greek products (notably Corinthian and East Greek pottery).

Paradoxically, whereas Euboean fine ware appears in many places for a period of time, Euboean transport amphoras are not easily identified, and so far they have not been used to trace exported agricultural products (wine, olive oil, grain). Although this situation is likely to change—thanks to research on Euboean SOS amphoras (Pratt 2015: 224–5) and the identification of new types produced in Chalcis or Eretria,[52] it is unlikely that Euboea will ever challenge other regions in terms of volume of exported containers (as well as contents).

### 2.8.4.2. Metals

Though hardly detectable in the archaeological record, raw metals probably weighed heavily in the cargo of Euboean ships. Despite the limited evidence, the search for metals is one of the most frequently cited reasons for Euboeans sailing to the north Aegean (Tiverios 2006–2008: 8–21) and southern Italy (Markoe 1992: 79–80; D'Agostino 2006–2008: 215, 22–4). The north Aegean was rich in gold (both in primary and placer deposits) and silver, while in Italy, Greeks had access to the products of Elba's iron ores and to Etruria's metalliferous inland.

The importance of metallurgy in the Euboean "sphere" is attested in textual sources, related to Euboean mythology. According to some authors, the Cretan Curetes (sometimes conflated with the Phrygian Corybantes) moved to Euboea and were the first to bring bronze weapons, manufactured by their mother Kombe or by themselves, to the island (Aristos of Salamis, *FGrH* 143 F5; Strabo 10.3.19; Nonnos *Dion.* 13, 135–8, 142–57).[53] According to another tradition, the Cyclopes were the first to manufacture weapons in a cave on Euboea (Istros *FGrH* 334 F71). Finally, Chalkodon, king of the Abantes (*Il.* 2.540–1) and specifically associated with Chalcis, evokes metallurgy by his very name ("he of the bronze teeth"), which alludes to the tongs of the blacksmith. All these sources are late, but they reflect the importance of metalworking and metallurgic craftsmen in Euboean Archaic society (Mele 1981).

Several sites on and away from the island (where the presence of Euboeans has been claimed) have yielded traces of metalworking in the form of residues and workshop facilities. Those sites include Lefkandi, Eretria (in the area of

---

52. Material from a potter's dump in Chalcis contains many completely painted amphoras (Johnston and Jones 1978: 112; for the context of discovery, see Charalambidou 2017a; Charalambidou 2017b; Charalambidou 2020).

53. We should add the name of the Δάκτυλοι (*daimones* associated with metallurgy), celebrated in a hymn inscribed on a Hellenistic *stēlē* from the Sanctuary of Apollo Daphnephoros in Eretria (*IG* XII.9.259; see Blakely 2006: 79–98).

the Sanctuary of Apollo and the West Quarter), Oropus, Pithecusae, and, most recently, Methone (Ridgway 1992: 91–6; Mazarakis Ainian 2012: 126–40; Verdan 2013: 145–51; Morris and Papadopoulos 2023). There is clear archaeological evidence that iron and bronze were worked in these places, and gold in some of them. The scale and nature of the production are difficult to ascertain, but there are strong hints of production of bronze tripods and gold jewellery at Lefkandi (Lemos 2002: 126–34), small bronzes and gold diadems at Eretria, iron tools and weapons at Oropus, and a variety of small bronzes at Methone. Evidence goes back to the Protogeometric period and continues into the Geometric period and through the beginning of the seventh century. Therefore, postulating the existence of an Early Iron Age metallurgical tradition involving Lefkandi, Eretria, and Chalcis is not outlandish. What remains unclear, however, is what happened to this tradition in the seventh and sixth centuries, a period for which evidence is currently lacking.

The strongest body of evidence relates to gold. Mention must first be made of an eighth-century hoard containing c. 500 g of gold found in a pot buried under the floor of a house in Eretria (Themelis 1983; Le Rider and Verdan 2002; Kroll 2012: 36). The gold is in the form of small oblong and round ingots as well as pieces of crafted items such as wires. These are half-finished products, belonging to an intermediate step of the *chaîne opératoire* and used in the production of finished objects, as wires are recut and welded for the creation of jewels. This material was originally taken to be the stock of a goldsmith but is now typically seen as pieces of precious metal cut into smaller pieces in order to be weighed on a scale, for commercial transactions (see below). Additionally, pottery sherds used in the melting of gold were discovered in the Sanctuary of Apollo Daphnephoros in Eretria (Verdan 2013: 149–9, 271–3). Although these finds are exceptional for the early Greek world, they are insufficient for unveiling Euboea's role in the circulation of gold in the Archaic period. The Eretrian hoard was originally hypothesized to be material that originated in the eastern Mediterranean and was acquired by a Greek merchant. However, recent discoveries at Methone (an Eretrian colony in the Thermaic Gulf) make the placer deposits of Macedonian rivers a more likely source, at least for part of the hoard; the large quantity of material found at Methone and linked to metalworking includes pottery sherds used in the melting of gold (similar to the Eretrian ones). This find shows that people in Methone were transforming local alluvial gold into small ingots, analogous to those discovered in the Eretrian hoard (Verdan 2023). It is, therefore, probable that the Eretrians enjoyed some privileges in this local chain of production.

Two points require clarification. First, the search for metals was only one of the many reasons for embarking on overseas ventures. Second, that search implied more actors and means than just a few individuals getting their hands on raw materials from natural sources for their own needs. The circulation of recycled metal, the redistribution of stock to various purchasers, and the trade of finished products were also part of the business.

Regarding circulation, the nature of the hoard from Eretria strongly suggests that bullion gold was used in monetary transactions, in the same way that silver was used in the contemporary Near East (Le Rider and Verdan 2002; Kroll 2012; Verdan and Heymans 2020; Heymans 2021: 203–12). Euboeans probably became acquainted with this practice when trading with Eastern partners and eventually adopted it, in a similar way to the Greek alphabet being concurrently adapted from the Phoenician model (see Section 2.12.1). The importance of the Euboic weight standard brings an additional argument to the discussion. It was adopted by the Athenians (hence its subsequent label "Euboic-Attic"), Samians, and Corinthians (Kroll 2008: 44–6) for their early coinage. According to Herodotus (3.89), the Euboic standard was used for measuring the tributes paid in gold to the Persian king, Darius. The Herodotus passage can be interpreted in different ways (see, e.g., Balcer 1989), but it establishes an explicit link between the Euboic weight system and gold in the Archaic period.[54]

There is currently a knowledge gap between the circulation of gold in Euboean networks during the Geometric and Early Archaic periods and the first Chalcidian and Eretrian coinage in the second half of the sixth century. To what extent the merchants from the two cities were also active in the circulation of silver, which became increasingly important during the Archaic period (Kroll 2012), is not known. However, ties with their north Aegean colonies may have favored access to ores,[55] resulting in the coining of silver from a relatively early period, both in the metropoleis and the colonies (for Eretria, see van Alfen 2015: 274).

Alongside precious metals, finished products may well have circulated. According to textual sources, metallurgy was a Euboean field of expertise from an early date. Local mythology is replete with references to bronze and iron working by *daimones* and heroes (Mele 1981; Breglia 2013). Chalcis features prominently in that mythology, and its iron blades were legendary. So far, however, no compelling series of metal objects has been recognized as typically Euboean. Nothing closely comparable to Peloponnesian bronzes, for instance, is known from the island at any period. Traces of metallurgical industry are discrete and certainly do not suggest concentrated activity in one place. Part of the debate has focused on the island's alleged metalliferous ores (see Section 2.8.1). Although ancient iron

---

54. It is worth noting here that the Persian tributes paid in silver were measured in Babylonian *talanta*, according to Herodotus.

55. Eretrians certainly played a role in Pisistratus' silver mining in the Pangaeus area (Viviers 1987).

ores have been authenticated, they are far from ubiquitous. Moreover, the availability of copper remains undocumented. Hence, doubts have been raised regarding the importance of Euboean cities in bronze and iron metallurgy. However, a renowned industry does not necessarily depend on the proximity of raw materials. Metals could have been imported as a response to the demand of Euboean workshops. As noted before, Euboean ventures overseas may have been partly motivated by the search for metals.

## 2.8.5. Coinage

In the pre-monetary period, the Euboeans were familiar with metals as a means of exchange, and to this day, the only known Greek pre-coinage hoard of precious metal is the aforementioned eighth-century hoard from Eretria (Themelis 1983; Le Rider and Verdan 2002; Kroll 2012: 36). In the Archaic period, many Greek states seem to have adopted the silver Euboic *mna* of 432–6 g for their silver coinage but subdivided it differently: 25 or 50 *statēres* to the *mna* in Euboea and Attica (and hence 17.2 or 8.64 g per *statēr*), 35 *statēres* to the *mna* (and hence 12.3 g per *statēr*) in Aegina (van Wees 2013b: 110–11). The early use of the Euboic *mna* is usually explained by the prominent role played by the Euboeans along the sea routes of the Mediterranean (van Wees 2013b: 110).

According to Psoma (2015: 98), the Euboeans first adopted a standard with a *statēr* at 17.2 g. This "Euboean standard" was used in the Chalcidian colonies in Sicily as well as in some of the earliest coinages of the Chalcidice peninsula, reflecting the relationships between Euboean foundations and their mother cities (Psoma 2015; Psoma 2017: 410). In their coinage, however, Chalcis and Eretria later adopted a *statēr* at 8.64 g, the so-called Euboic-Attic standard (Psoma 2015: 98–9). A weight of 8.79 g found at Pithecusae, where the Euboeans were particularly active, could be interpreted alternatively as the equivalent to half a Euboean *statēr* (van Wees 2013b: 110) or to one Attic-Euboic *statēr* (Kroll 2008: 45). Moreover, it has been argued that the Attic-Euboic *statēr* at 8.64 g might result from a slight increase to the Babylonian shekel at 8.40 g and that its use can be traced back to Lefkandi in the ninth century on the basis of stone balance weights found in a tomb there (Kroll 2008; Kroll 2012: 40). It is plausible that the Euboeans adopted at an early stage the weight standard of the Babylonians, possibly increasing it in order to facilitate equivalences between the Babylonian and Euboean *talanta*, as suggested by a passage of Herodotus (3.95) in which he uses Euboean *mnai* and *talanta* for converting the amount of tribute owed to Darius (Kroll 2008; Bresson 2017: 310). The origins of the "Euboean" and "Attic-Euboic" standards are difficult to trace, but their adoption outside Euboea attests to the prominent role played by Euboeans in maritime enterprise.

In the last decades of the sixth century, Chalcis and Eretria were among the first *poleis* of Central Greece to mint silver coins, after Aegina, Corinth, and Athens. Coins corresponding to the Athenian *Wappenmünzen* and dated to the third quarter of the sixth century have been assigned to Euboean metropoleis and to colonies in the north Aegean, but precise attributions are still a matter of discussion (Kraay 1976: 88–92, 134; van Alfen 2015). Among the types, those featuring a bovid, with its obvious allusion to the island's name, were particularly common (Kagan 1988). A substantial coin production in Chalcis and Eretria begins in the last quarter of the sixth century. These issues are two-sided and comparable to the famous "Athenian owl and Athena's head" *tetradrachma*. In Chalcis, an eagle on the obverse is associated with a wheel on the reverse, while Eretria has the cow and the octopus, symbols of its economic activities on land and sea.

Archaic coins from Chalcis and Eretria have been found in only a few hoards, and then in small quantities,[56] implying a modest volume of minting and mainly local circulation. Both cities certainly stopped minting during difficult times: Chalcis after the defeat of 506 (see Section 2.7.4.2), Eretria after the Persian siege of 490. However, this led to an only temporary interruption. Later in the fifth century, the growing economic power of Athens had a more radical effect on Euboean coinage, which eventually caused its suspension in 425 under Athenian dominance (Brunner and Spoerri Butcher 2010: 146).

## 2.9. Familial/Demographic History

Ancient population figures are notoriously scarce and untrustworthy. Eretria, in this respect, represents an exception. In the late fourth and early third centuries, Eretrians inscribed catalogs of fully enfranchised adult male citizens on a series of large *stēlai*, many of which are extant. Cumulatively, those *stēlai* record some 2,400 names with patronymics and demotics, making Eretria the best-known ancient *polis* population from a demographic point of view (Hansen 2006: 61; Knoepfler 1997: 371–3; Fachard 2012: 111–23). However, interpretation of the raw data is a matter of debate, resulting in population numbers varying by as much as 100%. Nonetheless, some of these figures can be compared with the figures we have for the late Archaic period. In this section, we offer some demographic reconstructions, followed by an overview of the evidence regarding familial history and prosopography.

---

56. There are three known hoards on Euboea itself (ICGH 3, 9, and 10), one in Athens (ICGH 2), one in Eleusis (ICGH 5), one in Isthmia (ICGH 11), one in Phoenicia (ICGH 1483), and three in Egypt (ICGH 1639, 1640, and 1644). See van Alfen 2015: 275–8.

## 2.9.1. Demography

For the Archaic period, we perforce rely on a few military figures, mostly unverifiable, and modern reconstructions. For 506, the military force of Chalcis has been estimated at 3,000 hoplites, and in 480, the city was able to launch 20 ships (triremes?) at the same time, which suggests a contingent of 4,000 sailors (see Section 2.7.3). According to standard demographic models, a force of 3,000–4,000 men ages 20–59 suggests that in late Archaic times, the free population (including males and females of all ages) of the entire *polis* of Chalcis was c. 12,340–16,454, which should be considered as a minimum.[57]

Strabo mentions a *stēlē* from the Sanctuary of Artemis at Amarynthos in the territory of Eretria recording a procession of 3,000 hoplites, 600 cavalrymen, and 60 chariots (10.1.10; see Section 2.7.1). This military force—incomplete since there is no mention of light-armed troops—suggests a total male population of over 7,600 and a free civilian population of over 15,000 (male and female) which appears to be incompatible with the population of Eretria (both the city and the chora) around 700 given the archaeological record (see below). It would fit better within a post-500 population.

For the eighth century, a population of 1,000–2,000 has been suggested for Eretria (Hall 2014b: 75, 134). The lower figure might be more reasonable for the settlement in c. 700. This is not as meager as it sounds: it equates to 160–230 families of four to five people living in an equal number of dwellings in the settlement area. We currently know two dozen possible "houses," so finding the remaining 140–200 would be archaeologically challenging. Nevertheless, if we think in terms of families, an estimated 160 households (c. 800–1,000 people) in Eretria around 700 provides a reasonable hypothesis (if not too high). If we adopt a 1% annual population growth (see Scheidel 2003), a population of 800–1,000 for the settlement of Eretria in 700 would have increased to c. 5,800–7,300 by c. 500.

If in 700, the total population of Eretria, Amarynthos, Tamynai, and Oichalia (the major settlements in what would become the Eretrian *chōra*; see Section 2.4.1.4) were 600–2,000, the total population of the entire *polis* of Eretria c. 500 would perhaps have reached 23,200–29,200 people (including males and females of all ages). This would provide a military force of men ages 20–59 of approximately 5,600–7,100. Since the higher end would exceed the available figures from the late Classical period,[58] a military roster of c. 4,000–5,000 and a free population of c. 20,000–21,000 seem more reasonable for 500.

---

57. Men ages 20–59 = 48.62% of the male population (Hansen 1985: 12).

58. Based on military catalogs and ephebic lists from the 340s, the Eretrian army has been estimated at 5,000 infantry and a 500-strong cavalry (Knoepfler 1997: 372). This is perhaps a maximum (Fachard 2012: 111–12).

## 2.9.2. Onomastics, Prosopography, and Marriage

Thanks in large part to the Eretrian catalogs of citizens, more than 2,000 names of citizens from the late Classical to early Hellenistic periods are known. Several of those names were already used in the late Archaic period, which demonstrates, to some extent, onomastic continuity.[59] A fascinating feature is the high proportion of names starting and ending in ἵππος, such as Philippos, Hippostratos, Telesippos, Erasippos, and so on (Bechtel 1900; Wallace 1947; Knoepfler 2014). This must surely reflect the prominent role of the horse in Euboean culture (see Section 2.5.2). While not every ἵππος name points to the existence of an aristocrat or a horse breeder, a high proportion of "equestrian" names in a region may nevertheless reflect favorable conditions for raising horses and suggests the economic, cultural, social, military, and even political importance of the animal for its local population. A look at the distribution of ἵππος names does indeed show that they are very rare in the southern districts of the Eretriad, while they are mostly concentrated in the central districts, which were among the best suited for hippotrophy and the most fertile of Euboea (Fachard 2012: 119–20).

Beyond a few Chalcidian and Eretrian tyrants (see Section 2.5.3), evidence for prominent families is available mostly for Eretria. Close ties between Eretrian and Athenian elites seem to emerge in the Geometric period, as imported vases conspicuously displayed on Eretrian tombs point to either shared funerary customs or intermarriages (see Section 2.4.3). The material evidence for the Archaic period still awaits a proper inquiry, but written sources portray Eretria as a welcoming place for prominent Athenians from various (and opposed) political sides and indicate that the links between the two cities remain predominantly (if not exclusively) a matter of family alliances rather than diplomatic contacts.

The Athenian *genos* of the Gephyraioi (whose most famous members were Harmodius and Aristogeiton) were allegedly from Eretria (Hdt. 5.57, 61; Gray 2007: 205–18); the fact that they were based in the region of Aphidna, on the vital road between Oropus and Athens, suggests that the Gephyraioi might have maintained links with both an Eretrian "outpost" at Oropus and Eretria itself. Lysanias from "flourishing Eretria" (Hdt. 6.127), who famously competed for the daughter of Cleisthenes of Sicyon, was undeniably of impeccable aristocratic stock (Lolos Forthcoming: Section 2.2.7.4). The pampered Koisyra (see Section 2.7.4.1) certainly belonged to a prominent Eretrian clan, regarded as of equal status to the Alcmeonids in Athens. More generally, the Eupatrids enjoyed links of

---

59. Several names from the deme of Styra listed in the Eretrian citizen catalogs from the late fourth and early third centuries are already found on the Styra lead tablets from c. 475 (Knoepfler 2014: 61; see Section 2.2.2).

friendship and hospitality with the Eretrian aristocracy, as echoed by an epitaph of c. 525 found in Eretria and naming a certain "Chairion of Athens, belonging to the Eupatrids" (*IG* I³.1516; Duplouy 2003: 4–5; Knoepfler 2008). Others might have enjoyed similar relationships, such as Pleistias of Sparta, whose epitaph detailed that he "earned a living in Athens" before he drew his last breath in Eretria in the final quarter of the sixth century (*IG* XII.9.286). Herodotus mentions several "esteemed" citizens; Aeschines son of Nothon, who "advised" the Athenian cleruchs to abandon Eretria (Hdt. 6.100), might have had dubious motives. Euphorbus son of Alkimachos and Philagros son of Kyneas opened the gates to the Persians in 490 (Hdt. 6.101).

## 2.10. *Social Customs and Institutions*
### 2.10.1. Symposium

The symposium played a central role in the social customs of Archaic Greek *poleis*. Some aspects of this convivial and highly ritualized practice can be illustrated by early discoveries coming from Euboea, such as drinking vessels bearing versified inscriptions. The best known of them is the "Cup of Nestor," a kotylē made at Teos but discovered at Pithecusae in a grave of the last quarter of the eighth century (Buchner and Ridgway 1993: 219, 745–59; Bartoněk and Buchner 1995: 146–54; Akurgal, Hertel, Kerschner, et al. 2002; Kadıoğlu, Özbil, Kerschner, et al. 2015; D'Acunto Forthcoming: Section 1.2.11A.2). The inscription (*SEG* 16.404), one of the earliest-known examples of Greek alphabetic writing, consists of three lines (the latter two of which are dactylic hexameters):

> I am Nestor's cup, good to drink from.
> Whoever drinks this cup empty, straightaway
> Desire for beautiful-crowned Aphrodite will seize him.[60]

This inscription is a digest of symposiac ingredients: relevant skills to master (writing and poetical composition), an allusion to the epic world, and an evocation of divinely inspired love. Another cup, of slightly later date and discovered at Methone, bears an iambic inscription of the same general type: "I am of Hakesandros. [Whoever . . .] will be deprived of his [ . . . ]" (Besios, Tzifopoulos, and Kotsonas 2012: 339–43; Tzifopoulos, Besios, and Kotsonas 2017: 372–4). In Eretria, two very fragmentary vases dated to the eighth century could bear similar

---

60. The text of the first line is damaged, and various emendations and appurtenant translations have been proposed. The relevant body of scholarly literature is extensive. See, for example, Lombardi 2003; Gerhard 2011.

inscriptions (Johnston and Andreiomenou 1989; Kenzelmann-Pfyffer, Theurillat, and Verdan 2005: 60–1, cat. 4). These vases provide strong evidence for symposiastic practices in Euboean society from an early date (Wecowski 2014).

## 2.10.2. Pederasty

According to later authors, the Chalcidians were renowned for their homoerotic practices, giving rise to the verb χαλκιδίζειν (Suda, Hesychius s.v.). The origin of this custom is reported by Plutarch (*Mor.* 760a–1b), who claims that Kleomachos (of Pharsalus or Thrace), prompted by his attachment to his Chalcidian *erōmenos*, victoriously led the Thessalian cavalry in battle against the Eretrians during the Lelantine War (see Section 2.7.1). In the aftermath of the battle, according to Plutarch, the Chalcidians consecrated a column to Kleomachos' memory in their agora (see Section 2.4.1.1) and became enthusiasts of pederasty. Although the historical veracity of this *aition* is open to question, it does suggest the existence of probably institutionalized homoerotic educational practices, similar to those attested for Sparta and Crete, going back to the period when Chalcis was governed by aristocrats (Mele 1975: 24).

## 2.10.3. Festivals and Associations

Several social events marked the rhythm of the Eretrian and Chalcidian calendars. The Amarynthos armed procession of 3,000 hoplites, 600 cavalrymen, and 60 chariots (see Sections 2.7.1, 2.11.2.6) was no doubt a grand event. Besides its military and political importance, it also bore considerable social significance and expressed the identity of the community. It is almost certain that the entire population took part in the procession, thus providing an occasion for social gathering and feasting. The event was one of the main social events of the Eretrian year and also bore importance for other Euboeans.

Athletic games and competitions were also held in both cities, although our evidence is slim. Games in honor of Heracles were organized in Eretria at least from the sixth century onward (see Section 2.11.2.4) and probably in Chalcis as well, given the importance of the hero there in later periods. Euboeans took part in the major Panhellenic games. Eryxias of Chalcis won the *stadion* at Olympia in 532 (Moretti 1957: #121), and Krokon of Eretria won the horse race at Olympia sometime around 492 (Moretti 1957: #177). Krokon commemorated his victory by means of the dedication of a small bronze horse (Pausanias 6.14.4).

Mention should be made of the ἀειναῦται, the "eternal sailors," attested at Eretria in the late fifth century (*SEG* 34.898; Knoepfler 2008: 604; van Wees 2013b: 56–7). They perhaps formed an association sharing seafaring interests, but the origin of the ἀειναῦται cannot be presently traced back to the Archaic period (*contra* Walker 2004: 127).

## 2.11. Religious Customs and Institutions

It would be erroneous to believe that the early stages of a *polis'* religious life were less rich and varied than the later stages. However, the former are more difficult to trace because they involved smaller groups and a correspondingly more limited collection of contemporary textual and material evidence. In order to give a broad overall picture of the religious life of an Archaic *polis*, a common approach consists of gathering later testimonies and estimating the probable antiquity of institutions and cults. However, this method is inadequate when the literary sources are scarce, as is the case with Archaic Euboea. For Chalcis, the current data are very limited. Only in Eretria is it possible to present the shrines and institutions that are attested for the period of our interest, but they nevertheless represent the tip of the iceberg in terms of data.

### 2.11.1. Chalcis

The absence of systematic archaeological work at Chalcis has left us with a very sketchy picture of its religious landscape. In fact, the first known intra muros shrine came to light only recently, dating back to the fourth century (Kalamara, Kosma, Boukaras, et al. 2015: 21–3). Extra muros, a rural shrine at Pei Dokou revealed an eighth-century votive deposit containing small bronzes, including 12 bull figurines and two male figurines (Kalamara, Kosma, Boukaras, et al. 2015: 30, 33). Therefore, we must rely on the limited collection of relevant literary evidence, mainly post-Classical in date. This is, of course, regrettable, as Heraclides Criticus, who visited Chalcis in the fourth century, mentions that sanctuaries were a remarkable feature of the city, along with other public buildings (1.26–9; see Section 2.4.1.1).

One cult site that seems quite likely to have existed in the Archaic period is a temenos dedicated to Athena that was evidently located in the Lelantine plain and that was linked with the Athenian cleruchy imposed in 506 (Aelian *VH* 6.1; *IG* XII.9.934; *SEG* 10.304.3; see Section 2.7.4.2). Later sources mention a heroic cult (of Archaic date?) honoring Kleomachos, who ostensibly died in the Lelantine War (see Section 2.4.1.1), and a column dedicated to him existed in the agora, perhaps surmounted by a sphinx, statue, or tripod (Bakhuizen 1976b; Psoma 2017). It is possible that the cult to Kleomachos was already in existence in the Archaic period, but that remains nothing more than a supposition, given the uncertainties surrounding the Lelantine War (see Section 2.7.1).

With respect to other cults, our earliest source is from the fifth century and mentions a Sanctuary of Zeus Olympios (*IG* I³.40.35.61–2). Five Doric capitals, discussed in Section 2.4.1.1 and dated to 500–470, belong to a temple tentatively associated with Zeus but without solid evidence. An inscription of the fourth century mentions a sanctuary of Athena (*IG* II².44.17), but its location is unknown. The nymph Arethusa was probably the object of a cult (Arjona-Perez 2017). The worship of Apollo Delphinios, Poseidon Euripios (located on the cemetery hill?), Chalcis Archegetis (located northeast of the city?), Hestia, Athena, Demeter, Dionysus, and Heracles are all attested for later periods (Bakhuizen 1985). These cults could have an Archaic origin, although this remains sheer speculation. Textual sources do not allow us to identify the patron deity of the city, but Zeus, whose eagle appears on Chalcis' Archaic coinage (Kraay 1976: 92), is a potential candidate.

## 2.11.2. Eretria

The literary sources bearing on religious activity in Eretria are not more abundant than those for Chalcis. In Eretria, however, excavation of three urban sanctuaries, where cult activity began in the eighth and seventh centuries, allows us to follow the development of sacred spaces and the evolution of Eretrian religious practices. As we will see, both in the urban center and in the *chōra*, Apollo and Artemis played a central role in Eretrian cultic activity.

### 2.11.2.1. Sanctuary of Apollo Daphnephoros

The most important urban shrine was dedicated to Apollo Daphnephoros. Along with his twin sister, Artemis, he can be considered to be the patron deity of the *polis* in the historical period. The site was identified thanks to inscriptions of the Hellenistic period that were discovered in situ and that mention the Sanctuary of Apollo Daphnephoros as the place where they were put on display. No inscription confirms the god's presence in earlier periods, but several arguments speak in favor of a continuity of cult stretching from the eighth century down to the end of the Hellenistic period (Verdan 2013: 29, 231–3).

Cult activity began in the first half of the eighth century, at which point the sanctuary contained a circular altar and four small round or apsidal buildings. Three monumental buildings succeed one another at the same spot: a temple built in the third quarter of the eighth century was replaced by a second one in the seventh century, and a Doric temple was erected at the end of the sixth century (see Sections 2.4.1.3.3–5). The activities taking place in the earliest phase of the sanctuary are poorly known, except for animal sacrifices and banquets, attested by large pottery assemblages (kratēres, drinking cups, etc.) buried in pits close to the buildings. For the Late Geometric period, a few images on vases and the offering of light arms suggest the existence of rites of integration for the city's young men, a context in which Apollo properly fits (Verdan 2013: 221–2). Religious acts practiced in the sanctuary, however, were certainly more varied. The *epiklēsis* of the god, Daphnephoros, as well as the probable existence of a month called Daphnephorion in the Eretrian calendar (Voutiras 2008: 785–6) encourage us to restore the existence of a feast honoring the god, in the course of which the festival of the Daphnephoria occurred; a festival by that name was also held in Thebes (Verdan 2013: 235–6).

The Sanctuary of Apollo was central to the religious and political life of Eretria, but it also evinces the city's connection with Athens. It is striking that the Eretrians, in the late sixth century, decided to place Athena and Theseus in the center of the west pediment of the temple of their patron deity Apollo (see Section 2.12.5). One is tempted to recognize the assertion of a special connection between both cities, at a time when democracy was established in Eretria (see Section 2.5.3.2).

The fall of Eretria to the Persians in 490 (see Section 2.7.5) is a dramatic event for the Sanctuary of Apollo if we are to believe Herodotus' testimony referring to the burning down of the city's shrines (Hdt. 6.101). This has given rise to much speculation about the real impact of these acts upon the Temple of Apollo. The matter is not satisfactorily resolved (Hall 2014a: 35–53), but one thing is certain: the sanctuary continued to function and retained its importance after 490, as attested by the display of decrees and civic documents.

### 2.11.2.2. *Northern Sacrificial Area and Worship of Artemis*

Another sacred area, with its own (circular) altar, is located north of the Sanctuary of Apollo (Huber 2003). The first traces of cultic activity here date to the eighth century, and the bones associated with the altar attest to the sacrifice of sheep and goats. A deep pit near the altar contained thousands of vases from the Archaic period. No inscription reveals the identity of the divinity, but the proximity of the Apollo sanctuary and the nature of the offerings suggest Artemis (Huber 2003: 154–6). Two types of vases were found in large quantities: miniature hydriai and high-necked jugs (some with paintings of women engaged in what seem to be cultic activities). Both shapes were probably associated with rituals carried out by women and are found elsewhere in Eretria and Amarynthos, testifying to religious practices that are common to several sanctuaries of the city (Huber 2013). The votive objects deposited in the Archaic period also include scarabs, seals, amulets, and fibulas from the Syrian-Phoenician coast, Egypt, and Italy. These reflect Eretrian connectivity.

### 2.11.2.3. *Acropolis and Worship of Athena*

A sanctuary was located on the plateau of the acropolis, perhaps as early as the late seventh century (Huber 2007; Huber and Maillard 2015). Its dedication to Athena is established on the basis of an engraved Cypro-Ionian statuette of a lion bearing the name of the goddess. The votive material indicates that the sanctuary was frequented by maidens and women, among others. For example, numerous objects are connected with the processing of wool, which refers also to Athena's patronage of crafts. Sixth-century architectural terracottas depicting armed riders and charioteers reflect the taste of the elite for horsemanship. They also illustrate Athena's well-known affection for horses. We speculate that Athena could have been celebrated as Athena Hippia (as in Athens; see Aristid. *Or.* 1.43; Camp 1998: 9).

### 2.11.2.4. *Heracles*

The worship of Heracles in Archaic Eretria is attested by several finds. Two inscriptions—one on a dinos from the middle of the sixth century (*IG* XII.9.257), the second on a bronze cauldron dating to the second half of the fifth century (*IG* XII.9.272)—indicate that games were held in his honor from the Archaic period onward (Altherr-Charon and Lasserre 1981; Themelis 1987; Nielsen 2018: 69–70). Further evidence for games to Heracles may come from an inscription, dated to c. 550–530, on a limestone votive column that presumably originally supported a bronze cauldron. The text of the inscription as restored by Antoinette Altherr-Charon and Lasserre in the *editio princeps* (*SEG* 31.806) reads as follows:

Τιμοκράτες ἀνέθεκε Διὸ[ς κούροι πένταθλον]
ἀνδρῶν νικέρας,[61] τοῖ χάριν ἀν[τιδιδούς]

Timokrates set <this monument> up to [the son] of Zeu[s] having won [the pentathlon] of the men, thus returning him the favor. (trans. T. Nielsen)

However, other scholars have suggested different restorations that remove any reference to Heracles; Knoepfler, for instance, suggests Διο[νύσωι] (Knoepfler 2010: 229; see further Nielsen 2018: 69–70). No shrine has yet been firmly associated with his cult, despite its seeming popularity in the Eretrian and Euboean pantheon. A sanctuary and a festival of Heracles are attested in a later source (*IG* XII.9.234; Chankowski 1993: 20–1).

---

61. See Section 2.12.2 for discussion of this dialectal form.

## 2.11.2.5. "Heroon"

Another significant hero, whose name is unknown, might have been the object of a cult in the city during the Archaic period, not far from the site where the West Gate was built. After a series of burials from the late eighth and early seventh centuries, the location of the graves was signaled on the ground by a large triangle made of stone slabs (see Section 2.4.4). Small buildings were erected nearby, defining a space that remained in continuous use throughout the Archaic period. The exceptional character of the graves, the layout of the Archaic buildings, and the material discovered in nearby pits (banquet ware, lamps, terracotta figurines) have led the excavators to identify this space as a heroon. One of the individuals buried in the necropolis, perceived as a hero-protector (and perhaps the founder of the city), was the object of a cult, according to Claude Bérard. This phenomenon would coincide with the process of *polis* formation (Bérard 1970; Bérard 1972; Bérard 1978; Antonaccio 1995: 228–35). However, no written evidence supports such a theory, and the material still needs to be studied in detail. Moreover, several questions remain unresolved. Is a "hero" honored here or just powerful ancestors? Do the rituals imply an entire *polis* or just an aristocratic group in particular? The social, political, and religious signification of the Eretrian "Heroon" remains controversial.

### 2.11.2.6. Great Rural Sanctuaries: Sanctuary of Artemis at Amarynthos and Sanctuary of Apollo at Tamynai

Sanctuaries of the *chōra* occupy a central place in the religious and political landscape of Greek *poleis*. In the Eretrian *chōra*, the most important of them was undoubtedly the (recently located) Sanctuary of Artemis Amarysia, which was situated at Amarynthos and hence c. 11 km east of Eretria (see Section 2.4.1.4). Later sources demonstrate that the Sanctuary of Artemis Amarysia at Amarynthos was one of the main sanctuaries of the Eretrian *polis*. It was, for instance, used for the display of decrees and treaties with other *poleis* (Knoepfler 1988). A text banning the use of missiles in combat, mentioned by Strabo, was supposedly displayed here (see Section 2.7.1). Once a year, during the festival of the Artemisia, a procession involving at some point 3,000 hoplites, 600 cavalrymen, and 60 chariots followed the sacred road leading from Eretria to Amarynthos. Evidence shows that other Euboeans gathered here as well, so the sanctuary was also regionally important. To the armed procession was added the *agōn* of the Pyrrhic, a dance in arms, perhaps following the Persian Wars (Knoepfler 1988: 386–7).

Another particularly important religious site in the Eretrian *chōra* was located at Tamynai. Dedicated to Apollo, this shrine was situated in the heart of the central Avlonari valley, in the richest farmland of the island, and in an area with important

Bronze Age remains. The sanctuary has not been found yet, but inscriptions from the Classical period reveal that it was the site of a festival (the Tamyneia) involving musical competitions (Dillon 1997: 139 Knoepfler and Ackermann 2012).

## 2.12. *Cultural History*

The very few windows one can open on the cultural histories of Chalcis and Eretria offer highly contrasting views. On the one hand, the Geometric period appears to be extremely dynamic for the Euboeans, as early users of the alphabet and potential agents of diffusion of Greek *mythoi* throughout the Mediterranean (Lane Fox 2008: 165–316). On the other hand, no native Eretrian or Chalcidian poet is known for the Archaic period. A decline of some sort in the seventh century, perhaps linked to the emergence of new sea routes (Broodbank 2013: 550), might provide at least part of an answer, but the causes of any decline that might have occurred were likely varied.

### 2.12.1. Alphabet

Euboeans were among the earliest users of alphabetic writing in Greece. Indeed, the largest corpora of eighth-century inscriptions come from the Euboean sphere: Eretria, Pithecusae, and Methone (Kenzelmann-Pfyffer, Theurillat, and Verdan 2005; Bartoněk and Buchner 1995; Besios, Tzifopoulos, and Kotsonas 2012; Papadopoulos 2016). Considering that the Euboeans were most active at sea during the Geometric period and thus had many occasions to meet Easterners commonly using writing, it has been argued that the adaptation of the Semitic alphabet to the Greek language was carried out by Euboeans, possibly in a place where merchants regularly met, such as Al-Mina, Pithecusae, or Methone (Jeffery 1990: 10–12; Powell 1991; Marek 1993; Papadopoulos 2016). Although this hypothesis is plausible, it must remain a hypothesis, as the chances of locating the exact moment and place of this "invention" are remote. Instead, let us state that the new system of writing was quickly adopted by Euboeans for various purposes. The material evidence reveals only a tiny part of the phenomenon, since it stems primarily from individuals, displaying their writing skills by scratching a few letters or words on vessels during banquets or cultic ceremonies. Writing, however, also played a role in commercial activities, and some inscriptions (e.g., on Nestor's and Hakesandros' cups; see Section 2.10.1) prove that it was used to write down poetry as well.

People from Chalcis and Eretria not only put the alphabet to good use, but they also contributed to its diffusion in the West. Both the Etruscan and the Latin alphabets follow the Euboean one (Boffa 2016). Additionally, numerical notations might have been transmitted through the same channels (Verdan 2017).

## 2.12.2. Language

Chalcidians and Eretrians spoke local forms of Ionic, best qualified as dialects. This means that many words were pronounced and spelled differently from in other parts of the Ionic linguistic sphere. For example, the conjunction ἰάν is a Euboean form for the Attic ἐάν (Dubois 2015: 55). The Eretrian dialect had a characteristic trait in the form of rhotacism, which is to say that the intervocalic sigma was altered to rho (Knoepfler 1981: 317; Knoepfler 2014: 55). So, for instance, the Eretrian name Hegerippus is a rhotacised form of Hegesippus. Rhotacism is first attested in the second half of the sixth century, in an epigram of Timokrates (*SEG* 31.806; see Section 2.11.2.4), in the form of a participle νικέρας (Dubois 2015: 55). Rhotacism was also a characteristic of Chalcidian dialect (Knoepfler 2000: 70), at least in the central and southern parts of its territory. It is interesting to note that it was also a characteristic of the dialect spoken at Oropus (Knoepfler 2000: 373; Knoepfler 2010: 88–9). Rhotacism disappears, both at Eretria and Oropus, at the end of the fourth century.

## 2.12.3. Literature

Not a single Archaic poet from Chalcis or Eretria was considered talented enough in later centuries to have his or her name come down to us. This does not mean, of course, that poets, whether locals or foreigners, were absent from Euboea. Hesiod himself reports having come to Chalcis to sing at King Amphidamas' funeral games and won a bronze tripod as a prize for a poetic contest (*Op.* 650–9). Elaborating further on this testimony, later authors constructed a poetic confrontation opposing Hesiod and Homer that was set in Chalcis (*Contest of Homer and Hesiod*; see Debiasi 2012). This fictional event aside, modern scholars have hypothesized that Homer's epics circulated among a Euboean audience and even that they were first written down at some place on the island (West 1988; Powell 1991: 231–3; Ruijgh 1997; Powell 2004: 30–44; Ruijgh 2004; Wathelet 2007; Janko 2015). These theories rest on linguistic evidence (i.e., the presence of West Ionic elements in Greek epic), the florescence of Euboean communities during the Geometric period, and the Euboeans' early use of the alphabet. As in the case of the birth of the Greek alphabet, the search for the exact moment and place of the writing down of Homer's epics is a vexed issue. However, Euboeans most probably contributed to the diffusion of heroic narratives along the sea lanes on which they sailed. Stories of homecoming (*nostoi*), such as that of Odysseus, especially echo their experiences as navigators, merchants, and colonists (Malkin

1998b). In fact, the first material traces of Greek literature originate from the Euboean sphere in the form of verse inscribed on objects by amateur poets during banquets (see Section 2.10.1).

## 2.12.4. Myths

Euboean sea journeys spread stories in addition to generating new ones, fueled by the discovery of new places, friendly or hostile contact with their inhabitants, and memorable accomplishments on sea and land (Lane Fox 2008: 165–316). This has prompted some scholars to restore a "Euboean spirit" behind the adventures of Odysseus (see Section 2.12.3) or in the stories of Heraclean exploits in the north Aegean and western Mediterranean (Tiverios 2013; Valenza Mele 1979).

Leaving aside the wealth of myths conveyed by Euboean seafarers, what of the mythology of their own island? The truth is, we know very little. Metallurgy features prominently in the exiguous sources bearing on Euboean mythology (see Section 2.8.4.2). A few legendary rulers have come down to us but without their biographies. Some of them bear names that were connected with the "pre-historical" population or geography of the island: Abas, eponymous hero of the legendary Abantes tribe, who took part in the Trojan War (*Il.* 2.536–45) and was considered by the Chalcidians and probably by other Euboeans as their mighty ancestor (on the Abantis tribe in Chalcis, see Section 2.5.3.1); Lelantos, said to have given his name to Euboea's main river; Chalkodon, linked to Chalcis by his very name.[62] The Euboeans also cultivated their own versions of myths that are better known in other regions of Greece. Narcissus, most often perceived as Boeotian, is deeply rooted in Amarynthos; Admetus the Thessalian is also placed at Tamynai (see Section 2.5.3.2). Different traditions situate Oichalia, destroyed by Heracles, in the Peloponnese, in Thessaly, or in Euboea (Breglia 2013: 42–52). Finally, we also hear of a Euboean version of Io's myth (Mitchell 2001). Coherence is not necessarily to be found in such incomplete documentation.

## 2.12.5. Sculpture and Pottery

Except for a few exceptional examples, Archaic sculpture from Chalcis and Eretria is scarcely known, not to mention almost entirely absent from other sites on the island (Touloupa 2002: esp. 77–91; Sapouna-Sakellaraki 2009: esp. 103–6). It is, therefore, difficult to assume the existence of a Euboean school, to say

---

62. Abas: Hes. *Cat.* F 244, 1 Merkelbach-West; Ephorus, *FGrH* 70, F 24. Lelantos: Schol. Callim. *Hymn* 6, 289; Hesychius, *Lexicon* Λ.859. Chalkodon: *Il.* 2.540–1; Hes., *Cat.* F 204, 52–4 Merkelbach-West; Soph. *Phil.* 488–9; Plut. *Mor.* 774c, 1–6; Paus. 9.17.3, 9.19.3.

nothing of a workshop. Based on style, the attribution of single pieces is debated, as some features point toward the Cyclades, others toward Attica, two regions where stone sculpture flourished early in the Archaic period. Euboean cities certainly made the most of this proximity, particularly by importing high-quality marbles, by inviting foreign artists, and by welcoming new ideas and techniques.

In Eretria, an unfinished *korē* and the head of a *kouros* in local marble hint at local production (Touloupa 2002: pl. 65, figs. 175–6). However, in the absence of a signature or literary text, both the identity and the origin of the sculptors working in the city remain open. This is best illustrated by the Amazonomachy from the west pediment of the Doric Temple of Apollo Daphnephoros at Eretria (Touloupa 2002; Persano 2017), which was built toward the end of the sixth century (see Section 2.4.1.3.5) (see Figure 2.15).[63] These masterpieces have been alternately attributed to an Athenian master (Antenor himself or a direct collaborator?), a Cycladic sculptor, and an Eretrian former apprentice from a renowned workshop.

Athena stands imposingly in the center of the pediment, while the main figure, who has been identified as Theseus, is shown in a chariot in the midst of kidnapping the Amazon queen Antiope. (Another chariot group, the occupant of which is unclear, stood on the other side of Athena.) This sculptural group has been seen as reflecting strong Athenian influence and perhaps some form of Athenian patronage, which would be consonant with other evidence for close links between Athens and Eretria in the sixth century (see Section 2.7.4.1). However, the composition of the pediment remains subject to debate, and a reference to an "unknown" Eretrian or Euboean mythological episode should not be discarded.

There is no absolutely firm consensus as to the date of these sculptures. It has been traditionally assumed that they decorated the temple destroyed by the Persians in 490. Some objections have been raised, however (Francis and Vickers 1983; debate summarized in Hall 2014a: 38–47), and the issue deserves further study. Ideologically, an Athenian motif on an Eretrian temple could well fit the post–Persian Wars spirit.

There is at present not sufficient evidence to identify a distinctive local Eretrian and Chalcidian sculptural style, if one ever existed (Langlotz 1927; Duplouy 2018: 44–5). However, the issue of local artistic styles in Euboea can be addressed with Geometric pottery. J. N. Coldstream hypothesized about the link between the diversification of Late Geometric pottery styles and the development of *poleis*. Although he attempted to correlate the most creative and coherent styles with the political autonomy that came into being along with the *polis*, as well as the influential role played by several urban centers, he noticed a "Euboean exception." Whereas, for example, the rivalry between Paros and Naxos seems to have led to the development of consciously different local artistic

---

63. The sculptures from the east pediment are extremely fragmentary.

**FIGURE 2.15.** Marble sculpture showing Theseus and Antiope, originally part of an Amazonomachy, from the west pediment of the Temple of Apollo Daphnephoros; last quarter of the sixth century; height in present form: 1.10 m. Archaeological Museum of Eretria 18053.

styles on those two islands (Croissant 2007), a similar phenomenon cannot be found in central Euboea.[64] In the second half of the eighth century, Chalcis and Eretria (as well as Lefkandi) seem to share a common pottery style despite the fact that they represent distinct, rivalrous polities (Coldstream 1983: 20, 25; see also Snodgrass 1999b: 26). Various hypotheses can be made in order to explain

---

64. New discoveries in Chalcis could potentially change this account.

THE OXFORD HISTORY OF THE ARCHAIC GREEK WORLD

this prominence of a regional style: a centralized organization of pottery production[65] or perhaps the desire to maintain a homogeneous style of pottery that was frequently distributed overseas to trading partners for whom the Euboean identity was more important than a distinction between Eretria and Chalcis. The issue remains open.

## 2.13. *Conclusion*

This study of Chalcis and Eretria will hopefully help the reader situate the two *poleis* in the wider Archaic Greek world. For both polities, the eighth and seventh centuries were a period of great dynamism, marked by close but frequently hostile relations on Euboea and by a sustained participation in Mediterranean trading networks. Chalcis and Eretria developed a peculiar Euboean identity and material culture and shared many traits with maritime-based economies and colonizing forces such as Paros or Corinth. With respect to colonization and maritime trading networks in particular, it appears that at the end of the eighth century, Eretria and Chalcis had little in common with their neighbors Athens and Boeotia.

By contrast, the sixth century marks a period of increased interaction between the two Euboean cities and their continental neighbors, yet with divergent trajectories, reflecting perhaps older divisions. Chalcis, due to its position, appears to have been politically closer to its Boeotian neighbors than it was to Attica. The events of 506 and the harsh resolutions imposed by Athens in Chalcidian territory show a deep hostility between the two *poleis*. On the other hand, Eretria enjoyed what seems to have been a consistently amicable relationship with Athens. The social and cultural links between the two polities' elites, attested in many aspects of Athenian and Eretrian society, created a strong *terrain d'entente*. Political emulation and the fast transmission of political and civic ideals provided additional points of convergence between the two *poleis* in the late Archaic period, and it is fascinating to see how democratic change at Athens and Eretria took place at roughly the same time.

After the Athenian conquest of Chalcis in 506, Eretria for the first time had no serious rival on the island. The sustained rise of Eretria in the sixth century (city walls, coinage, peripteral temple with sculpture, navy) culminated in its participation in the Ionian Rebellion alongside Athens and propelled the city as a regional maritime power—until the arrival of the Persian armada in the summer of 490. One can only imagine what the surviving Eretrians contemplated from their acropolis when the Persian ships set sail for Marathon after the siege. The

---

65. Workshops sourced the same clay in the Lelantine plain (Verdan, Kenzelmann-Pfyffer, and Theurillat 2014: 75–6; Kerschner and Lemos 2014: 191).

news had certainly reached a terror-stricken Athens. At this moment, few would have predicted a successful outcome for the Athenians. But what if the Persians had stopped at Marathon first? The story of Eretria and Euboea could have been quite different. Instead, an era came to an end.

Indeed, the Archaic period closed brutally for Chalcis and Eretria. In less than two decades, which saw the conquest of Chalcis by the Athenians and the fall of Eretria to the Persian armada, the Euboean momentum, stretching from Lefkandi's rise in the 11th to 9th centuries to the increasing domination of Chalcis and Eretria in the seventh and sixth centuries, was lost. When contemplating Chalcis and Eretria in the Archaic period, we can only agree with Broodbank (2013: 535) in seeing the period as "a culmination of much older initiatives rather than a point of origin."

For modern visitors standing on the Eretrian acropolis, the view of the quiet waters of the Euboean Gulf will evoke the voyages of Euboean seafarers to the shores of the north Aegean and southern Italy. The tell of Lefkandi, the cement factories of Chalcis, the ferries to Oropus, and the hill of Paleoekklisies above Amarynthos will call to mind the main actors of Euboea's early archaeohistory. The mountain chains of Attica and Boeotia in the foreground will remind them of the two giants with whom Euboea was variously but always interconnected, from the Late Bronze Age to the Classical period and beyond.

On their way down from the acropolis to the Eretria museum and then to the Temple of Apollo, the visitors will have the best glimpse of Euboean material culture of the Archaic Age. This statement is not intended to do injustice to Chalcis, which has been unfairly treated in modern times; without its adequate archaeological exploration, a big portion of the picture is still missing. It reminds us just how crucial archaeology is for our understanding of the past, and this chapter could not have been written without the results from the excavations of Lefkandi and Eretria.

Moreover, the sixth-century statue of Heracles fighting a centaur from Histiaia (Sapouna-Sakellaraki 2009), the Archaic *kouros* of Metochi (Papavasileiou 1902: 71–2; Fachard 2012: 199), and the participation of Carystians at the Artemisia of Amarynthos (Knoepfler 1972) all serve as powerful reminders that Euboea is much more than Chalcis and Eretria. Although progress has been made in the last decades (especially in the southern part of the island), this "Other Euboea" still remains, in many ways, an unknown land, hindering our understanding of a Euboean "identity," with all the caution that this evolving concept entails. In the sixth century, the inhabitants of Chalcis, Eretria, or Histiaia, while in Euboea, might have called themselves Chalcidians, Eretrians, and Histiaians. In the eighth century, away from home and mostly overseas, however, in storytelling and in interactions with foreigners in the greatly diverse and cosmopolitan trading towns of the wider Mediterranean, they perhaps identified themselves first as "Euboeans."

"The Euboeans are the great discovery of early Greek archaeology since World War II," wrote Anthony Snodgrass in 1994 (Snodgrass 2006: 145). A quarter of a century later, other regions might now claim this title, yet the Euboeans remain an ongoing discovery. Much is to be expected in the future from the promising excavations at Amarynthos, and when long-term, systematic, and targeted archaeological work is conducted at Chalcis, Archaic Euboean archaeohistory will surely be transformed.

## *Guide to Further Reading*

With respect to the bibliography, there is an imbalance between Chalcis and Eretria, as the former has never been systematically investigated from an archaeological point of view, while Eretria is among the most thoroughly excavated sites in Greece.

On Chalcis, the best starting place is found in the guide to the city authored by Kalamara, Kosma, Boukaras, et al. (2015). A survey of the textual evidence bearing on Chalcis can be found in Bakhuizen (1985), but the archaeological overview in that volume should be updated with the latest rescue excavations published in the *Archaiologikon Deltion*. A new, lavishly illustrated guide to the Chalcis archaeological museum was published in 2022 (Simossi 2022).[66]

Regarding Eretria, excavations have been carried out since the 19th century by the Athens Archaeological Society, the American School of Classical Studies at Athens, the Greek Archaeological Service, and the Swiss School of Archaeology in Greece (since 1964). The Swiss School has published so far 25 monographs in the Eretria series (which can be consulted online),[67] two guidebooks (Schefold and Auberson 1972; Ducrey, Fachard, Knoepfler et al. 2004), one exhibition catalog (Martin Pruvot, Reber, and Theurillat 2010 [French]; Kaltsas, Fachard, Psalti et al. 2010 [Greek]), and hundreds of scholarly articles which are compiled in a searchable online database.[68] The results of the Greek excavations are published in the *Archaiologikon Deltion*. Annual reports of the work of the Swiss School at Eretria are published in the journal *Antike Kunst* and are available for free online.[69]

---

66. https://www.latsis-foundation.org/eng/e-library.

67. https://www.esag.swiss/fr/eretria-series/.

68. https://www2.unil.ch/esag/database/login.php?function=show_login_form.

69. https://www.esag.swiss/fr/antike-kunst-reports/.

## Gazetteer

| Name | Map/Figure # | Grid Designation |
|---|---|---|
| Acropolis, Chalcis | Figure 2.1 | --- |
| Acropolis, Eretria | Figure 2.2 | --- |
| | Figure 2.6 | --- |
| Acte | Map 2.10 | inset |
| Aegina | Map 2.3 | E/F3 |
| Agia Paraskevi | Map 2.8 | E3 |
| Agios Ilias hill | Map 2.8 | E3 |
| Agios Ioannis, Chalcis | Figure 2.1 | |
| Agios Stephanos cemetery, Chalcis | Figure 2.1 | |
| Agios Vlassios | Map 2.9 | D2 |
| Agora, Eretria | Figure 2.6 | |
| Aidespos | Map 2.7 | B1 |
| Aigilia | Map 2.9 | C3 |
| Al-Mina | Map 2.5 | |
| Aliveri | Map 2.7 | E2 |
| | Map 2.9 | D3 |
| | Map 2.12 | E3 |
| Aliveri bay | Map 2.9 | D3 |
| Amarynthos | Map 2.2 | D3 |
| | Map 2.6 | D3 |
| | Map 2.7 | D2 |
| | Map 2.8 | G4 |
| | Map 2.12 | D3 |
| Andros | Map 2.4 | C3 |
| Anthedon | Map 2.2 | C3 |
| Aphidna | Map 2.2 | D4 |
| Aphytis | Map 2.10 | B2 |
| Archaic edifice, Sanctuary of Artemis Amarysia | Figure 2.8 | |
| Archaic temple, Sanctuary of Artemis Amarysia | Figure 2.8 | |
| Archaic well, Eretria | Figure 2.6 | |

| Name | Map/Figure # | Grid Designation |
|---|---|---|
| Archampolis valley | Map 2.12 | H5 |
| Arderrika | Map 2.5 | |
| Arethusa cemetery, Chalcis | Figure 2.1 | |
| Arethusa spring, Chalcis | Figure 2.1 | |
| Argos | Map 2.3 | D3 |
| Artemision | Map 2.2 | B1 |
| Athenai Diades | Map 2.2 | A2 |
| Athenaion, Eretria | Figure 2.6 | |
| Athens | Map 2.1 | D5 |
| | Map 2.2 | D5 |
| | Map 2.3 | F3 |
| Attica | Map 2.1 | D4/5 |
| Aulis | Map 2.2 | C3 |
| Avlonari river | Map 2.7 | E2 |
| | Map 2.12 | E2/3 |
| Axios river | Map 2.10 | A2 |
| Bay of Agios Stephanos, Chalcis | Figure 2.1 | |
| Bay of Liani Ammos, Chalcis | Figure 2.1 | |
| Boeotia | Map 2.1 | C4 |
| Boudoron river | Map 2.7 | C1 |
| Bouratza, Eretria | Figure 2.2 | |
| Campania | Map 2.11 | D/E/F2 |
| Canal, Eretria | Figure 2.6 | |
| Cape Kaphireus | Map 2.7 | F3 |
| Cape Lichada | Map 2.1 | B3 |
| | Map 2.7 | A1 |
| Carthage | Map 2.11 | A7 |
| Carystus | Map 2.2 | F4 |
| | Map 2.7 | F3 |
| Catana | Map 2.11 | F6 |
| Ceos | Map 2.4 | C3 |
| Chalcidice peninsula | Map 2.10 | inset |

| Name | Map/Figure # | Grid Designation |
| --- | --- | --- |
| Chalcis | Map 2.2 | C3, inset |
| | Map 2.3 | F2 |
| | Map 2.4 | B2 |
| | Map 2.6 | B3 |
| | Map 2.7 | C2 |
| | Map 2.8 | E4, inset |
| | Map 2.9 | A3 |
| | Map 2.10 | B4 |
| | Map 2.12 | B3 |
| Chios | Map 2.4 | D/E2 |
| Choireai | Map 2.9 | C3 |
| Corcyra | Map 2.11 | J4 |
| Corinth | Map 2.3 | D3 |
| Cumae | Map 2.11 | D/E3 |
| Curium | Map 2.5 | |
| Cyclades | Map 2.1 | G6 |
| Cyme | Map 2.4 | E2 |
| Delos | Map 2.4 | D3 |
| Diakres apo Chalkideon | Map 2.2 | D2 |
| | Map 2.8 | G2 |
| Diakrioi en Euboia | Map 2.2 | D3 |
| | Map 2.9 | C2 |
| Dikaia | Map 2.10 | A2 |
| Dion | Map 2.2 | A2 |
| Dystos | Map 2.7 | E2 |
| | Map 2.9 | D3 |
| East Stoa, Sanctuary of Artemis Amarysia | Figure 2.8 | |
| Eion | Map 2.10 | B2 |
| Elba | Map 2.11 | A1 |
| Eleusis | Map 2.2 | C4 |
| Elis | Map 2.3 | A/B3 |
| Elymnion (modern Limni) | Map 2.2 | B2 |
| | Map 2.8 | C2 |

| Name | Map/Figure # | Grid Designation |
|---|---|---|
| Ephesus | Map 2.4 | F3 |
| Eretria | Map 2.2 | D3 |
| | Map 2.3 | F2 |
| | Map 2.4 | B2 |
| | Map 2.6 | C3 |
| | Map 2.7 | D2 |
| | Map 2.8 | F4 |
| | Map 2.9 | B3 |
| | Map 2.10 | B4 |
| | Map 2.12 | C3 |
| Erythrae | Map 2.4 | E2 |
| Etruria | Map 2.11 | B/C1 |
| Euboea | Map 2.1 | C/D/E3–4 |
| | Map 2.3 | E/F/G1–2 |
| Euboean Gulf | Map 2.1 | C/D/E3–4 |
| | Map 2.2 | B/C/D/E2–4 |
| Euripos | Map 2.2 | inset |
| | Map 2.8 | inset |
| | Figure 2.1 | |
| Francavilla Marittima | Map 2.11 | G4 |
| Gallikos river | Map 2.10 | A1/2 |
| Grynchai (?) | Map 2.2 | E3 |
| | Map 2.9 | E3 |
| Gulf of Naples | Map 2.11 | E3 |
| Gyftika, Chalcis | Figure 2.1 | |
| Haliakmon river | Map 2.10 | A2 |
| Heroon, Eretria | Figure 2.2 | |
| | Figure 2.6 | |
| Histiaia | Map 2.2 | B2 |
| | Map 2.7 | B1 |
| | Map 2.8 | B1 |
| Hollows of Euboea | Map 2.7 | E/F2–3 |
| Hysiae | Map 2.2 | C4 |
| Isthmia | Map 2.3 | D3 |
| Kallimani hill, Chalcis | Figure 2.1 | |

| Name | Map/Figure # | Grid Designation |
|---|---|---|
| Kalogritsa hill, Chalcis | Figure 2.1 | |
| Kamaraki | Map 2.9 | B/C4 |
| Kamares hill, Chalcis | Figure 2.1 | |
| Karabournaki | Map 2.10 | A2 |
| Karavos | Map 2.9 | D3 |
| Kenaion | ancient name for modern Cape Lichada | |
| Kerinthos | Map 2.2 | C2 |
| | Map 2.7 | C1 |
| | Map 2.8 | D2 |
| Kotylaion | Map 2.9 | D2 |
| Kymi | Map 2.7 | E2 |
| | Map 2.9 | D2 |
| Lake of Dystos | Map 2.12 | E3 |
| Lamari | Map 2.8 | G3 |
| Lefkandi | Map 2.2 | D3, inset |
| | Map 2.7 | D2 |
| | Map 2.8 | F4, inset |
| | Map 2.9 | B3 |
| | Map 2.12 | C3 |
| Lelantine plain | Map 2.6 | B/C3 |
| | Map 2.8 | E/F4 |
| | Map 2.12 | B/C3 |
| Lelantos river | Map 2.2 | inset |
| | Map 2.6 | C2 |
| | Map 2.7 | D2 |
| | Map 2/8 | F/G3, inset |
| | Map 2.12 | C2 |
| Leontini | Map 2.11 | E6 |
| Lilas river | modern name for ancient Lelantos river | |
| Limni (modern site of ancient Elymnion) | Map 2.7 | B1 |
| Locris | Map 2.1 | B/C3 |
| Macedonia | Map 2.10 | A2 |

| Name | Map/Figure # | Grid Designation |
|---|---|---|
| Manika | Map 2.8 | E4 |
| Manikia gorge | Map 2.7 | E2 |
| Manikiatis river | Map 2.7 | E2 |
| | Map 2.12 | D/E2 |
| Marathon | Map 2.2 | D4 |
| Megara | Map 2.3 | E3 |
| Mende | Map 2.10 | B3 |
| Mesapios delta | Map 2.7 | C2 |
| Methone | Map 2.10 | A2 |
| Metochi | Map 2.12 | D2 |
| Miletus | Map 2.4 | F3 |
| Mouteri | Map 2.12 | E2 |
| Mt. Dirphys | Map 2.6 | C/D2 |
| | Map 2.7 | D2 |
| | Map 2.8 | G3 |
| | Map 2.9 | C2 |
| | Map 2.12 | D2 |
| Mt. Kandili | Map 2.6 | A1/2 |
| | Map 2.7 | C1/2 |
| | Map 2.8 | D2 |
| Mt. Ochi | Map 2.7 | F3 |
| Mt. Panagaion | Map 2.10 | C2 |
| Mt. Pixaria | Map 2.7 | C1 |
| Mt. Servouni | Map 2.6 | D3 |
| | Map 2.7 | D2 |
| | Map 2.8 | G4 |
| | Map 2.9 | C3 |
| Mt. Skotini | Map 2.7 | D/E2 |
| Mt. Telethrion | Map 2.7 | B1 |
| Mt. Vathrovouni | Figure 2.1 | |
| Naxos (island) | Map 2.4 | D3 |
| Naxos (Sicily) | Map 2.11 | F6, inset |
| Nea Lampsakos | Map 2.8 | inset |
| Neapolis | Map 2.10 | C2 |

| Name | Map/Figure # | Grid Designation |
|---|---|---|
| North Sacrificial Area, Eretria | Figure 2.2 | |
| North Stoa, Sanctuary of Artemis Amarysia | Figure 2.8 | |
| Northeast cemetery, Chalcis | Figure 2.1 | |
| Oichalia | Map 2.2 | E3 |
| | Map 2.9 | D2 |
| Oinoe | Map 2.2 | C4 |
| Olympia | Map 2.3 | B3 |
| Oreos | Map 2.7 | B1 |
| Orontes river | Map 2.5 | |
| Oropus | Map 2.2 | D4 |
| | Map 2.9 | B4 |
| | Map 2.12 | C4 |
| Paleoekklisies hill, Amarynthos | Figure 2.8 | |
| Palioura | Map 2.8 | F3 |
| Pallene | Map 2.10 | inset |
| Paros | Map 2.4 | D3 |
| Pass of Derveni | Map 2.7 | C1 |
| Pei Dokou | Map 2.8 | inset |
| Petaliai islands | Map 2.1 | E4/5 |
| | Map 2.7 | E3/4 |
| Pezonisi | Figure 2.6 | |
| Plain of Eretria | Map 2.6 | C3 |
| Plataea | Map 2.2 | B4 |
| Pharsalus | Map 2.1 | A2 |
| Philagra | Map 2.2 | F4 |
| Phthiotis | Map 2.1 | A3 |
| Pithecusae | Map 2.11 | D3 |
| Pontecagnano | Map 2.11 | E3 |
| Porthmos harbor | Map 2.9 | D3 |
| Posideion | Map 2.2 | B/C1–2 |
| Psachna | Map 2.7 | C2 |
| | Map 2.12 | B2 |

| Name | Map/Figure # | Grid Designation |
| --- | --- | --- |
| Psachna plain | Map 2.6 | B/C2 |
| | Map 2.8 | F3 |
| Rhegium | Map 2.11 | inset |
| Rhodes | Map 2.4 | F/G4–5 |
| Rovies | Map 2.8 | C2 |
| Salamis | Map 2.2 | C5 |
| Salganeus | Map 2.2 | C3 |
| Samos | Map 2.4 | E3 |
| Sanctuary of Apollo Daphnephoros, Eretria | Figure 2.2 | |
| | Figure 2.6 | |
| Sanctuary of Artemis Amarysia | Map 2.9 | C3 |
| Sarandopotamos river | Map 2.6 | D3 |
| | Map 2.7 | D2 |
| Sardis | Map 2.4 | G2 |
| Seaside Necropolis, Eretria | Figure 2.2 | |
| | Figure 2.6 | |
| Sicyon | Map 2.3 | D3 |
| Sindus | Map 2.10 | A2 |
| Sithonia | Map 2.10 | inset |
| Sparta | Map 2.3 | C4 |
| Sporades | Map 2.1 | D/E2–3 |
| | Map 2.4 | B/C1–2 |
| | Map 2.10 | B/C3–4 |
| Steni Diryphys | Map 2.6 | C/D2 |
| | Map 2.7 | D2 |
| Strait of Messina | Map 2.11 | inset |
| Strait of Otrano | Map 2.11 | I/J3–4 |
| Styra | Map 2.2 | E4 |
| | Map 2.7 | E3 |
| | Map 2.9 | E5 |

| Name | Map/Figure # | Grid Designation |
|---|---|---|
| Susa | Map 2.5 | |
| Sybaris | Map 2.11 | G4 |
| Tamynai | Map 2.2 | E3 |
| | Map 2.9 | D2/3 |
| Tanagra | Map 2.2 | C4 |
| Temenos (?) | Map 2.9 | B3 |
| Teos | Map 2.4 | E2 |
| Tharrounia | Map 2.9 | C2 |
| Thebes | Map 2.1 | C4 |
| | Map 2.2 | B4 |
| | Map 2.3 | E2 |
| Thermaic Gulf | Map 2.10 | A2 |
| Thesmophoreion, Eretria | Figure 2.6 | |
| Thessaly | Map 2.1 | A1 |
| | Map 2.10 | A3 |
| Thrace | Map 2.10 | B1/2 |
| Tinos | Map 2.4 | D3 |
| Torone | Map 2.10 | B2/3 |
| Triada | Map 2.8 | F3 |
| Tyrrhenian Sea | Map 2.11 | C/D/E4 |
| Vassiliko | Map 2.8 | inset |
| Viglatouri | modern name for site of ancient Oichalia | |
| Vourlaki | Map 2.8 | inset |
| Vrachos | Map 2.8 | inset |
| Vrisakia | Map 2.8 | E3 |
| West Gate, Eretria | Figure 2.6 | |
| Xiropotamos river | Map 2.7 | B1 |
| Zagora | Map 2.4 | C3 |
| Zancle | Map 2.11 | inset |

## BIBLIOGRAPHY

Akurgal, M., D. Hertel, M. Kerschner, et al. 2002. *Töpferzentren der Ostägäis: archäometrische und archäologische Untersuchungen zur mykenischen, geometrischen und archaischen Keramik aus Fundorten in Westkleinasien*. Ergänzungshefte zu den *Jahresheften des Österreichischen Archäologischen Institutes in Wien* 3. Vienna: Österreichisches Archäologisches Institut.

Altherr-Charon, A., and F. Lasserre. 1981. "Héraclès à Érétrie (Une nouvelle inscription agonistique archaïque)." *Études de lettres* 4: 25–35.

Andreiomenou, A. 1960. "Εὔβοια." *Αρχαιολογικόν Δελτίον* 16: 149–53.

Andreiomenou, A. 1972. "Ἔρευναι καὶ τυχαῖα εὑρήματα ἐν τῇ πόλει καὶ τῇ ἐπαρχίᾳ Χαλκίδος." *Αρχαιολογικόν Δελτίον* 27 A: 171–84.

Antonaccio, C. M. 1995. *An Archaeology of Ancestors: Tomb Cult and Hero Cult in Early Iron Age Greece*. Lanham, MD: Rowman & Littlefield.

Aravantinos, V. L. 2006. "A New Inscribed Kioniskos from Thebes." *Annual of the British School at Athens* 101: 369–77.

Arjona-Perez, M. 2017. "Η Αρέθουσα, ο Ποσειδώνας και η Ήρα. Ανάλυση και ερμηνεία ενός χαλκιδικού μύθου." In *An Island between Two Worlds: The Archaeology of Euboea from Prehistory to Byzantine Times, Proceedings of International Conference, Eretria, 12–14 July 2013*, edited by Ž. Tankosić, F. Mavridis, and M. Kosma, 403–8. Papers and Monographs from the Norwegian Institute at Athens 6. Athens: Norwegian Institute at Athens.

Auberson, P. E. 1968. *Temple d'Apollon Daphnéphoros: Architecture*. Eretria I. Bern: Francke.

Auberson, P. E. 1974. "La reconstruction du Daphnéphoréion d'Érétrie." *Antike Kunst* 17: 60–8.

Auberson, P. E. 1975a. "Chalcis, Lefkandi, Érétrie au VIIIe siècle." In *Contribution à l'étude de la société et de la colonisation eubéennes*, 9–14. Cahiers du Centre Jean Bérard 2. Naples: Centre Jean Bérard.

Auberson, P. E. 1975b. "A propos d'un puits public à Érétrie." *Bulletin de correspondance hellénique* 99: 789–99.

Bakhuizen, S. C. 1976a. *Chalcis-in-Euboea: Iron and Chalcidians Abroad*. Studies of the Dutch Archaeological and Historical Society 5. Leiden: Brill.

Bakhuizen, S. C. 1976b. "Ο Μέγας Κίων: The Monument for Kleomachos at Chalcis-in-Euboea." In *Festoen opgedragen aan A.N. Zadoks-Josephus Jitta bij haar zeventigste verjaardag*, edited by J. S. Boersma, 43–8. Scripta archaeologica Groningana 6. Groningen: Bussum.

Bakhuizen, S. C. 1985. *Studies in the Topography of Chalcis on Euboea: A Discussion of the Sources*. Studies of the Dutch Archaeological and Historical Society 11. Leiden: Brill.

Baladié, R., ed. 1996. *Strabon: Géographie, Tome VI (Livre IX)*. Paris: Les Belles Lettres.

Balcer, J. M. 1989. "Ionia and Sparda under the Achaemenid Empire, the 6th and 5th Centuries BC." In *Le tribut dans l'empire perse: Actes de la table ronde de Paris, 12–13 décembre 1986*, edited by P. Briant and C. Herrenschmidt, 1–28. Travaux de l'Institut d'Études Iraniennes de l'Université de la Sorbonne Nouvelle 13. Paris: Peeters.

Bartoněk, A., and G. Buchner. 1995. "Die ältesten griechischen Inschriften von Pithekoussai (2. Hälfte des VIII. bis 1. Hälfte des VII. Jhs." *Die Sprache: Zeitschrift für Sprachwissenschaft* 37: 129–231.

Bechtel, F. 1900. "Das Wort ἵππος in den eretrischen Personennamen." *Hermes* 15: 226–331.

Beck, H. Forthcoming. "Thebes." In *The Oxford History of the Archaic Greek World*, edited by P. Cartledge and P. Christesen, *The Oxford History of the Archaic Greek World, Volume 6*. New York: Oxford University Press.

Bérard, C. 1970. *L'Hérôon à la Porte de l'Ouest*. Eretria III. Bern: Francke.

Bérard, C. 1971. "Architecture érétrienne et mythologie delphique." *Antike Kunst* 14: 59–73.

Bérard, C. 1972. "Le sceptre du prince." *Museum Helveticum* 29: 219–27.

Bérard, C. 1978. "Topographie et urbanisme de l'Érétrie archaïque: L'Hérôon." In *Eretria VI*, 89–95. Eretria VI. Bern: Francke.

Bérard, C. 1982. "Récupérer la mort du prince: Héroïsation et formation de la cité." In *La mort, les morts dans les sociétés anciennes*, edited by G. Gnoli and J.-P. Vernant, 89–105. Cambridge: Cambridge University Press.

Bershadsky, N. 2018a. "Chariots on the Lelantine Plain and the Art of Taunting the Losers, Part 1: Riding into the Reenactment." *Classical Inquiries: Studies on the Ancient World from the Center for Hellenic Studies* 2018.05.17. https://classical-inquiries.chs.harvard.edu/chariots-on-the-lelantine-plain-and-the-art-of-taunting-the-losers/.

Bershadsky, N. 2018b. "Impossible Memories of the Lelantine War." *Mètis* 16: 191–213.

Besios, M., Y. Z. Tzifopoulos, and A. Kotsonas. 2012. *Μεθώνη Πιερίας Ι: Επιγραφές, χαράγματα και εμπορικά σύμβολα στη γεωμετρική και αρχαϊκή κεραμική από το 'Υπόγειο' της Μεθώνης Πιερίας στη Μακεδονία*. Thessaloniki: Κέντρο Ελληνικής Γλώσσας.

Blaineau, A. 2015. *Le cheval de guerre en Grèce ancienne*. Rennes: Presses Universitaires de Rennes.

Blakely, S. 2006. *Myth, Ritual and Metallurgy in Ancient Greece and Recent Africa*. Cambridge: Cambridge University Press.

Blandin, B. 2007. *Les pratiques funéraires d'époque géométrique à Érétrie: Espace des vivants, demeures des morts*. 2 vols. Eretria XVII. Gollion: Infolio.

Boardman, J. 1952. "Pottery from Eretria." *Annual of the British School at Athens* 47: 1–48.

Boardman, J. 1957. "Early Euboean Pottery and History." *Annual of the British School at Athens* 52: 1–29.

Boardman, J. 1980. *The Greeks Overseas: Their Early Colonies and Trade*. 3rd ed. London: Thames & Hudson.

Boardman, J. 1982. "The Islands. Euboea." In *The Cambridge Ancient History, Volume III, Part 1: The Prehistory of the Balkans, the Middle East and the Aegean World, Tenth to Eighth Centuries B.C.*, edited by J. Boardman, I. E. S. Edwards, N. G. L. Hammond, et al., 754–65. Cambridge: Cambridge University Press.

Boardman, J. 1990. "Al Mina and History." *Oxford Journal of Archaeology* 9: 169–90.

Boardman, J. 1998. *Early Greek Vase Painting: 11th–6th Centuries BC*. London: Thames & Hudson.

Boardman, J. 2006. "Early Euboean Settlements in the Carthage Area." *Oxford Journal of Archaeology* 25: 195–200.

Boffa, G. 2016. "'Prima colonizzazione' e 'primo alfabeto': Osservazioni su soggetti e modalità dell'interazione culturale fra le più antiche presenze greche in occidente e l'ambiente italico in riferimento alla scrittura." In *Contexts of Early Colonization, Acts of the Conference "Contextualizing Early Colonization: Archaeology, Sources, Chronology and Interpretative Models between Italy and the Mediterranean,"* edited by L. Donnellan, V. Nizzo, and G.-J. Burgers, 335–49. Papers of the Royal Netherlands Institute in Rome 64. Rome: Palombi Editori.

Breglia, L. 2013. "Titani, Cureti, Eracle: Mitopoiesi euboica e guerra lelantina." In *Tra mare e continente: L'isola di Eubea*, edited by C. Bearzot and F. Landucci, 17–65. Milan: Vita e Pensiero.

Brenne, S. 2002. "Die Ostraka (487–ca. 416 v. Chr.) als Testimonien." In *Ostrakismos–Testimonien I: Die Zeugnisse antiker Autoren, der Inschriften und Ostraka über das Athenische Scherbengericht aus vorhellenistischer Zeit (487–322 v. Chr.)*, edited by P. Siewert, 36–166. Stuttgart: Franz Steiner Verlag.

Bresson, A. 2014. "The Ancient World: A Climatic Challenge." In *Quantifying the Greco–Roman Economy and Beyond*, edited by F. de Callataÿ, 43–62. Bari: Edipuglia.

Bresson, A. 2016. *The Making of the Ancient Greek Economy: Institutions, Markets, and Growth in the City-States*. Princeton, NJ: Princeton University Press.

Bresson, A. 2017. "Money Exchange and the Economics of Inequality in the Ancient Greek and Roman World." In *Économie et inégalité: Ressources, échanges et pouvoir dans l'antiquité classique*, edited by P. Derron, 271–316. Entretiens sur l'antiquité classique 63. Vandoeuvres: Fondation Hardt.

Broodbank, C. 2013. *The Making of the Middle Sea: A History of the Mediterranean from the Beginning to the Emergence of the Classical World*. London: Thames & Hudson.

Brunner, M., and M. Spoerri Butcher. 2010. "Monnaies et monnayage à Érétrie." In *Cité sous terre: Des archéologues suisses explorent la cité grecque d'Érétrie, Exposition présentée à Bâle, à l'Antikenmuseum Basel und Sammlung Ludwig, du 22 septembre 2010 au 30 janvier 2011*, edited by C. Martin Pruvot, K. Reber, and T. Theurillat, 145–9. Gollion: Infolio.

Brunt, P. A. 1966. "Athenian Settlements Abroad in the Fifth Century B.C." In *Ancient Society and Institutions: Studies Presented to Victor Ehrenberg on His 75th Birthday*, edited by E. Badian, 71–92. Oxford: Blackwell.

Buchner, G., and D. Ridgway. 1993. *Pithekoussai I, La necropoli: Tombe 1–723 scavate dal 1952 al 1961*. 2 vols. *Monumenti antichi* 55, Serie monografica 4. Rome: Bretschneider.

Cairns, F. 1984. "XPHMATA DOKlMA: IG XII, 9, 1273 and 1274 and the Early Coinage of Eretria." *Zeitschrift für Papyrologie und Epigraphik* 54: 145–64.

Cairns, F. 1991. "The 'Laws of Eretria' (IG XII.9 1273 and 1274): Epigraphic, Legal, Historical, and Political Aspects." *Phoenix* 45: 296–313.

Calligas, P. 1990. "Η Πρώιμη αρχαία Χαλκίδα." In *Διεθνές Επιστημονικό Συνέδριο "Η πόλη της Χαλκίδας," Χαλκίδα, 24–27 Σεπτεμβρίου 1987*, 51–4. Athens: Εταιρεία Ευβοϊκών Σπουδών.

Cambitoglou, A., A. Birchall, J. J. Coulton, et al. 1988. *Zagora 2, Excavation of a Geometric Town on the Island of Andros: Excavation Season 1969, Study Season 1969–1970*. Athens: Η εν Αθήναις Αρχαιολογική Εταιρεία.

Camp, J. M. II. 1986. *The Athenian Agora: Excavations at the Heart of Classical Athens*. London: Thames & Hudson.

Camp, J. M. II. 1998. *Horses and Horsemanship in the Athenian Agora*. Excavations of the Athenian Agora Picturebook 24. Athens: American School of Classical Studies at Athens.

Chankowski, A. S. 1993. "Date et circonstances de l'institution de l'éphébie à Érétrie." *Dialogues d'histoire ancienne* 19: 17–44.

Charalambidou, X. 2006. "Συμβολή στην τοπογραφία της Ερέτριας των αρχαϊκών χρόνων." In *Αρχαιολογικό Έργο Θεσσαλίας και Στερεάς Ελλάδας, Conference Held in Volos (27.2–2.3 2003)*, edited by A. Mazarakis Ainian, 993–1018. Volos: Εργαστήριο Αρχαιολογίας Πανεπιστημίου Θεσσαλίας.

Charalambidou, X. 2017a. "Euboea and the Euboean Gulf Region: Pottery in Context." In *Interpreting the Seventh Century BC: Tradition and Innovation, Proceedings of the International Colloquium Conference Held at the British School at Athens, 9th–11th December 2011*, edited by X. Charalambidou and C. A. Morgan, 123–49. Oxford: Archaeopress.

Charalambidou, X. 2017b. "Viewing Euboea in Relation to Its Colonies and Relevant Sites in Northern Greece and Italy." In *Regional Stories: Towards a New Perception of the Early Greek World, Acts of an International Symposium in Honour of Professor Jan Bouzek, Volos 18–21 June 2015*, edited by A. Mazarakis Ainian, A. Alexandridou, and X. Charalambidou, 85–126. Volos: University of Thessaly Press.

Charalambidou, X. 2020. "Chalcidian Deposits and Their Role in Reconstructing Production and Consumption Practices and the Function of Space in Early Iron Age and Archaic Chalcis: Some First Thoughts." In *Euboica II: Pithekoussai and Euboea between East and West, Acts of the International Conference, Lacco Ameno,*

*Ischia, 14–17 May 2018, Volume I,* edited by T. E. Cinquantaquattro and M. D'Acunto, 55–72. *AION Annali di archeologia e storia antica* 27. Naples: Istituto Universitario Orientale di Napoli.

Clay, J. S., I. Malkin, and Y. Z. Tzifopoulos, eds. 2017. *Panhellenes at Methone: Graphê in Late Geometric and Protoarchaic Methone, Macedonia (ca 700 BCE).* Trends in Classics Supplementary Volume 44. Berlin: Walter de Gruyter.

Coldstream, J. N. 1983. "The Meaning of the Regional Styles in the Eighth Century B.C." In *The Greek Renaissance of the Eighth Century B.C.: Tradition and Innovation, Proceedings of the Second International Symposium at the Swedish Institute in Athens, 1–5 June, 1981,* edited by R. Hägg, 17–25. Skrifter Utgivna av Svenska Institutet i Athen 4° 30. Stockholm: Paul Åströms Förlag.

Coldstream, J. N. 1998. "The First Exchanges between Euboeans and Phoenicians: Who Took the Initiative?" In *Mediterranean Peoples in Transition, Thirteenth to Early Tenth Centuries BCE, in Honor of Professor Trude Dothan,* edited by T. K. Dothan, S. Gitin, A. Mazar, et al., 353–60. Jerusalem: Israel Exploration Society.

Coldstream, J. N. 2003. *Geometric Greece: 900–700 BC.* 2nd ed. University Paperbacks 680. London: Routledge.

Coldstream, J. N. 2008. *Greek Geometric Pottery: A Survey of Ten Local Styles and Their Chronology.* 2nd ed. Exeter: Bristol Phoenix Press.

Coulton, J. J. 2002. *The Fort at Phylla, Vrachos: Excavations and Researches at a Late Archaic Fort in Central Euboea.* British School at Athens Supplementary Volume 33. London: British School at Athens.

Crielaard, J. P. 1996. "How the West Was Won: Euboeans vs. Phoenicians." In *Akten des Internationalen Kolloquiums "Interactions in the Iron Age: Phoenicians, Greeks and the Indigenous Peoples of the Western Mediterranean" in Amsterdam am 26. und 27. März 1992,* 235–49. Mainz: Philipp von Zabern.

Crielaard, J. P. 1998. "Cult and Death in Early 7th-Century Euboea: The Aristocracy and the Polis." In *Nécropoles et pouvoir, Actes du colloque Théories de la nécropole antique (Lyon, janvier 1995),* edited by S. Marchegay, 43–58. Lyon: Maison de l'Orient et de la Méditerranée Jean Pouilloux.

Crielaard, J. P. 2006. "*Basileis* at Sea: Elites and External Contacts in the Euboean Gulf Region from the End of the Bronze Age to the Beginning of the Iron Age." In *Ancient Greece: From the Mycenaean Palaces to the Age of Homer,* edited by S. Deger-Jalkotzy and I. S. Lemos, 271–97. Edinburgh Leventis Studies 3. Edinburgh: Edinburgh University Press.

Crielaard, J. P. 2007. "Eretria's West Cemetery Revisited: Burial Plots, Social Structure and Settlement Organization during the 8th and 7th Centuries BC." In *Oropos and Euboea in the Early Iron Age: Acts of an International Round Table, University of Thessaly, June 18–20, 2004,* edited by A. Mazarakis Ainian, 169–94. Volos: University of Thessaly Press.

Crielaard, J. P. 2011. "The '*Wanax* to *Basileus* Model' Reconsidered: Authority and Ideology after the Collapse of the Mycenaean Palaces." In *The "Dark Ages" Revisited, Acts of an International Symposium in Memory of William D. E. Coulson, University of Thessaly, Volos, 14–17 June 2007*, edited by A. Mazarakis Ainian, 1: 83–112. 2 vols. Volos: University of Thessaly Press.

Croissant, F. 2007. "Style et identité dans l'art grec archaïque." *Pallas* 73: 27–37.

Cullen, T., L. E. Talalay, D. R. Keller, et al. 2013. *The Prehistory of the Paximadi Peninsula, Euboea*. Prehistory Monographs 40. Philadelphia: Institute of Aegean Prehistory Academic Press.

D'Acunto, M. Forthcoming. "Pithecusae and Cumae." In *The Oxford History of the Archaic Greek World*, edited by P. Cartledge and P. Christesen, In *The Oxford History of the Archaic Greek World*, Volume 3. New York: Oxford University Press.

D'Agostino, B. 2006–2008. "The First Greeks in Italy." In *Greek Colonisation: An Account of Greek Colonies and Other Settlements Overseas*, edited by G. R. Tsetskhladze, 1: 201–37. 2 vols. Leiden: Brill.

D'Agostino, B. 2014. "The Archaeological Background of the Analysed Pendent Semicircle Skyphoi from Pontecagnano." In *Archaeometric Analyses of Euboean and Euboean Related Pottery: New Results and Their Interpretations, Proceedings of the Round Table Conference Held at the Austrian Archaeological Institute in Athens, 15 and 16 April 2011*, edited by M. Kerschner and I. S. Lemos, 181–90. Vienna: Österreichisches Archäologisches Institut.

Debiasi, A. 2012. "Homer ἀγωνιστής in Chalcis." In *Homeric Contexts: Neoanalysis and the Interpretation of Oral Poetry*, edited by F. Montanari, A. Rengakos, and C. C. Tsagalis, 471–500. Berlin: Walter de Gruyter.

Denoyelle, M., and M. Iozzo. 2009. *La céramique grecque d'Italie méridionale et de Sicile: Productions coloniales et apparentées du VIIIe siècle au IIIe siècle av. J.–C.* Paris: Picard.

De Polignac, F. 1995. *Cults, Territory, and the Origins of the Greek City-State*. Translated by J. Lloyd. Chicago: University of Chicago Press.

Descoeudres, J.-P. 2002. "Al Mina across the Great Divide." *Mediterranean Archaeology* 15: 49–72.

Descoeudres, J.-P. 2006–2007. "Euboean Pottery Overseas (10th to 7th centuries BC)." In *Proceedings of the 25th Anniversary Symposium of the Australian Archaeological Institute at Athens, 2005*, edited by J.-P. Descoeudres and S. Paspalas, 3–24. *Mediterranean Archaeology* 19–20 (2006–2007). Sydney: University of Sydney.

De Souza, P. 1998. "Towards Thalassocracy? Archaic Greek Naval Developments." In *Archaic Greece: New Approaches and New Evidence*, edited by H. van Wees and N. Fisher, 271–94. London: Classical Press of Wales.

Dillon, M. 1997. *Pilgrims and Pilgrimage in Ancient Greece*. London: Routledge.

Dittenberger, W., and K. Purgold. 1896. *Die Inschriften von Olympia*. Olympia. Die Ergebnisse der von dem Deutschen Reich veranstalteten Ausgrabung, im *Aufträge des Königlich Preussischen Ministers der Geistlichen, Unterrichts– und Medicinal–Angelegenheiten* Textband 5. Berlin: Asher.

Domergue, C. 2008. *Les mines antiques: La production des métaux aux époques grecque et romaine.* Paris: Picard.

Domínguez, A. J. 2006–2008. "Greeks in Sicily." In *Greek Colonisation: An Account of Greek Colonies and Other Settlements Overseas,* edited by G. R. Tsetskhladze, 1: 253–357. 2 vols. Leiden: Brill.

Dubois, L. 2015. "Philologie et dialectologie grecques." *Annuaire de l'École Pratique des Hautes Études (EPHE), Section des Sciences Historiques et Philologiques* 146: 54–8.

Ducrey, P., and C. Brélaz. 2007. "Réalités et images de la fronde en Grèce ancienne." In *Les armes dans l'antiquité: De la technique à l'imaginaire, Actes du colloque international du SEMA, Montpellier, 20 et 22 mars 2003,* edited by P. Sauzeau and T. van Compernolle, 325–51. Montpellier: Presses Universitaires de la Méditerranée.

Ducrey, P., S. Fachard, D. Knoepfler, et al. 2004. *Érétrie: Guide de la cité antique.* Gollion: Infolio.

Duplouy, A. 2003. "Les Eupatrides d'Athènes, 'nobles défenseurs de leur patrie.'" *Cahiers du Centre Gustave Glotz* 14: 7–22.

Duplouy, A. 2006. *Le prestige des élites: Recherches sur les modes de reconnaissance sociale en Grèce entre les Xe et Ve siècles avant J.-C.* Histoire 77. Paris: Les Belles Lettres.

Duplouy, A. 2018. "Pathways to Archaic Citizenship." In *Defining Citizenship in Archaic Greece,* edited by A. Duplouy and R. Brock, 1–50. Oxford: Oxford University Press.

Duplouy, A. 2022. "Hippotrophia as Citizen Behaviour in Archaic Greece." In *From Homer to Solon: Continuity and Change in Archaic Greek Society,* edited by J. C. Bernhardt and M. Canevaro, 139–61. *Mnemosyne* Supplement 454. Leiden: Brill.

Esposito, A. 2012. "La question des implantations grecques et des contacts précoloniaux en Italie du Sud: Entre *emporia* et *apoikiai.*" *Pallas* 89: 97–121.

Fachard, S. 2004. "L'enceinte urbaine d'Érétrie: un état de la question." *Antike Kunst* 47: 91–109.

Fachard, S. 2012. *La défense du territoire d'Érétrie: Étude de la chora et de ses fortifications.* Eretria XXI. Gollion: Infolio.

Fachard, S. 2016. "Modelling the Territories of Attic Demes: A Computational Approach." In *The Archaeology of Greece and Rome: Studies in Honour of Anthony Snodgrass,* edited by J. L. Bintliff and N. K. Rutter, 192–222. Edinburgh: Edinburgh University Press.

Fachard, S. 2019. "Common Denominators? The Emergence of Territorial Organization in Athens and Eretria." In *From Hippias to Kallias: Greek Art in Athens and Beyond, 527–449 B.C., Proceedings of an International Conference Held at the Acropolis Museum, Athens, May 19–20, 2017,* edited by O. Palagia and E. P. Sioumpara, 160–9. Athens: Acropolis Museum.

Fachard, S. 2022. "Fieldwork of the Swiss School of Archaeology in Greece 2021." *Antike Kunst* 65: 1-23.

Fachard, S. and E. M. Harris, eds. 2021. *The Destruction of Cities in the Ancient Greek World. Integrating the Archaeological and Literary Evidence.* Cambridge: Cambridge University Press.

Fachard, S., D. Knoepfler, K. Reber, et al. 2017. "Recent Research at the Sanctuary of Artemis Amarysia in Amarynthos (Euboea)." *Archaeological Reports* 63: 167–80.

Fachard, S., A. Simossi, T. Krapf, et al. 2022. "The Artemision at Amarynthos: The 2021 Season." *Antike Kunst* 65: 128–36.

Fachard, S., T. Theurillat, A. Psalti, et al. 2017. "La nécropole du canal à Érétrie: Topographie et inscriptions." *Bulletin de correspondance hellénique* 141: 141–226.

Fehling, D. 1979. "Zwei Lehrstücke über Pseudo-Nachrichten (Homeriden, Lelantischer Krieg)." *Rheinisches Museum für Philologie* 122: 193–210.

Finné, M., K. Holmgren, H. S. Sundqvist, et al. 2011. "Climate in the Eastern Mediterranean, and Adjacent Regions, during the Past 6000 Years—A Review." *Journal of Archaeological Science* 38: 3153–73.

Flacelière, R. 1948. "Thémistocle, les Érétriens et le calmar." *Revue des études anciennes* 50: 211–17.

Francis, E. D., and M. J. Vickers. 1983. "Signa Priscae Artis: Eretria and Siphnos." *Journal of Hellenic Studies* 103: 49–67.

Frederiksen, R. 2011. *Greek City Walls of the Archaic Period, 900–480 BC*. Oxford: Oxford University Press.

Gagarin, M. 1986. *Early Greek Law*. Berkeley: University of California Press.

Gehrke, H.-J. 1994. "Mutmaßungen über die Grenzen von Chalkis." In *Stuttgarter Kolloquium zur Historischen Geographie des Altertums 4, 1990*, edited by E. Olshausen and H. Sonnabend, 335–45. Amsterdam: Adolf M. Hakkert.

Georgopoulou Melanidi, M., and N. Papadakis. 1974. "Αρχαϊκά και μεσαιωνικά ευρήματα εν Χαλκίδι." *Athens Annals of Archaeology* 7: 35–43.

Gerhard, Y. 2011. "La 'coupe de Nestor': Reconstitution du vers 1." *Zeitschrift für Papyrologie und Epigraphik* 176: 7–9.

Gex, K. 1993. *Rotfigurige und weissgrundige Keramik*. Eretria IX. Lausanne: Payot.

Ghilardi, M., M. Colleu, K. P. Pavlopoulos, et al. 2013. "Geoarchaeology of Ancient Aulis (Boeotia, Central Greece): Human Occupation and Holocene Landscape Changes." *Journal of Archaeological Science* 40: 2071–83.

Ghilardi, M., S. Fachard, K. P. Pavlopoulos, et al. 2012. "Reconstructing Mid-to-Recent Holocene Paleoenvironments in the Vicinity of Ancient Amarynthos (Euboea, Greece)." *Geodinamica Acta* 25: 38–51.

Ghilardi, M., T. Kinnaird, K. Kouli, et al. 2022. "Reconstructing the Fluvial History of the Lilas River (Euboea Island, Central West Aegean Sea) from the Mycenaean

Times to the Ottoman Period." *Geosciences* 12, no. 5: 204. https://doi.org/10.3390/geosciences12050204.

Ghilardi, M., S. Müller Celka, T. Theurillat, et al. 2016. "Évolution des paysages et histoire de l'occupation d'Érétrie (Eubée, Grèce) du Bronze ancien à l'époque romaine." In *Géoarchéologie des îles de Méditerranée*, edited by M. Ghilardi, 149–63. Paris: CNRS Editions.

Graham, A. J. 1982. "The Colonial Expansion of Greece." In *The Cambridge Ancient History, Volume III, Part 3: The Expansion of the Greek World, Eighth to Sixth Centuries B.C.*, edited by J. Boardman and N. G. L. Hammond, 83–162. 2nd ed. Cambridge: Cambridge University Press.

Gray, V. 2007. "Structure and Significance (5.55–69)." In *Reading Herodotus: A Study of the Logoi in Book 5 of Herodotus' Histories*, edited by E. K. Irwin and E. Greenwood, 202–21. Cambridge: Cambridge University Press.

Hall, J. M. 2006–2008. "Foundation Stories." In *Greek Colonisation: An Account of Greek Colonies and Other Settlements Overseas*, edited by G. R. Tsetskhladze, 2: 383–426. 2 vols. Leiden: Brill.

Hall, J. M. 2007. "Polis, Community, and Ethnic Identity." In *The Cambridge Companion to Archaic Greece*, edited by H. A. Shapiro, 40–60. Cambridge: Cambridge University Press.

Hall, J. M. 2014a. *Artifact and Artifice: Classical Archaeology and the Ancient Historian*. Chicago: University of Chicago Press.

Hall, J. M. 2014b. *A History of the Archaic Greek World, ca. 1200–479 BCE*. 2nd ed. Chichester, UK: Wiley-Blackwell.

Hansen, M. H. 1985. *Demography and Democracy: The Number of Athenian Citizens in the Fourth Century B.C.* Herning: Systime.

Hansen, M. H. 2006. *Studies in the Population of Aigina, Athens and Eretria*. Copenhagen: Kongelige Danske Videnskabernes Selskab.

Harris, E. M. 2006. *Democracy and the Rule of Law in Classical Athens: Essays on Law, Society, and Politics*. New York: Cambridge University Press.

Herrmann, P. 1998. *Inschriften von Milet Teil 2: Inschriften n. 407–1019*. Milet 6.2. Berlin: Walter de Gruyter.

Heymans, E. D. 2021. *The Origins of Money in the Iron Age Mediterranean World*. Cambridge: Cambridge University Press.

Hornblower, S. 1997. "Thucydides and 'Chalkidic' Torone (IV.110.1)." *Oxford Journal of Archaeology* 16: 177–86.

Howe, T. 2008. *Pastoral Politics: Animals, Agriculture and Society in Ancient Greece*. Claremont, CA: Regina Books.

Huber, S. 2003. *L'aire sacrificielle au nord du Sanctuaire d'Apollon Daphnéphoros: Un rituel des époques géométrique et archaïque*. Eretria XIV. Gollion: Infolio.

Huber, S. 2007. "Un mystère résolu: Athéna sur l'acropole d'Érétrie." *Antike Kunst* 50: 119–29.

Huber, S. 2012. "Pour une archéologie des cultes à Érétrie." In *30 Αρχαιολογικό Έργο Θεσσαλίας και Στερεάς Ελλάδας, Conference Held in Volos (12.3–15.3.2009)*, edited by A. Mazarakis Ainian, 845–61. Volos: Εργαστήριο Αρχαιολογίας Πανεπιστημίου Θεσσαλίας.

Huber, S. 2013. "Le cratère, l'hydrie et la cruche à haut col: Des céramiques au service des premiers rituels à Érétrie (Grèce)." In *La céramique dans les contextes rituels: Fouiller et comprendre les gestes des anciens, Table Ronde UMR 6566 CReAAH – Laboratoire LAHM, Université de Rennes 2, 16–17 juin 2010*, edited by M. Tuffreau–Libre and M. Denti, 75–93. Rennes: Presses Universitaires de Rennes.

Huber, S., and P. Maillard. 2015. "Cavaliers et dédicantes: Les terres cuites de l'Athénaion et la communauté civique d'Érétrie." In *Figurines en contexte: Iconographie et fonction(s), Actes du XXXVe Symposium International organisé par Halma–Ipel – UMR 8164 (Université Charles-de-Gaulle Lille 3, 7–8 décembre 2011, Lille)*, edited by S. Haxhi–Huysecom and A. Muller, 157–78. Villeneuve d'Ascq: Presses Universitaires du Septentrion.

Hurter, S. 2007. "The 'Octopus' Hoard: A Small Archaic Hoard Deposited in 478 BC." *Numismatica e antichità classiche* 36: 54–6.

Jacobsen, J. K. 2013. "Consumption and Production of Greek Pottery in the Sibaritide during the 8th Century BC." In *Vessels and Variety: New Aspects of Ancient Pottery*, edited by H. Thomasen, A. Rathje, and K. Boggild Johannsen, 1–24. *Acta Hyperborea* 13. Copenhagen: Museum Tusculanum Press.

Janko, R. 2015. "From Gabii and Gordion to Eretria and Methone: The Rise of the Greek Alphabet." *Bulletin of the Institute of Classical Studies* 58: 1–32.

Jeffery, L. H. 1976. *Archaic Greece: The City-States c. 700–500 B.C.* New York: St. Martin's Press.

Jeffery, L. H. 1990. *The Local Scripts of Archaic Greece: A Study of the Origin of the Greek Alphabet and Its Development from the Eighth to the Fifth Centuries B.C.* Rev. ed. with a supplement by Alan Johnston. Oxford: Oxford University Press.

Johnston, A. W., and A. Andreiomenou. 1989. "A Geometric Graffito from Eretria." *Annual of the British School at Athens* 84: 217–20.

Johnston, A. W., and R. E. Jones. 1978. "The 'SOS' Amphora." *Annual of the British School at Athens* 73: 103–41.

Kadıoğlu, M., C. Özbil, M. Kerschner, et al. 2015. "Teos im Licht der neuen Forschungen." In *Anatolien—Brücke der Kulturen: Aktuelle Forschungen und Perspektiven in den deutsch-türkischen Altertumswissenschaften, Tagungsband des Internationalen Symposiums "Anatolien—Brücke der Kulturen" in Bonn vom 7. bis 9. Juli 2014*, edited by Ü. Yalçın and H.-D. Bienert, 345–66. Bochum: Deutsches Bergbau-Museum Bochum.

Kagan, J. H. 1988. "Some Archaic Bovine Curiosities." *American Numismatic Society Museum Notes* 33: 37–44.

Kalamara, P. 2015. "Αρχαιολογικά δεδομένα του νομού Ευβοίας, 2009–2013." In *Αρχαιολογικές Συμβολές 3.3*, edited by S. Oikonomou, 151–64. Athens: Μουσείο Κυκλαδικής Τέχνης.

Kalamara, P., M. Kosma, K. Boukaras, et al. 2015. *The City of Chalkis*. Translated by D. Doumas. Athens: Kapon Editions.

Kaltsas, N. E., S. Fachard, A. Psalti, et al., eds. 2010. *Ερέτρια. Ματιές σε μια αρχαία πόλη*. Athens: Kapon Editions.

Kampouroglou, E. 1986. "Ελληνιστικό κτίριο και εμφανίσεις σιδηρομεταλλεύματος στο Ασπρόχωμα Ερέτριας." *Ανθρωπολογικά και Αρχαιολογικά Χρονικά* 1: 85–92.

Keller, D. R. 1984. "Archampolis: An Early Iron Age Settlement and Sanctuary in Southern Euboea." *American Journal of Archaeology* 88: 249.

Keller, D. R. 1985. "Archaeological Survey in Southern Euboea, Greece: A Reconstruction of Human Activity from Neolithic Times through the Byzantine Period." PhD diss., Indiana University.

Kenzelmann-Pfyffer, A., T. Theurillat, and S. Verdan. 2005. "Graffiti d'époque géométrique provenant du sanctuaire d'Apollon Daphnéphoros à Érétrie." *Zeitschrift für Papyrologie und Epigraphik* 151: 51–83.

Kerschner, M., and I. S. Lemos. 2014. "Production, Export and Imitation of Euboean Pottery: A Summary of the Results of the Workshop on the Provenance of Euboean and Euboean Related Pottery and Perspectives for Future Research." In *Archaeometric Analyses of Euboean and Euboean Related Pottery: New Results and Their Interpretations, Proceedings of the Round Table Conference Held at the Austrian Archaeological Institute in Athens, 15 and 16 April 2011*, edited by M. Kerschner and I. S. Lemos, 191–3. Vienna: Österreichisches Archäologisches Institut.

Knodell, A. R. 2017. "A Conduit between Two Worlds: Geography and Connectivity in the Euboean Gulf." In *An Island between Two Worlds. The Archaeology of Euboea from Prehistory to Byzantine Times, Proceedings of International Conference, Eretria, 12–14 July 2013*, edited by Ž. Tankosić, F. Mavridis, and M. Kosma, 195–213. Papers and Monographs from the Norwegian Institute at Athens 6. Athens: Norwegian Institute at Athens.

Knodell, A. R. 2021. *Societies in Transition in Early Greece: An Archaeological History*. Oakland: University of California Press.

Knoepfler, D. 1971. "La date de l'annexion de Styra par Érétrie." *Bulletin de correspondance hellénique* 95: 223–44.

Knoepfler, D. 1972. "Carystos et les Artémisia d'Amarynthos." *Bulletin de correspondance hellénique* 96: 283–301.

Knoepfler, D. 1981. "Argoura: Un toponyme eubéen dans la *Midienne* de Démosthène." *Bulletin de correspondance hellénique* 105: 289–329.

Knoepfler, D. 1985. "Les cinq-cents à Érétrie." *Revue des études grecques* 98: 243–59.

Knoepfler, D. 1988. "Sur les traces de l'Artémision d'Amarynthos près d'Érétrie." *Comptes rendus des séances de l'Académie des Inscriptions et Belles-Lettres* 132: 382–421.

Knoepfler, D. 1997. "Le territoire d'Érétrie et l'organisation politique de la cité (*dêmoi, chôroi, phylai*)." In *The Polis as an Urban Centre and the Political Community, Symposium August, 29–31 1996*, edited by M. H. Hansen, 352–449. Acts of the Copenhagen Polis Centre 4. Copenhagen: Munksgaard.

Knoepfler, D. 2000. *Décrets érétriens de proxénie et de citoyenneté*. Eretria XI. Lausanne: Payot.

Knoepfler, D. 2008. "Une cité au coeur du monde méditerranéen antique: Érétrie et son territoire, histoire et institutions." *L'annuaire du Collège de France* 108: 593–616.

Knoepfler, D. 2010. *La patrie de Narcisse: Un héros mythique enraciné dans le sol et dans l'histoire d'une cité grecque*. Paris: O. Jacob.

Knoepfler, D. 2014. "Anthroponymie et géographie régionales: Le cas des dèmes d'Érétrie." In *Institutions, sociétés et cultes de la Méditerranée antique: Mélanges d'histoire ancienne rassemblés en l'honneur de Claude Vial*, edited by C. Balandier and C. Chandezon, 51–75. Bordeaux: Ausonius Éditions.

Knoepfler, D. Forthcoming. *Eretria. Testimonia*.

Knoepfler, D., and G. Ackermann. 2012. "Phylè Admètis: Un nouveau document sur les institutions et les cultes de l'Érétriade découvert dans les fouilles de l'École Suisse d'Archéologie en Grèce." *Comptes rendus des séances de l'Académie des Inscriptions et Belles-Lettres* 156: 905–49.

Knoepfler, D., K. Reber, A. Karapaschalidou, et al. 2018. "L'Artémision d'Amarynthos 2017." *Antike Kunst* 61: 129–37.

Kosma, M. 2015. "Η τοπογραφία της αρχαίας Χαλκίδας υπό το πρίσμα της πρόσφατης έρευνας." In *Αρχαιολογικές Συμβολές 3.3*, edited by S. Oikonomou, 209–20. Athens: Μουσείο Κυκλαδικής Τέχνης.

Kosma, M., and Y. Chairetakis. 2017. "Η οχύρωση της Χαλκίδας. Η ανασκαφή στον χώρο ανέρεφσης του Νέου Γενικού Νοσοκομείου." In *An Island between Two Worlds. The Archaeology of Euboea from Prehistory to Byzantine Times, Proceedings of International Conference, Eretria, 12–14 July 2013*, edited by Ž. Tankosić, F. Mavridis, and M. Kosma, 359–70. Papers and Monographs from the Norwegian Institute at Athens 6. Athens: Norwegian Institute at Athens.

Kotsonas, A. 2012. "What Makes a Euboean Colony or Trading Station? Zagora in the Cyclades, Methone in the Thermaic Gulf, and Aegean Networks in the 8th Century BC." *Mediterranean Archaeology* 25: 243–57.

Kotsonas, A. 2020. "Euboeans & Co. in the North Aegean: Ancient Tradition and Modern Historiography of Greek Colonization." In *Euboica II: Pithekoussai and Euboea between East and West, Acts of the International Conference, Lacco Ameno, Ischia, 14–17 May 2018, Volume I*, edited by T. E. Cinquantaquattro and M.

D'Acunto, 301–24. *AION Annali di archeologia e storia antica* 27. Naples: Istituto Universitario Orientale di Napoli.

Kouli, K. 2012. "Vegetation Development and Human Activities in Attiki (SE Greece) during the Last 5,000 Years." *Vegetation History and Archaeobotany* 21: 267–78.

Kourou, N. 2002. "Phéniciens, Chypriotes, Eubéens et la fondation de Carthage." In *Hommage à Marguérite Yon, Actes du colloque international "Le temps des royaumes de Chypre, XIIIe–IVe s. av. J.–C.," Lyon, 20–22 juin 2002*, 89–111. *Cahiers du Centre d'Études Chypriotes* 32. Paris: De Boccard.

Kourou, N. 2017. "The Archaeological Background of the Earliest Graffiti and Finds from Methone." In *Panhellenes at Methone: Graphê in Late Geometric and Protoarchaic Methone, Macedonia (ca 700 BCE)*, edited by J. Strauss Clay, I. Malkin, and Y. Z. Tzifopoulos, 20–35. Trends in Classics Supplementary Volume 44. Berlin: Walter de Gruyter.

Kourou, N. 2020. "Euboean Pottery in a Mediterranean Perspective." In *Euboica II: Pithekoussai and Euboea between East and West, Acts of the International Conference, Lacco Ameno, Ischia, 14–17 May 2018, Volume I*, edited by T. E. Cinquantaquattro and M. D'Acunto, 9–35. *AION Annali di archeologia e storia antica* 27. Naples: Istituto Universitario Orientale di Napoli.

Kraay, C. M. 1976. *Archaic and Classical Greek Coins*. Berkeley: University of California Press.

Kramer-Hajós, M. T. 2008. *Beyond the Palace: Mycenaean East Lokris*. BAR International Series 1781. Oxford: Archaeopress.

Krapf, T. 2011. "Amarynthos in der Bronzezeit: Der Wissensstand nach den Schweizer Grabungen 2006 und 2007." *Antike Kunst* 54: 144–59.

Krentz, P. 2002. "Fighting by the Rules: The Invention of the Hoplite Agôn." *Hesperia* 71: 23–39.

Krentz, P. 2010. *The Battle of Marathon*. New Haven, CT: Yale University Press.

Kroll, J. H. 1998. "Silver in Solon's Laws." In *Studies in Greek Numismatics in Memory of Martin Jessop Price*, edited by R. H. J. Ashton and S. Hurter, 225–32. London: Spink.

Kroll, J. H. 2008. "Early Iron Age Balance Weights at Lefkandi, Euboea." *Oxford Journal of Archaeology* 27: 37–48.

Kroll, J. H. 2012. "The Monetary Background of Early Coinage." In *The Oxford Handbook of Greek and Roman Coinage*, edited by W. Metcalf, 33–42. Oxford: Oxford University Press.

Lane Fox, R. 2008. *Travelling Heroes: Greeks and Their Myths in the Epic Age of Homer*. London: Allen Lane.

Langlotz, E. 1927. *Frühgriechische Bildhauerschülen*. Nuremberg: Frommann.

Lemos, I. S. 2001. "The Lefkandi Connection: Networking in the Aegean and the Eastern Mediterranean." In *Italy and Cyprus in Antiquity: 1500–450 BC*, edited by L. Bonfante and V. Karageorghis, 215–26. Nicosia: Costakis and Leto Severis Foundation.

Lemos, I. S. 2002. *The Protogeometric Aegean: The Archaeology of the Late Eleventh and Tenth Centuries BC*. Oxford: Oxford University Press.

Lemos, I. S. 2005. "The Changing Relationship of the Euboeans and the East." In *Greeks in the East*, edited by A. C. Villing, 53–60. London: British Museum Press.

Lemos, I. S. 2014. "Communities in Transformation: An Archaeological Survey from the 12th to the 9th Century BC." *Pharos* 20: 161–91.

Lemos, I. S. 2020. "The Transition from the Late Bronze to the Early Iron Age in Euboea and the Euboean Gulf." In *Euboica II: Pithekoussai and Euboea between East and West, Acts of the International Conference, Lacco Ameno, Ischia, 14–17 May 2018, Volume I*, edited by T. E. Cinquantaquattro and M. D'Acunto, 37–53. *AION Annali di archeologia e storia antica* 27. Naples: Istituto Universitario Orientale di Napoli.

Lemos, I. S., and D. Mitchell. 2011. "Elite Burials in Early Iron Age Aegean: Some Preliminary Observations Considering the Spatial Organization of the Toumba Cemetery at Lefkandi." In *The "Dark Ages" Revisited, Acts of an International Symposium in Memory of William D. E. Coulson, University of Thessaly, Volos, 14–17 June 2007*, edited by A. Mazarakis Ainian, 2: 591–600. 2 vols. Volos: University of Thessaly Press.

Leone, B. 2015. "A Trade Route between Euboea and the Northern Aegean: Some Considerations." *Mediterranean Archaeology* 25: 229–41.

Le Rider, G., and S. Verdan. 2002. "La trouvaille d'Érétrie: Réserve d'un orfèvre ou dépôt monétaire?" *Antike Kunst* 45: 133–52.

Lolos, Y. Forthcoming. "Sicyon." In *The Oxford History of the Archaic Greek World*, edited by P. Cartledge and P. Christesen. *The Oxford History of the Archaic Greek World*, Volume 6. New York: Oxford University Press.

Lombardi, P. 2003. "Il 'bere di Nestore.'" In *Epigraphica, Atti delle Giornate di Studio di Roma e di Atene in memoria di Margherita Guarducci (1902–1999)*, 65–79. Opuscula Epigraphica 10. Rome: Quasar.

Luke, J. 2003. *Ports of Trade, Al Mina and Geometric Greek Pottery in the Levant*. Oxford: Archaeopress.

Malkin, I. 1994. "Inside and Outside: Colonization and the Formation of the Mother City." In *ΑΠΟΙΚΙΑ: I piu antichi insediamenti greci in Occidente: Funzioni et mode dell'organizzazione politice et sociale, Scritti in onore di Giorgio Buchner*, edited by B. D'Agostino and D. Ridgway, 1–10. *AION Annali di archeologia e storia antica* 1. Naples: Istituto Universitario Orientale di Napoli.

Malkin, I. 1998a. "Ithaka, Odysseus and the Euboeans in the Eighth Century." In *Euboica, l'Eubea e la presenza euboica in Calcidica e in Occidente, Atti del Convegno Internazionale di Napoli, 13–16 novembre 1996*, edited by M. Bats and B. D'Agostino, 1–10. Collections du Centre Jean Bérard 16. Naples: L'Arte Tipografica.

Malkin, I. 1998b. *The Returns of Odysseus: Colonization and Ethnicity*. Berkeley: University of California Press.

Malkin, I. 2002. "A Colonial Middle Ground: Greek, Etruscan, and Local Elites in the Bay of Naples." In *The Archaeology of Colonialism*, edited by C. L. Lyons and J. K. Papadopoulos, 151–81. Los Angeles: Getty Publications.

Malkin, I. 2009. "Foundations." In *A Companion to Archaic Greece*, edited by K. Raaflaub and H. van Wees, 373–94. Malden, MA: Wiley-Blackwell.

Manfredini, M. 1968. "La cleruchia ateniese in Calcide: Un problema storico e una questione di critica testuale (Hdt. V, 77)." *Studi classici e orientali* 17: 199–212.

Marek, C. 1993. "Euboia und die Entstehung des Alphabetschrifts." *Klio* 75: 27–44.

Markoe, G. E. 1992. "In Pursuit of Metals: Phoenicians and Greeks in Italy." In *Greece between East and West: 10th–8th Centuries BC, Papers of the Meeting at the Institute of Fine Arts, New York University, March, 1990*, edited by G. Kopcke and I. Tokumaru, 61–84. Mainz: Philipp von Zabern.

Martin Pruvot, C., K. Reber, and T. Theurillat, eds. 2010. *Cité sous terre: Des archéologues suisses explorent la cité grecque d'Érétrie, exposition présentée à Bâle, à l'Antikenmuseum Basel und Sammlung Ludwig, du 22 septembre 2010 au 30 janvier 2011*. Gollion: Infolio.

Masson, O. 1992. "Les lamelles de plomb de Styra IG XII 9, 56: Essai de bilan." *Bulletin de correspondance hellénique* 116: 61–72.

Mazarakis Ainian, A. 1997. *From Rulers' Dwellings to Temples: Architecture, Religion and Society in Early Iron Age Greece (1100–700 B.C.)*. Jonsered: Paul Åströms Förlag.

Mazarakis Ainian, A. 2007. "Architecture and Social Structure in Early Iron Age Greece." In *Building Communities: House, Settlement and Society in the Aegean and Beyond, Proceedings of a Conference Held at Cardiff University, 17–21 April 2001*, edited by R. Westgate, N. Fisher, and J. Whitley, 157–68. British School at Athens Studies 15. London: British School at Athens.

Mazarakis Ainian, A. 2012. "Des quartiers spécialisés d'artisans à l'époque géométrique?" In *Quartiers artisanaux en Grèce ancienne: Une perspective méditerranéenne*, edited by A. Esposito and G. M. Sanidas, 125–54. Villeneuve d'Ascq: Presses Universitaires du Septentrion.

Mazarakis Ainian, A. 2016. "Early Greek Temples." In *A Companion to Greek Architecture*, edited by M. M. Miles, 15–30. Malden, MA: Wiley-Blackwell.

Meiggs, R. 1982. *Trees and Timber in the Ancient Mediterranean World*. Oxford: Clarendon Press.

Meiggs, R., and D. M. Lewis. 1988. *A Selection of Greek Historical Inscriptions to the End of the Fifth Century B.C.* 2nd ed. Oxford: Clarendon Press.

Mele, A. 1975. "I caratteri della società eretriese arcaica." In *Contribution à l'étude de la société et de la colonisation eubéennes*, 15–26. Cahiers du Centre Jean Bérard 2. Naples: Centre Jean Bérard.

Mele, A. 1981. "I Ciclopi, Calcodonte e la metallurgia calcidese." In *Nouvelle contribution à l'étude de la société et de la colonisation eubéenne*, 9–33. Cahiers du Centre Jean Bérard 6. Naples: Centre Jean Bérard.

Mercuri, L. 2004. *Eubéens en Calabre à l'époque archaïque: Formes de contacts et d'implantation*. Bibliothèque des Écoles Françaises d'Athènes et de Rome 321. Rome: École Française de Rome.

Mitchell, L. G. 2001. "Euboean Io." *Classical Quarterly* 51: 339–52.

Moreno, A. 2007. *Feeding the Democracy: The Athenian Grain Supply in the Fifth and Fourth Centuries B.C.* Oxford: Oxford University Press.

Moretti, L. 1957. *Olympionikai: I vincitori negli antichi agoni olimpici*. Rome: Accademia Nazionale dei Lincei.

Morgan, C. A. 1998. "Euboians and Corinthians in the Area of the Corinthian Gulf?" In *Euboica, l'Eubea e la presenza euboica in Calcidica e in Occidente, Atti del Convegno Internazionale di Napoli, 13–16 novembre 1996*, edited by M. Bats and B. D'Agostino, 281–302. Collections du Centre Jean Bérard 16. Naples: L'Arte Tipografica.

Morris, S. P., and J. K. Papadopoulos, eds. 2023. *Ancient Methone, 2003–2013: Excavations by Matthaios Bessios, Athena Athanassiadou, and Konstantinos Noulas*. Monumenta Archaeologica 49. Los Angeles: Cotsen Institute of Archaeology Press.

Nielsen, T. H. 2018. *Two Studies in the History of Ancient Greek Athletics*. Scientia Danica, Series H, Humanistica, 8, Vol. 16. Copenhagen: Kongelige Danske Videnskabernes Selskab.

Niemeyer, H. G. 2004. "Phoenician or Greek: Is There a Reasonable Way out of the Al Mina Debate?" *Ancient West and East* 3: 38–50.

Niemeyer, H. G. 2006. "There is No Way out of the Al Mina Debate." *Ancient West and East* 4: 292–5.

Osborne, R. 1987. *Classical Landscape with Figures: The Ancient Greek City and its Countryside*. London: George Philip.

Osborne, R. 2023. "Athens." In *The Oxford History of the Archaic Greek World*, edited by P. Cartledge and P. Christesen. *The Oxford History of the Archaic Greek World*, Volume 2. New York: Oxford University Press.

Papadopoulos, J. K. 1996. "Euboians in Macedonia? A Closer Look." *Oxford Journal of Archaeology* 15: 151–81.

Papadopoulos, J. K. 1997. "Phantom Euboians." *Journal of Mediterranean Archaeology* 10: 191–219.

Papadopoulos, J. K. 2005. *The Early Iron Age Cemetery at Torone: Excavations Conducted by the Australian Institute at Athens in Collaboration with the Athens Archaeological Society*. 2 vols. Monumenta Archaeologica 24. Los Angeles: Cotsen Institute of Archaeology Press.

Papadopoulos, J. K. 2011. "'Phantom Euboians'—A Decade On." In *Euboea and Athens, Proceedings of a Colloquium in Memory of Malcolm B. Wallace (Athens 26–27 June*

*2009)*, edited by D. W. Rupp and J. E. Tomlinson, 113–33. Publications of the Canadian Institute in Greece 6. Athens: Canadian Institute in Greece.

Papadopoulos, J. K. 2016. "The Early History of the Greek Alphabet: New Evidence from Eretria and Methone." *Antiquity* 90: 1238–54.

Papavasileiou, G. A. 1900. "Ἀνασκαφαὶ ἐν Χαλκίδι." *Πρακτικὰ τῆς ἐν Ἀθήναις Ἀρχαιολογικῆς Ἑταιρείας* 55: 57–66.

Papavasileiou, G. A. 1902. "Εὐβοϊκαὶ Ἐπιγραφαί." *Ἀρχαιολογικὴ Ἐφημερίς* 1902: 98–123.

Papavasileiou, G. A. 1910. *Περὶ τῶν ἐν Εὔβοια ἀρχαίων τάφων*. Athens: Η ἐν Ἀθήναις Ἀρχαιολογικὴ Ἑταιρεία.

Papavasileiou, G. A. 1913. "Ἐρετρικὸς νόμος." *Ἀρχαιολογικὴ Ἐφημερίς* 1913: 210–11.

Parker, V. 1997. *Untersuchungen zum Lelantischen Krieg und verwandten Problemen der frühgriechischen Geschichte. Historia* Einzelschriften 109. Stuttgart: Franz Steiner Verlag.

Paspalas, S. A. 2012. "Greek Decorated Pottery II: Regions and Workshops." In *A Companion to Greek Art*, edited by T. J. Smith and D. Plantzos, 62–104. Malden, MA: Wiley-Blackwell.

Persano, P. 2017. "Scultura greca del tardo arcaismo: un nuovo esame delle sculture frontonali del tempio di Apollo Daphnephoros a Eretria." Ph.D. diss., Scuola Normale Superiore di Pisa.

Picard, O. 1979. *Chalcis et la confédération eubéenne: Étude de numismatique et d'histoire (IVe–Ier siècles)*. Paris: De Boccard.

Popham, M., P. Calligas, L. H. Sackett, et al. 1993. *Lefkandi II: The Protogeometric Building at Toumba, Part II, The Excavation, Architecture and Finds*. 2 vols. British School at Athens Supplementary Volume 23. Athens: British School at Athens.

Popham, M., L. H. Sackett, and P. Themelis. 1980. *Lefkandi I, The Iron Age: The Settlement, the Cemeteries*. London: Thames & Hudson.

Powell, B. 1991. *Homer and the Origin of the Greek Alphabet*. Cambridge: Cambridge University Press.

Powell, B. 2004. *Homer*. Malden, MA: Blackwell.

Pratt, C. 2015. "The 'SOS' Amphora: An Update." *Annual of the British School at Athens* 110: 213–45.

Psoma, S. E. 2015. "Corcyra's Wealth and Power." In *Prospettive corciresi*, edited by C. Antonetti and E. Cavalli, 145–67. Diabaseis 5. Pisa: Edizioni ETS.

Psoma, S. E. 2017. "Proud to Be Euboeans: The Chalcidians of Thrace." In *An Island between Two Worlds. The Archaeology of Euboea from Prehistory to Byzantine Times, Proceedings of International Conference, Eretria, 12–14 July 2013*, edited by Ž. Tankosić, F. Mavridis, and M. Kosma, 409–20. Papers and Monographs from the Norwegian Institute at Athens 6. Athens: Norwegian Institute at Athens.

Reber, K., M. H. Hansen, and P. Ducrey. 2004. "Euboia." In *An Inventory of Archaic and Classical Poleis*, edited by M. H. Hansen and T. H. Nielsen, 643–63. Oxford: Oxford University Press.

Reber, K., D. Knoepfler, G. Ackermann, et al. 2013. "Amarynthos 2012, Campagne de sondages." *Antike Kunst* 56: 100–7.

Renfrew, C. 1986. "Introduction: Peer Polity Interaction and Socio-Political Change." In *Peer Polity Interaction and Socio-Political Change*, edited by C. Renfrew and J. Cherry, 1–18. Cambridge: Cambridge University Press.

Rhodes, R. F. 2003. "The Earliest Greek Architecture in Corinth and the 7th-Century Temple on Temple Hill." In *Corinth, the Centenary: 1896–1996*, edited by C. K. Williams II and N. Bookidis, 85–94. Corinth 20. Princeton, NJ: American School of Classical Studies at Athens.

Ridgway, D. 1992. *The First Western Greeks*. Cambridge: Cambridge University Press.

Ridgway, D. 2007. "Some Reflections on the Early Euboeans and Their Partners in the Central Mediterranean." In *Oropos and Euboea in the Early Iron Age, Acts of an International Round Table, University of Thessaly, June 18–20, 2004*, edited by A. Mazarakis Ainian, 141–52. Volos: University of Thessaly Press.

Robinson, E. W. 1997. *The First Democracies: Early Popular Government outside Athens*. *Historia* Einzelschriften 107. Stuttgart: Franz Steiner Verlag.

Roller, D. W. 2018. *A Historical and Topographical Guide to the Geography of Strabo*. Cambridge: Cambridge University Press.

Ruijgh, C. J. 1997. "La date de la création de l'alphabet grec et celle de l'épopée homéri-que." *Bibliotheca orientalis* 54: 533–603.

Ruijgh, C. J. 2004. "The Source and the Structure of Homer's Epic Poetry." *European Review* 12: 527–42.

Sackett, L. H., R. J. Howell, T. W. Jacobsen, et al. 1966. "Prehistoric Euboea: Contributions toward a Survey." *Annual of the British School at Athens* 61: 33–112.

Saggini, T. Forthcoming. *Érétrie au tournant des époques archaïque et classique: Céramique en contextes*. Eretria XXVI.

Sampson, A. 1976. *Συμβολή στην τοπογραφία της αρχαίας Χαλκίδος*. Chalcis: Εταιρεία Ευβοϊκών Σπουδών.

Sapouna-Sakellaraki, E. 2009. *Σύμπλεγμα Ηρακλή με λέοντα από τους Ωρεούς Ιστιαίας*. Athens: Η εν Αθήναις Αρχαιολογική Εταιρεία.

Schefold, K., and P. E. Auberson. 1972. *Führer durch Eretria*. Bern: Francke.

Scheidel, W. 2003. "The Greek Demographic Expansion: Models and Comparisons." *Journal of Hellenic Studies* 123: 120–40.

Scott, L. 2005. *Historical Commentary on Herodotus Book 6*. Leiden: Brill.

Seyrig, H. 1950. "Poulpes et seiches sur les monnaies grecques." *Revue des études anci-ennes* 52: 372.

Shear, T. L. Jr. 1963. "Koisyra: Three Women of Athens." *Phoenix* 17: 99–112.

Simon, P. 2000. "Une campagne de prospection du territoire érétrien." *Antike Kunst* 43: 131–3.

Simon, P. 2001. "Nouvelles investigations dans le territoire de la cité d'Érétrie." *Antike Kunst* 44: 88–91.

Simon, P. 2002. "Nouvelles activités de prospection dans le territoire Érétrien." *Antike Kunst* 45: 125–7.

Simon, P. 2007. "Les environs d'Érétrie durant le premier Age du Fer: Un modèle d'occupation régionale?" In *Oropos and Euboea in the Early Iron Age, Acts of an International Round Table, University of Thessaly, June 18–20, 2004*, edited by A. Mazarakis Ainian, 153–69. Volos: University of Thessaly Press.

Simon, P., and S. Verdan. 2014. "Hippotrophia: Chevaux et élites eubéennes à la période géométrique." *Antike Kunst* 57: 3–24.

Simossi, A. 2022. *Arethousa: The Archaeological Museum of Chalkis*. Athens: John S. Latsis Public Benefit Foundation.

Slawisch, A. Forthcoming. "Miletus." In *The Oxford History of the Archaic Greek World*, edited by P. Cartledge and P. Christesen. *The Oxfor History of the Archaic Gerek World*, Volume 5. New York: Oxford University Press.

Snodgrass, A. M. 1999a. *Arms and Armor of the Greeks*. Baltimore: Johns Hopkins University Press.

Snodgrass, A. M. 1999b. "Centres of Pottery Production in Archaic Greece." In *Céramique et peinture grecques, modes d'emploi, Actes du colloque international École du Louvre, 26–28 avril 1995*, edited by M.-C. Villanueva-Puig, F. Lissarrague, P. P. Rouillard, et al., 25–33. Paris: La Documentation Française.

Snodgrass, A. M. 2006. *Archaeology and the Emergence of Greece: Collected Papers on Early Greece and Related Topics, 1965–2002*. Edinburgh: Edinburgh University Press.

Spence, I. G. 1993. *The Cavalry of Classical Greece*. Oxford: Clarendon Press.

Sprawski, S. 2008. "Aristotle on the History of Euboea? Remarks on the Author of Peri Euboias (*FGrH* 423)." *Journal of Classical Studies Matica Srpska* 10: 107–16.

Stissi, V. 2016. "Survey, Excavation and the Appearance of the Early *Polis*: A Reappraisal." In *The Archaeology of Greece and Rome: Studies in Honour of Anthony Snodgrass*, edited by J. L. Bintliff and N. K. Rutter, 31–54. Edinburgh: Edinburgh University Press.

Tankosić, Ž. 2017. "Fact or Fiction? Lithics-Only Prehistoric Sites in the Karystian Plain in Light of New Evidence from Southern Euboea." In *From Maple to Olive, Proceedings of a Colloquium to Celebrate the 40th Anniversary of the Canadian Institute in Greece, Athens, 10–11 June 2016*, edited by J. E. Tomlinson and D. W. Rupp, 239–52. Publications of the Canadian Institute in Greece 10. Athens: Canadian Institute in Greece.

Tankosić, Ž., and M. Chidiroglou. 2010. "The Karystian Kampos Survey Project: Methods and Preliminary Results." *Mediterranean Archaeology and Archaeometry* 10: 11–17.

Tankosić, Ž., F. Mavridis, and M. Kosma, eds. 2017. *An Island between Two Worlds: The Archaeology of Euboea from Prehistory to Byzantine Times, Proceedings of International Conference, Eretria, 12–14 July 2013*. Papers and Monographs from the Norwegian Institute at Athens 6. Athens: Norwegian Institute at Athens.

Themelis, P. 1969. "Νέα Λάμψακος Χαλκίδος ('Αρπάγιον)." *Athens Annals of Archaeology* 2: 163–5.

Themelis, P. 1979. "Ανασκαφή Ερέτριας." *Πρακτικά της εν Αθήναις Αρχαιολογικής Εταιρείας* 134: 40–55.

Themelis, P. 1983. "An 8th-Century Goldsmith's Workshop at Eretria." In *The Greek Renaissance of the Eighth Century B.C.: Tradition and Innovation, Proceedings of the Second International Symposium at the Swedish Institute in Athens, 1–5 June, 1981*, edited by R. Hägg, 157–65. Skrifter utgivna av Svenska Institutet i Athen 4° 30. Lund: Paul Åströms Förlag.

Themelis, P. 1987. "Ερετριακές λατρείες." In *Φίλια έπη εις Γεώργιον Ε. Μυλωνάν διά τα 60 έτη του ανασκαφικού του έργου*, 3, 106–25. Athens: Η εν Αθήναις Αρχαιολογική Εταιρεία.

Theodoropoulou, T. 2007. "'Gifts' from the Gulf: The Exploitation of Molluscs in the Geometric Artisan Site of Oropos." In *Oropos and Euboea in the Early Iron Age, Acts of an International Round Table, University of Thessaly, June 18–20, 2004*, edited by A. Mazarakis Ainian, 427–45. Volos: University of Thessaly Press.

Tiverios, M. 2006–2008. "Greek Colonisation in the Northern Aegean." In *Greek Colonisation: An Account of Greek Colonies and Other Settlements Overseas*, edited by G. R. Tsetskhladze, 2: 1–154. 2 vols. Leiden: Brill.

Tiverios, M. 2013. "The Presence of Euboeans in the North Helladic Region and the Myths of Heracles." In *De Antiquorum Artibus et Civilisatione: Estudia Varia Dedicated to Professor Ewdoksia Papouci-Władyka*, edited by J. Bodzek, 97–112. Studies in Ancient Art and Civilization 17. Krakow: Instytut Archeologii Uniwersytetu Jagiellonskiego.

Touloupa, E. 2002. *Τα εναέτια γλυπτά του ναού του Απόλλωνος Δαφνηφόρου στην Ερέτρια*. Athens: Η εν Αθήναις Αρχαιολογική Εταιρεία.

Touloupa, E., and M. Korres. 2002. "Το κεντρικό ακρωτήριο του ναού του Δαφνηφόρου Απόλλωνος στην Ερέτρια." In *Αρχαία Ελληνικά Γλυπτά, Αφιέρωμα στη μνήμη του γλύπτη Στέλιου Τριάντη*, edited by D. Damaskos, 73–82. Athens: Benaki Museum.

Tsetskhladze, G. R. 2006–2008. "Introduction: Revisiting Ancient Greek Colonisation." In *Greek Colonisation. An Account of Greek Colonies and Other Settlements Overseas*, edited by G. R. Tsetskhladze, 1: xiii–lxxxiii. 2 vols. Leiden: Brill.

Tzifopoulos, Y. Z., M. Besios, and A. Kotsonas. 2017. "Panhellenes at Methone, Pieria (c. 700 BC): New Inscriptions, Graffiti/Dipinti, and (Trade)marks." In *Interpreting the Seventh Century BC: Tradition and Innovation, Proceedings of the International Colloquium Conference Held at the British School at Athens, 9th–11th December 2011*, edited by X. Charalambidou and C. A. Morgan, 364–74. Oxford: Archaeopress.

Ure, A. D. 1973. "Observations on Euboean Black-Figure." *Annual of the British School at Athens* 68: 25–31.

Vacek, A. 2017. "Al Mina and Changing Patterns of Trade: The Evidence from the Eastern Mediterranean." In *Interpreting the Seventh Century BC: Tradition and*

*Innovation, Proceedings of the International Colloquium Conference Held at the British School at Athens, 9th–11th December 2011*, edited by X. Charalambidou and C. A. Morgan, 47–59. Oxford: Archaeopress.

Valenza Mele, N. 1979. "Eracle euboico a Cuma: La gigantomachia e la Via Heraclea." In *Recherches sur les cultes grecs et l'Occident*, edited by L. B. Brea, 19–51. Cahiers du Centre Jean Bérard 5. Naples: Centre Jean Bérard.

Van Alfen, P. 2015. "The Chalkid(ik)ian Beginnings of Euboian Coinage." In *Kairos: Contributions to Numismatics in Honor of Basil Demetriadi*, edited by U. Wartenberg and M. Amandry, 255–83. New York: American Numismatic Society.

Vanderpool, E., and W. P. Wallace. 1964. "The Sixth-Century Laws from Eretria." *Hesperia* 33: 381–91.

Van Effenterre, H., and F. Ruzé. 1994–1995. *Nomima: Recueil d'inscriptions politiques et juridiques de l'archaïsme grec*. 2 vols. Rome: École Française de Rome.

Van Wees, H. 2006. "Mass and Elite in Solon's Athens: The Property Classes Revisited." In *Solon of Athens: New Historical and Philological Approaches*, edited by J. Blok and A. P. M. H. Lardinois, 351–89. *Mnemosyne* Supplementum 272. Leiden: Brill.

Van Wees, H. 2010. "'Those Who Sail Are to Receive a Wage': Naval Warfare and Finance in Archaic Eretria." In *New Perspectives on Ancient Warfare*, edited by G. Fagan and M. Trundle, 205–26. History of Warfare 59. Leiden: Brill.

Van Wees, H. 2013a. "Farmers and Hoplites: Models of Historical Development." In *Men of Bronze: Hoplite Warfare in Ancient Greece*, edited by D. Kagan and G. Viggiano, 222–55. Princeton, NJ: Princeton University Press.

Van Wees, H. 2013b. *Ships and Silver, Taxes and Tribute: A Fiscal History of Archaic Athens*. London: I.B. Tauris.

Verdan, S. 2013. *Le sanctuaire d'Apollon Daphnéphoros à l'époque géométrique*. Eretria XXII. Gollion: Infolio.

Verdan, S. 2015a. "Geometric Eretria: Some Thoughts on Old Data." *Mediterranean Archaeology* 25: 181–9.

Verdan, S. 2015b. "Images, supports et contextes: sur quelques 'amphores funéraires' érétriennes." In *Pots, Workshops and Early Iron Age Society: Function and Role of Ceramics in Early Greece, Proceedings of the International Symposium (Université Libre de Bruxelles, 14–16 November 2013)*, edited by V. Vlachou, 127–37. Études d'archéologie 8. Brussels: CReA-Patrimoine.

Verdan, S. 2017. "Counting on Pots? Reflections on Numerical Notations in Early Iron Age Greece." In *Panhellenes at Methone: Graphê in Late Geometric and Protoarchaic Methone, Macedonia (ca 700 BCE)*, edited by J. Strauss Clay, I. Malkin, and Y. Z. Tzifopoulos, 105–22. Trends in Classics Supplementary Volume 44. Berlin: Walter de Gruyter.

Verdan, S. 2023. "Metallurgical Ceramics from the Hypogeion." In *Ancient Methone, 2003–2013: Excavations by Matthaios Bessios, Athena Athanassiadou,* and *Konstantinos Noulas*, edited by S. P. Morris and J. K. Papadopoulos, 545–562. Monumenta Archaeologica 49. Los Angeles: Cotsen Institute of Archaeology Press.

Verdan, S., and E. D. Heymans. 2020. "Men and Metals on the Move: The Case of Euboean Gold." In *Euboica II: Pithekoussai and Euboea between East and West, Acts of the International Conference, Lacco Ameno, Ischia, 14–17 May 2018. Volume I*, edited by T. E. Cinquantaquattro and M. D'Acunto, 279–300. *AION Annali di archeologia e storia antica* 27. Naples: Istituto Universitario Orientale di Napoli.

Verdan, S., A. Kenzelmann-Pfyffer, and C. Léderrey. 2008. *Céramique géométrique d'Erétrie. Eretria XX.* Gollion: Infolio.

Verdan, S., A. Kenzelmann-Pfyffer, and T. Theurillat. 2014. "'Euboean' Pottery from Early Iron Age Eretria in the Light of the Neutron Activation Analysis." In *Archaeometric Analyses of Euboean and Euboean Related Pottery: New Results and Their Interpretations, Proceedings of the Round Table Conference Held at the Austrian Archaeological Institute in Athens, 15 and 16 April 2011*, edited by M. Kerschner and I. S. Lemos, 71–90. Vienna: Österreichisches Archäologisches Institut.

Verdan, S., T. Theurillat, S. Fachard, et al. 2020. "Of Dykes and Men: Eretria in the Making." In *Opere di regimentazione delle acque in età arcaica: Grecia e Magna Grecia, Roma, Etruria e mondo italico*, edited by E. Bianchi and M. D'Acunto, 19–36. Rome: Quasar.

Verdan, S., T. Theurillat, T. Krapf, et al. 2020. "The Early Phases in the Artemision at Amarynthos in Euboea, Greece " In *Euboica II: Pithekoussai and Euboea between East and West, Acts of the International Conference, Lacco Ameno, Ischia, 14–17 May 2018. Volume I*, edited by T. E. Cinquantaquattro and M. D'Acunto, 73–118. *AION Annali di archeologia e storia antica* 27. Naples: Istituto Universitario Orientale di Napoli.

Viviers, D. 1987. "Pisistratus' Settlement on the Thermaic Gulf: A Connection with the Eretrian Colonization." *Journal of Hellenic Studies* 107: 193–5.

Voutiras, E. 2008. "La réconciliation des Dikaiopolites: Une nouvelle inscription de Dikaia de Thrace, colonie d'Érétrie." *Comptes rendus des séances de l'Académie des Inscriptions et Belles-Lettres* 152: 781–92.

Walker, K. G. 2004. *Archaic Eretria: A Political and Social History from the Earliest Times to 490 BC.* London: Routledge.

Wallace, W. P. 1947. "The Demes of Eretria." *Hesperia* 16: 115–46.

Wathelet, P. 2007. "Le rôle de l'eubéen et celui de l'Eubée dans l'épopée homérique." *Gaia: Revue interdisciplinaire sur la Grèce archaïque* 11: 25–52.

Wecowski, M. 2014. *The Rise of the Greek Aristocratic Banquet.* Oxford: Oxford University Press.

West, M. L. 1988. "The Rise of Greek Epic." *Journal of Hellenic Studies* 108: 151–72.

Westlake, H. D. 1948. "Athenian Food Supplies from Euboea." *Classical Review* 62: 2–5.

Wheeler, E. L. 1987. "Ephorus and the Prohibition of Missiles." *Transactions of the American Philological Association* 117: 157–82.

Wickens, J. M., S. I. Rotroff, T. Cullen, et al. 2018. *Settlement and Land Use on the Periphery: The Bouros-Kastri Peninsula, Southern Euboia*. Oxford: Archaeopress.

# 3

## *Chios–Lesbos–Samos*

*Paul Christesen, Giuseppe Lentini, Sarah Murray, and Matt Simonton*

### *List of Illustrations*

| | | |
|---|---|---|
| Map 3.1a: | Some key sites in the Aegean, Propontis, and eastern Mediterranean in the Archaic period mentioned in this essay. © Paul Christesen 2024. | 252 |
| Map 3.1b: | Some key sites in the eastern Aegean in the Archaic period mentioned in this essay. © Paul Christesen 2024. | 253 |
| Map 3.2: | Some key sites in mainland Greece, Crete, and North Africa mentioned in this essay. © Paul Christesen 2024. | 254 |
| Map 3.3: | Some key sites in Thrace and the Black Sea area mentioned in this essay. © Paul Christesen 2024. | 255 |
| Map 3.4: | Some key sites in southern Italy and Sicily mentioned in this essay. © Paul Christesen 2024. | 256 |
| Map 3.5: | Some key sites in the wider Mediterranean mentioned in this essay. © Paul Christesen 2024. | 257 |
| Map 3.6: | Some key sites on Chios in the Archaic period mentioned in this essay. © Paul Christesen 2024. | 258 |
| Map 3.7: | Topographic map of Chios. © Paul Christesen 2024. | 261 |
| Map 3.8: | Some key sites on Lesbos in the Archaic period mentioned in this essay. © Paul Christesen 2024. | 299 |
| Map 3.9: | Topographic map of Lesbos. © Paul Christesen 2024. | 302 |
| Map 3.10: | Some key sites on Samos and environs in the Archaic period mentioned in this essay. © Paul Christesen 2024. | 350 |
| Map 3.11: | Topographic map of Samos. © Paul Christesen 2024. | 353 |
| Figure 3.1: | Plan of Chios Town in the Archaic period. © Paul Christesen 2024. | 263 |

Paul Christesen, Giuseppe Lentini, Sarah Murray, and Matt Simonton, *Chios–Lesbos–Samos* In: *The Oxford History of the Archaic Greek World*. Edited by: Paul Cartledge and Paul Christesen, Oxford University Press.
© Oxford University Press 2024. DOI: 10.1093/oso/9780199383597.003.0003

246 THE OXFORD HISTORY OF THE ARCHAIC GREEK WORLD

Figure 3.2: Plan of Emporio in the Archaic period. © Paul Christesen 2024. 266

Figure 3.3: Chian chalice attributed to the Running Man Painter; c. 580–570; height: 14.4cm, diameter: 14.5 cm; from Camirus on Rhodes. Louvre Collection Salzmann, 1863 A 330 Bis. Photo by Egisto Sani. Reproduced under Creative Commons Attribution-NonCommercial-ShareAlike 2.0 Generic License (CC BY-NC-SA 2.0). https://www.flickr.com/photos/69716881@N02/24148942734 272

Figure 3.4: Plan of Mytilene in the Archaic period. © Paul Christesen 2024. 305

Figure 3.5: Plan of Methymna in the Archaic period. © Paul Christesen 2024. 312

Figure 3.6: Plan of Antissa in the Archaic period. © Paul Christesen 2024. 316

Figure 3.7: Plan of Eresus in the Archaic period. © Paul Christesen 2024. 319

Figure 3.8: Drawing of a trachyte Aeolic capital from Temple B at Klopedi; last quarter of the sixth century; height: 61 cm, width 88 cm. Based on Betancourt 1977: fig. 41. 347

Figure 3.9: Lesbian masonry walls at Apotheke on Lesbos. © Gabriel Kagialaris 2024; https://gkagialaris.files.wordpress.com/2017/06/nikon-l330-078-01.jpeg. Reproduced with permission.

Figure 3.10: Plan of Samos Town in the Archaic period. © Paul Christesen 2024. 357

Figure 3.11: The interior of the Eupalinos Tunnel; second half of sixth century. Photo by Tomisti. Reproduced under Creative Commons Attribution-Share Alike 4.0 International license; https://commons.wikimedia.org/wiki/File:Tunnel_of_Eupal inos_09.jpg. 360

Figure 3.12: Plan of the Samian Heraion in the first half of the eighth century. After H. Walter, Clemente, and Niemeier 2019: Zeichnung 3. Reproduced with permission. 367

Figure 3.13: Plan of the Samian Heraion, c. 680–630. After H. Walter, Clemente, and Niemeier 2019: Zeichnung 5. Reproduced with permission. 368

Figure 3.14: Plan of the Samian Heraion, c. 590–575. After H. Walter, Clemente, and Niemeier 2019: Zeichnung 8. Reproduced with permission. 372

Figure 3.15: Plan of the Samian Heraion in the mid-sixth century. © Paul Christesen 2024. 374

Figure 3.16: Plan of the Samian Heraion at the end of the sixth century. © Paul Christesen 2024.    378

Figure 3.17: Fikellura amphora; c. 540; height 29.10 cm, width 23.50 cm; from Camirus on Rhodes. British Museum 1861.0425.47. Photo by ArchaiOptix. Reproduced under Creative Commons Attribution-Share Alike 4.0 International license; https://commons.wikimedia.org/wiki/Category:Fikell ura#/media/File:Fikellura_Style_-_amphora_-_Altenburg_ Painter_-_Cook_III_12_-_Schaus_53_-_partridge_-_Lon don_BM_1861-0425-47.jpg.    384

Figure 3.18: Samian silver *drachmē*; c. 525; weight 3.48 g. American Numismatics Society 1977.158.383. Image in the public domain. http://numismatics.org/collection/1977.158.383?lang=en.    417

Figure 3.19: The Geneleos Group from the Samian Heraion; mid-sixth century. Archaeological Museum, Vathy. Photo by Tomisti. Reproduced under Creative Commons Attribution-Share Alike 4.0 International license; https://commons.wikime dia.org/wiki/Category:Geneleos_group#/media/File:Genel eos_group_1.jpg.    419

Figure 3.20: Bronze lion dedicated to Hera by the Spartiate Eumnastos at the Samian Heraion; c. 550; height: 10 cm, length: 16 cm; from the Samian Heraion. Archaeological Museum, Vathy, 1149/50. Photo by Dimitrios Pergialis, © photopedia.info. Reproduced with permission.    425

# List of Abbreviations

BNJ    *Brill's New Jacoby*. https://referenceworks.brillonline.com/browse/brill-s-new-jacoby.

FGrH    Jacoby, F. 1923–1958. *Die Fragmente der griechischen Historiker.* 3 v. in 14 vols. Berlin: Weidmann.

FHG    Müller, K. 1878–1885. *Fragmenta Historicorum Graecorum.* 5 vols. Paris: Didot. https://www.dfhg-project.org/.

IG    *Inscriptiones Graecae.* 1873–. Berlin: Walter de Gruyter.

LSJ    Liddell, H. G., R. Scott, H. S. Jones, et al. 1996. *A Greek-English Lexicon.* New York: Oxford University Press.

PEP Chios    McCabe, D. F. 1986. *Chios Inscriptions: Texts and Lists.* Princeton, NJ: Institute for Advanced Study. https://inscriptions.packhum.org/book/488?location=6.

SEG    *Supplementum Epigraphicum Graecum.* 1923–. Leiden: Brill.

## 3.1. Introduction

"They brought into the alliance the Samians, the Chians, the Lesbians, and the other islanders who had fought with the Greeks, binding them with pledges and oaths to abide in it and not desert."[1] So Herodotus (9.106.4) describes the aftermath of the Battle of Mycale in 479, when the Hellenic League (a modern term) greatly expanded its membership. This is the earliest attested instance of the trio of islands being named together as a noteworthy group. Herodotus could have listed all of "the other islanders" but settled on naming the three most prominent ones. They might have suggested themselves to him as a natural grouping because of their unique status in the Delian League—they were permitted by Athens to retain their own political systems and to contribute ships rather than money to what rapidly became the Athenian empire (Quinn 1981).

Whatever his reasoning, Herodotus' grouping of the three islands in the context of 479 echoes other Classical sources and was undoubtedly influenced by the later history of the Athenian empire.[2] This does not necessarily mean, however, that the grouping was unknown in the Archaic period, which, for our purposes, comprises the years between the middle of the eighth century, the date of the earliest textual sources for the three islands under discussion here, and the end of the Persian Wars and the creation of the Delian League. It was precisely because the three islands were already so powerful in the aftermath of 479 that they entered the Delian League with special privileges (Thuc. 1.19, 3.10; Plut. *Arist.* 23.4–5). Writing in a period when the three islands had been considerably humbled, the Classical sources allude to this one-time greatness: Herodotus famously dwells on the Greeks' "three greatest works of construction," all of which had been achieved on Archaic Samos (3.60.1–4), while Thucydides mentions the former (and even ongoing) power and prosperity of Lesbos (3.10) and Chios (8.24). We have some evidence to support these assessments. If Herodotus' figures (6.8) are correct, the three contributed the most ships of any of the islanders at the Battle of Lade in 494: Chios 100, Lesbos 70, and Samos 60. If the islands of the eastern Aegean in the Archaic period are the topic, then the three do indeed belong together.

At the same time, there is nothing very triune about this trinity. It is not clear what, if anything, unites the three apart from sheer prominence and geographical propinquity. All three islands were indeed flourishing by the end of the sixth century, but each for different reasons and largely in isolation from one another.

---

1. All translations from Herodotus' work in this essay are those of D. Grene. Unless otherwise indicated, all other translations are original, and all dates are BCE.

2. See further Thuc. 1.19, 2.9.5, 3.10.5; Arist. *Pol.* 1284a39–40; [Arist.] *Ath. Pol.* 24.2; Plut. *Arist.* 23.4; as well as Quinn 1981.

Samos and Chios were both members of the Panionion (see Section 3.10A), and, not knowing much about its rituals or institutions, we may be ignorant of many instances of interaction between the two *poleis*. Lesbos had little to do with either Chios or Samos, although it was perhaps controlled for a short period of time by Polycrates of Samos (Hdt. 3.39.4; see Section 3.7B).

Likewise, the three islands lack clear common archaeological features (although our understanding of the precise relationship among their material histories remains seriously hindered by an uneven record of exploration and research). Archaic Samos possessed massive fortifications, the engineering wonder that was the Eupalinos tunnel, and an extraordinarily wealthy sanctuary of Hera. Though this sanctuary entertained visitors from around the Aegean, hardly any Chian pottery (which is widespread elsewhere) can be found on Samos. The archaeological record of Chios is far humbler. Nonetheless, the widespread distribution of Chian pottery both throughout and beyond the Mediterranean raises the possibility that Chios had a thriving export economy that capitalized on its favorable location on maritime routes. Although Lesbos, too, is located on important East Greek trade routes, Lesbian material culture has its closest affinities in Anatolia rather than to the south and east. Overall, there are precious few points of similarity that bind the three islands together, and the inconsistency of the material cultural record across these major eastern Aegean *poleis* (one each on Chios and Samos, five—originally six—on Lesbos) is one of the most striking conclusions that can be drawn from studying them all together.

The divergences among Chios, Lesbos, and Samos in the Archaic period can be ascribed in part to patterns of activity that began in the Late Bronze Age. The *mythoi* that Greeks recounted about their early history included stories about substantial, organized groups of migrants leaving mainland Greece to settle in western Asia Minor and its offshore islands in some ill-defined era prior to the advent of historical writing; those movements of people have typically been called the Aeolian and Ionian migrations and assigned to the Early Iron Age in modern scholarship. Finds of significant quantities of Mycenaean cultural artifacts in western Asia Minor and its offshore islands, which indicate a long history of contact and exchange, helped reinforce belief in the essential historicity of those *mythoi*, and debate tended to center around the reliability of specific details, such as the geographic origins of the Greeks who settled any given site in Asia Minor.[3]

---

3. The discussion of the Aeolian and Ionian migrations offered here draws directly on H. Parker 2008; Rose 2008; Mokrišová 2016; Mac Sweeney 2017. See also see Bernstein 2019; Hall 1997: 51–6; Crielaard 2009; Vanschoonwinkel 2006–2008: 115–19, 21–30. For a general overview of the nature of Greek migrations in the eighth and seventh centuries, see the revisionist views articulated in Yntema 2011. On the formation of Ionian identity, see Section 3.10A.

More recently, however, scholars such as Brian Rose and Naoíse Mac Sweeney have persuasively argued that the relevant archaeological, linguistic, and literary evidence supports a different version of events that revolves around long-term, multidirectional cultural exchange and ongoing mobility of individuals and small groups. From this perspective, the Aeolian and Ionian migrations are historical fictions that greatly simplify and temporally compress a long and complicated process of contact, exchange, and movement. At present, it is impossible to securely identify large-scale, organized Greek colonizing ventures in western Asia Minor in either the Late Bronze Age or the Early Iron Age.[4] Starting in the Late Bronze Age and continuing into the Early Iron Age, people from the western and central Aegean, probably arriving in small groups, settled among preexisting populations in western Asia Minor (including on the islands of Chios, Lesbos, and Samos). Over the course of time, the gradual accretion of individuals from the western and central Aegean at particular sites created a situation in which Aegean cultural features came to play a predominant role in shaping local identities and traditions. The regional situation was, however, complex, as other sites in the vicinity of Aegeanizing ones are characterized by different material cultural styles and, probably, distinct traditions.

Over the course of time, and particularly in the seventh and sixth centuries, people living in certain communities in western Asia Minor began to develop collective identities, as members of a single, overarching cultural group, the Hellenes, and as members of regional groupings (Aeolians, Ionians, Dorians). *Mythoi* surrounding the Aeolian and Ionian migrations helped solidify those emergent identities and should be understood as stories that residents of communities such as Chios, Lesbos, and Samos (among others) told themselves about themselves, rather than as memories of a distant historical past. To the extent that any kernel of truth can be extracted from those stories, it is that their complexity and manifold contradictions reflect the fact that the communities in question had no single, straightforward moment or place of origin. It is, as a result, not surprising to find that the material culture and history of Chios, Lesbos, and Samos in the Archaic period manifest significant divergences—the communities in the eastern Aegean that came to understand themselves as culturally Greek were internally and collectively heterogeneous from the outset.

Any discussion of the history of Ionian communities in the Archaic period inevitably relies to a considerable extent on the narrative provided by Herodotus.

---

4. The material evidence suggests that Miletus and the area immediately to its south had an unusually close and perhaps highly organized relationship with the Greek mainland in the Late Bronze Age. See Mac Sweeney 2017: 388–9; Slawisch Forthcoming: Section 1.4.1 and the sources cited therein.

Scholarship on Herodotus is an industry unto itself, and it is impossible in the present context to examine in detail the full range of interpretations offered for each passage from the *Histories* discussed below. An enduring problem is that in the absence of competing literary accounts, it is possible to make many plausible claims about distortions and biases in specific parts of the *Histories* but very difficult to definitively establish any of those claims. That, in turn, has generated multiple, conflicting, and frequently mutually contradictory readings of even small portions of Herodotus' narrative. Our general approach has been to assume that the basic outline of events provided by Herodotus is reliable while remaining sensitive to the ways in which Herodotus' primarily oral sources and his own authorial proclivities shaped what he knew, what he considered worthy of recording, and how he presented events that he deemed worthy of recording.[5]

Insofar as the archaeohistory of Chios, Lesbos, and Samos evinces significant divergences, we have chosen to divide the following essay into three distinct sections, each devoted to one of the three islands. Within each of those sections, discussion is structured around the set of 11 rubrics that are common to all of the essays in *The Oxford History of the Archaic Greek World*. (See Maps 3.1–3.5.)

## Section A. Chios

## 3.2A. Sources for Archaic Chian History

Chios was not the subject of systematic archaeological investigation until 1914, when Konstantinos Kourouniotis initiated excavations at Latomi and Kato Phana (ancient Phanai) (Kourouniotis 1915; Kourouniotis 1916) and Dimitris Evangelidis did so at Nagos (Evangelidis 1921) (see Map 3.6).[6] Winifred Lamb conducted excavations on Chios in the 1930s, particularly at Kato Phana, while Edith Eccles produced early reports of an unsystematic survey of archaeological sites in the northern part of the island.[7] The majority of the material evidence for Archaic Chios, aside from occasional fortuitous finds by archaeologists working for the Greek Archaeological Service, is the result of work undertaken under the auspices of the British School at Athens, which received an anonymous donation

---

5. For discussion of many of the issues involved in the interpretation of Herodotus' work, see the articles collected in Bakker, de Jong, and van Wees 2002; Dewald and Marincola 2006; and Baron 2021.

6. See also Fustel de Coulanges 1856 for an earlier exploration of the vicinity of Chios Town and comments on Chian topography.

7. See summary in Merousis 2002: 51–3.

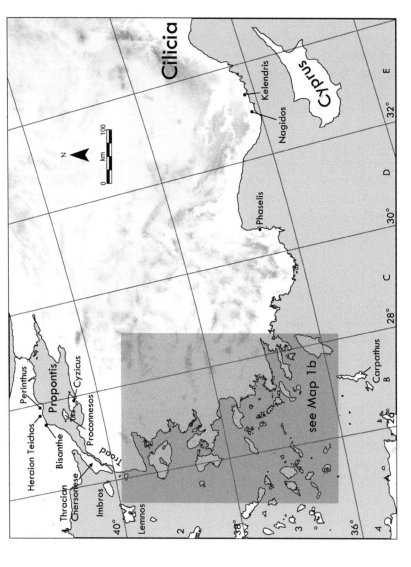

MAP 3.1A. Some key sites in the Aegean, Propontis, and eastern Mediterranean in the Archaic period mentioned in this essay.

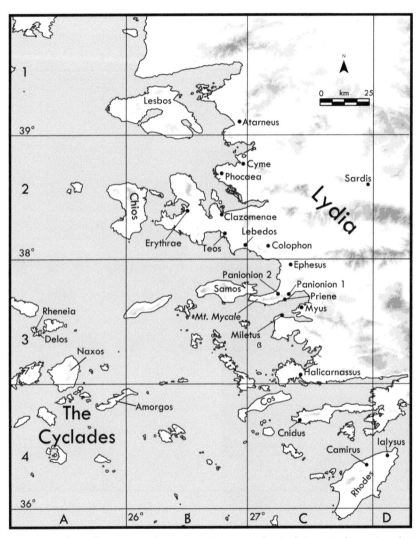

MAP 3.1B. Some key sites in the eastern Aegean in the Archaic period mentioned in this essay.

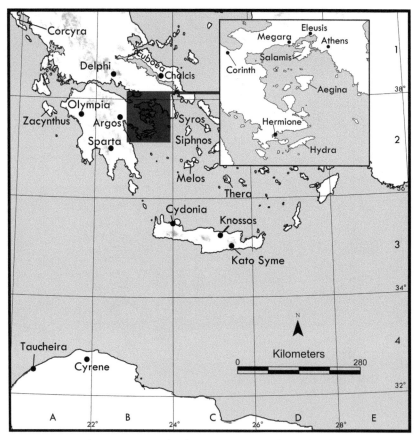

MAP 3.2. Some key sites in mainland Greece, Crete, and North Africa mentioned in this essay.

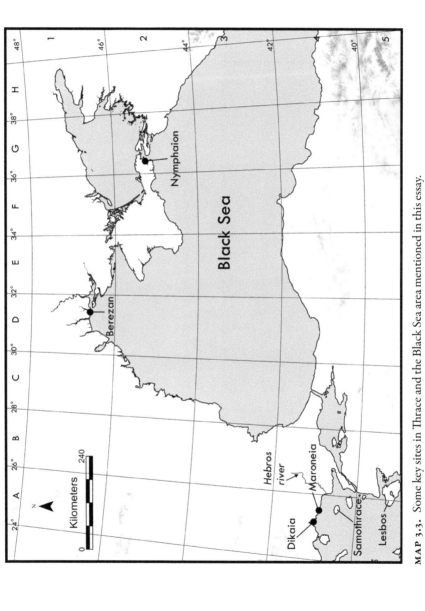

MAP 3.3. Some key sites in Thrace and the Black Sea area mentioned in this essay.

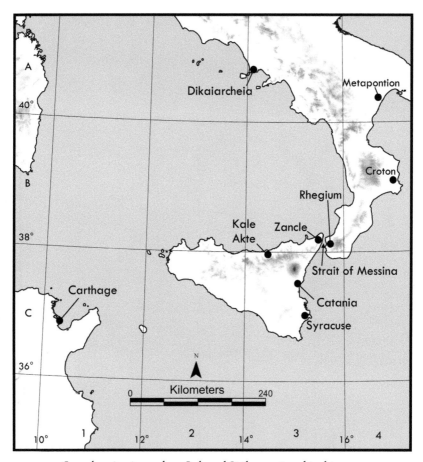

MAP 3.4. Some key sites in southern Italy and Sicily mentioned in this essay.

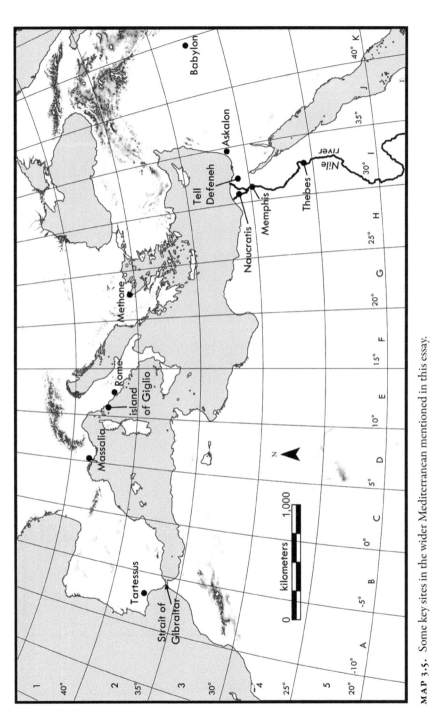

MAP 3.5. Some key sites in the wider Mediterranean mentioned in this essay.

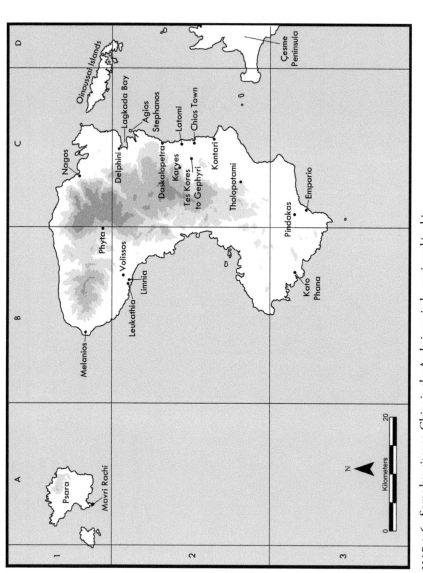

MAP 3.6. Some key sites on Chios in the Archaic period mentioned in this essay.

in the 1950s earmarked for research on Chios.[8] This work comprised excavations at the sites of the Kofina ridge outside of the modern town of Chios as well as at Emporio, Pindakas, and Delphini (ancient Delphinion); the results of those excavations were published gradually through the 1960s (see, for example, Boardman 1967). Since this flurry of activity, Eleftherios Yalouris has conducted a thorough survey of sites on the island, Lesley Beaumont has returned to Kato Phana to complete the study begun many decades earlier by Lamb and to conduct new excavations, and the Greek Archaeological Service has conducted a new campaign of fieldwork at Emporio between 2002 and 2006 (Leekley and Noyes 1975: 18–19; Yalouris 1986; Beaumont 2004; Roungou and Vouligea 2019).

Our knowledge of the Archaic history of Chios relies in no small part on epigraphic texts, as will become clear below. Several inscriptions, the most prominent being the so-called constitutional law (see Section 3.5A), provide important information about Chian political, legal, diplomatic, economic, and demographic history during the Archaic period. The standard collection of inscriptions from Chios is *PEP Chios*, the product of the Princeton Epigraphical Project, which was conceived by Christian Habicht and Glenn Bowersock at the Institute for Advanced Study in the 1980s and carried out by Donald F. McCabe. That project involved compiling lists of inscriptions from various sites in Ionia and Caria and creating digitized versions of the relevant texts. The results of that project were folded into the online database curated by the Packard Humanities Institute. At the time this essay was written, *IG* XII.6.3, a new collection of the inscriptions of Chios, was in preparation but not yet available.[9]

With respect to the literary sources, in addition to Herodotus, Archaic Chios was discussed by Classical historians whose works are quoted in fragmentary form in later sources. The most important of these, Ion the son of Orthomenes (*FGrH* 392), was born on Chios in the early decades of the fifth century and composed a "Foundation of Chios" (Χίου κτίσις).[10] Who exactly founded the Greek settlement(s) on Chios and when were often points of contestation among Classical writers, who were interested in the "ethnic" origins of the Greeks of the eastern Aegean and Asia Minor. One tradition included Chios among the settlements of the "Ionian Migration" led by the sons of Codros from Athens during

---

8. The circumstances are detailed by Hood in his preface to Boardman 1967: vi.

9. The inscriptions in *PEP Chios* can be accessed at https://inscriptions.packhum.org/book/488?location=6. For a good indication of the exciting new epigraphic publications we can expect from Chios, see Malouchou and Matthaiou 2006. For an overview of the epigraphical resources for the study of ancient Ionia, see Greaves 2010: 14–20.

10. On Ion, see the essays contained in Jennings and Katsaros 2007.

# 260 THE OXFORD HISTORY OF THE ARCHAIC GREEK WORLD

what corresponds to our eleventh century.[11] Many of the relevant literary sources are collected in the monumental *Bibliography of Chios from Classical Times to 1936* by the local historian and civic benefactor Philip Argenti (1940).

## 3.3A. Chian Natural Setting

The island of Chios is located approximately 7 km off the coast of Asia Minor. It is the fifth-largest island in the Aegean (826 sq km), stretching 51 km from its northernmost point (Cape Epanochori) to its southernmost point (Cape Masticho) and 29 km from east to west at its widest point. (On the Chian *peraia*, see Section 3.7A.) The landscape is generally mountainous (hence its Homeric epithet, *paipaloessa*, or rugged [*Od.* 3.170]), with a prominent central limestone ridge descending from the high point of Mt. Pelinaion (1,297 masl) (see Map 3.7). In the north, mountains truly predominate, villages are difficult to access, and agricultural produce is limited. In the south, mountains gradually give way to rolling hills and large, fertile plains; this is the current breadbasket of the island, as well as the center of its historic mastic industry (Zolotas 1921: 159–62; Higgins and Higgins 1996: 136–8).

The climate today is typical for an Aegean island, with long, dry summers and brief, cool winters, during which the island receives most of its rainfall (averaging approximately 520 mm annually).[12] Watercourses descend from the mountainous interior, with the longest, the Malagkiotis river, rising on the western slope of Mt. Pelinaion and running c. 15 km before entering the sea near the modern town of Limnia on the west coast of the island. Strong winds from the northeast (the meltemi) or from the southwest (the sirocco) frequently buffet the waters and coasts of the island and often make navigating difficult, especially in the strait between Chios and the Turkish coast (Purdy 1826: 253; Murray 1987).

There is little information available about the paleoenvironment of the island, so it is difficult to demarcate clear differences between the ancient and modern natural setting (Merousis 2002: 16–17). This would be a fertile area for future geo- and zoo-archaeological research, as the anthropogenic changes (especially the burning and destruction of forests) that have been wrought upon the island's natural environment between the Neolithic period (when humans first came to

---

11. Pherecydes *FGrH* 3 F155 (and, for the rest of the source passage for this fragment, Strabo 14.1.3); Hellanicus *FGrH* 4 F38; Hdt. 1.147.1. For the date of the migration, the Marmor Parium (*FGrH* 239 FA27) gives 1077/6; Eratosthenes (*FGrH* 241 F1a) 1044/3.

12. For weather data from Chios, see https://www.weather-atlas.com/en/greece/chios-climate#rainfall.

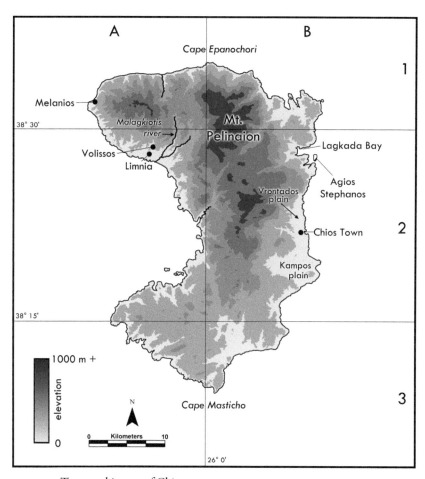

MAP 3.7. Topographic map of Chios.

Chios) and today have undoubtedly taken their toll. It is almost certainly true that Chios, like most other islands of the northeastern Aegean, would have been more heavily wooded in antiquity than today (see Strabo 13.1.8, who states that the Chios was originally called Pituoussa, "island of the pine trees"). We can tell from the presence of extensive waterworks at archaeological sites dating from the Neolithic period onward that access to water was always an issue (Boardman 1967: 59–60). Today there is little forestation overall, though the usual fragrant herbs such as *rigani* grow throughout the mountains (Merousis 2002: 20).

Cultivated agriculture is widespread, and citrus trees dominate the modern landscape in the Vrontados plain (north of ancient Chios Town/modern Chora) and Kampos plain (south of Chios Town/Chora) of central Chios. Olives are grown all over the island, though not in the same vast quantities as on neighboring Lesbos, and resin-producing mastic trees are encountered in the marginal hillsides of the south. Although Chian wine was famous in antiquity (see Section 3.8A.3), little trace of viticulture on the island survives today. Indeed, overall, the amount of fertile, cultivable land on the island is relatively limited, as are good water sources, especially in comparison with its neighbors in the northeastern Aegean, including Lesbos and Samos. While environmental determinism is rarely a productive approach to history, the suggestion that the relatively unforthcoming nature of the Chian environment encouraged its inhabitants in antiquity to pursue wealth through maritime endeavors is compelling (Sarikakis 1986: 121).

Good harbors on Chios are abundant (D. W. S. Hunt 1940–1945: 48–52). Chios' position at a midpoint on a major E–W coastal sea route ensured steady traffic through those harbors. In general, the east coast is far more hospitable than the steep and rocky west, though harbors at Volissos and Melanios make travel along the west coast possible.

## 3.4A. *Chian Material Culture*

The earliest evidence for habitation on Chios dates to the Neolithic period, and sites from the island that have produced Bronze Age material include Emporio, Kato Phana, Leukathia, Nagos, and the small island of Psara (located off the northwest coast) (Beaumont, Archontidou-Argyri, Beames et al. 2004; Vaessen 2014: 24–5). In the eighth century, substantial settlements existed at Emporio and at Mavri Rachi on Psara, and it is probable that Chios Town, the primary urban center of the island for much of its history, was already a significant site by that point.

Our understanding of the history of settlement at Chios Town has been greatly hindered by the fact that it lies underneath the modern town of Chora. The antiquities of the early periods of the city's history are thus poorly known (see Figure 3.1). The location, on the eastern coast of the central section of the

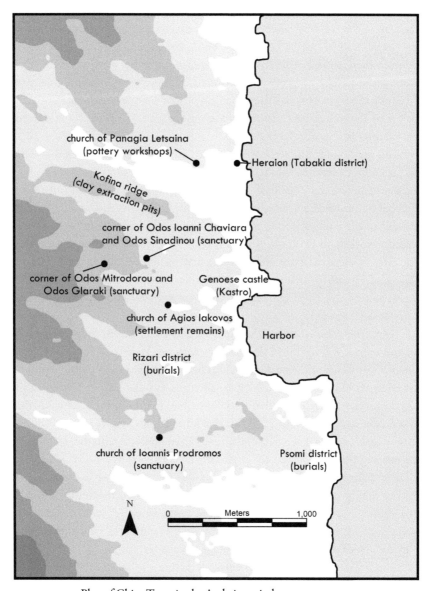

FIGURE 3.1. Plan of Chios Town in the Archaic period.

island, has been presumably favored from antiquity to the present because it offered a sheltered natural harbor and easy access to large tracts of relatively fertile land (Greaves 2010: 53). Scholars have generally assumed that the city was probably fortified from an early date, but the first mention of a city wall dates from the Classical period (Thuc. 8.40.2). No remains of the city wall have yet been found (Tsardaka 2010–2013: 486). The ancient acropolis probably lay beneath the Genoese castle (frequently referred to as the Kastro) on the north side of the harbor, as recently discovered building remains seem to suggest (Tsardaka 2010–2013: 490). The as-yet-unlocated Temple of Athena Poliouchos in Chios Town that is mentioned by Herodotus (1.160.3) was likely situated on that acropolis.

The only significant settlement deposit from the Archaic period that has so far come to light in Chios Town consists of a few seventh-century sherds excavated in the churchyard of Agios Iakovos (Homolle 1920: 412). Antonios Stephanou reported what he described as votive deposits to Demeter possibly datable to the Archaic period near that church (Stephanou 1958: 63). Multiple pottery workshops from the Archaic period have been found to the north of the city, in the area of the Kofina ridge and in the vicinity of the Church of Panagia Letsaina. In that same area, pits that seem to have been used for the extraction of clay starting in the Archaic period have been found (Tsardaka 2010–2013: 487–9).

Four sanctuaries that were active in the Archaic period have been found in and around Chios Town. A sanctuary with an Archaic building and votive deposit was found at the corner of Odos Ioanni Chaviara and Odos Sinadinou, probably within the walled area of the ancient city (Tsardaka 2010–2013: 499–501). Another sanctuary, with a curvilinear building from the Archaic period, was excavated at the corner of Odos Mitrodorou and Odos Glaraki, in the area known as Frangomachalas (Tsardaka 2010–2013: 499–502). To the north of the harbor, and probably outside the city walls, the remains of a Heraion (as apparent from inscribed dedications) have been found in the area known as Tabakia, with votives dating from the Archaic period through the fourth century (Tsardaka 2010–2013: 499–500). On the other side of town, excavations uncovered a sanctuary to a female deity, near the Church of Agios Ioannis Prodromos, again probably outside of the ancient walls (Tsardaka 2010–2013: 504).

Somewhat more evidence is available about the necropoleis of Archaic Chios Town. In the 1950s, more than 30 burials from the Archaic period were excavated in the area of Rizari on the southwest side of the city. Based on the excavated graves, it appears that burials began in the seventh century and continued through the Hellenistic period (Kontoleon 1952: 520–30; Kontoleon 1953: 268–74; cf. Lemos 1986; Lemos 1997; Phinphini 2015). A revetment from a sima decorated with a dog and with a horse's leg from 530–520, perhaps part of a burial sarcophagus, was found nearby (Simantoni-Bournia 1991: 75, 91–2). In the summer of 2014, the Greek Archaeological Service excavated a seventh- and sixth-century cemetery in the neighborhood of Psomi in the southern part of the urban core of the modern city. Other isolated tombs or small groups of graves are known.[13] Wolfram Hoepfner has argued, primarily on the basis of the location of tombs, that there were originally multiple distinct settlement clusters that grew into a single urban unit toward the end of the seventh century. He also suggests, on the basis of probability rather than solid archaeological evidence, that the city received fortification walls in the sixth century (Hoepfner and Tsakos 2011: 142–6; Hülden 2020: 107–9).

Archaeological information for Archaic Chios outside of Chios Town is drawn primarily from two sites, Emporio and Kato Phana.[14] Emporio was a settlement and sanctuary site located close to an excellent harbor in the southeast corner of the island (see Figure 3.2).[15] In the Final Neolithic period (fifth millennium) and the Bronze Age, the foot of a rocky hill on the south side of the harbor was the site of a sizable settlement. That settlement seems to have been abandoned sometime around 1100, but the finds from a sanctuary (the harbor sanctuary) on its western edge start in the Late Helladic IIIC period (12th/11th centuries) and seem to continue in an unbroken sequence down through the Roman period. When a new settlement came into being in the second half of the eighth century, it was centered on a 240-meter-high hill, now known as Prophitis Elias, just to the north of the harbor. By c. 600, the houses on Prophitis Elias had been abandoned (though activity at cult sites on Prophitis Elias continued), and settlement seems to have shifted for a time to a different site in the plain nearby.

The first phase of building activity on Prophitis Elias, in the second half of the eighth century, included a stone fortification wall (c. 800 m long and 1.6–2.5

---

13. https://chronique.efa.gr/?kroute=report&id=4748. From Phyta (seventh century; Kontoleon 1953: 274), Latomi (sixth century; Kourouniotis 1915: 67; D. W. S. Hunt 1940–1945: 32), Tes Kores to Gephyri (sixth century; Kourouniotis 1915: 67), Kontari (D. W. S. Hunt 1940–1945: 32–3), and Karyes (Kourouniotis 1915: 70). Hellenistic and Roman-era cemeteries have also been excavated, with the physical distribution of the different cemeteries indicating that the area of the ancient city shrank during the Roman period from its Archaic, Classical, and Hellenistic dimensions (Tsardaka 2010–2013: 505).

14. On the shrine for Cybele at Daskalopetra, see Section 3.11A.3.

15. The excavations and published finds are described in Boardman 1967. For the architecture of the settlement on Prophitis Elias, see Boardman 1967: 3–51; for the harbor sanctuary, see 52–96. Emporio is the modern name for the site. The ancient toponym is not known; see Boardman 1967: 254–6.

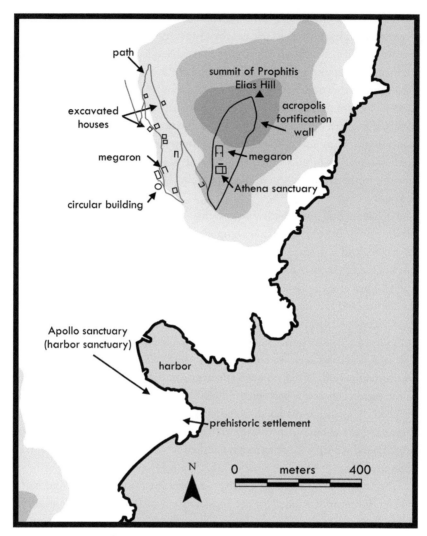

FIGURE 3.2. Plan of Emporio in the Archaic period.

m thick) that encircled the acropolis (to the south and just below the peak of Prophitis Elias) (Frederiksen 2011: 137–8; Hülden 2020: 106–7). Within the lines of that fortification wall and contemporary with it were just two architectural entities: a megaron and a Sanctuary to Athena. The megaron, measuring c. 18 x. 6.5 m and built entirely from stone, had a porch with two columns *in antis*, an interior axial colonnade, and a flat roof. The absence of interior finds makes it difficult to establish its function, but it has been plausibly interpreted as a town hall or chieftain's house (Mazarakis Ainian 1997: 197–8).

The Sanctuary to Athena originally consisted of a peribolos wall (which also functioned as a retaining wall) and a trapezoidal altar. In the sixth century, the sanctuary received a non-peripteral temple, measuring c. 10 x 6 m, built with rubble walls. That temple had both a pronaos and a cella. The eighth-century altar was enclosed in the cella, and a new altar was built on the temple's north side. The temple continued in use until the early fifth century, when it was destroyed, almost certainly as a result of Persian intervention on the island (see Section 3.7A). It was rebuilt in largely the same form in the fourth century, and offerings at the site continued in an unbroken sequence from the eighth down through the end of the fourth century.

To the west of the acropolis, approximately 50 houses, joined by a network of paths, were excavated on a series of terraces spilling down the slope of the hill. These houses seem to have been built in a haphazard manner, with each dwelling perched on its own diminutive, typically detached terrace. All of these dwellings were constructed from rough conglomerate stones, with an entrance typically on the north or south side (probably as a response to the strong prevailing winds). Roofs were flat, with horizontal beams and a protective coating made from clay, straw, and seaweed. The houses are mostly relatively small (c. 20–50 sq m), single-room buildings, rectangular or square in plan, with a courtyard. Some of the preserved interiors show significant differences in height, which may suggest that there were originally wooden floors that created multiple levels. The walls are insufficiently preserved to offer evidence for windows, but parallels elsewhere and vase paintings indicate that there were triangular openings high up on the walls. The interior spaces feature a small square hearth against one wall and benches at the back, presumably for sleeping.

The area of the site in which these houses were located also contained two rather different structures. One was a megaron that was constructed on a specially built terrace situated more or less in the center of the settlement. That building had two phases. In the first, it seems to have measured c. 17 x 7 m and had three interior spaces: a porch that gave way to a main chamber with an apsidal room behind it. The megaron was subsequently rebuilt in smaller form such that it became a two-room structure measuring c. 10 x 6 m, with a hearth in the larger room. What had been the apsidal room was walled off from the rest of the structure and became a separate space with its own entrance. Pottery finds date the later phase to the sixth century (Mazarakis Ainian 1997: 85–6). The other noteworthy structure was a circular building, c. 5 m in diameter, that seems to have served as a storage space.

The sanctuary on the western edge of the Bronze Age settlement on the south side of the harbor is typically referred to as the harbor sanctuary, because the deity to which it was dedicated was not clear until relatively recently, when an inscribed sherd dating to the sixth century and naming Apollo was found (Roungou 2012: 143, fig. 15). As noted above, the earliest finds from the sanctuary—figurines and ritual vessels—date to the Late Helladic IIIC and Protogeometric periods (Roungou and Vouligea 2019: 99–100). In the Archaic period, the sanctuary encompassed a series of terraces among which deposits were found, rich in votive objects dated to the eighth through sixth centuries. There is no trace of a cult building prior to the sixth century, and it is likely that for much of the Archaic period, the only architectural embellishment was a simple temenos wall with an entrance for a path leading up from the sea. By the sixth century, an enigmatic and apparently curvilinear or apsidal temple had been constructed, known solely from a few fragmentary architectural pieces (Boardman 1967: 65).

The early votive offerings from the harbor sanctuary are far more varied in origin than the locally produced offerings found at the Athena sanctuary on Prophitis Elias (Boardman 1967: 61–4). Early Corinthian, East Greek Wild Goat, and Attic ceramic wares from the seventh and sixth centuries are found in abundance, perhaps representing votives associated with passing merchant ships and their crews (Boardman 1967: 64). Although direct Archaic evidence for maritime networks is somewhat limited, the apparent remains of a seventh-century shipwreck, found near the islet of Agios Stephanos in Lagkada bay on the northeastern coast of Chios, provide powerful testimony to the connections between Chios and the rest of the Aegean in the Archaic period (Theodoulou, Kourkoumelis, Preka-Alexandri, et al. 2009: 145). Also noteworthy among the finds from the harbor sanctuary are three life-size marble statues (two *kouroi* and one *korē*) dating to the sixth century (Roungou 2012).

Other Archaic sanctuary remains on Chios are located at Phanai (modern Kato Phana) on the southwestern coast of the island. The finds from the excavations conducted at Phanai, which was primarily a cult site, point to the existence of a sanctuary dedicated to Apollo in the ninth century. The sanctuary lies a couple of hundred meters behind the current shoreline, but recent excavations have shown that the sea reached all the way up to the western side of the site in antiquity and that a torrent running past the north side of the site silted up what had been a good harbor. Phanai was an open-air cult site where a good deal of ritual feasting and drinking took place from the ninth to the seventh centuries. In the seventh century, a terrace wall that also served as a peribolos was constructed from rough limestone blocks on the western (seaward) side of the site. A stone staircase on the western side of the sanctuary seems to have been the main access point at that time (Kourouniotis 1915; Kourouniotis 1916; Lamb 1934–1935: 147–64; Beaumont 2004; Beaumont 2019).

In the first half of the sixth century, a new terrace/peribolos wall, built from rough limestone blocks, expanded the size of the sanctuary. The seventh-century entrance on the western side continued to be used, and a new entrance, accessed by double flights of stairs, was built on the north side. In the late sixth or early fifth century, the construction of a third terrace/peribolos wall, built from ashlar blocks of limestone, resulted in another significant extension of the sanctuary. The old western entrance (now likely taking the form of a walled dromos) continued to be in use, and the site also could be accessed by means of a staircase built into the northern side of the new wall. At some point in the sixth or early fifth century (the dating remains problematic), a marble temple, mostly destroyed except for partial remains of the *euthynteria*, was built. The finds from the late seventh and sixth centuries, like those of the harbor sanctuary at Emporio, derive from an unusually wide geographical range and are of relatively high value.

Leaving aside Chios Town, Emporio, and Phanai, a limited collection of evidence attests to activity at 15 sites on Chios during the Archaic period (Merousis 2002: 105).[16] This figure is much lower than the number of known Classical and Hellenistic sites but compares favorably with the apparent paucity of habitation during the Late Bronze Age.[17] These discrepancies could indicate anything from demographic change to variability in the relative visibility and preservation of remains to the particular research objectives of modern archaeologists. They need not lead us to posit that the island was sparsely populated in the Archaic period (see Section 3.9A). Given the uneven exploration of the island and a lack of chronological precision regarding local ceramic wares in the region, it is best to be conservative in terms of demographic extrapolations from the known site distribution.

We can nonetheless be certain that the island's population was not confined to Chios Town and Emporio. (On the Chian *peraia*, see Section 3.7A.) The settlement pattern on Chios during the Archaic period seems to have been largely determined by the geological makeup of the island, with a concentration of habitation in the fertile plains around Chios Town and Emporio (Evangelidis 1921). The sites outside of Chios Town were relatively small, subsidiary

---

16. The best existing overviews of sites from the island remain Yalouris 1976 and Yalouris 1986, but see also Merousis 2002 and now Tsardaka 2010–2013, summarizing the results of the excavations in modern Chora undertaken between 1985 and 2013.

17. Yalouris cataloged 34 Classical/Hellenistic sites and six sites dating to the Late Bronze Age (Yalouris 1976; Yalouris 1986: 166). Merousis (2002: 97–105) lists six Late Bronze Age sites and 48 Classical/Hellenistic ones, along with 15 certain and three possible Archaic sites.

settlements that formed part of a single *polis* that encompassed the entire island (see Section 3.5A). The size of the island and the existence of those subsidiary sites long after the island formed a single *polis* indicate that a significant fraction of the population of the *polis* resided in the *chōra*. In his account of the immediate aftermath of the Battle of Lade, Herodotus mentions a site on or near Chios called Polichne (6.26.2), which could be a fort or the proper name of a small town, possibly on the mainland. Chian slaves' personal knowledge of the countryside during the Athenian occupation of 412 (see Section 3.9A) likewise attests to rural settlements. Finally, we should note the mention by the Hellenistic historian Nymphodorus of Syracuse of the country estates (*agroikiai*) of the Chians, which he says were ravaged during a slave revolt (*FGrH* 572 F4).

Published evidence for Chian burial customs during the Archaic period comes from the necropoleis located at Latomi; in the area between the settlements of Latomi, Karyes, and Chios Town; and at Rizari and Psomi in Chios Town. Kourouniotis excavated at Latomi 30 Clazomenian-type terracotta sarcophagi dating to the sixth century (Kourouniotis 1915: 67-71; see also Hunt 1940-1945: 31-3). More recent excavations in the area between Latomi, Karyes, and Chios Town uncovered 176 tombs dated between the second half of the seventh and the end of the fourth century: 121 terracotta sarcophagi, 24 tile-roofed (κεραμοσκεπείς) tombs, 10 cists, 10 *enchytrismoi* in amphoras, 6 pits, and 5 stone sarcophagi. Forty-nine of the 121 terracotta sarcophagi contained grave goods, typically in the form of pottery, especially hydria (both full-sized and miniature). Metal objects (bronze mirrors, jewellery) were relatively uncommon (Demani 2019: 288-93).

At Rizari Kontoleon excavated a necropolis that was used in the Late Geometric and Archaic periods. He uncovered three inhumation burials in large local limestone sarcophagi containing offerings of local hydriai; the rest of the burials were placed in pithoi of local manufacture. In the center of the cemetery, surrounded by the sarcophagi and urn burials, was a funeral pyre dated to the seventh century by fragments of hydriai found among the carbonized remains (Kontoleon 1952: 520–30; Kontoleon 1953: 268–74; cf. Lemos 1986; Lemos 1997). Further burials of the same type were found in 1983 both at Rizari and near the church of Ioannis Prodromos, c. 500 m to the south of Rizari (Demani 2019: 294-300).[18]

---

18. Raftopoulou and Anetakis 2019: 313 mention the excavation of 261 tombs, some of which date to later periods, but no chronological breakdown.

Preliminary reports of the excavation of the cemetery at Psomi in Chios Town mention a total of 56 tombs. Burials took place in pithoi sealed with stone slabs, in Clazomenian-type terracotta sarcophagi, in trench graves with the bodies in extended or contracted position, and, in one case, in a stone sarcophagus. The existence of a horse buried within that cemetery is the first known equine burial from the northeastern Aegean, and demonstrates just how much we have yet to learn about the development of Chian society during the Archaic period.[19]

Mortuary conventions in Archaic Chios show influence from surrounding regions. Burials in terracotta sarcophagi, for example, are characteristic of the Anatolian coast around Clazomenae, while burials with horses are most common in Cyprus. Chian funerary practices during the Archaic period are, in general terms, characterized primarily by inhumations and by the side-by-side appearance of burials in stone or terracotta sarcophagi, terracotta vessels, and trench graves (Kourouniotis 1915: 67–70; Lemos 1997: 80–2; Merousis 2002: 144). Children are most often buried in jars. Hierarchy seems to be indicated by the elaboration or size of sarcophagi and vessels, rather than by ostentatious grave offerings. Given the patchy nature of the evidence for Archaic funerary customs on Chios, this summary stands to be revised as future work expands the available sample of evidence.

Pride of place among distinctive Chian products from the Archaic period must go to the island's pottery.[20] Chian pottery during the Archaic period should be understood within the wider context of East Greek pottery in general. The most prominent ceramic style of East Greece during the Archaic period is commonly called the Wild Goat Style because it features wild goats frolicking or grazing. Real and mythological creatures such as deer, lions, sphinxes, or sirens often accompany or are substituted for the goats, and these quadrupeds are usually surrounded by a plethora of filling ornaments, in a fashion typical of most orientalizing vase-painting styles. Wild Goat Style vessels are usually covered with a white or pale slip, with their interiors commonly coated in black slip.[21]

The Archaic Chian ceramic tradition operated within the wider world of the Wild Goat Style. The quintessential Chian shape is the chalice (see Figure 3.3), an evolution of the Geometric skyphos (Lemos 1991: vol. 1: 125–32; Boardman 1998: 145). Rare bespoke Chian shapes, such as a bull vase from Emporio, as

---

19. https://chronique.efa.gr/?kroute=report&id=4748; Demani 2019: 300–5.

20. Hermippus, the fifth-century Athenian comedian, praises the Chian kylix (Kock I 240 *apud* Athenaeus 480e). The only known Chian potter is Nikesermos, who signed a kalyx kratēr from Emporio (Boardman 1967: 251 pls. 34, 97, fig. 74).

21. For an introduction to Archaic Wild Goat style pottery, see Cook 1997: 109–33.

**FIGURE 3.3.** Chian chalice attributed to the Running Man Painter; c. 580–570; height: 14.4 cm, diameter: 14.5 cm; from Camirus on Rhodes. Louvre Collection Salzmann, 1863 A 330 Bis.

well as several phallus-shaped pots from Naucratis in Egypt, add variety and show a special spark and vitality among Chian potters (Lemos 1986: 244; D. W. Roller 2006: 127). The various Chian sub-styles of Wild Goat, including the Mature Animal Style, the Animal Chalice Style, and the Grand Style (which saw the introduction of human figures and the easing of ornamental fills) clearly developed from the general eastern Wild Goat Style, with similar iconographic concerns and superficial appearances (Lemos 1986: 163–75). The Chian slip was especially thick, white, and flaky, and the interior slip was relatively dull (Lemos 1991: vol. 1: 1–3; Bergeron 2014: 3). Decoration was added in black, with red, white, and purple highlights. Decorative elaboration is intricate and often floral, with general affinities to East Greek pottery overall but recognizable variation. Beginning in the seventh century but mainly after the middle of the sixth century, black-figure decoration replaced the East Greek Wild Goat Style, probably because of influence from mainland Greece (Laimou 1987–1988).

## 3.5A. Chian Political History

The Chians, as we know from both Ion of Chios and other independent accounts, claimed Oinopion, the son of Dionysus and Ariadne, as founder and first king of the *polis*.[22] The Oinopion (literally, "wine drinker") myth probably served as a way for the Chians to connect their *polis*' famous viticulture (see Section 3.8A.3) to gods and heroes. According to Ion, Oinopion's reign saw the introduction of Carians and Abantes to the island, while his sons were succeeded in the kingship by Amphiklos from Euboea. A descendant of the latter, Hector, also held the kingship and waged war on the island's non-Greek population. Ion's real innovation, however, was to make Oinopion a son of Theseus rather than of Dionysus. His account is a particularly direct and politicized example of mythographic attempts to make the Athenians the founders of the Ionian cities, typically for imperialistic purposes.[23]

Otherwise, the literary sources offer just a few scattered mentions of early kings, many of them probably later inventions. Most intriguing is the duo Polyteknos and Amphiklos, called tyrants in a fragment written by the (probably early Hellenistic) historian Hippias of Erythrae (*FGrH* 421 F1). Polyteknos has long been known as one of the eponyms of Chios' tribal system. A recently published inscription (*SEG* 56.1003; see below for further discussion) shows that Amphiklos was also a tribal eponym. The historicity of these figures is unclear. Amphiklos could be the king mentioned by Ion and would therefore "belong" to the eleventh century (i.e., would be mythical). Some modern historians, perhaps treating Hippias of Erythrae too uncritically as a source for Archaic history, put Polyteknos and Amphiklos in the seventh century (Berve 1967: vol. 1: 96; Huxley 1966: 26, 28; Carlier 1984: 444).[24]

---

22. Ion of Chios *FGrH* 392 F1; Critias fr. eleg. B2 West; Theopomp. *FGrH* 115 F276; Diod. Sic. 5.79.1, 5.84.3; cf. *PEP Chios* 499. For a cult building, the [Οἰν]οπιονεῖον, see *PEP Chios* 523. Previous political histories of Chios include O'Neil 1978–1979; Roebuck 1986; and Sarikakis 1998.

23. Cf. Solon F4a West; Hdt. 1.146.2, 1.147.2, 9.106.3; Thuc. 1.2.5–6, 2.15.4; Eur. *Ion* 74–5, 1575–89. See further Jacoby 1947: 4–7; Barron 1986; Olding 2007: 146–9; Mac Sweeney 2013: 80–91.

24. See Simonton 2018 for an extended analysis of the Hippias fragment.

274    THE OXFORD HISTORY OF THE ARCHAIC GREEK WORLD

By the end of the Archaic period, the entire island of Chios indubitably formed a single *polis* with its center at Chios Town, but the precise date of this political unification is difficult to establish, given the available evidence. It is possible that the abandonment of the settlement on Prophitis Elias at Emporio in c. 600 (see Section 3.4A) was the result of a process of centralization. Some have argued that the so-called constitutional law (see below for detailed discussion) was enacted as part of a process of political unification, which would suggest, but by no means definitively establish, a mid-sixth-century date (U. Walter 1993: 94; van Effenterre and Ruzé 1994–1995: vol. 1: 266).

The politics of Archaic Chios come alive for us for the first time with the aforementioned constitutional law from c. 550. The law is inscribed in boustrophedon on all four lateral faces of a slab of pinkish trachyte.[25] As Karl-Joachim Hölkeskamp (1999: 80–6) has argued, this document is not likely to have established the definition and competence of each Chian political and judicial institution, in the manner of a modern constitution or law code. Instead, and in line with much Archaic law (see Section 3.6A), it may have created some new bodies in an ad hoc fashion, in reaction to concrete infractions by magistrates that demanded a communal response. The misbehaving magistrates in question are the *dēmarchos* and the *basileus*, whose misdeeds seem to have required the involvement of a special council (the *dēmosiē bolē*).

We offer here a text and translation before discussing several difficulties presented by this document.[26]

A:     [- - -]κα: της Ιστιης δημο                    (1)
ρητρας:φυλασσω[ν? - - -]
[- - -]ον: ηρει: ημ μεν δεμαρ-
χων: η βασιλευων: δεκασ[θηι? - - -]
[- - -? τη]ς Ιστιης αποδοτω:δημα-          (5)

---

25. The stone was found in the Chian village of Tholopotami and published in 1909. Ottoman authorities had it transferred to Istanbul, where it remains in storage in the Archaeological Museum. Because the use of trachyte is otherwise unknown on Chios, Forrest (*apud* Meiggs and Lewis 1988: 38) suspected that the stone was a *pierre errante*, perhaps of Erythraean origin (cf. Hansen 1985). However, the dedication of Lykaithos (*PEP Chios* 152) originates, like the constitutional law, from Tholopotami and has similar letter forms (cross-theta rather than dot-theta, e.g.), and yet no one has questioned its Chian provenance. Therefore, in what follows, we treat the constitutional law as Chian. Important studies of the inscription include von Wilamowitz-Moellendorff 1909: 64–75 #25; Jeffery 1956; Meiggs and Lewis 1988: 38; van Effenterre and Ruzé 1994–1995: vol. 1: 62 (changing the order of the sides, putting D first); Robinson 1997: 90–101; Gagarin 2008: 56–8; Werlings 2010: 158–65.

26. The Greek text given here is taken from Jeffery 1956.

ρχεων·εξπρηξαι: τον ε[ξεταστην? - - -]
[- - -]εν δημο κεκλημενο
αλοιαι τιμη διπλησ[ιη? - - -]
[- - -]ν οσην παραλοιω[.]

B:    [ . . . ]ην δ' ηκκλητος δι[κη? - - -]                    (1)
[- - -]ην δε αδικηται: παρα
δημαρχωι: στατηρ[ας? - - -]

C:    εκκαλεσθω ες                                             (1)
βολην την δημ-
οσιην· τηι τριτηι
εξ εβδομαιων
βολη αγερεσθ-                                                  (5)
ω η δημοσιη ε-
πιθωιος λεκτ-
η πεντηροντ' απ-
ο φυλης· τα τ' αλ[λ]-
[α] πρησσετω τα δη-                                           (10)
μο και δικα[ς ο]-
[ρο]σαι αν εκκλ-
ητοι γενων[τ]-
[αι] το μηνος π-
ασας επι[ . . . ]                                            (15)
[ . . . ] σ ε ε ρ[ . . . ]

D:    [- - - Α]ρτημισιωνος vac.                               (1)
[- - -]ων ορκια επι-
ταμνετω ρω[μνυτω? - - -]
[- - - β]ασιλευσιν vac.

A: . . . of Hestia, watching over the ordinances [ῥῆτραι] of the people [δῆμος] . . .
if he, during his term as *demarch* or βασιλεύς, should [?take a bribe] . . . let him,
while serving as *demarch*, pay to [something or someone] of Hestia . . . the [indi-
vidual or institution beginning with the letter epsilon] is to exact the fine . . .
the people [δῆμος] having been called together; cases of assault: the penalty [is
to be] doubled . . .

B: . . . the appealed [?case] . . . if he should be mistreated in the presence of the
*demarchos* . . . . . . *statēres* . . .

276    THE OXFORD HISTORY OF THE ARCHAIC GREEK WORLD

C: Let him appeal to the council concerned with public matters [δημοσίη βολή; for this translation, see below]. On the third day after the Hebdomaia let the council be gathered, the one concerned with public matters, empowered to levy penalties [ἐπιθώϊος], selected [λεκτή] [according to] fifty [men] from a tribe. Let it exact any other property belonging to the people [δῆμος], and all those cases that were appealed during the month . . .

D: [the month of] Artemision . . . let him pledge [lit. "cut oath offerings"] and [?swear] . . . to the βασιλεῖς.

Because of the preponderance of words related to *dēmos* in the inscription, some scholars have speculated that something like democracy had emerged in Chios by the early sixth century (Robinson 1997: 90–101). The prominence of the *dēmos* in the law, however, is not necessarily precocious for its time. As Marie-Joséphine Werlings (2010) has shown, the *dēmos* played a significant role in many Archaic communities. Furthermore, the label *demosiē* does not necessarily mean a council "of the people," let alone a council created in opposition to an older, more "aristocratic" *boulē* (Ampolo 1983; Ruzé 1997: 364–6; Werlings 2010: 158–65). In the Archaic period, *dēmosios* most often has the sense "belonging to the community," sometimes with the narrower meaning "public property."[27] Given that the Chian law is explicitly concerned with bribes and fines and that the council is "empowered to levy penalties" (ἐπιθώϊος, C l. 6–7), it may be that *dēmosiē bolē* here means "the council concerned with public matters," especially public funds. On this understanding, the role of the council is not, as Lilian Jeffery argued, to "conduct [πρησσέτω] the other business of the people" (C l. 9–11) but rather to "exact [med. of πράσσω *LSJ* A.VI] any other property belonging to the δῆμος." Such powers would be fully in line with the numerous instances of *praxis* ("exaction of fines") by *polis* officials in Archaic law.[28]

    Whatever form of government is represented by the regime attested in the constitutional law, it probably stayed intact until the later sixth century, when the pro-Persian tyrant Strattis seized power (Hdt. 4.138.2, 8.132.2). Strattis was certainly in control of Chios by the time he took part in Darius' expedition against

---

27. *IG* IX.1².609.3; *IG* V.2.261.3; *SEG* 27.631A.4, 7, 631B.5. For literary instances, see, e.g., Xenophanes F2.8 West; Solon F4.12 West; Thgn. 50; Hipponax F128.4 West (paired with βουλή). For further discussion, see Fouchard 1998 and Werlings 2010: Annexe III Tableau B.

28. See, for example, van Effenterre and Ruzé 1994–1995: vol. 1: #97 lines 1, 7, 11; vol. 2: #80 line 3; Osborne and Rhodes 2017: #132 l.35. For exaction by officials at Chios, see *PEP Chios* 76, B.20, C.15–20. Earlier in the constitutional law, it is specified that an official will "exact" a penalty (A.6).

the Scythians in 513, but it is not likely that Strattis was installed as a tyrant by the Persians immediately following Cyrus' defeat of Croesus in 546. Instead, the tyrants enumerated by Herodotus at 4.138 seem to have come to power at different times, often based on their own enterprising initiative rather than by top-down Persian fiat (see Section 3.7A). Strattis was presumably deposed when the Ionian Rebellion began in 499 (Hdt. 5.38.2), but despite Herodotus' claim (6.43.3) that in 492, Mardonius "deposed all of the Ionian tyrants and established democracies in the *poleis*" (τοὺς γὰρ τυράννους τῶν Ἰώνων καταπαύσας πάντας ὁ Μαρδόνιος δημοκρατίας κατίστα ἐς τὰς πόλιας; translation our own), Strattis was in power in 480 when seven men formed (an ultimately futile) conspiracy to overthrow him (Hdt. 8.132.2). He must, therefore, have returned to power sometime after 494, presumably with Persian support. Strattis was presumably deposed after the Battle of Mycale, and an oligarchy came to power in Chios. That oligarchy lasted until 412 and receives praise from Thucydides for its moderation even during periods of prosperity (8.24.4; see Section 3.8A).

The so-called Dophitis inscription (Osborne and Rhodes 2017: #133), perhaps a product of this time, outlines the procedure for dealing with those who tamper with any of the 75 boundary stones that mark out a territory called Dophitis (the precise location of which on Chios remains unclear).[29] The "Guardians of the Boundary Stones" (ὁροφύλακες) are to exact a 100-*statēr* fine, but any negligence on their part is to be punished by the Fifteen (perhaps a subset of the Council, mentioned at B.3). The *dēmos* is not mentioned. If the Fifteen fail in their duty, the chain of responsibility falls not to any popular law court or volunteer prosecutor but to the gods: the Fifteen are to be cursed (Rubinstein 2003: 99). The *basileus* of the constitutional law reappears, this time cursing offenders (D.8), a religious function in line with what we know of this office's duties from later epigraphic sources.[30]

In terms of civic organization, the "constitutional law" decrees that the *demosiē bolē* should consist of 50 men from each of the tribes (*phylai*). Inscriptions dating to the fourth and third centuries show what appear to be tribes and other civic subdivisions. So far, four, possibly five, tribes have been identified: Totteidai, Chalazoi, Amphiklidai, Polyteknidai, and perhaps Oinopidai.[31] Listed under

---

29. For the text with the commentary, Matthaiou 2011: 13-34 and discussion at *SEG* 61.699. The inscription also deals with the sale of confiscated property, probably that of enemies of the state (Faraguna 2005).

30. For *basileis* in Chios, see further *SEG* 35.923B.2 (c. 400).

31. For a possible *phylē* of the Oinopidai, see the remarks of Forrest 1960: 188–9. With the publication of *SEG* 56.1003, it has become apparent that the Amphiklidai were a tribe. As we have seen, Amphiklos was considered a tyrant and contemporaneous with Polyteknos (*FGrH* 421 F1).

278    THE OXFORD HISTORY OF THE ARCHAIC GREEK WORLD

the tribes in the relevant inscriptions are other kinds of groupings with names that include patronymic suffixes. With the publication of a new inscription of this type (Malouchou 2006 = *SEG* 56.1003; late fourth/early third century), in which the famous *genos* of the Homeridai is one of the subordinate groups, the identification of the patronymic bodies with *genē* seems secure.[32] The remaining bodies, which follow the construction οἱ + the genitive of a masculine name, are likely newer civic bodies parallel to the *genē* rather than subdivisions of those *genē*.[33] It is striking that the new inscription *SEG* 56.1003 lists οἱ Παρμένοντος, since a military division of freed slaves called δεκὰς Παρμένοντος is known from a late fifth-century inscription (*PEP Chios* 62 B.11). It may be, then, that the *dekas Parmenontos* was incorporated into the civic body already in the late fifth century.[34] (See the discussion of the Chians' treatment of their slaves in Section 3.9A for more on the *dekas Parmenontos*.)

## *3.6A.  Chian Legal History*

Our understanding of Archaic Chian legal history is based largely on the so-called constitutional law and the Dophitis inscription, both discussed in Section 3.5A. The Dophitis inscription deals with disputes over confiscated and publicly sold property. The *polis* agrees to judge cases of disputed ownership and to pay any plaintiff who turns out to have had his possessions taken illegally. The potential problems surrounding confiscated property evinced by the inscription are common in the aftermath of *stasis*, as is known from later epigraphic examples.[35] It is striking that, outside of these first two examples, *leges sacrae* predominate in early Chian epigraphy, with eight examples from the fifth and fourth centuries.[36]

---

32. For the Homeridai as a *genos*, see Akousilaos *FGrH* 2 F2; Hellanicus *FGrH* 4 F20. For further discussion of the Homeridai, see Section 3.12A.

33. For alternative reconstructions, see Forrest 1960: 178; Malouchou 2006.

34. Forrest (Forrest 1963: 54 n. 8), with incredible prescience, asked, "Would . . . the δεκὰς Παρμένοντος remain a separate unit in the tribe—οἱ Παρμένοντος?" The new tribal list seems to confirm his suggestion.

35. See, for example, Rhodes and Osborne 2003: #84 (also Chios), 85, 101; *SEG* 51.1075 (fourth-century Chios); *IG* XII.4.132.

36. Two further sacred laws, both from the later fifth/earlier fourth century, are published in Matthaiou 2006 and R. Parker 2006. Parker (2006: 70) notes the remarkable abundance of these texts given the paucity of Chian inscriptions overall. They all date to the Classical period or later and thus lie outside our time period. This chronological distribution demonstrates well the relative lack of Archaic Chian inscriptions compared with, e.g., Samos.

## 3.7A. Chian Diplomatic History

The details of Chios' wars during the early Archaic period remain murky. The *polis* fought often with Erythrae (see, for example, Hdt. 1.18.3), which was located directly opposite Chios on the coast of Asia Minor. The casus belli evidently involved the contested territory of Leukonia (probably, but not certainly, located on the mainland and hence potentially part of Chios' *peraia*; Rubinstein 2004b: 1060). The wars between the two *poleis* provide the setting for a story on the courage of Chian women, related by both Polyaenus (8.66) and Plutarch (*Mor.* 244e–45b). The Milesians seem to have aided the Chians in the latter's hostilities with Erythrae, and, in return, the Chians lent assistance to the Milesians when they were attacked by the Lydian king Alyattes (Hdt. 1.18.3) sometime around 600.

Chios was one of the members of the Ionian League, which probably came into being in the first half of the sixth century. The members of the Ionian League all participated in the worship of Poseidon Helikonios at the Panionion and took part in collective political deliberations. It is, however, not evident that the Ionian League was at any point during the Archaic period responsible for organizing political interventions or military campaigns of any great note (see Section 3.10A).

The Chians and other Ionian islanders made pacts of *xenia* with Croesus c. 554 (Hdt. 1.27.5) and hence remained independent from the Lydians, though the islanders may have paid tribute to the Lydians (Hdt. 1.6.2). Herodotus says that following the Persian conquest of Lydia in 546, the islanders surrendered to Cyrus (σφέας αὐτοὺς ἔδοσαν Κύρῳ; 1.169.2), though he also says that "there was no danger for islanders, for the Phoenicians were not yet subjects of Persia, and the Persians themselves were no sailors" (Hdt. 1.143.1). The extent of Persian control over Chios was probably quite limited for a considerable period of time. As we have seen (see Section 3.5A), pro-Persian tyrannies developed gradually, and it is likely that the pro-Persian tyrant Strattis did not come to power in Chios until well after the Persian conquest of Lydia.[37]

Not long after 546, the Chians handed over Paktyes (a Lydian who had led a revolt against Persian rule) to the Persians, in exchange for which they received the city of Atarneus (located on the mainland of Asia Minor) (Hdt. 1.160.3–5). Atarneus represented most or all of Chios' *peraia*, which was among the smallest

---

37. Strattis first appears in the historical record in the context of Darius' expedition against the Scythians in 513 (see below). For Persian policy vis-à-vis the Greek tyrants, see D. F. Graf 1985; Austin 1990.

280   THE OXFORD HISTORY OF THE ARCHAIC GREEK WORLD

in the Greek world. It is likely that the presence of Erythrae on the coast directly opposite Chios made the development of a substantial *peraia* effectively impossible (Funke 1999: 64; Constantakopoulou 2007: 178–9, 241–2). Sometime before this, the Chians had also come to possess the Oinoussai islands (just off the northeast coast of Chios), which they refused to sell to the Phocaeans in 545 for fear that the resettled Phocaeans would inhibit the Chians' maritime commerce (Hdt. 1.165.1).

Strattis took part in Darius' expedition against the Scythians in 513 (Hdt. 4.138.2), which indicates that Chios had become a Persian dependency by that point in time, presumably under Strattis' direction. The Chians expelled Strattis and joined the Ionian Rebellion in 499, and it was to Chios that the former Milesian tyrant Histiaeus came upon his return to Ionia from Persia sometime around 496 (Hdt. 6.2.2).[38] The Chians initially confined Histiaeus because they suspected he had come to return Chios to Persian rule, but he persuaded them of his good intentions, and the Chians provided some limited assistance to Histiaeus in his failed attempts to restore himself to power in Miletus (Hdt. 6.5). At the Battle of Lade in 494, the Chians supplied 100 ships to the Ionian fleet, more than any other Greek city, and stationed 40 citizens on each ship to serve as marines (Hdt. 6.8.1, 15.1) (see Section 3.9A on the Chians' use of slaves as rowers). Herodotus claims that much of the Ionian fleet deserted the line of battle at Lade, while the Chians fought with notable bravery in a losing cause and retreated toward Chios with their surviving ships when the battle was over (Hdt. 6.14–15). A certain number of Chian ships were sufficiently damaged that they had to be beached at Mycale. The survivors set off on foot but were killed by the Ephesians, who mistook them for pirates (Hdt. 6.16). Histiaeus, who operated independently and with murky intentions for much of the Ionian Rebellion, attacked and conquered Chios in the aftermath of the Battle of Lade, for reasons that remain the subject of much speculation (Hdt. 6.26–7; D. Kienast 1994).[39]

In 493, the Persian fleet captured Chios and, according to Herodotus, rounded up the entire population of the island by "netting" them with a cordon of men, made some of the captured boys into eunuchs, and burned the city and various sanctuaries (Hdt. 6.31–2). The picture painted by Herodotus is one of catastrophic punishment, but such "nettings" were in all likelihood largely

---

38. For a more detailed account of the Ionian Rebellion, see Slawisch Forthcoming: Section 1.7.

39. It is possible, for instance, that Histaieus had it in mind to turn Chios over to the Persians in order to help secure his return to the Persian court (Heinlein 1909: 349–51).

symbolic and had limited long-term effects (Constantakopoulou 2007: 126–9). Herodotus does not say anything explicit about the Persians returning Strattis to power, but insofar as Strattis was ruling Chios in 480 (Hdt. 8.132.2), it is likely that he resumed the tyranny in 493.

When Strattis fell from power after the Battle of Mycale in 479, the Chians, along with the Lesbians and Samians, joined the Greek alliance (Hdt. 9.106.4). According to Plutarch, the Chians, Samians, and Lesbians approached Aristeides directly about switching allegiance from the Spartan regent Pausanias to him, and the Chian commander Antagores helped to discredit the Spartan in the eyes of the other allies (*Arist.* 23.4–5). In celebration of their emancipation from Persian control, the Chians dedicated an altar in front of the temple at Delphi (Hdt. 2.135.4; Daux 1943: 212). Chios was an enthusiastic supporter of the formation of the Delian League in 478/7 (Thuc. 1.96; [Arist.] *Ath. Pol.* 23.5, 24.2; Quinn 1981: 6–9, 39–49), and the Chians remained loyal subjects of the Athenian empire until 412.

Sometime before 650, the Chians undertook their only colonial venture (other than Naucratis, on which see Section 3.8A), founding Maroneia in Thrace (Ps.-Scymnus 675–8 with Philochorus *FGrH* 328 F43; cf. Tiverios 2006–2008: vol. 2: 99–104).[40] The place was supposedly named for Maron, the priest of Apollo at nearby Ismaros (Hom. *Od.* 9.197–8). Intriguingly, it is Maron who gives Odysseus the potent "dark wine" (μέλας οἶνος) that subdues the Cyclops. It is not difficult to imagine that the Chians, who believed that they themselves had invented *melas oinos* with help from Oinopion (see Section 3.8A.3), argued on the basis of epic poetry that they had a claim to the territory.

## 3.8A.  Chian Economic History

Chios had a reputation in the Classical period as being an unusually prosperous place. Thucydides notes that the Chians "flourished at the same time as they practiced prudence, and to the extent that their *polis* grew greater, they also ordered it more securely" (8.24.4; cf. 8.15.1, 8.45.4). Thucydides means his characterization to apply to the island as it developed after the Persian Wars, during which time its territory remained "undisturbed" (*apathēs*, 8.24.3). The evidence pertaining to the Archaic history of the island suggests, however, that this flourishing was more of a steady trend than a postwar divergence.

---

40. For an overview of the colonizing ventures undertaken by Greek communities in Asia Minor in the seventh and sixth centuries, see Tsetskhladze 2022.

## 3.8A.1. Agriculture and Animal Husbandry

Animal husbandry was not a significant part of the Chian economy during the Archaic period, but trade in agricultural produce was; see Section 3.8A.3 for more on trade in Chian wine.

## 3.8A.2. Natural Resources and Craft Activity

The Chians' notable prosperity was in no small part the result of their commercial activities. The Chians were concerned about losing their prominent place in maritime trade already around 545 (Hdt. 1.165.1; see Section 3.7A), and Aristotle (*Pol.* 1291b24) identifies Aegina and Chios as home to unusually large numbers of merchants.[41] Moreover, it is clear from the archaeological evidence that Chios was deeply entangled in the economic and cultural life of the eastern Aegean during the Archaic period. This conclusion is supported by three main lines of evidence: first, in the readily apparent presence of material originating from other eastern Aegean islands and other regions on Chios; second, in the clear and well-documented presence of Chians at Naucratis; and third, in the wide distribution of Chian pottery beyond the island's shores.

Within Chios itself, evidence of external influences on Chian material culture includes the affinity of some artworks—such as sixth-century lead griffin heads, terracotta bearded male figures, and a stone lion's head from Kato Phana (see Section 3.4A)—with similar works from Ephesus on the Asian mainland (Lamb 1934–1935: 148, 53). Similarly, stylistic affinities between Protocorinthian ceramic decorative regimes and East Greek Wild Goat and black-figure styles are well documented (Lemos 1986: 239; Lemos 1991: vol. 1: 10, 96, 136, 46, 69, 223–6).

## 3.8A.3. Commerce

Some of the most fascinating evidence for Chian engagement with the wider world comes from the Greek *emporion* of Naucratis in the Nile delta.[42] Although

---

41. Sarikakis (1986: 121) speculates on the motivations for Chian commercial activities.

42. Naucratis was first discovered by Flinders Petrie at the end of the 19th century, and investigation has continued sporadically during the 20th and 21st centuries. For excavation reports, see Petrie 1886; Gardner 1888; Hogarth, Edgar, and Gutch 1898–1899; Hogarth, Lorimer, and Edgar 1905; Coulson 1988; Coulson 1996; Leonard 1997; Leonard, Weiss, and Berlin 2001; Stacey, Cartwright, Tanimoto, et al. 2010. Other historical studies and research essays of note with relevance to the presence of Greeks, and specifically East Greeks, at Naucratis include Yoyotte 1993–1994; Möller 2000; Höckmann and Kreikenbom 2001; Villing and Schlotzhauer 2006; Schlotzhauer, Weber, and Mommsen 2012; Thomas and Villing 2013;

Herodotus (2.178) links the foundation of Naucratis to the pharaoh Amasis (reigned 570–526), the finds from the site indicate that Greeks were active there by the last quarter of the seventh century at the latest, and the *emporion* seems to have been attached to a preexisting Egyptian settlement just to the north. It is likely that Amasis facilitated the growth of the *emporion*, as the earliest-known architectural remains date to the middle of the sixth century.

Herodotus informs us that the most important sanctuary at Naucratis, the Hellenion, was jointly founded by Chios, Clazomenae, Cnidus, Halicarnassus, Mytilene, Phaselis, Phocaea, Rhodes, and Teos. Various Greek deities were worshipped at the Hellenion, and it was probably the administrative center for the *emporion*, since the *poleis* that founded the Hellenion had the exclusive right to appoint προστάται τοῦ ἐμπορίου. Herodotus also notes that the Aeginetans founded a sanctuary to Zeus, the Milesians founded one to Apollo, and the Samians founded one to Hera. Greek painted pottery with votive graffiti to Apollo and Aphrodite from the seventh century show that those deities were worshipped at Naucratis from its inception.

Among Greeks who left inscriptions at Naucratis, Chian ethnics are the most numerous (Austin 1970: 25), and Chian pottery from the late seventh- to mid-sixth-century deposits is noticeably greater in quantity than similar wares from Samos, Aegina, and other Aegean islands (D. Williams 2006; Johnston and Villing 2022: 392). The prominence of Chian pottery at Naucratis is, in fact, so noticeable that it was believed to have been produced there, before further work on Chios proved that both the clay and the ceramic style are native to the island (Kourouniotis 1915: 64–93; Kourouniotis 1916: 190–215; Lamb 1934–1935: 138–64; Boardman 1979: 288; Lemos 1991: vol. 1: 192–4). The Chian pottery at Naucratis consists almost entirely of fine, thin-walled drinking cups and phialai and is concentrated especially in the Sanctuary of Aphrodite. This has led some scholars to suppose that the Chians alone founded that cult (Austin 1970: 32), although, according to Herodotus, the Chians were involved only in the foundation of the common Hellenion. The discrepancy could indicate that Chian potters worked in the sanctuary producing bespoke votives for dedication to Aphrodite (Cook and Woodhead 1952: 51, 159–70; Boardman 1956: 56–9).[43]

---

Villing 2013; Johnston and Villing 2022. Due to the complex stratigraphy of the site and the early date of Petrie's excavations, our understanding of the precise cadence of occupation and nature of interaction between Greeks and Egyptians remains somewhat less than optimal (detailed comments at Möller 2000: 90–1).

43. If this was so, it would mean that raw clay rather than finished pottery was imported. It is difficult to choose between this seemingly inconvenient conclusion and the equally perplexing alternative, that cups were inscribed with a dedicant's name in Chios before being sent to

284    THE OXFORD HISTORY OF THE ARCHAIC GREEK WORLD

There remain many issues to confront when it comes to making sense of the precise role of the Chians at Naucratis, but the evidence is clear that Chian merchants were active in trade with Egypt from an early date.

One of the products that Chian merchants took with them was doubtless the wine for which their island was famous in antiquity (Greaves 2010: 73, 84). According to Athenaeus (26b–c), Theopompus, himself a native of the island, claimed that the Chians invented "dark wine":

> Theopompus says that dark wine [τὸν μέλανα οἶνον] was (discovered) by the Chians first, and that the Chians learned the cultivation of and care for vines from Oinopion son of Dionysus, who was a fellow resident of the island, and that they shared (this learning) with other people. (*FGrH* 115 F276; trans. W. S. Morison)

Chian wine enjoyed a reputation for unusual quality—in Aristophanes' *Ecclesiazusae*, a household slave praises a banquet at which there is "Chian wine . . . and lots of other good things" (1139–40; cf. Plut. *Demetr.* 19.4; Ath. 167e; Pliny *HN* 14.73). That reputation accounts for the high price that Chian wine evidently fetched in at least some times and places in antiquity (Plut. *Mor.* 470f; Sarikakis 1986: 122); it seems, for example, to have cost eight times as much as the less celebrated wine produced in Attica. Alain Bresson (2016: 171–2) has argued that in the late Archaic period, Chios became the first community in the Greek world to produce high-quality wine specifically for export and that, because viticulture was highly labor-intensive, Chians began using chattel slaves in large numbers at the same time (see Section 3.9A for further discussion of slavery in Chios). The popularity and broad dispersion of Chian chalices (see Section 3.4A) may well be linked to the Chians' deep involvement with viticulture (Burgemeister 2012).[44]

Further evidence for Chian maritime trade in wine (or something else that might go into an amphora; grain, wine, and/or preserved fish have been suggested; Roebuck 1986: 83) during the Archaic period is provided by the widespread distribution of Chian-made transport vessels in the Mediterranean and

---

Naucratis. A feature of the Chian pottery dedicated in the sanctuaries at Naucratis in the first half of the sixth century that might support the latter conclusion is the fact that only four dedicants (Zoilos, Mikis, Aristophanes, and Demophon) account for half of the dedicated pots. These Chians may have been career shipowners or traders who made frequent visits to Naucratis. The names likewise show up occasionally on dedications on Aegina, although never on Chios itself (Boardman 1986: 253).

44. On the importance of agriculture in the economy of ancient Ionia, see Greaves 2010: 69–94.

beyond.[45] Chian pithos amphoras traveled as far north as Berezan and a variety of other sites on the Black Sea (Vinogradov 1971; Sarikakis 1986: 123; Lemos 1997: 82; Monakhov [Monachov] and Kuznetsova 2017: 67–9) and found their way as far west as Massalia in France and as far south as Taucheira in Libya (Boardman and Hayes 1966; Boardman and Hayes 1973).

### 3.8A.4. Coinage

Chios minted coins beginning sometime around the middle of the sixth century at the latest (some unattributed electrum issues from the late seventh century could conceivably have been Chian) (Kraay 1976: 242–3, 53–5; Hardwick 1991; Hardwick 2010; Hardwick 2013; Wartenberg 2020: 599, 613–17). The sphinx was the predominant motif on Chian coins from the first issues through c. 300;[46] amphoras also appeared starting around c. 500. The earliest datable Chian coin, from the third quarter of the sixth century, is an electrum *hektē*, or one sixth of a *statēr* (*statēres* are mentioned in the "constitutional law" discussed in Section 3.5A), on the Chian standard (15.6 g), with a sphinx on the obverse and an incuse square on the reverse (Psoma 2016: 94). Starting c. 525, Chios issued electrum *statēres* and *hektai* on the Milesian standard and silver *statēres* and half- *statēres*. The electrum coins ceased c. 510, while silver issues continued. Nicholas Hardwick (1993: 213) argues that silver *statēr* production ceased c. 493, after the failure of the Ionian Rebellion. When minting resumed c. 490, Chian coins displayed a sphinx or an amphora on the obverse, appropriate for a city famous for its wine (Breitenstein 1946: 1539–55). (See Section 3.8C.4 for discussion of a coin series that may have been minted by the Greek cities that took part in the Ionian Rebellion.)

## 3.9A. Chian Familial/Demographic History

Evidence for Chian population levels during the Archaic period comes from Herodotus' description of the Battle of Lade in 494 (see Section 3.7A), in which

---

45. For Chian pottery in Aegina, see Johnston 1990: 38–40; for Carthage, see Bechtold and Docter 2010: 102; for Etruria, see Rizzo 1990: 22; for Miletus, see Pfisterer-Haas 1999 and Schaus 2020; for Samos, see Walter-Karydi 1973; for Catania, see Mommsen, Kerschner, and Pautasso 2009.

46. Sphinxes are found already on eighth-century ivory and faience seals from Emporio and Kato Phana. Hardwick (1991: 10–11, 17, 24) argues that the sphinx (associated with funerary rituals elsewhere in Greece) and amphora together allude to the cult worship of Oinopion, the mythical founder of Chios and inventor of viticulture. There is, however, no explicit connection anywhere between Oinopion and the sphinx.

## 286 THE OXFORD HISTORY OF THE ARCHAIC GREEK WORLD

the Chians contributed 100 ships, the most of any ally (6.8.1). From these numbers, Carl Roebuck estimated the total population of late Archaic Chios at 60,000–80,000, the highest of all the cities fighting at Lade (Roebuck 1986: 81; cf. Greaves 2010: 93, estimating 80,000). Some Chian families, at least, could trace (or could purport to trace) their ancestry back multiple generations: the gravestone of one Heropythos, dated conventionally to the first quarter of the fifth century, names 14 male ancestors going back to Kyprios (*PEP Chios* 369; see further Mac Sweeney 2013: 83). As the list contains no known heroic or divine individuals (in which case, it would likely represent an invented tradition), it may be a genuine genealogy preserved by Heropythos' *oikos*.[47]

One of the most remarked-upon features of the population of Chios has been its slaves. The story Herodotus tells about the Chian slave trader Panionios (see below) shows that Herodotus was aware of the importance of the slave trade to Chios (8.105–6), but Thucydides is the first extant literary source to focus on the island's reliance on slavery. In the course of describing Chios' revolt against the Athenian empire in 412, the historian writes:

> The slaves [οἰκέται] of the Chians were numerous—in fact, they were the most numerous of any single *polis* with the exception of the Lacedaemonians[48]—and by the same token, due to their numbers [πλῆθος], were punished quite harshly when they misbehaved. Thus when the Athenian force appeared to be firmly established in their territory with a fortified position, many of them immediately deserted to [the Athenians], and these men, knowing the lay of the land, did the greatest damage [to the Chians]. (8.40.2)

Despite his mention of the Spartans, an *obiter dictum* that has preoccupied scholars, Thucydides' primary purpose is to explain why the Chians were suffering so heavily from pillaging during the Athenians' siege. To this end, he points out not only the exceptional number of Chian slaves but also the repression prompted by their sheer numbers. The Chians clearly had extensive experience prior to 412 both dealing *in* slaves and dealing *with* them once purchased.[49]

---

47. Contrast, e.g., the Spartan king lists and the genealogy of Hecataeus of Miletus, which commenced with a god (Hdt. 2.143.1).

48. It is unclear whether Thucydides is referring here to a percentage of the population or an absolute number.

49. See *Etym. Magn.* 411.33, describing a ζήτρειον (treadmill) used to punish slaves on Chios (cf. Poll. 3.78; Ael. *VH* 14.18). For Thucydides' comparison of Chios with Sparta, see, e.g., Hornblower 2004: 82, 155–56.

The Chians' approach to their slave population was not, however, defined entirely by repression. Thucydides tells us that the Chians manned at least part of their naval fleet using their slaves (8.15.2). It is not clear how frequently the Chians employed this practice or what the terms of the slaves' service might have been. The most likely scenario is one in which, following attested Athenian practice, the Chians paid slaves (and thus their masters) for rowing (Xen. [*Ath. Pol.*] 1.11, 1.19; Thuc. 7.13.2 with Graham 1992). More exceptional must have been cases where the Chians promised freedom and possibly citizenship in exchange for service, again much as the Athenians did in preparation for the Battle of Arginusae in 407/6 (Hellanicus *FGrH* 323a F25). We possess epigraphic evidence for such a policy in a Chian military list dating to the end of the fifth century (*PEP Chios* 62 with Robert 1935: 453–9). Slaves, identifiable by their ethnic names (e.g. Syros, Kilikas, Phryx), are grouped according to "decades," with a man's name in the genitive heading each *dekas* (e.g., Parmenon, B.11). The first part of the inscription states that the *polis* "*ēle*" (l. 5); Louis Robert convincingly restored this as *ēle*[*otherōsen*], "freed them." The Chians would thus have employed the approach of "carrot and stick" in order to keep their slaves in order, a technique illuminated by the work of Peter Hunt (1998).

The sophistication of the Chians' treatment of their slaves in 412 hints at a long history of domination. The question is to what extent we find evidence for Chian slavery in the Archaic material and epigraphic record. As though to expand upon Thucydides' characteristically oblique description, Theopompus tells us that the Chians were the first Greeks after the Thessalians and the Lacedaemonians to make use of slaves but that they bought them on the market rather than conquering them in war (*FGrH* 115 F122). An unquestioning acceptance of this testimony would put Chian acquisition of chattel slaves in the Early Iron Age, but the large slave numbers Theopompus was familiar with probably started in the Archaic period.[50] Herodotus' story of Hermotimos of Pedasa (a settlement located near Halicarnassus) and the slave trader Panionios of Chios (8.104–6), dating from the time of the Ionian Rebellion, points to a long-established and lucrative slave trade on the island by 500. Panionios, who Herodotus says supported himself through "the most unholy deeds," was in the habit of castrating youths and selling them at Sardis and Ephesus for high prices. Hermotimos, one of his victims, later exacts terrible retribution from Panionios. Herodotus' moralizing notwithstanding, some Chians clearly recognized the profits to be had from slaving.[51]

---

50. For further discussion of the unreliability of the Theopompus fragment, see Lewis 2018: 145–6.

51. Hornblower (2003) sees the episode as allegorical, with the castration of Hermotimos representing the subjugation of the indigenous populations in the eastern Aegean by colonizing

288    THE OXFORD HISTORY OF THE ARCHAIC GREEK WORLD

A relevant piece of evidence here is an inscribed base from a now-lost dedicatory monument dating to the late sixth century (*PEP* Chios 154). In the inscription, Philes states that he has dedicated an object representing a tithe (*dekatē*) to an unnamed god. The last three words read, τῶν Ἀρίστωνος ἐξελεύθερος, "a freedman from the household of Ariston"; τῶν Ἀρίστωνος, however, could also continue to apply to Philes post-manumission as a kind of civic marker (Forrest 1963: 54–6). As we saw above (see Section 3.5A, discussing most notably the *dekas Parmenontos*), the construction οἱ+ genitive is well known as a civic subdivision from later Chian decrees. Groupings of this kind likely consisted of manumitted slaves who had been incorporated into tribes alongside more traditional *genē*. This practice may have existed already during the Archaic period. If so, the Philes dedication might show the earliest-known instance of the Chians enfranchising their ex-slaves.

## *3.10A. Chian Social Customs and Institutions*

The Chians fell under the broad heading of Ionians, but it is quite difficult to specify what being an Ionian meant to them and to others during the Archaic period. Herodotus (1.147.2) identifies the Ionians as an ethnic group defined on the basis of cult practice and descent, a definition that includes the residents of Athens. Whether that view had wide currency prior to the foundation of the Delian League remains unclear. A somewhat narrower conception identified the Ionians as Greeks living in Asia Minor and its offshore islands (see, for example, Aesch. *Pers.* 178; Hdt. 4.97; Thuc. 6.4.5). Finally, Ionians could be seen as the residents of the Greek communities that belonged to the Ionian League (Rubinstein 2004b: 1053–8; Crielaard 2009).

The Ionian League, sometimes referred to as the Ionian Dodecapolis, was a *koinon* comprising 12 Ionian *poleis*: ten on the coast of Asia Minor (Clazomenae, Colophon, Ephesus, Erythrae, Lebedos, Miletus, Myus, Phocaea, Priene, Teos) along with the two offshore islands of Chios and Samos (Hdt. 1.142). Herodotus tells us that the members of the Ionian League built a shrine for their own use, which they called the Panionion, excluding from it all the other Ionians (Hdt. 1.143.3). At this shrine, dedicated to Poseidon Helikonios and located on the peninsula of Mt. Mycale, the Ionians of the Dodecapolis celebrated a festival called the Panionia (Hdt. 1.148.1). By the end of the Archaic period, the Ionian League had both religious and political dimensions, and modern attempts to separate

---

Greeks and Panionios' name symbolizing the colonizers' assertion of superior and exclusivist identities.

those two spheres and identify one or the other as the dominant activity of the Ionian League overlook the fact that religion and politics were functionally inseparable.[52]

The Ionian League seems to have come into being in the first half of the sixth century. Later literary sources (not including Herodotus) claim that 12 Ionian *poleis* destroyed a city named Melie or Melite (variously described as Greek or Carian) and afterward built a common shrine, the Panionion, with a temple dedicated to Poseidon Helikonios. The main extant ancient source is Vitruvius, who states that 12 Ionian *poleis*, acting according to a "common resolution" (*communi consilio*, 4.1.4), destroyed a 13th Ionian city, Melie, due to the "arrogance of its citizens" (*civium adrogantiam*). (This conflict is regularly labeled in the ancient and modern sources as the Meliac War.) Vitruvius makes no mention of the Ionian League, but the fact that the 12 Ionian *poleis* he lists as the aggressors in the Meliac War are the same 12 *poleis* that were members of the Ionian League (Hdt. 1.142), along with his mention of a "common resolution," has been taken to mean that the Meliac War was an endeavor of the Ionian League.[53] Although it is impossible to establish the veracity of the details of the various extant accounts of the Meliac War, it would not be surprising if the prominent Greek communities closest to Melie—Samos, Priene, and Miletus—had joined together and destroyed Melie, with the conquered territory being divided among the victors. Both parties in that war may well have found allies in other nearby Greek communities.

The remains at the modern site of Çatallar Tepe, directly across from Samos on the coast of Asia Minor, have been plausibly identified by Hans Lohmann (2005; 2012a; 2017; 2022) as those of Melie.[54] Recent archaeological excavations

---

52. The discussion of the Ionian League offered here draws directly on Tausend 1992: 90–5; Rubinstein 2004a: 1053–8; Mac Sweeney 2013: 173–87; Mac Sweeney 2017; Lefèvre 2019. The relevant archaeological evidence is discussed in Lohmann 2012a; Hulek 2017; Lohmann 2017; Lohmann and Özgül 2017; Hulek 2018; Hulek 2019; Lohmann 2022.

53. For a thorough discussion of the passage from Vitruvius and of the other relevant literary and epigraphic sources, see Ragone 1986. On the various dates assigned to the Meliac War (von Wilamowitz-Moellendorff, for example, placed it in the eighth century), see Ragone 1986: 72–7.

54. For an alternative viewpoint, according to which (1) the Panionion was always located at Otomatik Tepe (see below), (2) the remains at Çatallar Tepe should be identified as Mykalessos, and (3) Melie should be identified with the remains at Kala Tepe near Otomatik Tepe, see Herda 2006. The remains on the summit of Kala Tepe include an oval structure dating to the seventh century, a rectangular structure dating to the sixth century, and a 530-m-long fortification wall that is tentatively dated to the seventh century. Another wall, this one more than 1400 m long but of less impressive thickness and presumably lower in height than that on the summit, was found on the lower slopes of Kala Tepe. The lower wall circuit has been tentatively dated to the late seventh or early sixth century. The relationship between the upper

## 290 THE OXFORD HISTORY OF THE ARCHAIC GREEK WORLD

at Çatallar Tepe have revealed a fortification wall that was built in the second half of the seventh century (Hülden 2020: 147–9) and what seems to have been a Carian settlement that was founded in the middle of the seventh century and destroyed sometime around 600. In the second quarter of the sixth century, a temple, presumably dedicated to Poseidon Helikonios, was built at Melie, over the remains of an earlier shrine.[55]

Many modern historians have taken the view that the Ionian League came into being to prosecute the Meliac War (Mac Sweeney 2013: 178–9). However, it seems more probable that the Meliac War was a local conflict involving some members of what became the Ionian League on both sides, rather than a grand coalition of 12 Ionian *poleis* against Melie (see Section 3.7C for further discussion of the Meliac War). The origins of the Ionian League can perhaps instead be traced, at least in part, to the negotiations attendant upon divvying up Melie's territory. However, given that the earliest relevant physical remains from the Panionion date to the second quarter of the sixth century and that the first reasonably well-attested functioning of the Ionian League is Herodotus' claim (1.141.4) that soon after the Persian conquest of Lydia in 546, the Ionians assembled at the Panionion to discuss how to respond to the emergent geopolitical realities, the Ionian League may not have coalesced until well after the destruction of Melie.

The Panionia festival may have been founded in the second quarter of the sixth century, at the same time the temple was built at the former site of Melie, but that remains speculative because we know almost nothing about the Panionia festival. It may have been a panegyris of some days' duration, if we can take other, better-known (Ionian) festivals such as the Panathenaia and the Delia as any guide. There is, in addition, the possibility that the festival was the venue

---

and lower settlements remains unclear (Kleiner, Hommel, and Müller-Wiener 1961: 110–16; Hülden 2020: 143–6). Lohmann argues that the remains of Kala Tepe should be equated with the settlement of Karion known from epigraphic evidence (see Section 3.7C).

55. That the Panionion was located on the former site of Melie is not explicitly stated in any of the extant ancient sources. Von Wilamowitz-Moellendorff (1908: 45–6 = 1935–1972: vol. 5.1: 136–7), based on his reading of the literary and epigraphical evidence available to him in the early 20th century, made that inference. A key piece of evidence was a second-century inscription (Hiller von Gaertringen 1906: #37–8) that recounts events in the Meliac War and that seems to mention a division of the territory of Melie at a meeting held at the Panionion (see Section 3.7C for discussion of that inscription). The layout of the site that has been identified as the location of Melie and of the Panionion matches a detail in Herodotus' description of the Panionion (1.148.1) and thus provides further support for von Wilamowitz-Moellendorff's inference (Lohmann 2012b: 111). Von Wilamowitz-Moellendorff also made the more speculative suggestion that there was at Melie a cult of Poseidon Helikonios that was taken over by the Ionian League; that suggestion may find some support from the existence of a small shrine underneath the temple built at the Panionion in the sixth century.

for performances of the Homeric poems in the early Archaic period (Frame 2009: 551–620; see Section 3.12A).

The temple at the former site of Melie was destroyed a decade or two after it was built, perhaps during the disturbances associated with the Persian conquest of Asia Minor. Afterward, the Panionion was moved c. 5 km west to a site near the modern village of Güzelçamli and the hill now known as Otomatik Tepe. This relocation put the Panionion significantly closer to the coast and thus made it easier to access. An altar (measuring c. 4 x 18 m) was built on the top of Otomatik Tepe at some point between the sixth and fourth centuries (the date is disputed), and in the fourth century, a *bouleutērion* was built on the lower slopes of that hill. No certainly Archaic structures are known at Güzelçamli or Otomatik Tepe, so the location of the Temple of Poseidon Helikonios after the destruction of the mid-sixth century remains unclear (Lohmann 2022).

The design of the sixth-century temple at Melie may offer some insight into the nature of the deliberative practices of the Ionian League during the Archaic period. The walls of that temple, a non-peripteral structure oriented E–W and measuring c. 28 x 8 m, were built from rammed earth on a stone foundation. The interior was divided into three rooms: a pronaos with a roof supported by a 2 x 4 colonnade, a naos with a roof supported by two columns, and a separate room in the western part of the cella that had a roof supported by three columns. Marble was used for the very top of the cella wall and the eastern ends of the pronaos walls. The interior columns, with Ionic capitals, were also marble. The superstructure of the building was wood, with a tile roof over it.

The west room in the cella was arranged as a dining space. The sole entrance to that part of the temple is an off-center door (framed by huge marble slabs) on the south side. The location of the door speaks to the room's function, as do the finds from within it, which include c. 300 ceramic vessels (primarily kylikes and plates) and ivory appliqués from couches. The discovery of iron spearheads, a sauroter, and part of a bronze cuirass indicate that the walls were decorated with weapons, presumably spoils of war (Lohmann and Özgül 2017; Lohmann 2022).

The elaborately equipped dining chamber in the Temple of Poseidon Helikonios at Melie may well have served as a deliberative space for representatives of the *poleis* constituting the Ionian League. There was no space in that chamber for a large gathering, but Herodotus (6.7) reports that the decision to fight a sea battle at Lade was made at the Panionion by *probouloi* from the *poleis* belonging to the Ionian League, so the deliberative mechanisms of the Ionian League may have involved relatively few individuals. The west room in the cella would thus be a predecessor of the fourth-century *bouleutērion* at the foot of Otomatik Tepe. Inscriptions from the fourth century found at Priene (Hiller von Gaertringen 1906: #139; *SEG* 55.1271) make reference to sacrifices at the Panionion to Zeus

Boulaios and the operation of a *boulē* presided over by a *prytanis* and a *basileus* equipped with a scepter.

Despite their construction of a common sanctuary, the extent of political cooperation among the *poleis* in the Ionian League in the Archaic period seems to have been limited. A plan formulated prior to the Persian conquest by Thales of Miletus, which would have entailed establishing a common council in Teos and treating the individual *poleis* in the Ionian League as demes, was never adopted (Hdt. 1.170.3; Asheri, Lloyd, and Corcella 2007: 190–1). The only known result of the meeting held at the Panionion after the Persian conquest of Lydia was that an embassy was sent to Sparta to ask for help (Hdt. 1.141.4). The *poleis* of the Ionian League failed to mount a unified opposition when Harpagus followed up the Persian conquest of Lydia in 546 by taking the Greek cities in Asia Minor one by one, and nothing came of the plan, offered by Bias of Priene at a meeting at the Panionion, that all of the residents of the communities in the Ionian League evacuate Asia Minor en masse and resettle in Sardinia (Hdt. 1.169–70). The Ionian Rebellion may have been fomented by members of the Ionian League, and the decision to fight a sea battle at Lade may have been made at the Panionion (Hdt. 6.7), but the so-called Ionian Rebellion involved both Greeks from outside the Ionian League and non-Greeks and can only be construed as an undertaking of the Ionian League with difficulty.[56]

The Ionian League did, however, serve as an important vehicle for the instantiation of a strong sense of Ionian ethnic identity. As we have seen, the term "Ionian" could take on a number of different meanings, and it is unlikely that all of the individuals who could conceivably be construed as Ionians ever understood themselves as belonging to a single, unified group.[57] However, many of the foundational elements of ethnic identity—a collective title, a belief in a shared history, association with a specific territory, a sense of solidarity—bound together the members of the Ionian League. Herodotus was evidently more than a little offended by the suggestion that the members of the Ionian League were "more Ionian that the other Ionians or are of nobler birth" (1.146.1; Dewald

---

56. The fate of the Ionian League in the immediate aftermath of the Ionian Rebellion is unknown. The scholarly consensus had been that it was dissolved by the Persians, but the current view is that it continued in operation. See the discussion at Lefèvre 2019: 359.

57. On the Ionian "ethnic construct," see Crielaard 2009. Crielaard emphasizes (2009: 72) that not all the Greeks living in and around Asia Minor who could be construed as Ionians were part of the Ionian League, so that we can safely think that regional interests came before "ethnic" unity. If we follow Hdt.1.147.2, a distinctive aspect of Ionian identity was the celebration of the religious festival of the Apatouria, but, Herodotus adds, Ephesians and Colophonians, who were part of the Ionian League, did not celebrate that festival.

and Munson 2022: 384), but the very fact that he felt obliged to rebut that suggestion indicates that the members of the Ionian League did indeed perceive themselves to belong to a single, exclusive group that could be construed as "the" Ionians.

## *3.11A. Chian Religious Customs and Institutions*
### 3.11A.1. Athena

As far as the cults directly attested for the Archaic Age are concerned, Herodotus mentions a Temple of Athena Poliouchos (Πολιοῦχος) in Chios Town while narrating the story of the Lydian Paktyes (1.160.3; the events in question date to the middle of the sixth century; see Section 3.7A).[58] The epithet suggests that she was the patron deity of the island, but caution is in order (on patron deities, cf. Cole 1995, specifically 301 on the use of the epithet *poliouchos*). The exact location of the temple is not known (F. Graf 1985: 44). Athena's cult is also attested at Emporio (F. Graf 1985: 45–6; see Section 3.4A). In the *Homeric Hymn to Apollo* 38 (sixth century; see Section 3.12A), Chios appears in a list of cult sites for Apollo. The sanctuary excavated at Kato Phana (F. Graf 1985: 50–3) was undoubtedly a primary center for the cult of this god (with the epithet of *phanaios*), but worship of Apollo also took place at the harbor sanctuary at Emporio (F. Graf 1985: 53–6) (see Section 3.4A). A cult of Artemis, alongside that of Apollo, is attested both at Kato Phana and at Emporio (F. Graf 1985: 54–6). Votive deposits to Demeter have been found also in the southern part of Chios Town (see Section 3.4A; F. Graf 1985: 69).

### 3.11A.2. Dionysus Omadios

One of the few Chian cults attested in literary sources is that of Dionysus Omadios, which involved "human" sacrifices (Porph. *Abst.* 2.55; these sacrifices were only symbolic, as we gather from Ael. *NA* 12.34). "Human" sacrifices to Dionysus are attested on Lesbos by Dosiadas (*FGrH* 458 F7, third century), and in a poem by Alcaeus, Dionysus has the epithet "eater of raw flesh," Ζόννυσον ὠμήσταν (F129.9 Lobel and Page), an epithet, it seems, from the same root as Omadios. A connection between the two epithets of the god and the corresponding cults has been suggested (F. Graf 1985: 44; *contra* Georgoudi 2011).

---

58. Relatively abundant material on religion in Archaic Chios comes from archaeological and epigraphical sources. This material, together with information scattered in literary texts, is thoroughly treated in F. Graf 1985: 11–146, 427–61.

### 3.11A.3. Cybele

The cult of Cybele, (possibly) identified at Daskalopetra (c. 6 km north of Chios Town; F. Graf 1985: 107–15; L. Roller 1999: 138; Roungou 2013: 107–8), has been discussed by scholars within the framework of the relationship between Greek and Anatolian (pre-Greek?) people in Greek Archaic settlements in Asia Minor.[59] The cult site at Daskalopetra is located alongside a spring and quite close to the sea. A limestone outcrop was cut back into a terrace, in the middle of which a protrusion of bedrock was carved into a cuboid shrine (c. 0.8 m high), the facade of which took the form of a niche with an enthroned female figure resting her feet on a stool. Accounts of early travelers suggest that the enthroned figure held a lion on her lap. The pillars framing the niche have bases in the form of lions' claws, and two striding lions are carved into the side "walls" of the shrine. The Daskalopetra shrine and related finds recall cult sites in Anatolia for the Phrygian mother goddess, whom the Greeks identified as Cybele, but they also have features suggesting that the Chians had both adopted and adapted Phrygian religious beliefs and practices. The worship of Cybele on Chios, Lesbos, and Lemnos seems to have begun in the middle of the sixth century, and the Daskalopetra shrine has been dated to the sixth century on stylistic grounds (Roungou 2013). Abundant traces of other cult sites for Cybele have recently emerged all across Ionia (Greaves 2010: 195–7, 99–200; see Section 3.11B for the cult in Lesbos). Finds of Archaic votives from Chios Town suggest that there was a shrine to Cybele on the north side of the city starting in the Archaic period (Roungou 2013: 106–12).

In the so-called constitutional law (see Section 3.5A), the goddess Hestia is mentioned twice (l. 1, 5), probably in her well-attested role (cf. Pind. *Nem.* 11.1) as "goddess of the Prytaneia" (F. Graf 1985: 139). As mentioned earlier, the Chians, together with the other members of the Ionian League, celebrated the festival called Panionia (see Section 3.10A).

## 3.12A. Chian Cultural History

The version of the Greek language spoken in Archaic Chios was the variety of Ionic dialect typical of Asia Minor (del Barrio 2014: 263–5). According to Herodotus (1.142.4), it was similar to that of Erythrae, but the distinctive

---

59. Daskalopetra ("Teacher's Stone") is a modern name; the ancient name of the site may have been Babrantion (Rubinstein 2004b: 1059). Daskalopetra is sometimes referred to as "Homer's rock" because of a story (which can be traced back no further than the 17th century CE) that Homer taught pupils there (Barron 1986: 24). See Section 3.12A for discussion of the ancient tradition connecting Homer to Chios.

characteristics Herodotus may have perceived are not immediately obvious to us. Some Aeolian characteristics of the dialect do seem to be present (F. Graf 1985: 3, with n. 14 and 16 for bibliography), but these do not seem to be limited to Chios (del Barrio 2014: 265). The Eastern Ionic alphabet was used, and texts from Chios demonstrate literacy by the first half of the seventh century at the latest (Jeffery 1990: 326–7, 36–8). Herodotus, in discussing the various misfortunes that befell the Chians toward the end of the Ionian Rebellion, mentions in passing that about that time, the roof collapsed on a school in Chios, killing all but one of the 120 children inside (Hdt. 6.27.2), which suggests a considerable degree of literacy toward the end of the Archaic period.

Chios seems to have played a major role in the early formation and transmission of the Homeric poems. Simonides quotes a line from the *Iliad* (6.146) and attributes it to the "man from Chios" (F19.1 West; Graziosi 2002: 63–4). Thucydides quotes several lines from the *Homeric Hymn to Apollo* in order to demonstrate the antiquity of the original festival in honor of Apollo in Delos, the Delia. Those lines describe a festival in Delos, attended by Ionians, with games and music (l. 146–55). Thucydides emphasizes that in that poem, Homer mentions himself. After praising the Delian maidens' choir, the singer begs of the maidens that, if asked about who is their favorite singer, they should respond (l. 172–3): "A blind man, and he lives in rocky Chios; all of his songs remain best afterward." Thucydides no doubt assumed that it was Homer himself speaking here.[60]

In other ancient sources, we find a strong connection between Chios and the Homeridae, the descendants of Homer (Graziosi 2002: 205).[61] Thucydides' digression on the *Hymn to Apollo* has been read in connection with a scholion to Pindar (Schol. Pind. *Nem.* 2.1c, 3, 29 Drachmann). This scholion comments on Pindar's incipit of *Nem.* 2, where the poet mentions the "Homeridae, singers of verses sewn together" (Ὁμηρίδαι | ῥαπτῶν ἐπέων . . . ἀοιδοί, clearly a paraphrase for the word ῥαψῳδός) and their habit of "starting from the *prooemium* of Zeus" (Διὸς ἐκ προοιμίου). It is worth quoting this scholion in full:

> Homeridae was the name given anciently to the members of Homer's family, who also sang his poetry in succession. But later it was also given to the rhapsodes, who no longer traced their descent back to Homer. Particularly

---

60. For thorough analyses of the passage from Thucydides, see Aloni 1989: 37–68; Nagy 2010: I§26–34.

61. The very existence of the Homeridai has been sometimes unjustifiably put in doubt. Quite intriguingly, they now appear as the name of a *genos* in a Chian inscription: *SEG* 56.1003 (fourth century). See Section 3.5A.

prominent were Cynaethus and his school, who, they say, composed many of the verses and inserted them into Homer's work. This Cynaethus came from a Chian family, and, of the poems that bear Homer's name, it was he who wrote the *Hymn to Apollo* and laid it to his credit. And this Cynaethus was the first to recite Homer's poems in Syracuse, in the 69th Olympiad (= 504/501), as Hippostratos says. (*FGrH* 568 F5m; trans. from West 2003: 9–10, with transliteration adjustments)[62]

A few words on the rhapsodes are in order. If we examine the relevant sources and also analyze the metaphor implicit in their name (that of "sewing songs"), we see that the *rhapsōdoi* were regularly connected with the public and agonistic recitation of epic songs, typically in festivals, and that they performed these songs in sequence, "by relay." The imposition of a stable, *fixed* order of performance for these (potentially independent) songs executed in sequence has been identified as the very principle determining the monumental design, as well as the basic unity, of the Homeric poems in the form we know them (Nagy 1996a: 65–112; Nagy 1996b: 59–86).

The author of the scholion quoted above identifies Cynaethus as the composer of the *Hymn to Apollo* attributed to Homer.[63] Building on the evidence offered by the scholion and on the bipartite nature of the Apollo hymn, which consists of two distinct sections, a Delian one and a Pythian one, Walter Burkert has convincingly identified the historical occasion for the actual original performance of the hymn (Burkert 1979; cf. Burkert 2004: 358–61 and Tsagalis 2018: 54–5).[64] Very close to the date of his death, in 523 or 522, the tyrant Polycrates of Samos organized a great festival in Delos in honor of Apollo as a magnificent display of his nautical power. It was then that he bound the island of Rheneia to Delos with a chain, thereby dedicating Rheneia to Apollo (Thuc. 3.104.2).[65] As specified by some late sources, this festival was *Pythia kai Dēlia*, both a Pythian and a Delian

---

62. On the interpretation of this compressed scholion, see Nagy 2010: I§157–66, as well as Graziosi 2002: 212–14 and Tsagalis 2018: 63–4. For other important sources on the Homeridae, see Graziosi 2002: 208–17; Nagy 2010: I§141–56. For discussion of the possibility that Cynaethus may not have come from Chios, see Abenstein 2021.

63. The scholion to Pindar seems to imply that Cynaethus was a forger and a "fake" member of the Homeridai. It may, however, simply reflect an "Aristarchaean" bias against the *neōteroi*, the notionally post-Homeric poets (Nagy 2010: I§158–62).

64. The recognition of the hymn as a conflation of two independent hymns is generally credited to D. Ruhnken, but cf. Martin 2000: 404.

65. According to Carty (2015: 201–3), Polycrates may have taken control of Rheneia and Delos as early as 528. She discusses the evidence on Polycrates' *Pythia kai Dēlia* but does not mention Burkert's hypothesis.

festival, so that a hymn to Apollo with Delian and Pythian sections would fit the occasion perfectly.[66]

A date in the last quarter of the sixth century for the *Hymn to Apollo* would tally well with the only temporal clue provided by the scholion to Pindar, namely, Cynaethus' first recitation of Homer in Sicily in the 69th Olympiad (504/501). The detail of this recitation being the first is also significant. It must refer to an institutional recitation of Homer, an authorized performance of the kind we know was adopted by the Pisistratids in Athens only a few years earlier (Càssola 1975: 101). In particular, in the *Hipparchus* (228b–c, attributed, probably erroneously, to Plato), we read that Pisistratus' son Hipparchus "was the first to bring over to this land [Athens] Homer's verses, and he forced the rhapsodes at the Panathenaia to go through these verses by relay in the right order just as they do even nowadays."

Here we have a definition of what has been called the "Panathenaic rule,"[67] an institutional intervention to correct what was considered a bad habit of the rhapsodes, performing "songs" from "Homer" without following the right sequential order.[68] The institution of such a rule presupposes the existence of such a fixed order. It presupposes, in other words, the very existence (in some form, physical or not) of a "work" with a recognized, fixed sequence of certain specific episodes.

It is particularly interesting that this passage speaks about Homer's verses being brought over (the verb used is κομίζω) to Athens. But brought over from where? And in what form? The Homeridae of Chios (together with the Kreophyleioi of Samos, on whom see Section 3.12C.2) have sometimes been mentioned in reference to these questions, with written texts invoked as the medium through which the poems traveled from Asia Minor to Athens (Janko 1994: 31). In Plato's *Ion*, we learn that the first prize in Homeric performance at the Panathenaia was awarded by the Homeridae (530d). This presumably means that the Athenians considered the Homeridae of Chios to be official regulators of the rhapsodic performances of the *Iliad* and the *Odyssey* at the Panathenaia. Based partly on this evidence, Gregory Nagy (2010: I§143–56; also 1996b: 179–80) has convincingly suggested that the narrative of Hipparchus "bringing over" Homer's poems "amounts to an aetiology explaining the function of the Homeridai as the authorizers of Homer in Athens." What Hipparchus "brings over," then, is the "correct" rule

---

66. Opinions among scholars differ widely on Cynaethus' exact role in the production of the *Hymn to Apollo*; see Janko 1982: 99–132; Aloni 1989; Martin 2000; West 2003: 10–11; Aloni 2004; Ferrari 2010a: 14–26.

67. Diogenes Laertius (1.57) credits Solon with the introduction of the same rule; cf. Nagy 1996b: 70–1 and Nagy 2010: I§37–40, who prefers to speak of Panathenaic regulation rather than rule.

68. On the reasons leading to such a "bad habit," see Martin 2000: 423–4.

for performing the Homeric poems, the so-called Panathenaic rule, rather than written texts. This rule was not invented in Athens; it was already operating elsewhere before Hipparchus, and it reached Athens by way of the Homeridae of Chios (Nagy 2010: I§53).[69] It is precisely through the Homeridae, it seems, that "authorized" versions of the Homeric poems reached Athens and later moved even farther west to Sicily (Ferrari 2010b: 30–2).

Ionia was generally at the forefront of developments in stone sculpture of the Archaic period, but the number of sculptures surviving from Chios itself is not large (Roungou 2012). Ernst Langlotz (1927; 1978–1979) tried to identify a Chian school of sculpture based on a collection of material, little of it found on Chios itself, from the second half of the sixth century. Much has subsequently been written about a Chian sculptural style during the Archaic period (see, for instance, Pedley 1982), but more recent scholarship has called the existence of such a school into question (Sheedy 1985).

Architecturally, there is little evidence for the reconstruction of a distinctive Chian style in the Archaic period.[70] Stone architectural fragments are known only from a few sites, so comparisons to other regional styles are necessarily tenuous but point to convergence with the Ionian style of the eastern Aegean. In particular, Helmut Kyrieleis (1986: 193–4) has suggested that limestone column fragments from Kato Phana may be based on a Samian prototype (though they also bear close similarities to the columns from the Temple of Artemis at Ephesus).

## Section B. Lesbos

### 3.2B. Sources for Archaic Lesbian History

A concrete elaboration of the material record in Lesbos continues to be hindered by a lack of excavation—few of the Archaic sites on the island have been thoroughly explored. The first systematic archaeological work on Lesbos was conducted by Robert Koldewey in 1885–1886; Koldewey surveyed antiquities across the island and excavated the Temple of Zeus, Hera, and Dionysus at Messa (ancient Messon) (see Map 3.8). Dimitris Evangelidis conducted work at Klopedi, site of

---

69. This is not often explicitly recognized, as accounts of the Pisistratid recitations tend to be Athenocentric in emphasizing the innovations supposedly introduced by the Pisistratids (see, for example, Aloni 2006: 93–9). Frame (2009: 551–620; followed by Nagy 2010: I§38, I§54) connects the rule of memorizing and performing the Homeric poems in the right order to possible complete recitations of the Homeric poems at the Panionia (see Section 3.10A) in the early Archaic period, before that tradition was monopolized by the Homeridai on Chios when mainland Ionia was attacked by the Lydians.

70. See, however, the comments in Boardman 1959.

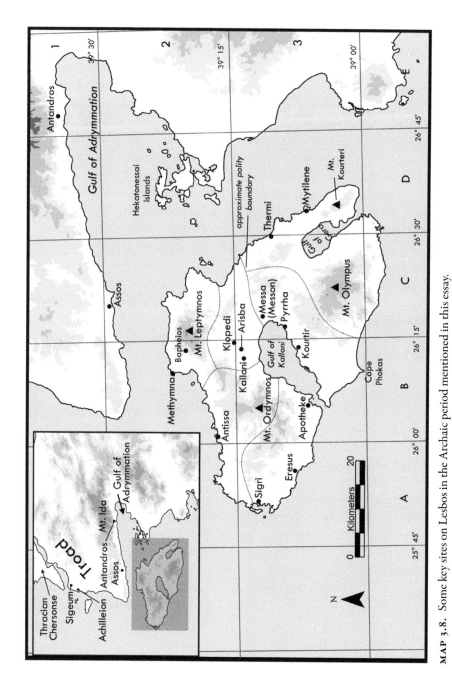

MAP 3.8. Some key sites on Lesbos in the Archaic period mentioned in this essay.

## 300 THE OXFORD HISTORY OF THE ARCHAIC GREEK WORLD

an important Archaic temple, in the 1920s but produced only brief publications on these excavations (1922–1925; 1927; 1928). Winifred Lamb worked extensively on the island (at Antissa, Thermi, and Methymna) in the 1920s and 1930s, but her progress was halted by the onset of World War II. Between 1983 and 1992, Caroline and Hector Williams collaborated with Aglaia Archontidou in excavating underneath the Byzantine-Genoese castle in Mytilene, and they also dug a site at Odos Nikomedias, near the North Harbor of Mytilene. Archaeological investigation by foreign archaeological missions on the island has, since the middle of the 20th century, otherwise been limited (Leekley and Noyes 1975: 20–1; Spencer 1995a: 270 n. 4; Spencer 1995b: 1–2).[71] However, throughout the later 20th century and increasingly in the 21st, a number of projects and rescue interventions by the Greek Archaeological Service have cast additional light on important sites across Lesbos, including Mytilene (Kourtzellis 2012; Kourtzellis and Panatsi 2019; Kourtzellis and Theotokis 2021), Messa (Acheilara 2002–2004), and the sanctuary at Klopedi (Roungou 2014b; Roungou, Douloumbekis, and Kossyphidou 2017).

The relevant textual evidence from literary sources starts with Homer, who intermittently mentions Lesbos because of its proximity to Troy. The most important literary sources for Archaic Lesbos can be found in the writings of contemporary residents of the island, the poets Sappho and Alcaeus, both of whom seem to have been born in the second half of the seventh century. A significant percentage of the extant poetry composed by Sappho and Alcaeus comes to us via quotations in later writers, and we must be sensitive to the potential for anachronizing distortion in how their verses were introduced, abridged, and paraphrased. Lesbos' prominence, its rich cultural traditions, and its involvement in the Ionian Rebellion mean that Herodotus discusses it repeatedly, providing information about its political, diplomatic, economic, and demographic history in the process. Thucydides also provides information about the status of Lesbos in the early Delian League. Lesbos was famous for its Classical and later historians, such as Hellanicus, the author of the first *Atthis*, but only bare fragments of their writings, many of which discussed Lesbian local history, survive (see *FGrH* 476–9 for writers of the local history of Lesbos, as well as Thomas 2019: 260–73).

Archaic epigraphic material from Lesbos is extremely meager. The surviving inscriptions tend to date from the Classical period and later, and no corpus has yet replaced James Paton's 1899 edition for *Inscriptiones Graecae* (XII.2), though

---

71. The only well-published excavations are Koldewey's work from Messa (1890: 47–61 and plates 18–26; see also Petrakos 1967c; Petrakos 1968c), Lamb's work at Antissa (Lamb 1930–1931; 1931–1932) and Thermi (Lamb 1936), and the work in Mytilene carried out with Archontidou by Williams and Williams (1985; 1986; 1987; 1988; 1989; 1990; 1991).

supplements to *IG* XII.2 were provided by Friedrich Hiller von Gaertringen in 1939 (#1–143 in *IG* XII Supplementum) and by Serapheim Charitonidis in 1968.

# 3.3B.  *Lesbian Natural Setting*

Lesbos, the third-largest island in the Aegean (1,614 sq km), stretches 70 km E–W and 45 km N–S, with 320 km of coastline. The island is separated from the mainland by a narrow (c. 12 km) strait and lies on an important trade route connecting the southern Aegean to the Hellespont and the Black Sea. Lesbos is roughly triangular in shape, with two major gulfs (Kalloni [ancient Gulf of Pyrrha] and Gera) intruding from the south and southeast, respectively (Naval Intelligence Division 1944–1945: 492–514; Philippson 1959: 233–44; Kontis 1978: 10–13, 17–21) (see Map 3.9).

Geography and geology divide Lesbos into distinct eastern and western halves. The Gulf of Kalloni, which runs 21 km roughly NE–SW, creates a physical separation between east and west that is reinforced by highly divergent landscapes in different parts of the island. The eastern half is dominated by strata of mica schists and gneiss granites, as well as limestones and marbles; the soil is deep and fertile, and the vegetation supports an abundance of animal life, along with extensive olive and grape cultivation (Green 1989: 48–9; Green 2005). The western half of the island is dominated by hard volcanic stones, especially andesite and basalt, and most of this part of the island is unsuitable for cultivation and is used today only as marginal grazing land (Hecht 1972; Schaus and Spencer 1994: 412 n. 2; Kontis 1978: 13–17; Higgins and Higgins 1996: 132–5).

The topography of Lesbos is generally hilly, with plains making up less than a third of the total surface area. There are four distinct mountain ranges: in the eastern part of the island are Mt. Olympus (967 masl, on the western side of the Gulf of Gera) and Mt. Kourteri (sometimes called Mt. Amali, 527 masl) (on the eastern side of the Gulf of Gera); in the western part of the island is Mt. Ordymnos (799 masl); and where the eastern and western halves join in the northern part of the island is Mt. Leptymnos (968 masl). Inland travel on Lesbos is, as a result, relatively complicated: in the 19th century CE, the 65-km-long journey from Mytilene to Methymna by road took two days. Communication was, however, simplified by the two large, sheltered gulfs, which facilitated travel by boat (Mason 1993: 225; Ellis-Evans 2019: 199–200).

The climate of Lesbos is mild; low temperatures and snowfall are exceedingly rare. As is the case across the eastern Aegean islands, research on the paleoclimate is lacking, but it is likely that the weather today, characterized by a favorable combination of plentiful rain (750 mm/year) and sunshine, does not differ markedly from that in antiquity (Kontis 1978: 19–42; see also Manning 2022

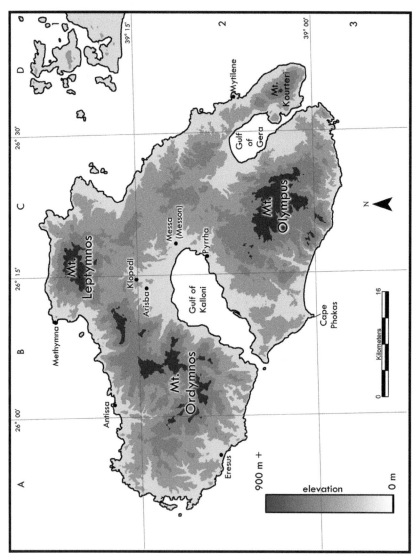

MAP 3.9. Topographic map of Lesbos.

for general observations on climatic changes over time in the Mediterranean).[72] There are numerous small watercourses on Lesbos, some of which are perennial. Lesbos was praised in antiquity as a place for retirement or refuge (Strabo 14.2.19; Diod. *Sic.* 17.29.2; Plin. *HN* 14.73; Cic. *Brut.* 85; Plut. *Pomp.* 74.1; Longus 1.1, 4.2.2–6).

## 3.4B. *Lesbian Material Culture*
### 3.4B.1. Early History of the Island

Lesbos was inhabited beginning in the Neolithic period, and there were substantial settlements on the island in the Bronze Age, most notably at Thermi on the east coast and at Kourtir on the Gulf of Kalloni. The material culture assemblage on Lesbos during the Bronze Age shows strong affinities with that of northwestern Anatolia, and Mycenaean influence seems to have been muted. Hittite documents suggest that from the 15th to 13th centuries, Lesbos constituted a region, known as Lazpa, that was under Hittite rule (Spencer 1995a: 273–5; Lambrianides and Spencer 1997; Kyriakopoulou and Roungou 2020).

Several ancient literary sources claim that settlers from the Greek mainland arrived on Lesbos as part of the so-called Aeolian migration during a nebulously defined era prior to the Archaic period (see Sections 3.1 and 3.5B). However, there are no discernible material traces of Late Bronze or Early Iron Age settlement disruption corresponding to major migrations from mainland Greece. Instead, the island seems to have been inhabited continuously from the Bronze Age, and Greek-speaking migrants to Lesbos evidently arrived gradually, rather than in a one-time colonizing venture. No precise chronology for that process of settlement can at present be supplied, but the archaeological record suggests that it began no later than c. 1000 (Kontis 1978: 116–24; Spencer 1995a: 275–7; Vanschoonwinkel 2006–2008: 119–20, 30–3; Rose 2008; Brown 2020).

Herodotus (1.151.2; cf. Ps.-Scylax 97 and Strabo 13.1.21) states that there were, in his time, five *poleis* on Lesbos but that (at an unspecified earlier period) there had been six until Arisba was destroyed and annexed by Methymna.[73] The five *poleis* in question, the so-called pentapolis, comprised Mytilene in the southeast, Pyrrha on the east shore of the Gulf of Kalloni, Methymna in the north, Antissa in the northwest, and Eresus in the southwest. Nigel Spencer's gazetteer (1995b)

---

72. For weather information on modern Lesbos, see http://www.weather.molyvos.eu/Bootstrap/history.html.

73. See Hansen, Spencer, and Williams 2004: 1018 for discussion of the problematic claim by Stephanus of Byzantium that there had been 13 *poleis* on Lesbos.

remains the only systematic attempt to come to terms with diachronic patterns of occupation. Spencer records 48 sites dating to the Archaic period, although his treatment of the evidence is not without problems.[74]

## 3.4B.2. Settlement Organization and *Chōra* of Mytilene

The urban core of Mytilene, the most important *polis* in Archaic Lesbos, was situated on an oval islet measuring roughly 1 km N–S and 800 m E–W (see Figure 3.4). That islet was separated from Lesbos by a c. 650-m-long, c. 30-m-wide channel known as the Euripos (Kontis 1978: 212, 15–6; Kourtzellis 2013b; Theodoulou and Kourtzellis 2019: 117–21). The basic layout of the city is briefly summarized by Diodorus (13.79.6):

> The old part of the city is a small island. The newer part was built nearby, opposite the old part of the city, on the island of Lesbos. In between the two parts of the city there is a narrow strait (εὔριπος), which helps make the city secure.

The Euripos was crossed by bridges (see, for example, Longus' *Daphnis and Chloe* 1.1), the remains of two of which (both post-Archaic) have been found (Acheilara 2012: 56 and n. 16; Kourtzellis and Theotokis 2021: 116).

The Euripos, which ran roughly along the line of the modern Odos Ermou, silted up in the medieval period and is no longer visible. The contours of the shoreline in the area have also changed, partially as the result of a c. 1- to 1.5-m rise in sea level (Theodoulou 2014: 495–6; Theodoulou and Kourtzellis 2019: 33). The highest point of the (former) islet, which seems to have served as the city's acropolis in antiquity, is currently crowned by a medieval fortress known as the Kastro. The flat, lower-lying area to the west of the acropolis is currently known as Epano Skala.

There were harbors on both the north and south sides of the islet, with the northern harbor serving primarily merchant ships and the southern for military vessels (Thuc. 3.6.1; Ps-Scylax 97; Strabo 13.2.2; Theodoulou and Kourtzellis

---

74. Many of Spencer's "Archaic" sites are dated solely based on the presence of distinctive Lesbian masonry construction in stone walls and terraces, which he argues always dates to the sixth century. This method of dating is problematic, since many examples of later building utilize the Lesbian style, as Spencer readily admits (see extended discussion in Spencer 1995b: 53–64). The number of Archaic sites on the island dated by something other than masonry style is significantly smaller.

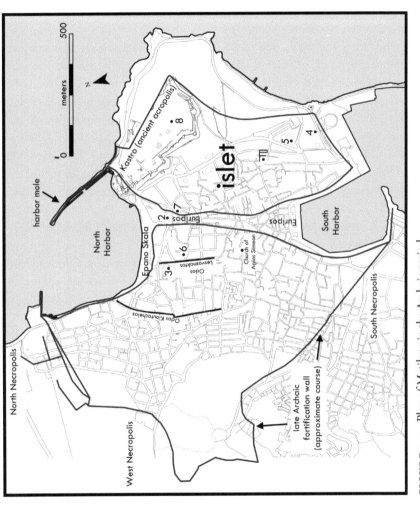

FIGURE 3.4. Plan of Mytilene in the Archaic period.

2019: 87–117; Kourtzellis and Theotokis 2021).[75] The modern city of Mytilene lies directly on top of its ancient predecessor, and archaeological exploration has accordingly been limited (Lang 1996: 247–9).

The site of Mytilene was occupied for much of the Bronze Age, after which there seems to have been a hiatus. The earliest traces of post–Bronze Age activity consist of a curvilinear building and nearby *bothros* with pottery, animal bones, and figurines dating from the ninth century BCE through the second century CE (excavated on Odos Longou, c. 250 m south of the current south shore of the North Harbor and 150 m west of the Euripos; #6 in Figure 3.4); two successive curvilinear buildings of unknown but possibly Protogeometric date found on the islet (in a rescue excavation at Odos Themidos; #1 in Figure 3.4); and scattered pottery finds and tombs. The curvilinear building at Odos Longou has been tentatively associated with the Sanctuary of Apollo Maloeis, mentioned by Thucydides (3.3.3), which was almost certainly already extant in the Archaic period (Spencer 1995a: 279 n. 51; Triantafyllidis 2015: 26–7; Kourtzellis 2019: 166; Kyriakopoulou and Roungou 2020: 55–6). The Hellenistic agora was located in this part of the city (Triantafyllidis 2015: 7; Kyriakopoulou and Roungou 2020: 119–23; #3 in Figure 3.4), and the Archaic agora (mentioned by Alcaeus, F130b.18 Lobel-Page) was likely situated directly to the east (and hence on the islet). The exiguous evidence uncovered to date suggests that the settlement was originally concentrated on the islet and near the North Harbor, but habitation spread onto the landward side of the Euripos at an early date (Spencer 1995a: 277–9 and fig. 3; Spencer 1995b: 9; Spencer 2000: 74–5; Hansen, Spencer, and Williams 2004: 1028; Kyriakopoulou and Roungou 2020: 54–5).

If we turn our attention to the Archaic period, excavations on the acropolis revealed a Sanctuary of Demeter and Persephone (#8 in Figure 3.4). The earliest structures associated with that sanctuary date to the fourth century, but there are pottery, lamps, and figurines that attest to cult activity starting in the sixth century at the latest (Cronkite 1997: 36–93). (For cult rituals at this sanctuary, see Section 3.11B.) A few hundred meters to the south, Archaic building remains under the Hellenistic Sanctuary of Aphrodite may speak to earlier cult activity (Kyriakopoulou and Roungou 2020: 60; #5 in Figure 3.4). The finds from the acropolis also include architectural remains, which have been dated to the mid-sixth century. Those remains were broken up and used as fill in the second century and so survive only in small fragments. Most of the fragments come from fluted Ionic columns and column bases; at least some of the bases seem to have been

---

75. Aristotle (*The Situations and Names of Winds* 973a) says that the northern harbor at Mytilene was called Maloeis, presumably after the Sanctuary of Apollo Maloeis that was located on its shores (see below). See also Strabo 13.2.2.

quite large (diameter of 0.83 m) and must have belonged to a substantial building of some kind (H. Williams 1993).

In the lower part of the city, there was a Sanctuary of Cybele (located on the east side of the current Odos Voutsina;[76] #7 in Figure 3.4). In antiquity, that site would have been on the east side of the Euripos, near the North Harbor. The cult building itself, enclosed in a temenos wall, went through at least two and possibly three construction phases starting perhaps as early as c. 700.[77] It is oval in shape (possibly apsidal in its original form) and oriented roughly N–S, measuring c. 8.3 x 14 m (Triantafyllidis 2015: 29–31). Finds from the site include two sixth-century figurines of Cybele as well as a sherd of sixth-century pottery inscribed ΑΠΟΛΛ-, suggesting that both Cybele and Apollo were worshipped there (Hatzi-Vallianou 1973: 515–17; Williams and Williams 1988; Spencer 1995a: 296–9; Mazarakis Ainian 1997: 89–90 and figs. 354–5; Roungou 2013: 41–4, 112–18; Kyriakopoulou and Roungou 2020: 59–60; the graffito is illustrated in Hatzi-Vallianou 1973: pl. 484γ).

Approximately 50 m to the north of the Cybele sanctuary, excavations at Odos Nikomedias (#2 in Figure 3.4) revealed a large Roman building that was situated on the southern shore of the North Harbor; under that structure lay successive strata that included stretches of Archaic walls (some of which may have formed part of harbor installations) and a considerable amount of seventh- and sixth-century locally produced and imported fine-ware pottery that may have been used in the Cybele sanctuary (Schaus 2017).[78]

Parts of an Archaic necropolis—or, more precisely, small clusters of burials that may have been intermingled among residential structures—have been found just to the west of the Euripos, in piecemeal excavations conducted in the area roughly delimited by the Church of Agios Simeon on the south, Odos Kioutacheias on the west, and the southern shore of the North Harbor on the north. A group of tombs (the number is uncertain) was discovered in 1928 during the construction of a bell tower at the Church of Agios Simeon (Acheilara 2012: 65 with earlier references). More recently, excavations on Odos Lesvonaktou, which runs north from the Church of Agios Simeon, uncovered 37 burials (Acheilara 1999). In addition, excavations across from the Church of

---

76. Odos Voutsina was known as Odos Achilleos when the sanctuary was excavated in the 1970s.

77. Spencer (1995a: 298–9) argues that the date of c. 700 suggested by the excavator is too early.

78. The few traces of domestic structures dating to the Archaic period are discussed in Williams and Williams 1988; Williams and Williams 1989; Williams and Williams 1991. The theater seems to date to the fourth century (Kourtzellis 2013a).

Agios Simeon brought another 40 or so burials to light (Acheilara 2012). A single cist tomb was found in the same general area (Acheilara 2012: 65). The finds associated with those burials indicate the necropolis was in use in the seventh and the first half of the sixth century. A limited number of burials of the same date have been found on the west shore of the North Harbor (Kyriakopoulou and Roungou 2020: 59–60).

Substantial necropoleis in use at the northern, western, and southern edges of the city started receiving burials in the late sixth or early fifth century (Kourtzellis and Panatsi 2019; Kyriakopoulou 2020: 109–11; list of relevant excavation reports in Kourtzellis 2020: 364 n. 4–5). The North and South Necropoleis were situated just beyond the ends of the North and South Harbors and outside newly constructed fortification walls (see below). A single Archaic tomb from the South Necropolis has been published (Acheilara 1987; Archontidou-Argyri 1989: 69–70; Spencer 1995a: 295 n. 157), and there is passing mention in archaeological reports of late Archaic tombs from the North Necropolis (Acheilara 2014). (See Section 3.4B.9 for further discussion of burial customs on Archaic Lesbos.)

The remains of what seems to have been a pottery workshop were excavated at Odos Argyri Ephtalioti, about 400 m to the south of the Cybele sanctuary, near the southeastern shore of the South Harbor (and hence on the islet that was the core of the ancient city of Mytilene; #4 in Figure 3.4). Six kilns, in use during the second half of the eighth and the first half of the seventh century, were abandoned in the second half of the seventh century, and a stone structure, measuring 8.70 x 4.52 m, was built. The excavator identified the structure as a sanctuary because its architecture bears some resemblance to the structure in the Cybele sanctuary, a basin was found set in the floor of the structure, and the head of a roughly life-size limestone representation of a male was built into the southern wall of the structure (and hence in secondary use) (Kourtzellis 2012: 215–20 and figs. 4–7). The head is roughly carved and probably formed part of an anthropomorphic *stēlē*. In its original form, that *stēlē* likely resembled examples from places such as Knossos and Thera that were found in funerary contexts (Kourou and Grammatikaki 1998; Koursoumis and Karapanagiotou 2010). It is likely, therefore, that there were pottery workshops on the south side of the city that were located near a cemetery and that a broken funerary *stēlē* from the necropolis was reused in constructing a ceramic workshop. The structure here identified as a workshop went out of use in the sixth century, and the general area around the workshop seems to have been renovated at the same time.

Some extant stretches of fortification wall in Lesbian masonry have been dated to the late sixth or early fifth century. It is likely that much of the islet was already fortified at some earlier date and that those fortifications included a wall running N–S down the east side of the Euripos, but no remains of earlier fortifications have been found (Frederiksen 2011: 173; Roungou 2013: 176 Eik. 5; Hülden 2020: 130-3). Koldewey, who mapped the stretches of wall visible in the 19th century CE, estimated that in the Classical and Hellenistic periods they enclosed an area of 140 ha (Koldewey 1890: 3–15 and pls. 1–3; Hansen, Spencer, and Williams 2004: 1029; Kyriakopoulou 2020: 111–14, with an updated plan in color pl. 6). There are extensive remains of an elaborate set of harbor moles (Kourtzellis 2008; Kourtzellis 2010; Kourtzellis 2013d; Kourtzellis 2013c; Theodoulou 2014: 495–6; Theodoulou 2017: 123–6; Theodoulou and Kourtzellis 2020: 78–83; Kourtzellis and Theotokis 2021: 112), which cannot presently be dated with any degree of precision (though see Spencer 1995a: 296 n. 171, who suggests that the earliest relevant structures date to the sixth century).

While any conclusions about the overall layout of Mytilene in the Archaic period are necessarily tentative, it is possible to sketch a plausible developmental trajectory. The original nucleus of the city was situated near the North Harbor, on both sides of the Euripos, and on the hill (acropolis/Kastro) above and to the east of the North Harbor. A necropolis on the western side of the Euripos, near the Church of Agios Simeon, was in use in the seventh and the first half of the sixth century, and in that same general time frame, the southeastern shore of the South Harbor was the site of a necropolis and ceramic workshops. In the second half of the sixth century, the city underwent a major transformation that included the building of fortification walls and harbor works, the abandonment of the necropolis on the west side of the Euripos, and the establishment of necropoleis at the northern, western, and southern extremes of the city. The pressure of a growing population and increasingly organized naval activity meant that the southern part of the city, where the military harbor was located, was redeveloped at the same time.

The *chōra* of Mytilene seems to have encompassed c. 500 sq km. Its eastern and southern limits were defined by the ocean; to the north and west, it bordered on the *chōrai* of Methymna and Pyrrha, respectively. The precise location of the northern frontier is debated; the western frontier lay in a pine forest on Mt. Olympus (Hansen, Spencer, and Williams 2004: 1018–19, 26). Mytilene also had an extensive *peraia* in the Archaic period, the possession of which helped make it the dominant *polis* on the island (see Section 3.5B).

## 3.4B.3. Settlement Organization and *Chōra* of Pyrrha

Mytilene shared the eastern half of the island with the *polis* of Pyrrha, which was situated on and around an oval hill on the east coast of the Gulf of Kalloni. A stream entered the gulf on the north side of the hill. The current shoreline has been much altered by a rise in sea level, as is clear from the existence of submerged buildings at the site, and the hill seems to originally have had harbors (now silted up) on both sides.

The extant excavated remains from the site are not extensive. The site was occupied in the Bronze Age, after the end of which there seems to have been a hiatus. Pottery and a burial date the beginning of the site's post–Bronze Age history to the tenth century. In the eighth century, an apsidal or oval stone and mud-brick structure of relatively diminutive dimensions (total surviving length c. 7 m, maximum width 6.6 m) was constructed on the hilltop. That building was modified and expanded on multiple occasions, including in the late seventh, the second half of the sixth, and the fifth century. The finds from the building indicate that it was a cult site, probably dedicated to Apollo, starting in the tenth century (Schiering 1989: 344, 67–74; Spencer 1995a: 281–3 and fig. 4; Spencer 1995b: 21–2; Mazarakis Ainian 1997: 92 and figs. 365–6; Hansen, Spencer, and Williams 2004: 1031; Amigues 2013: 72–86; Kyriakopoulou and Roungou 2020: 54). Many remains of what appear to be architectural members of Archaic buildings litter the site, suggesting that much significant architecture has yet to be discovered.

The extant traces of a fortification wall, which Koldewey reconstructed to encompass an area of 9.5 ha, have been dated by Spencer to the Archaic period on the basis of their polygonal masonry style (Koldewey 1890: 7–28 and pl. 11; Spencer 1995b: 21; Hansen, Spencer, and Williams 2004: 1031; Frederiksen 2011: 184; Hülden 2020: 138–9). Koldewey examined undated remains of ship-sheds in what had been the harbor on the north side of the hill and a jetty in what had been the south harbor (Theodoulou 2014: 506; Theodoulou 2017: 128; Theodoulou and Kourtzellis 2019: 149–53).

The *chōra* of Pyrrha consisted of the region between the east coast of the Gulf of Kalloni and Mt. Olympus. This is a relatively circumscribed area, suggesting a territory of c. 250 sq km. Its western and southern limits were defined by the Gulf of Kalloni and the ocean, and it bordered on Methymna to the north and Mytilene to the east (Hansen, Spencer, and Williams 2004: 1030). Messon, near the northern edge of Pyrrha's *chōra*, was the site of a sanctuary shared by all of the *poleis* at Lesbos (see Section 3.11B). At Cape Phokas on the southern coast of the island and within the *chōra* of Pyrrha, a sanctuary site was situated on a promontory. Although the Doric temple at Cape Phokas, at the southern limit of the *chōra* of Pyrrha, dates to the Roman period, the finds from the site, including stratified fine-ware pottery, suggest that cult activity was already taking place there in the Archaic period (Spencer 1995b: 17). Two inscribed dedications (*IG* XII.2.478; *SEG* 45.1094) from the site and a reference in Stephanus of Byzantium's *Ethnica* (s.v. Βρῖσα) show that Dionysus was worshipped there. Recent investigations revealed the remains of harbor works that seem to date to the Roman period, but two shipwrecks dating to the fifth and fourth centuries that were found in the waters near the sanctuary suggest that the harbor at Cape Phokas was active in the Classical period and perhaps earlier (Theodoulou 2014: 505–6; Theodoulou and Kourtzellis 2019: 117–21).

## 3.4B.4. Settlement Organization and *Chōra* of Methymna

Methymna, the second-most-powerful *polis* on Lesbos and a continual rival of Mytilene (Mason 1993), was situated on the western slopes of Mt. Leptymnos and hence in the western part of the island, both geographically and geologically (Higgins and Higgins 1996: 133 fig. 13.2). The urban core of ancient Methymna was located on a coastal promontory that runs E–W, with an acropolis on the highest point of the promontory (an area now occupied by a Genoese-Ottoman castle) (see Figure 3.5). The city surrounded the acropolis on all sides except the east. The site was occupied throughout the Bronze Age, and evidence for occupation in the 11th and tenth centuries has been found in the form of a small Protogeometric necropolis (Zachos 2017; Kyriakopoulou and Roungou 2020: 54).[79]

The limited collection of Archaic material from the site includes two residential areas: one located to the west of the acropolis and consisting of a paved street and houses from the eighth and seventh centuries and one located to the east of the acropolis and consisting of a paved street and houses from the seventh century. Small clusters of burials and two single tombs have been found in scattered locations to the west and north of the acropolis. On the northwest side of the city, an apsidal building with three consecutive floor deposits, dating from the Archaic to the Hellenistic period, has been recently excavated. The site appears to have been used for the production of clay figurines (Acheilara 2002–2004). In the Classical period, settlement concentrated on the west side of the acropolis, and the area to the east of the acropolis became a cemetery (Spencer 1995a: 283–5, 94 and fig. 5; Hansen, Spencer, and Williams 2004: 1025; Kourtzellis and Pappa 2020: 91–3, 95–7).

Koldewey traced the remains of fortifications that have been tentatively dated to the sixth century on the basis of their polygonal masonry style; he estimated that they enclosed an area of c. 30 ha (Buchholz 1975: 40–7, 61; Kontis 1978: 238–40; Hansen, Spencer, and Williams 2004: 1025; Frederiksen 2011: 168; Hülden 2020: 136–8; Kourtzellis and Pappa 2020: 93). Recent explorations have revealed

---

79. The extension of archaeological protection and concomitant rescue excavations that began in 1996 have rendered earlier scholarship on Methymna, most notably Buchholz 1975 and Kontis 1978: 261–99, largely obsolete. The best starting point for the study of the city is now Kourtzellis and Pappa 2020.

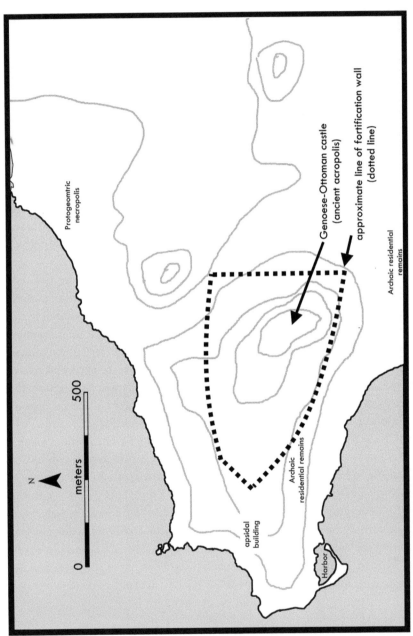

FIGURE 3.5. Plan of Methymna in the Archaic period.

the existence of substantial harbor works in the form of a long mole that formed a large, south-facing basin at the southwestern tip of the promontory. The extant structures seem to date to the Classical period but may have had Archaic predecessors (Theodoulou 2014: 495–6, 7–500; Theodoulou 2017: 126–7; Theodoulou and Kourtzellis 2019: 121–31; Theodoulou and Kourtzellis 2020: 73–5).

The *chōra* of Methymna, after its conquest and absorption of Arisba (see Section 3.4B.5), encompassed c. 400 sq km. Its western and northern edges were defined by the sea. To the southwest, it bordered on the *chōra* of Antissa, to the southeast on the *chōrai* of Pyrrha and Mytilene. The sanctuary at Messon, common to all of the *poleis* on Lesbos (see Section 3.11B), seems to have lain on the frontier between Methymna and Pyrrha (Hansen, Spencer, and Williams 2004: 1024). *Horoi* of Classical date near the modern village of Bapheios in the foothills of Mt. Leptymnos, and hence within the boundaries of the *chōra* of Methymna, demarcate a temenos of an unknown deity or hero; it is quite possible that the history of that temenos extended back into the Archaic period (Spencer 1995b: 45–6; Kourtzellis 2019: 165).

## 3.4B.5. Settlement Organization and *Chōra* of Arisba (and the Sanctuary at Klopedi)

As noted above (see Section 3.4B.4), Herodotus states that Methymna had at some unspecified earlier point conquered the *polis* of Arisba and annexed its territory (1.151.2; cf. Strabo 13.1.21). The site of Arisba has been located on a rise near the modern village of Kalloni, c. 3 km north of the current shoreline of the Gulf of Kalloni. Insofar as the site has never been systematically excavated, the long gap in known activity between the Middle Bronze Age and the Archaic period may well be filled at some future point. The most prominent features of the site are stretches of a 2-m-thick fortification wall that, as mapped by Koldewey, seems to have enclosed an area of c. 8 ha. The polygonal masonry from which that wall was built may suggest a sixth-century date, though Ioannis Kontis proposed a date at the end of the eighth century (Kontis 1978: 269, 88–90). Remains of houses at the site cannot be dated with any degree of precision (Koldewey 1890: pl. 13; Spencer 1995a: 287–8 and fig. 7; Spencer 1995b: 25–6, 64; Hansen, Spencer, and Williams 2004: 1022; Frederiksen 2011: 131).

The *chōra* of Arisba (and subsequently the *chōra* of Methymna) was the site of an important sanctuary located at modern Klopedi, near the village of Napi and c. 4 km north of the urban center of Arisba. That sanctuary quite possibly marked the border between Arisba and Methymna. Koldewey speculated that the sanctuary was dedicated to the cult of Apollo Napaios mentioned by Stephanus of Byzantium (s.v. Νάπη; cf. Strabo 9.4.5), and recent excavations, which uncovered a fragmentary plaque with the inscription [ . . . ]ΛΩΝΟΣ (Roungou, Douloumbekis, and Kossyphidou 2017: 119 and fig. 17; cf. Roungou 2014a), have at least partially confirmed that speculation.

There was a settlement at Klopedi in the Late Bronze Age, followed by what seems to be a period of abandonment (Douloumbekis and Kossyphidou 2014a; Kyriakopoulou and Roungou 2020: 50–1; Roungou 2020: 292–3).[80] In the late eighth or early seventh century, a curvilinear structure (measuring 13.6 x 8.6 m) was erected on top of the remains of the Bronze Age settlement. The finds from that structure, including jewellery, bovine terracotta figurines, weapons, and a 17-cm-tall head from a clay figure, indicate that it served cultic functions. A stretch of curved wall found to the south of the building, also dating to the eighth century, may be a temenos wall. Immediately outside that wall, a funerary pyre delimited by a low circular wall was excavated: the pottery from the pyre (including two gray-ware kratēres with incised decoration) shows that it was roughly contemporary with the aforementioned curvilinear structure (Roungou 2014a; Roungou 2014b; Roungou 2020: 293–5).

In the seventh century, a two-room rectangular structure containing a hearth was erected just to the south, superseding the eighth-century cult building. Prior to the end of the seventh century, a larger building with internal roof supports was erected on that same spot. The temenos wall was expanded at the same time. A contemporary inhumation burial in a pit grave covered with stone plaques was located just outside that temenos wall. Next to that grave were found pottery fragments and a hearth with ashes, outside of which were many gray-ware fragments, animal bones, and drinking vessels (Douloumbekis and Kossyphidou 2014b; Kyriakopoulou and Roungou 2020: 59). Sherds of amphoras and kratēres from the same area of the site show that it continued to be used for funerary purposes (and probably tomb or hero cult) through the middle of the sixth century.

Shortly after the middle of the sixth century, a temple (typically labeled Temple A) was built on top of the area of the site that had been used for funerary purposes. Only parts of the foundations of Temple A and some architectural members are preserved, but that is sufficient to show that it had a peristyle with Aeolic capitals, a tile roof, and red and white terracotta decoration in the superstructure. It was oriented E–W and had an entrance on the east side. The interior was divided into a deep pronaos, a naos, and a shallow opisthodomos. Temple A, which measured 29.20 x 18.70 m, was almost square in shape, likely because it

---

80. On Klopedi in general, see Betancourt 1977: 82–7; Spencer 1995a: 299–301; Spencer 1995b: 24; Roungou and Douloumbekis 2014; Roungou, Douloumbekis, and Kossyphidou 2017; {Roungou, 2019 #29889}.

was constructed in such a way as to avoid disturbing the earlier remains that lay underneath it (Douloumbekis 2014; Roungou 2020: 293–300).

In the last quarter of the sixth century, another temple (typically labeled Temple B) was constructed just to the north of Temple A. Temple B was more conventional in shape, measuring 16.90 x 38.15 m, and had an 8 x 17 peristyle. The (unfluted) columns and capitals were made from local trachyte, and the entablature seems to have been made of wood, with terracotta acroteria and antefixes and possibly a terracotta frieze of some kind. The existence of a square altar built from Lesbian polygonal masonry inside the cella of Temple B suggests a sequence of construction not unlike that observed at Emporio on Chios (see Section 3.4A), with a temple built around a platform that once served as the center of an open-air shrine. Temple B, perhaps best known for its elaborately carved Aeolic capitals, is an important example of a particular style of temple architecture that seems to have flourished on Lesbos (see Section 3.12B.3) (Kossyphidou 2014; Roungou 2020: 302–4).[81]

## 3.4B.6. Settlement Organization and *Chōra* of Antissa

The *polis* of Antissa lay to the southwest of Methymna and the north of Eresus. Its urban core was situated on and around a coastal promontory that is currently dominated by a Genoese-Ottoman castle (see Figure 3.6). The acropolis was located on a hill a few hundred meters to the south of the promontory, and the city surrounded the acropolis. There was a significant settlement at the site in the Late Bronze Age, followed by a hiatus that, on present evidence, lasted into the ninth century. Winifred Lamb excavated superimposed curvilinear buildings that went through three construction phases (Buildings III, IV-1, and IV-2) (the first measuring c. 17 x c. 6.5 m, the second c. 14 x c. 6 m) at the foot of the acropolis, each of which was modified on multiple occasions. Building III has been variously dated between the tenth and the early eighth centuries, Building IV to c. 700. The later building had walls of polygonal masonry and a hearth and seems to have continued in use through the seventh century. The finds from these buildings have led some to identify them as cult sites, but they have also been interpreted as houses (Fagerström 1988: 90; Spencer 1995a: 285–7 and fig. 6; Spencer 1995b: 62–3; Lang 1996: 245–7; Mazarakis Ainian 1997: 84–5, 91–2, and figs. 356.1, 58, 61a–b; Kyriakopoulou and Roungou 2020: 53–4). Just to the west of Buildings III–IV, another curvilinear building, tentatively dated to the Late Geometric period, was excavated in the 1970s (Hatzi-Vallianou 1973: 517–19;

---

81. For a lyrical discussion of the famous capitals from Temple B, see Scully 1969: 222–5.

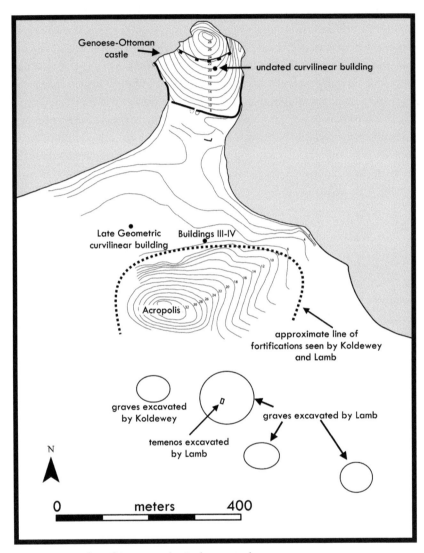

FIGURE 3.6. Plan of Antissa in the Archaic period.

Mazarakis Ainian 1997: 92 n. 490). A third curvilinear structure, located about 300 m north of Buildings III–IV, is marked on Koldewey's plan of the site (it is not noted on Lamb's plan), but no chronological indications are given (Mazarakis Ainian 1997: 108).

Koldewey and Lamb excavated Late Geometric through Classical graves to the south and southeast of the acropolis (E.-M. Mohr 2015: 211–12). The material found by Lamb was never fully published, but that material was restudied by Spencer (1995d). The most noteworthy feature of the burials is that they supply evidence for the existence of a tomb cult in the Archaic period. Two cist graves were, in the seventh century, surrounded by a stone wall that Lamb described as a temenos; the absence of finds from the cist graves makes it impossible to supply a more precise date than a terminus ante quem of the eighth century. Lamb's excavations of the area within the temenos uncovered an extensive collection of dedications that date from the seventh through the fifth centuries and consist of fine pottery, bronze figurines and fibulas, spindle whorls, and what seem to be votive terracottas (which were hung on the temenos wall) including miniature human legs. Three kilns dating to the sixth century were found nearby; finds indicate that they were used to produce amphoras and perhaps other vessels (Kyriakopoulou and Roungou 2020: 61).

Both Koldewey and Lamb documented stretches of fortification wall encircling the acropolis and enclosing a space of c. 18 ha; Lamb dated that wall to the sixth century on the basis of associated pottery finds (Koldewey 1890: 19–20, 23, and pl. 6; Frederiksen 2011: 129–30). The city faced onto a sheltered cove to the southeast of the promontory, and there are some indications that the sixth-century fortifications were connected to a harbor mole (Theodoulou 2014: 500–1; Theodoulou 2017: 127; Theodoulou and Kourtzellis 2019: 131–9; Theodoulou and Kourtzellis 2020: 75–6).

The *chōra* of Antissa extended from the coast into the highlands of Mt. Ordymnos, giving the *polis* a territory of c. 250 sq km. Its northern and western limits were defined by the sea, and it bordered on the *chōra* of Methymna to the northeast and that of Eresus to the south (Hansen, Spencer, and Williams 2004: 1021–2). Literary sources from the Hellenistic period and later (see, for example, the third-century historian Myrsilus of Methymna [*FGrH* 477 F2]) claim that after women in Thrace had dismembered Orpheus and thrown his remains into the Hebros river, his head washed ashore on Lesbos and was placed in a cave near Antissa and that his head, which retained the power of speech, gave oracles. An Attic red-figure hydria from c. 440 shows Orpheus' head in a crevice in a rock, along with a man holding ropes (presumably to climb down into a cave) and the Muses (Watson 2013). Although there is nothing on the hydria that incontrovertibly links the scene it depicts to Lesbos, it has been suggested that the hydria offers evidence for the existence of an oracular cult of Orpheus near Antissa in the Classical period and quite possibly the Archaic period as well (Ustinova 2009: 106–7; Kourtzellis 2019: 164).

### 3.4B.7. Settlement Organization and *Chōra* of Eresus

The urban center of the *polis* of Eresus was located at the edge of an extensive coastal plain and occupied the area on and around a low hill (Vigla hill) immediately behind the coast that served as the city's acropolis (see Figure 3.7). The shoreline in the area has evolved significantly since antiquity, and there is reason to believe that there was once a good harbor to the west of the hill (Schaus and Spencer 1994: 421–4). The agora was situated near that harbor in the late Classical and Hellenistic periods and may well have been in the same place in the Archaic period. The earliest-known signs of activity on the acropolis date to the Early Bronze Age; the earliest evidence for post–Bronze Age occupation dates to the Protogeometric period. The hill was surrounded by a fortification wall of polygonal masonry that encompassed an area of c. 5 ha. A modest surface scatter of Archaic sherds found within those walls, along with their polygonal style, may support an Archaic date for their construction (Schaus and Spencer 1994; Spencer 1995a: 288 and fig 8; Spencer 1995b: 29–30; Schaus 1996; Hansen, Spencer, and Williams 2004: 1024; Zachos 2010: 22–3; Frederiksen 2011: 138; Hülden 2020: 139–40; Kyriakopoulou and Roungou 2020: 54). An Archaic Aeolic capital found on the beach below the acropolis hill suggests that its heights may have hosted a temple of some kind (Spencer 1995b: 30 n. 135). In the flat area to the north of the acropolis, a complex of buildings dated to the late seventh and sixth centuries, constructed of unworked stones and apparently roofed with perishable materials, was excavated in 2006 and 2007 (Zachos 2010: 231–6). Metallurgical slag recovered from the complex suggests a possible industrial use. Rescue excavations in 2005 uncovered a late Archaic and early Classical cemetery containing a combination of cist tombs, pithos burials, and inhumations in Clazomenian sarcophagi (Zachos 2010: 228). Recent reports indicate some parts of the Archaic harbor works may also be coming to light (Theodoulou 2014: 503; Theodoulou 2017: 127; Theodoulou and Kourtzellis 2019: 117–21; Theodoulou and Kourtzellis 2020: 76–7).

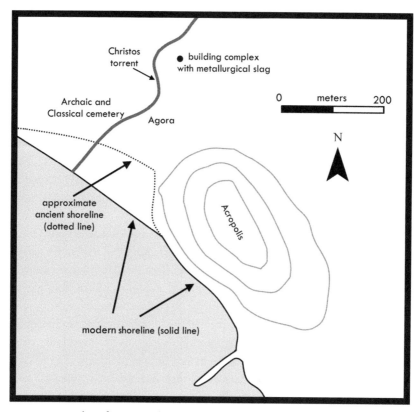

FIGURE 3.7. Plan of Eresus in the Archaic period.

The *chōra* of Eresus extended from the coast into the highlands of Mt. Ordymnos, giving the *polis* a territory of c. 225 sq km. Its southern and eastern limits were defined by the sea and the Gulf of Kalloni, and it bordered on the *chōra* of Antissa to the north (Hansen, Spencer, and Williams 2004: 1023). A series of stone-built structures were constructed near the borders of Eresus and of Methymna and along major routes of communication. These structures, which have been dated to the Archaic period on the basis of their polygonal masonry, were multifunctional and probably served as watchposts and refuge sites during periods of conflicts (Schaus and Spencer 1994; Koumarelas 2011: 93–112). One of them, located at the modern settlement of Apotheke (c. 15 km east of Eresus, on the southwest coast of the Gulf of Kalloni), consisted of a large (41.0 x 45.5 m) platform that was accessed by a ramp (see Figure 3.9

in Section 3.12B.3). The pottery scatter at the site, consisting almost entirely of fine wares, suggests that it had cultic functions (Kontis 1973: 81–2; Schaus and Spencer 1994: 216–17 and fig. 3; Kourtzellis 2019: 167–8; Theodoulou and Kourtzellis 2019: 117–21).

## 3.4B.8. Settlement Patterns on Lesbos

Although the evidence for settlement organization in Archaic Lesbos is insufficient to permit any generalizations, it is noteworthy that all five *poleis* were located at easily defensible coastal sites that included good harbors, and all (including Arisba) possessed immediate access to good agricultural land (Bresson 2000: 95–108).

In a similar vein, survey work carried out on Lesbos to date has not yielded enough evidence to permit definitive statements about the settlement pattern in the *chōra* of any of the *poleis* on the island. That said, as discussed above, a series of stone-built structures helped define the *chōra* of Eresus, and Spencer has argued that elaborate tower and enclosure complexes, which exist in some numbers in the central and western parts of the island, served similar purposes. Those structures are situated in highly visible locations on important routes, typically on the inland edge of coastal plains. In Spencer's view, they served a variety of functions, including conspicuous display of wealth by elites. He takes the absence of such structures in the eastern part of the island as a sign that elites in Mytilene founded their power and status on access to foreign exchange networks, rather than on symbolic control over distant parts of the *chōra*. Spencer sees this pattern of activity as already well established in the Archaic period, though some caution is in order, because the dating of the structures in question relies heavily on the assumption that polygonal masonry is sufficient evidence to postulate an Archaic date for any given structure (Spencer 1994; Spencer 1995c; Spencer 2000). As Lillian Acheilara (2020: 279–80) has pointed out, examples of Lesbian masonry on Lesbos date between the eighth and third centuries.

## 3.4B.9. Burial Customs on Lesbos

As is the case with Chios, a paucity of evidence makes it difficult to generalize confidently about Lesbian burial customs, although here we are in a better position because of the excavations of parts of an Archaic necropolis in Mytilene, as well as Lamb's work at Antissa and Spencer's restudy and republication of the cemeteries at that site (Lamb 1930–1931: 174–6; Spencer 1995d). Archaic burials have also come to light in Methymna (Evangelidis 1925–1926: 150–4; Acheilara and Archontidou-Argyri 1987: 482), and other mortuary evidence comes in the form of chance finds of cist and sarcophagus burials from Kalloni, Messa, and Eresus.[82]

Approximately 75 burials have been excavated in the Archaic necropolis on the west side of the Euripos in Mytilene (see Section 3.4B.2). Both cremation and inhumation were practiced with nearly equal frequency, with single burial being the norm. The cremation burials typically involved placing the ashes of the deceased in a gray-ware amphora (see Section 3.4B.10). The amphora holding the ashes was usually stood upright on the ground but was sometimes inserted into a narrow trench. Inhumation burials were placed in simple pit graves, cist graves, sarcophagi, and pots (the last of which, in many cases, held adults). Grave goods consisted primarily of smaller gray-ware vessels that were broken before being placed in the tomb, as well as *astragaloi*, limited amounts of bronze and gold jewellery, and imported pottery. At least some of the graves were marked by blank *stēlai* (Acheilara 1999; Acheilara 2012).

Burial practices in Archaic Lesbos seem to have been similar across the entire island and similar to those found in contemporary Greek communities in the eastern Aegean. The patterns evident at Mytilene are repeated elsewhere on the island, although sarcophagus burials seem to have been more common at Lesbian *poleis* other than Mytilene. That may, however, reflect diachronic change in that most of the sarcophagi from elsewhere on Lesbos seem to date to the sixth or early fifth century (Spencer 1995a: 293–6; Spencer 1995d; Acheilara 2012: 65–6). Insofar as the excavated necropolis at Mytilene went out of use in the mid-sixth century, further archaeological exploration may very well increase the number of sarcophagus burials from Mytilene. The mortuary evidence from Antissa and Klopedi (see Sections 3.4B.5–6) points to the existence of tomb cults of some sort at both sites.

## 3.4B.10. Lesbian Ceramics

Pottery production on Lesbos featured a distinctive gray ware made on the island from the Early Iron Age into the Hellenistic period. Lesbian gray ware is

---

82. Kalloni: Charitonidis 1964: 398. Messa: Petrakos 1967a: 72–5, figs. 73–6; Petrakos 1967b: 458–9; Petrakos 1967c: 96–102 pls. 74–84; Petrakos 1968a: 84–6; Petrakos 1968b: 80–2. Eresus (burials from vicinity of Vigla hill, the acropolis of ancient Eresus): Conze 1865: 27–39 pls. II.XII–XV; Koldewey 1890: 22–6 pls. 8–10; Laskaris 1960; Spencer 1995b: 30.

generally of high quality and was clearly valued within the island and overseas.[83] Recent excavations at Eresus have shown that the gray ware found on Lesbos is relatively uniform, but there are minor differences in style from one place to another on the island (Zachos 2012). Lesbian gray ware (often referred to as bucchero) is exceptional among other East Greek wares of the Archaic period in its lack of painted decoration. It seems that, for reasons that remain unclear, the Wild Goat and related styles of painted pottery that became popular in many other Greek communities in the eastern Aegean during the Archaic period were never favored on Lesbos (Cook 1997: 115–16). The surface of Lesbian gray ware is polished or washed instead of being painted and usually retains the silver-gray appearance of the clay itself. Decoration, when evident, is in the form of deep molded lines, relief, and stamped or freehand incisions. The presence of knobs and the color of the pottery suggest that it may have been influenced by metal prototypes. Representative shapes include dinoi (large bowls for mixing wine) along with their stands, dishes, and pouring vessels of various shapes. Lesbian gray-ware amphoras are found in burial contexts as well as votive deposits at sanctuaries (Spencer 1995d: 301–3). Similar ceramic traditions are evident at sites along the Turkish coast.

Outside of Lesbos and the northeastern Aegean, gray-ware amphoras have been discovered as far afield as Sicily, North Africa, and various ports on the Black Sea (Spencer 1995d: 301–2), testimony to the far-flung trade relations of the Lesbians. The recent discovery of a Lesbian gray-ware cup with vertical handles bearing an inscription, probably datable to the early Archaic period, in the *hypogeion* at the site of Methone may suggest that individual, entrepreneurial Lesbians were involved in northern Aegean trading communities. The inscription reads, "I am the cup of Philion" (Tzifopoulos 2013: 36–7; Archibald Forthcoming: Section 3.3.4). (On Lesbian amphoras, see Section 3.8B.3.)

## *3.5B. Lesbian Political History*

The political history of Lesbos can be considered both from the perspective of the relationship between the *poleis* on the island and from the perspective of the internal politics of the individual *poleis*. We will begin with the former.

It remains frustratingly unclear why the island of Lesbos, unlike Samos and Chios, did not develop a single, homonymous *polis* that encompassed the entire island but instead retained or developed multiple autonomous *poleis*, as

---

83. For studies of Aeolic gray-ware pottery, see Lamb 1932; Bayne 1963; Dupont 1982: 193–208. For Lesbian gray ware at Naucratis, see Kerschner 2006; Johnston and Villing 2022: 398.

enumerated in Section 3.4B. Cooperation among the various *poleis* on Lesbos was, nonetheless, not unknown, as is most evident from the Sanctuary of Zeus, Hera, and Dionysus at Messon (see Section 3.11B), which was shared by all of the Lesbian *poleis* during the Archaic period.[84] However, the centrifugal forces at work outweighed the centripetal ones straight through the fifth century and beyond. Potential factors at play might include the geography and resources of the island. The size and terrain of Lesbos make inland communication difficult (see Section 3.3B), and the island contains a considerably greater quantity of viable agricultural land and has generally more fertile soil than either Chios or Samos. It may be the case that the larger population these resources supported contributed to a more complex political geography. Aneurin Ellis-Evans (2019: 199–241) has recently argued that the *poleis* on Lesbos found ways to cooperate while, with the exception of Mytilene, taking active steps to inhibit the political unification of the island.

Mytilene was the outlier insofar as it seems to have had long-cherished ambitions to control the entirety of Lesbos, ambitions that came to a head in 427, when Methymna accused Mytilene of attempting to "synoecize" or politically unite the island by force (Thuc. 3.2.3). Mytilene was in a position to make a bid to control all of Lesbos in no small part because, unlike the other *poleis* on the island, it possessed a sizable *peraia*. The *poleis* of Lesbos did not found a considerable number of *apoikia* in far-off locales during the Archaic period, as the *poleis* on Euboea did, for example. The Lesbians did, however, found or conquer more than a dozen settlements along the coastlines of the Gulf of Adramyttion (to the northeast of Lesbos), the Troad, and the Thracian Chersonese (see Ellis-Evans 2019: map 4.1; and see Map 3.4 above). The nearness of Lesbos to Asia Minor (the two being separated by less than 10 km of sea at some points) and the generally muted winds and waves greatly simplified travel between Lesbos and the adjacent coast (Philippson 1959: 234). While all of the *poleis* on Lesbos may well have participated in that process in one fashion or another (Methymna was responsible for at least one foundation), Mytilene clearly played a leading role, coming to control much of the coastlines along the Gulf of Adramyttion and the Troad, and it found itself in a position to exclude the other *poleis* on Lesbos from those areas. A precise chronology cannot at present be established, but the Mytileneans certainly had a substantial *peraia* by the second half of the

---

84. The coin series that have been typically understood as a common coinage for Lesbos have now been reinterpreted as exclusively Mytilenean issues. See the discussion in Section 3.8B.4. Robert's argument (1969–1990: vol. 2: 818, 25) that there was some sort of formal political federation in Lesbos by the seventh century remains difficult to accept (Hansen, Spencer, and Williams 2004: 1019–20; Buraselis 2015: 370–5).

seventh century (Funke 1999: 62–3; Mason 1993: 226–9; Constantakopoulou 2007: 240–1).

Mytilene was tenacious in maintaining control over its *peraia*, as is evident from the extended hostilities between Mytilene and Athens over Sigeum. The Mytileneans founded Sigeum at a highly strategic location at the eastern side of the southern mouth of the Hellespont, but the Athenians, under their commander Phrynon, an Olympic victor of 636, expelled the Mytileneans sometime around 620. The Mytileneans seized it back in 607/6, when Pittacus (on whom see below) faced off against Phrynon in single combat and defeated him by employing a hidden net (Strabo 13.1.38; Diog. Laert. 1.74; Polyaenus 1.25; cf. Alc. F167 Lobel-Page; Isaac 1986: 163–6). In some battle during the broader conflict, Alcaeus threw his shield away, which was promptly put on display by the Athenians (Ἀττικοί in F428a Lobel-Page). The Athenians later recovered control of the site, to judge from Herodotus' claim that Pisistratus had wrested it from the Mytileneans and given it to his illegitimate son Hegesistratos (5.94.1; the chronology of this passage of Herodotus seems to be muddled, probably due to the vagueness of Herodotus' wording; see Hornblower 2013: 270–1).

Mytilene's relationship with the different parts of its *peraia* varied spatially and temporally. The coastline immediately opposite Mytilene was a direct agricultural dependency of Mytilene and lacked any substantial urban centers. Some communities in other parts of the *peraia*, such as Assos, seem to have become independent *poleis* by the early fifth century at the latest. However, most of the inhabitants in the Mytilenean *peraia* lived in communities that were controlled and economically dominated by Mytilene (Mason 1993: 226–9; Ellis-Evans 2019: 155–97).

The possession of an extensive *peraia* empowered and enriched Mytilene and helped make it the dominant *polis* on Lesbos. Mytilene's *peraia* was significantly larger in extent than its *chōra* on Lesbos and contained valuable resources, such as shipbuilding timber from Mt. Ida. In addition, the long stretches of coastline in the *peraia* lay along a sea route of primary importance and gave Mytilene a variety of opportunities to profit from maritime commerce. Moreover, as we will see (see Section 3.8B.4), Mytilene profited from producing a billon coinage that it imposed on the communities in its *peraia*.

There is some reason to believe that maritime COMMERCE played an important role in the internal dynamics of elite competition in Mytilene. Spencer (1994; 1995c; 2000), drawing on archaeological and literary evidence, has made the case that elites in Lesbian *poleis* other than Mytilene competed for status by establishing practical and symbolic control of land in the *chōra*, whereas status competition in Mytilene was built around access to foreign exchange networks (see Section 3.4B.8).

Dio Chrysostom (45.13) draws a direct connection between the Mytileneans establishing a *peraia* and their subsequent ambition to control all of Lesbos, and while Dio is less than an ideal source for the history of Archaic Lesbos, the causal link he suggests is certainly plausible. It is surely not coincidental that when the Athenians sought to render Mytilene harmless after the revolt of 428/7, they not only confiscated Mytilene's ships, dismantled its fortifications, and imposed a cleruchy but also took control of its *peraia* and sought to ensure that the communities in the *peraia* became firmly independent from Mytilene (Thuc. 3.50.1–3; Ellis-Evans 2019: 155–97).[85]

Although Methymna did not have a *peraia*, its position on the northern coast of Lesbos ensured that it maintained direct contact with the sea route running along the coast of Asia Minor. That, in turn, may have helped Methymna mount a stout resistance to Mytilene's ambitions to dominate all of Lesbos. Bresson (2000: 95–108) has argued that Mytilene and Methymna were the strongest *poleis* on Lesbos because they—unlike the other *poleis* on the island—had privileged access to maritime traffic. Hugh Mason (1993: 229–30) has made the case that Methymna's conquest of Arisba was a response to Mytilene's control of a *peraia*; shut out from the arable land on the mainland opposite to them, Methymna acquired territory by conquering a neighboring *polis* on Lesbos itself and thereby helped redress a growing power imbalance vis-à-vis Mytilene.

When we shift our attention to the internal politics of individual *poleis*, we find that the nature of the sources allows us to trace political developments in Mytilene during the Archaic period in some detail, but virtually nothing is known about contemporary events in the other *poleis* on the island. Homer calls Lesbos "the seat of Macar" (*Il.* 24.544), and one prominent strand of the foundation tradition emphasized this seemingly pre-Greek figure (Diod. *Sic.* 5.57.2; Alc. F34b Lobel-Page probably refers to "the [island] of Macar"). A separate set of *mythoi* traced the origins of the Greek settlers on Lesbos to Boeotia and Thessaly (see, for example, Strabo 9.2.3, 5; 13.1.1–4, 58; 13.2.1; 13.3.2–3; 13.3.5). A third prominent tradition connects Lesbos to the Peloponnese, specifically to the house of Atreus. Penthilos, the son of Orestes, is said to have settled Aeolis, including Lesbos (Hellanicus *FGrH* 4 F32; Strabo 9.2.3–5, 13.1.3; Paus. 3.2.1).[86]

---

85. For the purposes of assessing tribute, the Athenians grouped the communities in the former Mytilenean *peraia* under the heading of *Aktaiai poleis* ("coastal cities"). In 424, Mytilenean exiles seized Antandros in the former *peraia* as the first stage of an attempt to restore themselves by force (Thuc. 4.52.2–3).

86. For general discussions of the relevant sources, see Vanschoonwinkel 2006–2008: 119–20, 30–3; Rose 2008.

## 326 THE OXFORD HISTORY OF THE ARCHAIC GREEK WORLD

In the seventh century, a powerful family of Mytilenean elites, the Penthilidai, traced their lineage back to Penthilos, the son of Orestes. This "royal dynasty" (*basilikē dynasteia*) held power in Mytilene but was overthrown by one Megacles and his allies (Arist. *Pol.* 1311b27–9). At some later point in the seventh century, a Penthilid, Penthilos, was once again in control of Mytilene. Subsequently, continues Aristotle, a certain Smerdes (possibly Persian?) killed Penthilos for mistreating him.

The Penthilidai seem to have been just one (very prominent) clan among many in Mytilene, since we read elsewhere of the Kleanaktidai, Archeanaktidai, and Damoanaktidai (Alc. F112.23–4, 296b.1 Lobel-Page; cf. Sappho F98b.7 Lobel-Page). Political life in Archaic Mytilene was characterized by competition between small bands of the elite (*hetairoi*) linked by family (the *genos* or kin group) and friendship (*philia*). The chief location of group consolidation for these factions was the symposium (Rösler 1980; Bowie 1986). In the case of Alcaeus, his group included his brothers, Antimenidas (Strabo 13.2.3) and Kikis (F414 Lobel-Page). Yet there were also non-kin companions (*hetairoi*, F129.16; cf. 150.4) addressed in the poems: Melanippus (F38a.1 Lobel-Page; Hdt. 5.95.2), Agesilaidas (F130b.4 Lobel-Page), Bykchis (F335.3 Lobel-Page), and Aisimidas (F365 Lobel-Page). If each of these men had at least two brothers on the model of Alcaeus, we have a faction of at least 15 people.

Such men might boast connections with Near Eastern states such as Egypt, Lydia, and Babylon (FF48, 69 Lobel-Page; cf. Strabo 17.1.33). They emphasized the (perhaps fictionalized) noble, often heroic pedigree of their *genē*. Given that elite outsiders were frequently incorporated into local politics through alliances and marriage ties, elite status must have been largely constructed and fluid. It is doubtful that genealogical knowledge was secure beyond three or four generations.[87] Being of "bad patrilineage" (*kakopatris*; F67, 75, 106, 348 Lobel-Page) was the deadliest insult imaginable, but it was a contested term with no clear criteria; in many instances, the target merited it simply by betraying the speaker's faction. While the *hetairoi* were members of an economic and cultural elite, they claimed to act on behalf of the wider community, the *dēmos*, which sometimes asserted its own interests (FF70.12, 129.20 Lobel-Page; cf. λᾱός, 364.2).[88] The interaction of these social groups and factions created an explosive political climate.

---

87. Cf. F130b.20 Lobel-Page, where Alcaeus mentions the property of his "father and his father's father." For the fluidity of the Archaic elite, see Duplouy 2006.

88. Scholars have wondered about the representativeness of Alcaeus' political views. To many, he has appeared to be an incorrigible elitist doomed to live in changing times. Far from representing a dying view, however, Alcaeus' ideology was overwhelmingly common among the members of his class. The kind of snobbery Alcaeus expresses can still be found almost a century later in the remark allegedly directed against Maiandrios of Samos by Telesarchos, a member of the local elite: "You are not worthy [ἄξιος] to be our ruler, lowborn as you are and a scoundrel besides [γεγονώς ... κακῶς ... ὄλεθρος]" (Hdt. 3.142.5).

*Chios–Lesbos–Samos*

Shortly after the death of Penthilos, a series of strongmen emerged in Mytilene.[89] As Strabo put it, writing many centuries after the fact, "the *polis* was tyrannized over during those times by many men, due to the dissensions [διχοστασίαι] that occurred" (13.2.3). As he may well have read in the writings of one of the direct participants of the time, Alcaeus, the city was full of "heart-rending sedition and intestine battle" (F70.10–11 Lobel-Page). We have to be extremely careful in approaching the politics of late seventh-century Mytilene, given that words used by Alcaeus may have had different shades of meaning at the time and may have been misinterpreted by later authors.[90] Alcaeus' account of the situation is also intensely partisan and thus tendentious. All the same, his testimony, along with the use of Olympic dating by later sources, allows us to piece together the political history of Mytilene during the period c. 612–580 with a level of specificity unparalleled in either Chios or Samos.[91]

After the Penthilidai, the first dominant figure to emerge was Melanchros, whose main claim to fame is being overthrown by a coalition of Alcaeus' brothers and Pittacus in the 42nd Olympiad (612–609) (Alc. F331 Lobel-Page; Suda s.v. Πιττακός; Diog. Laert. 1.74). Alcaeus may have been too young to participate.[92] Pittacus was the son of a member of the Thracian elite and (presumably) a Mytilenean mother (Duris of Samos *FGrH* 70 F76; cf. Thuc. 4.107.3 for Pittacus as a non-Greek, Thracian name). Pittacus enhanced his position in Mytilenean society by marrying a daughter of the Penthilos who was killed by Smerdes, making himself a Penthilid and, by extension, a member of the Atreidai (Diog. Laert. 1.81; Alc. F70 Lobel-Page).[93]

The next *tyrannos* to arise was Myrsilus, with whom Pittacus partnered, to the fury of Alcaeus (F6, 70, 129, 208 Lobel-Page).[94] Alcaeus and his faction went into exile, with the poet himself going only as far as Pyrrha, just west of Mytilene (F114 Lobel-Page with schol.). The pan-Lesbian sanctuary at the nearby site of Messon

---

89. For what follows, see Andrewes 1956: 92–9; Spencer 2000; Forsdyke 2005: 36–48. For a study devoted to what is known about the constitutions of all the Lesbian *poleis* in the Archaic period, see now Dimopoulou-Piliouni 2015.

90. For further discussion of Alcaeus and his poetry, see Section 3.12B.

91. Absolute chronology is difficult here, since Olympic dating by Classical and later authors is not always reliable (Christesen 2007). The relative sequence of events is more certain.

92. Cf. F75 Lobel-Page; *POxy* 2506 F105 mentions Alcaeus and the 40th Olympiad (620–617), which may be the time of his birth.

93. Gagné 2009 argues that Alcaeus' description of Pittacus as having acquired an Atreid wife is pejorative and meant to associate him with the ancestral fault of Atreus' line.

94. Dale (2011) argues that Myrsilus is not a person but a title, known from Hittite documents (cf. Hdt. 1.7.2). He speculates (not altogether plausibly) that Alcaeus used this word to refer to both Melanchros and Pittacus.

(see Section 3.11B) provides the setting for F129. Alcaeus calls on a Fury to pursue Pittacus for his oath breaking, and he attacks Pittacus with the label "potbelly" (φύσγων), one of many colorful epithets he uses to insult his opponent's appearance and status (Diog. Laert. 1.81; Kurke 1994).

During this time, Alcaeus' brother Antimenidas fought as a mercenary in Nebuchadnezzar II of Babylon's campaign against Askalon, which ended in 604 (FF48, 350 Lobel-Page). Knowing this date, we can determine that Pittacus' double-cross and alignment with Myrsilus followed his distinguished performance at Sigeum, where he defeated the Athenian commander Phrynon in 607/6 (see Section 3.7B; cf. Alc. F167 Lobel-Page).

At some point after this, Myrsilus died, much to Alcaeus' delight (F332 Lobel-Page). However, there was no happy homecoming for Alcaeus—ever the also-ran—and his partisans. The Mytileneans turned to Pittacus out of fear of what might happen if the exiles returned. Historians date the beginning of Pittacus' period of sole rule to c. 590, in order to account for his death a further ten years after his "term" ended (570, according to Diog. Laert. 1.79; cf. 1.75).

Aristotle says that Pittacus' new position was called *aisymnētēs*, a kind of formal elective dictatorship, but there is no contemporary evidence for this, and he is probably theorizing too ambitiously (*Pol.* 1285a35–b3; Alc. F348 Lobel-Page; Romer 1982). We should believe Alcaeus' claim that a significant proportion of the Mytileneans voluntarily acclaimed Pittacus as some sort of leader, although they need not have referred to him as a *tyrannos* as Alcaeus does. Apollodorus (*FGrH* 244 F27a) claims that Pittacus resigned his position after ten years, which may suggest that a time limit was set when Pittacus was appointed.

The details of Pittacus' rule are mostly unknown to us. Alcaeus (F130b Lobel-Page) mentions an assembly and council (*agoras . . . kai bollas*) in a poem written during his period of exile (see Section 3.11B for the text), though how those bodies would have interacted with Pittacus is unclear. Pittacus likely used his period of predominance to establish laws in a fashion similar to that of Solon (see Section 3.6B). Theophrastus (F97 Wimmer) states that Pittacus required market sales (presumably over a certain threshold of value) to be made in the presence of *basileis* and a *prytanis* (παρὰ βασιλεῦσι καὶ πρυτάνει), which, if accurate, attests to the existence of officials with those titles in Archaic Mytilene. A *prytanis* in Mytilene appears in a pact between Mytilene and Phocaea dating to the second half of the fifth century (*SEG* 34.849.19; see Section 3.8B), and a *prytaneion*, in which Sappho's brother Larichos served as cupbearer to the magistrates, is known from literary testimony (Ath. 10.425a).

Pittacus was remembered fondly in popular discourse, to judge from a folk song preserved in Plutarch: "Grind [ἄλει], mill, grind; for Pittacus, too, grinds, ruling [βασιλεύων] over great Mytilene" (*Mor.* 157e). Some scholars have interpreted the song as pejorative, a reference either to Pittacus' tyrannical "grinding down" of Mytilene or to his excessive sexual activity ("grinding" taken *in sensu obscaeno*: Forsdyke 2012: 96, 101). The verb βασιλεύειν, however, suggests genuine praise. Pittacus himself might have employed grinding imagery as a populist gesture: the Peripatetic philosopher Clearchus knew a story that Pittacus took his exercise by grinding grain (ἀλεῖν, F71 Wehrli; cf. Ael. *VH* 7.4). Diodorus says that Pittacus allotted a large estate granted to him by the Mytileneans to his fellow citizens in equal portions, retaining only a modest plot for himself.[95] It is unclear whether this account reflects a historical act of land redistribution or simply affords Pittacus populist credentials retroactively (Diod. *Sic.* 9.12.1; cf. Diog. Laert. 1.75 [where the plot is called "Pittakeios"]). Pittacus' appearance among the ranks of the Seven Sages further attests to his positive reputation.

After Pittacus, Mytilenean political activity goes dark for more than half a century. As in the case of Chios and Samos (see Sections 3.5A and 3.5C), Lesbos does not appear to have had a tyrant imposed on it by the Persians as a matter of policy following Cyrus' defeat of Croesus in 546.[96] The political ramifications of Polycrates' conquest of Lesbos, sometime in the third quarter of the sixth century, in the aftermath of a naval battle in which Polycrates defeated ships from Lesbos and Miletus (see Section 3.7B), are unclear. According to Herodotus, during his Thracian campaign in 513, Darius received advice from Koes son of Erxandros, a Mytilenean general; Koes was subsequently rewarded for his service by being made tyrant of his *polis* (Hdt. 4.97.2–6, 5.11). The Persian commander Otanes had ships from Lesbos under his command during his conquest of Lemnos and Imbros sometime around 512 (Hdt. 5.26), and it is probable that the ships in question came at least in part from Mytilene, indicating that the Persians moved swiftly to put Koes in power. During the Ionian Rebellion, Koes was deposed by Aristagoras of Miletus, handed over to the Mytileneans, and stoned to death (Hdt. 5.37–8). Following the Persian Wars, Mytilene set up an oligarchy that lasted until its revolt against the Athenian empire in 427 (Thuc. 3.27).

---

95. An attempt by Pittacus to win the favor of the *dēmos* of Mytilene is not a priori implausible. Extreme views (e.g., Cawkwell 1995) that deny any involvement by non-elite citizens during the "age of the tyrants" must engage in special pleading against the prima facie evidence of Alcaeus and other sources (e.g., Solon F36–7 West); cf. Luraghi 2015: 80.

96. Cambyses' use of a Mytilenean ship to send a message during his campaign in Egypt in 525 (Hdt. 3.13.1) may imply that the city was by that point in time ruled by a pro-Persian tyrant, but the ship in question may simply have been a merchant vessel that happened to be in the area.

## 3.6B. Lesbian Legal History

Traditions about Pittacus' laws for Mytilene constitute our main, almost certainly unreliable source for Archaic Lesbian law. Aristotle says that Pittacus did not frame an entire constitution (*politeia*), only individual laws, but this is in keeping with our general picture of Archaic lawgivers, who did not develop systematic "codes" (Arist. *Pol.* 2.1274b18; Hölkeskamp 1999; Dimopoulou-Piliouni 2015: 55–135; Dimopoulou 2017). One stricture mentioned by multiple sources is his increase in penalties for crimes committed while intoxicated (Arist. *Pol.* 2.1274b18–20; Diog. Laert. 1.76). As we have seen (see Section 3.5B), Theophrastus (F97 Wimmer) claims that Pittacus required that market sales be made in the presence of *basileis* and a *prytanis*. Athina Dimopoulou (2017: 26–7) has argued that Pittacus wrote the laws of Mytilene on wooden boards that were posted in public.

## 3.7B. Lesbian Diplomatic History

Leaving aside Mytilene's establishment of a *peraia* (see Section 3.5B), very little is known about the diplomatic and military history of Lesbos prior to the sixth century. The story that the Greeks conquered Lesbos while at Troy (*Iliad* 9.128–32, 270–4) is far from a reliable piece of information. There is, however, some evidence for Lesbian mercenaries serving in Babylonia early in the Archaic period (Austin 1970: 15, though cf. Fantalkin 2022), and Mytilene participated in the founding of Naucratis in Egypt in the seventh century (see below).

In the sixth century, the Lesbians found themselves at the mercy of powerful outside forces. Herodotus states that Croesus compelled the Aeolians of the eastern Aegean (among others) to pay tribute (Hdt. 1.6.2), but he also reports (1.27) that Croesus was dissuaded from building a navy and instead formed ties of *xenia* with the Ionians living on islands (πειθόμενον παύσασθαι τῆς ναυπηγίης. καὶ οὕτω τοῖσι τὰς νήσους οἰκημένοισιʼἼωσι ξεινίην συνεθήκατο). The Persians were clearly a looming presence in the eastern Aegean after their conquest of Lydia in 546. As we have seen (Section 3.7A), the Persians did not immediately gain control, either directly or indirectly, over the offshore islands, but the Lesbians inevitably found themselves compelled to adjust to emergent geopolitical realities. The Lydian Paktyes led a failed revolt against Persian rule almost immediately after Cyrus left Sardis in 546, and when that revolt failed, he fled to the Greek city of Cyme as a suppliant. When the Persians demanded the Cymaeans hand over Paktyes, the Cymaeans, evidently reluctant either to anger the Persians or to surrender a suppliant, dispatched him to Mytilene. The Mytileneans did not share the Cymaeans' compunctions and began negotiating with the Persians about what rewards would be on offer for handing over Paktyes, but before those negotiations could come to fruition, the Cymaeans, hearing about what was afoot, sent a ship to Lesbos and moved Paktyes to Chios. Unfortunately for Paktyes, the Chians delivered him to the Persians in exchange for the city of Atarneus (see Section 3.7A; Hdt. 1.157–60; Charon of Lampsacus *FGrH* 262 F9; Briant 2002: #37). This story indicates that Lesbos was not under Persian control at the time of Paktyes' rebellion but that the Mytileneans were ready to treat with the Persians when it was to their advantage.

Sometime in the third quarter of the sixth century, Polycrates conquered Lesbos after the Lesbians had sent all of the ships at their disposal to aid the Milesians in a sea battle that Polycrates won. The Lesbian prisoners were put to work building fortifications on Samos (Hdt. 3.39.4; on those fortifications, see Section 3.4C.2).[97] The fact that Miletus was under Persian influence, if not out-right control, at that point in time may suggest that there was a close relationship between Persia and at least some *poleis* on Lesbos not long after 546 (Carty 2015: 133–4). Mytilene was surely pro-Persian under the rule of the tyrant Koes, who was installed in power by the Persians sometime around 513 and who controlled the city until he was deposed in 499 (see Section 3.5B). Ships from Lesbos formed part of the Persian fleet that conquered Lemnos and Imbros sometime around 512 (Hdt. 5.26).

Some or all of the *poleis* on Lesbos took part in the Ionian Rebellion.[98] Seventy ships from Lesbos fought on the Greek side at the Battle of Lade in 494, and it is likely that many, if not most, of those ships came from Mytilene (Hdt. 6.8.1). Herodotus claims that the contingent from Lesbos shirked its duties at Lade (6.14). When the Persians reasserted control over the eastern Aegean after Lade, they landed forces on Lesbos and, according to Herodotus, "netted" the entire population and burned cities and sanctuaries (6.31–2). As we have seen (see Section 3.7A), the effects of "netting" may not have been nearly as serious as Herodotus implies. Like the Samians and the Chians, the Lesbians joined the Greek alliance after the Battle of Mycale and, later, the Delian League, retain-ing special privileges (Hdt. 9.92.1, 9.106.4; Thuc. 1.96; [Arist.] *Ath. Pol.* 23.5, 24.2). The Mytileneans, who were oligarchically governed, complain in 428—in a speech delivered to the Spartans at Olympia—of having had to "court the

---

97. The chronology of events in Polycrates' reign is uncertain at best. See, for example, Carty 2015: 75–90. A reference in Polyaenus (6.45) to a war between the Samians and the Aeolians sometime in the early sixth century may suggest that there was a long-standing inimical rela-tionship between Samos and Lesbos (Shipley 1987: 53), though the term "Aeolians" could have several different meanings, some of which did not include Lesbos (Rubinstein 2004a: 1033–6). See Section 3.7C for further discussion.

98. See n. 38.

commons [κοινόν] and the leaders" of the Athenians to survive during the *penta-kontaetia* (Thuc. 3.11.7; cf. Xen. [*Ath. Pol.*] 1.18).

## 3.8B. *Lesbian Economic History*
### 3.8B.1. Agriculture and Animal Husbandry

As was the case throughout the ancient Greek world, agriculture played a funda-mental role in the economy of Archaic Lesbos. We have already had occasion to mention that the (original) six *poleis* on Lesbos were positioned in a fashion that gave each of them immediate access to good farmland (see Section 3.4B.8), and Methymna's conquest of Arisba was in all likelihood motivated, at least in part, by the desire to acquire arable land (some of the most fertile soil on Lesbos lay in the *chōra* of Arisba). Cicero lauds the fertility of Mytilene's *chōra* (*On the Agrarian Law* 2.16), and the fourth-century gourmand Archestratos, quoted by Athenaeus (111f–112a), praises the quality of grain produced in southwestern Lesbos:

> The best one can get and the finest of all, all sifted clean from highly pro-ductive barley, are in Lesbos, on the wave-girt breast where famous Eresus is located, whiter than heavenly snow. If the gods eat barley groats, it is from there that Hermes goes and buys it for them. (111f–112a; trans. S. D. Olson)

Like Chios (see Section 3.8A.3), Lesbos produced wine, almost certainly in considerable quantities, that was highly regarded and widely exported. Strabo (14.1.33), presumably drawing on the poetry of Sappho, claims that Sappho's brother Charaxos (see Section 3.8B.3) exported Lesbian wine to Naucratis, a statement that is reinforced by third-century papyri from Egypt recording the importation of Lesbian wine (see the listing of sources at Dzierzbicka 2015: 202 n. 4). Athenaeus (28e) offers an array of quotes from Athenian Middle Comedy playwrights praising Lesbian wine (for a full listing of relevant literary references, see Clinkenbeard 1982: 254–6). Finds of Lesbian amphoras (see Section 3.8B.3) provide evidence for the export of wine starting in the seventh century.

Some insight into the relative importance of different crops on Lesbos can be had from a series of inscriptions (*IG* XII.2.76–80) supplying details of tax cen-suses carried out in the late third or early fourth century CE. The inscriptions in question supply details of land use on estates, including the amounts of land dedicated to sown crops, vines, olives, and pasture. The general pattern is that the ratio of land given over to sown crops, vines, and olive trees is roughly 9:2:1; there is, however, considerable variation from one estate to the next, indicating that some estates specialized in particular crops. Although considerable caution must be exercised in retrojecting the information from these censuses almost a millennium backward into the Archaic period, the relatively small percentage of cultivated land given over to olives is surprising, given that in the current day, olive trees occupy more than half of the cultivated area of the island (Spencer 1996).

The Mytilenean *peraia* gave the city access to important timber resources, especially on and near Mt. Ida (see Section 3.5B and Ellis-Evans 2019: 57–108), and there were also forests on Lesbos itself. Mt. Olympus is currently the site of an extensive pine forest, and Theophrastus' reference to the "pine-covered Pyrrhaean mountain" (*Hist. Pl.* 3.9.5, cf. 3.18.13; cf. Pliny *HN* 16.19.46) indicates that the same part of the island was forested in antiquity (Spencer 1996: 253–9).

## 3.8B.2. Natural Resources and Craft Activity

Although the existence of considerable quantities of ceramics produced on Lesbos leaves no doubt that craft activity was well established in Archaic Lesbos, that activity has left little in the way of tangible traces. Six ceramic kilns from the eighth and seventh centuries were found in the southern part of the city of Mytilene (see Section 3.4B.2), three ceramic kilns from the sixth century were found at Antissa (see Section 3.4B.6), and a building in Methymna was used in the production of clay figurines from the Archaic through the Hellenistic periods (see Section 3.4B.4). A structure in Eresus dating to the seventh and sixth centuries may have been used for metallurgy (see Section 3.4B.7). There is some evidence for the existence of a silver mine in the Archaic period in the *chōra* of Methymna (Davies 1932: 985).

## 3.8B.3. Commerce

The inhabitants of the *poleis* of Lesbos, Mytilene in particular, engaged in maritime commerce from an early date. We have already seen (see Section 3.5B) that in the seventh century, Mytilene established a *peraia* that gave it access to major sea routes, and the importance of maritime commerce for the residents of Archaic Lesbos is also apparent in the poetry of Sappho and Alcaeus. In a recently published poem (Obbink 2014), Sappho speaks about the return of her brother Charaxos "with a full ship."[99] Charaxos, in line with what we know of him from

---

99. The publication of this poem by Dirk Obbink (the so called Brothers Poem), together with other fragments by Sappho, was sensational, but the papyrus containing them is, as of now, at the center of a fierce controversy regarding its extremely suspicious provenance (Sampson 2020; Hyland 2021), even if the authenticity of the fragments has been generally accepted by scholars. For a commented edition of the Brothers Poem, see now Neri 2021: F10.

later sources, has been abroad for the purposes of maritime trade. (As part of this activity, he seems to have freed the prostitute Rhodopis while in Naucratis, for which act, Herodotus tells us, he was harshly upbraided by his sister. The poem does not survive.)[100]

Mytilene was intimately involved in the founding of the *emporion* of Naucratis (on which, see Section 3.8A.3; Hdt. 2.178), and Lesbian pottery is well represented there.[101] The presence of Lesbian traders at that site is probably confirmed by several dedications in Aeolic dialect by Mityleneans (Austin 1970: 26; Möller 2000: 172–4). The interaction of Lesbos with the wider Aegean and Mediterranean is also evident from the ceramic record, particularly in transport amphoras. The amphoras produced on Lesbos are typically divided into two groups—gray and red—based on their fabric. The red-fabric examples are frequently fractional sizes of full-size examples in gray fabric. Both the gray- and the red-fabric amphoras have a distinctive feature: a ridge running from the base of the handle over the shoulder of the vessel, frequently referred to as a rat-tail motif. Both the color of these amphoras and the use of relief decoration display influences coming from northwestern Anatolia, mixed with Aegean traditions in the production of transport containers.

Petrographic and chemical analyses have shown that both gray and red amphoras were produced on Lesbos. The currently available data suggest that both gray and red amphoras were produced at Mytilene, whereas other pottery workshops on the island produced predominantly gray amphoras. That evidence also suggests that some red amphoras were produced at one or more as-yet-unlocated centers outside of Lesbos. The gray-fabric amphoras began to be produced no later than the last quarter of the eighth century and continued to be produced into the fourth century. The red-fabric amphoras may have entered production slightly later—the earliest-known examples are dated to the seventh century—and went out of production in the early fifth century. Both the gray- and the red-fabric amphoras were widely exported, but the patterning of their find-spots is not identical. Neither type is found in any quantity on the Greek mainland, but the gray-fabric examples appear in some numbers at sites in the eastern and western Mediterranean, where the red-fabric amphoras are significantly less common. On the other hand, red-fabric examples greatly outnumber gray-ware examples

---

100. Hdt. 2.135; Strabo 17.1.33; Ath. 13.596b; Sappho T1 Campbell. For elite reliance on overseas trade, see Hes. *Op.* 633–40; Solon F13.43–6 West; Semon. F1.15–16 West.

101. Petrie 1886: 49; Möller 2000: 144; Kerschner 2006; Johnston and Villing 2022: 398. Aeolian, probably Lesbian, pottery is also known from Tell Defenneh across the Suez Canal (Oren 1984; Möller 2000: 35).

in Asia Minor and around the periphery of the Black Sea (Clinkenbeard 1982; Dupont 1982: 201–3; Whitbread 1995: 154–64; Cook and Dupont 1998: 158–63; de Domingo and Johnston 2003: 35–6; Bîrzescu 2005; Dupont 2011; Lawall 2017: 292–7; Dupont 2021).

Although ceramic imports are rarely found in great quantity at sites on Lesbos, a particular class of amphora, typically gray in color and equipped with cylindrical handles with a tail that runs along the shoulder of the vessel, was produced in Lesbos between the seventh and fourth centuries; those amphoras are widespread at sites around Asia Minor (Clinkenbeard 1982). (See Section 3.4B.6 on kilns at Antissa used to produce these amphoras, Section 3.4B.10 for further discussion of Lesbian pottery, and Section 3.5B for discussion of the impact of maritime commerce on the power dynamic among the *poleis* on Lesbos.)

## 3.8B.4. Coinage

From the 520s down through the third quarter of the fifth century, substantial issues of billon (a bronze-silver alloy with less than 50% silver) coins in numerous denominations with widely variant iconography were minted on Lesbos. Some of those coins bear legends, including ΛΕΣ, ΛΕ, Μ, ΜΥ, and Α. The iconography can include a head of a calf or of a lion on the obverse, and an incuse square, sometimes with an eye or an amphora, on the reverse. These coins have typically been interpreted as a common coinage intended to be used throughout the island and authorized on a formal or informal basis by some sort of *koinon* of the Lesbians. From that perspective, the legends Μ, ΜΥ, and Α stand for Methymna, Mytilene, and Antissa, respectively, and the varied iconography reflects the placement on the coins of types linked to each of the five *poleis* on the island. Ellis-Evans has, however, recently and persuasively argued that the coins in question have nothing to do with any sort of *koinon* of the Lesbians (see Section 3.5B for further discussion of a possible Archaic Lesbian *koinon*), that they were all issued by Mytilene, and that they served in part to reinforce Mytilene's ambitions to be hegemon of the entire island (Ellis-Evans 2019: 224–7 with earlier references). Ellis-Evans suggests that the billon coins bore a face value that substantially exceeded the value of the metal they contained and that Mytilene turned a tidy profit by producing those coins in large numbers and mandating their use both in Mytilene itself and in the communities in the Mytilenean *peraia* (see Section 3.5B; Ellis-Evans 2019: 189–90).

In that respect, Mytilene's billon coins served the same function as some of its electrum issues. Starting in the 520s, Mytilene produced a series of electrum coins in collaboration with the city of Phocaea. A considerable amount of information about the production of those coins is supplied by an inscription (*IG* XII.2.1)

336    THE OXFORD HISTORY OF THE ARCHAIC GREEK WORLD

that was found at Mytilene. The inscription in question has been dated to somewhere around 400, but it is typically understood as a renewal of a long-standing pact between the two cities. The surviving part of the (damaged) inscription deals with issues such as the mixing of gold and silver to produce the metal for the coins, audits of the work done by the people involved in the minting process, and punishments for misbehavior (including the death penalty for deliberately debasing the mixture) (Figueira 1998: 487–9; Psoma 2020: 71–2).

The coins in question were produced in just one denomination, the *hektē* (one-sixth of a *statēr*) on the Phocaic weight standard (*statēr* of 16.5 g), meaning that they weighed c. 2.5 g. The iconography on those coins changed regularly (including obverses with a ram's head, a lion's head, Apollo, or Dionysus and reverses with a panther, a sphinx, or Persephone in an incuse square) and had no obvious links to either city. Most of the coins have no legends, and the ones that do, all seemingly issued by Mytilene, have M, ΛE, or A (cf. the legends on the billon coins discussed above). Finds of single coins and hoards show that they circulated in Mytilene and Phocaea but were more heavily used in the Propontis and the hinterland of Phocaea (Mackil and van Alfen 2006: 210–19).

Emily Mackil and Peter van Alfen have argued that the minting of these electrum coins was an intentionally profit-producing enterprise and that they were sold to merchants who used them to facilitate commercial transactions in the Propontis. The presence of gold in the electrum *hektai* meant that they had significant value, roughly the same as an Athenian silver *tetradrachmon*, so they were not particularly useful in everyday retail transactions. Electrum became an important medium of transaction in and around Asia Minor starting in the seventh century, and although silver emerged as the dominant metal for coinage in the Aegean in the sixth century, electrum seems to have retained its importance in certain parts of the Propontis and the Black Sea. The Persian Daric served as the primary gold coinage in Asia Minor during the period when Phocaea and Mytilene were minting electrum *hektai*, but the gold Darics (8.4 g) were very high-value coins, and fractions were lacking, and it seems that the *hektai* functionally served as Daric fractions (Bissa 2009: 76–7).

Electrum presented special opportunities for seigniorage because the proportions of gold and silver in naturally occurring electrum vary widely, and those proportions could be manipulated in the artificially created gold-silver alloys to mint coins with face values that exceeded the value of the metal in them. Considerable effort was involved in quantifying the precise proportions of gold and silver in any given electrum coin, and it was therefore easier to accept any reasonably unadulterated electrum coin at face value, whereas silver coins could easily be weighed and the value of the metal therein rapidly determined. The reasons for the long-term cooperation between Mytilene and Phocaea in producing these coins are unknown, but presumably, the joint commitment helped ensure the acceptance of their electrum *hektai* over a wide area.

Mytilene also produced electrum coins on its own in denominations other than the *hektē*, probably starting in the final quarter of the sixth century. The obverses show a bull, a lion, a boar, a head of Heracles, or a Gorgon; the reverses feature an incuse square (Bodenstedt 1981: 67–87, 97–125). These coins were based on a different, slightly lighter weight standard than the aforementioned *hektai* (Mackil and van Alfen 2006: 216 n. 54).[102]

Unlike Mytilene, which produced only billon and electrum coins prior to 427, Methymna minted silver coins on the Euboic standard (based on a *statēr* of 17.4 g) starting at some point in the second half of the sixth century. A range of denominations (*statēr*, *tetrōbolon*, *diōbolon*) is attested, with Athena and the Gorgoneion featuring in the iconography (Franke 1975; Psoma 2016: 98–9). The other *poleis* on Lesbos do not seem to have minted their own coins prior to the fourth century. (See Section 3.8C.4 for discussion of a coin series that may have been minted by the Greek cities that took part in the Ionian Rebellion.)

## 3.9B.  Lesbian Familial/Demographic History

Lesbos was during the Archaic period an island of at least five independent *poleis*. The number of Lesbian ships at Lade has been employed to estimate the total population at c. 62,000 (Roebuck 1959: 21–3; cf. the modern population of c. 86,000). Mytilene's population in the late Classical period has been estimated, on the basis of the walled area of the urban center and the size of its *chōra*, to have been 20,000–25,000, with roughly half of that number residing in the city itself (Hansen 2008: 269). The walled area of Mytilene was significantly larger than that of any of the other *poleis* on the island (140 ha vs. Methymna, the next biggest, at c. 30 ha), and the *chōra* of Mytilene was larger than that of Methymna and roughly twice the size of the *chōrai* of Antissa, Eresus, and Pyrrha (see Section 3.4B). The urban and rural inhabitants of the *polis* of Mytilene, therefore, may well have represented one-third of the total population of the island. A dossier of documents from Eresus pertaining to the trials of tyrants in the third quarter of the fourth century (*IG* XII.2.526) records that 883 votes were cast, which suggests a population of c. 1,000 adult male citizens and a total population of c. 4,000 (Hansen, Spencer, and Williams 2004: 1023–4). It is unlikely that the population

---

102. Those coins were studied in detail by Friedrich Bodenstedt (1981), but his conclusions, particularly regarding chronology, have been subject to serious criticism (see, for example, Wallace 1983), and further study is required (Ellis-Evans 2019: 190 n. 17).

of Eresus was significantly larger in the Archaic period, which reinforces the general sense that Mytilene was, by some margin, the most populous of the *poleis* on Lesbos.

## *3.10B. Lesbian Social Customs and Institutions*

Few Archaic inscriptions from Lesbos are extant (Jeffery 1990: 360), so our knowledge of Archaic Lesbos relies heavily on literary sources. These are largely connected to the poets Sappho and Alcaeus. The poetry of both Sappho and Alcaeus was originally composed for particular occasions and performed in front of specific audiences, so scholars have often attempted to reconstruct the social reality implied by their poems (see Sections 12B.1–2; on Alcaeus' *hetaireia*, see also Section 3.5B). The language used in the poems by Sappho and Alcaeus no doubt reflected, up to a certain point, the Aeolian dialect spoken on the island; however, it betrays the characteristics of a *Kunstsprache*, with Homerisms and other "artificial" features (Hodot 2014).

In today's Western culture, Lesbos is the emblem of female homoeroticism, and this is no doubt due to the figure of Sappho and her poetry. While it is hard to deny that Sappho's poems contain much that has to do with the expression of love for other (younger) women (see Section 3.12B.2), there is the risk of projecting our own categorizations of love and sex onto a totally different culture (Williamson 1995: 90–132; Most 1996).

## *3.11B. Lesbian Religious Customs and Institutions*

A cult common to all of the *poleis* on Lesbos was located at Messon (modern Messa), c. 5 km north of the urban center of Pyrrha (Spencer 1995b: 22).[103] This cult site is mentioned in Alcaeus F129.1–8 Lobel-Page, which, in its fragmentary form (it is known through a papyrus from Oxyrhynchus) begins as follows:

> . . . the Lesbians established this great conspicuous precinct to be held in common [εὔδειλον τέμενος μέγα ξῦνον κά[τε]σσαν], and put in it altars of the blessed immortals, and they entitled Zeus God of Suppliants and you, the Aeolian, Glorious Goddess, Mother of all [Αἰολήιαν [κ]υδαλίμαν θέον πάντων γενέθλαν], and this third they named Kemelios, Dionysus, eater of raw flesh. (trans. D. Campbell)

---

103. See Κ' Ἐφορεία Προϊστορικῶν καὶ Κλασικῶν Ἀρχαιοτήτων 2004: 26–40 on the history of excavations at this site.

Louis Robert (1960) convincingly identified the sanctuary described by Alcaeus with a site referenced in epigraphic sources as Messon—an apt name, since it is located more or less in the geographical center of the island and was shared by all of the *poleis* in Lesbos. Another important facet of its location is its position in a liminal space on the frontier between Methymna and Pyrrha. The proximity of Messon to the coast greatly simplified access to the site, an especially important feature given that the topography of the island made overland travel quite difficult (see Section 3.3B).

A fragment from Sappho (F17 Lobel-Page) indicates that the identity of the Aeolian goddess mentioned by Alcaeus was Hera;[104] the use of the deictic τυίδ(ε) ("here," l. 7) suggests that the poem in question was performed at Messon (Nagy 2007a: 24), presumably at a religious festival. Another fragment from Alcaeus (F130b Lobel-Page) describes an annual festival that almost certainly took place at Messon and that may well be the one to which Sappho implicitly refers:

> I, poor wretch, live with the lot of a rustic, longing to hear the assembly being summoned, Agesilaidas, and the council: the property in possession of my father and my father's father have grown old among these mutually destructive citizens, from it I have been driven, an exile at the back of beyond . . . to the precinct of the blessed gods . . . where Lesbian women with trailing robes go to and fro being judged for beauty, and around rings the marvelous sound of the sacred yearly shout of women. (trans. D. Campbell)

Several later authors (including Theophrastus, a native of Eresus and hence no doubt familiar with Messon on a firsthand basis) refer to Lesbos as a place known for its beauty contests (relevant sources collected at Page 1955: 168 n. 4), which seem to have been based not just on physical appearance but also on demonstration of *sophrosynē* (Amigues 2013: 104–8; Gherchanoc 2016: 97–102).

The annual festival at Messon would have been an opportunity for the residents of the habitually rivalrous *poleis* on Lesbos to mount competitive displays while also reinforcing and celebrating a collective Lesbian identity (Ellis-Evans 2019: 227–30). In the Hellenistic period, Messon served as the seat of a *koinon* of the Lesbians (Labarre 1994), and while, as we have seen (see Section 3.5B), there was no such formal political organization on Lesbos in the Archaic period, Messon must have played an important role in fostering peaceful interaction on

---

104. For detailed discussion of the identity of the Aeolian goddess, see Amigues 2013: 98–104, *contra* Spencer 1995a: 298 n. 186, who suggests that the goddess was Cybele.

Lesbos on an informal basis throughout its history. Alcaeus lived in the immediate vicinity of the sanctuary during his exile from Mytilene, and so Messon must also have served as a place of refuge and most likely as a site where negotiations about conflicts between *poleis* on Lesbos could be held. Little in the way of remains of dedications, such as honorary statues that one might expect from such a site, have been found. The absence of such material may say something important about how Messon functioned as a shared space, but any such conclusion is provisional in the absence of further excavations (Ellis-Evans 2019: 229).

The beginning of ritual activity at Messon may date as early as the eleventh century. In the Archaic period, an apsidal building was constructed, measuring c. 24 x c. 6 m and built from large blocks of volcanic (trachyte) stone. The existence of a circular clay altar within that building indicates that it was a cultic structure (Kourtzellis 2019: 170–3 and fig. 7). That structure was subsequently incorporated into the foundations of a large, pseudodipteral temple (cf. the situation at Klopedi, discussed in Section 3.4B.5) that has been variously dated to the late Classical or early Hellenistic period (Spencer 1995b: 22; Amigues 2013: 76–86).

Each *polis* on the island of Lesbos had its own cults, calendars, sanctuaries, and festivals, but the combination of limited excavations and meager epigraphic sources means that relatively little is known about the details of cult activity in Archaic Lesbos. We shall focus on cults attested as having existed in the Archaic period, even if later material might, in some cases, throw some light on earlier phases of Lesbos' religious customs. (For a still-useful survey of cults attested in ancient Lesbos, see Shields 1917). The scarcity of our sources does not encourage us to speculate about the patron deities of any of these *poleis* (in general, for the problematic identification of such deities, see Cole 1995 and Burkert 1995: 207–9).

As far as Mytilene is concerned, the sixth-century Temple of Cybele, where Apollo was also worshipped, has already been mentioned, and it is likely that the cult of Apollo Maloeis referenced by Thucydides (Thuc. 3.3.3) was already extant in the Archaic period (see Section 3.4B.2). The iconography on Mytilene's coins from the Archaic and Classical periods includes heads of Apollo, Dionysus, and the nymph Mytilene (Hansen, Spencer, and Williams 2004: 1029–30; see also Section 3.8B.4). Finds from the Demeter sanctuary on the acropolis of Mytilene—thousands of piglet bones, much dining ware, and many lamps—strongly suggest that the sanctuary hosted a Thesmophoria festival with nocturnal rites and communal feasting. It is impossible to specify precisely when that festival may have begun, but the sanctuary was in operation in the sixth century, and it is likely that a Mytilenean Thesmophoria existed before the end of the Archaic period (Cronkite 1997: 36–93; Ruscillo 2013).

In Pyrrha's territory, at Cape Phokas, a sanctuary to Dionysus, perhaps from the Archaic period, seems to have been present (see Section 3.4B.3). Apollo was worshipped at the sanctuary at Klopedi (originally in the *chōra* of Arisba, before that *polis* was absorbed by Methymna). Though our sources are late, it seems reasonable to posit the presence of a cult of Dionysus in Archaic Methymna (Paus. 10.19.3; see Casevitz and Frontisi-Ducroux 1989, as well as Lyons 2014). Athena appears on coins struck by Methymna starting from c. 500 (Head 1911: 560–1). A relief suggesting the existence of a cult to Cybele in the mid-sixth century has been found at Eresus (Spencer 1995a: 299; Roungou 2013: 116–17, 33), and a Cybele relief (dated to the Archaic period on stylistic grounds) was also found at Sigri, a coastal site that lay on the border of the *chōrai* of Eresus and Antissa (Roungou 2013: 117, 34; Kourtzellis 2015).

This is not an extensive collection of evidence on which to base any general statements about religious practice in Archaic Lesbos, but some provisional observations are perhaps in order. Strabo (13.2.5) states that Apollo was held in especially high esteem in the area around Lesbos, a claim that finds support in the cults of Apollo known from Mytilene and Klopedi and his appearance on the coins of Methymna and Mytilene. Spencer (1995a: 296–9) has argued that the presence of cults of Cybele in (at minimum) Mytilene and Eresus reflects a continuing Anatolian influence on cultural practices of all kinds in Lesbos.[105] The role of Zeus, Hera, and Dionysus as patrons of the sanctuary at Messon may suggest that those deities played a particularly important role on Lesbos in general, particularly with respect to a Lesbian collective identity.[106] The finds from both Klopedi and Antissa (see Sections 3.4B.5 and 3.4B.6) point to the existence of some sort of ancestor or hero cult from an early date. There may have been an oracular cult of Orpheus at Antissa in the Archaic period (see Section 3.4B.6).

## *3.12B.  Lesbian Cultural History*

The number of extant inscriptions of Archaic date from Lesbos is small (see Section 3.2B), and hence relatively little is known about the epichoric alphabet used on Lesbos (Jeffery 1990: 359–61). On the other hand, there is a substantial body of evidence showing that a musical and poetic tradition was already well established in early Archaic Lesbos. A certain Lesches of Pyrrha was credited with the authorship of the epic poem known as the *Little Iliad*, and from Lesbos came the legendary musicians Terpander of Antissa and Arion of Methymna (seventh

---

105. In general, on the cult of Cybele in Archaic Greece, see L. Roller 1999: 119–41.

106. See Pirenne-Delforge and Pironti 2014 for discussion of Zeus and Hera at Messon.

century).[107] The two Archaic Lesbian artists we know best, Alcaeus and Sappho, clearly worked in a flourishing poetic tradition.[108]

## 3.12B.1. Alcaeus

Herodotus mentions Alcaeus while discussing the Athenian presence in the Troad and Athens' long-lasting war against the Mytileneans in that area. According to Herodotus, the Athenians were based at Sigeum, the Mytileneans at Achilleion (5.94–5; see Section 3.5B). Alcaeus took part in the war, but during a battle, he had to abandon his shield in order to save his own life. Herodotus mentions a specific poem Alcaeus had composed about that occasion (F428 Lobel-Page) and states that Alcaeus sent his poem to Mytilene, announcing his misfortune to his comrade Melanippus (Μελανίππῳ ἀνδρὶ ἑταίρῳ). Herodotus' words lead us directly into the world that forms the background of Alcaeus' poetry: that of an elite *hetaireia*. The role of these groups in the history of Archaic Mytilene is treated in Section 3.5B. Here we must stress the importance of Alcaeus' group for his poetry since "there is no lyric poet Alcaeus without *hetaireia*" (Rösler 1980: 40).

Another important tidbit of information provided by Herodotus has to do with the perception of the heroic past in Lesbos and in Archaic Greece. Sigeum and Achilleion were places connected with the epic tradition of the Trojan War (Nagy 2010: II ch. 7). Herodotus (5.94.2) tells us that the Athenians justified their claim to Sigeum by stating that "Aeolians had no more share in the land of Ilium than themselves or any others among the Greeks who had taken part with Menelaus in avenging the rape of Helen." We see here a reference by the Athenians to the Panhellenic dimension of the Trojan War in an attempt to gain sanction for their hegemony over a site in the Troad. Whatever economic interests the Lesbians and Athenians had in seeking to occupy Achilleion and Sigeum, there was also a cultural element operating in the conflict.

Alcaeus' poetry itself can show us how this connection with the heroic past may have been perceived in the milieu of the Lesbian elite.[109] As we have seen, the *genos* of the Penthilidai in Mytilene proclaimed their origins from Agamemnon's son Orestes (see Section 3.5B). In F70.6–13, Alcaeus connects Pittacus' acquisition

---

107. See Beecroft 2010: 107–21 for the legendary nature of Terpander's biography. On Arion, see Dewald and Munson 2022: 214–19. On Lesches, see West 2013: 26–7, 34–7.

108. For a detailed treatment of Sappho and Alcaeus, see Yatromanolakis 2009. For briefer overviews, see Lardinois 2022 (on Sappho) and Spelman 2022 (on Alcaeus).

109. On myth in the poetry of Alcaeus and Sappho, see also Nagy 2007a.

of control at Mytilene (his being elected [?] *tyrannos* or *aisymnētēs*) with his marriage to a woman in the *genos* of the Penthilidai. This allows Alcaeus to express his wish to put an end to his fight against Pittacus using a reference to the epic world:

> Let that guy [*scil.* Pittacus], who married into the family of the Atreidai [Ἀτρεΐδα[ν] γ[ένει]], devour the city [δαπτέτω πόλιν] as he did with Myrsilus, until Ares wants to turn us to arms. But may we forget this anger [χόλω τῶδε], and let us relax from the heart-eating strife and civil strife [θυμοβόρω λύας ἐμφύλω τε μάχας], which one of the Olympians [τις Ὀλυμπίων] has aroused, leading the people to folly [ἀυάταν] and giving delightful power [κῦδος] to Pittacus.

After introducing the mythological reference to the Atreidai, Alcaeus goes on to interpret the political events in Mytilene along the lines provided by the narrative of the *Iliad*. Pittacus and his distant relative Agamemnon son of Atreus share the characteristic of "devouring" their subjects: the metaphor of δαπτέτω πόλιν parallels the epithet δημοβόρος ("devourer of the people") that Achilles attributes to Agamemnon in *Iliad* 1.231.

In fact, Alcaeus recasts the whole conflict between his own group and that of Pittacus according to the model provided by the Iliadic quarrel between Achilles and Agamemnon, as demonstrated by the occurrence of terms such as *cholos* and *auata* (= *atē*), two key motifs in the plot of the *Iliad*. The anger, *cholos* or *mēnis*, of Achilles directed at Agamemnon is the prime mover of the Iliadic narrative, at least up to Book 19. This anger is in turn brought about by the *atē*, the folly, of Agamemnon. Alcaeus' resolute tone at line 7 (δαπτέτω κτλ.) may recall that of Achilles in Book 9 of the *Iliad* (e.g., at l. 337 and 377). But by wishing to forget his anger (l. 9), Alcaeus seems rather to be echoing the reconciliation episode in *Iliad* 19, when Achilles publicly announces that he will put an end to his wrath (*Il.* 19.56–68). It is in the same episode that Agamemnon identifies the cause of his quarrel with Achilles: the intervention of the gods, who cast folly (*atē*) on his heart (*Il.* 19.86–9). In an extremely significant twist, however, in Alcaeus, the folly is attributed to the people (*damon*), even if, as in the Achaean camp of the *Iliad*, a god is considered the ultimate cause of events.[110]

Alcaeus has been said to have taken on the literary persona of a figure implacably opposed to tyranny, but the last, appeasing lines of this poem show us a

---

110. The god's intervention gives Pittacus *kudos*, here in the sense of "royal" charisma; cf. Nestor on Agamemnon's kudos in *Il.* 1.277–9. For the textual reconstruction and interpretation of the poem, see Lentini 2000. For the epic poems circulating in Archaic Lesbos, see West 2002.

## 344 THE OXFORD HISTORY OF THE ARCHAIC GREEK WORLD

partially different picture. It should be stressed that Alcaeus' (provisional) refusal in F70 concerns what he explicitly defines as "internal strife" (l. 9–10 ἐμφύλω . . . μάχας), commonly called *stasis* (on this concept, see Hansen and Nielsen 2004: 124–9). The elite Alcaeus has been considered a champion of an anti-*polis* ideology, as opposed to a "middling" *polis* ideology. Such a crude opposition, however, is inadequate to account for some contrasting hints we can find in what we read of his poetry.[111] For reasons of space, we must confine ourselves to discussing the remarkable case of F130b Lobel-Page (see Section 3.11B for the text), in which Alcaeus embraces the cause of the *polis* and refuses to engage in oppositional political activity (described, precisely, as *stasis*).

Inferences commonly drawn from this text are that the poetic "I" is in exile at Messon, where the beauty contests are being celebrated. In addition, it has often been assumed that the poem is a sort of verse epistle that Alcaeus, alone, without his companions, would have sent to a certain Agesilaidas (l. 4), who supposedly, despite being absent from Alcaeus' other fragments, was a companion back in Mytilene (Page 1955: 209; Rösler 1980: 272–85). In any case, on the basis of what we know of Alcaeus, his poetry, and his *hetaireia*, it is surprising that in F130b, we find no reference whatsoever to the common activities of his group. What we find, rather, is an insistence, expressed in a self-pitying tone, on the *polis*' deliberative activities (l. 3–5 ἀγόρας . . . βόλλας) and a refusal to engage in *stasis* (l. 11–12).[112] It is possible that Agesilaidas, not necessarily a close friend of Alcaeus, was meant to act as a go-between between Alcaeus and the people holding power in the *polis* at that time and to make use of Alcaeus' conciliatory poem to plead the exiled poet's cause.[113]

### 3.12B.2. Sappho

Echoing the discourse on Alcaeus, scholarly discussion of Sappho has been dominated by an interest in defining her social group and audience. Sappho's social milieu, however, is even more elusive and controversial than Alcaeus' *hetaireia*. Ulrich von

---

111. See in general Hammer 2004, with important criticisms of the influential theories of Morris and Kurke.

112. The text and interpretation of l. 11–14 are hotly contested. For the interpretation given here, see Lentini 2006: 234–7.

113. This hypothesis is based on analogies between this poem and the last section of Pindar *Pythian* 4 (l. 279–97), where Pindar pleads the exiled Damophilos' cause (compare in particular Alcaeus' refusal to countenance "fighting with the more powerful ones" at l. 11–12 and Damophilos οὐκ ἐρίζων ἀντία τοῖς ἀγαθοῖς in Pind. *Pyth.* 4.285). A hint at a possibly "civic" performance of the poem is in the deictic τωνδέων connected to πολίταν at lines 6–7 ("these citizens here"), which would notionally imply the presence of those very citizens.

Wilamowitz-Moellendorff authoritatively championed the idea of Sappho as a "schoolmistress," but this has been called into question by Holt Parker, who finds no evidence that Sappho's audience consisted of young, unmarried girls. Instead, in Parker's opinion, Sappho's songs must have been sung at banquets for other adult women, and Sappho's group then should be conceived of as a female counterpart to male groups like Alcaeus' *hetaireia* (H. Parker 1993; cf. also Stehle 1997: 262–318). In a long article, André Lardinois (1994) has objected that this theory fails to find support in extant fragments, and he posits, following some suggestions by Claude Calame, that Sappho was an instructor of young women's choruses. This theory, too, has been critiqued (Yatromanolakis 2009: 217–19). However, the notion that Sappho took care of the education of young girls, some from abroad, is supported by a body of evidence that is difficult to dismiss (Ferrari 2010b: 33–7).

The best source of information about Sappho's audience is her poetry itself, but the handling of this evidence is far from straightforward (D'Alessio 2018; Kivilo 2021). It seems wise to assume that her songs were performed mainly on festive occasions and could be executed by either a chorus or a solo singer. Her writings include songs performed by a chorus notionally for the whole community (e.g., wedding songs and other songs connected to religious festivities, such as F140 Lobel-Page on Adonis), in addition to poems suggesting a more restricted audience. Several are addressed, for example, to members of her own family (the Charaxos poem mentioned by Hdt. 2.135 [F202 Lobel-Page]; the ode to her daughter Kleis [F98 Lobel-Page]). These poems presuppose the existence of a regular group of Sapphic companions (which no doubt, *pace* Parker, included younger women) in competition with other groups within the civic community. This scenario is not unlike what can be said of Alcaeus' *hetaireia*. Regarding the occasions of performance of Sappho's songs, then, "it may be more fruitful to replace the concept of *context* with that of *contexts*" (Yatromanolakis 2009: 218).

Some remarks on Charaxos and the recently published Brothers Poem have been offered in Section 3.8B.3. The ode to Sappho's daughter Kleis (F98 Lobel-Page: cf. Ferrari 2010b: 1–16) shows how the familial dimension intersects with local politics and, in turn, with an international network. In particular, in this poem, there is a reference to luxury goods coming from Lydia, the place usually identified as the source of *habrosynē* (cf. the famous lines of Xenophanes F3 West). In F58.25, Sappho says she loves *habrosynē* (Ferrari 2010b: 66–71), and it seems natural to define Sappho's outlook as aristocratic, however elusive this category may be. Some of the noble families dominating the political arena of Mytilene, the same whom we know from Alcaeus' poems, appear also in Sappho's verses: apart from the Kleanaktidai (perhaps Sappho's *genos*? Ferrari 2010b: 17–18), the Penthilidai (F1 Lobel-Page) and the Polyanaktidai (F155 Lobel-Page) are mentioned in other poems in unequivocally polemical contexts. The rivalry of

Sappho with other women (in particular Gorgo and Andromeda; cf. Maximus of Tyre 18.9 = T20 Campbell) and their respective groups no doubt had a political dimension (Caciagli 2011: 212–32). We have, after all, a late report of an exile of Sappho in Sicily (*Marm. Par. FGrH* 239 FA36).

The religious dimension within Sappho's poems may reflect the fact that religious festivities were the most common occasions for their performance. Aphrodite is especially prominent in Sappho's songs. Indeed, the first poem in the Alexandrian edition of Sappho was one commonly identified as an ode to Aphrodite (F1 Lobel-Page). This religious dimension, however, has been explained both in a "private" sense (Aphrodite was worshipped by Sappho and her pupils; von Wilamowitz-Moellendorff 1913: 42 and others after him) and in a "public" and civic sense (Sappho as priestess of Aphrodite; e.g. Lasserre 1989: 113–18).[114] It has also been suggested that Aphrodite could have been the tutelary deity of Sappho's "clan" (Caciagli 2011: 242–84). Given the many uncertainties, it is not surprising that when it comes to imagining the actual occasions for the performance of the already mentioned ode to Aphrodite, scholars have contrasting ideas, due in part also to different textual interpretations or reconstructions.[115]

A rare glimpse into a ritual in honor of Aphrodite is offered by F2, in which the goddess is invited to manifest herself in an epiphany.[116] The setting is a *locus amoenus*: there is a grove of apple trees in which lay altars smoking with incense, a stream, and a meadow where horses graze and winds blow gently. The first line summons Aphrodite from Crete. This detail may suggest a connection with the goddess worshipped (together with Hermes) at Kato Syme in Crete and with the rites performed there by young men and young women (Ferrari 2011: 450–3).

## 3.12B.3. Architecture and Sculpture

Much less is known about the artistic traditions of Archaic Lesbos as manifested in more tangible media. It is clear, however, that the Aeolic style of architecture flourished on Lesbos during the Archaic period. That style had its roots in Syro-Palestine and found its defining element in the Aeolic capital, which features

---

114. Lasserre relies especially on an insecure textual reconstruction from a commentary first published in 1974 (Page and Lobel 1974: 261a.7 ff.), which would bear witness to Sappho's obtaining a προεδρία of the rites of Aphrodite in Mytilene. On Sappho and the rites of Aphrodite, see also Himer. *Or.* 9.4 (= F194 Lobel-Page), with Ferrari 2010a: 148–50.

115. Distinct approaches in Lasserre 1989: 205–14; Aloni 1997: X–XIV; Nagy 2007b: 25–7; Ferrari 2010a: 161–5.

116. On the text and interpretation of this fragment, see Ferrari 2010a: 151–4 and, with more details, Ferrari 2011.

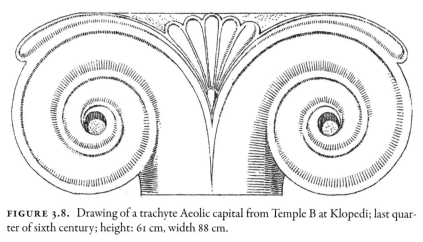

FIGURE 3.8. Drawing of a trachyte Aeolic capital from Temple B at Klopedi; last quarter of sixth century; height: 61 cm, width 88 cm.

two vertical volutes linked by a rising palmette (Betancourt 1977: 58–98). Aeolic architectural elements first appear on Lesbos in the ninth century (in the form of terracotta ornaments from the first curvilinear building at Antissa), and the style is employed on a large scale at Temple B at Klopedi, which dates to the last quarter of the sixth century (see Section 3.4B.5 and Figure 3.8). An Aeolic capital was also discovered on the acropolis of Mytilene and was probably originally used in a votive or funerary context (Mendel 1912–1914: vol. 2: #276). Another Aeolic capital is known from Eresus and likely comes from an otherwise unattesed temple (Kontis 1946–1948: 24–6; Betancourt 1977: 88). Spencer has made the case that the popularity of the Aeolic style on Archaic Lesbos is an indication of the island's strong Eastern orientation during that period (Spencer 1995a: 299–301).

A major feature of Archaic material cultural style on Lesbos is so-called Lesbian polygonal masonry (see Figure 3.9a–b), in which stones (either chiseled to a fine finish or left roughly surfaced) are cut with curved edges that fit tightly against one another in dry-stone construction. Aristotle (*Eth. Nic.* 1137b29–32) describes the way in which the blocks were shaped, with a "leaden rule that is fitted to the shape of the stone and is not fixed." The most famous example of Lesbian polygonal masonry in the Greek world is found in the terrace wall at Delphi, but there are many noteworthy examples on the island of Lesbos itself (Spencer 1995a: 51–64 reviews them). The origin of the style is uncertain, although it has been argued that it was invented on Lesbos and represents a stylized imitation of the curved natural stones used to create the earliest terraces and fortifications on the island (Mason 2001).

The quantity of Archaic sculpture excavated from sites on Lesbos is small but continues to grow. We have already had occasion to mention the roughly carved

**FIGURE 3.9A.** Lesbian masonry walls at Apotheke on Lesbos.

**FIGURE 3.9B.** Lesbian masonry walls at Apotheke on Lesbos.

limestone head of a life-size representation of a male from what was probably an anthropomorphic funerary *stēlē* (see Section 3.4B.2). The head was found in secondary usage and so must be dated stylistically; the comparanda suggest it should be placed in the late seventh century (Kourou and Grammatikaki 1998; Koursoumis and Karapanagiotou 2010; Kourtzellis 2012: 215–20 and figs. 4–7). Although the quality of the work is not high, the fact that it was carved out of limestone indicates that it was made locally and that some life-size sculpture was being produced on Lesbos from an early date. Excavations in Mytilene also produced a marble horse's head (a fragment of a larger sculpture) and a relief of the nymphs, both from the late Archaic period. Fragments of a marble *kouros* came to light in Eresus (Kourtzellis 2012: 220–6).

Coroplasts were active on Lesbos starting in the early Archaic period at the latest and continuing through the Roman period. Representations of females predominate among the terracotta figurines from Lesbos in all eras. The figurines from the Archaic period predominantly show simple, frontal, individual figurines (Acheilara 2006: vol. 1: 173 and passim).

# Section C. Samos

## 3.2C. Sources for Archaic Samian History

In antiquity, the appellation of Samos was applied both to the island and to the main urban center on the island (Rubinstein 2004b: 1094). In the interests of clarity, the island is here referred to as Samos and the ancient city as Samos Town (the modern settlement of Pythagoreio sits on top of Samos Town). The vast majority of the archaeological exploration carried out on the island of Samos has taken place at just two sites—the ancient city of Samos in the southeastern part of the island and the sanctuary of Hera (the Samian Heraion) c. 6 km to the west of the ancient city of Samos (see Map 3.10). The remains of the Samian Heraion were known to early travelers, but systematic investigation of the site began only in the late 19th century CE, with the excavations conducted by the Greek archaeologists Panagiotis Kavvadias and Themistocles Sophoulis. Theodor Wiegand and a team from the German Archaeological Institute worked at the site between 1910 and 1914. Members of the German Archaeological Institute returned to the Heraion in 1925 and have been active at the site since then (with a hiatus from 1939 to 1952). The primary publication venue for the results of those very fruitful excavations is the *Samos* series, which currently runs to 30 volumes.[117]

---

117. See Kyrieleis 1993: 126–9; Tsakos and Viglaki-Sofianou 2012: 19–22; Walter, Clemente, and Niemeier 2019: 1–26 for summaries of the history of excavations at the Heraion.

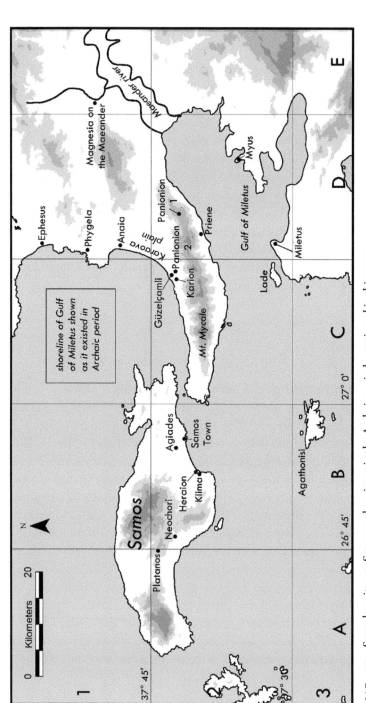

MAP 3.10. Some key sites on Samos and environs in the Archaic period mentioned in this essay.

The modern town of Pythagoreio overlies the primary urban center of ancient Samos, but because the modern town is smaller than the ancient city, it has been possible to conduct systematic excavations on the fringes of the ancient city (especially on its western side), as well as rescue excavations in the center of the modern town. Those excavations, which were carried out in earnest starting after World War II, revealed details of the Eupalinos tunnel, city walls, harbor works, urban sanctuaries, and cemeteries (Leekley and Noyes 1975: 22). While Graham Shipley has compiled information about several sites with possible Archaic remains in the *chōra*, little excavation or formal, team-based survey has been carried out, making it difficult to say much about overall population or settlement patterns on the rest of the island (Shipley 1987: 249–68).

Excavations in Samos, particularly those at the Heraion, have yielded a rich harvest of epigraphic material, including one of the earliest-known inscriptions from Ionia (Jeffery 1990: 328), 13 epitaphs from the seventh and sixth centuries, and close to 100 Archaic graffiti. All of the epigraphic material from Samos has recently been collected and edited by Klaus Hallof and Angelos Matthaiou in *IG* XII.6.1–2.[118]

During the Archaic period, Samos produced or hosted a number of authors— Asius and Anacreon, for example—whose work, unfortunately, survives only in fragments. Our chief source for the political, legal, diplomatic, economic, and even demographic history of Archaic Samos is undoubtedly Herodotus, who devoted several important segments of his *Histories* to the island. He considered it one of the foremost states among both Greeks and non-Greeks of the later sixth century (3.139.1), admired the "magnificence" (μεγαλοπρέπεια) of the tyrant Polycrates (3.125.2), and drew attention to its engineering marvels (3.60). He was clearly personal friends with Samian citizens of his time and visited the Heraion.[119] Several later writers, including Thucydides (1.13, 3.104), Diodorus (10.16.4), and Polyaenus (*Strat.* 1.23), display interest in Polycrates' colorful career. The Aristotelian *Constitution of the Samians* (FF570–8 Rose) and Duris of Samos' history of the island (*FGrH* 76 F21–6, 60–71, 96; Gattinoni

---

118. The Greek text (and German translation) of 433 of the inscriptions from *IG* XII.6 can be accessed online at http://telota.bbaw.de/ig/editionindex.html.

119. For Herodotus and Samos, see Mitchell 1975; Irwin 2009; Pelling 2011. Herodotus' informants about Samian history seem to have been from the group of Samians who opposed both tyranny and Medism, attitudes that are reflected in the stories they told Herodotus (Cartledge 1982: 260). For Herodotus' familiarity with the Heraion, see, for example, his description of the bronze cauldron dedicated by Kolaios (4.152.4), discussed in Section 3.4C.4.3. It is salutary to bear in mind that our understanding of Archaic history sometimes comes from Classical sources' (idiosyncratic) interpretations of earlier dedications or from what temple attendants told them: see Thonemann 2016: 160–1.

1997: 207–16; Thomas 2019: 277–83), both of which seem to have had much to say about Archaic Samos, have come down to us only in fragmentary form.

A list of historians who wrote about Archaic Samos is included in an inscription from the second century recording the results of Rhodian arbitration of a dispute between Samos and Priene over the possession of territory near Mt. Mycale (Hiller von Gaertringen 1906: #37–8; Magnetto 2008). The historians named in that inscription—Duris, Eualkes of Ephesus (*FGrH* 418), Euagon of Samos (*FGrH* 535), Kreophylos of Ephesus (*FGrH* 417),[120] Maiandrios of Miletus (*FGrH* 535), Olympichos of Samos (*FGrH* 537), Ouliades of Samos (*FGrH* 538), and Theopompus of Chios (*FGrH* 115)—all discussed a war, typically dated to the early part of the Archaic period, in which the city of Melie was destroyed and its territory distributed to its conquerors, including Samos (see Section 3.7C for further discussion of the second-century inscription and the war against Melie). Euagon was evidently active prior to the Peloponnesian War (Dion. Hal. *Thuc.* 5) and seems to be cited in the Aristotelian *Constitution of the Samians*. Theopompus was active in the fourth century, Duris c. 300, and Kreophylos in the Hellenistic period. The inscription from Priene provides the primary chronological information, in the form of a terminus ante quem, for Eualkes, Maiandrios, Olympichos, and Ouliades. Unfortunately, the work of all of those authors survives only in fragments, most of which offer minimal insight into Archaic Samos.

We also have rather more informative fragments from other historians who wrote about the early history of Samos: Menodotos of Samos (*FGrH* 541) produced *A Register of Notable Things in Samos* and *On Objects at the Temple of the Samian Hera*, while Alexis of Samos (*FGrH* 539) wrote *Samian Chronicles*. Both authors seem to have been active in the Hellenistic period. The literary sources for ancient Samos are conveniently collected in Meyer (2012).

## 3.3C.  Samian Natural Setting

Samos is separated from Asia Minor by the Mycale Strait, which is less than 2 km wide at its narrowest point. The island measures 45 km E–W and 19 km N–S, giving it a total surface area of c. 470 sq. km. It is the 12th-largest island in the Mediterranean. The terrain of Samos is dominated by two major mountains, Kerkis (ancient Kerketeus, highest point 1433 m) in the western part of the island and Karvounis (ancient Ampelos, highest point 1153 m) in the central part of the island (see Map 3.11). Together, these mountains occupy more than half of the surface area of Samos, and they were home to large forests in antiquity.

---

120. Not to be confused with the homonymous Samian poet, on whom see Section 3.12C.2.

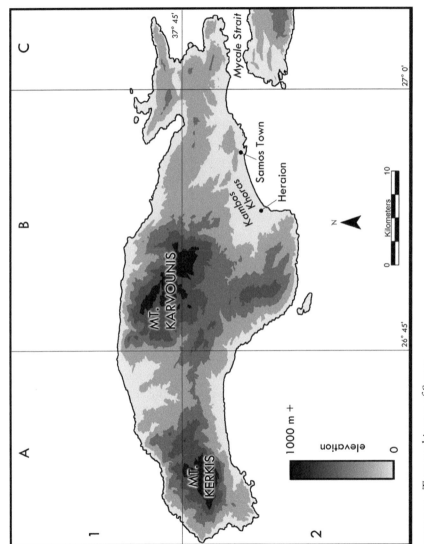

MAP 3.11. Topographic map of Samos.

Aristotle described Samos as *druoussa* (oaken) (F570 Rose; cf. Plin. *HN* 5.135), and Aristokritos of Miletus (second–first century) as *kyparissa* (cypress-clad) (*FGrH* 493 F4).[121]

Whereas the north coast of Samos is steep and rocky, the southern side of the island has less dramatic topography, and its coastline features a number of good harbors sheltered from the prevailing northerly winds. The waters to the south and east of Samos are remarkably shallow for the Aegean, at only c. 200 m deep. Between Samos and Chios, the depth of water is more than five times as great, reaching 1,200 m (Philippson 1959: 260–1, 99). This means that conditions for mariners during storms would have been much more severe to the north of the island than to the south.

The largest plains on Samos are found in the southeastern part of the island, and extensive lowlands also exist in the region between Kerkis and Karvounis. A considerable fraction of the coastal lowlands on the island was marshy in antiquity and hence unsuitable for agriculture, but the smaller inland plains and the lower slopes of the mountains offered prime farmland with good soil.

Compared with many Aegean islands, Samos has plentiful rainfall. The northern side of the island, which is directly exposed to the northerly, rain-bearing winds, currently receives an average annual total of 918 mm of rain, whereas the south side receives 709 mm.[122] The climate in the Archaic period seems to have been roughly the same as it is in the modern day (though see the caveats in Manning 2022), and Samos enjoyed a reputation in antiquity for being particularly well watered. It is, for example, described as *hydrēlē* ("watery") in the *Homeric Hymn to Apollo* (l. 41; cf. Callim. *Hymn 4* 48–50; Heschyius s.v. ἄστυ Νυμφέων). Streams, most of which are seasonal, run from the mountains down to the coast, and the many perennial springs on the island were an invaluable resource for its inhabitants. The perennial spring near the modern village of Agiades was, in the sixth century, channeled through the tunnel of Eupalinos (see Section 3.4C.2) to provide drinking water for the city of Samos. Temperatures are mild throughout the year.

## 3.4C. Samian Material Culture

The archaeological record of Archaic Samos is overwhelmingly dominated by two sites on the southern coast of the island, Samos Town and the Samian Heraion, which are located at the eastern and western ends, respectively, of the

---

121. Shipley 1987: 5–12 offers a concise summary of the natural setting of Samos.

122. For weather data from Samos, see https://www.samosin.gr/climateofsamosisland/.

Kambos Khoras (or simply Kambos or Khora), the largest plain on Samos.[123] The south side of the island seems to have been the focus of occupation during the Archaic period (Shipley 1987: 234 fig. 11), presumably because that is where the best farmland on the island was found and because the southern coast was more hospitable than the often aggressively windswept northern shore (see Section 3.3C). The emergence of the main habitation center at Samos Town, on the eastern edge of the Kambos Khoras, can be attributed in part to its strategic position vis-à-vis the Mycale Strait.

Information about other Archaic sites on the island is scanty due to lack of excavation or systematic survey in the *chōra*.[124] The existence of an Archaic cemetery at Klima, in the area of the Heraion, indicates what could have been plausibly assumed—that there must have been substantial secondary settlements on the island. A sixth-century inscription found at the modern village of Neochori (c. 15 km west of Samos Town) records the construction of a bridge on the primary land route giving access to the lowland between Kerkis and Karvounis, which suggests that the Samians invested resources in the Archaic period to link together the settlements on the island (Shipley 1987: 259 #03030).[125]

## 3.4C.1. Settlement Organization of Samos Town

The nucleus of Samos Town was a low (c. 20 masl) hill that served as the city's acropolis (see Figure 3.10). That hill, currently occupied by a Byzantine castle and the Church of Metamorphosis tou Sotiros, takes its modern name, Kastro, from the Byzantine castle; it seems to have been called Astypalaia in antiquity (Tölle-Kastenbein 1974).[126] In the Archaic period, there were harbors to both the east and the west of Kastro hill. The western harbor, which lay c. 600 m west of Kastro hill and was situated just to the west of the western edge of the city's fortification

---

123. The smaller plain to the east of Samos Town is sometimes referred to as Miso Kambos or Meso Kambos in the present day.

124. Though see the gazetteer in Shipley 1987: 234–5 fig. 11.

125. There is also some evidence for small fortresses, presumably to guard against seaborne incursions, dating to the late Archaic period in the western part of the island (Shipley 1987: 95 and n. 94).

126. On the name of the hill, see Shipley 1987: 76 n. 39, who elsewhere in that same work expresses some skepticism that Kastro hill was in fact the acropolis of the ancient city (Shipley 1987: 193 n. 47 *contra* Tölle-Kastenbein 1979). An alternative suggestion for the location of the acropolis is the northwestern corner of the fortifications, which occupy the highest point on Ampelos hill.

356    THE OXFORD HISTORY OF THE ARCHAIC GREEK WORLD

walls, served as the primary harbor of the city for much of the Archaic period. It has, since antiquity, silted up, though a small wetland with two lakes (Mikri and Megali Glyphada) has remained in place to the present day (Tsakos 2003: 316–17; Tsakos 2006: 301). After the Samians installed elaborate moles in the inlet on the east side of Kastro hill (see below), probably at some point in the second half of the sixth century, that became the main harbor of the city. The agora was located on the northwestern side of Kastro hill and was thus easily accessible from both harbors. An extensive set of fortifications encompassed Kastro hill, all of another low hill (Kastelli) to the northeast of Kastro hill, and much of a significantly higher (240 masl) and steeper hill (Ampelos) that ran E–W along the shore to the north and northwest of Kastro hill.[127] The area within those fortifications was roughly rectangular and measured c. 1.2 km E–W and c. 800 m N–S (Lang 1996: 217–22). Herodotus (3.60.1–3) claims that the Samians were responsible for the three greatest building projects carried out anywhere in the Greek world: the Eupalinos tunnel, the harbor moles in the city of Samos, and the Temple of Hera at the Heraion. At least some remains of all three have survived. (On the question of whether Polycrates was responsible for the harbor works and the Eupalinos tunnel, see Section 3.5C.2; see Meyer 2012: 277–91, 305–26, for a listing of ancient literary sources on Samos Town.)

Even though it is not at present possible to provide a detailed, diachronic account of the development of the urban fabric of Samos Town, a general sketch can be offered. The earliest-known remains at Samos Town were found on Kastro hill and date to the Neolithic period; a settlement and sanctuary occupied the same location in the Middle and Late Bronze Age (Felsch 1988). Finds of Protogeometric and Geometric material suggest that starting in the tenth century, the core of the settlement was the area of the later agora, along the banks of a stream that descended from the hills to the northeast of Samos Town, ran behind (i.e., on the north side of) Kastro hill, then entered the sea on its west side. That torrent has been tentatively identified as the Chesios river mentioned in some literary sources (Shipley 1987: 281–2). A necropolis, c. 400 m to the west of the later agora and located in a sandy area (underneath the Hellenistic gymnasium) near the coastline, was the site of a substantial number of burials starting in the tenth century (see Section 3.4C.5), but three Geometric-era burials were also found in the general vicinity of the later agora. A somewhat mysterious feature of Samos Town is the existence of numerous shallow pits, found in the area of the

---

127. Ampelos hill takes its name from the fact that it is in some sense a foothill of Mt. Ampelos (modern Karvounis, see Section 3.3C). Ampelos hill is sometimes called Spiliani or Mt. Kastro; the latter nomenclature tends to create confusion between it and Kastro hill.

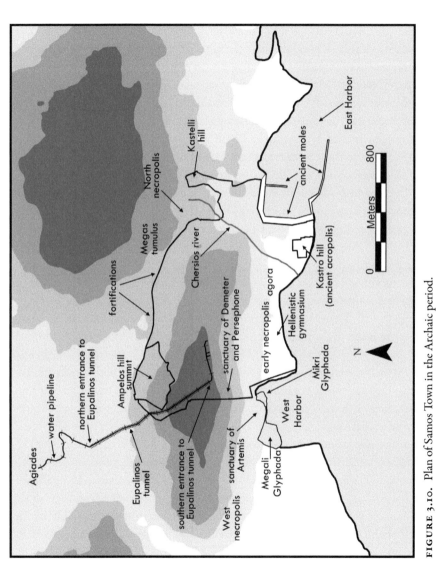

FIGURE 3.10. Plan of Samos Town in the Archaic period.

358 THE OXFORD HISTORY OF THE ARCHAIC GREEK WORLD

later agora and on Kastro hill, filled with Geometric and Archaic pottery, soil, and stones, perhaps related in some way to construction or ceramic production (Tsakos 2007: 190–2; Tsakos 2011).

On the acropolis of Samos Town (Kastro hill), Hellenistic terracing swept away nearly all the Archaic and Classical structures (Tölle-Kastenbein 1979), although a seated Archaic statue of Polycrates' father, Aiakes, testifies to the fact that this must have been an important site for elite display in the seventh and sixth centuries (Duplouy 2006: 244–6; Carty 2015: 53–66). Recent excavations have revealed evidence for a subsurface sanctuary on Kastro hill that was active in the Archaic period (Giannouli 2001–2004: 50–2). Herodotus (3.146.2) claims that Polycrates' successor Maiandrios was confident that he could flee Samos anytime he wished because he had built a secret passage from the acropolis in Samos Town to the sea (ἐπεποίητο γὰρ οἱ κρυπτὴ διῶρυξ ἐκ τῆς ἀκροπόλιος φέρουσα ἐπὶ θάλασσαν). If one takes that claim seriously, it would suggest that Maiandrios had a home on the acropolis. According to Herodotus (3.123.1), Maiandrios dedicated at the Heraion the furnishings from the *andron* in Polycrates' house (τὸν κόσμον τὸν ἐκ τοῦ ἀνδρεῶνος τοῦ Πολυκράτεος ἐόντα ἀξιοθέητον ἀνέθηκε πάντα ἐς τὸ Ἥραιον). This may imply that Maiandrios inherited both Polycrates' position as leader and his house, which would in turn indicate that Polycrates had a lavishly furnished house on the acropolis of Samos Town (cf. 3.42.2, where a fisherman brings an unusually large fish to Polycrates' house rather than taking it to the agora to sell). Herodotus' recounting of the brief Persian occupation of Samos after the death of Polycrates suggests that the acropolis was separately fortified (3.146.2–3, 3.147.2, cf. 3.143.1).

Most of the excavated remains from the agora, which lies underneath the center of the modern city, date to the Roman period. However, recent excavations in the area of the new archaeological museum revealed houses and large cisterns dating to the Archaic period (Tsakos 1996: 121), as well as deposits of Archaic figurines and pottery that almost certainly came from a sanctuary (Viglaki-Sofianou 1999). The orientation of the houses indicates that the basic layout of the road network of modern Pythagoreio closely follows that of Samos Town in the Archaic period (Tsakos 2007: 193–4). Plutarch's story (*Mor.* 303f–304c) of Samian generals overthrowing the oligarchic government, probably in the early sixth century, mentions a *bouleutērion* and a large hall of some kind in or near the agora of Samos (see Section 3.5C.1 for further discussion of this story). According to Herodotus (6.14.3), the names and patronymics of the Samians who had distinguished themselves at the Battle of Lade were inscribed on a *stēlē* that was set up in the agora of Samos Town. Clearchus of Soli (F44 Wehrli; see Shipley 1987: 76 n. 36 for further sources) claimed that Polycrates built an alley or bazaar (*laura*) that served as a red-light district for Samos Town. Nothing is known about the location of this alley, but it may well have been situated near the agora.[128]

## 3.4C.2. Fortifications and Water Engineering

In the second half of the sixth century, the Samians built an elaborate set of fortifications that ran for c. 6.5 km. Those fortifications were rebuilt twice, once at the end of the fourth century and again in the early second century, but the course of the walls remained largely the same because it was, already in the sixth century, highly adapted to the terrain of the site and to the location of the West Harbor (at that point the main harbor). The walls as originally constructed consisted of a c. 3-m-thick stone base in polygonal limestone masonry, on top of which mudbricks were laid. The fortifications enclosed an area of c. 103 ha, but, because the terrain of the site played a key role in determining the course of the walls, it is far from certain that the entire area within the walls was densely settled in the sixth century (H. J. Kienast 1978; Lang 1996: 218–20; Tsakos 2006; Frederiksen 2017: 184–5; Hülden 2020: 171–8).

The Samians' capacity to withstand a siege rested in part on a concealed water pipeline that ran through the famous Eupalinos tunnel (see Figure 3.11). That pipeline connects an abundant perennial spring (producing c. 400 cubic meters of water daily) at Agiades (c. 2.5 km northwest of Samos Town in a straight line) to the city. Insofar as Agiades was on the north side of Ampelos hill, the pipeline had to either run along the northern edge of Ampelos and then descend into the city, or it could take a shorter but much more difficult route via a tunnel cut through Ampelos. The latter solution had two advantages: it restricted access to the majority of the pipeline, helping to protect it against hostile action, and it ensured that the water arrived near the city at a relatively high point (Agiades is only 52 m above sea level), which helped create sufficient pressure to pipe the water into and around the city.[129] The spring was channeled at its source into a large underground reservoir, the roof of which was supported by an array of marble pillars. Terracotta pipes were laid in an 890-m-long channel

---

128. Athenaeus (13.602d), quoting the third-century philosopher Hieronymos of Rhodes (F34 Wehrli), claims that Polycrates destroyed all of the *palaistrai* in Samos Town because they were sites of resistance against his rule. The veracity of that claim is open to question, and in any case, the location of the *palaistrai* in Samos Town is not specified.

129. There is an extensive and continuously growing collection of scholarship on the Eupalinos tunnel. The discussion provided here is based primarily on Kienast and Meissner 1995; Jantzen 2004; H. J. Kienast 2005; Zambas 2017; Angistalis, Dounias, Tsokas, et al. 2018: 197–8; H. J. Kienast 2020b.

FIGURE 3.11. The interior of the Eupalinos tunnel, second half of sixth century.

(740 m of trench cut into the bedrock and roofed with stone slabs and 150 m of narrow tunnel) that took a circuitous course, following the contours of the terrain, from the reservoir to the northern end of the Eupalinos tunnel. This part of the pipeline, which lay outside the city's fortifications, was its most vulnerable section, but it was not easily found because it was entirely underground when completed.

The next section of the pipeline was laid in a tunnel that runs for 1,036 m underneath Ampelos hill. Herodotus (3.60.3) states that it was designed by Eupalinos of Megara. One of the more remarkable features of that tunnel is that it was cut simultaneously from both ends (Herodotus calls it *amphistomon*), an approach that no doubt considerably accelerated construction but also entailed serious engineering challenges. Eupalinos had to make sure that each mouth of the tunnel (separated spatially and visually by the mass of Ampelos hill) was at precisely the same height, that each part of the tunnel was dug along a trajectory such that they would meet, and that elevation and alignment were maintained throughout the difficult work of digging through the limestone of Ampelos hill using nothing but hand tools. Further complications arose because the trajectory of the north tunnel led into a section of unstable rock so that the tunnel had to take a dogleg and then return to its original course.

Eupalinos overcame all of those challenges with remarkable skill: the mouths of the two tunnels differ in level by only 4 cm, the difference in elevation between the two parts of the tunnel where they meet 170 m below the surface of Ampelos hill is a mere 60 cm (a discrepancy of less than 0.125% over the distance traveled), and the alignment between the two parts of the tunnel is virtually perfect.[130] The means by which Eupalinos achieved that astonishing degree of precision continues to be a subject of lively scholarly debate (see, for example, Apostol 2004; Olson 2012; Senseney 2016: 66–70; H. J. Kienast 2020b: 75–7). The process of digging the tunnel, which has an average cross section of 1.8 x 1.8 m, likely took several years.

Eupalinos had to overcome yet another unforeseeable difficulty because the area around the Agiades spring evidently subsided after it had been channeled into the underground reservoir. The original plan seems to have been to run terracotta pipes in a shallow open trench, dug into the eastern side of the floor of the Eupalinos tunnel, that begins just below the floor level of the northern end of the tunnel and slopes gradually downward as it runs south. By the time the subsidence became apparent, the tunneling under Ampelos hill had already begun. As a result, the pipeline leading from the spring met the northern mouth of the Eupalinos tunnel approximately 4 m lower than the floor of the tunnel, so the pipes from the spring could not be connected to pipes in the trench in the floor of the tunnel. That problem was addressed by digging a (second) tunnel directly underneath the floor of the open trench in the Eupalinos tunnel; that second, lower tunnel was dug by sinking vertical shafts down from the floor of the trench in the Eupalinos tunnel roughly every 10 m and then digging horizontally from the bottom of those shafts to connect them into a new tunnel. Terracotta pipes, connected directly to those leading from the spring to the northern mouth of the Eupalinos tunnel, were laid in the lower, smaller tunnel. The lower tunnel slopes so that it is approximately 4 m below the northern mouth of the main tunnel and approximately 8 m below its southern mouth.

The southern mouth of the tunnel is situated on the side of Ampelos hill, approximately 1 km northwest of the city center and safely within the city's

---

130. The tunnels meet at close to right angles, because near their meeting point, both tunnels were dug at angles from their primary trajectory (the tunnel leading from the northern mouth bent left, and the tunnel leading from the southern mouth turn bent right) to heighten the chances that they would not miss each other completely. The measuring and construction had been carried out so precisely that this precaution was unnecessary.

fortifications. The lower tunnel diverges from the main tunnel just before it reaches the southern mouth of the main tunnel and joins a rock-cut channel in which terracotta pipes were laid—the same system as that used for the northern end of the pipeline. That section of the pipeline, which has been traced for only part of its length, led into the city, where it branched out to supply water to various parts of the city and fed fountain houses and cisterns (Tölle-Kastenbein 1975: 213–14; Giannouli 1996; Giannouli 2001–2004: 35–8; Tsakos 2007: 193; H. J. Kienast 2020b: 72–3). The total length of the pipeline from Agiades to the city center was well more than 3 km and required more than 5,000 terracotta pipes.

The date of the construction of the tunnel has been securely established by pottery finds as c. 540. Given that security seems to have been a major concern in the construction of the pipeline and that its southern mouth lies just within the western edge of the city's fortifications, it is likely that the pipeline and the fortifications were planned and built at roughly the same time.

Herodotus (3.60.3) states that the Samians, at some unspecified time, built harbor moles that were two *stadia* (c. 360 m) long and 20 *orguai* (c. 36 m) deep. While the accuracy of the dimensions supplied by Herodotus is probably suspect, it is clear that the Samians went to some lengths to improve their harbor facilities (H. J. Kienast 2004: 74–6; Asheri, Lloyd, and Corcella 2007: 455–7). Built structures that could plausibly belong to the Archaic period have been identified underwater in the inlet to the east of Kastro hill, but since the harbor works were maintained and updated over the course of the centuries, assigning a precise date to these has proven challenging (Simossi 1991; Baika 2015: 450). By the Hellenistic period, at the latest, there were two moles: a long one starting from the southwestern corner of the inlet and running more or less E–W into the open water and a shorter one starting from the northern part of the inlet and running more or less N–S. Together, those moles created a large, sheltered basin that, in part because the ancient shoreline was up to 150 m farther north and west than it is at present, was roughly double the size of the current harbor. Both moles were tied into the fortifications of the city, and the mole on the southern side of the harbor ended in a large (c. 70 x 90 m) platform (Lang 1996: 220–1). Herodotus' (3.54.4) account suggests that this platform could have served as a foundation for shipsheds during Polycrates' reign.

### 3.4C.3. Sanctuaries and Cemeteries in Samos Town

The evidence for Archaic sanctuaries in Samos Town is relatively limited. A Sanctuary of Artemis was located just outside the western walls, near the modern lakes of Megali and Mikri Glyphada. Excavations at that site uncovered only scanty architectural remains but did reveal three substantial votive deposits containing materials from the sixth century, including several objects with dedicatory inscriptions naming Artemis (Tsakos 1980; Tsakos 2003). Herodotus (3.48) relates a story, set in the generation before Polycrates, that boys from Corcyra, who were being sent against their will to Sardis to be made into eunuchs, took refuge in a sanctuary of Artemis after the ship on which they were sailing put in at Samos (see Section 3.7C). The aforementioned votive deposits are located in the area of the West Harbor, which, at the time in which the story is set, served as the main harbor of Samos, and the excavated remains have been plausibly connected to the Artemis sanctuary mentioned by Herodotus. Among the most notable features of the finds from the Artemis sanctuary is the presence of significant quantities of Laconian ceramics (Pipili 2001), which could be related to a purportedly close relationship between Samos and Sparta (see Section 3.7C).

A Sanctuary of Demeter and Persephone was found c. 200 m to the north of the Sanctuary of Artemis. Most of the material from the relevant excavations dates to the Hellenistic period, but there are exiguous building remains from earlier periods, as well as a considerable amount of Archaic material including pottery (primarily cups from the sixth century), a *korē* figurine, and two stone molds for a terracotta *korē* figurine (Touratsoglou and Tsakos 2008: 108 n. 14; Tsakos and Giannakopoulos 2014: 233).

As we have seen (see Section 3.2C), recent excavations have uncovered evidence for Archaic sanctuaries on Kastro hill and in the agora. A rescue excavation near the modern harbor uncovered part of the stylobate of a building, dated to the Archaic period and built from large blocks of limestone, that was probably a temple (Tsakos 2007: 193). According to Herodotus (3.142), Polycrates' successor Maiandrios built an altar and temenos for Zeus Eleutherios that was located in the suburbs (*proasteion*) of the city and was still in place in Herodotus' time.

Several Archaic necropoleis have come to light around the ancient city, on the west, north, and northeast outskirts beyond the walls. On the west side of the city, a necropolis located c. 400 m west of Kastro hill ("early necropolis" in Figure 3.10) received burials from the tenth through the early seventh centuries. Around the time this cemetery went out of use, a new one came into being another 400 m farther west (just outside the line of the sixth-century fortifications). Burials in that cemetery, typically called the West Necropolis, tailed off sharply in the last quarter of the sixth century, after which time new necropoleis seem to have come into being farther to the west and north of the city. Other cemeteries that have received only cursory excavation existed on the north and east sides of the city (see Section 3.4C.5 for further discussion).

## 3.4C.4. The Heraion

### 3.4C.4.1. Introduction

As impressive as the Archaic remains from Samos Town might be in another context, they are overshadowed by the wealth of archaeological evidence from the Heraion, located approximately 6 km west of Samos Town.[131] Samos Town and the Heraion were linked by a Sacred Road that was built c. 600 and ran along the coast. In earlier periods, the main entrance to the sanctuary was from the coast, and most visitors presumably arrived by boat (Kyrieleis 1993: 130; M. Mohr 2013: 40–9). The Imbrasos river enters the sea near the sanctuary, and the marshy site was said to be where Hera was born, underneath a lygos (willow) tree (Paus. 7.4.4). Menodotos of Samos' *Register of Notable Things in Samos* (third or second century) offered a detailed aetiology of the origin of the cult that suggests that the lygos played an ongoing role in the rituals held at the sanctuary (*FGrH* 541 F1; see Section 3.11C.1). The sanctuary was heavily quarried starting in the medieval period, and most of the extant structures at the site exist solely at the foundation level. A single column from the late sixth-century Temple of Hera was left standing, likely as a navigational aid for ships coming to the sanctuary to carry off stone.

The Samian Heraion was extraordinarily richly endowed with offerings of all shapes, materials, and types from across the entire Mediterranean. As Kyrieleis (1993: 145) has pointed out, "No other archaeological exploration in Greece has . . . produced anything like the number and variety of imports found in the Archaic sanctuary of Hera in Samos." The find-spots of most of the objects uncovered by early excavations at the site are not known, but much of the votive material from more recent excavations comes from the marshy southeastern part of the temenos, and that part of the site seems to have been used for the disposal of votives from an early date. Fill from disused wells has also produced a large number of votives. The wet conditions in which many of the Heraion's votives were found mean that a wider variety of materials, including wood, are preserved than is typical from Greek sanctuaries (see, for instance, Kopcke 1967; Kyrieleis 2020b).

---

131. Concise histories of the exploration of the site can be found in Kyrieleis 1993: 126–9; Tsakos and Viglaki-Sofianou 2012: 19–22; Walter, Clemente, and Niemeier 2019: 1–26. New insights and evidence from the sanctuary continue to emerge from German excavations and study of the site; see, e.g., Clemente 2010; Niemeier and Maniatis 2010; H. J. Kienast 2016; H. J. Kienast 2017; Henke 2022. An up-to-date overview of what is known about the early history of the site down through the sixth century can be found in Walter, Clemente, and Niemeier 2019. The relevant ancient literary sources are collected in Meyer 2012: 292–304.

The number and variety of the extant votives from the Heraion, most of which are Archaic in date, make it impossible to provide anything resembling a full treatment here. In general terms, the post–Bronze Age votives start with locally made terracotta figurines (mostly cattle and horses) in the tenth century (Jarosch 1994). A major shift occurs in the second half of the eighth century, when terracotta figurines of humans appear in significant numbers for the first time, dedications of bronze objects begin, and votives produced outside of Samos become an important element in the offerings made at the sanctuary (Kyrieleis 1993; Walter, Clemente, and Niemeier 2019: 163–4).

In the seventh century, large bronze protome cauldrons, initially imported from northern Syria but soon imitated locally, appear as the first form of monumental dedication (Gehrig 2004; Walter, Clemente, and Niemeier 2019: 165–6; Papalexandrou 2021: 27–43). Around the same time, Cypriot-style terracotta figurines, initially imported from Cyprus but soon imitated locally, become the dominant form of terracotta figurine at the site (see Section 3.8C.3), and dedications of significant numbers of Egyptian and Egyptianizing objects (including Egyptian bronzes that are rarely found at other Greek sanctuaries as well as items in faience and ivory) begin (see Section 3.11C.1). In the late seventh or early sixth century, dedications of life-size stone statues begin, and over the course of the sixth century, close to 50 marble *korai* and *kouroi* were erected (see Section 3.12C.1). Particular categories of votives that illuminate aspects of Samian architectural, economic, and religious history will be treated in more detail in the discussion that follows. (For discussion of ritual activity at the Heraion, see Section 3.11C.1.)

### 3.4C.4.2. Early History of the Site to c. 675

The site that became the Heraion was occupied starting in the second half of the fourth millennium, and it developed into a sizable settlement during the Early and Middle Bronze Ages (Milojcic 1961; Isler 2021). The settlement seems to have been abandoned toward the end of the Middle Bronze Age, and in the 17th century, a sanctuary came into existence in the general vicinity of where the Great Altar later stood. In its first phase, this sanctuary included a paved square (Pavement A) with a mud-brick altar. Locally produced imitations of Minoan cups were found placed upside down on the pavement (a standard part of Minoan cult practice as known from Crete), and ritual equipment in the form of incense burners formed part of the finds. In the middle of the 15th century, a new pavement (Pavement B) was laid on top of the earlier one (Walter, Clemente, and Niemeier 2019: 27–34, 145–53). (See Section 3.4C.4.3 for discussion of the possibility that a tree cult existed at the site of the Heraion in the Late Bronze Age.)

366 THE OXFORD HISTORY OF THE ARCHAIC GREEK WORLD

The next phase of the site begins with the construction above Pavement B of the first of a series of six altars,[132] each of which encased its predecessor. Altar 1 (c. 2 x c. 1 m) was a rectangular construction with an earth and rubble core around which stones were laid as an outer skin. This altar was surrounded by a round stone platform c. 15–16 m in diameter that presumably facilitated the activities of people making sacrifices or provided a space to stand for people witnessing activities taking place at the altar. Not long after Altar 1 was constructed, four wells (A–D) were dug c. 20 m to the southwest of the altar (Rupp 1983: 102 and figs. 9–10; Walter, Clemente, and Niemeier 2019: 35–7, 61–2, 154–65, Taf. 4–6, Zeichn. 2).

The date of Altar 1 has been the subject of much debate. Some researchers place its construction around 1000 (Walter, Clemente, and Niemeier 2019: 35–7). Other researchers have suggested that Altar 1 was built in the late tenth or early ninth century (see, for example, Reimer 2005: 186 and n. 416) or the late ninth century (Mazarakis Ainian 2016: 22). If Altar 1 is down-dated, the earliest evidence for post–Bronze Age cult activity at the site likely consists primarily of terracotta animal figurines, the earliest of which have been dated to the tenth century (Jarosch 1994; Coldstream 2003: 52–4).

Altar 1 remained in use until the first half of the eighth century, when it was replaced by Altar 2 (c. 3 x c. 2 m), which encased Altar 1 and, like its predecessor, was constructed of an earth and rubble core around which stones were laid as an outer skin (see Figure 3.12). Sometime around 760, shortly after the construction of Altar 2, a new pavement was built around the new altar. This pavement, in the form of a rounded square, was smaller (c. 7 m in diameter) than the pavement built around Altar 1. The new pavement was connected to two paved paths, one of which (Ostweg 1) was c. 2 m wide, led southeast to the beach, and hence provided an access path for visitors arriving at the site by sea (the primary means of accessing the sanctuary at this time). The second path (Westweg), which was wider (c. 3.5 m) and led westward, incorporated a round platform (c. 1.3 m in diameter) that may have served as the base for a cult statue that was put on display during festivals. It is possible that the second path continued farther westward to an as-yet-undiscovered cult building in which the cult statue was stored (Buschor and Schleif 1933; Kyrieleis 1993: 135–7; Walter, Clemente, and Niemeier 2019: 37–9, 62, Taf. 4–5, Zeichn. 3).

In the middle of the eighth century, Altar 2 was replaced by Altar 3 (c. 4.0 x 3.4 m), which had a fundamentally different design: it consisted of an elevated platform surrounded by a parapet on three sides and accessed via a step on the west side. The construction technique differed as well: Altar 3 was built from

---

132. Restudy of the remains of those altars has reduced the number of distinct phases from seven to six.

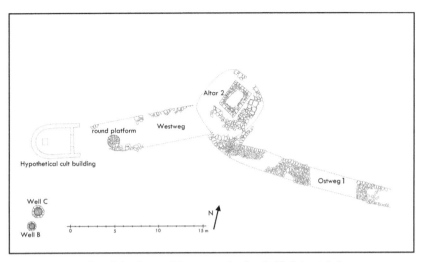

FIGURE 3.12. Plan of the Samian Heraion in the first half of the eighth century.

nicely cut ashlar masonry (Rupp 1983: 102–3 and figs. 11–12). Wells A and D went out of use prior to the construction of Altar 2, while Wells B and C continued to be used into the early part of the seventh century. At about the time Altar 3 was built, two new wells (E and F) were dug: E was close to the altar, F c. 50 m to the southwest (Walter, Clemente, and Niemeier 2019: 39, 62–3, Taf. 3–6, Zeichn. 4).

The period when Altar 3 was constructed also saw a shift in the material of the votives dedicated at the site. Prior to the middle of the eighth century, those votives were primarily locally made objects, typically in the form of terracotta figurines. In the second half of the eighth century, bronze figurines and votives produced outside of Samos appear among the dedications.

### 3.4C.4.3. Monumentalization of the Sanctuary in the First Half of the Seventh Century

The architecture and votives at the site became monumental in scale starting in the seventh century. Sometime around 675, the first-known major temple, Hekatompedon 1, was constructed (see Figure 3.13).[133] That structure measured 32.86 x 6.5 m, or 100 x 20 Ionic feet, and was thus a "hundred-footer" (ἑκατόμπεδον).

---

133. The date of the construction of Hekatompedon 1 has been the subject of much discussion, but recent excavations seem to anchor it firmly in the first half of the seventh century. See Walter, Clemente, and Niemeier 2019: 12–14, though cf. the critiques in H. J. Kienast 2020a and the response in Niemeier 2021.

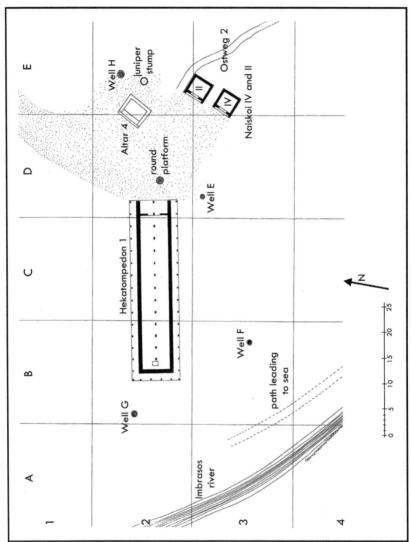

FIGURE 3.13. Plan of the Samian Heraion, c. 680–630.

Its walls were built entirely from limestone ashlar blocks and were decorated with an incised and painted frieze showing a procession of warriors.[134] Extant stretches of stone paving just outside the western and southern cella walls have led some scholars to argue that Hekatompedon 1 was peripteral, a position that has been strongly rejected by others (Figure 3.13 shows the structure with a peripteros).[135] The interior held 13 axially placed wooden columns on stone bases supporting a thatch roof. In the back of the cella, a rubble base probably held a wooden statue (*xoanon*) of Hera (see below). The finds from the interior include the remains of a substantial collection of iron *oboloi* (Walter, Clemente, and Niemeier 2019: 70–5, 77–83, 88–9; Niemeier 2021).

At roughly the same time that Hekatompedon 1 was being built, the area around Altar 3 was renovated. A new pavement, in the form of large pebbles, was laid down (covering the path that had previously led west), and a new path (Ostweg 2), running from the pebbled pavement around Altar 3 directly south to the beach, was built to replace the previous path (Ostweg 1) that ran in a more southeasterly direction.

Naiskos II was built on the edge of the pebbled pavement (and there may have been an earlier structure, Naiskos I, near the altar; Walter, Clemente, and Niemeier 2019: 93). Naiskos IV (located just to the south of Naiskos II) was built shortly thereafter (Walter, Clemente, and Niemeier 2019: 93). Two new wells (G and H) were dug at roughly the same time. Not long after the pebble pavement had been built, Altar 4 was constructed to replace Altar 3, and another layer of pebbles was laid down. The design of the altar remained the same, though its size (4.9 x 3.9 m) increased slightly (Rupp 1983: 104 and fig. 13; Walter, Clemente, and Niemeier 2019: 39–44, 62–4, Taf. 3–5, Zeichn. 5–6).

The second layer of pebble pavement associated with the construction of Altar 4 had a striking feature: the stump of a juniper tree was placed in a pit, the bottom of which lay 30–40 cm below the level of that pavement (Walter, Clemente, and Niemeier 2019: 42). Dendrochronological dating shows that the tree in question was felled sometime around 670, and saw marks on the stump

---

134. Though see also the skeptical comments in H. J. Kienast 2001, who doubts that this frieze was associated in any way with the Hera temple.

135. Early reconstructions assumed a *hekatompedon* built c. 800, a peristyle added c. 700, and a similar replacement built c. 660, after destruction due to flooding (Buschor 1930: 34; H. J. Kienast 1996: 16). Alfred Mallwitz argued instead that evidence for an early peristyle was lacking. He reconstructed a single, aperipteral building from the first half of the seventh century, to which a peripteros was appended after 650 (Mallwitz 1981: 624–33). More recently, Hermann Kienast has argued that no phase of the early *hekatompedon* had an exterior colonnade (H. J. Kienast 1996: 20–4; H. J. Kienast 2004; see also H. J. Kienast 2020a). The various arguments are summarized at Walter, Clemente, and Niemeier 2019: 14–17 and in Niemeier 2021.

demonstrate that the tree originally grew elsewhere and was placed in the pavement after it was cut down (Niemeier and Maniatis 2010). It has been argued that this is the stump of the tree from which a *xoanon* of Hera was carved as the cult statue for the new temple, Hekatompedon 1 (Walter, Clemente, and Niemeier 2019: 19).[136] Callimachus states that the cult statue of Hera on Samos was originally a simple piece of wood (F100 Harder). Pausanias (8.17.2) mentions a cult statue of Hermes in Arcadia carved from juniper, and because of confusion in the relevant terminology, it is likely that other cult statues that have sometimes been understood as being carved from cypress were in fact made from juniper, which had a reputation for strongly resisting rot (Frazer 1913: vol. 4: 245–7). A wooden figurine dating to the mid-seventh century from the Heraion that shows a female wearing a high *polos* may reflect the form of the Archaic cult statue (Kopcke 1967: 102–7 and pl. 43–7).

The earliest large-scale votives from the Heraion, in the form of bronze cauldrons with griffin protomes, began in the first half of the seventh century. More than 300 griffin protomes from the period between 690 and 620 have been found at the Heraion (Herrmann 1979: 155–67; Treister 1996: 129; Gehrig 2004; Walter, Clemente, and Niemeier 2019: 165–6; Papalexandrou 2021: 27–43). The first examples were imported from northern Syria, but imitations were soon produced locally. The most famous of these cauldrons is that dedicated by the Samian merchant Kolaios (on whom see Section 3.8C.3). According to Herodotus (4.152), this cauldron was decorated with griffins' heads (πέριξ δὲ αὐτοῦ γρυπῶν κεφαλαὶ πρόκροσσοί εἰσι) and was supported by kneeling bronze figures, each of which was 7 cubits high (*heptapēchus*), which suggests a dedication that was nearly 5 m tall. There is some reason to believe that Herodotus saw this cauldron at the Heraion and based his account in part on its dedicatory inscription (Asheri, Lloyd, and Corcella 2007: 679; Papalexandrou 2021: 143–59). A small round base (W3), located close to where the path to the beach (Ostweg 2) joined the pebbled pavement around Altar 3, may have supported a dedication of a large tripod cauldron.

In this phase of the Heraion's history, most visitors seem to have arrived by sea. Those visitors could enter the sanctuary using a pebbled path (Ostweg 2). There was also a path leading from the sea into the sanctuary that ran along the eastern side of the branch of the Imbrasos river that formed the western border of the sanctuary. The edges of that branch of the Imbrasos seem to have been defined by a boulder wall in the second quarter of the seventh century, and pottery finds from alongside the eastern bank suggest that commercial activity took place in that part of the sanctuary in the first half of the seventh century. There

---

136. On the evidence for the form of this *xoanan*, see O'Brien 1993: 18–25.

was also an entrance to the northeast of Altar 4 (Walter, Clemente, and Niemeier 2019: 42–4). However, no temenos wall seems to have existed prior to the mid-sixth century (see Section 3.4C.4.5).

### 3.4C.4.4. Regularization and Further Monumentalization of the Sanctuary in the Second Half of the Seventh Century and the First Quarter of the Sixth Century

A new phase in the architectural history of the sanctuary began around 630 (Walter, Clemente, and Niemeier 2019: 44–50, Taf. 1 and 3, Zeichn. 7). The most important building project dated to this period was the construction of Hekatompedon 2 (see Figure 3.14). The reasons for the replacement of Hekatompedon 1 are unclear, but it is possible that Hekatompedon 1 was intentionally burned to make way for a new temple. Hekatompedon 2 was built on top of the foundations of its predecessor and, like Hekatompedon 1, had walls constructed from ashlar limestone blocks. However, Hekatompedon 2 had a tile rather than thatch roof, and the lower pitch of the roof made an internal colonnade in the cella superfluous. There is some inconclusive evidence that Hekatompedon 2 had a peristyle, perhaps consisting of tetragonal wooden columns on stone bases arranged in a 6 x 18 pattern around the building (Walter, Clemente, and Niemeier 2019: 75–9, 83–9).

Altar 5 (11.5 x 4.4 m), much larger than its predecessor, was constructed in front of the new temple (Rupp 1983: 104 and fig. 14; Walter, Clemente, and Niemeier 2019: 64–5). Three *naiskoi* (III, IV, V) stood at the edges of the pebbled pavement around Altar 5. Naiskos IV had been built earlier, while Naiskoi III and V were new constructions (Walter, Clemente, and Niemeier 2019: 92–4).

Two new paths (the Südweg and the Südwestweg) led from the western edge of the pebble pavement around Altar 5 to the beach. Beginning in the late seventh century or very shortly thereafter, impressive and often monumental votive dedications were set up alongside these paths (see Section 3.12C.1 for further discussion). These dedications included at least two examples of entire ships, perhaps pentecoters (Walter and Vierneisel 1959: 11–13; Höckmann 1995: 210–12). The discovery of approximately 40 small (c. 40 cm long) wooden boat models dating to the seventh century indicate that ship-shaped votives of all sizes were dedicated (Baumbach 2004: 163; Kyrieleis 2020a: 20–1). At the same time, the path at the western edge of the sanctuary, alongside the Imbrasos river, continued to be used, and a long stoa (the South Stoa), measuring c. 70 x 6 m, was built on the western side of that path. The South Stoa seems to have been damaged by flooding not long after its construction, and, c. 620–610, the branch of the Imbrasos running behind the South Stoa was canalized behind a large (c. 1 m high and 2 m thick) wall (Gruben 1957; Walter, Clemente, and Niemeier 2019: 43–4).

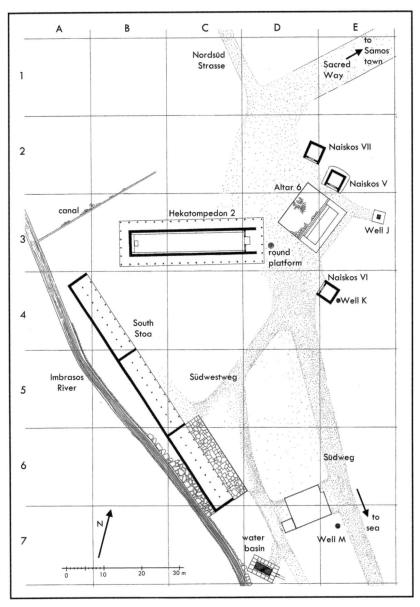

FIGURE 3.14. Plan of the Samian Heraion, c. 590–575.

Over the course of the seventh century, most of the wells in the sanctuary were gradually filled with votives and remains of old sacrifices, including crocodile skulls and horns from African antelopes (Kyrieleis 1993: 135–8; Ekroth 2018) (though Well J, to the east of the altar, remained in use). The wells were replaced with built stone water basins that worked like artesian wells; one such basin was built just to the south of the South Stoa (Walter, Clemente, and Niemeier 2019: 99–106). Others were found in the southeastern part of the sanctuary (Kyrieleis 2020a: 9–13).

Construction at the sanctuary continued in the early sixth century. Sometime around 600, a road was built connecting the Heraion to Samos Town, the Sacred Way (M. Mohr 2013: 40–9). The Sacred Way entered the temenos on the northeast side of the sanctuary and ended near what became the northeastern corner of Dipteros 2, where it joined a road (the Nordsüd Strasse) that ran north and out of the sanctuary. Large stone pylons marked the places where the Sacred Way and the Nordsüd Strasse entered the sanctuary (H. J. Kienast 2007; Kienast, Moustaka, Großschmidt, et al. 2017). The land route became the primary means of accessing the Heraion, and the sides of the parts of the Sacred Way and the Nordsüd Strasse in the sanctuary itself rapidly became highly desirable locations for the dedication of impressive votives such as life-size statues.

At roughly the same time, the branch of the Imbrasos river that ran to the west of the South Stoa was diverted 100 m to the west, and the sanctuary was expanded so that the perimeter of the temenos was triple its previous length and encompassed an area of 7 ha. A fence supported on stone posts marked the new western border of the sanctuary (Gruben and Kienast 2014: 173 and n. 303), but there is no trace of a temenos wall at this point in time (Walter, Clemente, and Niemeier 2019: 191).

Sometime around 590, Altar 6 was erected, the final in the series of altars that began with Altar 1, each enclosing its predecessors. Altar 6, measuring c. 6 x 13 m, had a paved forecourt. Naiskoi V, VI, and VII stood at the edges of the pavement around Altar 6 (Walter, Clemente, and Niemeier 2019: 50–2, 65–6, 92–4; Henke 2022).

### 3.4C.4.5. *Onset of Gigantism in the Second Quarter of the Sixth Century*

The second quarter of the sixth century at the Heraion was marked by the onset of gigantism. The temple built starting c. 575, Dipteros 1, was spectacularly bigger than its predecessor, Hekatompedon 2 (see Figure 3.15). In order to make room for Dipteros 1, Hekatompedon 2 and the South Stoa were demolished. Dipteros 1 is sometimes known as the Rhoikos temple because ancient literary sources (listed in Svenson-Evers 1996: 7–66; Meyer 2012: 333–42) identify someone named Rhoikos (or Rhoikos working with Theodorus) as its architect.

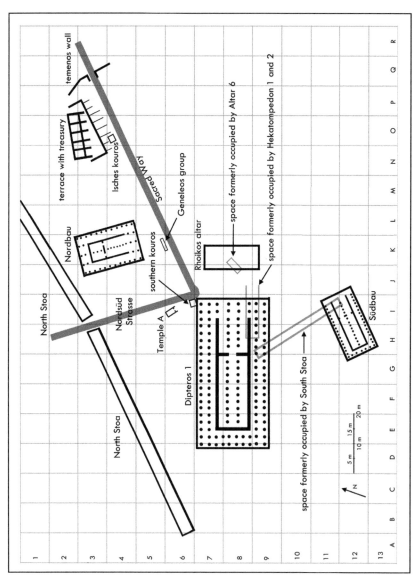

**FIGURE 3.15.** Plan of the Samian Heraion in the mid-sixth century.

Dipteros 1 measured c. 105 x 52 m, equivalent to 200 x 100 Samian cubits, meaning that the temple was twice as long as a *hekatompedon*. The cella alone was 100 Samian cubits long (c. 52 x 25 m). The temple was dipteral on all four sides, with 21 columns on the outside of the long sides, eight columns across the east facade, and ten columns across the west facade. A further double colonnade ran the length of the cella. The columns were c. 18 m high and represent one of the earliest-known manifestations of canonical Ionic style, including bases and capitals.[137] The walls were built of ashlar limestone blocks, and the superstructure consisted of a wooden entablature covered with terracotta roof tiles. The roof was embellished with elaborate terracotta palmette antefixes and terracotta acroteria in the form of sphinxes (Hendrich 2007; Moustaka 2009: 170–9; Ohnesorg 2009: 64–77; H. J. Kienast 2012: 6–11; Walter, Clemente, and Niemeier 2019: 172).

It is evident that a great deal of economic investment in the form of labor and material outlay was required for the construction of this temple. Its floor area was 12 times that of Hekatompedon 1, and its volume was 100 times greater. The columns consisted of c. 5,000 separate drums, and the roof required something on the order of 20,000 tiles (H. J. Kienast 2004: 70–2; H. J. Kienast 2012: 16). Dipteros 1 was a striking departure in scale from any Greek building that came before it, and it seems to have inspired emulation at other sites such as Ephesus. Dipteros 1 was probably completed in the span of about 25 years (Walter, Clemente, and Niemeier 2019: 172). The construction of Dipteros 1 has been interpreted as a project of Syloson, the son of Kalliteles, who may have ruled Samos as a tyrant in this period, based on the speculative notion that only a tyrant could have mustered the necessary resources to complete such an ambitious project in a relatively brief period of time (Walter, Clemente, and Niemeier 2019: 174–5; see Section 3.5C.1 for further discussion of Syloson).

Temple A, which may have served as a temporary home for the cult statue while work proceeded on Dipteros 1, was built on the north side of Dipteros 1 (Ziegenaus 1957b: 88–95, 142–6; H. Walter 1990: 121; Walter, Clemente, and Niemeier 2019: 48–9). Contemporary with Temple A are a paved area built to the north of Altar 6 and two short-lived *naiskoi* (Naiskoi VIII and IX) on the northern edge of that paved area (the *naiskoi* were demolished to make space for the Rhoikos altar; see below; Walter, Clemente, and Niemeier 2019: 52–6, 94–5).[138]

---

137. Much of the material from Dipteros 1 was reused in Dipteros 2, with the result that it is difficult to establish many of the details of Dipteros 1, including the precise height of its columns.

138. The remains of Naiskoi VIII and IX were at one point interpreted as a propylon, a phantom building that appears on some older plans of the Heraion (Walter, Clemente, and Niemeier 2019: 54).

The emerging importance of the land route to the sanctuary is reflected in the placement of two nearly identical colossal *kouroi* (just under 5 m high) (Kyrieleis 1996; H. Walter, Clemente, and Niemeier 2019: 172–4). Those *kouroi* seem to have been erected shortly before the completion of Dipteros 1. One, which carried the inscription "Isches son of Rhesis dedicated [this]" (*IG* XII.6.2.560) on its left thigh, was placed just inside the northeastern entrance to the temenos (hence, it is called either the Isches or Eastern Kouros). The other abutted the northeastern edge of the Rhoikos temple, near where the Sacred Road intersected the Nordsüd Strasse (hence, it is sometimes called the Southern Kouros).[139] (See Section 3.5C.1 for discussion of the possible political significance of these *kouroi*.)

Sometime in the second quarter of the sixth century, a new altar was erected, typically called the Rhoikos altar (Schleif 1933; Walter, Clemente, and Niemeier 2019: 52; Henke 2022). The Rhoikos altar was on a scale commensurate with the new temple at the site: it measured 38 x 18 m (200 times the size of the earliest altar) and featured a 5-m-high enclosure wall and a full flight of steps on the west side. Its orientation was altered so that, for the first time, the altar was axially aligned with the temple.

The design and scale of Dipteros 1 as well as the two stone colossi and the Rhoikos altar—all of which seem to have formed part of a single building program—almost certainly reflect the influence of Egyptian architecture and art on Samians, who were visiting Egypt with considerable regularity in this period (Hoffmann 1953: 194–5; Walter, Clemente, and Niemeier 2019: 174). (See Section 3.8C.3 for further discussion of Samian mobility.)

The mid-sixth century also saw the investment of considerable resources in monumentalizing the entrances to and delimiting the edges of the sanctuary (Kienast, Moustaka, Großschmidt, et al. 2017; Walter, Clemente, and Niemeier 2019: 191–2). It was at this point in time that the first temenos wall was built. Along the northern edge of the sanctuary, in the area where the Nordsüd Strasse entered the temenos, a new stoa (the North Stoa) was erected, presumably a replacement for the demolished South Stoa. The North Stoa was gradually extended until it was some 200 m long and framed the northern entrance to the sanctuary.

At the same time, what seems to have been a treasury was built just inside the sanctuary's northeastern entrance, on the north side of the Sacred Way and behind the Isches Kouros (H. J. Kienast 2017). The treasury measured c. 28 x 8.5 m and had four chambers of equal size. It was built on top of a 1-m-high podium

---

139. There has been considerable discussion of the dates of these *kouroi*. The base of the *kouros* abutting the temple actually interrupts the temple's steps, which may indicate that at least that *kouros* antedated the temple. However, the steps of the temple were seemingly the last part of the building to be constructed, and it is possible that a miscalculation of some sort was made.

created by a terrace wall that ran for c. 40 m parallel to the Sacred Way. Two staircases were built to provide access to the building on top of the podium.

In the southern face of the terrace wall forming the treasury's podium, unused limestone column drums from Dipteros 1, c. 1.70 m in diameter, were placed so as to form eight projecting spur walls. The spur walls were perpendicular to the terrace wall and were evenly spaced over the length of the 40-m-long terrace. Four of the eight spur walls (positioned at the ends of the terrace wall) consisted of one column drum, and four of the spur walls (positioned in the central part of the terrace wall) consisted of two column drums joined together. The column drums stood on their curved outer edges so that the large, circular, flat surfaces that would normally be hidden were visible. The exposed large, circular, flat surfaces of the drums were decorated with incised and painted designs. The only two preserved examples come from spur walls consisting of two column drums, with the decoration taking the form of a Gorgon extending over both drums (so that one eye appeared on each drum).

Also built in the sanctuary during the mid-sixth century were the Nordbau and the Südbau, which were located to the northeast and southeast of the Temple of Hera. The Nordbau was originally built as a non-peripteral tristyle prostyle structure measuring 34 x 20 m, with an interior colonnade and an interior space divided into two rooms by a cross wall with two doors. In the second half of the sixth century, an Ionic peristyle was added to the Nordbau, making it a pseudo-dipteral building (H. J. Kienast 1989; Walter, Clemente, and Niemeier 2019: 174–5, 80). The Südbau was originally designed as a peripteral building measuring c. 45 x 23 m. However, this version of the building was never completed, and at the same time that the Nordbau was rebuilt as a pseudodipteral building, the Südbau was reconfigured so that it featured an Ionic peristyle on three sides but no columns at all on the eastern facade (Buschor 1930: 59–67; Ziegenaus 1957a; Kyrieleis 1981: 91–4; Walter, Clemente, and Niemeier 2019: 174–5, 80). These buildings looked like and may have served as temples.[140]

### 3.4C.4.6. The Heraion in the Time of Polycrates

In the second half of the sixth century, presumably after the completion of Dipteros 1, yet another wave of construction was carried out in the Heraion (see Figure 3.16). The extent to which that activity can be attributed to Polycrates, who was tyrant of Samos for much, if not all, of the third quarter of the sixth century, remains an open question (see Section 3.5C.2).

---

140. For example, Buschor (1957: 84) suggested that the Südbau was a temple to Aphrodite and Hermes (who appear in a fourth-century inventory inscription from the Heraion)

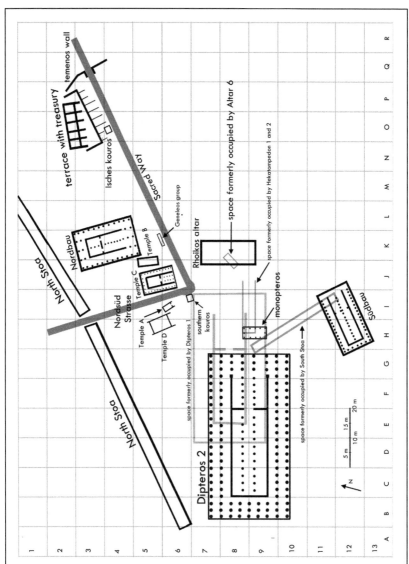

**FIGURE 3.16.** Plan of the Samian Heraion at the end of the sixth century.

Three smaller buildings (Temples B, C, and D) were erected in the northern part of the sanctuary in the second half of the sixth century (Ziegenaus 1957b). They should be considered alongside the various *naiskoi* that were built in the Heraion during the Archaic period, insofar as all of these structures share certain architectural features with temples, but their functions remain ambiguous. The chronology of their construction has been the subject of much debate (Kyrieleis 1993: 131–2; Walter, Clemente, and Niemeier 2019: 91–8). It is possible that they represent treasuries or architectural votives, but it is not clear who their dedicants may have been. Prominent local elite families, the wealthy *proxenoi* of trading partners, or ambitious individuals may all be candidates for the agents behind the construction of these buildings, although surely more research into the precise nature of the differences between temples (which were often used to store votives), treasuries (which look like temples), and votives (of which temples have been conceived as one variety) is necessary before this question can be answered with any certainty.

The biggest single building project in the Heraion in the second half of the sixth century began when Dipteros 1 (the Rhoikos temple) was demolished, just a few decades after it was completed. The reasons for the short period of use of Dipteros 1 continue to be much debated (Walter, Clemente, and Niemeier 2019: 176–7); one possibility is that the ground underneath the building proved to be incapable of supporting its great weight (H. J. Kienast 2002: 5). In the 530s, the construction of a new temple, Dipteros 2, was initiated. The east facade of Dipteros 2 was shifted c. 40 m to the west of that of Dipteros 1. Dipteros 2 is frequently called the Polycrates temple because it was begun when Polycrates was in power and presumably at his behest. This Ionic temple, which was never completed, measured 108 x 55 m, slightly larger than its predecessor.[141] It was intended to be dipteral on the long sides and tripteral on the short sides, with eight columns on the east facade, nine on the west facade, and 24 on the north and south facades; the height of the columns was c. 21 m. The remains currently visible at the Heraion, including the one standing column, belong to Dipteros 2 (Hellner 2009; Gruben and Kienast 2014; Walter, Clemente, and Niemeier 2019: 179–80, 93–6).

When Dipteros 1 was demolished to make way for Dipteros 2, a small (11.88 x 7.44 m) monopteros with wooden columns in a 3 x 5 arrangement was built, c. 10 m to the east of the east facade of Dipteros 2. In the early fifth century, that monopteros was replaced by a second, slightly larger (13.29 x 8.33 m) version with

---

141. Herodotus (3.60.4) describes Dipteros 2 as "the greatest temple [νηὸς μέγιστος] that I have ever seen."

stone columns. The monopteros stood over the area that had been occupied by the west end of Hekatompedon 1 and 2, and it was originally interpreted as a structure designed to cover the remains of the cult statue base from those earlier structures, which had been enclosed within the pronaos of the Rhoikos temple but which was now exposed to the elements. More recently, Hans Walter and Angelika Clemente have argued that the building held the cult statue when it was put on display during festivals (Walter and Clemente 1986).

Although the Heraion had a long history that stretched into the early Christian period, building activity decreased significantly after c. 500. A downward shift in investment at the site probably reflects the permanent decline in Samos' economic and political fortunes that occurred after the reign of Polycrates.

### 3.4C.5. Samian Burial Customs

As discussed in Section 3.4C.1, there was during the Geometric period a necropolis in Samos Town that was situated on a flat and sandy site close to the shoreline c. 400 m west of Kastro hill and within the circuit of the sixth-century fortifications; burials continued in that necropolis into the seventh century (Viglaki-Sofianou 2004; Viglaki-Sofianou 2013). The necropolis contained burials of both subadults and adults. Subadults were buried in pots, while adults were usually cremated, although a small number of inhumations in pits and one cist grave have also been excavated. After cremation, bones and ashes were collected in large pithoi, amphoras, or hydriai and deposited in pits dug in the sand, with the pots typically laid on their sides with their mouths closed by stone or clay plaques. The burials were placed within circular periboloi (four of which have been excavated) 3.5–5.0 m in diameter that were delimited by c. 1-m-high limestone walls. Each peribolos was covered by a tumulus of soil, pebbles, stones, and fragments of terracotta.

Grave goods consisted of both coarse- and fine-ware pottery (miniature vessels, cups, and oinochoai), terracotta figurines, and metal objects. Some graves were marked by blank stone plaques, and one pyre was surmounted by a cuboid structure built from stone plaques. The periboloi remained in use over long periods of time. A stone enclosure was formed by the intersection of the walls of three periboloi, and a low, straight wall held the ashes left over from pyres and seems to have been used communally. The presence of burned bronze fibulas, bronze rings, and olive pits among the pyre remains shows that corpses were cremated while dressed and that offerings of food were made. Finds of substantial quantities of dining pottery and animal bones in and around the pyres suggest that a ritual meal formed part of the funerary rites.

This necropolis went out of use in the early seventh century and seems to have been replaced by the West necropolis, which was located c. 400 m farther west, just outside the western edge of the fortifications built in the sixth century. In the late 19th century CE, Johannes Boehlau excavated 161 graves in the West Necropolis, 50 of which have been fully published (Boehlau 1898: 10–32; Löwe 1996). Smaller numbers of additional graves from the same necropolis were uncovered in subsequent excavations (Tsakos 1996). One of the oldest excavated graves in the West Necropolis contains the remains of a woman who was cremated in the early part of the seventh century while wearing ivory jewellery, bronze bow fibulas, and a bronze Phrygian belt (Tsakos 1996: 124). By the third quarter of the sixth century, the standard practice had become to inter adults in limestone (or occasionally marble or terracotta) sarcophagi, including some examples with lids carved with human features (so-called Phoenician-type sarcophagi). Almost all of the sarcophagi contain a single burial, and they have no consistent orientation because their placement is dictated by the details of the terrain. One of the earliest sarcophagi is also the most elaborate: it is carved from marble and its exterior features a depiction of an Aeolic colonnade with pilasters on square bases in low relief (Freyer-Schauenburg 1974: 183–4 and Taf. 76). The West Necropolis also contains some cist graves built of stone plaques that seem designed to imitate the appearance of sarcophagi. Subadults were buried in large pots (amphoras and hydriai) or in small cist graves.

Some of the graves in the West Necropolis were marked with *cippi* or with *stēlai* crowned by anthemia; four *stēlai* carry inscriptions supplying the name of the deceased (Tsakos 2001). In two instances (Tombs 29 and 36), a small, rectangular stone building was erected over the shaft into which the sarcophagus was sunk. Boehlau suggested that a square stone attached to the south side of the building over Tomb 29 held a funerary *kouros* (Boehlau 1898: 26). There is some evidence for the existence of tumuli, though it is not clear how common they were. Burials were arranged in clusters delimited by terrace walls and periboloi.

Of the 50 thoroughly published graves excavated by Boehlau, 40 were supplied with grave goods (typically relatively meager), primarily in the form of one or two terracotta figurines or pieces of pottery (Löwe 1996; Mariaud 2015a). The vases that appear with the greatest frequency are black-glaze kylikes and lekythoi from East Greek workshops, though Corinthian amphoriskoi, aryballoi, lydia, and pyxides also appear. The pots or cists holding subadults were habitually without grave goods, but in some instances, objects were placed on stone slabs or in shallow pits next to the grave. Laconian vases, terracotta masks, and metal objects were discovered in some graves, but the distribution of these goods suggests that they were restricted to a limited group of individuals (Mariaud 2015a). (See Section 3.7C for further discussion of the nature of the relationship between Samos and Sparta in the sixth century.)

Burials in the West Necropolis become sparser after c. 520. The few graves dated to the end of the sixth century have little in the way of grave goods, and no tumuli are evident. Finds of late sixth- and early fifth-century *stēlai* with elaborately carved marble anthemia in areas to the west and north of Samos Town indicate that burial grounds probably shifted farther outside the urban center.

Another necropolis with burials dated to the sixth century is located on the north side of Samos Town. Boehlau spent a few days exploring this necropolis and recording the remains he uncovered. These primarily consisted of two large stone circles that both probably served as the retaining walls for Archaic tumuli. Close to the stone circles, Boehlau found two fragmentary *kouroi* that he interpreted as grave markers. Other Archaic burials (inhumations) were discovered a short distance away, on rocky and rough terrain along the path toward the city (Karo 1933: 252).

The remains of one of the stone circles Boehlau found to the north of Samos Town have recently been restudied in some detail by Olivier Mariaud (2015b; for the location of this tumulus, see Figure 3.10 here). The structure contained a cremation burial in an amphora placed at the center of a tumulus that was approximately 6 m in diameter. The retaining wall was surmounted by a votive column and a fragmentary *kouros* carved from gray Samian marble (Freyer-Schauenburg 1974: #53). The base of the *kouros* carried the following inscription (*IG* XII.6.2.626): "Megas, son of E[ . . . ], son of Exakos, son of Xenos, son of Pyrraithos." The style of amphora and *kouros* indicate a date of c. 540 for the burial. Both the genealogical inscription and the usage of a *kouros* as a grave marker make this tomb of particular interest.[142]

The use of *kouroi* as grave markers is relatively unusual in the Greek world (Fullerton 2016: 60–1), but there is some evidence to suggest that they were used in that way at least occasionally on Samos. A second fragmentary *kouros* was found in the same area as the one marking Megas' tomb (Freyer-Schauenburg 1974: #56). The base attached to the building over Tomb 29 in the West Necropolis may have held a *kouros*.

We cannot say much about the purported "East Necropolis," because it is known only from some scattered sarcophagus fragments, which may or may not be Archaic, observed to the east of the city (Kleemann 1962; Mariaud 2015b: 262–3).

The only other significant Archaic cemetery known from Samos is located north of the Heraion at Klima, where burials took place between 630 and 590

---

142. Mariaud has suggested a reconstruction of rival funerary strategies, distinct between the West and North Necropoleis (Mariaud 2015b). The latter might have been characterized by cremation burials covered by tumuli and marked with statues.

(Marthari 1982). Thirty-two tombs were excavated: 12 *enchytrismos* burials, 18 cist tombs, and two inhumations in sarcophagi. Grave offerings were nearly non-existent (aside from a few ceramic vessels) in the *enchytrismos* burials but were more abundant in the cist tombs, where they included imported Corinthian and Laconian wares, as well as bronze jewellery. The sarcophagi were unfortunately "found in a particularly bad state of repair" (Marthari 1982: 352), and it is not clear from reports which finds came from these burials.

## 3.4C.6. Samian Pottery

The many contacts with the East that Samos maintained throughout its early history (see Sections 3.7C and 3.8C.3) made themselves apparent in the forwardly orientalizing style of Samian art. Samian pottery is interesting because it appears to have absorbed very few traditions from Attica or Corinth, adhering primarily to East Greek models and specifically to the local style of the far southeastern Aegean (Rhodes and Miletus are the best comparanda). However, within the constellation of pottery produced at Greek sites in the eastern Aegean in the Archaic period, Samos' was not a particularly distinguished ceramic tradition, and workshops with an eye to export seem to have been mostly nonexistent (Shipley 1987: 43; Cook 1997: 117).

Most regularly associated with the island is the Fikellura Style, which has been found in abundance on Samos and was originally known as "Samian" (Cook 1933–1934: 1), although chemical analysis suggests that many of the finest pieces were made at Miletus (Dupont 1983).[143] Fikellura pottery shares some features with southern Aegean Wild Goat, including the characteristics of the clay, the paint, and the slip, but it differs in shapes and decoration. The typical shape is a short, plump amphora with decoration, usually purely vegetal or linear but sometimes also incorporating groups of animals (boars and birds are popular choices) or men (Cook 1933–1934; Schaus 1986) (see Figure 3.17). Usually, the decoration on the body of the pot is divided into zones, but occasional experiments with a free field exist (see, for example, Cook 1997: pl. 32a for the famous "running man" amphora [BM 1864, 1007.156]). Samian amphoras and their distribution are discussed in Section 3.8C.1. An interesting specimen from Camarina in Sicily with an Egyptianizing scene of oryx sacrifice speaks to the cosmopolitan connections of Samos in the Archaic period (Grace 1979: 118, n. 57, pl. 35.1–2).

---

143. The name Fikellura comes from a site on Rhodes.

FIGURE 3.17. Fikellura amphora; c. 540; height: 29.10 cm, width: 23.50 cm; from Camirus on Rhodes. British Museum 1861.0425.47.

## 3.5C. Samian Political History

### 3.5C.1. Early History and Foundation

It is a cruel irony of history that despite knowing the names of so many local Samian historians (see Section 3.2C), we are not particularly well informed about the early political history of the island. Mythological foundation accounts began to emerge in the seventh century,[144] and over the course of time, a number of different, internally contradictory traditions came into being. One version, which seems to have been popular among the Samians themselves, was recounted by the sixth-century Samian poet Asius and is summarized by Pausanias as follows:

> Asius . . . says . . . that Phoenix had two daughters, Astypalaia and Europa, by Perimede, daughter of Oeneus; that Astypalaia had by Poseidon a son Ankaios, who reigned over the Leleges, as they are called; that Ankaios married Samia, daughter of the river Maeander, and had by her Perilaus, Enoudos, Samos, Alitherses, and also a daughter Parthenope . . . (7.4.1; trans. J. G. Frazer)

This version of events gives the eponymous Samos an illustrious heritage connected both to the sea (Poseidon) and the river Maeander, the mouth of which was located on the mainland opposite Samos. The importance of the Maeander to the Samians is further demonstrated by the number of potamophoric or perhaps theophoric Maiandr- and Mandro- names from the island, many of which we will encounter below.[145] King Ankaios appears in other early texts as an Argonaut, giving the island a prominent place in Panhellenic poetry (Simonides the Genealogist *FGrH* 8 F2).

Other traditions about the arrival of Greeks in Samos placed the foundation in the context of the Ionian Migration. The story went that Ion's descendant Prokles, exiled from Epidaurus, came to Samos and married a Carian woman and that during the reign of Prokles' son Leogoros, Ephesians, under the leadership of Androklos (the son of the last king of Athens), seized control of the island for ten years, before themselves being driven out by Leogoros (Paus. 7.4.2–3). The

---

144. The title of a lost poem, *On the Archaeology of the Samians*, by the seventh-century poet Semonides of Amorgos, is known (*FGrH* 534 T1). On the foundation accounts of Samos, see Mac Sweeney 2013: 91–102; Beck-Schachter 2019.

145. See Thonemann 2006 for the importance of the Maeander river for the Ionians generally and for Miletus, Samos, and Magnesia in particular.

386    THE OXFORD HISTORY OF THE ARCHAIC GREEK WORLD

*Etymologicum Magnum* (s.v. Ἀστυπαλαία) cites the historian Themistagoras of Ephesus (*FHG* IV pg. 512 #1) as a source for the story that Prokles and Tembrion brought Greek colonists to Samos and reached an agreement with the indigenous Carians, who lived in a place called Astypalaia.[146] The terms of the agreement were that the Greek colonists would settle close to Astypalaia, along the banks of the Schesios river (or, in some manuscripts, the Chesios), and that the Carians and Greeks would form a single community divided into two tribes named after Astypalaia and the (S)chesios.[147]

Moving from the legendary to a more historical past, the relevant sources make mention of a handful of political figures in Samos prior to the mid-sixth century without offering much in the way of absolute or relative chronology. Herodotus (3.59.4) refers to a *basileus*, Amphikrates, who led the Samians in war against the Aeginetans. According to Plutarch (*Mor.* 303f–304c), a *monarchia* under the rule of Demoteles existed in Samos until he was assassinated by the Geomoroi ("landowners"),[148] who set up an oligarchic government. Plutarch adds that the Geomoroi were themselves overthrown by nine Samian generals who led a successful attack on Megarian forces that had invaded the Samian colony of Perinthus. After the battle, the generals persuaded their Megarian captives to lend assistance in overthrowing the oligarchic government on Samos. The generals returned to Samos and, leading the Megarian captives in fetters that were intentionally not secured, went to the agora, where the generals and the captives killed the oligarchs, who were meeting in the *bouleutērion*. The generals subsequently built a large hall (*oikos*) in which they dedicated the fetters from the Megarian captives. The 13th-century CE writer Theodorus Metochites (*Miscell.* pp. 668–9) claims that Phoibias held the office of *aisymnētēs* (a kind of formal elective dictatorship; cf. Pittacus in Mytilene [see Section 3.5B]) in Samos. According to Polyaenus (*Strat.* 6.45), Syloson the son of Kalliteles was a Samian general during a war against the Aeolians and seized control of the government when most of the population was at a festival at the Heraion.

Even if one accepts the historicity of all of these figures and events, the paucity of chronological indicators means that they can be put in any number of

---

146. Themistagoras is cited by Athenaeus and two later authors; the period when he was active is unknown.

147. Diodorus (5.81.8) characterizes Samos as a colony of Lesbos.

148. The title is known from elsewhere, especially Syracuse (De Angelis and Mignosa Forthcoming: Section 3.5). Their name should mean that they claimed to be descendants of the first settlers at Samos (cf. the definition at Hsch. s.v. γαμόροι).

continuous or discontinuous sequences. Some helpful temporal parameters are that Perinthus was founded c. 600 (Loukopoulou and Laitar 2004: 920) and that Syloson may have been an ancestor of the dynasty of tyrants that ruled Samos in the second half of the sixth century (Shipley 1987: 68). One of many possible scenarios is that kings (including Amphikrates) ruled Samos until c. 700, after which an oligarchy of Geomoroi controlled the *polis*. The Geomoroi were subsequently overthrown by Demoteles, who made himself tyrant and was in due course assassinated by the Geomoroi. However, the Geomoroi, once restored to power, were sufficiently unpopular as to prompt the appointment of Phoibias as *aisymnētēs* before the end of the seventh century. By the early sixth century, the Geomoroi were back in power but were overthrown by a populist coup led by nine generals. The government that came into being after that coup was short-lived and gave way to Syloson the son of Kalliteles, who became tyrant sometime in the first quarter of the sixth century.[149]

The Geomoroi certainly still existed in the late fifth century and played a prominent role in the oligarchic regime that was overthrown in 412 (Thuc. 8.21). Their existence and influence in the Archaic period are less clear, and it should concern us that Herodotus never mentions them. Samos' elite was undoubtedly important, both during and outside of periods of tyrannical rule. This is perhaps most evident in the remarkable series of stone statue dedications that start in the late seventh century, primarily at the Heraion but also elsewhere on Samos. The statue dedications from the Heraion dating to the first half of the sixth century include (but are not limited to) (a) two identical, colossal *kouroi*, one of which bears an inscription naming Isches the son of Rhesis as the dedicator (*IG* XII.6.2.560); (b) a group of six statues (the so-called Geneleos group) set on a long base with an inscription naming -ilarches as the dedicator (*IG* XII.6.2.559F); and (c) three *kourai* and one *kouros* bearing dedicatory inscriptions from Cheramyes (*IG* XII.6.2.558A–D). All of those individuals are otherwise unknown, but their ability to erect large and costly dedications at prominent spots in the Heraion attests to the existence of wealthy and powerful elites who were actively competing among themselves for social position and influence (Duplouy 2006: 185–203, 36–49; Franssen 2011; see Section 3.9C for further discussion of the Geneleos group and Cheramyes' dedications). We should, however, be wary of identifying Samian elites of all periods with the

---

149. This scenario is implicitly embedded in Shipley's discussion of the political history of Archaic Samos (Shipley 1987: 37–65). Modern scholars have suggested a significant number of different versions of the political history of Samos prior to Polycrates. See, for example, Carty 2015: 23–73. Syloson the son of Kalliteles has been seen as the driving force behind the construction of Dipteros I in the Samian Heraion (see Section 3.4C.4.5).

## 388   THE OXFORD HISTORY OF THE ARCHAIC GREEK WORLD

Geomoroi and of seeing the latter's hand behind various political acts of the sixth century.

### 3.5C.2. The Sixth Century and Polycrates

We find ourselves on firmer ground once we move into the second half of the sixth century and the tyranny of Polycrates and his family.[150] Even here, however, there are uncertainties. Polyaenus (*Strat.* 6.45) tells a story about Syloson, who, upon having been appointed to be the Samians' general in a war against the Aeolians, seized control of Samos Town. That story does not mesh with the circumstances in which Polycrates' brother Syloson came to power (see below), and the Syloson in question has been understood to be Polycrates' grandfather (Shipley 1987: 69–73).

The *Suda* (s.v. Ἴβυκος) claims that the poet Ibycus traveled from Rhegium to Samos in the 54th Olympiad (564–561), when Polycrates' father Aiakes was tyrant of Samos. However, both the date offered and the claim that Polycrates' father was tyrant of Samos have been called into question, and the text of the entry has been variously emended (Giannini 2004: 52–3; Ornaghi 2008; Wilkinson 2013: 6–8; Carty 2015: 50–2, 82–4).[151]

A fragmentary poem from an Oxyrhynchus papyrus (*POxy* 15.1790) that is addressed to a Polycrates has been regularly attributed to Ibycus (F282; Wilkinson 2013: 49–50) and taken as an encomium of the famous Samian by that name. Since the poem praises the beauty of the addressee (l. 46) and invokes the figure of Troilus as a foil, it was presumably written when Polycrates was a boy (Hutchinson 2001: 232). That Polycrates would receive such attention from a well-known poet implies that his family enjoyed some sort of special status in Samos. Further evidence for the assertion that Polycrates' father and possibly grandfather held the tyranny before him can perhaps be found in the fact that Aiakes dedicated a statue on the acropolis of Samos Town (see Section 3.4C.1).

Herodotus, however, makes no mention of Polycrates' forebears as tyrants and specifically states that Polycrates, along with his brothers Syloson and Pantagnotos, organized a violent revolt (ἐπαναστάς, 3.39.1; cf. 3.120 and

---

150. For the ancient testimonia on Polycrates, see Meyer 2012: 80–132. On the tyranny of Polycrates and his family members, see Berve 1967: vol. 1: 107–14; Shipley 1987: 69–99; Carty 2015.

151. See also Burkert 2004: 355–6, discussing Ibycus' presence at the court of Polycrates in the novel *Metiochos and Parthenope* (first century?).

Polyaenus *Strat.* 1.23) against the government in Samos.[152] The historian Alexis of Samos (probably Hellenistic period) claimed that "before becoming tyrant, he [Polycrates] had provided himself with expensive draperies and cups that he furnished to people who were celebrating marriages and very big receptions" (*FGrH* 539 F2; trans. A. d'Hautcourt). There may be something to that story (it is hard to see what purpose its invention would have served), which is much more consonant with a wealthy and ambitious private person ladling out patronage than the young son of an established tyrant biding his time before taking over for his father. The aforementioned statue of Aiakes has carved on it an inscription (*IG* XII.6.561) that mentions *sylē* (the import of the inscription as a whole, and the meaning of *sylē* in the inscription, remain unclear), and Aileen Carty has argued that Polycrates' father Aiakes was not a tyrant but did hold a powerful magistracy that gave him control over tax collection on the proceeds from piratical ventures (Carty 2015: 53–66).

In sum, if Polycrates' forebears had indeed held power, it would appear that they had been overthrown by the time of Polycrates' coup. It has proven difficult to establish the precise date of that event, but it must have taken place sometime around 540. Polycrates soon thereafter put his brother Pantagnotos to death and exiled his other brother, Syloson (Hdt. 3.39.2).

Unlike some of Herodotus' Greek tyrants, particularly Periander, Polycrates is not represented in the extant sources as prone to transgressive, gratuitous violence (see, for example, Alexis of Samos *FGrH* 539 F2), and there is good reason to believe that he achieved a considerable degree of popularity among the Samian populace (Shipley 1987: 90). Herodotus implies that Polycrates and his brothers gained control of Samos with a tiny force of men (3.120.3; though cf. Polyaenus *Strat.* 1.23), which suggests that the regime he overthrew was not held in high esteem and that Polycrates' rule came as a welcome change. Polycrates evidently took at least some populist measures: Duris (*FGrH* 76 F63) claims that Polycrates required wealthy Samian citizens to support the mothers of men who had been killed in battle (see Section 3.6C).[153]

---

152. Polyaenus, *Strat.* 1.23.2, states that the tyrant Lygdamis of Naxos helped Polycrates to become tyrant. The veracity of that claim is impossible to verify, but it is highly likely that Polycrates and Lygdamis knew and perhaps supported each other in their tyrannies.

153. The mention of a tyrant together with women recalls the charge frequently lodged against single rulers that they forced themselves on citizen women. The fact that Alexis explicitly denied that Polycrates sent for women and children suggests that this aspect of Polycrates' tyranny was contested in later traditions, and Duris' statement about Polycrates' treatment of mothers who had lost their sons in battle may be Duris' attempt to put a positive spin on an attack on the tyrant's reputation.

390   THE OXFORD HISTORY OF THE ARCHAIC GREEK WORLD

Polycrates may well have achieved a considerable degree of popularity in part because he established a sort of piratical thalassocracy that brought significant amounts of wealth to Samos. Herodotus begins his account of Polycrates' reign by stating:

> Polycrates' fortunes rose so high that they were cried up throughout Ionia and the rest of Greece. Whenever he decided to strike in a campaign, everything went well for him. He got himself 100 penteconters and 1,000 archers, and he harried and plundered every state without distinction. He said that he would win more gratitude by giving back to a friend what he had taken than never having seized it in the first place. He captured a great number of the islands and many of the towns on the mainland. (3.39.3–4; cf. Polyaenus *Strat.* 1.23.1)

In recounting Polycrates' death, Herodotus observes:

> Polycrates is the first of the Greeks we know to lay plans for mastery of the sea, except for Minos of Knossos and any of those that before him were lords of the sea. But Polycrates is the first of the human race to do so, and he had high hopes of mastering Ionia and the islands. (3.122.2)[154]

Herodotus implies that Polycrates directly ruled over numerous places in Asia Minor and islands other than Samos. Van Alfen, noting that Thucydides describes Polycrates as having made many of the islands "subject allies" (ὑπηκόους, 1.13.6), has argued that Polycrates did indeed build something of a miniature empire along the coast of Asia Minor. He suggests that Polycrates exerted power in part by building numerous examples of a new type of warship, the *samaina*, that had two banks of oars (as opposed to the single bank of oars found on a penteconter) and was equipped with a ram and a distinctive boar's head prow.[155] Van Alfen links Polycrates' preference for the *samaina* with coins issued by Samos, Ialysus, and Cyzicus and likely other cities in Asia Minor showing a boar's head on the obverse and a quadripartite incuse square on the reverse. Those coins were, in van Alfen's view, minted by Polycrates' subject allies as a sort of cooperative coinage that facilitated trade and the payment of tribute (van Alfen 2004).

---

154. Eusebius' *Chronicon* supplies a list of successive thalassocracies from the fall of Troy to 480; Samos is listed as thassalocrat from 540 to 516. See the discussion in de Souza 1998: 287–8.

155. On the *samaina*, see also Morrison and Coates 1996: 181–4; Kuciak 2020: 54–60. Wallinga's (1993: 93–9) argument that the *samaina* was designed to ferry mercenaries to Egypt and to bring back grain is appropriately critiqued by van Alfen.

There may well be something to van Alfen's argument, but it seems improbable that the Persians, who were a looming presence after their conquest of the Lydian kingdom in 546, would have tolerated Samian hegemony over coastal sites in Asia Minor such as Cyzicus in the 530s and 520s. A perhaps more plausible approach is to interpret Polycrates' actions in light of the seafaring tradition that Polycrates inherited. The Samians had a long history of maritime activity prior to Polycrates' rule (see Section 3.8C.3), and while much of that activity involved peaceful commerce, Samians, like many other Greeks and non-Greeks who frequented the seaways of the Mediterranean in the Archaic period, were not averse to engaging in piracy when opportunities presented themselves. As Thomas Figueira (2015: 507) puts it, "commercial voyages possessed a belligerent dimension." The Samians' early interest in establishing outposts on the coast of Cilicia (see Section 3.7C), an area that later became a notorious lair for pirates, is quite possibly significant in that regard (Braun 1982: 15).

What set Polycrates apart is that he seems to have taken piracy to a new level by transforming it into a highly organized, large-scale, state-sponsored enterprise (Shipley 1987: 94–5; Carty 2015: 144–48; though cf. the doubts expressed in Luraghi 2001). Piracy may well have been a family business for Polycrates: as we have seen, Polycrates' father Aiakes may have held a magistracy charged with collecting taxes on the proceeds of piratical booty, and the uncommon name of Polycrates' brother Syloson contains the word for "seized goods," *sylē*. Although Polycrates could put to sea a significant number of ships, *samainai* and triremes (Hdt. 3.44.2), equipped with rams and intended primarily for ship-to-ship combat, he also had at his disposal 100 penteconters, which were much better suited to piratical raids. Polycrates thus maintained two separate naval fleets, one intended for organized naval warfare and one intended for his program of "corsair adventuring writ large" (Shipley 1987: 95).[156] This activity seems to be reflected in an inscription, found at the Heraion and dated to the second half of the sixth century, that records a dedication made by an Amphidemos upon the capture of multiple ships (*IG* XII.6.2.543; Dunst 1972: 106–10).

Antoine Deramaix (2014) has argued that Samian piracy shaded into something resembling formal hegemony. He points to the significant investments that Samians made in their fleet and fortified port facilities and their capacity to intervene on the island of Rheneia (see below) and notes that, according to Diodorus:

> Polycrates the tyrant of the Samians, used to dispatch triremes to the most suitable places and plunder all who were on the seas, and he would return

---

156. See Jackson 2000: 141–9 for the contrary argument, namely that the Samians were not particularly committed to piracy.

the booty which he had taken only to those who were allies of his [ἀπεδίδου δὲ μόνοις τοῖς συμμάχοις τὰ ληφθέντα]. (10.16.1; trans. C. H. Oldfather)

This account clearly draws on Herodotus, but whereas Herodotus discusses Polycrates' *philoi*, Diodorus mentions his *symmachoi*. All of that evidence is suggestive, but nothing more than that. We can, however, be confident that whatever form Samian power took during Polycrates' reign, piracy was a primary component.

The wealth that piracy brought to Samos made it possible to fund, among other things, the sixth-century building projects (the Eupalinos tunnel, fortifications, and a massive temple at the Heraion) that so impressed Herodotus (3.60, see Section 3.4C). The difficulties involved in supplying precise starting dates for those projects and for Polycrates' reign make it impossible to say for certain that Polycrates was responsible for them (Shipley 1987: 74–80; Walter, Clemente, and Niemeier 2019: 177–9). Herodotus does not explicitly connect any of them to Polycrates, though later writers did (Arist. *Pol.* 1313b24; Suet. *Calig.* 21). It is probable that if Polycrates did not set one or more of those projects in motion, he at least helped usher them to completion.

The wave of wealth that washed ashore on Samos in the second half of the sixth century also facilitated cultural production of other kinds. Herodotus states that "except for the tyrants of Sicily alone, there is not one of the rest of the Greek despots who is worthy to be compared with Polycrates for magnificence" (3.125.2). Later sources claim that Polycrates imported luxury goods from abroad and offered financial emoluments that attracted famous poets, most notably Anacreon, and skilled craftsmen to Samos (see, for example, Alexis of Samos *FGrH* 539 F2; Klytos of Miletus *FGrH* 490 F2; Ael. *VH* 9.4). According to Aristotle's student Clearchus of Soli, Polycrates built an alley or bazaar (*laura*) in Samos Town, modeled on a similar area in Sardis, which was the haunt of male and female prostitutes who also produced various kinds of luxury items, especially textiles (F44 Wehrli; see Shipley 1987: 76 n. 36 for further sources). (Discussion of cultural life in Archaic Samos can be found in Section 3.12C.)

Polycrates' ambitions extended well beyond Samos, and he clearly wanted to promote both himself and his *polis* before a Panhellenic audience. This is most evident from his engagement with Delos. Sometime around 525, Polycrates gained control of Rheneia, dedicated it to Apollo, and made a symbolic connection between Rheneia and Delos by joining the two islands with a chain (Thuc. 1.13.6, 3.104.2). Polycrates also founded a festival at Delos, presumably on the occasion of the dedication of Rheneia (Suidas s.v. Πύθια καὶ Δήλια; Constantakopoulou 2007: 47–9; see Section 3.12A).

Polycrates' actions were thus fully in line with the traditional actions of tyrants such as Pisistratus, who had intervened at Delos before Polycrates, but Polycrates may have been more influenced by non-Greek models. David Asheri remarked that Polycrates "imitated more the Persian satraps than the Greek tyrants of his age" (Asheri, Lloyd, and Corcella 2007: 509). We hear of alliances and *xenia* with Amasis of Egypt (Hdt. 3.39–43), Cambyses of Persia (Hdt. 3.44), and the satrap Oroites (Hdt. 3.120–5), but Polycrates did not cultivate ties, marriage-based or otherwise, with fellow Greeks.

## 3.5C.3. Overthrow of Polycrates

Despite his evident popularity and notable magnificence, Polycrates' rule met with considerable opposition among certain segments of the population of Samos. A fragmentary poem by Anacreon and the ancient commentary on that poem suggest that there was active resistance to Polycrates on Samos, perhaps organized by an elite-led faction that went by the name of the Halieis (Shipley 1987: 92).[157] According to Herodotus (3.44), when Polycrates heard in c. 525 that Cambyses was going to attack Egypt, he sent the Persians support in the form of 40 triremes, crewed by those whom Polycrates "most suspected to rise against him," and directed Cambyses to see to it that they never returned. Those crews went on board their ships but did not sail to Egypt. Instead, they went to Sparta to ask for help in overthrowing Polycrates (see Section 3.7C). When Polycrates learned about this act of sedition, he sought to minimize desertions to the would-be coup leaders by imprisoning the families of some Samian citizens in shipsheds in Samos Town and threatening to burn alive the family members of anyone switching sides (Hdt. 3.45.4). The Spartans sent a military expedition to support the crews of the Samian triremes; when that expedition ended in failure, the Samians on the losing side left the island and founded a settlement at Cydonia in Crete (Perlman 2004: 1170–2; see Section 3.7C). A separate group of Samian exiles seem to have founded the settlement of Dikaiarcheia in southern Italy during the period of Polycrates' rule (Fischer-Hansen, Nielsen, and Ampolo 2004: 256), and Pythagoras may have departed for southern Italy at roughly the same time (see Section 3.12C.2).

In any event, Polycrates was overthrown not by internal opposition but by Persian plotting (see Section 3.7C). After Oroites, the satrap of Lydia, murdered Polycrates in 522, power transferred to the tyrant's secretary, Maiandrios son of

---

157. For a different interpretation, in which Polycrates is the leader of the faction of the Halieis, see Carty 2015: 121–7.

394    THE OXFORD HISTORY OF THE ARCHAIC GREEK WORLD

Maiandrios (Hdt. 3.123).[158] According to Herodotus, Maiandrios initially wanted to abdicate the tyranny, going so far as to establish a cult to Zeus Eleutherios and to declare *isonomia*, or equality under the law, and freedom (*eleutheria*) to the assembled Samians (3.142.2–4). The mention of *isonomia* in this context is historically plausible, although it should be read more as an elite slogan consonant with rule by a tightly restricted group rather than as a synonym for democracy (Raaflaub 2004: 110). The *eleutheria* Maiandrios had in mind was almost certainly freedom from tyranny and perhaps Persian rule (Mitchell 1975: 86).[159] However, Maiandrios doubled down on his autocratic rule when he realized that someone else would take his place if he gave up the tyranny. His faction was ousted sometime c. 517 by Syloson, the brother of Polycrates, who had the backing of a Persian army (Hdt. 3.142–7; Shipley 1987: 103–5).[160] Although Herodotus says the Persians slaughtered the population of Samos (3.147; cf. Arist. F574 Rose for the expression "thanks to Syloson there is plenty of room"), this is probably an exaggeration (Constantakopoulou 2007: 126–9).

## 3.5C.4.  Ionian Rebellion and the Fifth Century

Syloson's son Aiakes inherited the tyranny and was among the Persian-backed tyrants who accompanied the Persian army on the expedition to Scythia in 513 (Hdt. 4.138.2).[161] Though deposed at the beginning of the Ionian Rebellion in 499, he was reinstated by Darius after the Battle of Lade in 494 (Hdt. 5.38.2, 6.13.2, 6.25). When the Persians determined in 492 that the Ionians would be more loyal to them under regimes such as those Herodotus labeled *dēmokratiai*, Aiakes' reign came to an end (6.43.3). We hear little about the political activity

---

158. For Maiandrios, see Mitchell 1975: 85–7; Roisman 1985. Herodotus likely saw Maiandrios' dedications of the furnishings from Polycrates' house (3.123.1) in the Heraion (see Section 3.4C.1).

159. See Raaflaub 2004: 110–11 for the argument that the cult of Zeus Eleutherios was not founded until after 479.

160. The fact that Otanes made Maiandrios' brother Lykaretos tyrant of Lemnos after the Persian conquest of that island c. 512 (Hdt. 5.26–7; see Section 3.5B) may suggest that Maiandrios faced opposition from within his own family.

161. It is interesting to note that the Heraion continued to function as a site of self-promotion for members of the Samian elite during Aiakes' tyranny. Herodotus presumably saw in person the dedication of Mandrokles the architect, who built a pontoon bridge for Darius across the Bosporos in 513. Mandrokles' vaunting epigram (Hdt. 4.88.2) describes his accomplishment as a "crown" for himself and *kudos* for the Samians but does not mention Aiakes. Note that this is the third Maiandr- or Mandro- name we have encountered among the individuals making dedications in the Heraion.

of the (nominally) democratic regime that followed, but Samians fought on the side of the Persians at Salamis in 480. One of the Samian trierarchs, Theomestor the son of Androdamas, captured enemy ships in the battle and was rewarded by Xerxes with tyrannical rule over the island (Hdt. 8.85). Theomestor's tyranny lasted only to 479, when he was deposed in the aftermath of the Battle of Mycale.

Samos was ruled by an oligarchic regime during the *pentekontaetia*, interrupted only when the government was briefly suppressed in 441/0 and a (probable) democracy was installed (Thuc. 1.115.2–3). We know little about the oligarchy's institutions or laws. As is to be expected, the regime had generals, the most famous of whom was the (Eleatic School) philosopher Melissus son of Ithagenes (Plut. *Per.* 26.2).

Our knowledge of the structure of the Samian government in the Archaic period is limited, due in large part to the fact that the earliest extant public enactments from Samos date to the fourth century. Herodotus states that Maiandrios summoned an assembly of all the citizens in order to announce his abdication (ἐκκλησίην συναγείρας πάντων τῶν ἀστῶν, 3.142.2) and that a *koinon* of the Samians made arrangements to commemorate the deeds of the loyalist ship captains at Lade (6.14.3; see Section 3.7C), but neither of those passages provides definitive evidence for the existence of a formal assembly or, if there was such an assembly, what powers it might have had. A *boulē* is mentioned in an inscription from 405 (*IG* I³.127.8), and Plutarch, in a story set in the Archaic period, refers to a *bouleutērion* (*Mor.* 304b).

The Samian citizen body was divided into two tribes, the Astypalaieis and the Chesieis, for much of the Hellenistic period, but the Samian colony of Perinthus had the standard four Ionian tribes. It seems probable, therefore, that at some point after the foundation of Perinthus in c. 600 and before the earliest attestation of a system with just two tribes (c. 330), there was a reform of the tribal system in which the number of tribes was cut in half and their names changed. Inscriptions from the Hellenistic period show there were civic subdivisions smaller than tribes, *chiliastyes*, *hekatostyes*, and *genē*, and it seems likely that at least some of those subdivisions came into being as the result of the aforementioned tribal reform (Jones 1987: 195–9; Shipley 1987: 289–92).

## 3.6C. Samian Legal History

The lack of inscribed legal documents from Archaic Samos makes reconstruction of its legal history difficult. Zenobius cites the historian and tyrant Duris (*FGrH* 76 F63) for an explanation of the local Samian proverb "Polycrates distributes the mothers": the tyrant assembled the mothers of those who had been killed in war and handed them over to wealthy citizens to support. Such a policy resembles

396 THE OXFORD HISTORY OF THE ARCHAIC GREEK WORLD

the rearing of war orphans attributed to Solon (Diog. Laert. 1.55) and practiced by Classical democracies ([Arist.] *Ath. Pol.* 24.4; *SEG* 57.820; Diod. *Sic.* 20.84.3).

## 3.7C. Samian Diplomatic History

According to Herodotus, Samos sided with Chalcis in the Lelantine War of c. 700 (5.99.1; cf. Thuc. 1.15.3). The nature of the Lelantine War—and whether such a conflict ever took place—has been the subject of long-running and still lively scholarly debate (see, for example, Tausend 1987; V. Parker 1997; Hall 2014: 4–8). As Sylvian Fachard and Samuel Verdan have recently argued, the most likely scenario is that the Lelantine War consisted of a series of skirmishes fought over pasturelands on Euboea. To the extent that soldiers from outside Euboea were involved in that conflict, they were present not as part of organized armies sent by their respective *poleis* but as individuals bound by ties of *xenia* to individuals in one Euboean community or another (Fachard and Verdan in this volume: Section 2.7.1).[162]

Similarly fraught is the question of the "Meliac War," supposedly fought by the members of the Ionian League against the community of Melie. The ancient sources (the most important of which is Vitruvius 4.1.4) claim that the 12 *poleis* that belonged to the Ionian League destroyed Melie because of the arrogance of its inhabitants and subsequently built a common shrine and meeting place (the Panionion) on the site of Melie, with a temple dedicated to Poseidon Helikonios. The Meliac War has typically been understood as the foundational act of the Ionian League. Making sense of the various bits of information about this war is complicated, in part because the ancient sources disagree as to whether Melie was a Greek or Carian community and because, according to some sources, Ionian Greek communities were involved on both sides of the conflict (Tausend 1992: 70–8; Mac Sweeney 2013: 178–87).

The relevant evidence is discussed in detail in Section 3.10A above and need not be repeated here. It is, however, worth noting as preface to what follows that excavation at Çatallar Tepe on Mt. Mycale (in Asia Minor immediately to the east of Samos; see below) uncovered the remains of what seems to be a Carian settlement that was destroyed c. 600 and, on top of that settlement, a Greek temple dating to the second quarter of the sixth century. It is probable that the Carian settlement should be identified with Melie and the temple with the Temple of Poseidon Helikonios that was located at the Panionion. The temple at the

---

162. If Samians did indeed fight as Sparta's allies in the Messenian Wars, as Herodotus says the Samians themselves claimed (3.47.1), that would likely be another instance of individual rather than communal initiative.

Panionion was destroyed sometime around the middle of the sixth century, perhaps during the Persian conquest of Asia Minor, after which the sanctuary seems to have been moved to a new location near the modern village of Güzelçamli, on a hill currently known as Otomatik Tepe, 5 km to the west of Çatallar Tepe (and thus closer to the coast). (These sites are labeled as Panionion 1 and 2 on Map 3.6.) The material remains cannot, of course, resolve the question of the motivations for the war or the combatants involved in it.

The various traditions about the Meliac War are firmly grounded in geopolitical realities in the sense that Samians had a long-running interest in establishing control over the coastline opposite their island. The dominant feature of that coastline is the steep-sided peninsula of Mt. Mycale (the highest peak of which is nearly 1,300 masl). The Maeander river debouches into the (now mostly silted-up) Gulf of Miletus (sometimes called the Gulf of Latmos) on the southern side of Mt. Mycale, and the *poleis* of Priene and Miletus were located on the northern and southern banks of that river, respectively. The northern slopes of Mt. Mycale give way to the coastal Karaova plain; Melie was situated in the hills behind the Karaova plain and directly to the east of Samos. Magnesia on the Maeander was located c. 30 km northeast of Melie (and hence well inland), Ephesus on the coast c. 30 km north of Melie. The Samian *peraia* fluctuated in extent, but it was always centered around the north side of Mt. Mycale and the Karaova plain (Shipley 1987: 31–7; Funke 1999: 62–3; Constantakopoulou 2007: 242–3). Anaia, a coastal settlement in the Karaova plain (Rubinstein 2004b: 1063–4), was consistently the most important site in the Samian *peraia*.

Although it is impossible to establish the veracity of the details of the various extant accounts of the Meliac War, it would not be surprising if Samos, at some early point in its history, made common cause with Priene and perhaps some other Ionian communities and destroyed Melie, with the conquered territory being divided among the victors. The "Meliac War" was, in other words, probably a local dispute and did not involve anything resembling a "Panionian" coalition (Roebuck 1955: 32). Later accounts that present the war as a Panionian undertaking offered a unifying foundation myth for the Ionian *poleis* of the region and for the Ionian League that met at the significantly named Panionion (Crielaard 2009: 60; Mac Sweeney 2013: 178–87). As we have seen (see Section 3.10A), there is some reason to believe that the Ionian League came into being in the aftermath of the Meliac War.

The destruction of Melie did not in any way resolve the tensions between Samos, Priene, Magnesia, and Ephesus over the territory on and around Mt. Mycale and the Karaova plain. Samos and Priene (which controlled the northern and southern slopes of Mt. Mycale, respectively), in particular, found themselves

398   THE OXFORD HISTORY OF THE ARCHAIC GREEK WORLD

at loggerheads for centuries (Magnetto 2009). The Samians and Prienians repeatedly resorted to arbitration to resolve their differences, and we are fortunate in having inscriptions that record the results of two arbitrations that took place in the Hellenistic period. Those inscriptions offer glimpses into the history of the Samian *peraia* and perhaps into the diplomatic history of Samos in the Archaic period and hence merit thorough discussion.[163]

One of the inscriptions, cut into the cella walls of the Temple of Athena Polias in Priene, is a lengthy text (more than 200 lines long) that supplies a detailed summary of the findings of Rhodian arbitrators from c. 180 (Hiller von Gaertringen 1906: #37–8; Magnetto 2008). In making their case to the arbitrators, the Samians cited numerous historians to buttress their claim that the Ionians awarded them control over several sites on the mainland after the Meliac War. The most immediately relevant sections of text read as follows:

> The Samians provided testimonies of historians . . . trying to prove that Karion and the area around it were allotted to them, and that at the time when they divided the land of Melie, they themselves obtained Karion and Dryoussa, according to the record [about this?] in the *Histories* ascribed to Maiandrios of Miletus, to the effect that the Samians obtained Karion and Dryoussa, and after their Battle at the Oak against the Prienians, they gained the judgment by their victory, and they obtained the land through the treaty: for they marked out their territory against them [sc. the Prienians] following the courses of rivers: and they produced the historians to give evidence for them—Maiandrios to prove that they obtained Karion after the Meliac War, and Euagon [*FGrH* 535 F3], Olympichos [*FGrH* 537 F2], and Duris [*FGrH* 76 F25] to prove that they marked out their boundary against the Prienians following the courses of rivers. (l. 118–23)
>
> . . .
>
> Seeing all the other writers about the Meliac War and the land distribution allege that the Samians obtained Phygela from the distribution—although four of them are Samians, namely Ouliades [*FGrH* 538 F1],

---

163. A number of sources, starting with Aristophanes (*Peace* 363), refer to someone named Kallikon or Killikon who was said to have betrayed his community to its enemies, with various combinations of hometown and enemy being given. Those combinations include Kallikon betraying Samos to the Prienians and Syros to the Samians (Theopompus *FGrH* F111/404a, Suda s.v. πόνηρος). No specific historical context is given in any of the extant references to Kallikon/Killikon, and it is impossible to recuperate any factual information from the relevant stories.

Olympichos [*FGrH* 537 F2], Duris [*FGrH* 76 F25], and Euagon [*FGrH* 535 F3], and two of them are Ephesians, namely Kreophylos [*FGrH* 417 F2] and Eualkes [*FGrH* 418 F1], and Theopompus is a Chian [*FGrH* 115 F59, 305], all of whom we [sc. the Rhodian arbitrators] find in their histories recorded that the Samians obtained Phygela—but only in the *Histories* ascribed to Maiandrios of Miletus is it recorded that the Samians obtained Karion and Dryoussa, [histories] which many authors oppose, claiming they are pseudepigraphical [i.e., not by Maiandrios] [- - -] . . . (l. 101–11; trans. N. Sato from *BNJ* 491 F1)

This inscription shows that in the second century, there were strong disagreements as to who had gotten precisely what after the end of the Meliac War.[164] For example, the Rhodian arbitrators noted that Samian, Ephesian, and Chian historians agreed that Samos had received the coastal site of Phygela but that only Maiandrios of Miletus claimed that Samos had received Karion and Dryoussa. Karion has been plausibly identified with a fortified site at Kala Tepe, near the modern village of Güzelçamli and not far from the site of the later Panionion at Otomatik Tepe (Lohmann 2022: 145; on Kala Tepe/Karion, see Section 3.10A); Dryoussa remains unlocated. One of the Samian historians cited in that inscription for information about the division of Melie's territory after the Meliac War, Euagon of Samos, seems to have been active in the fifth century (see Section 3.2C), and so Samian claims to territory in Asia Minor can be traced back into the Classical period.

The second inscription was cut into a *stēlē*, found in Samos, that records the results of King Lysimachos' intervention in 283/2 in a dispute between Samos and Priene over a part of the Karaova plain known as the Batinetis ("the Brambles"; its precise location is unknown) (*IG* XII.6.1.155; Welles 1934: #7 with Greek text and English translation). The inscription is only partially preserved, but it shows that in 283/2, representatives from Samos and Priene cited, among other things, accounts by (unnamed) historians arguing about the course of events some years after the end of the Meliac War. (Thus, though this arbitration occurred a century earlier than the Rhodian arbitration discussed above, what we know of it pertains primarily to events after those featuring in the inscription pertaining to the Rhodian arbitration.)

The extant section of text preserves the beginning of the inscription, a summary of the arguments made by the Prienian envoys, and the beginning of the

---

164. For detailed discussions of the text of this inscription, see Magnetto 2008 and Polito 2009: 116–36, as well as the commentary by Noboru Sato in the *BNJ* (491 F1).

arguments made by the Samian envoys. The most immediately relevant sections of text read as follows:

> The envoys from Priene tried to prove by means of the histories and the other testimonials and documents . . . that the original possession of the Batinetis had been theirs. . . . When Lygdamis invaded Ionia with his army, they left the Batinetis and the Samians withdrew to the island. Lygdamis, after occupying the land three [?] years, returned them the same lots, and the Prienians took them over; no Samian was there at all unless one happened to be among them in the character of a resident alien and placed his crops at the disposal of Priene. Later the Samians seized the land forcibly, and consequently Bias was sent from Priene with full powers to conclude a peace with Samos, and he concluded the peace, and the Samian settlers left the Batinetis. The envoys, then, argued that affairs had remained in this state in former times and up to quite recently they had been in possession of the land. . . . Your [the Samians'] envoys declared that you had received your existing possession of the Batinetis from your ancestors. They admitted that, after the invasion of Lydgamis, the Samians like the rest left the land and retired to the island. Afterward . . . 1,000 Samian settlers . . . (trans. C. B. Welles, including Welles' restorations, with modifications)

The envoys from Priene thus claimed that they had been given the Batinetis after the Meliac War but that, when the Cimmerians under King Lygdamis invaded Asia Minor, Priene lost control of the Batinetis, and the Samians abandoned their *peraia* at the same time. According to the Prienians, after the Cimmerians left, Priene regained possession of the Batinetis, and the only Samians present were resident aliens, but the Samians subsequently gained control of the Batinetis by force. Bias of Priene then negotiated a treaty with Samos under the terms of which the Samians restored the Batinetis to Priene, which had maintained control of it until not long before the arbitration. Although the text breaks off just where the Samiains' counterclaims are recorded, it is evident that the Samians argued that they had received the Batinetis after the Meliac War, that they had left the mainland during the Cimmerian invasion, and that they had reoccupied the Batinetis shortly after the departure of the Cimmerians. The discovery of the *stēlē* on Samos and Lysimachos' tone in describing the dispute leave little doubt that he decided in favor of Samos.

The conflicts between Samos and Priene referenced in the aforementioned inscriptions are also discussed by Plutarch (*Mor.* 296a–b):

When the Samians and the Prienians were at war with each other, on the other occasions they suffered injuries and inflicted injuries to a moderate degree only, but when a great battle took place, the people of Priene slew 1,000 Samians. Six years later the Prienians engaged the Milesians at a place called the Oak, and lost practically all the best and the foremost of their citizens. At this time also the sage Bias was sent on an embassy from Priene to Samos and won high repute. For the women of Priene this was a cruel experience and a pitiable calamity, and it became established as a curse and an oath in the most important matters to swear by "the darkness by the Oak," because of the fact that there their sons, their fathers, and their husbands had been slaughtered. (trans. F. C. Babbitt, slightly modified)

An abbreviated version of the same story is recounted by Zenobius (*Proverbs* 6.12), who cites the Aristotelian *Constitution of the Samians* as his source, and it is likely that Plutarch also derived his information from that same source (both texts are listed under F576 in Rose's collection of Aristotelian fragments). Neither the inscriptions nor Plutarch offers precise temporal indicators, but references to the Cimmerian invasion and Bias have been used to generate various relative and absolute chronologies.

One of many possible scenarios is that sometime around the middle of the seventh century, the Cimmerians expelled both the Samians and the Prienians from the Karaova plain. When the Cimmerians departed not long after their incursion, the Prienians returned, but the Samians did not. Sometime around 600, the Samians participated in a conflict that led to the destruction of the Carian city of Melie and the division of its territory, some of which fell to Samos. Priene made an initially successful attempt to deprive Samos of its newly acquired possessions in Asia Minor, and sometime around 590, the Samians launched a major expedition and fought a battle in which the Prienians defeated the Samians and killed 1,000 Samian soldiers. Sometime around 585, the Prienians themselves suffered a crushing defeat at the hands of the Milesians, who had perhaps formed an alliance with the Samians, and in the aftermath of that defeat, the Prienians were forced to cede control of some or all of the Karaova plain to Samos (Shipley 1987: 29–54). Although the extant sources do not make it possible to trace hostilities between Samos and Priene over the Karaova plain for the remainder of the Archaic period, the arbitrations of the Hellenistic period suggest that the two *poleis* continued to dispute control of that territory.

The Samians were actively engaged in founding overseas settlements outside their *peraia* from an early date. At some point in the late eighth or the seventh century, they established outposts at Kelendris and Nagidos in Cilicia (directly opposite Cyprus) (Keen and Fischer-Hansen 2004: 1218–20).[165] These outposts (which eventually developed into *poleis* but probably did not start as such) facilitated both piratical raiding (see Section 3.5C.2) and commercial exchange. The Suda (s.v. Σιμμίας, Ῥόδιος) characterizes the three *poleis* on the island of Amorgos (c. 125 km southwest of Samos) as Samian foundations, with the poet Semonides as oikist (Reger 2004: 734).[166] In addition, the calendar used by Minoa on Amorgos shared some month names with that used on Samos (Loukopoulou 1989: 116–17 and n. 2). However, other sources (Stephanus of Byzantium *Ethnica* α 275; scholiast to Dionysius Periegete 525) characterize the *poleis* on Amorgos as Naxian foundations, and there is no clear archaeological evidence that would suggest Samos colonized Amorgos. It is likely that the ostensible colonial connections between Samos and Amorgos were Hellenistic fabrications (Constantakopoulou 2014).

In the late seventh and sixth centuries, the Samians turned their attention north and founded a chain of settlements (Bisanthe, Heraion Teichos, and Perinthus) on the west coast of the Propontis. Those settlements seem to have developed into autonomous communities at a relatively early date, but Samos did send a military expedition to support Perinthus not long after its foundation (Loukopoulou and Laitar 2004: 914–15, 18–21).[167] An inscription from the Samian Heraion, dating to the first half of the sixth century (*IG* XII.6.577), records two Perinthians dedicating several objects to Hera. The text is vexed, but they seem to describe themselves as *oikēioi* (l. 3–4), which A. J. Graham (1983: 162–3) interpreted to mean "kinsmen." Dikaia in Thrace, Samothrace, and Nymphaion in the Black Sea have all been identified as possible Samian colonies (Avram, Hind, and Tsetskhladze 2004: 948; Loukopoulou 2004: 878–8; Reger 2004: 769–71).

Farther afield, the Samians participated in the foundation of Naucratis in Egypt (on which see Section 3.8A.3) in Egypt and built their own sanctuary of Hera there (Hdt. 2.178.3) in the late seventh or early sixth century. They also evidently founded their own settlement at Oasis, somewhere in the general vicinity of Egyptian Thebes (Austin 2004: 1240).

There are some indications that the Samians' activities in the Propontis brought them into conflict with the inhabitants of Megara and Lesbos, both of

---

165. The fact that dedications of Cypriot figurines at the Heraion start around 670 (see Section 3.8C.3) may offer some indication of when Kelendris and Nagidos were founded.

166. The ostenible Samian colonization of Amorgos has been seen as the result of the loss of Samian *peraia* or of internal political strife (Shipley 1987: 49–51).

167. The Samians may have also seized the island of Proconnesos (originally settled by Miletus) at roughly the same time (Shipley 1987: 51–2).

which had a significant presence in the Propontis and nearby regions. As we have seen (see Section 3.5C.1), Plutarch (*Mor.* 303f–304c) claims that the Samians sent a fleet of 30 ships commanded by nine generals to the aid of Perinthus, which had been attacked by the Megarians. Polyaenus (6.45) claims that Syloson was appointed as the Samians' commander in a war against the Aeolians (which seems to refer to the Lesbians in general or the Mytileneans in particular). If the aforementioned events did indeed take place, they can plausibly be placed in the first quarter of the sixth century (Shipley 1987: 52–4).

Samos was a member of the Ionian League, which probably came into being in the first half of the sixth century. The Ionian League served as a venue for collective deliberation by its members, and important events in Samos' diplomatic history may have unfolded there. However, the few extant references to the activities of the Ionian League during the Archaic period indicate that it did not serve as the vehicle for significant political or military undertakings (see Section 3.10A).

The Samians, like the Chians and Lesbians (see Sections 3.7A and 3.7B, respectively), may have been bound to Lydia by ties of *xenia* and may have had to pay tribute to the Lydians (Hdt. 1.6.2, 1.27). The Samians did not, however, seem to have understood themselves to be in a particularly subservient relationship with Lydia. According to Herodotus (3.48–53), Periander, tyrant of Corinth, in order to punish the people of Corcyra for the killing of his son Lycophron, took 300 boys from leading families on Corcyra and loaded them onto a ship to be taken to the Lydian king Alyattes at Sardis, where they would be made into eunuchs. When the ship put in at Samos, the Samians, upon hearing of the purpose of the voyage, helped the boys flee to the nearby sanctuary of Artemis, where they were received as suppliants. When the Corinthians tried to starve the boys out of the sanctuary, the Samians instituted a festival as an excuse to bring quantities of food to the sanctuary, and the Corinthians eventually departed, leaving the Samians free to send the boys back to Corcyra.

This story, which is set in the first quarter of the sixth century by virtue of its connection to Periander and Alyattes, suggests that Samians were not concerned about intervening in a way that could conceivably have angered a Lydian monarch. In the same vein, Herodotus reports (1.70) that when the Spartans and Croesus concluded an alliance, the former sent the latter a massive bronze kratēr as a gift. However, the kratēr never reached Sardis. According to the Spartans, the Samians seized the ship carrying the kratēr and took it as booty; according to the Samians, the Spartans transporting the kratēr heard upon their arrival in Ionia that Lydia had been conquered by the Persians and so sold it to certain individuals in Samos (who then dedicated it at the Heraion) but then returned home and claimed that it had been stolen. Herodotus does not explicitly state which version of events he takes to be more trustworthy, but at

3.48.1, he says that the Samians' rescue of the 300 Corcyraean boys took place at about the same time as the "robbery of the kratēr" (κρητῆρος τῇ ἁρπαγῇ).[168] Here again, the implication is that the Samians felt that they had little to fear from the Lydians.

The Samians, like the Chians and the Lesbians, were not immediately affected, at least in terms of their sovereignty, by the Persian conquest of the Lydian kingdom in 546. Despite Herodotus' assertion that the Ionians of the island surrendered to Cyrus in 546 (1.169.2), Samos remained free of Persian subjection until the end of Polycrates' tyranny. Herodotus himself indicates (3.120.3) that Samos was not under Persian control prior to Polycrates' death, and he notes that even after the Persian conquest of Lydia, "there was no danger for the islanders, for the Phoenicians were not yet subjects of Persia, and the Persians themselves were no sailors" (1.143.1). Indeed, Polycrates felt himself free to make an alliance with the Persians' enemy, Amasis, the ruler of Egypt (Hdt. 3.39.1), and hence linked himself to a place where the Samians had long engaged in profitable commerce (see Section 3.8C.3).

The key issue in all of this was, as Herodotus notes, that the Persians lacked naval forces and thus did not represent a significant threat to Polycrates. That made it possible for the Samians under Polycrates' leadership to engage in piracy on a large scale and in a highly organized fashion (see Section 3.5C.2). Polycrates' policy of pillaging everyone and everything possible undoubtedly made him unpopular not only with the Persians but also with the Greeks who suffered from his depredations. As we have seen (see Section 3.7B), Polycrates conquered Lesbos after he defeated the combined fleets of Lesbos and Miletus in a sea battle. The Lesbian prisoners ended up digging a moat around the fortifications of Samos Town (Hdt. 3.39.4; on those fortifications, see Section 3.4C.2). Miletus was effectively under Persian control during this period, and it may well be that the Milesians and the Lesbians were acting as Persian proxies (supplying naval forces that the Persians lacked) when they were defeated by Polycrates and the Samians.[169]

---

168. The synchronization of trhe freeing of the Corcyraean boys being sent to Alyattes and the seizure of the kratēr being sent to Croesus creates major chronological difficulties. See Asheri, Lloyd, and Corcella 2007: 446 for further discussion.

169. Two Byzantine authors, John Malalas (sixth century CE; *Chronographia* 6.200–20) and Georgius Cedrenus (11th century CE; *Historia compendium* 138), both citing Sextus Julius Africanus as a source (second–third century CE; Christesen 2007: 14–15, 153–6, 250–76), claim that not long after 546, the Persians and Samians fought a naval battle in which Cyrus was killed (Shipley 1987: 80). Insofar as Cyrus was probably killed while campaigning in Central Asia (Briant 2002: 49–50), one might be inclined to dismiss the story of a Persian-Samian naval battle entirely.

*Chios–Lesbos–Samos* 405

The basic parameters under which Polycrates and the Samians operated changed radically once the Phoenicians were incorporated into the Persian empire. That shift put substantial naval forces at the disposal of the Persians, and Polycrates' position became much more fragile. The Persians notionally became the rulers of Phoenicia in 539 by virtue of their conquest of Babylonia, though it was probably some time before they had effective control of the Phoenician cities and their fleets. The Phoenicians' participation in the conquest of Egypt in 525 shows that they were Persian subjects by that point in time (Briant 2002: 51). Polycrates abrogated his alliance with Amasis and sent forces to support the Persian attack on Egypt in 525 (Hdt. 3.40–4)—a strong indication that Polycrates was finding it necessary to accommodate himself to the wishes of the Persians.[170]

Polycrates' decision to send forces to support the Persian attack on Egypt led indirectly to a Spartan military intervention in Samos sometime around 524 (see Carty 2015: 180 on the date).[171] Polycrates dispatched a fleet of 40 triremes to Egypt and, according to Herodotus (3.44.2), manned those ships with individuals he believed to be most likely to be plotting against him and sent a request to the Persian king Cambyses to ensure that those ships' crews never made it back to Samos. Herodotus (3.45) reports multiple different versions of the events that ensued—one in which the Samians on the triremes disobeyed orders and stopped at the island on Carpathus before sailing to Sparta to seek assistance, and another in which they went as far as Egypt before turning back, fighting a losing battle against Polycrates and the remaining Samian forces and then sailing to Sparta to seek assistance. The Spartans, with help from the Corinthians, sent an expeditionary force that launched an unsuccessful frontal attack on the fortifications of Samos Town, followed by a futile 40-day siege (Hdt. 3.54–6).

Herodotus (3.47) reports two different reasons the Spartans responded to the Samians' request for assistance. According to the Samians, it was because the Samians had aided the Spartans during the Messenian Wars. According to the Spartans, it was because they wanted to avenge the Samians' theft of not only the kratēr the Spartans had tried to send to Croesus but also an elaborate gold-embroidered linen breastplate that Amasis had tried to send to Sparta just a year after the kratēr had been stolen. Herodotus adds (3.48) that the Corinthians took part in the expedition because they sought revenge for the Samians' actions in freeing the 300 Corcyraean boys that Periander had tried to send to Lydia.

---

170. Herodotus reports that Amasis broke off the treaty because he was concerned by Polycrates' unremitting good fortune, a story that conceals Polycrates' betrayal of his ally (Shipley 1987: 96).

171. On Herodotus' account of Polycrates' tyranny, see Forsdyke 2002: 524–8.

Authors starting with Plutarch (*Mor.* 859e–860c) have found it difficult to accept that the Spartans and Corinthians would have undertaken a major military venture to avenge relatively minor Samian interventions that had taken place 20 years earlier—not least because the Spartans had not to that point in time shown any interest in projecting power overseas. It has instead been argued that the true reason for the Spartan-Corinthian expedition lay in the Spartans' desire to curb tyranny, to extend their hegemony outside the Peloponnese, to take preemptive action in the face of Persian expansion (insofar as Polycrates had, by sending ships to Egypt, openly allied himself with the Persians) (Cartledge 1982: 256–8), or to punish the Samians for interfering with the Spartans' lucrative slave trade with Lydia and Egypt (Carty 2015: 175–95).

Paul Cartledge, after reviewing most of those possibilities, argued that a crucial factor was the existence of close ties between prominent families in Sparta and Samos. He suggests that those ties might have gone back to the seventh century, when individual Samians may have come to the aid of the Spartans in their conflicts with the Messenians. He also highlights the fact that, starting in the last quarter of the seventh century, substantial quantities of pottery and luxury items produced in Laconia wound up on Samos, either as dedications at the Heraion or as grave goods in the West Necropolis (on which see Section 3.4C.3) (Cartledge 1982: 252–6; see also now Stibbe 1997; Pipili 2001; Pipili 2004; Carty 2015: 66–73 and the cautionary notes in Schaus 2018). That the objects in question were not simply exchanged through a process of depersonalized commerce is evident from a bronze cauldron attachment in the form of a couchant lion, found at the Samian Heraion and dated to c. 550, which bears the inscription "Eumnastos, a Spartiate, to Hera" (*IG* XII.6.2.540; see Figure 3.20 below). As we have seen, the Laconian objects from the West Necropolis come from a limited number of graves, which led Mariaud to argue that the graves in question belonged to a particular group of individuals who had a special interest in highlighting a strong connection to Sparta (Mariaud 2015a).[172]

It is thus probable that certain Samians from influential families could call upon long-standing relationships with equally influential individuals in Sparta. Those Samians, who may have both disliked Polycrates and been opposed to a rapprochement with the Persians, persuaded the Spartans and their Corinthian allies to intervene on their behalf against Polycrates. In an Archaic context, gratitude and revenge seem entirely appropriate grounds for action (Baragwanath 2008: 88–96).

---

172. It is interesting to note that the Aristotelian *Constitution of the Lacedaemonians* (F611.10 Rose; cf. Plut. *Lyc.* 4.4) claims that Lycurgus went to Samos and received there the text of the Homeric poems. See Section 3.12C.2.

Political turmoil on Samos led to further overseas ventures. In the period of Polycrates' reign, two separate groups of exiles founded settlements at Dikaiarcheia in southern Italy (Fischer-Hansen, Nielsen, and Ampolo 2004: 256) and at Cydonia in Crete (Perlman 2004: 1170–2). The history of the latter group is particularly illustrative of the fine line between settlers and pirates (de Souza 1999: 22–6). We have seen (see Section 3.5C.2) that the Samians (and not just Polycrates) were experienced freebooters. Following the Spartans' unsuccessful attempt to restore them, the Samian exiles, who had originally been dispatched on triremes to Egypt and hence had warships at their disposal, raided the wealthy *polis* of Siphnos and wrested an island, Hydra, from the *polis* of Hermione. Although their ultimate plan was to expel the Zacynthians and take over their land, they settled in Crete and founded Cydonia (Hdt. 3.58–9). There they became such a nuisance that the Aeginetans and Cretans attacked them, defeated them in a naval battle, and enslaved the survivors (Harvey 1988).

Although Polycrates managed to defeat the expeditionary force sent by Sparta and Corinth, his reign came to an end shortly thereafter. Polycrates' display of piety at Delos in conquering and dedicating Rheneia and founding a festival (see Section 3.12A) may have been a response to the increasing pressure he felt from the Persians and part of an attempt to build support in the Greek world. The end came sometime around 522, as a result of intrigues set in motion by Oroites, a Persian satrap based in Sardis. According to Herodotus, the only substantive source for this part of Samian history, Oroites sent a Lydian to Polycrates with the message that Oroites was in ill favor with Cambyses and that he wished to flee to Samos, with the promise that he would enrich Polycrates from the funds at his disposal and with the offer to receive an envoy from Polycrates who could confirm that Oroites was wealthy. Polycrates thereupon sent his secretary Maiandrios to Oroites, who tricked Maiandrios by showing him chests mostly filled with stones, on top of which Oroites placed a thin layer of gold. Polycrates was ensnared by Oroites' plot and went to the mainland to meet him, despite advice to the contrary from seers, family, and friends. Oroites took Polycrates prisoner, killed him in some horrible but unspecified fashion, and crucified him (3.122–5).

Herodotus' account of the motivations of both parties leaves something to be desired.[173] He says that most believed that Oroites was angry because he had been taunted by another satrap about his inability to conquer Samos (3.120.2–4) and that some believed that Polycrates had intentionally or unintentionally insulted a herald sent by Oroites (3.121). Herodotus then adds that Oroites knew that Polycrates' ambition was to establish a thalassocracy (θαλασσοκρατέειν ἐπενοήθη;

---

173. See Carty 2015: 208–20 for a detailed analysis of the relevant sections of Herodotus' work.

3.122.1–2), which implies that Oroites' motives were political rather than personal. As for Polycrates, Herodotus explicitly states that he "was . . . very fond of money" (ἱμείρετο . . . χρημάτων μεγάλως; 3.123.1). That meshes with a story told by Diodorus (10.16) to the effect that Polycrates (presumably shortly after the Persian conquest in 546) welcomed a group of wealthy suppliants from Lydia but subsequently slaughtered them and confiscated their possessions (see also Section 3.8C.4 on issues of lead coins by Samos, possibly to discharge state debt). Polycrates may have had similar plans for Oroites, but it is also possible that Polycrates hoped to exploit Oroites' position and influence to foment a rebellion against the Persians.

After Polycrates' death, the tyranny passed to Maiandrios, and it has been suggested that since Oroites did not invade Samos upon killing Polycrates, Maiandrios must have actively plotted with Oroites to remove Polycrates (Carty 2015: 217–21). Sometime around 517, Maiandrios, who initially seems to have wished to abdicate the tyranny (see Section 3.5C.4), was removed, and Polycrates' brother Syloson, with Persian aid, became tyrant instead.[174] The Persian army that came to Samos to install Syloson in power evidently inflicted substantial casualties (Hdt. 3.147; Arist. F574 Rose; though cf. Constantakopoulou 2007: 126–9).

With Syloson holding the tyranny, Samos came under Persian control for the first time, and Syloson's son and successor Aiakes took part in Darius' campaign in Scythia in 513 (Hdt. 4.138.2). It is noteworthy that the exiled Cyrenaean monarch Arcesilas III, who Medized after the conquest of Egypt in 525, came to Samos during Syloson's tyranny to recruit troops to help restore him to the throne (Hdt. 3.13.3–4, 4.162–4; Schaus Forthcoming: Section 1.3).

The Samians joined the Ionian Rebellion in 499 and deposed Aiakes (6.13.2).[175] Samian ships fought with distinction in a sea battle against the Phoenicians, off the coast of Cyprus in 497 (Hdt. 5.112.1). Although the Samians sent 60 triremes to the Battle of Lade (Hdt. 6.8.1), most of the Samian captains, concerned about the Ionians' prospects, seem to have deserted their posts and sailed away (Hdt. 6.13–14)—perhaps an indication of considerable internal dissension in Samos about the wisdom of revolting against the Persians. Aiakes, who had sent a messenger to the Samian fleet at Lade to encourage desertion, was returned to power

---

174. Oroites seems to have allied himself with the losing side in the power struggle in the Persian court that followed Cambyses' death in 522, and the newly installed Darius may have wished to remove Maiandrios to ensure that a loyal subordinate was in charge of Samos (Briant 2002: 97–106; Carty 2015: 218). Maiandrios eventually ended up at Sparta, where he (unsuccessfully) asked for assistance (Hdt. 3.148) so he could regain the tyranny.

175. See n. 38.

by the Persians, and Samos escaped punishment from the Persians because of the desertion of the Samian fleet at Lade (Hdt. 6.25.1). Sometime after 479 and a change of regime in Samos, the small group of Samian trierarchs that had insisted on fighting at Lade received an honorific monument in the agora of Samos Town (Hdt. 6.14.3).

After the Battle of Lade, a group of Samians responded to a request for settlers from the inhabitants of Sicilian Zancle, who were planning to found a colony at Kale Akte on the north coast of Sicily. However, Anaxilas, the tyrant of Rhegium (on the other side of the Strait of Messina from Zancle), convinced the Samians to seize Zancle while its citizens were away at war (Hdt. 6.22–4; cf. Arist. *Pol.* 5.1303a35–6). The obverses of Zanclaian coins dated to the years 494/3–489/7 feature types taken from Samian coinage (see Section 3.8C.4), and the Samian *samaina* (see Section 3.5C.2) appears on the reverses (Barron 1964: 40–3).

Although the Persians seem to have removed the tyrants ruling over the Greek cities in Ionia in 492 (see Section 3.5C.4), Samos remained firmly in the Persian empire, and Samians fought on the Persian side at the Battle of Salamis. One of the Samian trierarchs at Salamis, Theomestor, was rewarded for distinguished service at Salamis by being made tyrant of Samos (Hdt. 8.85). Behind Xerxes' back, an embassy of Samian elites approached the Greek fleet at Delos and convinced the Spartan king Leotychidas to initiate the campaign that led to the Battle of Mycale in 479 (Hdt. 9.90.1–92.1). In making their dispositions for that battle, the Persian commanders suspected the loyalty of the Samians, who had at some earlier point released 500 Athenian prisoners taken captive by the Persian army while it was in Attica. As a result, the Samian soldiers were disarmed before the battle, and in the fighting, the Samians supplied assistance of some unspecified kind to the Greek forces (Hdt. 9.99.1–2, 9.103.2). After the battle, the Greek fleet sailed to Samos, where the Chians, Lesbians, and Samians (among others) became sworn members of the Hellenic League; they subsequently joined the Delian League at its formation (Hdt. 9.92.1, 9.106.4; Thuc. 1.96; [Arist.] *Ath. Pol.* 23.5, 24.2).

## *3.8C. Samian Economic History*
### 3.8C.1. Agriculture and Animal Husbandry

Strabo reports that Samos was fertile but, unlike Chios and Lesbos, not a noted source of fine wine:

> The island does not produce good wine, although good wine is produced by the islands all round, and although most of the whole of the adjacent mainland produces the best of wines, for example, Chios and Lesbos and

Cos. . . . Now Samos is not altogether fortunate in regard to wines, but in all other respects it is a blest country, as is clear from the fact that it became an object of contention in war, and also from the fact that those who praise it do not hesitate to apply to it the proverb, that "it produces even birds' milk," as Menander somewhere says. (14.1.5; trans. H. L. Jones; see Meyer 2012: 359–70 for a listing of ancient literary sources on agriculture on Samos)

Despite its fertility, the size and topography of Samos (see Section 3.3C) placed inherent limitations on agricultural production, and given what is known about population levels (see Section 3.9C), it is likely that cereal imports were already a necessity by the end of the Archaic period (see Bissa 2009: 197–8 for detailed calculations).[176]

The Samian *peraia* was a key source of grain for the island's inhabitants in the Hellenistic period and almost certainly in the Archaic and Classical periods as well. A Samian decree from c. 200 (*IG* XII.6.1.172) records the establishment of a capital endowment, the funds in which were to be loaned out at interest and the proceeds used to purchase wheat. The wheat in question came in the first instance from the grain collected via a 5% in-kind tax imposed on cereal production in the *peraia* and payable to the overseers of the Heraion. Further purchases could be made either from the *peraia* or from elsewhere (Shipley 1987: 218–21; Osborne 1987: 97). The ferocity with which the Samians defended their mainland possessions (see Section 3.7C) from an early period can be traced in part to the agricultural importance of the *peraia*. The hilly terrain of Samos and of Mt. Mycale in its *peraia* did, however, provide ample pasturage for flocks (Shipley 1987: 18–19).[177]

We can assume, therefore, that the Samians did not export grain, but the large number of Samian transport amphoras discovered throughout the Mediterranean suggests that the Samians did produce some agricultural goods for export. The amphoras are distinctive (Grace 1971; cf. Dupont 2001), characterized by an ovoid body and a beveled ring foot as well as by their fabric, and have an interesting distribution pattern. While Samian amphoras dated to the sixth century are regularly found in Italy (Etruria and Sicily) and the western Mediterranean, they also appear in the Black Sea and eastern Aegean (Cook and Dupont 1998: 164–5; Monakhov [Monachov] and Kuznetsova 2017: 67–9). Anacreon's lyrics make

---

176. For an overview of agricultural production on Samos, see Shipley 1987: 15–20.

177. The various animals that Polycrates is reported as having collected (see, for example, Alexis *FGrH* 539 F2) were probably intended more for display than as a means of promoting economic growth (Shipley 1987: 82–3; Günther 1999; though cf. Galvagno 1994: 26–30).

mention of Samos' olive trees (F443 Page), Aeschylus describes Samos as "olive-planted" (*Pers.* 882), and Athenaeus (66f) recalls that either Antiphanes or Alexis (both of whom were active in the fourth century) praised Samian olive oil as the "clearest of all." One of the papyri (56015r) in the Zenon archive (from third-century Egypt) records the arrival of a pricey shipment of olive oil from Samos, and it is generally presumed that Samian amphoras were exported full of olive oil from an early date.

## 3.8C.2. Natural Resources and Craft Activity

Both Samos and its *peraia* contained valuable natural resources. Strabo describes Mt. Mycale as *eudendron*, and building accounts from Eleusis (*IG* II$^2$.1672.62–5, 93–4; Meiggs 1982: 211, 434–5) show that timber (probably pine or oak) was shipped from Samos to Attica in the fourth century. Samos was also the site of substantial emery quarries (Stamatakis and Malegiannaki 2018). It is probable that Samians exploited and exported both timber and emery during the Archaic period. A large quarry found at Agiades, c. 2.5 km northwest of Samos Town, was the source of much of the *poros* limestone used in Archaic building projects in Samos Town and at the Heraion (H. J. Kienast 2012–2013; Tziligkaki and Stamatakis 2018).

Samos was also the source of a product known as "Samian earth" (*Samia gē*). Theophrastus describes Samian earth as "greasy, dense, and smooth" and supplies information about how it was extracted:

> It is not possible to stand upright while digging in the pits of Samos, but a man has to lie on his back or his side. The vein stretches for a long way and is about two feet in height, though much greater in depth. It is surrounded on both sides by stones and is taken out from the space between them. It has a stratum right through the middle, and this is better than the parts on the outside; and then it has another stratum, and still another, up to four ... [hiatus in the manuscript]. The innermost earth is called "the star." This earth is used mainly or solely for clothes. (*De lapidibus* 62–4; trans. E. Caley and J. Richards)

Later writers (Dioscorides *De materia medica* 5.171; Pliny *HN* 35.191; and Galen *De simplicium medicamentorum temperamentis ac facultatibus* 9) make it clear that *kollourion* was a variety of Samian earth that differed from "the star" (*kollourion* presumably came from the outer sections of the relevant veins). Ancient literary sources and modern research suggest that Samian earth was mined in the western part of the island, near the modern town of Platanos (Shipley 1987: 277–8).

The material that Theophrastus calls Samian earth was probably bentonite clay in which small quantities of boron were present. Bentonite is relatively common in the Aegean (the island of Melos is currently the site of one of the largest bentonite mines in the world), but boron-based minerals are rare. Bentonite is a highly absorptive material, and in the present day, it is used in (among many other things) pharmaceuticals, cosmetics, detergents, stain removers, paints, and paper. Theophrastus mentions its use in clothes (as a whitening and cleaning agent), whereas other sources (e.g., the Hippocratic *On the Nature of Women* 50; see Meyer 2012: 345–58 for full references) state that it was used to treat a range of medical conditions including bleeding, inflammation, and eye pain. Recent experiments have shown that the boron in the bentonite clays from Samos gives Samian earth strong antibacterial properties (Photos-Jones, Keane, Jones, et al. 2015; Koutsopoulou, Christos, and Marantos 2016). The rarity of boron in the Aegean meant that Samian earth was a rather special version of an otherwise common mineral.

The particular properties of Samian earth seem to have made it a valuable commodity. Ephorus (*FGrH* 70 59a–b) states that a Samian named Mandroboulos discovered a "mine of earth" (*geōphanion*, almost certainly a site for the mining of Samian earth) on the island and that he made a successively diminishing series of dedications (presumably at the Heraion), starting with a large gold ram and ending with a small bronze ram (see the commentary by Victor Parker at *BNJ* 70 F59b). The appearance of Samian earth in the Hippocratic corpus indicates that its medicinal qualities were prized from an early date, and it is possible that some of the small, closed vessels exported from Samos in the Archaic period contained cosmetics or medicines made with Samian earth.

A diverse collection of evidence bears witness to considerable craft activity on Samos during the Archaic period. Pottery produced in Samos was shipped to various parts of the Mediterranean, and excavations at the Heraion have shown that pottery workshops were present in that part of Samos in the Archaic period (Kyrieleis 1993: 111 with references). Molds for terracotta *korai* figurines found at the Sanctuary of Demeter and Persephone on the west side of Samos Town attest to the existence of coroplastic workshops on Samos in the Archaic period (Touratsoglou and Tsakos 2008: 108 n. 14; Tsakos and Giannakopoulos 2014: 233). The dedications of numerous stone statues (starting in the sixth century) carved from Samian marble in the Heraion and elsewhere on Samos demonstrate that quarrying and sculpting of high-quality stone took place on the island (see Section 3.12C.1 for further discussion of Rhoikos, Theodorus, and Archaic statuary from Samos).

Finds from Samos Town and the Heraion of stone molds for the manufacture of bronze fibulas and waste metal from bronze casting show that metalworking was carried out on the island starting in the Late Geometric period at the latest. This may also be suggested by the presence of dedications of bronze ingots at the Heraion (Kyrieleis 1990: 23–4; Touratsoglou and Tsakos 2008: 107). Pausanias, writing in the second century CE, asserts at several points in his *Description of Greece* (8.14.5–8; 9.9.41.1; 10.38.6; cf. Pliny *HN* 35.152) that the Samians Rhoikos and Theodorus were instrumental in the introduction of lost-wax bronze casting to the Aegean world (see discussion in Kyrieleis 1990). This tradition is not supported by the archaeological evidence, which demonstrates clearly that Crete maintained a continuous tradition of lost-wax bronze casting from the Middle Bronze Age through the Early Iron Age. Pausanias describes the use of the lost-wax technique as following an era characterized by the use of the *sphyrelaton* technique, which involved hammering and piecing bronze elements together and which postdates the production of small, lost-wax cast statuettes by several centuries. On this evidence, it seems reasonable to suggest that Pausanias is crediting the Samians with developing a technique for creating large (i.e., life-size or larger) statues by melting and casting bronze, rather than with developing the method of lost-wax casting more generally. Samos' proximity to Egypt and Mesopotamia, both with long traditions of lost-wax bronze casting, may have facilitated a technological transfer at an early date. Archaeological evidence for the prominent role of Samians in pioneering craft traditions related to large-scale indirect lost-wax casting is ambiguous. The quality of small-scale cast bronzes, especially griffin protomes (see Section 3.4C.4.3) and anthropomorphic and zoomorphic figurines, found at the Heraion is indeed impressive, but no fragments of large bronze statues dated to the Archaic period survive (Kyrieleis 1990: 20–9). In any case, the later traditions probably represent a garbled memory of a period during which Samians were respected as skilled metallurgists.

The Samians' maritime activity, both commercial and military, was predicated on a ready supply of ships, and there can be little doubt that the building and maintenance of ships occupied more than a few Samians throughout the Archaic period. Thucydides (1.13.3) claims that the Corinthian shipwright Ameinokles went to Samos sometime around 700 and oversaw the construction of four warships,[178] and the Samians themselves invented a bireme, the *samaina* (Morrison and Coates 1996: 181–4). The size of the fleet at Polycrates' disposal (100 penteconters and at least 40 triremes, see Section 3.5C.2) makes it very likely that Samos was equipped with dockyards in the sixth century, and there is some literary evidence for shipsheds in Samos Town during Polycrates' reign (see Section

---

178. Whether or not the warships in question were triremes remains the subject of ongoing debate (see, for example, Wallinga 1993: 13–15; Figueira 2015).

## 3.8C.3. Commerce

Samos is located where the main cross-Aegean sea route intersected with the main sea route along the coast of Asia Minor. As a result, the island was "the pivot of navigation for Western Asia Minor" (Roebuck 1959: 6). The Samians were in a prime position to profit in a variety of ways from maritime activity, and Ioannis Touratsoglou and Konstantinos Tsakos are well justified in highlighting the Samians' "intensive mobility" starting in the eighth century (Touratsoglou and Tsakos 2008: 106). That mobility is reflected in dedications of full-size and model boats at the Heraion (see Section 3.4C.4.4) and in the remarkable range of provenances of the votives deposited at the Heraion during the Archaic period. Imma Kilian-Dirlmeier's study of eighth- and seventh-century dedications at the Heraion showed that more than two-thirds of the objects that did not come from Samos itself were probably manufactured outside of the region generally identified as culturally Greek during the Archaic period (Kilian-Dirlmeier 1985: 235–43, 48–53; see also Mylonopoulos 2008: 368–70).

As we have seen (see Section 3.5C.2), the overseas ventures of the Samians often took the form of piracy, but Samians were also energetic merchants from an early date. The Samian merchant who stands out in the extant ancient sources is Kolaios, who, according to Herodotus (4.152; cf. 1.163), was blown off course during a trading voyage to Egypt and found himself at Tartessus, on the southern coast of Iberia, just beyond the Strait of Gibraltar. The cargo on Kolaios' ship found a ready market at Tartessus, and he returned to Samos after having turned an immense profit (Herodotus says 60 *talanta*), a tithe of which he and his crew used to dedicate an enormous bronze cauldron at the Heraion.[179] Herodotus synchronizes Kolaios' journey with the foundation of Cyrene, and hence it can be dated to the later decades of the seventh century (see Schaus Forthcoming: Section 1.3.4 for the foundation date of Cyrene).

Kolaios' journey is presented by Herodotus as a fortuitous event, but the archaeological evidence shows that there was a major change in trade networks in the western Mediterranean in the late seventh and early sixth centuries, when goods from Ionia (including Samian cups, hydriai, and amphoras)

---

179. There is no good reason to believe that any of the extant ship dedications at the Heraion can be ascribed to Kolaios; see Section 3.4C.4.4. See Section 3.4C.4.3 for discussion of Kolaios' dedication at the Heraion.

begin to appear in significant quantities for the first time. The dedication at the Samian Heraion in the late seventh century of luxury objects (e.g., ivory combs) produced in Phoenician workshops in Iberia is a reflection of the emergence of new commercial connections (Freyer-Schauenburg 1966a: 104–10; Freyer-Schauenburg 1966b). The presence of Etruscan pottery at coastal sites in Iberia and in Ionia (including the Samian Heraion; Naso 2000) suggests that at least some of that commerce was carried on by Etruscan intermediaries (Aubet 2007).

Some sense of how such commerce worked can be had from a shipwreck found near the island of Giglio (located off the west coast of Italy, c. 140 km northwest of Rome) (Bound 1991). That wreck can be dated by its contents to the first quarter of the sixth century. The cargo consisted of a mixture of luxury and utilitarian goods, including pottery (both fine-ware and transport amphoras), unfinished granite anchor stocks, several auloi, a highly ornate wooden couch, a silver jug, iron spits, and copper and lead ingots. Some of the objects recovered from the wreck were almost certainly the personal possessions of the crew. Of particular note in the present context are the four distinct groups of amphoras among the cargo: Etruscan, East Greek, Phoenician Punic, and Samian. Some of the Etruscan amphoras contained olives, others pitch. A reasonable presumption is that the Samian amphoras on the ship contained olive oil (see Section 3.8C.1). It is possible that some or all of the 28 Corinthian and six Laconian aryballoi found on the ship were filled with unguents or medicines produced with Samian olive oil or with Samian earth (Shipley 1987: 61). The ship and crew have been variously identified as Etruscan or East Greek (see, for example, Cristofani 1992–1993).

Although the evidence leaves no doubt that Samians had commercial connections that stretched to the western Mediterranean, the focus of their maritime activities in the Archaic period was in the eastern Mediterranean.[180] Cyprus played a key role in these activities from an early date. The outposts the Samians established in Cilicia early in the Archaic period probably served as helpful waypoints on journeys to Cyprus (see Section 3.7C). The importance of Cyprus to Samos is reflected in the discovery at the Heraion of more than 1,000 limestone and terracotta Cypriot and Cypriot-style figurines dating to the seventh century (Schmidt 1968: 54–67, 99–103; Kyrieleis 1989; Henke 2019: 251–61). It seems that Cypriot and Cypriot-style figurines were the predominant type of figurine dedicated in the Heraion during this period, almost completely replacing the

---

180. For a general study of the commodities exchanged between the Aegean and the Levant in the sixth through fourth centuries, see van Alfen 2002.

local style of figurines produced on Samos in the eighth century. The appearance on Samos of a substantial amount of such material starting around 670 strongly hints at close connections between the residents of the two islands.

The Samians no doubt found much of value on Cyprus,[181] but it also probably served as an important way station on voyages to Egypt. Most of the terracotta figurines produced on Cyprus and found at the Heraion come from the southeastern part of Cyprus (Karageorghis, Kourou, Kilikoglou, et al. 2009), which may offer some indication of the patterns of seaborne movement. Samians and other Greeks of the eastern Aegean and Asia Minor were active at the *emporion* of Naucratis in Egypt that was founded in the late seventh century (Shipley 1987: 56–9; see Section 3.8A.3 for further discussion of the foundation and organization of Naucratis).

Unlike the Chians and the Mytileneans, Samians were not involved with the Hellenion sanctuary at Naucratis and so presumably were not represented among the overseers (*prostatai*) of the *emporion*. They did, however, manage their own sanctuary which was dedicated, appropriately, to Hera (Hdt. 2.178). The presence in Naucratis of vases with *dipinti* to Hera that precisely match vases found at the Samian Heraion indicates that something akin to a direct transfer of cult may have taken place (Schlotzhauer 2006: 311–13). Samian contact with Egypt through Naucratis is also reflected in the finds from the Heraion, including faience figurines (Webb 2016; Webb 2021) and two colossal *kouroi* (see Sections 3.4C.4.5 and 3.5C.1) that have strong Egyptian antecedents. Herodotus (2.182) states that the pharaoh Amasis sent two wooden statues of himself to the Samian Heraion and that they were still standing in the Temple of Hera in his time. Egyptian influence is also evident in onomastics, with names based on the Nile river appearing on Samos in the Archaic period and later.[182] Alain Duplouy posits the existence of what he calls an "*égyptomanie ambiante*" on Samos in the sixth century (Duplouy 2006: 203).

---

181. Plutarch (*Mor.* 303c) preserves stories about a Samian named Dexicreon, who is characterized as being either a sorcerer or a ship captain who, in obedience to instructions from Aphrodite, put a great deal of water on board his ship before setting off on a voyage to Cyprus. When the winds suddenly died and stranded many ships on the open sea, Dexicreon made a fortune selling them water and afterward made a dedication to Aphrodite.

182. E.g., *IG* XII.6.2.631 (Nelon son of Herophilos, early fifth century). Although they fall outside of the chronological scope of this study, it is worth noting the honorific epigram (*IG* XII.6.1.279 = Osborne and Rhodes 2017: 110a) for Hegesagoras son of Zoilos, who fought in the Egyptian campaign waged by the Delian League in the mid-fifth century (Thuc. 1.104) and captured 15 Phoenician ships at Memphis, and the remarkable honorific inscription granted by King Inaros of Egypt himself to Leokritos the son of Iphi-, presumably a Samian (*IG* XII.6.2.468 = Osborne and Rhodes 2017: 110b), both from the Heraion.

## 3.8C.4. Coinage

The Samians struck both electrum and silver coins in the Archaic period (Barron 1966: 14–39; Konuk 2005; Psoma 2016: 94–5; Gitler, Goren, Konuk, et al. 2020: 385). The electrum mintages date to c. 600–c. 525 and came in denominations starting at the *statēr* and going down to 1/64th of a *statēr*. Unlike most of the electrum coinage produced in Ionia in the Archaic period, the Samian electrum issues were on the Euboic standard (based on a 17.4-g *statēr*) rather than the Milesian standard (based on a 14.2-g *statēr*). The obverses of the Samians' electrum coins were marked by an eagle, a duck, or the head of a lioness (or panther); the reverses were marked by an incuse square or two incuse rectangles (with the varying markings on the reverse serving as indications of the denomination of the coin). Although the weights of Samian electrum coins are consistent, the relatively limited number of known examples show a wide range of composition, with the percentage of the total weight coming from gold varying from less than 50% to more than 80%. An inscription from the Heraion on a marble *stēlē* dated to c. 580 (*IG* XII.6.2.577.15–19) records a series of votives that the dedicants (from the Samian colony of Perinthus) purchased for the sum of 212 Samian *statēres* (along with the *stēlē* itself).

Sometime around 525, the Samians phased out the minting of electrum and began issuing silver coins on the Euboic standard, in denominations of *tetradrachmon*, *triōbolon*, and *obolos*. The most common set of markings on those coins was initially a winged boar on the obverse and a lion mask on the reverse, a pairing that was superseded by a lion's mask on the obverse and a bovid head on the reverse (see Figure 3.18). The lion and the bovid were both closely linked to Hera. The story

FIGURE 3.18. Samian silver *drachmē*; c. 525; weight: 3.48 g. American Numismatics Society 1977.158.383.

that Ankaios, the legendary first king of Samos, was killed by a boar (Aristotle F571 Rose), perhaps inspired the winged boar (Barron 1966: 1–5, 19–39), though that iconography may alternatively have referenced a type of ship developed in Samos, the *samaina*, which had a boar's-head prow (see Section 3.5C.2).

A series of electrum coins on the Milesian standard has been interpreted as an alliance coinage minted by the Greek cities that took part in the Ionian Rebellion. All of these coins feature an incuse square on the reverse and a variety of obverses that may reflect types associated with particular cities, including the bovid found on many Samian coins (Konuk 2012: 55). Serious doubts have been raised about that reading of the coins (Wartenberg 2020), and van Alfen has more recently interpreted those coins as part of a series issued as a cooperative coinage by Samos and subject allies under the leadership of Polycrates (see Section 3.5C.2).

Herodotus (3.56.2) reports, but dismisses, a story to the effect that the Spartans who laid siege to Samos Town (see Section 3.7C) were bought off by Polycrates using gilded lead coins. Lead coins, evidently without any trace of gilding, have been found in Samos and its *peraia*. Those coins, which seem to have been produced over an extended period of time in the sixth century (presumably with intermittent minting), starting well before Polycrates' tyranny, show a wide variety of types on the obverses (e.g., Chimaera, dog, and lotus flowers) and two incuse rectangles on the reverse (Barron 1966: 17–18; Konuk 2012: 54). It is probable that these lead coins, like the billon coins issued by Mytilene (see Section 3.8B.4), served as a locally valid token coinage that was perhaps issued in order to discharge debts owed by the *polis* at a lower cost than would otherwise have been possible (Furtwängler 2010). The Samians' creative financial maneuvers were not limited to the production of token coinage, since there is reason to believe that they purposefully added copper to their electrum coinages to make it appear to have more gold than it in fact did and thereby raise its value (Konuk 2005).

## 3.9 C. Samian Familial/Demographic History

The total population of the island of Samos in the early fifth century has been estimated at c. 50,000, based on the number of ships supplied at Lade in 494 (Roebuck 1959: 21–3; Shipley 1987: 14–15; Hansen 2008: 270; Greaves 2010: 93).[183] According to the Aristotelian *Constitution of the Samians* (F575 Rose), the Samians, having been crushed (καταπονηθέντες) by tyrants, offered

---

183. Insofar as there is reason to believe that much of the space within its sixth-century fortification walls was unoccupied (see Section 3.4C.1), it is impossible to produce anything resembling an accurate estimate of the population of Samos Town in the Archaic period.

FIGURE 3.19. The Geneleos group from the Samian Heraion; mid-sixth century. Archaeological Museum, Vathy.

to enroll slaves among the citizen body in return for a payment of five *statēres*. This fragment is preserved in the work of Photius (ninth century CE), and the passage from which it comes offers no specific chronological indications. It can perhaps be most plausibly assigned to the second half of the sixth century (Carty 2015: 204), when the population of Samos was reduced by, among other things, the departure and ultimate exile of the crews of 40 triremes sent to Egypt by Polycrates (see Section 3.5C.2) and by the casualties inflicted by the Persians when they took control over the island after the death of Polycrates (see Section 3.7C).

Little is known about any Samian family from the Archaic period outside of the tyrannical dynasty. However, the Heraion, through the so-called Geneleos monument, affords us a glimpse into Samian family life (see Figure 3.19). This group of six statues on a single base, dating to the mid-sixth century, originally stood along the north side of the Sacred Way (Freyer-Schauenburg 1974: 58–63). The group takes its name from the signature inscribed on the far left figure (from the viewer's perspective), that of a seated female: "Geneleos made us." That figure also has an inscribed name: Phileia (*IG* XII.6.2.559A). The two statues to the right of Phileia survive only in highly fragmentary condition. The statue immediately next to Phileia has been identified by some scholars as a young boy holding an aulos; the next statue to the right seems to have been a standing *korē*. The next two statues to the right, both largely intact, are almost identical, approximately life-size (1.6 m high without plinth) standing *korai*, carrying inscriptions

420   THE OXFORD HISTORY OF THE ARCHAIC GREEK WORLD

that identify them as Philippe and Ornithe (*IG* XII.6.2.559D–E). A fragmentary reclining figure rounds out the group, literally and figuratively: in addition to occupying the far right space on the base, it possesses a markedly lumpy physique, with ample stomach and chest protruding from beneath its clothing. That statue carries a damaged inscription that seems to read: [— c. 4–5 —]|. αρχης ἡμέ[α]ς ἀ[ν]έθηκε τῆι Ἥρηι. (*IG* XII.6.2.559F).

For reasons of appearance, this statue was originally interpreted as female, and the entire group was thought to be a college of priestesses of Hera. The *communis opinio*, however, now reads the name ending of the last figure as masculine -αρχης and the group as a family, with the mother and father flanking their four children, three daughters and a son (see, for example, Duplouy 2006: 195–7; Baughan 2011; Fullerton 2016: 34–6). The male head of the household, -αρχης, would then be responsible for making the dedication. He reclines because he is a symposiast, as further indicated by the drinking horn in his hand and the wineskin serving as a pillow beneath him. His rotund figure is not a mark of femininity but is instead a proud declaration of his luxurious lifestyle, in line with ancient stereotypes about Ionian *habrosynē* (Kurke 1992).[184]

As noted above (see Section 3.5C.1), Cheramyes dedicated four statues at the Heraion in the first half of the sixth century. Each statue carries a complete dedicatory inscription naming Cheramyes as the donor (*IG* XII.6.2.558A–D). Two of those statues are identical, greater than life-size (1.92 m without base) *korai*; one is an approximately life-size (1.67 m without base) *korē* clutching a hare; and one is a now-fragmentary *kouros* that would have been more than 2 m tall in its original state.[185] None of those statues was found in its original position in the sanctuary, so it is impossible to know for certain where they originally stood or whether they were grouped together in a single place in the sanctuary. Some have interpreted them as a family group, along the lines of the Geneleos group, that once stood on a single base, but others have rejected that interpretation because two of the *korai* are greater than life-size (and therefore have been interpreted as representations of Hera) and because the repetition of full dedicatory inscriptions on each statue suggests that they could not all be viewed at the same time (Bumke 2004: 90–5; Duplouy 2006: 197–203).

We can be tolerably certain that the Samians' "intensive mobility" (see Section 3.8C.3) during the Archaic period resulted in a certain number of Samians taking

---

184. Note also Herodotus occasionally calling the wealthy "the thick," οἱ παχέες: 5.30.1, 5.77.2, 6.91.1, 7.156.2.

185. Fragments of another *korē* from the Heraion have been speculatively identified as another dedication by Cheramyes; see Moustaka 2001.

spouses from outside Samos. Here again, the finds from the Heraion are relevant, because they include an Egyptian bronze mirror from the third quarter of the seventh century with incised decoration showing an Egyptian temple in which a robed woman stands before an enthroned goddess (Jantzen 1972: 33–5 B432). The mirror has a two-line dedicatory inscription in Egyptian hieroglyphics: "A dedication of the servant of Mut, Mistress of Heaven. She gives life, salvation, and health. [Anat . . .]. Your mother is [ . . . ]" (trans. P. Munro). The dedicator was a female and possibly, like the figure depicted in the temple, a priestess of Mut, the closest Egyptian equivalent to Hera. Katja Weiss has suggested that the mirror was dedicated by the wife of a Samian mercenary who had married while working in Egypt (Weiss 2012: 510; though cf. the cautionary comments at Villing 2017: 568–9).

## *3.10 C. Samian Social Customs and Institutions*

The male figure in the Geneleos group (see Section 3.9C) is represented in the act of participating in a banquet, which is consonant with the fact that during the Archaic period, Samian elites, like their peers elsewhere in Ionia, had a reputation for living well (Kurke 1992). The lifestyle of those Samians is eloquently described by the poet Asius of Samos:

> And they would go like that, when they had combed their locks, to Hera's precinct, wrapped in fine garments, in snowy tunics reaching down to the ground(?) [the Greek is corrupt]; there were gold brooches on them, like crickets; their hair floated in the wind, bound in gold; round their arms there were ornate bracelets. (F13 Bernabé *apud* Ath. 12.525e–6a, quoting the Samian historian Duris (*FGrH* 76 F60); trans. M. L. West)

Much is uncertain about this fragment, starting with the date of its author, but it can most plausibly be placed in the sixth century (Veneri 1984; Casadio 2004: 138–9; Condello 2020).

As one would expect, Samians seem to have engaged regularly in athletics during the Archaic period. At least one of the festivals held at the Heraion (see Section 3.11C.1) included athletic contests, almost certainly starting in the Archaic period (Nielsen 2018: 78–9, 149–50). A fragment from the third-century philosopher Hieronymos of Rhodes (F34 Wehrli) suggests that there were *palaistrai* in Samos in the sixth century. The second-century CE author Zenobius claims (6.15) that when Polycrates dedicated Rheneia to Delos, he also founded an *agōn* (no further details are given) that presumably formed part of the festival he established (see Section 3.12A).

Samians participated in the Olympics from an early date. The first-known Samian Olympic victor is Pythagoras son of Crates (not the philosopher, on whom see Section 3.12C.2), who achieved a victory in boxing in 588. According to Erastothenes, Pythagoras wore his hair long and dressed in a purple robe and was the first Greek athlete to box "scientifically" (ἐντέχνως) (*FGrH* 241 F11a; Moretti 1957: #88). Euthymenes of Samos won an Olympic victory in one of the combat-sport events in 532 (Moretti 1957: #123).

The finds from the Samian Heraion include many sherds from Panathenaic prize amphoras, most dating to the first quarter of the fifth century. Presuming that the amphoras in question were dedicated by Samian athletes who had been victorious at the Panathenaic Games, the finds from the Heraion attest to Samian athletes competing in running events, wrestling, and the pentathlon, as well as in horse and chariot races (Kreuzer 2017: 1–48).

The Samians were members of the Ionian League and took part in the Panionia festival hosted at the Sanctuary of Poseidon Helikonios. The Samians, like the Chians, probably had a strong sense of Ionian identity that derived from membership in the Ionian League (see Section 3.10A).

## 3.11C. Samian Religious Customs and Institutions
### 3.11C.1. Cult of Hera and the Heraion

The most prominent Samian cult was that of Hera. That she was the patron deity of Samos is not explicitly stated by our sources in the Archaic period, but Hera represents the *polis* of Samos in an Athenian document relief of 405/4 (Meiggs and Lewis 1988: 283–4; Lawton 1995: 88–9 #12) and is designated as ἀρχηγέτις τῆς πόλεως in later inscriptions (e.g., *IG* XII.6.1.7 l. 46, second century; on the epithet, cf. Cole 1995: 305).[186]

The most important festival celebrated at the Heraion was the Toneia (or Tonaia or Tonea; the form of the name is uncertain).[187] Our main source for the Toneia is Athenaeus 15.671e–4b. In a passage devoted to the explanation of Anacreon F352 Page, he quotes a long aetiological excerpt on the festival from Menodotos of Samos (third/second century). Menodotos (*FGrH* 541 F1) connects Hera's Samian sanctuary with Argos (cf. Paus. 7.4.4) and tells a story in

---

186. For a list of cult sites and of cults attested in ancient Samos, see Shipley 1987: 279–83.

187. On Hera's cult in Samos and the Toneia, see F. Graf 1985: 93–6; Baumbach 2004: 170–3; Casadio 2004; Larson 2007: 31–3; Pirenne-Delforge and Pironti 2015: 44–5. Some ancient sources mention a festival at the Heraion called the Heraia (see, for example, Duris of Samos *FGrH* 76 F71). It is unclear whether the Heraia and the Toneia are different names for the same festival, two distinct parts of the same festival, or two separate festivals.

Chios–Lesbos–Samos

which Carians and Tyrrhenian pirates play an important role, together with the branches of the lygos tree (*agnus castus*; see Section 3.4C.4.1 for further discussion of the lygos). The ritual act of wrapping the statue of the goddess with lygos branches seems to be reflected in the very name of the festival, which means something like "binding."[188] Rites also included a seaside purification of the statue and offerings of barley cakes (Ath. 15.672d–e). The meaning of the rituals associated with the Toneia has been much disputed (Larson 2007: 33). However, given that the lygos tree usually evoked chastity, those rituals seem to have been connected with the characteristics of a "virgin goddess" (Casadio 2004).

Textual and archaeological evidence suggests that during the Archaic period, part of the Toneia was a ritual meal that was consumed in the sanctuary by participants reclining on the ground on mats made from lygos branches (Kron 1988). The wet conditions prevailing in the southeastern part of the sanctuary have preserved, to an unusual degree, organic remains, which show that the seventh century saw a wide range of plants consumed in the sanctuary, including barley, wheat, olives, lentils, pomegranates, grapes, figs, peaches, and melons (Kučan 1995). The animal remains from the Heraion indicate that bovines were the preferred sacrificial animal. Thigh bones are conspicuously absent from those remains; they were probably burned on altars and hence did not form part of the meals associated with sacrifices. The Archaic finds also include large quantities of dining pottery, including many goblets, cups, and mugs (Kyrieleis 1993: 135–40). The strong connection between Hera and cattle is also reflected in the fact that terracotta figurines of cattle were the most common form of dedication at the Heraion in the ninth and first half of the eighth centuries (see the useful graph at Averett 2007: 288).

Varro (*apud* Lactant. *Div. Inst.* 1.17.8) and Augustine (*De civ. D.* 6.7.3) speak of a sacred marriage between Jupiter and Juno celebrated on Samos. A wooden relief, which seems to have formed part of a wooden couch and dates to the seventh century, of a couple embracing with an eagle between their heads may indicate that a sacred marriage of some kind was celebrated at the Heraion in the Archaic period (Ohly 1953: 77–83). However, this relief has also been interpreted as a kourotrophic scene (Fridh-Haneson 1988), and it does not seem to fit easily with what we know about the Toneia. It is possible that we are dealing with two different festivals, related to two different periods of the Samian religious calendar (Casadio 2004: 142).[189]

---

188. Because of her statue "bound with lygos," Artemis in Sparta was also called *Lygodesma*, as Paus. 3.16.11 informs us. On other "fettered gods," see F. Graf 1985: 81–96.

189. F. Graf 1985: 96 suggests instead that this is a mistake by Varro. Ath. 15.673b, however, quotes an epigram by the Hellenistic poet Nikainetos of Samos (l. 2703–10 in Gow and

The variety and wealth of Archaic votives from the Heraion (see Section 3.4C.4.1 for a summary) provide insight into cult practices at the site.[190] The finds suggest that Hera's role as a tutelary deity of women and children may have been an important aspect of worship at the Samian Heraion during the Archaic period. Terracotta female figurines holding doves in front of their breasts are common dedications, and the presence of a few faience figurines of Isis nursing Horus and 26 marble *korai* may provide additional evidence for a prominent female presence among worshipers. A concern with fertility is evident from the finds of pomegranate and poppy seeds and pine cones among the plant remains from the sanctuary and from the many dedications of terracotta and ivory representations of pomegranates and poppy pods.[191] A more general sense of Hera as protector of families and households is perhaps apparent from the 35 limestone and terracotta house models found at the Heraion (on which see Walter, Clemente, and Niemeier 2019: 123–34).

The Archaic votives and the literary sources indicate that Hera—or one of the other deities venerated at the Heraion—could also be associated with traditionally masculine spheres of activity such as warfare and maritime commerce.[192] More than 70 miniature terracotta and bronze shields, some with decoration showing armed warriors, were found at the Heraion (Kyrieleis 2020a: 18). According to Herodotus (4.152), the Samian merchant Kolaios (see Section 3.8C.3) and his crew, after a spectacularly successful trading voyage, spent the enormous sum of six *talanta* dedicating a bronze griffin protome cauldron at the Heraion (on that cauldron, see Section 3.4C.4.3). The dedications of full-size and model ships at the Heraion (see Section 3.4C.4.4) show that Kolaios was not the only seagoing Samian to offer votives to Hera. More generally speaking, the 21 marble *kouroi* and many terracotta figurines of males found at the Heraion can probably be attributed to male worshipers and may, in at least some cases, have been connected to young men coming of age.

---

Page 1965: vol. 1: 146) mentioning a Samian festival within a matrimonial context; see Pirenne-Delforge and Pironti 2015: 45.

190. The discussion in this and the following paragraph draws directly on Baumbach 2004: 153–68, which includes citations of the relevant excavation reports. On the archaeobotanical material, see Kučan 2000.

191. Pine trees did not grow in the wet soil of the site, and so the pine cones must have intentionally been brought there.

192. The Heraion, in addition to a series of increasingly gigantic temples to Hera, was also the site of large, temple-like structures that cannot be certainly associated with particular deities. See Section 3.4C.4.5 for further discussion, including the possibility that the structure known as the Südbau was a temple dedicated to Hermes and Aphrodite.

FIGURE 3.20. Bronze lion dedicated to Hera by the Spartiate Eumnastos at the Samian Heraion; c. 550; height: 10 cm, length: 16 cm; from the Samian Heraion. Archaeological Museum, Vathy, 1149/50.

The Archaic votives from the Heraion include large numbers of exotic items (e.g., a crocodile skull; Kyrieleis 1993: 135–8; Ekroth 2018) from across the Mediterranean. Some of those votives were dedicated by individuals who were not from Samos (e.g., the couchant lion dedicated by a Spartiate; *IG* XII.6.2.540, see Figure 3.20). It is a near certainty, therefore, that the Heraion attracted substantial numbers of visitors from outside the island, and the Heraion may have developed into a sort of pan-Mediterranean mother cult that built on the popularity of Cybele in Asia Minor and was visited by worshipers hoping for safe maritime passage. We might also consider the possibility that exotic objects dedicated at the Heraion were brought there by Greeks, either mercenaries returning from service in Egyptian or Babylonian armies,[193] or (perhaps

---

193. At least a few of the dedications in the Heraion from Egypt must have been heirlooms by the time they reached Samos (see comments at Carty 2015: 38 n. 7).

more likely) the booty of Samian pirates (on Samian piracy, see Section 3.5C.2) (Schmidt 1968; Jantzen 1972; Kyrieleis 1986: 189; Kyrieleis 1993: 143–8). In any case, the contrast between the dedications at most Archaic Greek sanctuaries, both in terms of the sorts of votive objects dedicated and the immense variety of origins of those objects, should compel serious contemplation about the nature of the cult of Hera on Samos and how it differed from traditional Greek religious practice.

Along these lines, the dedication at the Heraion of hundreds of religious objects from Egypt and Cyprus, as well as imitations of those objects produced in Samos or elsewhere in Ionia, may suggest that a variety of different cult practices or beliefs were enacted within the context of worship at the Heraion. Egyptian imports include well more than 100 bronze figurines of priests, male and female deities, and sacred animals, ranging in size from 2 to more than 50 cm. There are, in addition, hundreds of Egyptian and Egyptianizing objects in faience (particularly falcons and other animals and human figures; Jantzen 1972; Bianchi 1990; Tanner 2003: 118–21; Weiss 2005; Ebbinghaus 2006: 187–202; Weiss 2012: vol. 1: 493–511; Webb 2016; Webb 2021). The finds of Egyptian bronzes are particularly notable, since such objects are rarely found in Greek sanctuaries (Hölbl 2007: 451; Villing 2017: 567–74). Most prominent among the Cypriot material are hundreds of terracotta and limestone figurines (see Section 3.8C.3). Both the Egyptian and Cypriot material started arriving at the Heraion in the seventh century.

Much of this large collection of material may have been dedicated by Samians, but the extent to which cult practice at the Heraion was influenced by Egyptian and Cypriot cult practice remains a subject of lively scholarly debate. Faience had powerful associations with protective magic and fertility in Egypt, and the iconography of many of the faience objects found at the Heraion (e.g., amulets and Bes talismans) indicates that the dedicants in Samos were aware of those associations. At the same time, the iconography of some of the faience objects from the Heraion mix together elements that do not occur together in Egyptian art. For example, the finds from the Heraion include faience vases in the form of a kneeling woman with tightly curled hair, a baby on her back, and an ibex on her lap. In an Egyptian context, the kneeling position would signal a pharaoh making an offering to a god (or a lesser being in the presence of a greater one), the tightly curled hair would indicate a Nubian, carrying a baby on one's back would indicate a Syrian, and the ibex would be a tutelary animal. These vases were probably intended for a non-Egyptian clientele, and, as Virginia Webb notes, "the workshop which produced these vases was keen to access Egyptian ideas of beneficence and good luck, and was not overly concerned when combining concepts in an over-elaborate and nonsensical way" (Webb 2016: 37–43, quote at 38). Greek women frequently gave birth in a kneeling position, and it is likely that the dedicants at the Heraion chose this particular type of votive because they saw it as resonating with Hera's connections to fertility, childbirth, and protection (Baumbach 2004: 154–5). The Samians' religious customs were certainly affected by their extensive foreign contacts but in ways that defy simple characterization (Hölbl 2005; Hölbl 2007; Greaves 2010: 193–7; Hölbl 2014; Henke 2019: 267–74; Webb 2019; Webb 2021).[194]

### 3.11C.2. Artemis

The existence of a cult of Artemis in the urban center is demonstrated by the sanctuary uncovered at Samos Town (see Section 3.4C.1) and by Herodotus (3.48.3), who connects the institution of a festival for Artemis to the successful attempt by the Samians to rescue the 300 children from Corcyra whom Periander had sent to Sardis to be made into eunuchs. Polycrates evinced an interest in the cult of Apollo at Delos (see Section 3.12A), and Pausanias (2.31.6) mentions an ancient sanctuary of Pythian Apollo on Samos.

### 3.11C.3. Zeus Eleutherios

Herodotus (3.142.2) attributes to Maiandrios the institution of a cult of Zeus Eleutherios (together with the foundation of a shrine in a suburb of the town still visible in his own times) after Polycrates' death in 522 (see Section 3.4C.3). This piece of information, however, has been doubted and the cult dated to no earlier than the autumn of 479, when Samos was liberated from both Persian and tyrannical rule (Raaflaub 2004: 110–11 believes that Herodotus, or his source, fabricated a "historicizing fiction," projecting onto Maiandrios a course of action that was imaginable only in his own times).

### 3.11C.4. Panionia

Like Chios, Samos was one of the 12 cities of the Ionian League celebrating the Panionia festival at Mycale (see Section 3.10A).

---

194. Other votives from the Heraion have been interpreted along similar lines. For example, the dedications of pine cones have been seen as a reflection of Assyrian cult practice (Kyrieleis 1988: 219).

## 3.12C. Samian Cultural History
### 3.12C.1. Sculpture and Architecture

Samos was the site of innovative sculptural work in the Archaic period.[195] The earliest life-size stone sculptures from Samos, three *korai* from the Heraion that date to the end of the seventh century (Freyer-Schauenburg 1974: #1–3), were carved from Naxian marble, presumably by Naxian sculptors. More than 50 marble *kouroi* and *korai* dating to the sixth century have been found on Samos, primarily at the Heraion but also at the North Necropolis in Samos Town (see Section 3.4C.5) and elsewhere on the island. (Some of the more well-known pieces of that sculpture—the so-called Geneleos group and the dedications of Cheramyes—are discussed in Section 3.9C.) The use of Samian marble in many of those statues suggests that there was a local sculptural school, and Samian sculptors seem to have played a leading role in the early sixth century in the carving of drapery on *korai* in such a way as to highlight rounded folds and the substance of the cloth rather than embroidered patterns on the surface of the cloth (Fullerton 2016: 32–3). The Archaic sculptures of males produced on Samos reflect styles diffused throughout Ionia, and the sculptural finds from the Heraion include (as part of the Geneleos group) a corpulent male banqueter that embodies a style absent from much of the Greek world (Baughan 2011).

In the sixth century, Samos was the site of some of the most ambitious architectural and engineering projects anywhere in the Greek world. Of particular note are Dipteros 1 at the Heraion, the earliest-known truly monumental temple in the Greek world, and the tunnel of Eupalinos (see Sections 3.4C.4.5 and 3.4C.2, respectively). There is plentiful evidence from Herodotus and from the finds at Naucratis and Samos that Samians were active in Egypt starting in the seventh century (cf. Herodotus 2.163; 3.138; 4.152), and we might consider the possibility that the Samians responsible for constructing the Temple of Hera in Naucratis (see Section 3.8A.3) learned methods of colossal stone construction in Egypt and later had a hand in the erection of Dipteros 1. Herbert Hoffmann has argued that the altar constructed to go with Dipteros 1 in the sixth century was modeled on Egyptian mortuary and public temples (Hoffmann 1953).

The two most famous craftsmen from sixth-century Samos, Rhoikos and Theodorus, are both linked in one way or the other to the Heraion (see Svenson-Evers 1996: 7–66; Meyer 2012: 333–42 for a listing of relevant ancient literary sources). According to Herodotus (3.60.3), the first architect of the Temple at

---

195. An updated version of the catalog of Samian sculptures presented in Freyer-Schauenburg 1974 can be found in Franssen 2011. On the cult statue in the Temple of Hera at the Heraion, see Section 3.4C.4.3.

Hera at the Heraion was a Samian, Rhoikos, son of Philes; this reference has been taken to mean that Rhoikos designed Dipteros 1 (which had been demolished and replaced by Dipteros 2 when Herodotus was writing his *Histories*). Rhoikos was closely associated in later sources with another Samian, Theodorus the son of Telekles, whom Herodotus mentions as the maker of a huge silver bowl that Croesus sent to Delphi (1.51.1–2) and an elaborate emerald seal ring worn by Polycrates (3.41.1). Pliny (*HN* 36.19.90) claims that Smilis, Rhoikos, and Theodorus built a labyrinth with 150 columns in Lemnos, which seems to be a garbled reference to the Samian Heraion (Dinsmoor 1950: 124 n. 1). Pausanias (8.14.8, 10.38.6) claims that Rhoikos and Theodorus invented bronze casting (see Section 3.8C.2). Diodorus (1.98.5–9), who describes Rhoikos and Theodorus as brothers, says that Rhoikos and Theodorus, in the course of carving a wooden statue of Pythian Apollo for the Samians, created the two halves of the statue separately, but using the same system of proportions derived from Egypt, and found that the two halves of the statue fit together perfectly.

Theodorus is repeatedly referenced without any mention of Rhoikos in numerous literary texts. Plato (*Ion* 533a–b) describes him as a sculptor. Vitruvius (7.Preface 12) states that Theodorus wrote a book about the Temple of Hera at Samos. Pliny claims that Theodorus produced a portrait statue in brass and invented the carpentry square, the level, the lathe, and the key (*HN* 7.57.198, 34.19.83). Pausanias characterizes Theodorus as the architect of a building known as the Skias in Sparta and as the sculptor of a statue in the Artemision at Ephesus (3.12.10, 10.38.6). Diogenes Laertius credits Theodorus with coming up with the idea of stabilizing the foundations of the Artemision in Ephesus by spreading charcoal on the damp ground on which the temple would be built (2.103). Athenaeus credits Theodorus with making a gold kratēr for the palace of the Persian king (514f).

Most of the references to Rhoikos and Theodorus are of dubious reliability, but both men do seem to be firmly grounded in sixth-century Samos. The most likely scenario is that Rhoikos designed Dipteros 1 and that Theodorus designed Dipteros 2 (though see Svenson-Evers 1996: 7–66 for a different interpretation of the evidence);. Theodorus may well have written a book about his work on Dipteros 2 and probably also produced some notable kratēres in precious metals (Shipley 2003).

## 3.12C.2. Literature and Philosophy

Herodotus places the Samian dialect in a fourth group, apart from all the other members of the Ionian League (on which see Section 3.10A). Jeffery argued that Herodotus may have considered Samos' dialect the purest Ionic, but the basis

430 THE OXFORD HISTORY OF THE ARCHAIC GREEK WORLD

of Herodotus' classification of the Ionic dialects of Asia Minor is not immediately obvious to us. The eastern Ionic alphabet was used on Samos (Jeffery
1990: 326–31).

The earliest poet associated with Samos is the shadowy figure of Kreophylos.
The Suda (s.v. Κρεώφυλος; cf. Proclus *Life of Homer* 5) states that Kreophylos was
an epic poet from Chios or Samos, that Kreophylos was variously characterized
as Homer's son-in-law or friend, and that Homer, in recompense for hospitality
offered by Kreophylos, had written and given to Kreophylos a poem, the *Capture
of Oichalia*, which was subsequently attributed to Kreophylos. Strabo (14.1.18)
describes Kreophylos as a Samian who might have been Homer's teacher and
cites Callimachus (Epigram 6 Pfeiffer) in trying to decide whether Kreophylos or
Homer composed the *Capture of Oichalia*. The *Capture of Oichalia* is quoted and
referenced by other authors (see, for example, Paus. 4.2.3), and so a work by that
name was clearly in circulation, but it is far from certain that it was composed by a
Samian who was a contemporary and associate of Homer (see Bernabé 1987: 157–
64 for all of the relevant sources).

Whoever Kreophylos was and whatever his relationship to Homer, several
ancient authors claimed that a group of rhapsodes known as the Kreophyleioi
descended from Kreophylos and orally preserved Homer's poetry.[196] For example,
the Aristotelian *Constitution of the Lacedaemonians* says that the Spartan lawgiver Lycurgus went to Samos, where he "received the poetry of Homer from the
descendants of Kreophylos" (τὴν Ὁμήρου ποίησιν παρὰ τῶν ἀπογόνων Κρεοφύλου
λαβών, F611.10 Rose; cf. Plut. *Lyc.* 4.4). Burkert has argued that the Kreophyleioi
did in fact exist and played some role in preserving Homer's poetry. The role of
the Kreophyleioi as transmitters of Homer put them in direct competition with
the Homeridae of Chios (see Section 3.12A).

The Kreophyleioi were associated in later sources with one of the more
famous Samians of the Archaic period, Pythagoras.[197] The nature of the evidence
for Pythagoras is sufficiently problematic that almost everything pertaining to
his life and thought remains the subject of ongoing scholarly debate. Pythagoras
probably did not produce any written works, his followers from his own lifetime
did not create detailed accounts of his life and thought, and the comments of his
contemporaries and near contemporaries on his ideas survive only in fragments.

---

196. On Kreophylos and the Kreophyleioi and their relationship with "Homer" and the
Homeridae, Burkert 1972 is enlightening but (unavoidably) also very speculative; see also Nagy
1990: 23, 74; and (discussing the evidence in the Homeric *Vitae*) Nagy 2010: E§57–60.

197. The discussion of Pythagoras provided here draws directly from Huffman 2018 and
Huffman 2019, which offer thorough treatments of the relevant ancient sources and modern
scholarship.

These problems are compounded by the fact that by the fifth century, thinkers who were somehow connected with Pythagoras had developed a body of philosophy that may have diverged in significant ways from Pythagoras' views (Aristotle calls those thinkers the "so-called Pythagoreans," possibly to highlight that divergence). Over the course of time, a significant number of works falsely ascribed to Pythagoras went into circulation, and Pythagoras came to be seen by some as the originator of most of the basic strands in Greek philosophical thought. The most detailed accounts of Pythagoras' life and thought—those of Diogenes Laertius, Porphyry, and Iamblichus, all of whom wrote in the third century CE— were shaped by centuries of accretions and cannot be read as anything like reliable accounts.

All of that said, a basic outline of Pythagoras' career can be sketched with some degree of confidence. He was born on Samos c. 570 and emigrated to the *polis* of Croton in southern Italy c. 530. Sometime around 510, Pythagoras and his followers were driven out of Croton, whereupon Pythagoras found refuge in Metapontion, where he died c. 490. In his own lifetime, Pythagoras does not seem to have enjoyed any sort of reputation as a mathematician or as a cosmologist but rather was known for his views on the fate of the soul after death (he evidently argued that the soul was immortal and experienced successive reincarnations), his expertise in religious ritual, and his insistence that his followers pursue a highly rigorous lifestyle that included dietary restrictions.[198]

The nature of the sources is such that it is nearly impossible to say anything certain about Pythagoras' activities on Samos prior to his departure for southern Italy. Some of the relevant parts of the biographical tradition—such as the claim that Polycrates gave a letter of introduction to Pythagoras so that the latter could meet the pharaoh Amasis—are at best improbable. In a similar vein, although Pythagoras and his followers seem to have wielded considerable political influence in some Greek communities in southern Italy, claims (see, for example, Iambl. *VP* 5.20, 6.28) that Pythagoras played a prominent role in Samian politics need to be treated with great caution. The same can be said about ostensible connections between Pythagoras and the Kreophyleioi, for example, the notion that Pythagoras was the pupil of a Kreophyleios named Hermodamas (Neanthes *FGrH* 84 F29 [= Porph. *Vita Pythagorae*]; cf. Burkert 1972: 77).

Although Pythagoras does not seem to have produced any written works, either in Samos or in southern Italy, other figures active on Samos in the Archaic

---

198. On the (different) Pythagoras of Samos who won an Olympic victory in boxing, see Section 10C.

432    THE OXFORD HISTORY OF THE ARCHAIC GREEK WORLD

period were authors of some note. The poets Semonides and Asius were both born on Samos. Semonides (seventh century), the author of a well-known satiric attack on women in iambic trimeters (F7 West), was, according to the Suda (s.v. Σιμμίας, Ῥόδιος), sent by his fellow citizens to guide the colonization of Amorgos, to which he is generally connected in our sources (in general, and also for the interpretation of the problematic biographical sources, see Zimmerman 2011: 148–53). He was also the author of an entirely lost *On the Archaeology of the Samians* (cf. Bowie 1986: 31). We have already mentioned (see Section 3.10C) the observations on the luxury of the Samians found in a passage by the poet Asius of Samos (? sixth century; succinct information on him can be found in Zimmerman 2011: 73, 94). Asius composed epic poems with genealogical content and was evidently interested in Samian local traditions.

There is some reason to believe that Ibycus traveled from Rhegium to Samos in the sixth century and composed an encomium for a young Polycrates (see Section 3.5C.2). Some modern scholars have seen a markedly anti-Homeric, anti-Chian bias in that poem, for example, in the poet's insistence on dwelling on figures such as Kyanippos, Zeuxippos, and Troilos (l. 36–45), who have a nonexistent or limited role in the Homeric poems (Bowra 1961: 254; Barron 1964: 224–6; Giannini 2004: 57–8; Carty 2015: 73, 83, 99). The extent to which the contents of the poem should be considered deliberately and specifically anti-Homeric remains difficult to ascertain, and it is even more tenuous to speculate that such a peculiarity betrays a polemical intention against Chios and the Homeridae (Giannini 2004: 58).[199] Yet it does not seem out of place to wonder whether a relationship exists between the heroic themes hinted at in the poem and the inherently Samian epic tradition connected with Kreophylos and his *apogonoi*.[200]

Polycrates made Samos a pole of attraction for foreign celebrities and pursued what can be called a cultural policy (Berve 1967: vol. 1: 111–12, vol. 2: 585–6; Shipley 1987: 69–99). The famous doctor Democedes of Croton (on whom see Hdt. 3.125; 129–38) became his personal physician. Even more remarkable is the presence of the poet Anacreon at his court. In a memorable passage, Herodotus (3.121) describes Polycrates, not long before his death, lying in the men's apartments (that is, celebrating a symposium) in the company of Anacreon, paying no

---

199. The fact, for example, that it has been possible to identify both a pro-Spartan and an anti-Spartan (pro-Argive) bent in the poem demonstrates the shaky foundations on which such hypotheses rest.

200. It is a pity that we can only wonder at the fact that it was the Chian Cynaethus, and not a Samian "descendant of Kreophylos," who was called to perform in Homeric style at the Πύθια καὶ Δήλια of 523 or 522 (see Section 3.12A).

heed to the herald sent by the Persian satrap Oroites (cf. Burkert 2004: 354–5). In Polycrates of Samos, we see emerging for the first time a partnership between dynast and poet.[201]

Strabo (14.1.16) goes so far as to claim that all of Anacreon's poetry was full of mentions of Polycrates. Judging from the remains of Anacreon's poetry, this sounds like hyperbole. Moreover, Anacreon's poetic activity and production were not exclusively linked to Samos. In fact, in comparison to earlier sympotic poetry (Archilochus, Alcaeus, Theognis, etc.), it has been argued that Anacreon's poetry is much less definite in time and place, since it contains strikingly "little political or military language, no references to genealogical descent or the social status of the symposiasts, and no assertion of a firm fellowship." In his poetry, we find an almost exclusive attention to the themes of love, youth, and wine, and "while the audiences of the poets preceding Anacreon are clearly aristocratic, the latter's audience is unidentifiable and, at best, ambiguous socially," so that his poetry looks "generic and inclusive enough to accommodate a wider range of audiences" (Kantzios 2004–2005: 228, 39, 42).

We should perhaps concede, however, that the indefiniteness we perceive in Anacreon's poetry might, at least in part, be a product of its ancient reception and that specific references to the actual circumstances of the songs' production and execution may have appeared more clearly and more frequently in his poetry than we can recognize today.[202] Difficulties in the interpretation of F353 Page, for example, with its mention of μυθιῆται ("talkers"? or rather "rebels," as suggested by the Homeric scholion quoting the lines?) in the island having control of the sacred city (ἱρὸν ἄστυ), are also due to its allusion to specific circumstances of the political situation in Samos (Vetta 1998; Carty 2015: 121–7).

It is also true, as has been recently pointed out, that Anacreon's poetry seems to be thoroughly private, with very few allusions to cult beyond ritual practice that was integrated into private symposia (Budelmann 2009b: 228, 32). However, both F501.6 Page, which attributes *partheneia* (songs sung by a chorus of maidens) to Anacreon, and Critias' references to Anacreon's "women's songs" and "female choruses" (Critias F8 Gow and Page) compel us to be cautious in restricting the range of Anacreon's poetry to the private sphere. Recently, new readings in an ancient commentary on Anacreon (*POxy* 54.3722, F15

---

201. On tyrants and poets, see further the bibliography in Budelmann 2009a: 228 n. 5. For a recent treatment of Anacreon, see Budelmann 2009a.

202. On Anacreon's late Archaic and Classical reception in Athens, see Burkert 2004: 353–4; Shapiro 2012.

col. i, 15–18) have made it possible to identify an invocation to the Eleusinian god Eubouleus in a poem Anacreon would have composed while in Samos (Bernsdorff 2011: 29–31).

Polycrates' horrible death put an end to his grand plans. Later on, the city of Athens assumed the naval power over the Aegean that Polycrates had striven to seize for Samos. And it was again Athens that became the central site for the maintenance and production of Ionian cultural traditions. In the same passage from the *Hipparchus* attributed to Plato, in which it is said that Hipparchus brought over to Athens the Homeric poems for performance at the Panathenaia (cf. Section 3.12A), it is also said that he sent a penteconter to Ionia to bring over Anacreon (from Samos, arguably) together with Simonides of Ceos (228c). Not only the epic tradition but also the tradition of Ionian lyric moved west to Athens.[203]

## 3.13. *Conclusion*

Although conventionally grouped together, each of the three islands treated here possessed distinctive features unparalleled in the other two, differences remarked upon already by the ancient sources. Chios enjoyed remarkable material prosperity, underpinned by a massive slave population, although this prosperity seems not to have translated into identifiable monumental architecture. Lesbos had its reputation for poetry: writing in the fourth century for a newly established oligarchy at Mytilene, Isocrates says that the *polis* was "agreed upon by all to be the most devoted to *mousikē*, with the most famous practitioners of it being born there" (*Epistle* 8.4). Samos, finally, hosted the strikingly singular Heraion sanctuary, unique among the islands and equipped with a series of remarkable temples. Society, culture, architecture, and religion are just a few categories in which the three differed. Politically, too, they appear to have taken divergent routes. Samos is now best known for Polycrates' tyrannical dynasty, Lesbos for the period of internecine chaos documented by Alcaeus and for the writings of Sappho, and Chios for its good order, institutional precocity, and wine.

Yet these differences conceal some common strands, which emerge when we move beyond the "greatest hits" of each *polis* (as Herodotus might say, their μεγάλα ἔργα) to broader themes. Mytilene, after all, also experienced tyranny, first under Pittacus and later under the Persian-backed general Koes. Meanwhile, if we

---

203. See Nagy 2007a: 226–7; Nagy 2010: I§144. On Hipparchus' cultural initiatives and his "East Ionian" connection, see especially Aloni 2000; also Burkert 2004: 353–4.

are to believe Herodotus, the tyrant Strattis controlled Chios for the great majority of the more than 30-year span between 513 and 480. So all three islands experienced significant periods of tyrannical rule. It is Herodotus' decision to focus on the figure of Polycrates that has guaranteed his outsize prominence. A productive approach for political historians going forward would be to look for similarities among the islands as well as among other *poleis*, in the pursuit of understanding "Archaic elite political culture" more generally.[204]

It is noteworthy, for example, in the case of Chios, Lesbos, and Samos that all three produced sworn bands of elites united against tyrants (Hdt. 8.132.2; Alc. F129; Hdt. 9.90)—and that these factions closely resembled the conspiracy formed by the Athenian tyrannicides Harmodius and Aristogeiton, down to the fellow conspirator who betrayed the group.[205] The accounts together illustrate the importance of oaths in attempting to overcome the considerable barriers to cooperation among elites, as well as the incentives that managed to induce many sworn conspirators to defect from plots.[206] On the other hand, in a marked departure from the Athenian experience, all three islands emerged from the Persian Wars not as emboldened democracies but as oligarchies.[207] Despite their differing constitutional paths up to that point, the three "autonomous" members of the Delian League converged on the rule of the few as their preferred regime type, thus auguring the hardening opposition between *dēmokratia* and *oligarchia* over the course of the fifth century.[208]

## Guide to Further Reading

Chian material culture is summarized in Merousis (2002), which is a convenient resource for those able to read modern Greek. Boardman (1967) presents the

---

204. This has sometimes been attempted, albeit often indirectly, as a byproduct of discussions about tyranny or exile; see, e.g., Anderson 2005; Forsdyke 2005: 30–78. Directly concerned with the Archaic elite are Stein-Hölkeskamp 1989 and Duplouy 2006. In a more geopolitical vein, it could be useful to pursue further questions about the different islands' mainland holdings; for an excellent start on this, see Carusi 2003.

205. Compare Thuc. 6.57.2 ("when they saw one of the conspirators speaking in a friendly manner with Hippias . . . they were afraid and thought they had been informed on") with Alc. F129.22–3 (Pittacus "trampled upon the [conspiratorial] oaths with his feet") and Hdt. 8.132.2 ("the plotters were revealed when one of the participants disclosed the attempt").

206. For the use of oaths in conspiracies, see Sommerstein and Bayliss 2013: 120–8 (Pittacus and the Athenian tyrannicides are discussed but not the Chian and Samian examples).

207. Note, however, that by the later fifth century, Methymna on Lesbos had become a democracy; Thuc. 3.2 and 8.100.

208. The subject of Classical Greek oligarchy is treated in Simonton 2017.

results of the British excavations at Emporio, while Roungou and Vouligea (2019) is an update on more recent excavations. Beaumont (2004) is a good source for Kato Phana. For other sites, Lemos (1997; on Rizari) and Evangelidis (1921; on Nagos) are helpful. The most authoritative treatment of Chian pottery is Lemos (1991). For Chian political and social history, see many of the contributions contained in Jennings and Katsaros (2007). Ionian identity is treated in Mac Sweeney (2013). New Chian epigraphical discoveries are found in Malouchou and Matthaiou (2006). For Archaic elite politics in general, see Anderson (2005; on tyranny) and Duplouy (2006). On Chios' cults, see F. Graf (1985). On the Homeridai of Chios, within a wide-ranging discussion of the formation and fixation of the Homeric poems in the Archaic age, see Nagy 2010; on Cynaethus of Chios, see Burkert (1979) and Aloni (1989).

An overview of archaeological evidence from Archaic Lesbos is available in the form of Spencer's gazetteer (1995b), and his historiographical and archaeological summary in (Spencer 1995a) is a useful resource as well. Schaus (2017) reviews some new finds of Lesbian pottery from Mytilene and provides an updated discussion of Lesbian gray ware in general. For those able to read modern Greek, the more recent publications listed in the bibliography by Acheilara, Kourtzellis, Roungou, and colleagues present various aspects of the archaeological record that have come to light since the 1990s. On the social, political, and historical background of Alcaeus' poetry, Rösler (1980) is fundamental, but see also the important qualifications by Nagy (2004). Dimopoulou-Piliouni (2015) provides an overview of Lesbian constitutional and legal development. Greene (1996) offers a well-balanced selection of contemporary approaches to Sappho; on Sappho's community and audience as well as for the textual reconstructions of many fragments, see Ferrari (2010b); also D'Alessio (2018). Neri (2021) provides a monumental commented edition of the fragments of Sappho's poetry.

Thirty volumes in the DAI's *Samos* series cover the material remains of the Heraion and Pythagoreio in impressive detail. A brief summary of finds at the Heraion is presented in Kyrieleis (1996). Excellent photographs and concise treatments of many of the votive offerings there can be found in Tsakos and Viglaki-Sofianou (2012). Shipley (1987) remains the standard political history of Samos. Carty (2015) revisits Polycrates' tyranny. A rich collection of essays on literature, culture, and religion in ancient Samos from the Archaic age onward is Cavallini (2004). For the connection between East Ionia and the Athens of the Pisistratids, see Aloni (2000).

*Chios–Lesbos–Samos*

## Gazetteer

| Name | Figure/Map # | Grid Designation |
| --- | --- | --- |
| Achilleion | Map 3.8 | inset |
| Aegina | Map 3.2 | inset |
| Agathonisi | Map 3.10 | B3 |
| Agiades, Samos | Map 3.10 | B2 |
| | Figure 3.10 | |
| Agios Stephanos, Chios | Map 3.6 | C2 |
| | Map 3.7 | B2 |
| Altar 2, Samian Heraion | Figure 3.12 | |
| Altar 4, Samian Heraion | Figure 3.13 | D/E2 |
| Altar 6, Samian Heraion | Figure 3.14 | D/E3 |
| | Figure 3.15 | J/K8 |
| | Figure 3.16 | J/K8 |
| Amorgos | Map 3.1b | B3 |
| Ampelos hill, Samos Town | Figure 3.10 | |
| Anaia | Map 3.10 | D1 |
| Antandros | Map 3.8 | E1, inset |
| Antissa, Lesbos | Map 3.8 | B2 |
| | Map 3.9 | B1 |
| Apollo sanctuary, Emporio | Figure 3.2 | |
| Apotheke, Lesbos | Map 3.8 | B3 |
| apsidal building, Methymna | Figure 3.5 | |
| Argos | Map 3.3 | B2 |
| Arisba, Lesbos | Map 3.8 | B3 |
| | Map 3.9 | B2 |
| Archaic and Classical cemetery, Eresus | Figure 3.7 | |
| Archaic residential remains, Methymna | Figure 3.5 | |
| Askalon | Map 3.5 | I3 |
| Assos | Map 3.8 | C2, inset |
| Astypalaia, Samos Town | ancient name for Kastro hill | |
| Atarneus | Map 3.1b | B1 |

| Name | Figure/Map # | Grid Designation |
| --- | --- | --- |
| Athena sanctuary, Emporio | Figure 3.2 | |
| Athens | Map 3.2 | inset |
| Babylon | Map 3.5 | K3 |
| Bapheios | Map 3.8 | B2 |
| Berezan | Map 3.3 | D1 |
| Bisanthe | Map 3.1a | B1 |
| Building III, Antissa | Figure 3.6 | |
| Building IV, Antissa | Figure 3.6 | |
| Camirus | Map 3.1b | C4 |
| Cape Epanochori, Chios | Map 3.7 | A/B1 |
| Cape Masticho, Chios | Map 3.6 | B3 |
| Cape Phokas, Lesbos | Map 3.8 | B3 |
| | Map 3.9 | B2 |
| Carpathus | Map 3.1a | B4 |
| Carthage | Map 3.4 | C1 |
| Catania | Map 3.4 | C3 |
| Çatallar Tepe | see Panionion 1 | |
| Çesme peninsula | Map 3.6 | D2 |
| Chalcis | Map 3.2 | B1 |
| Chesios river, Samos Town | Figure 3.10 | |
| Chios | Map 3.1b | A/B2 |
| (topography) | Map 3.6 | B/C1–3 |
| | Map 3.7 | |
| Chios Town, Chios | Map 3.6 | C2 |
| | Map 3.7 | B2 |
| Chora, Chios | modern name for Chios Town | |
| Christos torrent, Eresus | Figure 3.7 | |
| Church of Agios Iakovos, Chios Town | Figure 3.1 | |
| Church of Agios Simeon, Mytilene | Figure 3.4 | |
| Church of Ioannis Prodromos, Chios Town | Figure 3.1 | |
| Church of Panagia Letsaina, Chios Town | Figure 3.1 | |

| Name | Figure/Map # | Grid Designation |
|---|---|---|
| Cilicia | Map 3.1a | F3 |
| circular building, Emporio | Figure 3.2 | |
| clay extraction pits, Chios Town | see Kofina ridge | |
| Clazomenae | Map 3.1b | B2 |
| Cnidus | Map 3.1b | C4 |
| Colophon | Map 3.1b | C2 |
| Corcyra | Map 3.2 | A1 |
| Corinth | Map 3.2 | inset |
| corner of Odos Ioanni Chaviara and Odos Sinadinou, Chios Town | Figure 3.1 | |
| corner of Odos Mitrodorou and Odos Glaraki, Chios Town | Figure 3.1 | |
| Cos | Map 3.1b | C4 |
| Croton | Map 3.4 | B4 |
| curvilinear buildings, Antissa | Figure 3.6 | |
| curvilinear building, Mytilene | Figure 3.4 (#1) | |
| Cyclades | Map 3.1b | A4 |
| Cydonia | Map 3.2 | C3 |
| Cyme | Map 3.1b | B2 |
| Cyrene | Map 3.2 | A4 |
| Cyzicus | Map 3.1a | B1 |
| Daskalopetra, Chios | Map 3.6 | C2 |
| Delos | Map 3.1b | A3 |
| Delphi | Map 3.2 | B1 |
| Delphini, Chios | Map 3.6 | C2 |
| Delphinion, Chios | ancient name for modern Delphini | |
| Dikaia | Map 3.3 | A4 |
| Dikaiarcheia | Map 3.4 | A3 |
| Dipteros 1, Samian Heraion | Figure 3.15 | D7 to I9 |
| | Figure 3.16 | D7 to I9 |
| Dipteros 2, Samian Heraion | Figure 3.16 | B7 to G10 |
| early necropolis, Samos Town | Figure 3.10 | |
| East Harbor, Samos Town | Figure 3.10 | |

| Name | Figure/Map # | Grid Designation |
|---|---|---|
| Eastern Kouros, Samian Heraion | alternative name for Isches Kouros | |
| Eleusis | Map 3.2 | inset |
| Emporio, Chios | Map 3.6 | C3 |
| Epano Skala, Mytilene | Figure 3.4 | |
| Ephesus | Map 3.1b | C3 |
| | Map 3.10 | D1 |
| Eresus, Lesbos | Map 3.8 | A3 |
| | Map 3.9 | A2 |
| Erythrae | Map 3.1b | B2 |
| Euboea | Map 3.2 | B/C1–2 |
| Eupalinos tunnel, Samos | Figure 3.10 | |
| Euripos, Mytilene | Figure 3.4 | |
| Geneleos Group, Samian Heraion | Figure 3.15 | K5 |
| --- | Figure 3.16 | K5 |
| Genoese castle, Chios Town | Figure 3.1 | |
| Genoese-Ottoman castle, Antissa | Figure 3.6 | |
| Genoese-Ottoman castle, Methymna | Figure 3.5 | |
| Giglio, island of | Map 3.5 | E1 |
| Gulf of Adrymmation | Map 3.8 | D2, inset |
| Gulf of Gera, Lesbos | Map 3.8 | C/D3 |
| | Map 3.9 | C/D2 |
| Gulf of Kalloni, Lesbos | Map 3.8 | B/C3 |
| | Map 3.9 | B/C2 |
| Gulf of Latmos | alternative name for Gulf of Miletus | |
| Gulf of Miletus | Map 3.10 | D2 |
| Gulf of Pyrrha, Lesbos | ancient name for Gulf of Kalloni | |
| Güzelçamli | Map 3.10 | C2 |
| Halicarnassus | Map 3.1b | C3 |
| Harbor Sanctuary, Emporio | see Apollo sanctuary, Emporio | |
| Hebros river | Map 3.3 | B4 |
| Hekatompedon 1, Samian Heraion | Figure 3.13 | B/C/D2 |
| | Figure 3.15 | H8/H9/I8/I9/J8/J9 |
| | Figure 3.16 | H8/H9/I8/I9/J8/J9 |

*Chios–Lesbos–Samos* 441

| Name | Figure/Map # | Grid Designation |
| --- | --- | --- |
| Hekatompedon 2, Samian Heraion | Figure 3.14 | B/C/D3 |
| | Figure 3.15 | H8/H9/I8/I9/J8/J9 |
| | Figure 3.16 | H8/H9/I8/I9/J8/J9 |
| Hekatonessai Islands | Map 3.8 | D2 |
| Heraion, Samos | Map 3.10 | B2 |
| | Map 3.11 | B2 |
| Heraion (Tabakia district), Chios Town | Figure 3.1 | |
| Heraion Teichos | Map 3.1a | B1 |
| Hermione | Map 3.2 | inset |
| Hydra | Map 3.2 | inset |
| Ialysus | Map 3.1b | D4 |
| Imbrasos river | Figure 3.13 | A3 |
| | Figure 3.14 | A5 |
| Imbros | Map 3.1a | A1 |
| Isches Kouros, Samian Heraion | Figure 3.15 | O4 |
| | Figure 3.16 | O4 |
| juniper stump, Samian Heraion | Figure 3.13 | E2 |
| Kala Tepe | hill near modern village of Güzelçamli, Turkey, likely site of ancient Karion | |
| Kale Akte | Map 3.4 | C3 |
| Kalloni, Lesbos | Map 3.8 | B3 |
| Kambos Khoras, Samos | Map 3.11 | B2 |
| Kampos plain, Chios | Map 3.7 | B2 |
| Karaova plain | Map 3.10 | D1/2 |
| Karion | Map 3.10 | C2 |
| Karyes | Map 3.6 | C2 |
| Kastelli hill, Samos Town | Figure 3.10 | |
| Kastro, Chios Town | see Genoese castle, Chios Town | |
| Kastro, Mytilene | Figure 3.4 | |
| Kastro hill, Samos Town | Figure 3.10 | |
| Kato Phanai, Chios | Map 3.6 | B3 |
| Kato Syme, Crete | Map 3.2 | C3 |
| Kelendris, Cilicia | Map 3.1a | E3 |

| Name | Figure/Map # | Grid Designation |
| --- | --- | --- |
| Klima, Samos | Map 3.10 | B2 |
| Klopedi, Lesbos | Map 3.8 | B2 |
| | Map 3.9 | B1 |
| Knossos | Map 3.2 | C3 |
| Kofina ridge, Chios Town | Figure 3.1 | |
| Kontari, Chios | Map 3.6 | C2 |
| Kourtir, Lesbos | Map 3.8 | B3 |
| Lade | Map 3.10 | C2 |
| Lagkada bay, Chios | Map 3.6 | C2 |
| | Map 3.7 | B2 |
| late Archaic fortification wall, Mytilene | Figure 3.4 | |
| Latomi, Chios | Map 3.6 | C3 |
| Lebedos | Map 3.1a | B2 |
| Lemnos | Map 3.1a | A2 |
| Lesbos | Map 3.1b | B1 |
| (topography) | Map 3.3 | A/B 5 |
| | Map 3.8 | |
| | Map 3.9 | |
| Leukathia, Chios | Map 3.6 | B2 |
| Limnia, Chios | Map 3.6 | B2 |
| | Map 3.7 | A2 |
| Lydia | Map 3.1b | C2/3 |
| Maeander river | Map 3.10 | E1/2 |
| Magnesia on the Maeander | Map 3.10 | E1 |
| Malagkiotis river, Chios | Map 3.7 | A1–2 |
| Maloeis, Mytilene | see North Harbor, Mytilene | |
| Maroneia | Map 3.3 | A4 |
| Massalia | Map 3.5 | D1 |
| Mavri Rachi, Psara island | Map 3.6 | A1 |
| Megali Glyphada, Samos Town | Figure 3.10 | |
| Megara | Map 3.2 | inset |
| Megaron, Emporio | Figure 3.2 | |
| Megas Tumulus, Samos Town | Figure 3.10 | |

| Name | Figure/Map # | Grid Designation |
|---|---|---|
| Melanios, Chios | Map 3.6 | B1 |
| | Map 3.7 | A1 |
| Melos | Map 3.2 | C2 |
| Memphis, Egypt | Map 3.5 | I4 |
| Messa, Lesbos | Map 3.8 | C3 |
| | Map 3.9 | C2 |
| Messon, Lesbos | ancient name for Messa | |
| Metapontion | Map 3.4 | A4 |
| Methone | Map 3.5 | G1 |
| Methymna, Lesbos | Map 3.8 | B2 |
| | Map 3.9 | B1 |
| Mikri Glyphada, Samos Town | Figure 3.10 | |
| Miletus | Map 3.1b | C3 |
| | Map 3.10 | D2 |
| monopteros, Samian Heraion | Figure 3.16 | H8/9 |
| Mt. Amali, Lesbos | alternative name for Mt. Kourteri | |
| Mt. Ampelos, Samos | ancient name of Mt. Karvounis | |
| Mt. Ida | Map 3.8 | inset |
| Mt. Karvounis, Samos | Map 3.11 | B1 |
| Mt. Kastro, Samos Town | alternative name for Ampelos hill | |
| Mt. Kerketeus, Samos | ancient name of Mt. Kerkis | |
| Mt. Kerkis, Samos | Map 3.11 | A2 |
| Mt. Kourteri, Lesbos | Map 3.8 | D3 |
| | Map 3.9 | D2 |
| Mt. Leptymnos, Lesbos | Map 3.8 | C2 |
| | Map 3.9 | B/C1 |
| Mt. Mycale | Map 3.1b | C3 |
| | Map 3.10 | C2 |
| Mt. Olympus, Lesbos | Map 3.8 | C3 |
| | Map 3.9 | C2 |
| Mt. Ordymnos, Lesbos | Map 3.8 | B3 |
| | Map 3.9 | B2 |
| Mt. Pelinaion, Chios | Map 3.7 | B1 |
| Mycale Strait | Map 3.11 | C2 |

| Name | Figure/Map # | Grid Designation |
|---|---|---|
| Mytilene, Lesbos | Map 3.8 | D3 |
| | Map 3.9 | D2 |
| Myus | Map 3.1b | C3 |
| | Map 3.10 | D2 |
| Nagidos, Cilicia | Map 3.1a | E3 |
| Nagos, Chios | Map 3.6 | C1 |
| Naiskos II, Samian Heraion | Figure 3.13 | E3 |
| Naiskos IV, Samian Heraion | Figure 3.13 | E3 |
| Naiskos V, Samian Heraion | Figure 3.14 | E2 |
| Naiskos VI, Samian Heraion | Figure 3.14 | E4 |
| Naiskos VII, Samian Heraion | Figure 3.14 | D2 |
| Naucratis | Map 3.5 | I3 |
| Naxos (island) | Map 3.1b | B3 |
| Neochori, Samos | Map 3.10 | B2 |
| Nordbau, Samian Heraion | Figure 3.15 | K3/4 |
| | Figure 3.16 | K3/4 |
| Nordsüd Strasse, Samian Heraion | Figure 3.14 | C1 |
| | Figure 3.15 | I4 |
| | Figure 3.16 | I4 |
| North Harbor, Mytilene | Figure 3.4 | |
| North Necropolis, Mytilene | Figure 3.4 | |
| North Necropolis, Samos Town | Figure 3.10 | |
| North Stoa, Samian Heraion | Figure 3.15 | E4 |
| | Figure 3.15 | E4 |
| Nymphaion | Map 3.3 | G2 |
| Odos Kioutacheias, Mytilene | Figure 3.4 | |
| Odos Lesvosnaktos, Mytilene | Figure 3.4 | |
| Oinoussai Islands | Map 3.6 | C/D1 |
| Olympia | Map 3.2 | A2 |
| Ostweg 1, Samian Heraion | Figure 3.12 | |
| Ostweg 2, Samian Heraion | Figure 3.13 | E3 |
| Otomatik Tepe | see Panionion 2 | |
| Panionion 1 | Map 3.1b | C3 |
| | Map 3.10 | D2 |

| Name | Figure/Map # | Grid Designation |
| --- | --- | --- |
| Panionion 2 | Map 3.1b | C3 |
| | Map 3.10 | C2 |
| Perinthus | Map 3.1a | B1 |
| Phanai, Chios | ancient name for modern Kato Phana | |
| Phaselis | Map 3.1a | D3 |
| Phocaea | Map 3.1b | B2 |
| Phygela | Map 3.10 | D1 |
| Phyta, Chios | Map 3.6 | B/C1 |
| Pindakas, Chios | Map 3.6 | C3 |
| Platanos, Samos | Map 3.10 | A2 |
| Polycrates Temple, Samian Heraion | see Dipteros 2 | |
| pottery workshop, Mytilene | Figure 3.4 (#4) | |
| pottery workshops, Chios Town | see church of Panagia Letsaina | |
| Priene | Map 3.1b | C3 |
| | Map 3.10 | D2 |
| Proconnesos | Map 3.1a | B1 |
| Prophitis Elias hill, Emporio | Figure 3.2 | |
| Propontis | Map 3.1a | B/C1 |
| Protogeometric necropolis, Methymna | Figure 3.5 | |
| Psara | Map 3.6 | A1 |
| Psomi district, Chios Town | Figure 3.1 | |
| Pyrhha, Lesbos | Map 3.8 | C3 |
| | Map 3.9 | C2 |
| Pythagoreio, Samos | modern town located at ancient Samos Town | |
| Rhegium | Map 3.4 | B3 |
| Rheneia | Map 3.1b | A3 |
| Rizari district, Chios Town | Figure 3.1 | |
| Rhodes | Map 3.1b | C/D4 |
| Rhoikos altar, Samian Heraion | Figure 3.15 | K7–9 |
| | Figure 3.16 | K7–9 |
| Rhoikos Temple, Samian Heraion | alternative name for Dipteros 1 | |

| Name | Figure/Map # | Grid Designation |
| --- | --- | --- |
| Rome | Map 3.5 | E1 |
| round platform, Samian Heraion | Figure 3.12 | D2 |
| | Figure 3.13 | D3 |
| | Figure 3.14 | |
| Sacred Way, Samos | Figure 3.14 | E1 |
| | Figure 3.15 | M5 |
| | Figure 3.16 | M5 |
| Salamis | Map 3.2 | inset |
| Samos | Map 3.1b | B3 |
| (topography) | Map 3.10 | A1/B1/C1/A2/B2/ |
| | Map 3.11 | C2 |
| Samos Town, Samos | Map 3.10 | B3 |
| | Map 3.11 | B2 |
| Samothrace | Map 3.3 | A4 |
| Sanctuary of Aphrodite, Mytilene | Figure 3.4 (#5) | |
| Sanctuary of Apollo Maloeis, Mytilene | Figure 3.4 (#6) | |
| Sanctuary of Artemis, Samos Town | Figure 3.10 | |
| Sanctuary of Cybele, Mytilene | Figure 3.4 (#7) | |
| Sanctuary of Demeter and Persephone, Mytilene | Figure 3.4 (#8) | |
| Sanctuary of Demeter and Persephone, Samos Town | Figure 3.10 | |
| Sardis | Map 3.1b | D2 |
| Sigeum | Map 3.8 | inset |
| Sigri, Lesbos | Map 3.8 | A3 |
| Siphnos | Map 3.2 | C2 |
| South Harbor, Mytilene | Figure 3.4 | |
| South Necropolis, Mytilene | Figure 3.4 | |
| South Stoa, Samian Heraion | Figure 3.14 | B4 |
| | Figure 3.15 | H10 |
| | Figure 3.16 | H10 |
| Southern Kouros, Samian Heraion | Figure 3.15 | I6 |
| | Figure 3.16 | I6 |
| Sparta | Map 3.2 | B2 |

| Name | Figure/Map # | Grid Designation |
|---|---|---|
| Spiliani hill, Samos Town | alternative name for Ampelos hill | |
| Strait of Gibraltar | Map 3.5 | A2 |
| Strait of Messina | Map 3.4 | B3 |
| Südbau, Samian Heraion | Figure 3.15 | H/I/J12 |
| | Figure 3.16 | H/I/J12 |
| Südweg, Samian Heraion | Figure 3.14 | E6 |
| Südwestweg, Samian Heraion | Figure 3.14 | C5 |
| Syracuse | Map 3.4 | C3 |
| Syros | Map 3.2 | C2 |
| Tartessus | Map 3.5 | A2 |
| Taucheira | Map 3.2 | A4 |
| Tell Defeneh | Map 3.5 | I3 |
| Temenos, Antissa | Figure 3.6 | |
| temenos wall, Samian Heraion | Figure 3.15 | P2/Q3 |
| | Figure 3.16 | P2/Q3 |
| Temple A, Samian Heraion | Figure 3.15 | I6 |
| | Figure 3.16 | I6 |
| Temple B, Samian Heraion | Figure 3.16 | J5 |
| Temple C, Samian Heraion | Figure 3.16 | J5/6 |
| Temple D, Samian Heraion | Figure 3.16 | H5/6 |
| Thebes | Map 3.5 | I4 |
| Thera | Map 3.2 | C2 |
| Teos | Map 3.1b | B2 |
| terrace with treasury, Samian Heraion | Figure 3.15 | N2/N3/O2/O3 |
| | Figure 3.16 | N2/N3/O2/O3 |
| Tes Kores to Gephyri, Chios | Map 3.6 | C2 |
| Thermi, Lesbos | Map 3.8 | C3 |
| Tholopotami, Chios | Map 3.6 | C2 |
| Thracian Chersonese | Map 3.1a | B1 |
| | Map 3.8 | inset |
| Troad | Map 3.1a | B1–2 |
| | Map 3.8 | inset |
| Volissos, Chios | Map 3.6 | B2 |
| | Map 3.7 | A2 |

| Name | Figure/Map # | Grid Designation |
| --- | --- | --- |
| Vrontados plain, Chios | Map 3.7 | B2 |
| Water basin, Samian Heraion | Figure 3.14 | D7 |
| Water pipeline, Samos Town | Figure 3.10 | |
| Well B, Samian Heraion | Figure 3.12 | |
| Well C, Samian Heraion | Figure 3.12 | |
| Well E, Samian Heraion | Figure 3.13 | D3 |
| Well F, Samian Heraion | Figure 3.13 | B3 |
| Well G, Samian Heraion | Figure 3.13 | B2 |
| Well H, Samian Heraion | Figure 3.13 | E2 |
| Well J, Samian Heraion | Figure 3.14 | E3 |
| Well K, Samian Heraion | Figure 3.14 | E4 |
| Well M, Samian Heraion | Figure 3.14 | E7 |
| West Harbor, Samos Town | Figure 3.10 | |
| West Necropolis, Mytilene | Figure 3.4 | |
| West Necropolis, Samos Town | Figure 3.10 | |
| Westweg, Samian Heraion | Figure 3.12 | |
| Zacynthus | Map 3.2 | A2 |
| Zancle | Map 3.4 | B3 |

## BIBLIOGRAPHY

Abenstein, C. 2021. "Wer ist Kynaithos von Chios?" *Hermes* 149: 4–18.

Acheilara, L. 1987. "Οδός Μανιάτη 11 (οικόπεδο Μ. Αποστολέλη)." *Αρχαιολογικόν Δελτίον* 42 B2: 479.

Acheilara, L. 1999. "Επάνω Σκάλα, Οδός Λεσβώνακτος." *Αρχαιολογικόν Δελτίον* 54 B2: 745–9.

Acheilara, L. 2002–2004. "Μήθυμνα." *Αρχαιολογικόν Δελτίον* 59 B6: 4–5.

Acheilara, L. 2006. *Η Κοροπλαστική της Λέσβου.* 2 vols. Mytilene: Υπουργείο Πολιτισμού, Κ' Εφορεία Προϊστορικών και Κλασικών Αρχαιοτήτων.

Acheilara, L. 2012. "Τα γκριζόχρωμα αγγεία από το αρχαϊκό νεκροταφείο της Μυτιλήνης: η περίπτωση του οικοπέδου Χ. Κρικλάνη -Δ. Κουτσοβίλη." In *Η κεραμικη της αρχαϊκης εποχης στο Βορειο Αιγαιο και την περιφερεια του (700–480 π.Χ.): Πρακτικά Αρχαιολογικής Συνάντησης Θεσσαλονίκη, 19-22 Μαΐου 2011*, edited by M. Tiverios, V. Misailidou-Despotidou, E. Manakidou, et al., 55–68. Thessaloniki: Αρχαιολογικό Ινστιτούτο Μακεδονικών και Θρακικών Σπουδών.

Acheilara, L. 2014. "Τα νέα ευρήματα κοροπλαστικής από τη βόρεια νεκρόπολη τη Μυτιλήνης." In *Κοροπλαστική και μικροτεχνία στον αιγιακό χώρο από τους γεωμετρικούς χρόνους έως και τη ρωμαϊκή περίοδο, Διεθνές συνέδριο στη μνήμη της Ηούς Ζερβουδάκη, Ρόδος, 26–29 Νοεμβρίου 2009*, edited by A. Giannikouri, 1: 261–74. 2 vols. Athens: Υπουργείο Πολιτισμού και Αθλητισμού.

Acheilara, L. 2020. "The Lesbian Masonry on the Island of Lesbos." In *Urbanism and Architecture in Ancient Aiolis: Proceedings of the International Conference from 7th–9th April 2017 in Çanakkale*, edited by E.-M. Mohr, K. Rheidt, and N. Arslan, 279–90. Asia Minor Studien 95. Bonn: Rudolf Habelt.

Acheilara, L., and A. Archontidou-Argyri. 1987. "Μήθυμνα." *Αρχαιολογικόν Δελτίον* 42 B2: 482–3.

Aloni, A. 1989. *L'aedo e i tiranni: Ricerche sull' Inno omerico a Apollo*. Rome: Edizioni dell'Ateneo.

Aloni, A. 1997. *Saffo: Frammenti*. Florence: Giunti.

Aloni, A. 2000. "Anacreonte e Atene: Datazione e significato di alcune iscrizioni tiranniche." *Zeitschrift für Papyrologie und Epigraphik* 81: 81–94.

Aloni, A. 2004. "L' ira di Era: Tracce di committenza samia nell' 'Inno omerico a Apollo.'" In *Samo: Storia, letteratura, scienza*, edited by E. Cavallini, 13–29. Pisa: Istituti Editoriali e Poligrafici Internazionali.

Aloni, A. 2006. *Da Pilo a Sigeo: Poemi, cantori e scrivani al tempo dei tiranni*. Alessandria: Edizioni dell'Orso.

Amigues, S. 2013. "Pyrrha de Lesbos dans les textes et dans les faits." *Journal des savants*: 71–109.

Ampolo, C. 1983. "La Βουλή δημοσίη di Chio: un consiglio 'popolare'?" *La parola del passato* 38: 401–16.

Anderson, G. 2005. "Before *Turannoi* Were Tyrants: Rethinking a Chapter of Early Greek History." *Classical Antiquity* 24: 173–222.

Andrewes, A. 1956. *The Greek Tyrants*. London: Hutchinson.

Angistalis, G., G. Dounias, G. Tsokas, et al. 2018. "The Walls of Eupalinos Aqueduct, Samos Island, Greece: Description, Pathology and Proposed Restoration Measures." *Bulletin of the Geological Society of Greece* 53: 193–228.

Apostol, T. 2004. "The Tunnel of Samos." *Engineering and Science* 1: 30–40.

Archibald, Z. H. Forthcoming. "Macedonia." In *The Oxford History of the Archaic Greek World*, edited by P. Cartledge and P. Christesen, *The Oxford History of the Archaic Greek World*, Volume 4. New York: Oxford University Press.

Archontidou-Argyri, A. 1989. "Χρονικά της Κ' Εφορείας Προϊστορικών και Κλασικών Αρχαιοτήτων έτους 1986-1987." *Lesbiaka* 12: 56–76.

Argenti, P. 1940. *Bibliography of Chios from Classical Times to 1936*. Oxford: Clarendon Press.

Asheri, D., A. B. Lloyd, and A. Corcella. 2007. *A Commentary on Herodotus: Books I–IV*. Oxford: Oxford University Press.

Aubet, M. E. 2007. "East Greek and Etruscan Pottery in a Phoenician Context." In *"Up to the Gates of Ekron": Essays on the Archaeology and History of the Eastern Mediterranean in Honor of Seymour Gitin*, edited by S. White Crawford and A. Ben-Tor, 447–60. Jerusalem: Israel Exploration Society.

Austin, M. M. 1970. *Greece and Egypt in the Archaic Age: Proceedings of the Cambridge Philological Society*, Supplement 2. Cambridge: Cambridge Philological Society.

Austin, M. M. 1990. "Greek Tyrants and the Persians, 546-479 B.C." *Classical Quarterly* 40: 289–306.

Austin, M. M. 2004. "From Syria to the Pillars of Herakles." In *An Inventory of Archaic and Classical Poleis*, edited by M. H. Hansen and T. H. Nielsen, 1233–49. Oxford: Oxford University Press.

Averett, E. W. 2007. "Dedications in Clay: Terracotta Figurines in Early Iron Age Greece (c. 1100–700 BCE)." PhD diss., University of Missouri.

Avram, A., J. Hind, and G. R. Tsetskhladze. 2004. "The Black Sea Area." In *An Inventory of Archaic and Classical Poleis*, edited by M. H. Hansen and T. H. Nielsen, 924–73. Oxford: Oxford University Press.

Baika, K. 2015. "Ancient Harbour Cities: New Methodological Perspectives and Recent Research in Greece." In *Harbors and Harbor Cities in the Eastern Mediterranean from Antiquity to the Byzantine Period: Recent Discoveries and Current Approaches*, edited by S. Ladtstätter, F. Pirson, and T. Schmidts, 445–91. Istanbul: Deutsches Archäologisches Institut.

Bakker, E., I. de Jong, and H. van Wees, eds. 2002. *Brill's Companion to Herodotus*. Leiden: Brill.

Baragwanath, E. 2008. *Motivation and Narrative in Herodotus*. Oxford: Oxford University Press.

Baron, C., ed. 2021. *The Herodotus Encyclopedia*. 3 vols. Hoboken, NJ: Wiley-Blackwell.

Barron, J. P. 1964. "The Sixth-Century Tyranny at Samos." *Classical Quarterly* 14: 210–29.

Barron, J. P. 1966. *The Silver Coins of Samos*. London: Athlone Press.

Barron, J. P. 1986. "Chios in the Athenian Empire." In *Chios: A Conference at the Homereion in Chios*, edited by C. E. Vaphopoulou-Richardson and J. Boardman, 89–103. Oxford: Clarendon Press.

Baughan, E. P. 2011. "Sculpted Symposiasts of Ionia." *American Journal of Archaeology* 115: 19–53.

Baumbach, J. D. 2004. *The Significance of Votive Offerings in Selected Hera Sanctuaries in the Peloponnese, Ionia, and Western Greece*. BAR International Series 1249. Oxford: Archaeopress.

Bayne, N. 1963. "The Grey Wares of North-West Anatolia in the Middle and Late Bronze Age and the Early Iron Age and Their Relation to Early Greek Settlements." PhD diss., Oxford University.

Beaumont, L., A. Archontidou-Argyri, H. Beames, et al. 2004. "Excavations at Kato Phana, Chios: 1999, 2000 & 2001." *Annual of the British School at Athens* 99: 201–55.

Beaumont, L. A. 2019. "Shaping the Ancient Religious Landscape at Kato Phana, Chios." In *Listening to the Stones: Essays on Architecture and Function in Ancient Greek Sanctuaries in Honour of Richard Alan Tomlinson*, edited by E. Partida and B. Schmidt-Dounas, 182–90. Oxford: Archaeopress.

Bechtold, B., and R. F. Docter. 2010. "Transport Amphorae from Punic Carthage: An Overview." In *Motya and the Phoenician Ceramic Repertoire between the Levant and the West 9th–6th Century BC*, edited by L. Nigro, 85–116. Quaderni di archeologia fenicio-punica 5. Rome: University of Rome La Sapienza.

Beck-Schachter, A. 2019. "The Tonaia and Samian Identity." In *Religious Convergence in the Ancient Mediterranean*, edited by S. Blakely and B. J. Collins, 437–54. Studies in Ancient Mediterranean Religions 2. Atlanta: Lockwood Press.

Beecroft, A. 2010. *Authorship and Cultural Identity in Early Greece and China: Patterns of Literary Circulation*. Cambridge: Cambridge University Press.

Bergeron, M. 2014. "Chian Pottery." In *Naukratis: Greeks in Egypt*, edited by A. C. Villing, M. Bergeron, G. Bourogiannis, et al., www.britishmuseum.org/pdf/Bergeron_Chian_Pottery.pdf. London: British Museum Press.

Bernabé, A., ed. 1987. *Poetae Epici Graeci: Testimonia et Fragmenta*. Leipzig: Teubner.

Bernsdorff, H. 2011. "Notes on *P.Oxy.* 3722 (Commentary on Anacreon)." *Zeitschrift für Papyrologie und Epigraphik* 178: 29–34.

Bernstein, F. 2019. "'Ionische Migration' vs. 'Große Kolonisation der Griechen': Kategorien und Konsquenzen." *Historia* 68: 258–84.

Berve, H. 1967. *Die Tyrannis bei den Griechen*. 2 vols. Munich: C. H. Beck.

Betancourt, P. 1977. *The Aeolic Style in Architecture: A Survey of Its Development in Palestine, the Halikarnassos Peninsula, and Greece, 1000–500 B.C.* Princeton, NJ: Princeton University Press.

Bianchi, R. S. 1990. "Egyptian Metal Statuary of the Third Intermediate Period (circa 1070–656 B.C.) from Its Egyptian Antecedents to Its Samian Examples." In *Small Bronze Sculpture from the Ancient World: Papers Delivered at a Symposium Organized by the Departments of Antiquities and Antiquities Conservation and Held at the J. Paul Getty Museum, March 16–19, 1989*, 61–84. Malibu, CA: J. Paul Getty Museum.

Bîrzescu, I. 2005. "Die Handelsamphoren der 'Lesbos Rot'-Serie in Istros." *Mitteilungen des Deutschen Archäologischen Instituts, Athenische Abteilung* 120: 45–69.

Bissa, E. M. A. 2009. *Governmental Intervention in Foreign Trade in Archaic and Classical Greece. Mnemosyne* Supplementum 312. Leiden: Brill.

Boardman, J. 1956. "Chian and Naucratite." *Annual of the British School at Athens* 51: 55–62.

Boardman, J. 1959. "Chian and Early Ionic Architecture." *Antiquaries Journal* 39: 170–218.

Boardman, J. 1967. *Excavations in Chios, 1952–1955: Greek Emporio*. British School at Athens Supplementary Volume 6. London: Thames & Hudson.

Boardman, J. 1979. "The Problems of Analyses of Clays and Some General Observations on Possible Results." In *Les céramiques de la Grèce de l'Est et leur diffusion en Occident*, edited by G. Vallet, 281–90. Paris: CNRS Éditions.

Boardman, J. 1986. "Archaic Chian Pottery at Naucratis." In *Chios: A Conference at the Homereion in Chios*, edited by C. E. Vaphopoulou-Richardson and J. Boardman, 250–8. Oxford: Clarendon Press.

Boardman, J. 1998. "The Ragusa Group." In *In memoria di Enrico Paribeni*, edited by G. Capecchi, E. Paribeni, and O. Paoletti, 59–65. Archaeologica 125. Rome: Bretschneider.

Boardman, J., and J. W. Hayes. 1966. *Excavations at Tocra 1963–1965: The Archaic Deposits I*. British School at Athens Supplementary Volume 4. London: Thames & Hudson.

Boardman, J., and J. W. Hayes. 1973. *Excavations at Tocra 1963–1965: The Archaic Deposits II and Later Deposits*. British School at Athens Supplementary Volume 10. London: Thames & Hudson.

Bodenstedt, F. 1981. *Die Elektronmünzen von Phokaia und Mytilene*. Tübingen: Wasmuth.

Boehlau, J. 1898. *Aus Ionischen und italischen Nekropolen*. Leipzig: Teubner.

Bound, M. 1991. *The Giglio Wreck: A Wreck of the Archaic Period (c. 600 BC) off the Tuscan Island of Giglio: An Account of Its Discovery and Excavation, a Review of the Main Finds. Enalia* Supplement 1. Athens: Hellenic Institute of Marine Archaeology.

Bowie, E. L. 1986. "Early Greek Elegy, Symposium and Public Festival." *Journal of Hellenic Studies* 106: 13–35.

Bowra, C. M. 1961. *Greek Lyric Poetry, from Alcman to Simonides*. 2nd ed. Oxford: Clarendon Press.

Braun, T. F. R. G. 1982. "The Greeks in the Near East." In *The Cambridge Ancient History, Volume III, Part 1: The Prehistory of the Balkans, the Middle East and the Aegean World, Tenth to Eighth Centuries B.C.*, edited by J. Boardman, I. E. S. Edwards, N. G. L. Hammond, et al., 1–31. Cambridge: Cambridge University Press.

Breitenstein, N. 1946. *Sylloge Nummorum Graecorum: The Royal Collection of Coins and Medals, Danish National Museum, Part 24: Ionia, Pt. 3: Smyrna–Teos; Islands*. Copenhagen: Munksgaard.

Bresson, A. 2000. *La cité marchande*. Bordeaux: Ausonius Éditions.

Bresson, A. 2016. *The Making of the Ancient Greek Economy: Institutions, Markets, and Growth in the City-States*. Princeton, NJ: Princeton University Press.

Briant, P. 2002. *From Cyrus to Alexander: A History of the Persian Empire*. Translated by P. T. Daniels. Winona Lake, IN: Eisenbrauns.

Brown, A. 2020. "Anatolia." In *A Companion to Greeks across the Ancient World*, edited by F. De Angelis, 221–45. Hoboken, NJ: Wiley-Blackwell.

Buchholz, H.-G. 1975. *Methymna. Archäologische Beiträge zur Topographie und Geschichte von Nordlesbos*. Mainz: Philipp von Zabern.

Budelmann, F. 2009a. "Anacreon and the Anacreontea." In *The Cambridge Companion to Greek Lyric*, edited by F. Budelmann, 227–39. Cambridge: Cambridge University Press.

Budelmann, F., ed. 2009b. *The Cambridge Companion to Greek Lyric*. Cambridge: Cambridge University Press.

Bumke, H. 2004. *Statuarische Gruppen in der frühen griechischen Kunst*. Berlin: Walter de Gruyter.

Buraselis, K. 2015. "Federalism and the Sea: The *Koina* of the Aegean Islands." In *Federalism in Greek Antiquity*, edited by H. Beck and P. Funke, 358–76. Cambridge: Cambridge University Press.

Burgemeister, K. 2012. "Chiische Chalikes: Wein und Ritual, Überlegungen zur Verwendung eines archaischen Trinkgefässes." In *Tryphe und Kultritual im archaischen Kleinasien—ex oriente luxuria?*, edited by L.-M. Günther, 126–38. Wiesbaden: Harrassowitz.

Burkert, W. 1972. "Die Leistung eines Kreophylos: Kreophyleer, Homeriden und die archäische Heraklesepik." *Museum Helveticum* 29: 74–85.

Burkert, W. 1979. "Kynaithos, Polycrates, and the Homeric Hymn to Apollo." In *Arktouros: Hellenic Studies Presented to Bernard M. W. Knox on the Occasion of His 65th Birthday*, edited by M. Putnam, W. Burkert, and G. W. Bowersock, 53–62. Berlin: Walter de Gruyter.

Burkert, W. 1995. "Lydia between East and West or How to Date the Trojan War: A Study in Herodotus." In *The Ages of Homer: A Tribute to Emily Townsend Vermeule*, edited by J. P. Carter and S. P. Morris, 139–48. Austin: University of Texas Press.

Burkert, W. 2004. "Policrate nelle testimonianze letterarie." In *Samo: Storia, letteratura, scienza*, edited by E. Cavallini, 351–61. Pisa: Istituti Editoriali e Poligrafici Internazionali.

Buschor, E. 1930. "Heraion von Samos: Frühe Bauten." *Mitteilungen des Deutschen Archäologischen Instituts, Athenische Abteilung* 55: 1–99.

Buschor, E. 1957. "Aphrodite and Hermes." *Mitteilungen des Deutschen Archäologischen Instituts, Athenische Abteilung* 72: 77–86.

Buschor, E., and H. Schleif. 1933. "Heraion von Samos: Der Altarplatz der Frühzeit." *Mitteilungen des Deutschen Archäologischen Instituts, Athenische Abteilung* 58: 146–73.

Caciagli, S. 2011. *Poeti e società: Comunicazione poetica e formazioni sociali nella Lesbo del VII/VI secolo a.C.* Amsterdam: Adolf M. Hakkert.

Carlier, P. 1984. *La royauté en Grèce avant Alexandre*. Strasbourg: AECR.

Cartledge, P. 1982. "Sparta and Samos: A Special Relationship?" *Classical Quarterly* 32: 243–65.

Carty, A. 2015. *Polycrates, Tyrant of Samos: New Light on Archaic Greece*. Stuttgart: Franz Steiner Verlag.

Carusi, C. 2003. *Isole e peree in Asia Minore: Contributi allo studio dei rapporti tra poleis insulari e territori continentali dipendenti*. Pubblicazioni della Classe di Lettere e Filosofia, Scuola Normale Superiore Pisa 28. Pisa: Scuola Normale Superiore.

Casadio, G. 2004. "Il culto di Hera a Samo." In *Samo: Storia, letteratura, scienza*, edited by E. Cavallini, 135–55. Pisa: Istituti Editoriali e Poligrafici Internazionali.

Casevitz, M., and F. Frontisi-Ducroux. 1989. "Le masque du 'Phallen': Sur une épiclèse de Dionysos à Méthymna." *Revue de l'histoire des religions* 206: 115–27.

Càssola, F., ed. 1975. *Inni Omerici*. Milan: Mondadori.

454 THE OXFORD HISTORY OF THE ARCHAIC GREEK WORLD

Cavallini, E., ed. 2004. *Samo: Storia, letteratura, scienza*. Pisa: Istituti Editoriali e Poligrafici Internazionali.

Cawkwell, G. L. 1995. "Early Greek Tyranny and the People." *Classical Quarterly* 45: 73–86.

Charitonidis, S. 1964. "Αρχαιότητες καὶ μνημεῖα νήσων Αἰγαίου: Λέσβος." *Αρχαιολογικόν Δελτίον* 19 B3: 396–400.

Charitonidis, S. 1968. *Αι Επιγραφαί Τῆς Λέσβου: Συμπλήρωμα*. Βιβλιοθήκη της εν Αθήναις Αρχαιολογικής Εταιρείας 60. Athens: Η εν Αθήναις Αρχαιολογική Εταιρεία.

Christesen, P. 2007. *Olympic Victor Lists and Ancient Greek History*. Cambridge: Cambridge University Press.

Clemente, A. 2010. "Zur Basis der Geneleos-Gruppe." *Mitteilungen des Deutschen Archäologischen Instituts, Athenische Abteilung* 125: 133–42.

Clinkenbeard, B. G. 1982. "Lesbian Wine and Storage Amphoras: A Progress Report on Identification." *Hesperia* 51: 248–68.

Coldstream, J. N. 2003. *Geometric Greece: 900–700 BC*. 2nd ed. University Paperbacks 680. London: Routledge.

Cole, S. G. 1995. "Civic Cult and Civic Identity." In *Sources for the Ancient Greek City-State*, edited by M. H. Hansen, 292–325. Acts of the Copenhagen Polis Centre 2. Copenhagen: Munksgaard.

Condello, F. 2020. "Asius fr. 13 Davies (= Bernabé = West = Tsagalis): Note testuali e proposta di esegesi (con qualche osservazione su Duride)." *Athenaeum* 108: 5–57.

Constantakopoulou, C. 2007. *The Dance of the Islands: Insularity, Networks, the Athenian Empire, and the Aegean World*. Oxford: Oxford University Press.

Constantakopoulou, C. 2014. "Semonides of Samos or of Amorgos? The *Archaeology of the Samians* and the Question of the Archaic Colonization of Amorgos Reconsidered." In *Pouvoirs, îles et mer: Formes et modalités de l'hégémonie dans les Cyclades antiques (viie s. a.C.–iiie s. p.C.)*, edited by G. Bonnin and E. Le Quéré, 257–68. Scripta Antiqua 64. Bordeaux: Ausonius Éditions.

Conze, A. 1865. *Reise auf der Insel Lesbos*. Hanover: Carl Rümpler.

Cook, R. M. 1933–1934. "Fikellura Pottery." *Annual of the British School at Athens* 34: 1–98.

Cook, R. M. 1997. *Greek Painted Pottery*. 3rd ed. London: Routledge.

Cook, R. M., and P. Dupont. 1998. *East Greek Pottery*. London: Routledge.

Cook, R. M., and A. G. Woodhead. 1952. "Painted Inscriptions on Chiot Pottery." *Annual of the British School at Athens* 47: 159–70.

Coulson, W. D. E. 1988. "The Dark Age Pottery of Sparta II: Vrondama." *Annual of the British School at Athens* 83: 21–4.

Coulson, W. D. E. 1996. *Ancient Naukratis II.1: The Survey at Naukratis*. Oxford: Oxbow Books.

Crielaard, J. P. 2009. "The Ionians in the Archaic Period: Shifting Identities in a Changing World." In *Ethnic Constructs in Antiquity: The Role of Power and*

*Tradition*, edited by N. Roymans and T. Derks, 37–84. Amsterdam: Amsterdam University Press.

Cristofani, M. 1992–1993. "Un naukleros greco-orientale nel Tirreno: Per un'interpretazione del relitto del Giglio." *Annuario della Scuola Archeologica di Atene e delle Missioni Italiane in Oriente* 70: 205–32.

Cronkite, S.-M. 1997. "The Sanctuary of Demeter at Mytilene: A Diachronic and Contextual Study." PhD diss., University College London.

Dale, A. 2011. "Alcaeus on the Career of Myrsilos: Greeks, Lydians and Luwians at the East Aegean–West Anatolian Interface." *Journal of Hellenic Studies* 131: 15–24.

D'Alessio, G. B. 2018. "Fiction and Pragmatics in Ancient Greek Lyric: The Case of Sappho." In *Textual Events. Performance and the Lyric in Early Greece*, edited by F. Budelmann and T. Phillips, 31–62. Oxford: Oxford University Press.

Daux, G. 1943. *Inscriptions depuis le Trésor des Athéniens jusqu'aux Bases de Gélon.* Fouilles de Delphes III.3. Paris: De Boccard.

Davies, O. 1932. "Bronze Age Mining Round the Aegean." *Nature* 130: 985–7.

De Angelis, F. and V. Mignosa. Forthcoming. "Syracuse." In *The Oxford History of the Archaic Greek World*, edited by P. Cartledge and P. Christesen, *The Oxford History of the Archaic Greek World*, Volume 6. New York: Oxford University Press.

De Domingo, C. A., and A. W. Johnston. 2003. "A Petrographic and Chemical Study of East Greek and Other Archaic Transport Amphorae." *Ευλιμένη* 4: 27–60.

Del Barrio, M. L. 2014. "Ionic." In *Encyclopedia of Ancient Greek Language and Linguistics*, edited by G. K. Giannakis, 2: 260–7. 3 vols. Leiden: Brill.

Demani, S., V. Boura, D. Tsardaka, *et al.* 2019. "Οι νεκροπόλεις της αρχαίας πόλεως Χίου. Έθιμα ταφής και πρακτικές ενταφιασμού από τον 7ο έως τον 4ο αι. π.Χ." In *Σωστικές ανασκαφές της Αρχαιολογικής Υπηρεσίας. Ι, Τα νεκροταφεία. Χωροταξική οργάνωση - ταφικά έθιμα - τελετουργίες*, edited by E. Kountouri and A. Gadolou, 3: 281-311. 3 vols. Athens: Ταμείο Αρχαιολογικών Πόρων και Απαλλοτριώσεων.

Deramaix, A. 2014. "Une thalassocratie samienne au vie s. a.C.?" In *Pouvoirs, îles et mer: Formes et modalités de l'hégémonie dans les Cyclades antiques (viie s. a.C.–iiie s. p.C.)*, edited by G. Bonnin and E. Le Quéré, 25–43. Scripta Antiqua 64. Bordeaux: Ausonius Éditions.

De Souza, P. 1998. "Towards Thalassocracy? Archaic Greek Naval Developments." In *Archaic Greece: New Approaches and New Evidence*, edited by H. van Wees and N. Fisher, 271–94. London: Classical Press of Wales.

De Souza, P. 1999. *Piracy in the Graeco-Roman World.* Cambridge: Cambridge University Press.

Dewald, C., and J. Marincola, eds. 2006. *The Cambridge Companion to Herodotus.* Cambridge: Cambridge University Press.

Dewald, C., and R. V. Munson, eds. 2022. *Herodotus Histories Book I.* Cambridge: Cambridge University Press.

Dimopoulou, A. A. 2017. "'The Lion and the Sage': Writing the Law in Archaic Lesbos." *Rivista di diritto ellenico* 7: 19–36.

456 THE OXFORD HISTORY OF THE ARCHAIC GREEK WORLD

Dimopoulou-Piliouni, A. A. 2015. *Λεσβίων Πολιτεία. Πολίτευμα, θεσμοί και δίκαιο των πόλεων της Λέσβου (αρχαϊκοί, κλασικοί, ελληνιστικοί ρωμαϊκοί χρόνοι*. Athens: Eurasia.

Dinsmoor, W. B. 1950. *The Architecture of Ancient Greece*. 3rd ed. London: Batsford.

Douloumbekis, N. 2014. "Η οικοδόμηση των Ναών Α και Β." In *Αιολικό Ιερό Κλοπεδής Λέσβου*, edited by K. Roungou and N. Douloumbekis, 41–50. Mytilene: Εφορεία Αρχαιοτήτων Λέσβου.

Douloumbekis, N., and G. Kossyphidou. 2014a. "Η περίοδος πριν από την ίδρυση του Ιερού: προς το τέλος της 2ης π.Χ. χιλιετίας." In *Αιολικό Ιερό Κλοπεδής Λέσβου*, edited by K. Roungou and N. Douloumbekis, 26–9. Mytilene: Εφορεία Αρχαιοτήτων Λέσβου.

Douloumbekis, N., and G. Kossyphidou. 2014b. "Η περίοδος των πρώιμων Αρχαϊκών χρόνων (7ος π.Χ. αιώνας)." In *Αιολικό Ιερό Κλοπεδής Λέσβου*, edited by K. Roungou and N. Douloumbekis, 37–9. Mytilene: Εφορεία Αρχαιοτήτων Λέσβου.

Dunst, G. 1972. "Archaische Inschriften und Dokumente der Pentekontaetie aus Samos." *Mitteilungen des Deutschen Archäologischen Instituts, Athenische Abteilung* 87: 99–163.

Duplouy, A. 2006. *Le prestige des élites: Recherches sur les modes de reconnaissance sociale en Grèce entre les Xe et Ve siècles avant J.-C.* Histoire (Les Belles Lettres, Paris) 77. Paris: Les Belles Lettres.

Dupont, P. 1982. "Amphores commerciales archaïques de la Grèce de l'Est." *La parola del passato* 37: 193–209.

Dupont, P. 1983. "Classification et détermination de provenance des céramiques grecques orientales archaïques d'Istros: Rapport préliminaire." *Dacia* 27: 19–46.

Dupont, P. 2001. "Amphores 'Samiennes' archaïques: Sources de confusion et questionnements." In *Ceràmiques jònies d'època arcaica: Centres de producció i comercialització al Mediterrani occidental, Actes de la Taula Rodona celebrada a Empúries, els dies 26 al 28 de maig de 1999*, edited by P. Cabrera Bonet and M. Santos Retolaza, 57–62. Monografies Emporitanes 11. Barcelona: Museu d'Arqueologia de Catalunya.

Dupont, P. 2011. "Données archéometriques préliminaires sur les amphores du type de Lesbos." In *PATABS II: Production and Trade of Amphorae in the Black Sea, Acts of the International Round Table Held in Kiten, Nessebar, and Sredetz, September 26–30, 2007*, edited by C. Tzochev, 171–8. Sofia: Bulgarian Academy of Sciences.

Dupont, P. 2021. "Lesbos Wine: ΟΙΝΟΣ ΑΥΘΙΓΕΝΗΣ or Regional Vintage Spread throughout the Lesbian Sphere?" *Materiale și Cercetări Arheologice* 17: 71–85.

Dzierzbicka, D. 2015. "Import of Wine to Egypt in the Graeco-Roman Period." In *Olive Oil and Wine Production in Eastern Mediterranean during Antiquity: International Symposium Proceedings, 17–19 November 2011, Urla, Turkey*, edited by A. Diler, A. K. Şenol, and U. M. Aydınoğlu, 201–8. Ege Universitesi Edebiyat Fakültesi yayınları 189. Izmir: Ege Universitesi Edebiyat Fakültesi Yayınları.

Ebbinghaus, S. 2006. "Begegnungen mit Ägypten und Vorderasien im archaischen Heraheiligtum von Samos." In *Stranieri e non cittadini nei santuari greci: Atti del convegno internazionale, Firenze*, edited by A. Naso, 187–229. Studi Udinesi sul Mondo Antico 2. Florence: Le Monnier.

Ekroth, G. 2018. "The Crocodile on Samos, or Africa in the Aegean." In *The Resilience of Heritage: Cultivating a Future of the Past, Essays in Honour of Professor Paul J. J. Sinclair*, edited by C. Isendahl, A. Ekblom, and K.-J. Lindholm, 61–8. Studies in Global Archaeology 23. Uppsala: Uppsala Department of Archaeology and Ancient History.

Ellis-Evans, A. 2019. *The Kingdom of Priam: Lesbos and the Troad between Anatolia and the Aegean*. Oxford: Oxford University Press.

Evangelidis, D. 1921. "Ἀνασκαφὴ Ναγοῦ Χιω." *Ἀρχαιολογικὴ ἐφημερίς*: 45–52.

Evangelidis, D. 1922–1925. "Ἀνασκαφαὶ ἐν Λέσβῳ." *Ἀρχαιολογικὸν Δελτίον, Παράρτημα*: 41–4.

Evangelidis, D. 1925–1926. "Ἀνασκαφικαὶ ἔρευναι ἐν Λέσβῳ." *Πρακτικὰ τῆς ἐν Ἀθήναις Ἀρχαιολογικῆς Ἑταιρείας*: 147–56.

Evangelidis, D. 1927. "Ἀνασκαφαὶ ἐν Λέσβῳ." *Πρακτικὰ τῆς ἐν Ἀθήναις Ἀρχαιολογικῆς Ἑταιρείας*: 57–9.

Evangelidis, D. 1928. "Ἀνασκαφὴ Κλοπεδῆς Λέσβου." *Πρακτικὰ τῆς ἐν Ἀθήναις Ἀρχαιολογικῆς Ἑταιρείας*: 126–37.

Fagerström, K. 1988. *Greek Iron Age Architecture: Developments through Changing Times*. Studies in Mediterranean Archaeology 81. Gothenburg: Paul Åströms Förlag.

Fantalkin, A. 2022. "Did Ionian or Other Greek and Carian Mercenaries Serve in the Neo-Assyrian Army?" In *Ionians in the West and East: Proceedings of the International Conference "Ionians in East and West," Museu d'Arqueologia de Catalunya-Empuries, Empuries/L'Escala, Spain, 26–29 October, 2015*, edited by G. R. Tsetskhladze, 441–66. Colloquia Antiqua 27. Leuven: Peeters.

Faraguna, M. 2005. "Terra pubblica e vendite di immobili confiscati a Chio nel V secolo a.C." *Dike: Rivista di storia del diritto greco ed ellenistico* 8: 89–99.

Felsch, R. 1988. *Das Kastro Tigani: die spätneolithische und chalkolithische Siedlung*. Samos 2. Bonn: Rudolf Habelt.

Ferrari, F. 2010a. "Introduzione." In *Inni Omerici*, edited by S. Poli, 9–34. Torino: UTET.

Ferrari, F. 2010b. *Sappho's Gift: The Poet and Her Community*. Translated by B. Acosta-Hughes and L. Prauscello. Ann Arbor: Michigan Classical Press.

Ferrari, F. 2011. "Da Kato Simi a Mitilene: Ancora sull'ode dell'ostrakon fiorentino." *La parola del passato* 66: 442–63.

Figueira, T. J. 1998. *The Power of Money*. Philadelphia: University of Pennsylvania Press.

Figueira, T. J. 2015. "Archaic Naval Warfare." *Historiká: Studi di storia greca e romana* 5: 499–514.

Fischer-Hansen, T., T. H. Nielsen, and C. Ampolo. 2004. "Italia and Kampania." In *An Inventory of Archaic and Classical Poleis*, edited by M. H. Hansen and T. H. Nielsen, 249–320. Oxford: Oxford University Press.

Forrest, W. G. 1960. "The Tribal Organization of Chios." *Annual of the British School at Athens* 55: 172–89.

458 THE OXFORD HISTORY OF THE ARCHAIC GREEK WORLD

Forrest, W. G. 1963. "The Inscriptions of South-East Chios, I." *Annual of the British School at Athens* 58: 53–67.

Forsdyke, S. 2002. "Greek History c. 525–480 BC." In *Brill's Companion to Herodotus*, edited by E. Bakker, I. de Jong, and H. van Wees, 521–49. Leiden: Brill.

Forsdyke, S. 2005. *Exile, Ostracism, and Democracy: The Politics of Expulsion in Ancient Greece*. Princeton, NJ: Princeton University Press.

Forsdyke, S. 2012. *Slaves Tell Tales and Other Episodes in the Politics of Popular Culture in Ancient Greece*. Princeton, NJ: Princeton University Press.

Fouchard, A. 1998. "'Dèmosios' et 'dèmos': Sur l'état grec." In *Public et privé en Grèce ancienne: Lieux, conduites, pratiques*, edited by F. de Polignac and P. Schmitt Pantel, 59–70. *Ktèma* 23. Strasbourg: Centre de Recherches sur le Proche-Orient et la Grèce Antiques.

Frame, D. 2009. *Hippota Nestor*. Cambridge, MA: Harvard University Press.

Franke, P. R. 1975. "Zur Münzpragung von Methymna." In *Methymna: Archäologische Beitrage zur Topographie und Geschichte von Nordlesbos*, edited by H.-G. Buchholz, 163–76. Mainz: Philipp von Zabern.

Franssen, J. 2011. *Votiv und Repräsentation: Statuarische Weihungen archaischer Zeit aus Samos und Attika*. Archäologie und Geschichte 13. Heidelberg: Verlag Archäologie und Geschichte.

Frazer, J. G., ed. 1913. *Pausanias's Description of Greece*. 2nd ed. 6 vols. London: Macmillan.

Frederiksen, R. 2011. *Greek City Walls of the Archaic Period, 900–480 BC*. Oxford: Oxford University Press.

Frederiksen, R. 2017. "Fortifications in the Seventh Century: Where and Why?" In *Interpreting the Seventh Century BC: Tradition and Innovation, Proceedings of the International Colloquium Conference Held at the British School at Athens, 9th–11th December 2011*, edited by X. Charalambidou and C. A. Morgan, 186–92. Oxford: Archaeopress.

Freyer-Schauenburg, B. 1966a. *Elfenbeine aus dem samischen Heraion: Figürliches, Gefäße und Siegel*. Abhandlungen aus dem Gebiet der Auslandskunde (Universität Hamburg) 70. Hamburg: Cram.

Freyer-Schauenburg, B. 1966b. "Kolaios und die Westphönizischen Elfenbeine." *Madrider Mitteilungen* 7: 89–108.

Freyer-Schauenburg, B. 1974. *Bildwerke der archaischen Zeit und des strengen Stils*. Samos 11. Bonn: Rudolf Habelt.

Fridh-Haneson, B. M. 1988. "Hera's Wedding on Samos: A Change of Paradigm." In *Early Greek Cult Practice: Proceedings of the Fifth International Symposion at the Swedish Institute at Athens, 26.–29. June 1986*, edited by R. Hägg, N. Marinatos, and G. Nordquist, 205–13. Skrifter Utgivna av Svenska Institutet i Athen 4° 38. Stockholm: Swedish Institute at Athens.

Fullerton, M. D. 2016. *Greek Sculpture*. Malden, MA: Wiley-Blackwell.

Funke, P. 1999. "PERAIA: Einige Überlegungen zum Festlandbesitz griechischer Inselstaaten." In *Hellenistic Rhodes: Politics, Culture, and Society*, edited by V.

Gabrielsen, 55–75. Studies in Hellenistic Civilization Volume 9. Aarhus: Aarhus University Press.

Furtwängler, A. E. 2010. "Herodot 3,56: Polykrates als Falschmünzer? Zu neuen Münzfunden und Finanzmanipulationen im archaischen Ionien." In *Studia Hellenistica et Historiographica: Festschrift für Andreas Mehl*, 159–70. Gutenbberg: Computus.

Fustel de Coulanges, N. D. 1856. "Memoire sur l'ile de Chio." *Archives des Missions Scientifiques et Littéraires* 5: 481–642.

Gagarin, M. 2008. *Writing Greek Law*. Cambridge: Cambridge University Press.

Gagné, R. 2009. "Atreid Ancestors in Alkaios." *Journal of Hellenic Studies* 129: 39–43.

Galvagno, E. 1994. "L'economia del tiranno: Il caso di Policrate di Samo." *Rivista storica dell'antichità* 24: 7–47.

Gardner, E. 1888. *Naukratis II*. London: Trübner.

Gattinoni, F. L. 1997. *Duride di Samo*. Monografie Centro Ricerche e Documentazione sull'Antichita Classica 18. Rome: Bretschneider.

Gehrig, U. 2004. *Die Greifenprotomen aus dem Heraion von Samos*. Samos 9. Bonn: Rudolf Habelt.

Georgoudi, S. 2011. "Sacrificing to Dionysos: Regular and Particular Rituals." In *A Different God? Dionysos and Ancient Polytheism*, edited by R. Schlesier, 47–60. Berlin: Walter de Gruyter.

Gherchanoc, F. 2016. *Concours de beauté et beautés du corps en Grèce ancienne: Discours et pratique*. Bordeaux: Ausonius Éditions.

Giannini, P. 2004. "Ibico a Samo." In *Samo: Storia, letteratura, scienza*, edited by E. Cavallini, 51–64. Pisa: Istituti Editoriali e Poligrafici Internazionali.

Giannouli, V. 1996. "Neue Befunde zur Wasserversorgung der archaischen Stadt Samos." *Archäologischer Anzeiger*: 247–57.

Giannouli, V. 2001–2004. "Σάμος." *Αρχαιολογικόν Δελτίον* 56-9 B6: 33–56.

Gitler, H., Y. Goren, K. Konuk, et al. 2020. "XRF Analysis of Several Groups of Electrum Coins." In *White Gold: Studies in Early Electrum Coinage*, edited by P. van Alfen and U. Wartenberg, 379–422. New York: American Numismatic Society.

Gow, A. S. F., and D. L. Page, eds. 1965. *The Greek Anthology: Hellenistic Epigrams*. 2 vols. Cambridge: Cambridge University Press.

Grace, V. 1971. "Samian Amphoras." *Hesperia* 40: 52–95.

Grace, V. 1979. *Amphoras and the Ancient Wine Trade*. Excavations of the Athenian Agora Picture Book 6. Princeton, NJ: American School of Classical Studies at Athens.

Graf, D. F. 1985. "Greek Tyrants and Achaemenid Politics." In *The Craft of the Ancient Historian: Essays in Honor of Chester G. Starr*, edited by J. W. Eadie and J. Ober, 79–123. Lanham, MD: University Press of America.

Graf, F. 1985. *Nordionische Kulte: Religionsgeschichtliche und epigraphische Untersuchungen zu den Kulten von Chios, Erythrai, Klazomenai und Phokaia*. Rome: Schweizerisches Institut in Rom.

Graham, A. J. 1983. *Colony and Mother City in Ancient Greece*. 2nd ed. Chicago: Ares Publishers.

Graham, A. J. 1992. "Thucydides 7.13.2 and the Crews of Athenian Triremes." *Transactions of the American Philological Association* 122: 257–70.

Graziosi, B. 2002. *Inventing Homer: The Early Reception of Epic*. Cambridge: Cambridge University Press.

Greaves, A. M. 2010. *The Land of Ionia: Society and Economy in the Archaic Period*. Chichester, UK: Wiley-Blackwell.

Green, P. 1989. "Lesbos and the Genius Loci." In *Classical Bearings*, edited by P. Green, 45–62. Berkeley: University of California Press.

Green, P. 2005. "Early Travellers to Lesbos." *Arion* 13: 61–72.

Greene, E., ed. 1996. *Reading Sappho: Contemporary Approaches*. Berkeley: University of California Press.

Gruben, G. 1957. "Die Südhalle." *Mitteilungen des Deutschen Archäologischen Instituts, Athenische Abteilung* 72: 52–64.

Gruben, G., and H. J. Kienast. 2014. *Der Polykratische Tempel im Heraion von Samos*. Samos 27. Wiesbaden: Reichert Verlag.

Günther, L.-M. 1999. "Alles von überall her . . .: Handel und Tryphe bei Polykrates von Samos." *Münstersche Beiträge zur Antiken Handelsgeschichte* 18: 48–56.

Hall, J. M. 1997. *Ethnic Identity in Greek Antiquity*. Cambridge: Cambridge University Press.

Hall, J. M. 2014. *A History of the Archaic Greek World, ca. 1200–479 BCE*. 2nd ed. Chichester, UK: Wiley-Blackwell.

Hammer, D. 2004. "Ideology, the Symposium, and Archaic Politics." *American Journal of Philology* 125: 479–512.

Hansen, M. H. 1985. *Demography and Democracy: The Number of Athenian Citizens in the Fourth Century B.C.* Herning, Denmark: Systime.

Hansen, M. H. 2008. "An Update on the Shotgun Method." *Greek, Roman, and Byzantine Studies* 48: 259–86.

Hansen, M. H., and T. H. Nielsen, eds. 2004. *An Inventory of Archaic and Classical Poleis*. Oxford: Oxford University Press.

Hansen, M. H., N. Spencer, and H. Williams. 2004. "Lesbos." In *An Inventory of Archaic and Classical Poleis*, edited by M. H. Hansen and T. H. Nielsen, 1018–32. Oxford: Oxford University Press.

Hardwick, N. M. M. 1991. "The Coinage of Chios from the Sixth to the Fourth Century B.C." PhD diss., University of Oxford.

Hardwick, N. M. M. 1993. "The Coinage of Chios from the VIth to the IVth Century BC." In *Actes du XIe Congrès International de Numismatique: Organisé à l'occasion du 150e anniversaire de la Société Royale de Numismatique de Belgique, Bruxelles, 8–13 septembre 1991*, edited by T. Hackens and G. Moucharte, 211–22. Louvain-la-Neuve: Association Professeur Marcel Hoc.

Hardwick, N. M. M. 2010. "The Coinage of Chios 600–300 BC: New Research Developments 1991–2008." In *Το νόμισμα στα νησιά του Αιγαίου: Νομισματοκοπεία, κυκλοφορία, εικονογραφία, ιστορία, Πρακτικά συνεδρίου της Ε' Επιστημονικής Συνάντησης, Μυτιλήνη, 16–19 Σεπτεμβρίου 2006*, edited by P. Tselekas, 1: 217–45. 2 vols. Athens: Έκδοση των Φίλων του Νομισματικού Μουσείου.

Hardwick, N. M. M. 2013. "'The Coinage of Chios 600–300 BC: New Research Developments 1991–2008': Correction." *Journal of the Oriental Society of Australia* 43: 116–17.

Harvey, F. D. 1988. "Herodotus and the Man-Footed Creature." In *Slavery and Other Forms of Unfree Labor*, edited by L. J. Archer, 42–52. London: Routledge.

Hatzi-Vallianou, D. 1973. "Ἀρχαιότητες καί μνημεῖα νησῶν Αἰγαίου." *Ἀρχαιολογικόν Δελτίον* 28 B2: 507–20.

Head, B. V. 1911. *Historia Numorum: A Manual of Greek Numismatics*. 2nd ed. Oxford: Clarendon Press.

Hecht, J. 1972. "Zur Geologie von Südost-Lesbos." *Zeitschrift der Deutschen Geologischen Gesellschaft* 123: 423–32.

Heinlein, S. 1909. "Histaios von Milet." *Klio* 9: 341–51.

Hellner, N. 2009. *Die Säulenbasen des zweiten Dipteros von Samos: Grundlage für die Rekonstruktion des Tempels in seinen Bauphasen*. Samos 26. Bonn: Rudolf Habelt.

Hendrich, C. 2007. *Die Säulenordnung des ersten Dipteros von Samos*. Samos 25. Bonn: Rudolf Habelt.

Henke, J.-M. 2019. "Cypriot Terracotta Figurines in the East Aegean as Evidence for a Technical and Cultic Innovation Transfer?" *British Museum Studies in Ancient Egypt and Sudan* 24: 248–80.

Henke, J.-M. 2022. "New Excavations in the Altar Area of the Sanctuary of Hera on Samos: First Results concerning Ritual Practices and Deposition Customs of Sacrificial Debris in the Late 7th Century BC." In *Ionians in the West and East: Proceedings of the International Conference "Ionians in East and West," Museu d'Arqueologia de Catalunya-Empuries, Empuries/L'Escala, Spain, 26–29 October, 2015*, edited by G. R. Tsetskhladze, 303–32. Colloquia Antiqua 27. Leuven: Peeters.

Herda, A. 2006. "Panionion-Melia, Mykalessos-Mykale, Perseus und Medusa: Überlegungen zur Besiedlungsgeschichte der Mykale in der frühen Eisenzeit." *Istanbuler Mitteilungen* 56: 43–102.

Herrmann, H.-V. 1979. *Die Kessel der Orientalisierenden Zeit. 2: Kesselprotomen und Stabdreifüße*. Olympische Forschungen 11. Berlin: Walter de Gruyter.

Higgins, M. D., and R. A. Higgins. 1996. *A Geological Companion to Greece and the Aegean*. London: Duckworth.

Hiller von Gaertringen, F. 1906. *Inschriften von Priene*. Berlin: G. Reimer.

Höckmann, O. 1995. "Some Thoughts on the Greek Pentekonter." In *Tropis III: 3rd International Symposium on Ship Construction in Antiquity*, edited by H. E. Tzalas, 207–20. Athens: Hellenic Institute for the Preservation of Nautical Tradition,.

462   THE OXFORD HISTORY OF THE ARCHAIC GREEK WORLD

Höckmann, U., and D. Kreikenbom, eds. 2001. *Naukratis: Die Beziehungen zu Ostgriechenland, Ägypten und Zypern in archaischer Zeit, Akten der Table Ronde in Mainz, 25.–27. November 1999*. Möhnesee: Bibliopolis.

Hodot, R. 2014. "Lesbian." In *Encyclopedia of Ancient Greek Language and Linguistics*, edited by G. K. Giannakis, 2: 228–31. 3 vols. Leiden: Brill.

Hoepfner, W., and K. Tsakos. 2011. *Ionien: Brücke zum Orient*. Stuttgart: Theiss.

Hoffmann, H. 1953. "Foreign Influence and Native Invention in Archaic Greek Altars." *American Journal of Archaeology* 57: 189–95.

Hogarth, D., C. C. Edgar, and C. Gutch. 1898–1899. "Excavations at Naukratis." *Annual of the British School at Athens* 5: 22–97.

Hogarth, D., H. L. Lorimer, and C. C. Edgar. 1905. "Naukratis 1903." *Journal of Hellenic Studies* 25: 105–36.

Hölbl, G. 2005. "Ägyptisches Kulturgut in der griechischen Welt im frühen ersten Jarhtausend vor Christus (10.–6. Jahrhundert v. Chr.)." In *Ägypten, Griechenland, Rom: Abwehr und Berührung, Städelsches Kunstinstitut und Städtische Galerie 26. November 2005–26. Februar 2006*, edited by H. Beck, P. Bol, and M. Bückling, 114–32. Tübingen: Wasmuth.

Hölbl, G. 2007. "Ionien und Ägypten in archaischer Zeit." In *Frühes Ionien: Eine Bestandsaufnahme, Panionion-Symposion Güzelçamli, 26. September–1. Oktober 1999*, edited by J. Cobet, V. von Graeve, and W.-D. Niemeier, 447–61. Milesische Forschungen 5. Mainz: Philipp von Zabern.

Hölbl, G. 2014. "Ägyptisches Kulturgut in Ionien im 7. Jh. v. Chr.: Der Beitrag Milets zu einem religionhistorischen Phänomenon." In *Der Beitrag Kleinasiens zur Kultur- und Geistesgeschichte der griechisch-römischen Antike: Akten des Internationalen Kolloquiums, Wien, 3.–5. November 2010*, edited by J. Cobet, 181–209. Archäologische Forschungen 24. Vienna: Verlag der Österreichischen Akademie der Wissenschaften.

Hölkeskamp, K.-J. 1999. *Schiedsrichter, Gesetzgeber und Gesetzgebung im archaischen Griechenland*. *Historia* Einzelschriften 131. Stuttgart: Franz Steiner Verlag.

Homolle, T. 1920. "Chronique des fouilles et découvertes archéologiques dans l'Orient hellénique (novembre 1919–novembre 1920)." *Bulletin de correspondance hellénique* 44: 367–415.

Hornblower, S. 2003. "Panionios of Chios and Hermotimos of Pedasa (Hdt. 8. 104–6)." In *Herodotus and His World: Essays from a Conference in Memory of George Forrest*, edited by P. Derow and R. Parker, 37–57. Oxford: Oxford University Press.

Hornblower, S. 2004. *Thucydides and Pindar: Historical Narrative and the World of Epinikian Poetry*. Oxford: Oxford University Press.

Hornblower, S. 2013. *Herodotus Histories Book V*. Cambridge: Cambridge University Press.

Huffman, C. A. 2018. "Pythagoras." In *The Stanford Encyclopedia of Philosophy*, https://plato.stanford.edu/archives/win2018/entries/pythagoras.

Huffman, C. A. 2019. "Pythagoreanism." In *The Stanford Encyclopedia of Philosophy*, https://plato.stanford.edu/archives/fall2019/entries/pythagoreanism.

Hülden, O. 2020. *Das griechische Befestigungswesen der archaischen Zeit: Entwicklungen, Formen, Funktionen*. Sonderschriften des Österreichischen Archäologischen Institutes in Wien 59. Vienna: Holzhausen.

Hulek, F. W. 2017. "The Architecture of the Middle Archaic Temple at Mount Çatallar Tepe." In *Αρχαία Ελίκη και Αιγιάλεια. Ποσειδών. Ο θεός των σεισμών και των υδάτων. Λατρεία και ιερά*, edited by D. Katsonopoulou, 77–98. Helike V. Athens: Εταιρεία Φίλων της Αρχαίας Ελίκης.

Hulek, F. W. 2018. *Der hocharchaische Tempel am Çatallar Tepe: Architektur und Rekonstruktion*. Forschungen in der Mykale III.1; Asia Minor Studien 89. Bonn: Rudolf Habelt.

Hulek, F. W. 2019. "Temple and *Hestiatorion*: The Combined Edifice on Mount Çatallar Tepe (Turkey)." In *Listening to the Stones: Essays on Architecture and Function in Ancient Greek Sanctuaries in Honour of Richard Alan Tomlinson*, edited by E. Partida and B. Schmidt-Dounas, 223–32. Oxford: Archaeopress.

Hunt, D. W. S. 1940–1945. "An Archaeological Survey of the Classical Antiquities of the Island of Chios Carried Out between the Months of March and July 1938." *Annual of the British School at Athens* 41: 29–52.

Hunt, P. 1998. *Slaves, Warfare, and Ideology in the Greek Historians*. Cambridge: Cambridge University Press.

Hutchinson, G. O. 2001. *Greek Lyric Poetry: A Commentary on Selected Larger Pieces*. Oxford: Oxford University Press.

Huxley, G. L. 1966. *The Early Ionians*. New York: Humanities Press.

Hyland, B. D. 2021. "A Note on the Provenance of the Sappho Fragments P.GC. inv. 105." *Zeitschrift für Papyrologie und Epigraphik* 218: 1–16.

Irwin, E. K. 2009. "Herodotus and Samos: Personal or Political?" *Classical World* 102: 395–416.

Isaac, B. 1986. *The Greek Settlements in Thrace until the Macedonian Conquest*. Studies of the Dutch Archaeological and Historical Society 10. Leiden: Brill.

Isler, H. P. 2021. *Ausgrabungen in der frühbronzezeitlichen Siedlung im Heraion von Samos 1966*. Samos 30. Berlin: Reichert Verlag.

Jackson, A. H. 2000. "Sea-Raiding in Archaic Greece with Special Attention to Samos." In *The Sea in Antiquity*, edited by G. J. Oliver, R. Brock, T. J. Cornell, et al., 133–49. BAR International Series 899. Oxford: Archaeopress.

Jacoby, F. 1947. "Some Remarks on Ion of Chios." *Classical Quarterly* 41: 1–17.

Janko, R. 1982. *Homer, Hesiod and the Hymns: Diachronic Development in Epic Diction*. Cambridge: Cambridge University Press.

Janko, R. 1994. *Iliad: A Commentary, Volume 4, Books 13–16*. Cambridge: Cambridge University Press.

Jantzen, U. 1972. *Ägyptische und orientalische Bronzen aus dem Heraion von Samos*. Samos 8. Bonn: Rudolf Habelt.

Jantzen, U. 2004. *Die Wasserleitung des Eupalinos: Die Funde.* Samos 20. Bonn: Rudolf Habelt.

Jarosch, V. 1994. *Samische Tonfiguren des 10. bis 7. Jahrhunderts v. Chr. aus dem Heraion von Samos.* Samos 18. Bonn: Rudolf Habelt.

Jeffery, L. H. 1956. "The Courts of Justice in Archaic Chios." *Annual of the British School at Athens* 51: 157–67.

Jeffery, L. H. 1990. *The Local Scripts of Archaic Greece: A Study of the Origin of the Greek Alphabet and Its Development from the Eighth to the Fifth Centuries B.C.* Rev. ed. Oxford: Oxford University Press.

Jennings, V., and A. Katsaros, eds. 2007. *The World of Ion of Chios.* Leiden: Brill.

Johnston, A. W. 1990. "Aegina, Aphaia-tempel XIII: The Storage Amphorae." *Archäologischer Anzeiger*: 37–64.

Johnston, A. W., and A. Villing. 2022. "Southward Ho! A Journey from Ionia to Egypt." In *Ionians in the West and East: Proceedings of the International Conference "Ionians in East and West," Museu d'Arqueologia de Catalunya-Empuries, Empuries/L'Escala, Spain, 26–29 October, 2015*, edited by G. R. Tsetskhladze, 383–406. Colloquia Antiqua 27. Leuven: Peeters.

Jones, N. F. 1987. *Public Organization in Ancient Greece: A Documentary Study.* Memoirs of the American Philosophical Society 176. Philadelphia: American Philosophical Society.

Κ' Εφορεία Προϊστορικών και Κλασικών Αρχαιοτήτων. 2004. *Ἐν τῷ ἵρω τῷ ἐμ Μέσσω.* Mytilene: Κ' Εφορεία Προϊστορικών και Κλασικών Αρχαιοτήτων.

Kantzios, I. 2004–2005. "Tyranny and the Symposion of Anacreon." *Classical Journal* 100: 227–45.

Karageorghis, V., N. Kourou, V. Kilikoglou, et al., eds. 2009. *Terracotta Statues and Figurines of Cypriote Type Found in the Aegean: Provenance Studies.* Nicosia: A. G. Leventis Foundation.

Karo, G. 1933. "Archäologische Funde von mai 1932 bis juli 1933, Griechenland und Dodekanes." *Jahrbuch des Deutschen Archäologischen Instituts* 48: 191–261.

Keen, A. G., and T. Fischer-Hansen. 2004. "The South Coast of Asia Minor (Pamphylia, Kilikia)." In *An Inventory of Archaic and Classical Poleis*, edited by M. H. Hansen and T. H. Nielsen, 1211–22. Oxford: Oxford University Press.

Kerschner, M. 2006. "On the Provenance of the Aiolian Pottery." In *Naukratis: Greek Diversity in Egypt, Studies on East Greek Pottery and Exchange in the Eastern Mediterranean*, edited by A. C. Villing and U. Schlotzhauer, 109–26. British Museum Research Publication 162. London: British Museum Press.

Kienast, D. 1994. "Die Auslösung des Jonischen Aufstandes und das Schicksal des Histiaios." *Historia* 43: 387–401.

Kienast, H. J. 1978. *Die Stadtmauer von Samos.* Samos 15. Bonn: Rudolf Habelt.

Kienast, H. J. 1989. "Das Bauwerk." In *Der Nordbau im Heraion von Samos*, edited by A. E. Furtwängler and H. J. Kienast, 15–62. Samos 3. Bonn: Rudolf Habelt.

Kienast, H. J. 1996. *Samos.* Bonn: Rudolf Habelt.

Kienast, H. J. 2001. "Der Kriegerfries aus dem Heraion von Samos." In *Άγαλμα: μελέτες για την αρχαία πλαστική προς τιμήν του Γιώργου Δεσπίνη*, edited by D. Pandermalis and E. Voutyras, 13–20. Thessaloniki: Υπουργείο Πολιτισμού.

Kienast, H. J. 2002. "Topography and Architecture of the Archaic Heraion at Samos." In *Excavating Classical Culture: Recent Archaeological Discoveries in Greece*, edited by M. Stamatopoulou and M. Yeroulanou, 317–25. BAR International Series 1031. Oxford: Archaeopress.

Kienast, H. J. 2004. "Die Tyrannis inszeniert sich: Großbauten auf der Insel Samos." In *Macht der Architektur–Architektur der Macht: Bauforschungskolloquium in Berlin vom 30. Oktober bis 2. November 2002 veranstaltet vom Architektur-Referat des DAI*, edited by E.-L. Schwandner and K. Rheidt, 69–78. Diskussionen zur Archäologischen Bauforschung 8. Mainz: Philipp von Zabern.

Kienast, H. J. 2005. *The Aqueduct of Eupalinos on Samos*. Athens: Υπουργείο Πολιτισμού.

Kienast, H. J. 2007. "Wege und Tore im Heraion von Samos." In *Frühes Ionien: Eine Bestandsaufnahme, Panionion-Symposion Güzelçamli, 26. September–1. Oktober 1999*, edited by J. Cobet, V. von Graeve, and W.-D. Niemeier, 201–9. Milesische Forschungen 5. Mainz: Philipp von Zabern.

Kienast, H. J. 2012. "Die Dipteroi im Heraion von Samos." In *Dipteros und Pseudodipteros: Bauhistorische und archäologische Forschungen, Internationale Tagung, 13.11.–15.11.2009 an der Hochschule Regensburg*, edited by T. Schulz and H. J. Kienast, 5–17. Byzas 12. Istanbul: Ege Yayınları.

Kienast, H. J. 2012–2013. "Die Poros-Steinbrüche von Samos." *Mitteilungen des Deutschen Archäologischen Instituts, Athenische Abteilung* 127–128: 143–60.

Kienast, H. J. 2016. "Die sogennante Nordhalle im Heraion von Samos: Ein spuren-suche." *Mitteilungen des Deutschen Archäologischen Instituts, Athenische Abteilung* 129–130: 95–123.

Kienast, H. J. 2017. "Eine monumentale Terrasse im Heraion von Samos." *Mitteilungen des Deutschen Archäologischen Instituts, Athenische Abteilung* 131–132: 79–98.

Kienast, H. J. 2020a. "Review of H. Walter, A. Clemente, and W.-D. Niemeier, *Ursprung und Frühzeit des Heraion von Samos. Teil 1: Topographie, Architektur und Geschichte*." *Gnomon* 92: 737–43.

Kienast, H. J. 2020b. "The Tunnel of Eupalinos Reconsidered." In *Opere di regimentazione delle acque in età arcaica: Grecia e Magna Grecia, Roma, Etruria e mondo italico*, edited by E. Bianchi and M. D'Acunto, 71–82. Rome: Quasar.

Kienast, H. J., and B. Meissner. 1995. *Die Wasserleitung des Eupalinos auf Samos*. Samos 19. Bonn: Rudolf Habelt.

Kienast, H. J., A. Moustaka, K. Großschmidt, et al. 2017. "Der archaischer Osttor des Heraion von Samos: Bericht über die Ausgrabungen der Jahre 1996 und 1998." *Archäologischer Anzeiger*: 125–212.

Kilian-Dirlmeier, I. 1985. "Fremde Weihungen in griechischen Heiligtümern vom 8. bis zum Beginn des 7. Jahrhunderts v. Chr." *Jahrbuch des Romisch-Germanischen Zentralmuseums Mainz* 32: 215–54.

Kivilo, M. 2021. "Sappho's Lives." In *The Cambridge Companion to Sappho*, edited by P. J. Finglass and A. Kelly, 11–21. Cambridge: Cambridge University Press.

Kleemann, I. 1962. "Der archaische Sarkophag mit Säulendekoration in Samos." In *Festschrift für Friedrich Matz*, edited by N. Himmelmann-Wildschütz and H. Biesantz, 44–55. Mainz: Philipp von Zabern.

Kleiner, G., P. Hommel, and W. Müller-Wiener. 1961. *Panionion und Melie. Jahrbuch des Deutschen Archäologischen Instituts* Ergänzungsheft 23. Berlin: Walter de Gruyter.

Koldewey, R. 1890. *Die antiken Baureste der Insel Lesbos*. Berlin: G. Reimer.

Kontis, I. 1946–1948. "Capitello eolico di Eresso." *Annuario della Scuola Archeologica di Atene e delle Missioni Italiane in Oriente* 8–10: 25–36.

Kontis, I. 1973. *Λεσβιακὸ Πολύπτυχο*. Athens: Aiolida.

Kontis, I. 1978. *Λέσβος και η Μικρασιατική της περιοχή*. Αρχαίες ελληνικές πόλεις 24. Athens: Athens Center of Ekistics.

Kontoleon, N. M. 1952. "Ἀνασκαφή ἐν Χίῳ." *Πρακτικά της εν Ἀθήναις Ἀρχαιολογικῆς Ἑταιρείας*: 520–30.

Kontoleon, N. M. 1953. "Ἀνασκαφή ἐν Χίῳ." *Πρακτικά της εν Ἀθήναις Ἀρχαιολογικῆς Ἑταιρείας*: 268–74.

Konuk, K. 2005. "The Electrum Coinage from Samos in Light of a Recent Hoard." In *Neue Forschungen Zu Ionien: Fahri Isik Zum 60, Geburtstag Gewidmet*, edited by E. Schwertheim and E. Winter, 42–55. Asia Minor Studien 54. Bonn: Rudolf Habelt.

Konuk, K. 2012. "Asia Minor to the Ionian Revolt." In *The Oxford Handbook of Greek and Roman Coinage*, edited by W. H. Metcalf, 43–60. Oxford: Oxford University Press.

Kopcke, G. 1967. "Neue Holzfunde aus dem Heraion von Samos." *Mitteilungen des Deutschen Archäologischen Instituts, Athenische Abteilung* 82: 100–48.

Kossyphidou, G. 2014. "Ο Ναὸς Β." In *Αιολικό Ιερό Κλοπεδῆς Λέσβου*, edited by K. Roungou and N. Douloumbekis, 51–6. Mytilene: Εφορεία Αρχαιοτήτων Λέσβου.

Koumarelas, V. K. 2011. *Ερεσίων χώρα*. Mytilene: Πρωτοβουλία Ερεσού, Περιβαλλοντικός Κοινωνικός Σύλλογος.

Kourou, N., and E. Grammatikaki. 1998. "An Anthropomorphic Cippus from Knossos." In *Archäologische Studien in Kontaktzonen der antiken Welt*, edited by R. Rolle and K. Schmidt, 237–49. Göttingen: Vandenhoeck & Ruprecht.

Kourouniotis, K. 1915. "Ἀνασκαφαὶ καὶ ἔρευναι ἐν Χίῳ." *Ἀρχαιολογικόν Δελτίον* 1: 64–93.

Kourouniotis, K. 1916. "Ἀνασκαφαὶ καὶ ἔρευναι ἐν Χίῳ 2." *Ἀρχαιολογικόν Δελτίον* 2: 190–215.

Koursoumis, S. S., and A. B. Karapanagiotou. 2010. "Anthropomorphic *Stele* from Levidi, Arcadia: A Typological and Interpretative Study." In *Honouring the Dead in the Peloponnese: Proceedings of a Conference Held at Sparta 23–25 April 2009*, edited by H. Cavanagh, W. G. Cavanagh, and J. Roy, 371–90. CSPS Online Publication 2. Nottingham: University of Nottingham, Centre for Spartan and Peloponnesian Studies.

Kourtzellis, Y. 2008. "Τοπογραφία παράκτιας ζώνης πόλεως Μυτιλήνης. Από την αρχαιότητα έως σήμερα." In *Πρακτικά του 4ου Πανελληνίου Συνεδρίου "Διαχείριση και Βελτίωση Παράκτιων Ζωνών": Μυτιλήνη, 23–27 Σεπτεμβρίου 2008*, 213–22. Athens: Εργαστήριο Λιμενικών Έργων.

Kourtzellis, Y. 2010. "Νομίσματα από τις αρχαίες λιμενικές εγκαταστάσεις του βόρειου λιμένα της Μυτιλήνης." In *Το νόμισμα στα νησιά του Αιγαίου: νομισματοκοπεία, κυκλοφορία, εικονογραφία, ιστορία: πρακτικά συνεδρίου της Ε' Επιστημονικής Συνάντησης: Μυτιλήνη, 16–19 Σεπτεμβρίου 2006*, edited by P. Tselekas, 1: 185–200. 2 vols. Athens: Έκδοση των Φίλων του Νομισματικού Μουσείου.

Kourtzellis, Y. 2012. "Ανασκαφική έρευνα στην αρχαϊκή πόλη της Μυτιλήνης: Ευρήματα πλαστικής." In *Neue Funde Archaischer Plastik aus griechischen Heiligtümern und Nekropolen: Internationales Symposion Athen, 2.–3. November 2007*, edited by G. Kokkorou-Alevras and W.-D. Niemeier, 213–28. *Athenaia 3*. Munich: Hirmer.

Kourtzellis, Y. 2013a. "The Ancient Theatre." In *Mytilene: Unique Approaches*, edited by Z. Myroyianni, 23–5. Mytilene: Chamber of Lesvos.

Kourtzellis, Y. 2013b. "The Euripus–Ermou Str." In *Mytilene: Unique Approaches*, edited by Z. Myroyianni, 29–31. Mytilene: Chamber of Lesvos.

Kourtzellis, Y. 2013c. "The Northern Harbour." In *Mytilene: Unique Approaches*, edited by Z. Myroyianni, 10–15. Mytilene: Chamber of Lesvos.

Kourtzellis Y. 2013d. "The Southern Harbour." In *Mytilene: Unique Approaches*, edited by Z. Myroyianni, 47–9. Mytilene: Chamber of Lesvos.

Kourtzellis, Y. 2015. "Οι αρχαιότητες της περιοχής του Σιγρίου." In *Οδηγός Πάρκου Απολιθωμένου Δάσους Νησιώτης*, 28–31. Lesbos: Μουσείο Φυσικής Ιστορίας.

Kourtzellis, Y. 2019. "The Sanctuaries on the Island of Lesbos from an Architectural and Topographical Perspective." In *Listening to the Stones: Essays on Architecture and Function in Ancient Greek Sanctuaries in Honour of Richard Alan Tomlinson*, edited by E. Partida and B. Schmidt-Dounas, 162–81. Oxford: Archaeopress.

Kourtzellis, Y. 2020. "Επιτύμβιο άγαλμα νεαρού θλιμμένου ήρωα από τη Νότια Νεκρόπολη της Μυτιλήνης." In *Τέχνης εμπειρία. Νέα Αρχαιολογικά Ευρήματα και Πορίσματα. Τιμητικός Τόμος για την Καθηγήτρια Γεωργία Κοκκορού-Αλευρά*, edited by K. Kopanias and G. Doulphis, 363–86. Athens: Καρδαμίτσα.

Kourtzellis, Y., and A. Panatsi. 2019. "Ερυθρόμορφες πελίκες από τη Νότια Νεκρόπολη της Μυτιλήνης." In *Η κεραμική της Κλασικής Εποχής στο Βόρειο Αιγαίο και την περιφέρειά του (480-323/300 π.Χ.): Πρακτικά του Διεθνούς Αρχαιολογικού Συνεδρίου, Θεσσαλονίκη 17-20 Μαΐου 2017*, edited by H. Manakidou and A. Avramidou, 559–72. Thessaloniki: University Studio Press.

Kourtzellis, Y., and M. Pappa. 2020. "Methymna: Tracing the Development of a Great City of Lesbos from the Geometric to the Roman Periods." In *Urbanism and Architecture in Ancient Aiolis: Proceedings of the International Conference from 7th–9th April 2017 in Çanakkale*, edited by E.-M. Mohr, K. Rheidt, and N. Arslan, 89–108. Asia Minor Studien 95. Bonn: Rudolf Habelt.

Kourtzellis, Y., and T. Theotokis. 2021. "Lesbos' Harbour Network: A Case Study of Mytilene's North Harbour and Its Development in a Micro-Regional Context." In *Hafen, Stadt, Mikroregion: Beiträge der Arbeitsgruppe 5 "Hafenorte" des*

*Forschungsclusters 6 "Connecting Cultures: Formen, Wege und Räume kultureller Interaktion" und einer Tagung am 26. und 27. Mai 2017 an der Abteilung Istanbul des DAI*, edited by U. Mania, 109–18. Studien aus den Forschungsclustern des Deutschen Archäologischen Instituts 18. Wiesbaden: Harrassowitz.

Koutsopoulou, E., G. E. Christos, and I. Marantos. 2016. "Mineralogy, Geochemistry and Physical Properties of Bentonites from the Western Thrace Region and the Islands of Samos and Chios, East Aegean, Greece." *Clay Minerals* 51: 563–88.

Kraay, C. M. 1976. *Archaic and Classical Greek Coins*. Berkeley: University of California Press.

Kreuzer, B. 2017. *Panathenäische Preisamphoren und rotfigurige Keramik aus dem Heraion von Samos*. Samos 23. Wiesbaden: Reichert Verlag.

Kron, U. 1988. "Kultmahle im Heraion von Samos archaischer Zeit. Versuch einer Rekonstruktion." In *Early Greek Cult Practice: Proceedings of the Fifth International Symposion at the Swedish Institute at Athens, 26.–29. June 1986*, edited by R. Hägg, N. Marinatos, and G. Nordquist, 135–48. Skrifter Utgivna av Svenska Institutet i Athen 4° 38. Stockholm: Swedish Institute at Athens.

Kučan, D. 1995. "Zur Ernährung und dem Gebrauch von Pflanzen im Heraion von Samos im 7. Jahrhundert v. Chr." *Jahrbuch des Deutschen Archäologischen Instituts* 110: 1–64.

Kučan, D. 2000. "Rapport synthétique sur les recherches archéobotaniques dans le sanctuaire d'Héra de l'île de Samos." *Pallas* 52: 99–108.

Kuciak, J. 2020. "The Fleet as the Basis for Polycrates of Samos' Thalassocracy." *Electrum* 27: 45–66.

Kurke, L. 1992. "The Politics of *Habrosunê* in Archaic Greece." *Classical Antiquity* 11: 91–120.

Kurke, L. 1994. "Crisis and Decorum in Sixth-Century Lesbos: Reading Alkaios Otherwise." *Quaderni urbinati di cultura classica* 47: 67–92.

Kyriakopoulou, T. 2020. "Public and Private Space in Hellenistic and Roman Mytilene: A Summary of Current Research." In *Urbanism and Architecture in Ancient Aiolis: Proceedings of the International Conference from 7th–9th April 2017 in Çanakkale*, edited by E.-M. Mohr, K. Rheidt, and N. Arslan, 109–42. Asia Minor Studien 95. Bonn: Rudolf Habelt.

Kyriakopoulou, T., and K. Roungou. 2020. "The Island of Lesbos from the Late Bronze Age to the Archaic Period: Trends and General Lines of Settlement Development." In *Urbanism and Architecture in Ancient Aiolis: Proceedings of the International Conference from 7th–9th April 2017 in Çanakkale*, edited by E.-M. Mohr, K. Rheidt, and N. Arslan, 47–69. Asia Minor Studien 95. Bonn: Rudolf Habelt.

Kyrieleis, H. 1981. *Führer durch das Heraion von Samos*. Athens: Krene Verlag.

Kyrieleis, H. 1986. "Chios and Samos in the Archaic Period." In *Chios: A Conference at the Homereion in Chios*, edited by C. E. Vaphopoulou-Richardson and J. Boardman, 187–204. Oxford: Clarendon Press.

Kyrieleis, H. 1988. "Offerings of 'the Common Man' in the Heraion at Samos." In *Early Greek Cult Practice: Proceedings of the Fifth International Symposion at the Swedish Institute at Athens, 26.–29. June 1986*, edited by R. Hägg, N. Marinatos, and G. Nordquist, 215–22. Skrifter Utgivna av Svenska Institutet i Athen 4° 38. Stockholm: Swedish Institute at Athens.

Kyrieleis, H. 1989. "New Cypriot Finds from the Heraion of Samos." In *Cyprus and the East Mediterranean in the Iron Age: Proceedings of the Seventh British Museum Classical Colloquium, April 1988*, edited by V. Tatton-Brown, 52–4. London: British Museum Press.

Kyrieleis, H. 1990. "Samos and Some Aspects of Archaic Greek Bronze Casting." In *Small Bronze Sculpture from the Ancient World: Papers Delivered at a Symposium Organized by the Departments of Antiquities and Antiquities Conservation and Held at the J. Paul Getty Museum, March 16–19, 1989*, 15–30. Malibu, CA: J. Paul Getty Museum.

Kyrieleis, H. 1993. "The Heraion at Samos." In *Greek Sanctuaries: New Approaches*, edited by N. Marinatos and R. Hägg, 99–122. London: Routledge.

Kyrieleis, H. 1996. *Der grosse Kuros von Samos*. Samos 10. Bonn: Rudolf Habelt.

Kyrieleis, H. 2020a. *Ausgrabungen im südostgebiet des Heraion von Samos*. Samos 28. Wiesbaden: Reichert Verlag.

Kyrieleis, H. 2020b. "Eine frücharchaische Holz-Figur aus dem Heraion von Samos." In *Σπονδή: Αφιέρωμα στη μνήμη του Γιώργου Δεσπίνη*, edited by A. Delivorrias, E. Vikela, A. Zarkadas, et al., 1: 65–9. 2 vols. Μουσείο Μπενάκη Supplement 12. Athens: Μουσείο Μπενάκη.

Labarre, G. 1994. "ΚΟΙΝΟΝ ΛΕΣΒΙΩΝ." *Revue des études anciennes* 96: 415–46.

Laimou, A. 1987–1988. "Κορινθιακές καὶ Λακωνικές Ἐπιδράσεις στὰ Χιακὰ Ἀγγεῖα." In *Πρακτικὰ του Γ' Διεθνούς Συνεδρίου Πελοποννησιακῶν Σπουδῶν, Καλαμάτα, 8–15 Σεπτεμβρίου 1985*, 2: 71–80. 3 vols. Πελοποννησιακὰ Παράρτημα 13. Athens: Εταιρεία Πελοποννησιακῶν Σπουδῶν.

Lamb, W. 1930–1931. "Antissa." *Annual of the British School at Athens* 31: 166–78.

Lamb, W. 1931–1932. "Antissa." *Annual of the British School at Athens* 32: 41–67.

Lamb, W. 1932. "Grey Wares from Lesbos." *Journal of Hellenic Studies* 52: 1–12.

Lamb, W. 1934–1935. "Excavations at Kato Phana in Chios." *Annual of the British School at Athens* 35: 138–64.

Lamb, W. 1936. *Excavations at Thermi in Lesbos*. Cambridge: Cambridge University Press.

Lambrianides, K., and N. Spencer. 1997. "Unpublished Material from the Deutsches Archäologisches Institut and the British School at Athens and Its Contribution to a Better Understanding of the Early Bronze Age Settlement Pattern on Lesbos." *Annual of the British School at Athens* 92: 73–107.

Lang, F. 1996. *Archaische Siedlungen in Griechenland. Struktur und Entwicklung*. Berlin: Akademie Verlag.

Langlotz, E. 1927. *Frühgriechische Bildhauerschülen*. Nuremberg: Frommann.

Langlotz, E. 1978–1979. "Kore in Malibu." *J. Paul Getty Museum Journal* 6–7: 193–5.

Lardinois, A. P. M. H. 1994. "Subject and Circumstance in Sappho's Poetry." *Transactions of the American Philological Association* 124: 57–84.

Lardinois, A. P. M. H. 2022. "Sappho." In *A Companion to Greek Lyric*, edited by L. Swift, 261–74. Hoboken, NJ: Wiley.

Larson, J. 2007. *Ancient Greek Cults: A Guide*. New York: Routledge.

Laskaris, G. 1960. "Τὰ λεῖψανα τῆς ἀρχαίας Ἐρεσοῦ." *Lesbiaka* 3: 67–74.

Lasserre, F. 1989. *Sappho: Une autre lecture*. Padua: Antenore.

Lawall, M. L. 2017. "Regional Styles of Transport Amphora Production in the Archaic Aegean." In *Material Koinai in the Greek Early Iron Age and Archaic Period: Acts of an International Conference at the Danish Institute at Athens, 30 January–1 February 2015*, edited by S. Handberg and A. Gadolou, 289–311. Monographs of the Danish Institute at Athens 22. Aarhus: Aarhus University Press.

Lawton, C. L. 1995. *Attic Document Reliefs: Art and Politics in Ancient Athens*. Oxford: Clarendon Press.

Leekley, D., and R. Noyes. 1975. *Archaeological Excavations in the Greek Islands*. Park Ridge, NJ: Noyes Press.

Lefèvre, F. 2019. "Observations sur l'histoire et les institutions du koinon des Ioniens." *Journal des savants*: 353–94.

Lemos, A. 1986. "Archaic Chian Pottery on Chios." In *Chios: A Conference at the Homereion in Chios*, edited by C. E. Vaphopoulou-Richardson and J. Boardman, 233–49. Oxford: Clarendon Press.

Lemos, A. 1991. *Archaic Pottery of Chios: The Decorated Styles*. 2 vols. Oxford: Oxbow Books.

Lemos, A. 1997. "Rizari: A Cemetery in Chios Town." In *Greek Offerings: Essays on Greek Art in Honour of John Boardman*, edited by O. Palagia, 73–85. Oxford: Oxbow Books.

Lentini, G. 2000. "Pittaco erede degli Atridi: Il fr. 70 V. di Alceo." *Studi Italiani di Filologia Classica* 18: 3–14.

Lentini, G. 2006. "Un lamento 'da' donna: Il fr. 10 V. di Alceo (ἔμε δείλαν), alla luce dei frr. 6 e 130b V." *Seminari romani di cultura greca* 9: 219–42.

Leonard, A. 1997. *Ancient Naukratis: Excavations at a Greek Emporium in Egypt I*. Atlanta: Scholars Press.

Leonard, A., M. Weiss, and A. M. Berlin. 2001. *Ancient Naukratis: Excavations at a Greek Emporium in Egypt II, The Excavations at Kom Hadid*. Boston: David Brown.

Lewis, D. M. 2018. *Greek Slave Systems in Their Eastern Mediterranean Context, c.800–146 BC*. Oxford: Oxford University Press.

Lohmann, H. 2005. "Melia, das Panionion und der Kult des Poseidon Helikonios." In *Neue Forschungen Zu Ionien. Fahri Isik Zum 60. Geburtstag Gewidmet* edited by E. Winter and E. Schwertheim, 57–91. Asia Minor Studien 54. Bonn: Rudolf Habelt.

Lohmann, H. 2012a. "Ionians and Carians in the Mycale: The Discovery of Carian Melia and the Archaic Panionion." In *Landscape, Ethnicity and Identity in* the *Archaic Mediterranean Area*, edited by G. Cifani and S. Stoddart, 32–50. Oxford: Oxbow Books.

Lohmann, H. 2012b. "Melia und das archaische Panionion am Çatallar Tepe in der Mykale." In *Anatolian Metal 6*, edited by Ü. Yalçin, 109–22. *Der Anschnitt* Beiheft 25. Bochum: Selbstverlag des Deutschen Bergbau-Museums.

Lohmann, H. 2017. "The Discovery of the Sanctuary of Poseidon *Helikonios* in the Mycale (Dilek Daglari)." In *Αρχαία Ελίκη και Αιγιάλεια. Ποσειδών. Ο θεός των σεισμών και των υδάτων. Λατρεία και ιερά*, edited by D. Katsonopoulou, 77–98. Helike V. Athens: Εταιρεία Φίλων της Αρχαίας Ελίκης.

Lohmann, H. 2022. "Where the Bull Groaned: Melia and the Temple of Poseidon Helikonios on Mt. Mycale (Dilek Dağları/Aydin)." In *Ionians in the West and East: Proceedings of the International Conference "Ionians in East and West," Museu d'Arqueologia de Catalunya-Empuries, Empuries/L'Escala, Spain, 26–29 October, 2015*, edited by G. R. Tsetskhladze, 143–68. Colloquia Antiqua 27. Leuven: Peeters.

Lohmann, H., and Ö. Özgül. 2017. "The Fortified Carian Settlement of Melia at Çatallar Tepe." In *Αρχαία Ελίκη και Αιγιάλεια. Ποσειδών. Ο θεός των σεισμών και των υδάτων. Λατρεία και ιερά*, edited by D. Katsonopoulou, 59–76. Helike V. Athens: Εταιρεία Φίλων της Αρχαίας Ελίκης.

Loukopoulou, L. D. 1989. *Contribution à l'histoire de la Thrace propontique durant la période archaïque*. Μελετήματα 9. Athens: Κέντρον Ελληνικής και Ρωμαϊκής Αρχαιότητος, Εθνικό Ίδρυμα Ερευνών.

Loukopoulou, L. D. 2004. "Thrace from Nestos to Hebros." In *An Inventory of Archaic and Classical Poleis*, edited by M. H. Hansen and T. H. Nielsen, 870–84. Oxford: Oxford University Press.

Loukopoulou, L. D., and A. Laitar. 2004. "Propontic Thrace." In *An Inventory of Archaic and Classical Poleis*, edited by M. H. Hansen and T. H. Nielsen, 912–23. Oxford: Oxford University Press.

Löwe, W. 1996. "Bestattungssitten und Funde." In *Samos: Die Kasseler Grabung 1894 in der Nekropole der archaischen Stadt von Johannes Boehlau und Edward Habich*, edited by A. von Dieter, 92–107. Kataloge der Staatlichen Museen Kassel 24. Kassel: Staatliche Museen.

Luraghi, N. 2001. "Samo arcaica: Storie di pirati e di tiranni." In *Atti del Congresso Storiografia Locale e Storiografia Universale: Forme di acquisizione del sapere storico nella cultura antica (Bologna, 16–18 dicembre 1999)*, 119–38. Como: Edizioni New Press.

Luraghi, N. 2015. "Anatomy of the Monster: The Discourse of Tyranny in Ancient Greece." In *Antimonarchic Discourse in Antiquity*, edited by H. Börm, 67–84. Stuttgart: Franz Steiner Verlag.

Lyons, D. 2014. "Arion the Methymnian and Dionysos Methymnaios: Myth and Cult in Herodotus' Histories." In *Approaching the Ancient Artifact: Representation, Narrative, and Function, A Festschrift in Honor of H. A. Shapiro*, edited by A. Avramidou and D. Demetriou, 425–33. Berlin: Walter de Gruyter.

Mackil, E., and P. van Alfen. 2006. "Cooperative Coinage." In *Agoranomia: Studies in Money and Exchange Presented to John H. Kroll*, edited by P. van Alfen, 201–47. New York: American Numismatic Society.

Mac Sweeney, N. 2013. *Foundation Myths and Politics in Ancient Ionia*. Cambridge: Cambridge University Press.

Mac Sweeney, N. 2017. "Separating Fact from Fiction in the Ionian Migration." *Hesperia* 86: 379–421.

Magnetto, A. 2008. *L'arbitrato di Rodi fra Samo e Priene: Edizione critica, commento e indici*. Testi e Commenti 8. Pisa: Edizioni della Normale.

Magnetto, A. 2009. "La querelle territoriale entre Samos et Priène: Propositions pour un débat." *Topoi* 16: 7–17.

Mallwitz, A. 1981. "Kritisches zur Architektur Griechenlands im 8. und 7. Jahrhundert." *Archäologischer Anzeiger*: 599–642.

Malouchou, G. E. 2006. "Νέα ἐπιγραφή γενῶν." In *Χιακὸν Συμπόσιον εἰς μνήμην W. G. Forrest*, edited by G. E. Malouchou and A. P. Matthaiou, 81–94. Athens: Ἑλληνικὴ Ἐπιγραφικὴ Ἑταιρεία.

Malouchou, G. E., and A. P. Matthaiou, eds. 2006. *Χιακὸν Συμπόσιον εἰς μνήμην W. G. Forrest*. Athens: Ἑλληνικὴ Ἐπιγραφικὴ Ἑταιρεία.

Manning, S. W. 2022. "Climate, Environment, and Resources." In *The Cambridge Companion to the Ancient Greek Economy*, edited by S. von Reden, 373–91. Cambridge: Cambridge University Press.

Mariaud, O. 2015a. "Formes et fonctions des terres cuites dans les tombes archaïques de Samos." In *Figurines de terre cuite en Méditerranée grecque et romaine 2: Iconographie et contextes*, edited by A. Muller and E. Lafli, 297–304. Villeneuve d'Ascq: Éditions du Septentrion.

Mariaud, O. 2015b. "A Samian Leopard? Megas, His Ancestors, and Strategies of Social Differentiation in Archaic Samos." In *"Aristocracy" in Antiquity: Redefining Greek and Roman Elites*, edited by N. Fisher and H. van Wees, 259–86. Swansea: Classical Press of Wales.

Marthari, M. 1982. "Ηραιο: αρχαικό νεκροταφείο." *Αρχαιολογιχόν Δελτίον* 37 B2: 351–2.

Martin, R. P. 2000. "Synchronic Aspects of Homeric Performance: The Evidence of the *Hymn to Apollo*." In *Una nueva visión de la cultura griega antigua hacia el fin del milenio*, edited by M. González de Tobia, 403–32. La Plata: Editorial de la Universidad Nacional de La Plata.

Mason, H. J. 1993. "Mytilene and Methymna: Quarrels, Borders and Topography." *Echos du monde classique* 37: 225–50.

Mason, H. J. 2001. "*Lesbia Oikodomia*: Aristotle, Masonry, and the Cities of Lesbos." *Mouseion* 3: 31–53.

Matthaiou, A. P. 2006. "Τρεῖς ἐπιγραφὲς Χίου." In *Χιακὸν Συμπόσιον εἰς μνήμην W. G. Forrest*, edited by G. E. Malouchou and A. P. Matthaiou, 103–36. Athens: Ἑλληνικὴ Ἐπιγραφικὴ Ἑταιρεία.

Matthaiou, A. P. 2011. *Τὰ ἐν τῆι στήληι γεγραμμένα: Six Greek Historical Inscriptions of the Fifth Century B.C.* Athens: Ελληνική Επιγραφική Εταιρεία.

Mazarakis Ainian, A. 1997. *From Rulers' Dwellings to Temples: Architecture, Religion and Society in Early Iron Age Greece (1100–700 B.C.).* Jonsered, Sweden: Paul Åströms Förlag.

Mazarakis Ainian, A. 2016. "Early Greek Temples." In *A Companion to Greek Architecture*, edited by M. M. Miles, 15–30. Malden, MA: Wiley-Blackwell.

Meiggs, R. 1982. *Trees and Timber in the Ancient Mediterranean World.* Oxford: Clarendon Press.

Meiggs, R., and D. M. Lewis. 1988. *A Selection of Greek Historical Inscriptions to the End of the Fifth Century B.C.* 2nd ed. Oxford: Clarendon Press.

Mendel, G. 1912–1914. *Catalogue des sculptures grecques, romaines et byzantines.* 3 vols. Rome: Bretschneider.

Merousis, N. 2002. *Χίος, φυσικό περιβάλλον και κατοίκηση: Από τη νεολιθική εποχή μέχρι το τέλος της αρχαιότητας.* Chios: Papyros.

Meyer, K. 2012. *Samos, die wasserreiche: Die Insel in der antiken Literatur.* Möhnesee: Bibliopolis.

Milojcic, V. 1961. *Die prähistorische Siedlung unter dem Heraion: Grabung 1953 und 1955.* Samos 1. Bonn: Rudolf Habelt.

Mitchell, B. M. 1975. "Herodotus and Samos." *Journal of Hellenic Studies* 95: 75–91.

Mohr, E.-M. 2015. *Eisenzeitliche Nekropolen im westlichen Kleinasien: Struktur und Entwicklung zwischen dem 9. und 6. Jh. v. Chr.* Byzas 21. Istanbul: Ege Yayinlari.

Mohr, M. 2013. *Die Heilige Strasse: Ein 'Weg der Mitte'? Soziale Gruppenbildung im Spannungsfeld der archaischen Polis.* Zürcher Archäologische Forschungen 1. Rahden: Verlag Marie Leidorf.

Mokrišová, J. 2016. "Minoanisation, Mycenaeanisation, and Mobility: A View from Southwest Anatolia." In *Beyond Thalassocracies: Understanding Processes of Minoanisation and Mycenaeanisation in the Aegean*, edited by E. Gorogianni, P. Pavúk, and L. Girella, 43–57. Oxford: Oxbow Books.

Möller, A. 2000. *Naukratis: Trade in Archaic Greece.* Oxford: Oxford University Press.

Mommsen, H., M. Kerschner, and A. Pautasso. 2009. *Stipe votiva del Santuario di Demetra a Catania 2: La ceramica greco-orientale.* Rome: Consiglio Nazionale delle Ricerche.

Monakhov [Monachov], S. I., and E. V. Kuznetsova. 2017. "Overseas Trade in the Black Sea Region from the Archaic to the Hellenistic Period." In *The Northern Black Sea in Antiquity: Networks, Connectivity, and Cultural Interactions*, edited by V. Kozlovskaya, 59–99. Cambridge: Cambridge University Press.

Moretti, L. 1957. *Olympionikai: I vincitori negli antichi agoni olimpici.* Rome: Accademia Nazionale dei Lincei.

Morrison, J. S., and J. F. Coates. 1996. *Greek and Roman Oared Warships.* Oxbow Monograph 62. Oxford: Oxbow Books.

474 THE OXFORD HISTORY OF THE ARCHAIC GREEK WORLD

Most, G. W. 1996. "Reflecting Sappho." In *Re-reading Sappho: Reception and Transmission*, edited by E. Greene, 11–35. Berkeley: University of California Press.

Moustaka, A. 2001. "Θραῦσμα μιας νέας σαμιακῆς κόρης." In *Ἄγαλμα: Μελέτες για την αρχαία πλαστική προς τιμήν του Γιώργου Δεσπίνη*, edited by D. Pandermalis and E. Voutyras, 21–7. Thessaloniki: Υπουργείο Πολιτισμού.

Moustaka, A. 2009. "Großplastik aus Ton aus dem Heraion von Samos." *Mitteilungen des Deutschen Archäologischen Instituts, Athenische Abteilung* 124: 179–86.

Murray, W. M. 1987. "Do Modern Winds Equal Ancient Winds?" *Mediterranean Historical Review* 2: 139–67.

Mylonopoulos, J. 2008. "'Fremde' Weihungen in Heiligtümern der Ostägäis im 7 und 6. Jh. v. Chr." In *Tagung Austausch von Gütern, Ideen und Technologien in der Ägäis und im östlichen Mittelmeer: Von der prähistorischen bis zu der archaischen Zeit; 19.–21.05.2006 in Ohlstadt/Obb. Deutschland*, edited by A. Kyriatsoulis, 363–86. Weilheim: Verein zur Förderung der Aufarbeitung der hellenischen Geschichte.

Nagy, G. 1990. *Pindar's Homer: The Lyric Possession of an Epic Past*. Baltimore: Johns Hopkins University Press.

Nagy, G, 1996a. *Homeric Questions*. Austin: University of Texas Press.

Nagy, G. 1996b. *Poetry as Performance: Homer and Beyond*. Cambridge: Cambridge University Press.

Nagy, G. 2004. "Transmission of Archaic Greek Sympotic Songs: From Lesbos to Alexandria." *Critical Inquiry* 31: 26–48.

Nagy, G. 2007a. "Did Sappho and Alcaeus Ever Meet? Symmetry of Myth and Ritual in Performing the Songs of Ancient Lesbos." In *Literatur und Religion 1: Wege zu einer mythisch-rituellen Poetik bei den Griechen*, edited by A. Bierl, R. Lämmle, and K. Wesselmann, 211–69. Berlin: Walter de Gruyter.

Nagy, G. 2007b. "Lyric and Greek Myth." In *The Cambridge Companion to Greek Mythology*, edited by R. D. Woodard, 19–51. Cambridge: Cambridge University Press.

Nagy, G. 2010. *Homer the Preclassic*. Berkeley: University of California Press.

Naso, A. 2000. "Materiali Etruschi e Italici nell'Orientemediterraneo." In *La Magna Grecia e Oriente mediterraneo prima dell'età ellenistica: Atti del Trentanovesimo Convegno di studi sulla Magna Grecia, Taranto, 1–15 ottobre 1999*, 1: 165–85. 2 vols. Taranto: Istituto per la Storia e l'Archeologia della Magna Grecia.

Naval Intelligence Division. 1944–1945. *Greece*. 2nd ed. 3 vols. B.R. 516, 516A, 516B. London: Naval Intelligence Division.

Neri, C. 2021. *Saffo, testimonianze e frammenti: Introduzione, testo critico, traduzione e commento*. Texte und Kommentare 68. Berlin: Walter de Gruyter.

Nielsen, T. H. 2018. *Two Studies in the History of Ancient Greek Athletics*. Scientia Danica, Series H, Humanistica 8, Vol. 16. Copenhagen: Kongelige Danske Videnskabernes Selskab.

Niemeier, W.-D. 2021. "Zur Datierung des Hekatompedos I im Heraion von Samos." *Archäologischer Anzeiger*: 10–36.

Niemeier, W.-D., and Y. Maniatis. 2010. "Der Heilige Baum und Kultkontinuität im Heraion von Samos." *Mitteilungen des Deutschen Archäologischen Instituts, Athenische Abteilung* 125: 99–118.

Obbink, D. 2014. "Two New Poems by Sappho." *Zeitschrift für Papyrologie und Epigraphik* 189: 32–49.

O'Brien, J. V. 1993. *The Transformation of Hera: A Study of Ritual, Hero, and the Goddess in the Iliad*. Lanham, MD: Rowman & Littlefield.

Ohly, D. 1953. "Holz." *Mitteilungen des Deutschen Archäologischen Instituts, Athenische Abteilung* 68: 77–126.

Ohnesorg, A. 2009. "Die Dachterrakotten aus dem Heraion von Samos." *Mitteilungen des Deutschen Archäologischen Instituts, Athenische Abteilung* 124: 19–167.

Olding, G. 2007. "Ion the Wineman: The Manipulation of Myth." In *The World of Ion of Chios*, edited by V. Jennings and A. Katsaros, 139–54. Leiden: Brill.

Olson, Å. 2012. "How Eupalinos Navigated His Way through the Mountain: An Empirical Approach to the Geometry of Eupalinos." *Anatolia Antiqua* 20: 25–34.

O'Neil, J. L. 1978–1979. "The Constitution of Chios in the Fifth Century B.C." *Talanta* 10–11: 66–73.

Oren, E. 1984. "Migdol: A New Fortress on the Edge of the Eastern Nile Delta." *Bulletin of the American Schools of Oriental Research* 256: 7–44.

Ornaghi, M. 2008. "I policrati ibicei: Ibico, Anacreonte, Policrate e la cronografia dei poeti della 'corte' di Samo." *Annali Online di Ferrara, Lettere* 3: 14–72.

Osborne, R. 1987. *Classical Landscape with Figures: The Ancient Greek City and Its Countryside*. London: George Philip.

Osborne, R., and P. J. Rhodes, eds. 2017. *Greek Historical Inscriptions, 478–404 BC*. Oxford: Oxford University Press.

Page, D. L. 1955. *Sappho and Alcaeus: An Introduction to the Study of Ancient Lesbian Poetry*. Oxford: Oxford University Press.

Page, D. L., and E. Lobel, eds. 1974. *Supplementum lyricis Graecis: Poetarum lyricorum Graecorum fragmenta quae recens innotuerunt*. Oxford: Clarendon Press.

Papalexandrou, A. C. 2021. *Bronze Monsters and the Cultures of Wonder: Griffin Cauldrons in the Preclassical Mediterranean*. Austin: University of Texas Press.

Parker, H. 1993. "Sappho Schoolmistress." *Transactions of the American Philological Association* 123: 309–51.

Parker, H. 2008. "The Linguistic Case for the Aiolian Migration Reconsidered." *Hesperia* 77: 431–64.

Parker, R. 2006. "Sale of a Priesthood on Chios." In Χιακόν Συμπόσιον εἰς μνήμην W. G. Forrest, edited by G. E. Malouchou and A. P. Matthaiou, 67–79. Athens: Ἑλληνικὴ Ἐπιγραφικὴ Ἑταιρεία.

Parker, V. 1997. *Untersuchungen zum Lelantischen Krieg und verwandten Problemen der frühgriechischen Geschichte. Historia* Einzelschriften 109. Stuttgart: Franz Steiner Verlag.

Pedley, J. G. 1982. "A Group of Early Sixth Century Korai and the Workshop on Chios." *American Journal of Archaeology* 86: 183–91.

Pelling, C. B. R. 2011. "Herodotus and Samos." *Bulletin of the Institute of Classical Studies* 54: 1–18.

Perlman, P. 2004. "Crete." In *An Inventory of Archaic and Classical Poleis*, edited by M. H. Hansen and T. H. Nielsen, 1144–95. Oxford: Oxford University Press.

Petrakos, B. 1967a. "Ἀνασκαφὴ τοῦ ναοῦ τῶν Μέσων Λέσβου." *Πρακτικά της εν Αθήναις Αρχαιολογικής Εταιρείας*: 96–102.

Petrakos, B. 1967b. "Ἀρχαιότητες καὶ μνημεῖα νήσων Αἰγαίου: Μυτιλήνη." *Αρχαιολογικόν Δελτίον* 22 B2: 445–62.

Petrakos, B. 1967c. "Μέσα Λέσβου." *Τὸ Ἔργον της εν Αθήναις Αρχαιολογικής Εταιρείας*: 72–5.

Petrakos, B. 1968a. *Ho Oropos kai to Ieron tou Amphiariou*. Athens: Papadogianni.

Petrakos, B. 1968b. "Ἀνασκαφὴ τοῦ ναοῦ τῶν Μέσων Λέσβου." *Πρακτικά της εν Αθήναις Αρχαιολογικής Εταιρείας*: 84–6.

Petrakos, B. 1968c. "Μέσα Λέσβου." *Τὸ Ἔργον της εν Αθήναις Αρχαιολογικής Εταιρείας*: 80–2.

Petrie, W. 1886. *Naukratis I*. London: Trübner.

Pfisterer-Haas, S. 1999. "Funde aus Milet VI: Die Importkeramik." *Archäologischer Anzeiger*: 263–71.

Philippson, A. 1959. *Die griechischen Landschaften: Eine Landeskunde, Band 4: Das agaische Meer und seine Inseln*. Frankfurt: Klostermann.

Phinphini, M. 2015. "Περιοχή Ριζάρη, πάροδος Ιωάννη Μουτάφη (οικόπεδο Μ. Στάθη)." *Αρχαιολογικόν Δελτίον* 70 B2: 1193–5.

Photos-Jones, E., C. Keane, A. X. Jones, et al. 2015. "Testing Dioscorides' Medicinal Clays for Their Antibacterial Properties: The Case of Samian Earth." *Journal of Archaeological Science* 57: 257–67.

Pipili, M. 2001. "Samos, the Artemis Sanctuary: The Laconian Pottery." *Jahrbuch des Deutschen Archäologischen Instituts* 116: 17–102.

Pipili, M. 2004. "Lakonische Vasen aus der Westnekropole von Samos: Ein erneuter Blick auf alte Funde." *Mitteilungen des Deutschen Archäologischen Instituts, Athenische Abteilung* 119: 91–105.

Pirenne-Delforge, V., and G. Pironti. 2014. "Héra et Zeus à Lesbos: Entre poésie lyrique et décret civique." *Zeitschrift für Papyrologie und Epigraphik* 191: 27–31.

Pirenne-Delforge, V., and G. Pironti. 2015. "Many vs. One." In *The Oxford Handbook of Ancient Greek Religion*, edited by E. Eidinow and J. Kindt, 39–47. Oxford: Oxford University Press.

Polito, M. 2009. *Milesiaka Volume 1, Meandrio: Testimonianze e frammenti*. Frammenti degli Storici Greci 4. Tivoli: Edizioni Tored.

Psoma, S. E. 2016. "Choosing and Changing Monetary Standards in the Greek World during the Archaic and Classical Periods." In *The Ancient Greek Economy: Markets, Households, and City-States*, edited by E. M. Harris, D. M. Lewis, and M. Woolmer, 90–115. Cambridge: Cambridge University Press.

Psoma, S. E. 2020. "White Gold and Electrum in Literary Sources and Inscriptions." In *White Gold: Studies in Early Electrum Coinage*, edited by P. van Alfen and U. Wartenberg, 65–82. New York: American Numismatic Society.

Purdy, J. 1826. *The New Sailing Directory for the Mediterranean Sea, the Adriatic Sea, or Gulf of Venice, the Archipelago and Levant, the Sea of Marmara, and the Black Sea.* London: R. H. Laurie.

Quinn, T. J. 1981. *Athens and Samos, Lesbos, and Chios, 478–404 B.C.* Manchester: Manchester University Press.

Raaflaub, K. 2004. *The Discovery of Freedom in Ancient Greece.* 2nd ed. Chicago: University of Chicago Press.

Ragone, G. 1986. "La guerra meliaca e la struttura originaria della lega ionica in Vitruvio 4, 1, 3-6." *Rivista di filologia e di istruzione classica* 114: 173–205.

Raftopoulou, M. and M. Anetakis. 2019. "Ένας παιδικός τάφος του 4ου αι. π.Χ. από το Ριζάρι της Χίου." In *Σωστικές ανασκαφές της Αρχαιολογικής Υπηρεσίας. I, Τα νεκροταφεία. Χωροταξική οργάνωση - ταφικά έθιμα - τελετουργίες*, edited by E. Kountouri and A. Gadolou, 3: 313–29. 3 vols. Athens: Ταμείο Αρχαιολογικών Πόρων και Απαλλοτριώσεων.

Reger, G. 2004. "The Aegean." In *An Inventory of Archaic and Classical Poleis*, edited by M. H. Hansen and T. H. Nielsen, 732–93. Oxford: Oxford University Press.

Reimer, H. 2005. *Die Aschenaltäre aus dem Reitia-Heiligtum von Este im mitteleuropäischen und mediterranen Vergleich.* Studien zu Vor- und Frühgeschichtlichen Heiligtümern 4; Il Santuario di Reitia a Este 3. Mainz: Philipp von Zabern.

Rhodes, P. J., and R. Osborne, eds. 2003. *Greek Historical Inscriptions: 404–323 BC.* Oxford: Oxford University Press.

Rizzo, M. A. 1990. *Le anfore de trasporto e il commercio etrusco arcaico.* Rome: De Luca Edizioni d'Arte.

Robert, L. 1935. "Sur des inscriptions de Chios (suite)." *Bulletin de correspondance hellénique* 59: 453–70.

Robert, L. 1960. "Recherches épigraphiques V: Inscriptions de Lesbos." *Revue des études anciennes* 62: 285–315.

Robert, L. 1969–1990. *Opera minora selecta: Epigraphie et antiquités grecques.* 7 vols. Amsterdam: Adolf M. Hakkert.

Robinson, E. W. 1997. *The First Democracies: Early Popular Government Outside Athens.* *Historia* Einzelschriften 107. Stuttgart: Franz Steiner Verlag.

Roebuck, C. A. 1955. "The Early Ionian League." *Classical Philology* 50: 26–40.

Roebuck, C. A. 1959. *Ionian Trade and Colonization.* New York: Archaeological Institute of America.

Roebuck, C. A. 1986. "Chios in the Sixth Century BC." In *Chios: A Conference at the Homereion in Chios*, edited by C. E. Vaphopoulou-Richardson and J. Boardman, 81–8. Oxford: Clarendon Press.

478 THE OXFORD HISTORY OF THE ARCHAIC GREEK WORLD

Roisman, J. 1985. "Maiandrios of Samos." *Historia* 34: 257–77.

Roller, D. W. 2006. *Through the Pillars of Herakles: Greco-Roman Exploration of the Atlantic.* London: Routledge.

Roller, L. 1999. *In Search of God the Mother: The Cult of Anatolian Cybele.* Berkeley: University of California Press.

Romer, F. 1982. "The Aisymneteia. A Problem in Aristotle's Historic Method." *American Journal of Philology* 103: 25–46.

Rose, C. B. 2008. "Separating Fact from Fiction in the Aiolian Migration." *Hesperia* 77: 399–430.

Rösler, W. 1980. *Dichter und Gruppe: Eine Untersuchung zu den Bedingungen und zur historischen Funktion früher griechischer Lyrik am Beispiel Alkaios.* Munich: Fink.

Roungou, K. 2012. "Ἀρχαϊκὰ γλυπτὰ ἀπό το ιερό του λιμανιού στο εμποριό της χίου." In *Neue Funde Archaischer Plastik aus griechischen Heiligtümern und Nekropolen. Internationales Symposion Athen, 2.–3. November 2007,* edited by G. Kokkorou-Alevras and W.-D. Niemeier, 133–46. *Athenaia* 3. Munich: Hirmer.

Roungou, K. 2013. "Η λατρεία της Κυβέλης στο βορειοανατολικό Αιγαίο: Λέσβος, Χίος, Λήμνος." PhD diss., University of Ioannina.

Roungou, K. 2014a. "Ζητήματα Λατρείας." In *Αιολικό Ιερό Κλοπεδή Λέσβου,* edited by K. Roungou and N. Douloumbekis, 58–60. Mytilene: Εφορεία Αρχαιοτήτων Λέσβου.

Roungou, K. 2014b. "Η αρχή του Ιερού και η οικοδόμηση του πρώτου λατρευτικού κτιρίου (8ος π.Χ. αιώνας)." In *Αιολικό Ιερό Κλοπεδή Λέσβου,* edited by K. Roungou and N. Douloumbekis, 30–6. Mytilene: Εφορεία Αρχαιοτήτων Λέσβου.

Roungou, K. 2020. "Das aiolische Heiligtum von Klopedi auf Lesbos." In *Urbanism and Architecture in Ancient Aiolis: Proceedings of the International Conference from 7th–9th April 2017 in Çanakkale,* edited by E.-M. Mohr, K. Rheidt, and N. Arslan, 291–311. Asia Minor Studien 95. Bonn: Rudolf Habelt.

Roungou, K., and N. Douloumbekis, eds. 2014. *Αιολικό Ιερό Κλοπεδή Λέσβου.* Mytilene: Εφορεία Αρχαιοτήτων Λέσβου.

Roungou, K., N. Douloumbekis, and G. Kossyphidou. 2017. "Νέα ευρήματα από το αιολικό ιερό στην Κλοπεδή Λέσβου." In *Το Αρχαιολογικό Έργο στα Νησιά του Αιγαίου. Διεθνές Επιστημονικό Συνέδριο (Ρόδος, 27 Νοεμβρίου–1 Δεκεμβρίου 2013),* edited by K. Birtacha, P. Triantaphyllides, K. Sarantidis, et al., 2: 111–22. 3 vols. Mytilene: Η Εφορεία Αρχαιοτήτων Λέσβου.

Roungou, K., and E. Vouligea. 2019. "Greek Emporios in Chios: The Archaeological Data from the Excavations of the Last Decades." In *Greek Art in Motion: Studies in Honour of Sir John Boardman on the Occasion of His 90th Birthday,* edited by R. Morais, D. F. Leão, and D. Rodríguez Pérez, 93–105. Oxford: Archaeopress.

Rubinstein, L. 2003. "Volunteer Prosecutors in the Greek World." *Dike: Rivista di storia del diritto greco ed ellenistico* 6: 87–113.

Rubinstein, L. 2004a. "Aiolis and South-Western Mysia." In *An Inventory of Archaic and Classical Poleis,* edited by M. H. Hansen and T. H. Nielsen, 1033–52. Oxford: Oxford University Press.

Rubinstein, L. 2004b. "Ionia." In *An Inventory of Archaic and Classical Poleis*, edited by M. H. Hansen and T. H. Nielsen, 1053–107. Oxford: Oxford University Press.

Rupp, D. W. 1983. "Reflections on the Development of Altars in the Eighth Century B.C." In *The Greek Renaissance of the Eighth Century B.C.: Tradition and Innovation, Proceedings of the Second International Symposium at the Swedish Institute in Athens, 1–5 June, 1981*, edited by R. Hägg, 101–7. Skrifter Utgivna av Svenska Institutet i Athen 4° 30. Stockholm: Paul Åströms Förlag.

Ruscillo, D. 2013. "*Thesmophoriazousai*: Mytilenean Women and Their Secret Rites." In *Bones, Behaviour, and Belief: The Zooarchaeological Evidence as a Source for Ritual Practice in Ancient Greece and Beyond*, edited by G. Ekroth and J. Wallenstein, 181–95. Skrifter Utgivna av Svenska Institutet i Athen. 4° 55 Stockholm: Swedish Institute at Athens.

Ruzé, A. 1997. *Délibération et pouvoir dans la cité grecque: De Nestor à Socrate*. Paris: Publications de la Sorbonne.

Sampson, C. M. 2020. "Deconstructing the Provenances of P. Sapph. Obbink." *Bulletin of the American Society of Papyrologists* 57: 143–69.

Sarikakis, T. 1986. "Commercial Relations between Chios and Other Cities in Antiquity." In *Chios. A Conference at the Homereion in Chios*, edited by C. E. Vaphopoulou-Richardson and J. Boardman, 121–7. Oxford: Clarendon Press.

Sarikakis, T. 1998. *Η Χίος στην Αρχαιότητα*. Athens: Eryfili.

Schaus, G. 1986. "Two Fikellura Vase Painters." *Annual of the British School at Athens* 81: 251–95.

Schaus, G. 1996. "An Archaeological Field Survey at Eresos, Lesbos." *Echos du monde classique* 40: 27–74.

Schaus, G. 2017. "Archaic Imported Fine Wares from the Lower Town Site at Mytilene, Lesbos." In *From Maple to Olive: Proceedings of a Colloquium to Celebrate the 40th Anniversary of the Canadian Institute in Greece, Athens, 10–11 June 2016*, edited by J. E. Tomlinson and D. W. Rupp, 265–302. Publications of the Canadian Institute in Greece 10. Athens: Canadian Institute in Greece.

Schaus, G. 2018. "Laconia and East Greece: Cultural Exchange in the Archaic Period." In *Archaic and Classical Western Anatolia: New Perspectives in Ceramic Studies*, edited by R. G. l. Gürtekin-Demir, H. Cevizoğlu, Y. Polat, et al., 285–302. Colloquia Antiqua 19. Leuven: Peeters.

Schaus, G. 2020. *Funde aus Milet V, Teil 4: Laconian and Chian Fine Ware Pottery at Miletus*. Wiesbaden: Harrassowitz.

Schaus, G. Forthcoming. "Cyrene." In *The Oxford History of the Archaic Greek World*, edited by P. Cartledge and P. Christesen, *The Oxford History of the Archaic Greek World*, Volume 4. New York: Oxford University Press.

Schaus, G., and N. Spencer. 1994. "Notes on the Topography of Eresos." *American Journal of Archaeology* 98: 411–30.

Schiering, W. 1989. "Pyrrha auf Lesbos: Nachlese einer Grabung." *Archäologischer Anzeiger*: 339–77.

Schleif, H. 1933. "Der grosse Altar der Hera von Samos." *Mitteilungen des Deutschen Archäologischen Instituts, Athenische Abteilung* 58: 173–210.

Schlotzhauer, U. 2006. "Griechen in der Fremde: Wer weihte in den Filialheiligtümern der Samier und Milesier in Naukratis." In *Stranieri e non cittadini nei santuari greci: Atti del convegno internazionale, Firenze*, edited by A. Naso, 292–324. Studi Udinesi sul Mondo Antico 2. Florence: Le Monnier.

Schlotzhauer, U., S. Weber, and H. Mommsen. 2012. *Griechische Keramik des 7. und 6. Jahrhunderts v. Chr. aus Naucratis und anderen Orten in Ägypten*. Archäologische Studien zu Naucratis 3. Worms: Werner.

Schmidt, G. 1968. *Kyprische Bildwerke aus dem Heraion von Samos*. Bonn: Rudolf Habelt.

Scully, V. 1969. *The Earth, the Temple, and the Gods*. Revised ed. New Haven, CT: Yale University Press.

Senseney, J. R. 2016. "The Greek East: Temples and Engineering." In *A Companion to Greek Architecture*, edited by M. M. Miles, 60–74. Malden, MA: Wiley-Blackwell.

Shapiro, H. A. 2012. *Re-Fashioning Anakreon in Classical Athens*. Munich: Fink.

Sheedy, K. A. 1985. "The Delian Nike and the Search for Chian Sculpture." *American Journal of Archaeology* 89: 619–26.

Shields, E. L. 1917. *The Cults of Lesbos*. Menasha, WI: George Banta.

Shipley, D. G. J. 1987. *A History of Samos, 800–188 B.C.* Oxford: Clarendon Press.

Shipley, D. G. J. 2003. "Rhoikos and Theodoros." In *Grove Art Online*, https://doi.org/10.1093/gao/9781884446054.article.T071806.

Simantoni-Bournia, E. 1991. "Πλίνθοι και κέραμοι στάκτως ερριμένα Πήλινα αρχιτεκτονικά ανάφλυφα από τη Χίο." *Αρχαιολογική Εφημερίς*: 71–109.

Simonton, M. 2017. *Classical Greek Oligarchy: A Political History*. Princeton, NJ: Princeton University Press.

Simonton, M. 2018. "The Local History of Hippias of Erythrai: Politics, Place, Memory, and Monumentality." *Hesperia* 87: 497–543.

Simossi, A. 1991. "Underwater Excavation Research in the Ancient Harbour of Samos: September–October 1988." *International Journal of Nautical Archaeology and Underwater Exploration* 20: 281–98.

Slawisch, A. Forthcoming. "Miletus." In *The Oxford History of the Archaic Greek World*, edited by P. Cartledge and P. Christesen, *The Oxford History of the Archaic Greek World*, Volume 5. New York: Oxford University Press.

Sommerstein, A. H., and A. Bayliss. 2013. *Oath and State in Ancient Greece*. Berlin: Walter de Gruyter.

Spelman, H. 2022. "Alcaeus." In *A Companion to Greek Lyric*, edited by L. Swift, 275–89. Hoboken, NJ: Wiley.

Spencer, N. 1994. "Towers and Enclosures of Lesbian Masonry in Lesbos: Rural Investment in the *Chora* of Archaic *Poleis*." In *Structures rurales et sociétés antiques*, edited by P. Doukellis and L. G. Mendoni, 207–13. Paris: Les Belles Lettres.

Spencer, N. 1995a. "Early Lesbos between East and West: A 'Grey' Area of Aegean Archaeology." *Annual of the British School at Athens* 90: 269–306.

Spencer, N. 1995b. *A Gazetteer of Archaeological Sites in Lesbos.* Oxford: Tempus Reparatum.

Spencer, N. 1995c. "Multi-Dimensional Group Definition in the Landscape of Rural Greece." In *Time, Tradition and Society in Greek Archaeology: Bridging the "Great Divide,"* edited by N. Spencer, 29–42. London: Routledge.

Spencer, N. 1995d. "Respecting Your Elders and Betters: Ancestor Worship at Antissa, Lesbos." *Echos du monde classique* 39: 45–60.

Spencer, N. 1996. "Τὸ Πυρραίων ὄρος τὸ πιτυωδες": An Archaeological and Epigraphical Approach to a Topographical Problem." *Zeitschrift für Papyrologie und Epigraphik* 112: 253–62.

Spencer, N. 2000. "Exchange and Stasis in Archaic Mytilene." In *Alternatives to Athens: Varieties of Political Organization and Community in Ancient Greece*, edited by R. Brock and S. Hodkinson, 68–81. Oxford: Oxford University Press.

Stacey, R., C. Cartwright, S. Tanimoto, et al. 2010. "Coatings and Contents: Investigations of Residues on Some 6th Century BC Vessel Sherds from Naukratis (Egypt)." *British Museum Technical Research Bulletin* 4: 19–26.

Stamatakis, M., and I. Malegiannaki. 2018. "The Exploitation of Emery on the Island of Samos: Existing Data and Research Perspectives." *Bulletin of the Geological Society of Greece* 53: 1–27.

Stehle, E. 1997. *Performance and Gender in Ancient Greece: Nondramatic Poetry in Its Setting.* Princeton, NJ: Princeton University Press.

Stein-Hölkeskamp, E. 1989. *Adelskultur und Polisgesellschaft: Studien zum griechischen Adel in archaischer und klassischer Zeit.* Stuttgart: Franz Steiner Verlag.

Stephanou, A. 1958. *Χιακα Μελετήματα.* Chios: Eleutheria.

Stibbe, C. M. 1997. "Lakonische Keramik aus dem Heraion von Samos." *Mitteilungen des Deutschen Archäologischen Instituts, Athenische Abteilung* 112: 25–142.

Svenson-Evers, H. 1996. *Die griechischen Architekten archaischer und klassischer Zeit.* Archäologische Studien 11. Frankfurt: Peter Lang.

Tanner, J. 2003. "Finding the Egyptian in Early Greek Art." In *Ancient Perspectives on Egypt*, edited by R. Matthews and C. Roemer, 115–43. London: University College London Press.

Tausend, K. 1987. "Der Lelantinische Krieg, ein Mythos?" *Klio* 59: 499–514.

Tausend, K. 1992. *Amphiktyonie und Symmachie: Formen zwischenstaatlicher Beziehungen im archaischen Griechenland.* Stuttgart: Franz Steiner Verlag.

Theodoulou, T. 2014. "Recording the Harbour Network of Ancient Lesbos (2008–2009)." In *Häfen und Hafenstädte im östlichen Mittelmeerraum von der Antike bis in byzantinische Zeit: Neue Entdeckungen und aktuelle Forschungsansätze, Istanbul, 30.05.–01.06.2011*, edited by S. Ladstätter, F. Pirson, and T. Schmidts, 493–508. Byzas 19; Sonderschriften Österreichisches Archäologisches Institut 52. Istanbul: Ege Yayınları.

Theodoulou, T. 2017. "Recording the Harbour Network of Ancient Lesbos (2007 Mission)." In *Το Αρχαιολογικό Έργο στα Νησιά του Αιγαίου. Διεθνές Επιστημονικό Συνέδριο (Ρόδος, 27 Νοεμβρίου–1 Δεκεμβρίου 2013)*, edited by K. Birtacha, P. Triantaphyllides, K. Sarantidis, et al., 2: 123–30. 3 vols. Mytilene: Η Εφορεία Αρχαιοτήτων Λέσβου.

Theodoulou, T., D. Kourkoumelis, K. Preka-Alexandri, et al. 2009. "Υποβρύχιες αρχαιολογικές έρευνες στην περιοχή της Χίου. Η εξέλιξη της υποβρύχιας επισκόπησης 1954–2008." In *9 Πανελλήνιο Συμπόσιο Ωκεανογραφίας & Αλιείας, 13–16 Μαΐου 2009, Πανεπιστήμιο Πατρών, Πάτρα, Πρρακτικά*, edited by T. Dailianis, C. S. Tsigenopoulos, C. Dounas, et al., 1: 140–5. 2 vols.

Theodoulou, T., and Y. Kourtzellis. 2019. *Ενάλια Λέσβος - Το αρχαίο λιμενικό δίκτυο— Lesbos Underwater: The Ancient Harbour Network*. Mytilene: Δημοτικο Λιμενικό Ταμείο Λέσβου.

Theodoulou, T., and Y. Kourtzellis. 2020. "Structural Characteristics of the Ancient Harbours of Lesbos." In *Urbanism and Architecture in Ancient Aiolis: Proceedings of the International Conference from 7th–9th April 2017 in Çanakkale*, edited by E.-M. Mohr, K. Rheidt, and N. Arslan, 71–87. Asia Minor Studien 95. Bonn: Rudolf Habelt.

Thomas, R. 2019. *Polis Histories, Collective Memories and the Greek World*. Cambridge: Cambridge University Press.

Thomas, R., and A. C. Villing. 2013. "Naukratis Revisited 2012: Integrating New Fieldwork and Old Research." *British Museum Studies in Ancient Egypt and Sudan* 20: 81–125.

Thonemann, P. 2006. "Neilomandros: A Contribution to the History of Greek Personal Names." *Chiron* 36: 11–43.

Thonemann, P. 2016. "Croesus and the Oracles." *Journal of Hellenic Studies* 136: 152–67.

Tiverios, M. 2006–2008. "Greek Colonisation in the Northern Aegean." In *Greek Colonisation: An Account of Greek Colonies and Other Settlements Overseas*, edited by G. R. Tsetskhladze, 2: 1–154. 2 vols. Leiden: Brill.

Tölle-Kastenbein, R. 1974. *Das Kastro Tigani: Die Bauten und Funde griechischer, römischer und byzantinischer Zeit*. Samos 14. Bonn: Rudolf Habelt.

Tölle-Kastenbein, R. 1975. "Miszellen zur Topographie der Stadt Samos." *Mitteilungen des Deutschen Archäologischen Instituts, Athenische Abteilung* 90: 189–214.

Tölle-Kastenbein, R. 1979. "Excavations on the Acropolis of Samos." *Archaeology* 32: 6–14.

Touratsoglou, I., and K. Tsakos. 2008. "Economy and Trade Routes in the Aegean: The Case of Samos (Archaic to Hellenistic Times)." In *Sailing in the Aegean: Readings on the Economy and Trade Routes*, edited by C. Papageorgiadou-Banis and A. Giannikouri, 105–37. Μελετήματα 53. Athens: Κέντρον Ελληνικής και Ρωμαϊκής Αρχαιότητος, Εθνικό Ίδρυμα Ερευνών.

Treister, M. Y. 1996. *The Role of Metals in Ancient Greek History*. Mnemosyne Supplementum 156. Leiden: Brill.

Triantafyllidis, P. 2015. *Ενοποίηση των Αρχαιολογικών Χώρων της Πόλης της Μυτιλήνης*. Mytilene: Εφορεία Αρχαιοτήτων Λέσβου.

Tsagalis, C. C. 2018. "Performance Contexts for Rhapsodic Recitals in the Archaic and Classical Periods." In *Homer in Performance: Rhapsodes, Narrators, Characters*, edited by J. L. Ready and C. C. Tsagalis, 29–75. Austin: University of Texas Press.

Tsakos, K. 1980. "Ein Heiligtum der Artemis auf Samos." *Athens Annals of Archaeology* 13: 305–18.

Tsakos, K. 1996. "Stadt und Nekropolen: Samos in der archaischen Epoche (6. Jh.)." In *Samos: Die Kasseler Grabung 1894 in der Nekropole der archaischen Stadt von Johannes Boehlau und Edward Habich*, edited by A. von Dieter, 120–31. Kataloge der Staatlichen Museen Kassel 24. Kassel: Staatliche Museen.

Tsakos, K. 2001. "Die archaischen Gräber der Westnekropole von Samos und die Datierung der samischen Anthemienstelen." *Archäologischer Anzeiger*: 451–66.

Tsakos, K. 2003. *Samos: Historischer und archäologischer Führer*. Athens: Hesperos.

Tsakos, K. 2006. "Σάμος, αρχαία πόλη: Νεότερα από το δυτικό μέτωπο της οχύρωσης." In *Γενέθλιον: Αναμνηστικός τόμος για την συμπλήρωση είκοσι χρόνων λειτουργίας του Μουσείου Κυκλαδικής Τέχνης*, edited by N. Stampolidis, 295–303. Athens: Μουσείο Κυκλαδικής Τέχνης.

Tsakos, K. 2007. "Die Stadt Samos in der geometrischen und archaischen Epoche." In *Frühes Ionien: Eine Bestandsaufnahme, Panionion-Symposion Güzelçamli, 26. September–1. Oktober 1999*, edited by J. Cobet, V. von Graeve, and W.-D. Niemeier, 189–99. Milesische Forschungen 5. Mainz: Philipp von Zabern.

Tsakos, K. 2011. "Πρωτογεωμετρική κεραμική από τη Σάμο και οι φιλολογικές μαρτυρίες " In *Ταξιδεύοντας στην κλασική Ελλάδα: τόμος προς τιμήν του καθηγητή Πέτρου Θέμελη*, edited by P. Valavanis, 325–43. Athens: Εταιρεία Μεσσηνιακών Αρχαιολογικών Σπουδών.

Tsakos, K., and G. Giannakopoulos. 2014. "Κοροπλαστική από το ιερό της Δήμητρας Θεσμοφόρου στη Σάμο." In *Κοροπλαστική και μικροτεχνία στον αιγιακό χώρο από τους γεωμετρικούς χρόνους έως και τη ρωμαϊκή περίοδο: Διεθνές συνέδριο στη μνήμη της Ηούς Ζερβουδάκη, Ρόδος, 26–29 Νοεμβρίου 2009*, edited by A. Giannikouri, 1: 231–46. 2 vols. Athens: Υπουργείο Πολιτισμού και Αθλητισμού.

Tsakos, K., and M. Viglaki-Sofianou. 2012. *Samos: The Archaeological Museum*. Athens: John S. Latsis Public Benefit Foundation.

Tsardaka, D. 2010–2013. "Συμβολή στην ιστορική τοπογραφία της αρχαίας πόλεως Χίου: Νέα στοιχεία από τις σωστικές ανασκαφές των ετών 1985-2013." *Όρος: ένα Αρχαιογνωστικό Περιοδικό* 22–25: 481–517.

Tsetskhladze, G. R. 2022. "Introduction: Ionians Overseas." In *Ionians in the West and East. Proceedings of the International Conference "Ionians in East and West," Museu d'Arqueologia de Catalunya-Empuries, Empuries/L'Escala, Spain, 26–29 October, 2015*, edited by G. R. Tsetskhladze, 1–71. Colloquia Antiqua 27. Leuven: Peeters.

Tzifopoulos, Y. Z. 2013. *Letters from the "Underground": Writing in Methone, Pieria, Late 8th, Early 7th Century BC.* Thessaloniki: Υπουργείο Πολιτισμού.

Tziligkaki, E., and M. Stamatakis. 2018. "Underground Quarries in the Area of Agiades, Samos Island, Greece: Notes on Historical Topography and Chronology." *Bulletin of the Geological Society of Greece* 53: 161–92.

Ustinova, Y. 2009. *Caves and the Ancient Greek Mind: Descending Underground in the Search for Ultimate Truth.* Oxford: Oxford University Press.

Vaessen, R. 2014. "Cultural Dynamics in Ionia at the End of the Second Millennium BCE." PhD diss., University of Sheffield.

Van Alfen, P. 2002. "*Pant'Agatha*: Commodities in the Levantine-Aegean Trade during the Persian Period, 6–4th C. B.C." PhD. diss, University of Texas.

Van Alfen, P. 2004. "Financing a Late 6th C. B.C. Greek Fleet: A Reassessment of Polykrates and His Thalassocracy." Lecture delivered at Princeton University (February 2004). https://www.academia.edu/11696570/Financing_a_late_6th_c_ B_C_Greek_fleet_a_reassessment_of_Polykrates_and_his_thalassocracy.

Van Effenterre, H., and F. Ruzé. 1994–1995. *Nomima: Recueil d'inscriptions politiques et juridiques de l'archaïsme grec.* 2 vols. Rome: École Française de Rome.

Vanschoonwinkel, J. 2006–2008. "Greek Colonisation in the Northern Aegean." In *Greek Migrations to Aegean Anatolia in the Early Dark Age*, edited by G. R. Tsetskhladze, 1: 115–41. 2 vols. Leiden: Brill.

Veneri, A. 1984. "Asio e la τρυφή dei Samii." *Quaderni urbinati di cultura classica* 17: 81–93.

Vetta, M. 1998. "Anacreonte e i cospiratori di Samo (fr. 21 G.)." *Rivista di cultura classica e medioevale* 40: 321–7.

Viglaki-Sofianou, M. 1999. "Οικόπεδο I. Μενελάου (Ο.Τ. 8, αριθ. οικ. 120)." *Αρχαιολογικόν Δελτίον* 54 B2: 806–10.

Viglaki-Sofianou, M. 2004. "Γεωμετρική νεκρόπολη Αρχαίας Σάμου." In *Το Αιγαίο στην πρώιμη εποχή του σιδήρου: Πρακτικά του Διεθνούς Συμποσίου; Ρόδος, 1–4 Νοεμβρίου 2002*, edited by N. Stampolidis and A. Giannikouri, 189–96. Athens: Panepistimio Kritis.

Viglaki-Sofianou, M. 2013. "Ανάδειξη της Γεωμετρικής νεκρόπολης των τύμβων της αρχαίας πόλης της Σάμου." In *Νησιωτικές Ταυτότητες: Η συμβολή της Γενικής Γραμματείας Αιγαίου και Νησιωτικής Πολιτικής στην έρευνα και ανάδειξη του πολιτισμού του αρχιπελάγους*, edited by M. Alvanou, 21–3. Mytilene: Geniki Grammateia Aigaiou kai Nisiotikis Politikis.

Villing, A. C. 2013. "Egypt as a 'Market' for Greek Pottery: Some Thoughts on Production, Consumption and Distribution in an Intercultural Environment." In *Pottery Markets in the Ancient Greek World (8th–1st Centuries B.C.): Proceedings of the International Symposium Held at the Université libre de Bruxelles, 19–21 June 2008*, edited by A. Tsingarida, D. Viviers, and Z. Archibald, 73–101. Études d'Archéologie 5. Brussels: CReA-Patrimoine.

Villing, A. C. 2017. "Greece and Egypt: Reconsidering Early Contact and Exchange." In *Regional Stories: Towards a New Perception of the Early Greek World, Acts of an International Symposium in Honour of Professor Jan Bouzek, Volos 18–21 June 2015*, edited by A. Mazarakis Ainian, A. Alexandridou, and X. Charalambidou, 563–96. Volos: University of Thessaly Press.

Villing, A. C., and U. Schlotzhauer, eds. 2006. *Naukratis: Greek Diversity in Egypt, Studies on East Greek Pottery and Exchange in the Eastern Mediterranean*. British Museum Research Publication 162. London: British Museum Press.

Vinogradov, Y. 1971. "Drevneishee grecheskoe pis'mo s ostrova Berezan." *Vestnik Drevnej Istorii* 4: 74–100.

Von Wilamowitz-Moellendorff, U. 1908. "Panionion." *Sitzungsberichte der Königlich Preussischen Akademie der Wissenschaften zu Berlin* 30: 38–57.

Von Wilamowitz-Moellendorff, U. 1909. *Nordionische Steine*. Berlin: Akademie der Wissenschaften.

Von Wilamowitz-Moellendorff, U. 1913. *Sappho und Simonides: Untersuchungen über griechische Lyriker*. Berlin: Weidmann.

Von Wilamowitz-Moellendorff, U. 1935–1972. *Kleine Schriften*. 5 vols. Berlin: Weidmann.

Wallace, M. B. 1983. "Review of Friedrich Bodenstedt's *Die Elektronmünzen von Phokaia und Mytilene*." *American Journal of Archaeology* 87: 286–7.

Wallinga, H. T. 1993. *Ships and Sea-Power before the Great Persian War. Mnemosyne* Supplementum 121. Leiden: Brill.

Walter, H. 1990. *Das griechische Heiligtum: Dargestellt am Heraion von Samos*. Stuttgart: Urachhaus.

Walter, H., and A. Clemente. 1986. "Zum Monopteros im Heraion von Samos." *Mitteilungen des Deutschen Archäologischen Instituts, Athenische Abteilung* 101: 137–47.

Walter, H., A. Clemente, and W.-D. Niemeier. 2019. *Ursprung und Frühzeit des Heraion von Samos, Teil 1: Topographie, Architektur und Geschichte*. Samos 21.1. Berlin: Reichert Verlag.

Walter, H., and K. Vierneisel. 1959. "Heraion von Samos: Die Funde der Kampagnen 1958 und 1959." *Mitteilungen des Deutschen Archäologischen Instituts, Athenische Abteilung* 74: 10–34.

Walter, U. 1993. *An der Polis teilhaben: Bürgerstaat und Zugehörigkeit im archaischen Griechenland*. Stuttgart: Franz Steiner Verlag.

Walter-Karydi, E. 1973. *Samische Gefässe des 6. Jahrhunderts V. Chr. Landschaftsstile ost-griechischer Gefässe*. Samos 6.1. Bonn: Rudolf Habelt.

Wartenberg, U. 2020. "Was There an Ionian Revolt Coinage? Monetary Patterns in the Late Archaic Period." In *White Gold: Studies in Early Electrum Coinage*, edited by P. van Alfen and U. Wartenberg, 569–640. New York: American Numismatic Society.

Watson, S. B. 2013. "Muse of Lesbos or (Aeschylean) Muses of Pieria? Orpheus' Head on a Fifth-Century Hydria." *Greek, Roman, and Byzantine Studies* 53: 441–60.

Webb, V. 2016. *Faience Material from the Samos Heraion Excavations*. Samos 13. Wiesbaden: Reichert Verlag.

Webb, V. 2019. "The Significance of Faience in the Religious Practices at Naukratis and Beyond." *British Museum Studies in Ancient Egypt and Sudan* 24: 313–40.

Webb, V. 2021. "Faience Found in the Recent Excavations to the East of the Great Altar in the Samos Heraion." *Archäologischer Anzeiger* 1: 237–80.

Weiss, K. 2005. "Ägyptische Bronzevotive in griechischen Heligtümern." In *Ägypten Griechenland Rom: Abwehr und Berührung, Städelsches Kunstinstitut und Städtische Galerie 26. November 2005–26. Februar 2006*, edited by H. Beck, P. C. Bol, and M. Bückling, 133–7. Tübingen: Wasmuth.

Weiss, K. 2012. *Ägyptische Tier- und Götterbronzen aus Unterägypten: Untersuchungen zu Typus, Ikonographie und Funktion sowie der Bedeutung innerhalb der Kulturkontakte zu Griechenland*. 2 vols. Ägypten und Altes Testament 81. Wiesbaden: Harrassowitz.

Welles, C. B. 1934. *Royal Correspondence in the Hellenistic Period*. New Haven, CT: Yale University Press.

Werlings, M.-J. 2010. *Le dèmos avant la démocratie: Mot, concepts, réalités historiques*. Nanterre: Presses Universitaires de Paris Ouest.

West, M. L. 2002. "The View from Lesbos." In *'Epea pteroenta': Beiträge zur Homerforschung*, edited by A. Rengakos and M. Reichel, 207–19. Stuttgart: Franz Steiner Verlag.

West, M. L. 2003. *Homeric Hymns, Homeric Apocrypha, Lives of Homer*. Cambridge, MA: Harvard University Press.

West, M. L. 2013. *The Epic Cycle: A Commentary on the Lost Troy Epics*. Oxford: Oxford University Press.

Whitbread, I. K. 1995. *Greek Transport Amphorae: A Petrological and Archaeological Study*. Fitch Laboratory Occasional Paper 4. Athens: British School at Athens.

Wilkinson, C. L. 2013. *The Lyric of Ibycus. Introduction, Text, and Commentary*. Berlin: Walter de Gruyter.

Williams, C., and H. Williams. 1985. "Excavations on the Acropolis of Mytilene, 1984." *Echos du monde classique* 29: 225–33.

Williams, C., and H. Williams. 1986. "Excavations on the Acropolis of Mytilene, 1985." *Echos du monde classique* 30: 141–54.

Williams, C., and H. Williams. 1987. "Excavations at Mytilene (Lesbos), 1986." *Echos du monde classique* 31: 247–62.

Williams, C., and H. Williams. 1988. "Excavations at Mytilene (Lesbos), 1987." *Echos du monde classique* 32: 135–49.

Williams, C., and H. Williams. 1989. "Excavations at Mytilene, 1988." *Echos du monde classique* 33: 167–81.

Williams, C., and H. Williams. 1990. "Excavations at Mytilene, 1989." *Echos du monde classique* 34: 181–93.

Williams, C., and H. Williams. 1991. "Excavations at Mytilene, 1990." *Echos du monde classique* 35: 175–91.

Williams, D. 2006. "The Chian Pottery from Naukratis." In *Naukratis: Greek Diversity in Egypt. Studies on East Greek Pottery and Exchange in the Eastern Mediterranean*, edited by A. C. Villing and U. Schlotzhauer, 127–32. British Museum Research Publication 162. London: British Museum Press.

Williams, H. 1993. "Archaic Architectural Fragments from Ancient Mytilene." In *Les grands ateliers d'architecture dans le monde égéen du VIe siècle av. J.-C.: Actes du Colloque d'Istanbul, 23–25 mai 1991*, edited by J. des Courtils and J.-C. Moretti, 83–7. Varia Anatolica 3. Paris: De Boccard.

Williamson, M. 1995. *Sappho's Immortal Daughters*. Cambridge, MA: Harvard University Press.

Yalouris, E. 1976. "The Archaeology and Early History of Chios." PhD diss., Oxford University.

Yalouris, E. 1986. "Notes on the Topography of Chios." In *Chios: A Conference at the Homereion in Chios*, edited by C. E. Vaphopoulou-Richardson and J. Boardman, 141–68. Oxford: Clarendon Press.

Yatromanolakis, D. 2009. "Alcaeus and Sappho." In *The Cambridge Companion to Greek Lyric*, edited by F. Budelmann, 204–26. Cambridge: Cambridge University Press.

Yntema, D. G. 2011. "Archaeology and the *Origo* Myths of the Greek *Apoikiai*." *Ancient West and East* 10: 243–66.

Yoyotte, J. 1993–1994. "Les contacts entre Égyptiens et Grecs." *Annuaire du Collège de France* 94: 679–94.

Zachos, G. 2010. "New Evidence on the Topography of Ancient Eresos: Bridging the Gap." *Mitteilungen des Deutschen Archäologischen Instituts, Athenische Abteilung* 125: 221–42.

Zachos, G. 2012. "Αρχαϊκή κεραμική από την Ερεσό της Λέσβου." In *Η κεραμικη της αρχαϊκης εποχης στο Βορειο Αιγαιο και την περιφερεια του (700–480 π.Χ.): Πρακτικά Αρχαιολογικής Συνάντησης Θεσσαλονίκη, 19–22 Μαΐου 2011*, edited by M. Tiverios, V. Misailidou-Despotidou, E. Manakidou, et al., 305–19. Thessaloniki: Αρχαιολογικό Ινστιτούτο Μακεδονικών και Θρακικών Σπουδών.

Zachos, G. 2017. "Ένα πρωτογεωμετρικό νεκροταφείο στη Μήθυμνα της Λέσβου." In *Το Αρχαιολογικό Έργο στα Νησιά του Αιγαίου. Διεθνές Επιστημονικό Συνέδριο (Ρόδος, 27 Νοεμβρίου–1 Δεκεμβρίου 2013)*, edited by K. Birtacha, P. Triantaphyllides, K. Sarantidis, et al., 2: 91–110. 3 vols. Mytilene: Η Εφορεία Αρχαιοτήτων Λέσβου.

Zambas, C. 2017. "More Light in the Tunnel of Eupalinos." *Mitteilungen des Deutschen Archäologischen Instituts, Athenische Abteilung* 131–132: 99–145.

Ziegenaus, O. 1957a. "Der Südbau. Ergänzende Untersuchungen." *Mitteilungen des Deutschen Archäologischen Instituts, Athenische Abteilung* 72: 65–86.

Ziegenaus, O. 1957b. "Die Tempelgruppe im Norden des Altarplatzes." *Mitteilungen des Deutschen Archäologischen Instituts, Athenische Abteilung* 72: 87–151.

Zimmerman, B., ed. 2011. *Handbuch der griechischen Literatur der Antike, Erster Band, Die Literatur der archaischen und klassischen Zeit*. Munich: C. H. Beck.

Zolotas, G. 1921. *Ιστορία της Χίου*. Athens: Η εν Αθήναις Αρχαιολογική Εταιρεία.

# 4

# *Corcyra*

*Hans-Joachim Gehrke and Philip Sapirstein*

## *List of Illustrations*

| | | |
|---|---|---|
| Map 4.1: | Topography of Corfu and some key sites on and near Corfu mentioned in this essay. © Paul Christesen 2024. | 498 |
| Map 4.2: | Some key sites in the general vicinity of Corfu mentioned in this essay. © Paul Christesen 2024. | 500 |
| Map 4.3: | Some key sites and regions in the wider Mediterranean mentioned in this essay. © Paul Christesen 2024. | 551 |
| Figure 4.1: | Plan of ancient Corcyra and modern Corfu Town with topography. © Paul Christesen 2024. | 492 |
| Figure 4.2: | Plan of the urban center of Corcyra showing modern Corfu Town. © Philip Sapirstein 2024. | 495 |
| Figure 4.3: | Plan of the urban center of Corcyra. © Philip Sapirstein 2024. | 504 |
| Figure 4.4: | Reconstruction of the west facade of the Temple of Artemis; c. 580. Drawn by Hans Schleif (Schleif, Rhomaios, and Klaffenbach 1940: plate 26). Image in public domain. | 514 |
| Figure 4.5: | Photograph of the center of the pediment of the Temple of Artemis; c. 580. Archaeological Museum of Corfu. Photo by Philip Sapirstein. © Ελληνική Δημοκρατία, Υπουργείου Πολιτισμού και Αθλητισμού-ΟΔΑΠ (Hellenic Republic Ministry of Culture and Sports, Agency for the Management and Development of Cultural Resources). Reproduced with permission of the Εφορεία Αρχαιοτήτων Κέρκυρας (Ephorate of Antiquities of Corfu). | 515 |

Hans-Joachim Gehrke and Philip Sapirstein, *Corcyra* In: *The Oxford History of the Archaic Greek World.*
Edited by: Paul Cartledge and Paul Christesen, Oxford University Press. © Oxford University Press 2024.
DOI: 10.1093/oso/9780199383597.003.0004

Figure 4.6: Reconstruction of the center of the west pediment of the Temple of Artemis; c. 580. Drawn by Hans Schleif (Schleif, Rhomaios, and Klaffenbach 1940: plate 26). Image in the public domain. 515

Figure 4.7: Photograph of the south corner of the west pediment of the Temple of Artemis; c. 580. Archaeological Museum of Corfu. Photo by Philip Sapirstein. © Ελληνική Δημοκρατία, Υπουργείου Πολιτισμού και Αθλητισμού-ΟΔΑΠ (Hellenic Republic Ministry of Culture and Sports, Agency for the Management and Development of Cultural Resources). Reproduced with permission of the Εφορεία Αρχαιοτήτων Κέρκυρας (Ephorate of Antiquities of Corfu). 516

Figure 4.8: Reconstruction of the terracotta roof of the temple at Mon Repos; c. 610. From Sapirstein 2012: Figure 28. © Philip Sapirstein 2024. 519

Figure 4.9: The Dionysus pediment; c. 500. Archaeological Museum of Corfu. Photo by Philip Sapirstein. © Ελληνική Δημοκρατία, Υπουργείου Πολιτισμού και Αθλητισμού-ΟΔΑΠ (Hellenic Republic Ministry of Culture and Sports, Agency for the Management and Development of Cultural Resources). Reproduced with permission of the Εφορεία Αρχαιοτήτων Κέρκυρας (Ephorate of Antiquities of Corfu). 521

Figure 4.10: Burial pithos from the Bali Plot in the necropolis in the modern suburb of Garitsa; first half of the sixth century; height: 1.42 m, maximum diameter: 1.14 m. Photo courtesy of Museum of Palaiopolis-Mon Repos. © Ελληνική Δημοκρατία, Υπουργείου Πολιτισμού και Αθλητισμού-ΟΔΑΠ (Hellenic Republic Ministry of Culture and Sports, Agency for the Management and Development of Cultural Resources). Reproduced with permission of the Εφορεία Αρχαιοτήτων Κέρκυρας (Ephorate of Antiquities of Corfu). 529

Figure 4.11: Tomb of Menecrates; first half of the sixth century. Photo by Larry Koester. Reproduced under Creative Commons Attribution 2.0 Generic License; https://creativecommons.org/licenses/by/2.0/. 531

Figure 4.12: Limestone sculpture known as the Lion of Menecrates; last quarter of seventh century; plinth of statue is 122 cm long. Archaeological Museum of Corfu. Photo by Sarah Murray. © Ελληνική Δημοκρατία, Υπουργείου Πολιτισμού και Αθλητισμού-ΟΔΑΠ (Hellenic Republic Ministry of Culture and Sports,

Agency for the Management and Development of Cultural Resources). Reproduced with permission of Sarah Murray and the Εφορεία Αρχαιοτήτων Κέρκυρας (Ephorate of Antiquities of Corfu). 533

Figure 4.13: Terracotta figurines from the "Small Artemis Sanctuary;" sixth through fifth centuries. Archaeological Museum of Corfu. Photo by Philip Sapirstein. © Ελληνική Δημοκρατία, Υπουργείου Πολιτισμού και Αθλητισμού-ΟΔΑΠ (Hellenic Republic Ministry of Culture and Sports, Agency for the Management and Development of Cultural Resources). Reproduced with permission of the Εφορεία Αρχαιοτήτων Κέρκυρας (Ephorate of Antiquities of Corfu). 563

Figure 4.14: Terracotta sima and geison revetment from the Temple of Artemis; c. 580; height 80.5 cm. Archaeological Museum of Corfu. Photo by Philip Sapirstein. © Ελληνική Δημοκρατία, Υπουργείου Πολιτισμού και Αθλητισμού-ΟΔΑΠ (Hellenic Republic Ministry of Culture and Sports, Agency for the Management and Development of Cultural Resources). Reproduced with permission of the Εφορεία Αρχαιοτήτων Κέρκυρας (Ephorate of Antiquities of Corfu). 580

## List of Abbreviations

| | |
|---|---|
| *Cf-el* | *Chronique des fouilles en ligne.* chronique.efa.gr. |
| *FGrH* | Jacoby, F. 1923–1958. *Die Fragmente der griechischen Historiker.* 3v. in 14 vols. Berlin: Weidmann. |
| *FHG* | Müller, K. 1878–1885. *Fragmenta historicorum graecorum.* 5 vols. Paris: Didot. https://www.dfhg-project.org/. |
| *IG* | *Inscriptiones Graecae.* 1873–. Berlin: Walter de Gruyter. |
| *SEG* | *Supplementum Epigraphicum Graecum.* 1923–. Leiden: Brill. |

## *4.1. Introduction*

Greeks have inhabited the island of Corfu since c. 730, when settlers arrived as part of a larger wave of immigration organized by Corinth.[1] The ancient name

---

1. All dates are BCE unless otherwise indicated. A monograph by Selene Psoma (2022) treating the history of Corcyra between its colonization to the Roman era appeared in print just as this chapter was going to press. We have been able to cite its major contributions but, due to the timing, were unable to engage with this work in its entirety.

for the island is the same as both the name of the urban center founded by those settlers—Κορκού[ρα], Κόρκυρα, or Κέρκυρα— and the name for the polity that encompassed the entire island (Gehrke and Wirbelauer 2004: 361). In the interests of avoiding confusion, the island as a whole is here designated with its modern name, Corfu, whereas the ancient urban center and polity are called Corcyra. The primary modern city, here referred to as Corfu Town (see Figure 4.1), is situated c. 2 km north of the ancient urban center.

The town of Corcyra was founded on the east coast of Corfu, on the Kanoni peninsula, which had excellent natural harbors on its northern and western sides (the Alcinous and Hyllaic harbors, respectively). A defensible acropolis takes the form of an undulating plateau running along the eastern side of the peninsula: this high ground is frequently described as Analipsis hill after a chapel near its midpoint. The modern suburb of Garitsa, which is dominated by Soter hill, lies between the ancient and modern urban centers. As Corfu was ruled by Venice between 1386 and 1797, many of its topographical features have both Greek and Italian names; Soter hill, for example, is sometimes called San Salvatore. The British, who controlled Corfu from 1814 to 1864, also left their mark on the island, most notably in the form of the villa of Mon Repos, located on the peninsula of Kanoni, which was built by a British High Commissioner in 1828–31. Two Archaic sanctuaries have been found on the spacious grounds surrounding this villa.

As was common in many foundations (*apoikiai*) in the Archaic period, the immigrants who arrived on Corfu in the eighth century developed their own political community with some elements fashioned after their "mother city" (metropolis). For more than 150 years, relations between Corinth and Corcyra fluctuated between friendship and hostility, dominance (by the metropolis) and independence (of the *apoikia*). Shortly after the beginning of the sixth century, the Corcyraeans achieved complete freedom from Corinth and adopted a moderately democratic form of governance.

The Greeks living on Corfu took full advantage of everything the island had to offer. Blessed with excellent natural resources and fertile soil and located at a key point on the maritime route between Greece and Italy, the polity developed magnificently and built a powerful fleet. By the end of the Archaic period, Corcyra belonged among the leading Greek *poleis*.

With respect to the temporal parameters of the Archaic period on Corfu, the obvious starting point is the foundation of the Corinthian *apoikia* c. 730. The conventional end date for the Archaic period, 480/79, is maintained here. Although the Corcyraeans participated in the Persian Wars (see Section 4.7.5), the island was not directly impacted by the invasion and appears to have prospered without interruption until destructive civil wars in the latter part of the fifth century.

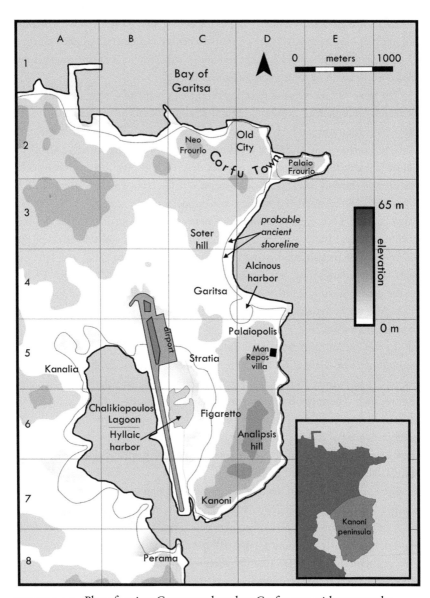

**FIGURE 4.1.** Plan of ancient Corcyra and modern Corfu town with topography.

*Corcyra* 493

The chronology of Archaic Corcyra is inextricably intertwined with that of Corinth and, more precisely, Corinth's ruling tyrannical family, the Cypselids. This essay follows the "higher" chronology, which was favored by one of the authors of this essay (Gehrke 1990) and which seems to be "today almost universally accepted" (Dubbini 2011: 52 n. 31). That chronology suggests the following dates for the reigns of Cypselus and his descendants:

Cypselus 657/6–627/6
Periander 627/6–587/6
Psammetichus-Cypselus 587/6–584/3.[2]

The relevant dates appear to be in part schematic—for example, the precisely 30- and 40-year-long reigns of Cypselus and Periander, respectively—but it is possible to confirm them *grosso modo*, and they cannot be more than a few years off in one direction or the other. The high chronology works well with the most commonly accepted date for the foundation of the Corinthian *apoikia* on Corfu, 734/3 (see Section 4.5.2).[3]

## 4.2. Sources
### 4.2.1. Textual Sources

The earliest literary sources offering information about Corcyra date to the Classical period.[4] Herodotus preserves several relevant oral traditions, though in his own particular narrative form.[5] Thucydides and Xenophon report, at times in quite some detail, about conflicts that played themselves out in the city and on the island. Even though those conflicts did not occur until the later fifth and fourth centuries, the two historians do provide important information about the geographic, topographic, economic, and social circumstances of Corcyra, some of which may also be extrapolated back to earlier eras. Later geographic writers,

---

2. On this chronology, see especially Servais 1969 and Lapini 1996: 79-147; cf. Gehrke 1990: 34–8, and now Dubbini 2011: 51–9; Fantasia 2017: 19 n. 41 ("l'unica cronologia dei Cipselidi accettabile").

3. The high chronology is independently and indirectly confirmed by Thucydides' dating of the first sea battle between Corcyra and Corinth; see Section 4.7.2.

4. For a useful compilation of the literary sources for Corcyra, see Riemann 1879–1880: vol. 1: 10–15.

5. On this, see the articles in Luraghi 2001 (especially the contributions of O. Murray and N. Luraghi).

494   THE OXFORD HISTORY OF THE ARCHAIC GREEK WORLD

especially Strabo, are also particularly rich sources. Furthermore, possible reflections of the perspectives of settlers or colonizers may be sought in passages of the *Odyssey* (e.g., 9.130–9), and other Homeric passages paint a picture of a city that perhaps looks something like Corcyra did near the time of its foundation (e.g., *Od.* 6.262–6). These are, however, at best indirect testimonies that can be used only to make more vivid or plausible our hypothetical reconstructions.

Inscriptions from Corfu are collected in *Inscriptiones Graecae* IX.1² fascicle 4, published in 2001, which supersedes Dittenberger's 1897 edition (*SEG* 51.665).[6] *IG* IX.1² fascicle 4 includes about two dozen texts datable to the Archaic period. Five monumental epigrams survive from the decades around 600 (*IG* IX.1².4.878–82), of which two are reproduced below due to their relevance to the political organization and history of early Corcyra (see Sections 4.5.3 and 4.7.5). Also noteworthy are eight lead tablets (*IG* IX.1².4.865–72), datable as early as c. 500, that seem to be receipts for private financial transactions (see Sections 4.5.4 and 4.8.4). One might also note a concentration of fifth-century dedications from a small sanctuary to Apollo Corcyraios (*IG* IX.1².4.822–33; see Section 4.4.2.7.2).

## 4.2.2. Excavation and Surveys

Corfu has received less systematic and sustained excavation than have some other regions of Greece. The ancient urban center was extensively disrupted by later building and stone looting prevalent under Byzantine, Venetian, and British rule (Metallinou 2010: 11–12), but modern excavations have been able to clarify its general layout. The earliest work on the archaeological remains consists of descriptions written by travelers and local scholars in the late 18th and early 19th centuries CE.[7] In 1822, British engineers carrying out work on the Kardaki spring on the northeastern slope of Analipsis hill uncovered the remains of a temple now dated to the last quarter of the sixth century (see Section 4.4.2.7.3 and Figure 4.2).

Starting in the second half of the 19th century CE, Corfu began attracting the attention of scholars interested in the possibility that it was the Homeric Scheria, the homeland of the Phaeacians. Hence the island was visited and described by Heinrich Schliemann (who believed that the Phaeacians' capital was situated on the Kanoni peninsula), Victor Bérard, and Wilhelm Dörpfeld, among others (Leekley and Noyes 1975: 1–2; see here Sections 4.4.2 and 4.5.2). When the

---

6. *Inscriptiones Graecae* IX.1² fascicle 4 is freely available online at http://telota.bbaw.de/ig/; for a recent index of all inscriptions pertaining to the island, see Psoma 2022, part B: 659–76.

7. On the history of archaeological excavations on Corfu, see Riemann 1879–1880: vol. 1: 15–41; Schmidt 1890: 47–50; Rhomaios 1925; Leekley and Noyes 1975: 1–3; Carter 1996; Kanta-Kitsou 1996: 104 n. 36; Metallinou 2010: 12; Preka-Alexandri 2010: 87–91.

# Corcyra

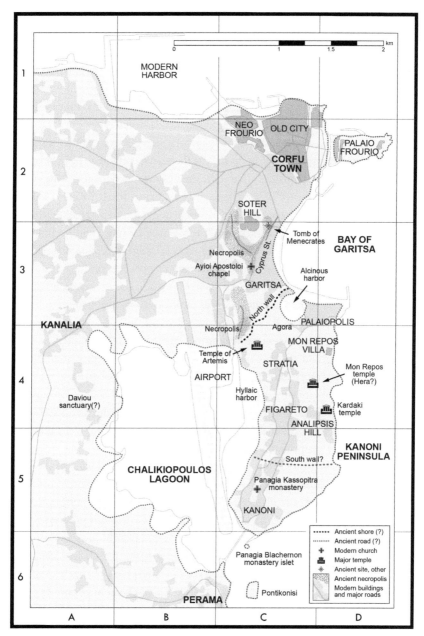

FIGURE 4.2. Plan of the urban center of Corcyra showing modern Corfu town.

496    THE OXFORD HISTORY OF THE ARCHAIC GREEK WORLD

Venetian fortifications surrounding Corfu Town were demolished in the mid-19th century CE, important remains, including an Archaic necropolis, came to light on Soter hill in the southeastern part of the modern city, and other antiquities were discovered in the area of the agora of the ancient city on the Kanoni peninsula at around the same time (Schmidt 1890: 26–32).

The first sustained excavations took place in the early 20th century CE and focused on the northern half of the Kanoni peninsula, as has much of the archaeological work undertaken on Corfu since. In 1910, farmers discovered the famous pediment from the Temple of Artemis in the northwestern part of the peninsula, near the monastery of Agioi Theodoroi,[8] and the site was excavated the following year by Federiko Versakis on behalf of the Greek Archaeological Society. Kaiser Wilhelm II, who owned a summer palace on Corfu, sought and received permission from the Greek government to continue excavations overseen by Dörpfeld and Konstantinos Rhomaios (Ephor of Antiquities from 1908–1922). Their exploration was cut short by the outbreak of World War I, but supplementary work was carried out in 1919–1920 (Dörpfeld 1914; Rhomaios 1925; Schleif, Rhomaios, and Klaffenbach 1940: 9–13). Detailed publications with the results of the excavations appeared in 1939–1940 (Rodenwaldt 1939; Schleif, Rhomaios, and Klaffenbach 1940).

During his last excavation campaign in Corfu, Dörpfeld explored a temple at Kardaki spring and another nearby temple that was located to the north of Analipsis chapel (Dörpfeld 1914: 170–5). Although both of these temples are located within the extensive grounds of the 19th-century CE villa of Mon Repos, the temple near the Kardaki spring is typically described as the Kardaki Temple, whereas the site north of Analipsis chapel is typically identified as the temple at Mon Repos (and was probably dedicated to Hera).

Archaeological explorations conducted by the Greek Archaeological Service and international collaborators starting in the second half of the 20th century CE have greatly expanded our knowledge of the ancient urban center. Early campaigns returned to the Archaic sanctuaries, beginning with the excavations in 1962–1967 at the Mon Repos temple directed by Giorgos Dontas (who was succeeded by Peter Calligas in 1967) and in 1976–1978 at the Kardaki Temple by Dontas and Alfred Mallwitz. A late Archaic pediment from a temple very likely dedicated to Dionysus was discovered at the southern end of the Kanoni peninsula on the Giovane-Kolla properties in 1973, and the site was explored in 1974 and 1977–1978 (see Section 4.4.2.7.4). Ongoing investigations have encountered stretches of the fortifications encircling the ancient city of Corcyra (see Section 4.4.2.3). The same holds true for the ancient city's harbor facilities, the excavation of which

---

8. The location is described as Garitsa in some publications, although the sanctuary is within the Kanoni peninsula.

is now being supplemented by geophysical survey, especially in the area of the so-called harbor of Alcinous (see Section 4.4.2.4). Intermittent excavations have also taken place in the Archaic necropolis in the area of Soter hill (see Section 4.4.2.8).

Much of the archaeological evidence from Corfu has yet to be published beyond the annual reports by the Greek archaeological service issued in the *Archaiologikon Deltion* and related venues, and there are comparatively few available syntheses (see, e.g., Kanta-Kitsou 1996; Lang 1996: 299–301; Dontas 1997; Metallinou 2010; Preka-Alexandri 2010; Baika 2013; Hernandez 2017: 217–19).

No intensive survey on Corfu has yet been conducted and published.

## 4.3. Natural Setting

Corfu is a relatively long, narrow island that runs roughly N–S (see Map 4.1). A bay on the east coast gives the island a contour that resembles a sickle, in keeping with ancient testimony that the island was once known as Drepane.[9] The northern end of Corfu is roughly oval in shape, running c. 25 km E–W and c. 10 km N–S. The remainder of the island is a long, narrow spit of land that runs roughly NW–SE for c. 45 km, gradually curving in parallel to the mainland and tapering from north to south, with its width varying from c. 10 km to c. 4 km. The total surface area is 585 sq km.

Corfu is divided into three topographical zones. The northern part of the island is dominated by a high, rugged plateau that rises to the highest peak on the island, Pantokrator (914 masl).[10] A lower set of hills, reaching their highest elevation at Agioi Deka (567 masl), occupies the central part of the island. A low, rocky spine forms the long, narrow southern extension of the island. In the 19th century CE, the traditional names for those three zones were (from north to south): Oros (the northern, most mountainous part of the island), Mese (the rugged central zone between Pantokrator and Agioi Deka), and Aleuki (the southern part of the island, to the south of Agioi Deka).[11]

---

9. Or "sickle"; see Aristotle FF1, 3–4 Gigon; Timaeus *FGrH* 566 F79; Callimachus F14 Pfeiffer; Stephanus Byzantinus s.v. Φαίαξ. The name was at some point linked with the mytho-historical interpretation that the island hid the sickle with which Ouranos was castrated. The ancestry of the Phaeacians is traced back to the droplets of Ouranos' blood in the writings of Alcaeus (F441 Lobel Page) and Acusilaus (*FGrH* 2 F4). Also see Lane Fox 2008: 274–7.

10. On the geology and topography of the island, Partsch 1887 remains fundamental; see also Riemann 1879–1880: vol. 1: 6–8; Matton 1960: 12–23; and the short remarks in Meyer 1975: 305 and Higgins and Higgins 1996: 101.

11. So Schmidt 1890: 8–18, who connects the name Aleuki with Leukimme (93 n. 63). Philippson 1958: 427 has a fourfold division because he subdivides the middle area into a northern hill zone and a southern mountain zone.

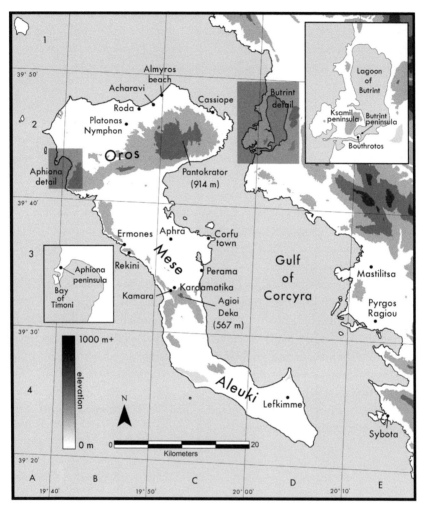

MAP 4.1. Topography of Corfu and some key sites on and near Corfu mentioned in this essay.

The mountainous zone in the north has stretches of relatively flat, elevated terrain, especially in the northwest, in which tertiary materials, especially marl, and alluvial land provide good conditions for agriculture. The northern part of the middle zone is especially favored by its more extensive, low-elevation plains (Schmidt 1890: 19; Bürchner 1922: 1403–4, 1408; Philippson 1958: 447–8). The primary urban center was located at a coastal site on the eastern edge of the middle zone, and the main area of cultivation in its vicinity must be that described by Xenophon (*Hell.* 6.26). Clay deposits are evident immediately north of the ancient town of Corcyra in what is today the suburb of Garitsa (see Figure 4.2) (Bürchner 1922: 1407; Preka-Alexandri 1992: 50; Finocchiaro, Barone, Mazzoleni, et al. 2018). The southern third of the island lies at low elevation and offers additional potential farmland, though the island is quite narrow here and thus adds relatively little territory compared with the middle and northern zones.

The climatic conditions, which have not fundamentally changed between antiquity and today (Manning 2022), were also beneficial for agriculture and hence promoted the general development of the island. The climate in Corcyra is decidedly maritime and moderate in comparison with the conditions generally encountered elsewhere in Greece. In the summer, cool northern winds (known in the present day as Maïstros, and as Skiros in antiquity) predominate, while the winter cold is tempered by the sirocco, or the ancient Euros, winds (Partsch 1887: 52; Bürchner 1922: 1404). Corfu has relatively high precipitation, and the island is generally well watered (Bürchner 1922: 1404, 1409; cf. Hammond 1967: 17).

Corfu's geographical situation is also favorable. It is located both near the point where the Greek mainland most closely approaches the Italian peninsula; the distance between the west coast of Corfu and the Italian peninsula is c. 100 km (see Map. 4.2) and at the southern end of the Adriatic Sea. Furthermore, the island is separated from the Greek mainland by a relatively narrow, sheltered body of water. The result is that Corfu is a natural waypoint for maritime journeys from the Greek mainland to both Italy and the Adriatic. Here one must take into account the special features of ancient seafaring, which favored coastal travel. A journey up to Corfu, from which one could reach the coast of Apulia with relative ease by taking advantage of the prevailing currents and winds, was generally preferred to the direct route from the Peloponnese to Sicily (and one would have sailed the same route when traveling in the opposite direction). When Thucydides emphasized that the Corfu "lies nicely on the route of the coastal voyage to Italy and Sicily," his point is about the island's strategic naval position, but it nevertheless mirrors the general maritime situation (Thuc. 1.36.2, cf. 1.44.3;

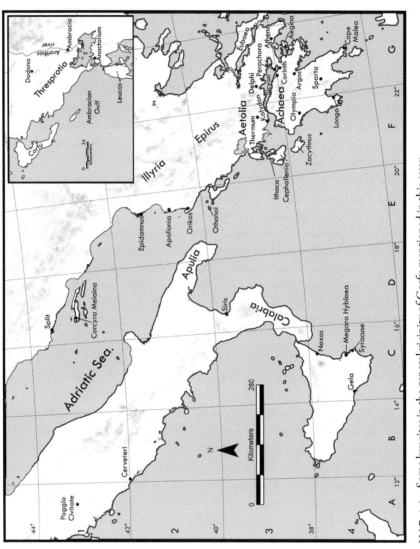

MAP 4.2. Some key sites in the general vicinity of Corfu mentioned in this essay.

see also Xen. *Hell.* 6.2.6; Hornblower 1991–2008: vol. 1: 80).[12] At the same time, Corfu is also an ideal point for staging journeys into the more northerly regions of the Adriatic (Kiechle 1979; see here Sections 4.4 and 4.8).

Corfu's natural advantages also present themselves at a local level. Thanks both to the narrowness of the straits that separate the northern and southern extremities of the island from the mainland and to the gently concave curve of the coastline between them, the gulf separating Corfu and the mainland (the Gulf of Corcyra) is something like an "inland lake," a large area sheltered from the western and northern winds (see Map 4.1). The contrast with the western side of the island makes this especially clear; indeed, the waters to the west of the island were later called *agriopelago* or *agriothalassa* ("wild sea") (Schmidt 1890: 19), and Corfu's west coast, particularly at its north, is dominated by steep defiles and cliffs barring passage between land and sea. But in the east, the sea invited fishing and seafaring, connecting more than it divided.

The land controlled by Corcyra on the opposite mainland (probably from a very early period of its history onward), its *peraia*, is both relatively flat and separated from areas farther inland by mountain ranges that run parallel to the coast. The *peraia* thus is oriented to the west, opening toward the sea and Corfu, while remaining comparatively closed to the mainland farther east (Hammond 1967: 35; Carusi 2011: 99).[13]

## 4.4. Material Culture
### 4.4.1. Corfu up to the Arrival of the Greeks

Archaeological finds indicate that Corfu was occupied since the Lower Paleolithic era, when it was connected to the mainland during the glacial maximums (Sordinas 1969; Souyoudzoglou-Haywood 1999: 6; Arvanitou-Metallinou 2007; Sordinas 2007; Preka-Alexandri 2010: 16–24). In the Bronze Age, there is evidence for close ties with Epirus as well as with the small islands off Corfu's northwest shores, such as Othonoi (Hammond 1967: 377; Hammond 1972: 255; Arvanitou-Metallinou 2017; *Cf-el* #899, 1618–20, 2611–12, 3284, 3297–99, 4071, 5044). The degree of contact with Mycenaean Greece appears to have been fairly limited (Calligas 1982: 58; Morgan 1998: 293 n. 83; Souyoudzoglou-Haywood 1999: 11–13; Preka-Alexandri 2010: 24, 143–4).[14]

---

12. Unless otherwise indicated, all translations of Thucydides in this essay are taken from Martin Hammond's translation in the Oxford World's Classics series (published in 2009).

13. On *peraiai* in general, see Funke 1999.

14. Mycenaean pottery recently excavated near Ermones (on the west coast of the island, due west of the ancient urban center of Corcyra) suggests at least some trade contact (Preka-Alexandri 2010: 24).

502    THE OXFORD HISTORY OF THE ARCHAIC GREEK WORLD

We know comparatively little about what was happening on Corfu during the Early Iron Age, in part due to a preference for handmade pottery that is difficult to date with any precision (Hammond 1967: 363–5; Calligas 1982: 58–60; Morgan 1998: 286 n. 33).[15] The Protogeometric finds from the southern Ionian islands, especially Ithaca, are not paralleled on Corfu (Souyoudzoglou-Haywood 1999: 142–3).

The earliest Greek artifacts from the island originate from the main urban center of Corcyra. The great majority of these artifacts were found not in clearly stratified contexts but rather mixed with later objects in contexts created or disrupted by later activity, and so they need to be dated purely on a stylistic basis. After reviewing the collection in the Corfu archaeological museum, Bruno D'Agostino (D'Agostino 2012: 296) confirmed the consensus in the previous scholarship (Hammond 1967: 414; Kallipolitis 1982; Riginos, Bouligea, Spanodimos, et al. 2007: 797; *Cf-el* #3289) that a few sherds of cups date to the third quarter of the eighth century and that the first concentrations of decorated Greek pottery belong in the final quarter of that century. Several votive bronzes of the Late Geometric period (and hence roughly contemporary with the first Greek pottery) found near the Mon Repos temple and a short distance to its west are the earliest signs of cult activity in the urban center (see Section 4.4.2.7.2). The restriction of such early finds to the urban center of Corcyra and the absence of any identifiable Greek material from previous centuries suggest that there had been little prior interaction between Greeks and the indigenous inhabitants of Corfu.

As discussed at more length in the context of the island's political history (see Section 4.5), these finds have been interpreted through the lens of the ancient literary accounts attributing its colonization to Corinthians, perhaps following an earlier contingent of Euboeans. The archaeological finds indicate that a Greek settlement was developing in Corcyra at about the same time as Syracuse, a contemporary Corinthian foundation according to the later traditions.

The lack of any stratigraphy or architecture from the eighth century hinders physical reconstruction of the first decades of the *apoikia*. The aforementioned finds of bronze dedications at the Mon Repos temple attests to cult activity before the seventh century (see Section 4.4.2.7.2); the earliest in situ remains are

---

15. It has been suggested that the Late Bronze Age cemetery at the Mexa Plot, located between Ermones and Rekini, on the western coast of Corfu, might have continued to have been used into the Early Iron Age (*Cf-el* #1619). Our knowledge of what was happening on Corfu during the Early Iron Age might be significantly increased by a systematic archaeological survey; the recent survey of Thesprotia has identified numerous sites from the Early Iron Age (Georgiadou and Tzortzatou 2009).

early seventh-century graves in what would develop into the primary necropolis of Corcyra (see Section 4.4.2.8). At present, the archaeological evidence does not provide much insight into the nature of the relationship between the indigenous population of the island and the Greek settlers, though the literary sources (discussed in the context of political history in Section 4.5.2) make some mention of that subject.

## 4.4.2. Settlement Organization
### *4.4.2.1. Layout of the City*

The Corinthian settlers built their primary urban center on what is known today as the Kanoni peninsula, which is roughly rectangular in shape and measures c. 2 km N–S and c. 1.3 km E–W (see Figure 4.3).[16]

The peninsula was joined to the rest of the island on its northern side. The Gulf of Corcyra lay to the east and south of the peninsula, the lagoon of Chalikiopoulos to its west. The northern part of the peninsula is today known as Palaiopolis, homonymous with an early Christian church in that part of the site, where there is a concentration of other Late Antique buildings (Kanta-Kitsou 1996: 82 n. 7). The lower ground along the western side of the peninsula facing the lagoon of Chalikiopoulos is known as Figareto, after one of its better-known modern neighborhoods. The terrain rises as it moves to the east, forming a plateau of considerable area interrupted at places by low hills and valleys. Along its eastern edge, it drops sharply into the sea. This high ground is often called Analipsis, after the aforementioned chapel. Thucydides (3.72.3), in discussing events in Corcyra during the *stasis* between the *damos* and the oligarchs during the Peloponnesian War, mentions that at one point, members of the *damos* took refuge in "the acropolis and higher parts of the city" (ἀκρόπολιν καὶ τὰ μετέωρα τῆς πόλεως); the acropolis and the *meteōra* must together correspond to what is today called Analipsis hill (Schmidt 1890: 27–8). Besides the sanctuaries located within the Mon Repos park, we lack sufficient archaeological evidence to conclude how the elevated terrain of Analipsis hill was used in antiquity, although a water source is available in the form of the Kardaki spring. Since only the perimeter of the settlement seems to have been walled (see below), the acropolis and *meteōra* were not clearly demarcated from the rest of the city. Corcyra had two main harbors—the Alcinous harbor, on its northern side, and the Hyllaic harbor,

---

16. The name, derived from a battery once situated at the southern end of the peninsula (Schmidt 1890: 88 n. 91), is also used to refer just to the southern tip of the peninsula. The peninsula is occasionally described as Analipsis, which, in this discussion, is reserved for the hill in the southeastern part of the peninsula rather than the whole peninsula.

504 THE OXFORD HISTORY OF THE ARCHAIC GREEK WORLD

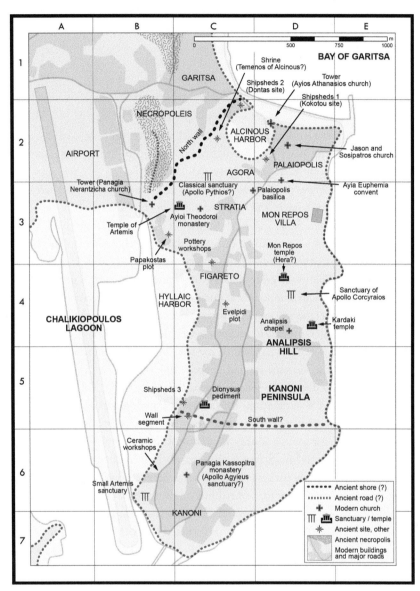

FIGURE 4.3. Plan of the urban center of Corcyra.

located somewhere along the Chalikiopoulos lagoon to its west—and potentially a third (see Section 4.4.2.4).

After the seventh century CE, the urban center of Corcyra was abandoned, and the population eventually resettled in Corfu Town, c. 2 km to the north, below two fortified peaks, which inspired the Italianized name Corfú (from the Byzantine Κορυφώ; see Riemann 1879–1880: vol. 1: 8; Preka-Alexandri 2010: 8–9). The area to the north of Corcyra town and to the south of Corfu Town is known as Garitsa, named after the bay to its east. Extensively quarried during the Byzantine and Venetian eras, the ancient urban center was largely abandoned until the modern city expanded south to reoccupy Garitsa and parts of the Kanoni peninsula.

There can be little doubt as to the reasons for the Greeks' choice to settle on the Kanoni peninsula: it offers ample space (roughly 250 ha), excellent natural harbors, and an isthmus that simplified the defense of the urban center. The situation is reminiscent of the town of the Phaeacians, as described by Nausicaa in Homer's *Odyssey*:

> There's a lofty tower around it, and on either side of the city a fine harbor and a narrow entrance. Double-oared ships are drawn upon the way, for all have a slip for each. (6.262–5; trans. J. Huddleston)

The correspondence of Homer's description with the layout of urban Corcyra, along with the island's location, helps explain why the Corcyraeans have been equated since antiquity with the Phaeacians, even if the connection is fanciful.[17]

### 4.4.2.2. *Urban Development of Corcyra in the Archaic Period*

As reviewed in the following sections, a considerable amount of evidence from the Archaic period has been found in Kanoni. It is, however, not yet possible to present a detailed diachronic sketch of the development of the urban center of Corcyra, and the discussion that follows is organized around types of spaces (harbors, sanctuaries, etc.). However, some general observations on the history of the city can be offered.

Some of the earliest graves, dated to the late eighth century and located in the central part of the Kanoni peninsula, were soon built over as the settlement

---

17. The starting point of the modern debate is von Wilamowitz-Moellendorff 1884: 170–2; see also Riemann 1879–1880: vol. 1: 9–10; Hornblower 1991–2008: vol. 1: 70, 469, with further evidence. The localizations by Victor Bérard (sketched in Matton 1960: 24–39) constitute an extreme form of later work along the same lines. All such attempts are, in the end, little more than speculation. The point here is not to identify Corfu with Homeric Scheria, but rather to account for the connections made between the Corcyraeans and the Phaeacians.

expanded (Metallinou 2010: 21; Preka-Alexandri 2010: 120). By the second half of the seventh century, the main cemetery was located just to the north of the Kanoni peninsula, in what is now the suburb of Garitsa (see Section 4.4.2.8). The location of that cemetery suggests that by the seventh century, the Archaic urban center had extended into the isthmus linking Kanoni to the rest of the island.

Three ancient roads led from the urban center toward the interior of the island. One ran west and two ran north, along either side of Soter hill. By the end of the seventh century, larger tombs were being set up along the roads leading north. Because such tombs tend to be located at highly visible positions, we may surmise that a considerable amount of traffic was moving north along the two roads flanking Soter hill, toward the headland now occupied by Corfu Town. Indeed, a suburban development in this region is attested by a late Archaic sanctuary and sixth- to fifth-century domestic architecture discovered in plots to the west of Corfu Town (see Section 4.4.3). The northern half of the Kanoni peninsula appears to have been already extensively built up in Archaic times, with residences, workshops, and various public monuments, although much is hidden by later and, in particular, early modern construction.

Extensive remains of Classical and Hellenistic houses oriented to an orthogonal system of roads, alleys, and drainage systems provide a clear indication of urban planning on the Kanoni peninsula by the fifth century (Kanta-Kitsou 1996: 84–5; Metallinou 2010: 21; Baika 2013: 321–2). Since the relevant archaeological work primarily took the form of intermittent rescue excavations conducted in small plots, and since those excavations are for the most part published only in cursory fashion, it is unclear how much of the urban infrastructure known from later periods had been established by the Archaic period.[18] Foundations discovered at lower levels and at a different orientation to Classical-era shipsheds (see Section 4.4.2.4) may indicate that the urban grid was instituted later in the settlement's history (Baika 2014: 481).

### 4.4.2.3. Fortifications

Xenophon (*Hell.* 6.2.3–26), in his account of the Spartan siege led by Mnasippos in the fourth century, describes Corcyra's city walls and towers, which we can potentially connect to excavated remains that date primarily to the Classical period. In light of the topographical situation, one would expect that securing the isthmus uniting the peninsula with the island was an early priority for the urban

---

18. Useful summaries may be found in Preka-Alexandri (2010: 38–9, 120–5), including some domestic sectors with traces of walls as early as c. 500. Recent reports of the Greek Archaeological Service provide additional documentation of domestic and other architectural finds, notably Riginos, Bouligea, Spanodimos et al. 2007; Metallinou, Provata, and Nakou 2008.

residents of Corcyra. Portions of the opposite ends of a wall crossing the isthmus have been identified at various points (Dierichs 2004: 40; Baika 2013: 323).

Near the Hyllaic harbor, coursed masonry from a Classical tower and gate is preserved up to a height of 6 m within the walls of the Panagia Nerantzicha church (Schleif, Rhomaios, and Klaffenbach 1940: 15–16; Dontas 1965b: 140), and stretches of wall along the Chalikiopoulos lagoon include a recently excavated tower, built from partly worked fieldstones, which, in light of the finds associated with the tower and its simpler masonry, might have originated in the Archaic period (Metallinou, Provata, and Nakou 2008: 832–4, 36 nn. 35–6; Metallinou 2010: 19-20; Baika 2014: 481).

The isthmus fortifications logically would have terminated at the Alcinous harbor, where the foundations and lower masonry courses of a tower stratigraphically dated to the fifth or fourth century are extant under the Church of Agios Athanasios (Dontas 1965a: 66–70). However, this tower is located at the west end of a spur wall, meaning that it would have protected the eastern side of the harbor, rather than connecting to the wall crossing the isthmus. More likely, this feature was part of a wall circuit running along the eastern shores of the peninsula, where traces of submerged fortifications have been identified as far south as the shoreline at the Kardaki spring (Dontas 1978; Baika 2013: 323).

Additional stretches of walls have been exposed along the west side of Kanoni and crossing the peninsula near its southern end (Baika 2014: 481). In sum, besides the well-documented masonry integrated into the Nerantzicha and Athanasios churches, too little has been published to comment on how Corcyra's fortifications developed, although a circuit was probably in place by the Classical period at the latest.

### 4.4.2.4. Harbors and Port Facilities

The city's harbors were among its most distinctive topographical features (see Figure 4.3). In his account of the *stasis* in Corcyra, Thucydides (3.72.3; cf. 3.81.2) speaks of two harbors: one near the agora, facing the mainland, and another called the "Hyllaic" (cf. Ap. Rhod. *Argon.* 4.1125). The one near the agora was called the Alcinous harbor, presumably after a sanctuary situated there dedicated to the legendary king of the Phaeacians in the *Odyssey*.[19] However, the

---

19. The name of the harbor is preserved in the Homeric scholia and in Eustathius' commentary on line 492 of the geographical work of Dionysius of Alexandria (Müller 1855–1861: vol. 2: 310). The Homeric scholia call the other harbor "the one of Hyllus." Thucydides (3.70.4) mentions a temenos of Alcinous without giving its location, which is usually believed to have been located near the harbor of the same name. For further discussion, see Kanta-Kitsou 2001b: 442; Baika 2013: 320-1.

geographer pseudo-Scylax (29) speaks of three harbors, one of which was allegedly closable (*kleistos*). Bernhard Schmidt (Schmidt 1890: 19–26) first clarified the location and orientation of the harbors of ancient Corcyra (cf. Bürchner 1922: 1410; Dontas 1965b: 142–4; Metallinou 2010: 19 n. 58). While his reconstruction still leaves some questions open, the basic picture has been confirmed by later archaeological investigations.[20] Today there is no doubt that the two named harbors were located on opposite sides of the Kanoni peninsula. The northern harbor, the Alcinous, was a basin (now entirely filled with silt) opening into the Bay of Garitsa. The Hyllaic harbor, entered from the south, lay within the Chalikiopoulos lagoon. The location of the possible third harbor and which of the three might have been closable remain unknown.

Recent archaeological and geomorphological research by Kalliopi Baika, Claudia Finkler, and Andreas Vött has provided valuable insight into the configuration of Corcyra's harbors and their facilities.[21] The coastline has changed significantly since antiquity due to the combined action of seismic events, which resulted in an uplift of the coast, and the accumulation of silt in the shallow basins of the ancient harbors (Baika 2013: 322; Finkler, Fischer, Baika, et al. 2017; Finkler, Baika, Rigakou et al. 2018: 106–8; Finkler, Baika, Rigakou et al. 2017). Deposits from the ancient harbor are today found about a meter above sea level and significantly inland from the modern coast.

Baika's recent syntheses (2013; 2014: 478–83) distinguish three different sets of shipsheds in urban Corcyra. "Corcyra 1," located on the southeastern side of the Alcinous harbor, consists of three parallel rows of foundations for piers and a common rear wall, indicating at least four slipways, with traces of a quay wall in front of the sheds (Baika 2013: 323–5; Finkler, Baika, Rigakou, et al. 2018).[22] A second complex, "Corcyra 2," located in the northwestern part of Alcinous harbor, consists of a single row of pier foundations for a minimum of two adjacent slipways (Dontas 1966a: 85–7; Baika 2013: 326).

The foundations of the shipsheds at "Corcyra 1" are dated near the beginning of the Classical period (Baika 2013: 329–30: Baika 2014: 481). The purpose of an ill-preserved Archaic building with a different orientation, detected underneath, is unknown. A lead tablet from the site, from the second half of the fifth

---

20. Gomme offers a very different reconstruction that has since been refuted by archaeological findings (Gomme, Andrewes, and Dover 1945–1981: vol. 2: 370–2).

21. The geophysical survey began in 2012 and was recently completed; we thank Andreas Vött (Mainz) for his invaluable assistance and Claudia Finkler (Mainz) for sharing their work.

22. Additional slipways to the east have been reported from rescue excavations preceding the construction of the Arion hotel (1997–2000) (Baika 2013: 328–9).

century (*IG* IX.1².4.874), records the delivery of wooden beams and tiles, possibly for repairing the roof of the shipsheds. The structures on the other side of the Alcinous harbor (Corcyra 2) are dated generally to the fifth century (Baika 2013: 329–31).

On the opposite side of Kanoni, "Corcyra 3" would have been accessed from the Hyllaic harbor (Kanta-Kitsou 2001a: 284–7; Baika 2013: 326, 31–2). Irregularities in its two rows of piers reflect modifications and repairs over its life span. Baika raises some doubts over the chronology proposed in earlier reports, but the area appears to have been in use by the late seventh or sixth century (Baika 2013: 327–9). At that point in time, the facilities possibly took the form of unroofed slipways, with roofed shelters being constructed in the early fifth century and modified in the Hellenistic era.

The existence of other harbor facilities is apparent from textual evidence. First, Thucydides (3.74.2) mentions a *neōrion* (a dockyard or arsenal) at the Alcinous harbor, which would suggest that, like the Kantharos in the Athenian Piraeus, this harbor had both commercial and military functions (Schmidt 1890: 24–6; Bürchner 1922: 1410; Gomme, Andrewes, and Dover 1945–1981: vol. 2: 363; Baika 2014: 479, 482–3). It is probably the same *neōrion* described as being encroached upon by a private house in a second-century inscription (*IG* IX.1².4.794 = *IG* IX.1.692; *SEG* 13.384, 1.8–12). Second, the aforementioned inscription also references the roof of a *skeuothēkē*, evidently a warehouse, whose location is unknown, although the building mentioned in this inscription has been connected to late fifth-century walls from the site of Corcyra 2 on the Alcinous harbor (Dontas 1966a: 87–92). The presence of at least one tower at the east of the entrance to that harbor (see Section 4.4.2.3) is also consistent with a military function.

As for the additional information from pseudo-Scylax (29), the closable harbor has been argued to have been the Alcinous, based on geomorphological evidence that the Bay of Garitsa was indented more deeply in the southwest than it is today (Partsch 1887: 65; Baika 2013: 321–3; Baika 2014: 481; Finkler, Fischer, Baika, et al. 2017; Finkler, Baika, Rigakou, et al. 2018; Finkler, Baika, Rigakou, et al. 2017). The third harbor is conjectured to have been located somewhere along the eastern edge of the peninsula (Finkler, Baika, Rigakou, et al. 2018: 94).[23]

---

23. Schmidt (1890: 22–3, 34–6 with n. 117) suggested the third harbor was located in Corfu town in the area north of the Palaio Frourio. Metallinou (2010: 19–20) argues for a location closer to the Alcinous harbor (see Figure 4.2). See also Baika 2013: 321, 28–9; Finkler, Baika, Rigakou, et al. 2018. If a third harbor was built in the fourth or third century, that would explain the discrepancy between the two harbors known to Thucydides and the three to Pseudo-Scylax.

## 4.4.2.5. *Agora*

That the agora was located in the northern part of Corcyra between the two harbors, but closer to the Alcinous harbor, is clear from Thucydides' description of the *stasis* in Corcyra in the 420s:

> When night came on the people retreated to the acropolis and the higher parts of the city, gathering their forces there and establishing their position: they also held the Hyllaic harbor. The other party took over the agora, where most of them lived, and the adjacent harbor facing the mainland. . . . A day passed, and then there was another battle, won this time by the people, who had the stronger positions and the greater numbers: they also had the enterprising support of their women, who pelted the enemy with tiles from their houses and faced the fray with a courage beyond their nature. The oligarchs' defeat came late in the afternoon, and their immediate fear was that the people would advance to take the dockyard unopposed and finish them off: they therefore set fire to the houses surrounding the agora and the tenement buildings, to prevent any way through. In this arson they spared neither their own property nor anyone else's, with the result that much merchants' stock was consumed by fire, and the whole city was in danger of destruction, if a wind had arisen to carry the flames in that direction. (3.72.3–74.2)

Since the agora, in this account, is located by a harbor that was opposite the mainland and distinct from the Hyllaic, it must have been adjacent to the Alcinous harbor.

Additional evidence places the agora adjacent to the harbor. An inscription in the Basilica of Palaiopolis (located c. 400 m south of the current shoreline of Garitsa Bay and c. 200 m south of the southern end of the now-silted-up Alcinous harbor) reports that Bishop Jovian (first half of the fifth century CE) "built this holy temple after he had destroyed the sanctuaries [temenē] and altars of the Hellenes" (*IG* IX.1².4.1191 II).[24] Although neither the agora nor the site of the temenē is mentioned, it is reasonable to assume that the church itself had replaced the latter, and the agora is a fitting locale for multiple sanctuaries and altars. Excavations around the basilica have also revealed the remains of large public structures of the sort that we would expect to find in and around an agora (Preka-Alexandri 2010: 97–101). Below the northeast side of the basilica

---

24. On the bishop, also see *IG* IX.1².4.1192. On the impressive ruins of the church, which had two additional phases of construction, see Riemann 1879–1880: vol. 1: 32–3; Schmidt 1890: 32.

*Corcyra* 511

is a large foundation (c. 40 m in diameter) that has been identified as the cavea of a *bouleutērion*, *prytaneion*, or *odeion* complex from the Severan period, which apparently was built over a Hellenistic predecessor (Speich and Speich 1982: 125; Dierichs 2004: 38–9; Baika 2013: 321–2; Baika 2014: 482).[25] A large Roman mosaic was uncovered in 1846 on the other side of the basilica, and Schmidt observed many fragments of ancient columns farther north (Schmidt 1890: 32). Roman baths from Severan times are located to the northwest (Preka-Alexandri 2010: 102–6; Baika 2013: 321). A bronze tablet, which was discovered just to the east of the basilica, with drilled holes for mounting on a wall, bears an early Hellenistic proxeny decree (*IG* IX.1².4.786), which would presumably have been displayed near the agora (Schmidt 1890: 26).

With respect to chronology, the testimony of Thucydides indicates that the agora was located in this general area by the fifth century. Although we have no direct evidence that an agora was located there as early as the Archaic period, the early importance of maritime activity, both mercantile and naval, in Corcyra suggests that it probably would have been established in the area of the harbors by the sixth century, if not earlier.

### 4.4.2.6. Workshops

By the sixth century, a workshop district had developed in the area to the southwest of the agora.

The best-known installation was found in the Figareto neighborhood, at a site c. 350 m from the agora, where a range of structures relating to the production of ceramics were found, including at least 13 kilns from various periods, several clay-processing basins, and two wells (see Figure 4.3) (Preka-Alexandri 1992; Preka-Alexandri 2010: 112–20). Among the finds from that installation are a significant number of bronze, bone, and ceramic implements for shaping and decorating pottery (Kourkoumélis and Démesticha 1997). The huge number of sherds, including some misfires, and clay molds attest to a specialization in transport amphoras and terracotta figurines, but the installation at Figareto also produced smaller plain and fine vessels, roof tiles, and lamps. The preponderance of the finds from the later Classical and early Hellenistic periods, with lesser quantities of late Archaic material, is perhaps attributable to periodic cleaning and removal of older debris. At the east of the site, a small shrine with a limestone *korē*, half of life-size, has been tentatively linked to Artemis Epiklivanios, the guardian of the kiln (Preka-Alexandri 2010: 82, 116–17, fig. 23; Preka-Alexandri 2016: 232; see here Sections 4.4.2.7.1 and 4.11.1). The statue, probably from around the middle

---

25. A *prytaneion* is attested for the year 208/7: *IG* IX.1².4.1196: 40, 42.

512 THE OXFORD HISTORY OF THE ARCHAIC GREEK WORLD

of the sixth century, indicates that by its day, production had grown enough to merit investment in a permanent shrine—one that would continue to be maintained for the next three centuries.

Another ceramics workshop was recently excavated in the Stratia district at the Papakostas Plot, roughly midway between the aforementioned installation at Figareto and the fortification wall at the Nerantzicha church (Riginos, Bouligea, Spanodimos, et al. 2007: 806–10). The production of pottery is confirmed by basins for mixing clay, drying areas, and a well. Most of the remains are Classical, but ceramic production clearly began earlier, as attested by misfired sherds, unfired clay, and workshop tools in Archaic deposits. The kilns must have been located nearby but outside the excavated perimeter, since overfired clay from the lining of a kiln and equipment for stacking vessels were recovered within the plot.

A little more than 1 km to the south, additional workshop activity is probably attested from a rescue dig in the Demesianou Plot, near the Panagia Kassopitra Monastery in the southern part of the Kanoni peninsula (Agallopoulou 1976: pl. 183–4; Preka-Alexandri 2010: 40–1). Excavations revealed several rows of intact pan tiles set vertically, as if stockpiled in a workshop yard,[26] and buried in a fill containing a portable terracotta altar, pithos fragments, and pottery, all of which were reportedly Archaic. About 40 m farther south, an extensive layer made up of lamps, primarily of one Archaic form, as well as detached handles, had evidently been discarded from a nearby workshop.

### 4.4.2.7. Sanctuaries

The Archaic period was the heyday for the construction of sacred architecture in the urban center of Corcyra, the residents of which built a series of monumental temples on the Kanoni peninsula that would not be surpassed in scale in later times. Additional cult sites have been located on the basis of discoveries of open-air altars or votive deposits, and still other cult sites are known via epigraphic and literary references. The evidence for identifying the deities worshipped at these sites is reviewed in Section 4.11, and the art-historical significance of the finds from these sanctuaries is reviewed in Section 4.12. Although the primary deity of the sanctuaries is often debatable, the identifications assumed in most scholarship are followed here for the sake of simplicity. The description here concentrates on five sites (the Temple of Artemis [Artemision], the temple at Mon Repos

---

26. In the excavation photographs, the pans are configured as if they had been repurposed as lining for a water channel, and thus the site may not be a tile workshop.

*Corcyra* 513

[Hera?], the Kardaki Temple, the Sanctuary of Dionysus, and the Sanctuary of Apollo Agyeius) that have yielded remains of monumental architecture, moving from north to south, with glances at other signs of cult activity in the vicinity of each principal area.

#### 4.4.2.7.1. ARTEMISION AND NEARBY SANCTUARIES

The best-known sanctuary from Corcyra is the Artemision, located in the northwestern part of the Kanoni peninsula. Despite the central importance of the Corcyraeans' Temple of Artemis to the scholarship on early Greek architecture and sculpture, we are largely in the dark about many basic questions about the sanctuary, such as when cult activity at the site began and for how long it was maintained. Much of the stonework of the temple was removed by looters after the sanctuary's abandonment, and the monastery of Agioi Theodoroi overlies its eastern and southern parts. The digging of trenches and construction of an artillery bastion by the French military in the early 19th century CE disrupted the area as well (Rhomaios 1925: 193–208), and the first archaeologists who cleared the site in 1910–1914 paid little attention to stratigraphy or small finds.[27] The final publications of the excavated remains of the Artemis temple and the associated finds, issued under the direction of Gerhart Rodenwaldt, are admirable tours de force of both *Bauforschung* and sculptural analysis, yet pottery and other votives that might allow us to reconstruct cult activity are virtually absent from these volumes (Rodenwaldt 1939; Schleif, Rhomaios, and Klaffenbach 1940). Even the identification of the primary deity as Artemis, while taken as a matter of faith in most scholarship, is not absolutely certain (Rignanese 2016; see Section 4.11.1).

The earliest well-documented sign of cult activity from the Artemis sanctuary is in fact the temple itself (see Figure 4.4),[28] which is noteworthy as one of the earliest-known Doric buildings with a peristyle constructed entirely from stone from foundation to cornice (Barletta 1990: 47; Barletta 2001: 77-9; Mertens 2006: 132–4; Marconi 2007: 11–14).[29] Relatively little has survived from its

---

27. See Rignanese 2016: 450–2, with additional bibliography, on the excavations overseen by Federico Versakis, Konstantinos Rhomaios, and Wilhelm Dörpfeld.

28. However, see Preka-Alexandri (2010: 128, 130–1), on reported traces of a peribolos wall that might have preceded the temple.

29. Dörpfeld (d 1914: 164–6) hypothesized an earlier wooden temple on the basis of roof tiles that have since been demonstrated to belong to the stone temple (Schleif, Rhomaios, and Klaffenbach 1940: 119–26).

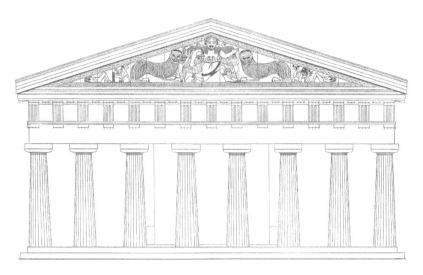

FIGURE 4.4. Reconstruction of the west facade of the Temple of Artemis; c. 580.

foundations, and the superstructure is attested by just a few surviving limestone fragments of each element. The stylobate can be restored at c. 23.8 x 49.0 m with an 8 x 17 colonnade around a comparatively narrow cella building, which suggests a pseudo-dipteral layout (Schleif, Rhomaios, and Klaffenbach 1940: 17–61). A paved path led from the east end of the building to a monumental altar, roughly the width of the temple's facade and decorated with a triglyph frieze on all four of its sides (Schleif, Rhomaios, and Klaffenbach 1940: 62–73; Wilson Jones 2014: 71).

Much of the western pediment is preserved, with the fragments of its sculpted slabs discovered as they had fallen (Rodenwaldt 1939). In its center, the Gorgon is presented in *Knielaufschema* with her offspring Pegasus (partially preserved to the left) and probably Chrysaor (to the right) (see Figures 4.5 and 4.6).[30] The central group is flanked by two stylized panthers with leonine

---

30. Stucchi (1981: 33–45) proposed Perseus instead, who was a popular figure at the time, whereas Chrysaor was rare in any period. His hypothesis, while still viable, has found little acceptance; see Mertens-Horn 1995: 261; Marconi 2007: 148–9.

FIGURE 4.5. Photograph of the center of the pediment of the Temple of Artemis; c. 580.

FIGURE 4.6. Reconstruction of the center of the west pediment of the Temple of Artemis; c. 580.

features, or "leopanthers." Next comes a pair of two-person groups whose compositions mirror each other. Each starts with a standing figure brandishing a weapon and attacking a seated (left) or kneeling (right) victim, the latter followed by a symbol indicating the setting: a masonry wall (left) and a tree (right) (see Figure 4.7). Fallen warriors occupy the edges (see Section 4.12.2 for further

FIGURE 4.7. Photograph of the south corner of the west pediment of the Temple of Artemis; c. 580. Archaeological Museum of Corfu.

discussion of the significance of this pediment and its iconography). Little remains of the eastern pediment, but fragments survive of another apotropaic Gorgon at its center (Rodenwaldt 1939: 108–12).

Lacking any documented stratified finds, the Artemis temple is dated by the style of its architecture and sculpture. A date range of 590/580–570 for the inauguration and completion of the building allows for the possibility that Corinthian tyrants had a role in its patronage.[31] However, most or all of the

---

31. A date before 590 is untenable, since it must postdate some monumental Doric projects from the first decade of the century (Barletta 2001: 58, 63–4, 70, 77–9, 83, 174 n. 4). More precisely, it should have followed the Heraion at Olympia, dated by stratified pottery no earlier than c. 600 (Sapirstein 2016a: 570–1), the Temple of Apollo at Syracuse from the beginning of the sixth century (Mertens 2006: 104–10, 32–4; Marconi 2007: 49–50), and the first Sicilian monuments with sima tiles and geison revetments, introduced during the first quarter of the sixth century, upon which the Artemision eaves tiles are modeled (Wikander 1990; Winter 1993: 299).

*Corcyra* 517

project's execution is more realistically placed in the years immediately after Corcyra became independent from Corinth (see Section 4.7), and its best comparanda are dated c. 580–570/60.[32] The iconography and significance of the architecture and sculpture are revisited in Sections 4.11 and 4.12.

In 1973 and 1979, a monumental altar and small temple (c. 6.5 x 13.5 m) were excavated c. 150 m northeast of the Artemision (Spetsieri-Choremi 1980b). Although the architecture dates to the latter part of the fifth century, the finds suggest that the cult, probably to Apollo Pythios, could have been established as early as the second half of the sixth century (see Section 4.11.1).

Traces of two private sanctuaries were identified to the south of the Artemision (see Figure 4.3). The first was in the Stratia quarter north of the Figareto workshop. Among the remains of later residences and workshops, a cache of 43 broken, albeit well-preserved, objects include terracotta figurines of enthroned or dancing females, musicians, and protomes (Spetsieri-Choremi 1991). Bronze vessels and fine pottery, including many imports and miniature vessels, were also recovered. Most objects date c. 550–490, evidently having been deposited after the cleaning of a shrine at some point before the end of the first quarter of the fifth century. By analogy to late Archaic workshop cults in Corinth (Williams II 1981; Spetsieri-Choremi 1991: 207–8), we might imagine that a family or private organization patronized the Stratia shrine. The evidence for the second private sanctuary is the *korē* installed near a kiln in the Figareto workshop (see Section 4.4.2.6). This sanctuary has been hypothetically connected with Artemis Epiklivanios, guardian of the kiln, due to its location and to the fact that figurines of Artemis were popular among the terracottas manufactured there (Preka-Alexandri 2010: 116–17).

### 4.4.2.7.2. TEMPLE AT MON REPOS AND SANCTUARY OF APOLLO CORCYRAIOS

Another important cult site was excavated within the grounds of the Mon Repos Villa on a low hill a short distance north of Analipsis chapel. The earliest finds

---

32. The pediment has typically been dated in the 580s, though in part this was based on an intertwined pair of conjectures: that it was the work of Corinthian sculptors and that it was commissioned under Periander before his death in 588/7 (see Sections 4.5.1 and 4.7.4 for further discussion). The former premise is unsupported for reasons laid out in Section 4.12.1. The proportions in the Doric entablature are similar to those of the early Temple of Aphaia at Aegina, dated in the later 570s (Schwandner and Riederer 1985: 113, 23–4, 28–9). Ridgway (1977: 193–4) identifies several sophisticated aspects of the sculpture as indicating a relatively advanced date in the 570s. Payne (1931: 241–2, 244) recognized but downplayed comparanda with low dates. For a thorough discussion of style and dating, see Dontas 1997: 97–121, 68. Note the recent (and quite unconvincing) arguments for dating the pediment to the time of Periander by Cigaina (2015: 47–52).

518    THE OXFORD HISTORY OF THE ARCHAIC GREEK WORLD

from the Mon Repos sanctuary—in particular two Geometric bronzes (a figurine of a horse and a fragmentary tripod leg)—suggest that it was founded shortly after the establishment of the *apoikia* (Dontas 1966b: 320–1; Preka-Alexandri 2010: 25–6, 31–3). It is now generally believed that the primary deity was Hera, although this identification is debatable, and the votives demonstrate that other gods were also worshipped within the temenos (see Section 4.11.2).

In keeping with its evident early importance to Corcyra, the oldest monumental architecture from the island was discovered at the Mon Repos sanctuary. A large temple is known from thousands of architectural fragments buried behind a peribolos wall from the second half of the fifth century. Those fragments come from massive roof tiles and some stone architectural members, the latter bearing telltale signs that they had been recut for secondary use (Dontas 1976: 122–30; Sapirstein 2012: 34–7).[33] The foundation trenches of a Classical temple appear to have obliterated any in situ traces of the Archaic temple, and no signs of an associated altar have been identified (Sapirstein 2012: 33–7).[34] The early temple has been dated to c. 610 by the style of its terracotta roof, whose molded decoration and architectural significance are reviewed in Section 4.12.1 (see Figure 4.8).[35]

Smaller structures were erected within the area of the sanctuary's peribolos over the course of the sixth and fifth centuries. Architectural members from various small later Archaic structures, votives, and pottery mixed in with the early monumental roof, along with traces of burned material, attest to a conflagration that swept through the sanctuary in the second half of the fifth century. Notable small finds include the head of a limestone *kouros* dated in the last quarter of the sixth century, several finely crafted bronze sculptures and vessels, and more than 400 female terracotta figurines of types similar to those found elsewhere in Kanoni (Calligas 1968: 303–9; Dontas 1976: 130–1; Dontas 1997: 55–89; Preka-Alexandri 2016: 225–6).

Discovered in 1967 just south of the peribolos wall of the Mon Repos sanctuary, an open-air altar dedicated to Apollo Corcyraios is identifiable by several inscriptions and votives dating as early as the end of the sixth century (Calligas

---

33. While the dimensions of the Archaic temple are unknown, its foundations may have been the same as those of its Classical replacement, which, at c. 20 x 43 m, approaches the scale of the Artemision (Sapirstein 2012: 41).

34. A recent campaign of excavations was undertaken at the site, but a preliminary report has yet to appear. Besides two relatively well-preserved marble lionhead waterspouts, the blocks from the Classical temple are ill preserved (Dörpfeld 1914: 172; Calligas 1968: 308–8; Sapirstein 2012: 33–4).

35. Sapirstein 2012: 37–42, 66–7, with citations to previous literature; that study demonstrated that all the large terracottas must have been installed together in a single roof, not the two or three partial systems proposed in previous studies (e.g., Dontas 1976: 126; Winter 1993: 115–19).

*Corcyra* 519

FIGURE 4.8. Reconstruction of the terracotta roof of the temple at Mon Repos; c. 610.

1968: 309–13; Calligas 1969: 54–8; see Section 4.11.1). This precinct, too, was destroyed in the later fifth century.

#### 4.4.2.7.3. KARDAKI TEMPLE

A third site preserving substantial remains of Archaic architecture was located a little more than 200 m southeast of the Mon Repos sanctuary, at the Kardaki spring (Schmidt 1890: 39–30; Johnson 1936: 46; Dinsmoor Jr. 1973; Dontas 1977; Barletta 2001: 71; Preka-Alexandri 2010: 32–3, 110–11; Andrikou 2017). The discovery of terracotta votives datable as early as the seventh century indicates that this cult was established within a few generations of that at the Mon Repos sanctuary (Rodenwaldt 1939: 173; Arafat and Morgan 1995: 37). The Kardaki sanctuary would have been prominently visible to ships sailing along Corfu's eastern shores by the last quarter of the sixth century, when a small Doric temple was built on a 30-m-high bluff so close to the sea that its eastern third has since been lost to erosion.

The peripteral temple, restored with 6 x 12 columns for overall stylobate dimensions of c. 25.6 x 11.9 m,[36] would have occupied just a quarter of the area of

---

36. There is some uncertainty over the length of temple due to the loss of the eastern part of the cella (Dinsmoor Jr. 1973: 167–8).

520　THE OXFORD HISTORY OF THE ARCHAIC GREEK WORLD

the Temple of Artemis. Several monolithic column shafts in limestone remain in situ; the many preserved blocks fallen from the architrave and geison level indicate that the canonical Doric triglyph-metope frieze was omitted (see Section 4.12.1). There remains considerable uncertainty about the deity to which this temple was dedicated, but the suggestion that it was dedicated to Apollo has some merit (see Section 4.11.1).

Excavations around the foundations of the Kardaki Temple in 1976, which unfortunately remain unpublished, identified a c. 4.7 x 2.3 m structure crossing the interior of the cella as an *eschara* (Dontas 1977: 156–7), rather than the statue base assumed previously (e.g., Dinsmoor Jr. 1973: 173; Preka-Alexandri 2010: 111). The structure has a facing of orthostates and is hollow inside, which would make it unsuitable for supporting statuary, and it is also located directly over an older structure of the same dimensions. The identification of the latter as an altar seems certain due to the animal bones and ash excavated around it, which had been preserved underneath the floor of the later temple.

### 4.4.2.7.4. SANCTUARY OF DIONYSUS

A fourth cult site was found c. 700 m southwest of the Kardaki Temple, halfway between it and the southern tip of the Kanoni peninsula. The key evidence for and from this cult site is the so-called Dionysus Pediment (or Later Corfu Pediment), discovered in 1973, which preserves a roughly 3 m high x 1 m wide fragment from the left side of a limestone sculpted pediment depicting a feast: Dionysus reclines with a boy on a couch, under which are a dog, a lion, and a kratēr (see Figure 4.9) (Choremis 1973–1974: 634–5; Choremis 1974; Cremer 1981). The pediment is datable to the end of the sixth century.

Although the associated building has not been located, excavations in the area uncovered a pavement and a sunken altar established in the sixth century. Around the pavement, an earthen floor was dated to the latter half of the seventh century, as was a nearby wall (Choremis 1973–1974: 642–4; Choremis 1977: 181; Preka-Alexandri 2010: 35–6). Bases for an Archaic statue and possibly for a votive column were found to the south, the latter suggested by a Doric capital with a flaring early Archaic profile that was later upended and recut in order to serve as a statue base. The iconography on the pediment and the discovery of a head from an Archaic statue of Dionysus strengthen the identification of this area as the sanctuary to that deity mentioned by Thucydides (3.81.5).

### 4.4.2.7.5. (POSSIBLE) SANCTUARY OF APOLLO AGYIEUS AND "SMALL ARTEMIS SANCTUARY"

A fifth area yielding Archaic religious architecture is located toward the southern end of the Kanoni peninsula, near the Panagia Kassopitra Monastery,

FIGURE 4.9. The Dionysus pediment; c. 500. Archaeological Museum of Corfu. Photo by Philip Sapirstein.

whose church stands on top of ancient masonry walls. Explorations in 1915 by Rhomaios in the cloister's grounds turned up several blocks from the architrave of an Archaic Doric structure, possibly a small temple (Rodenwaldt 1939: 173; Kanta-Kitsou 1996: 83; Kanta-Kitsou 2001a: 449, fig. 4; Preka-Alexandri 2010: 126–7). The proportions of the taenia and regula suggest the original structure was completed by the middle of the sixth century. More recent excavations to the west uncovered a 20-m-long segment of a stone-lined water channel and the torso of a less-than-life-size marble *kouros* dated c. 530 or slightly earlier. A limestone base that appears to have supported an unfluted pillar was discovered in a nearby Hellenistic house (Kanta-Kitsou 1996: 88–94; Kanta-Kitsou 2001b: 452–4). The latter find suggested to its excavator that the monastery overlies a sanctuary to Apollo Agyieus, whose cult was aniconic (see Section 4.11.1).

Yet another cult site was found c. 150 m to the southwest of the remains of the possible sanctuary of Apollo Agyieus. This site, the so-called "small Artemis sanctuary," is hypothetically connected with Artemis Agrotera (Lechat 1891; Kanta-Kitsou 1996: 84, 105 n. 42; Preka-Alexandri 2016: 224–5). This identification

522    THE OXFORD HISTORY OF THE ARCHAIC GREEK WORLD

is made on the basis of the roughly 3,500 terracotta figurines, many of Artemis, that were discovered there in the late 19th century CE (see Figure 4.13 in Section 4.8.3). The exact whereabouts of the sanctuary from which this cache originated remains unknown, although the figurines show it must have been established by the late Archaic period and was active through much of the fifth century.

#### 4.4.2.7.6. OTHER CULT SITES IN URBAN CORCYRA

A few additional cult locations should be mentioned. In 2006–2008, a two-room building was excavated west of the Alcinous harbor. The finds date the building to the sixth century and suggest that it functioned as a shrine (Riginos, Bouligea, Spanodimos, et al. 2007: 810–12; *Cf-el* #2607). Its identification with the temenos of Alcinous mentioned by Thucydides (3.70.4; Metallinou 2010: 20) is speculative, since Thucydides does not specify the location of that temenos, and the finds from the site do not link it to a specific god or hero.

Two further cult sites were located immediately outside the Kanoni peninsula (Preka-Alexandri 2010: 43). Votives excavated on the west side of the Chalikiopoulos lagoon indicate the existence of a small sanctuary there. At the Kaskati Plot in Daviou, Kanalia—a neighborhood west of modern Corfu Town (see Figure 4.2)—Laconian antefixes decorated with reliefs and a palmette, both types datable to the latter half of the sixth century, probably originated from a small temple. Graves from the Archaic through Hellenistic periods were also found at that site (Riginos, Bouligea, Spanodimos, et al. 2007: 814–17).

### 4.4.2.8. Necropoleis

The locations and chronology of Corcyra's cemeteries are reviewed here, while burial customs are discussed in a more synthetic manner in Section 4.4.6. Some of the earliest finds from the Greek settlement of Corfu come from graves. Those in the Evelpidi Plot, which is located toward the western edge of the central part of the Kanoni peninsula, date to the late eighth century and were found beneath domestic architecture, indicating that by the later Archaic period, the urban area had expanded over what was once a burial site (Dontas 1966b: 322; Dontas 1967: 367; Dontas 1968).[37] A fourth-century tomb excavated near the southern tip of Kanoni suggests that this part of the peninsula may have been outside the city (Agallopoulou 1972).

---

37. Two bronze animal figurines and pottery sherds, all from the Late Geometric period, were recently discovered at the same site (Riginos, Bouligea, Spanodimos, et al. 2007: 797).

The main cemetery of Corcyra was located to the north of the isthmus, in the modern neighborhood of Garitsa. Already in 1843, roadworks east of Soter hill revealed inscribed epitaphs, sculpted grave markers, and built tombs (Dierichs 2004: 50–2; Preka-Alexandri 2010: 41–3, 135–8). Over the course of the 20th century, many graves were discovered in various plots in the area. Rescue excavations conducted between the years 2000 and 2007 on the grounds of the law courts and opera house of Corfu exposed more than 1,000 burials, leaving no doubt that this was the primary necropolis for the ancient city (Riginos and Spanodimos 2009; Lazari, Riginos, Spanodimos, et al. 2018). The area had already begun to attract burials by the first half of the seventh century—that is, within two generations of the foundation of the *apoikia*—and continued as the primary cemetery for the next seven centuries (Georgiadou and Tzortzatou 2009; Lazari, Riginos, Spanodimos, et al. 2018).

### 4.4.3. Settlement Pattern

Due in large part to the incomplete and sporadic exploration of the island, little is known about Archaic sites on Corfu outside the main urban center (Bonelou 2018: 695–6).[38] The remains of three rural sanctuaries have been identified in the area to the west and southwest of the main urban center.

First, just 2 km from the Kanoni peninsula, above the modern seaside village of Perama (see Map 4.1), a small bronze statue datable to the late Archaic period was discovered among fragments of decorated pottery on the apex of the small hill of Rachonas (Kourkoumelis 1995: 257–62; Kanta-Kitsou 1996: 87). A votive inscription on the statue's leg (*IG* IX.1².4.850) indicates that the finds belonged to a small Archaic sanctuary, which must have been hypaethral, in light of the lack of any indication of buildings—though walls encircling parts of the hill could have belonged to a temenos.

Second, another sanctuary appears to have been located in the vicinity of Kardamatika, a hamlet on the northwestern flanks of Mt. Agioi Deka, c. 7 km from the main urban center. At least four small Doric capitals from the Classical period were reused in the chapel of the Archangels Michael and Gabriel at that site, and the altar table of the adjacent church of Agios Blasios incorporates a well-preserved Doric capital, datable to the middle of the sixth century, from either a votive column or a relatively large cult building (Calligas 1968: 315, 17;

---

38. The ancient toponym of Euboea mentioned by Strabo (10.1.15) as within the Corcyraean *chōra* has not been located. It may have been an area that had especially good conditions for animal husbandry.

524 THE OXFORD HISTORY OF THE ARCHAIC GREEK WORLD

Preka-Alexandri 2010: 53 figs. 73–4). The Doric column capital from Agios Blasios finds good parallels among votive capitals from the sanctuaries of Artemis and Hera (at Mon Repos) in the town of Corcyra.[39] In addition to other possibilities, both locales have been entertained as the ancient site of Istone, a hill occupied by the Corcyraean oligarchs during the *stasis* of 427 (Thuc. 3.85.4; 4.46.1–2; Steph. Byz. s.v. Ἰστώνη; Kourkoumelis 1995: 262–5).[40]

Third, the discovery in the early 20th century of a pair of Laconian antefixes decorated with *gorgoneia* near the village of Aphra, 5.5 km west of modern Corfu Town, points to the existence of a rural sanctuary (Schleif, Rhomaios, and Klaffenbach 1940: 141–2; Preka-Alexandri 2010: 43). These antefixes are similar to those found at the Kaskati Plot in Daviou, Kanalia (see Section 4.4.2.7.6) and are probably late Archaic or early Classical in date.

Additional evidence for Archaic activity was found along the northern coast of Corfu. A small peripteral temple (with 6 x 11 monolithic columns) and altar, both dating to the Classical era (Papadimitriou 1939), are situated in the modern village of Roda. Although the sanctuary appears to have been active by the Archaic period, no earlier architectural phases have been identified.[41] Elena Bonelou has recently reviewed the findings of rescue excavations in the environs of Roda, between Acharavi and Platonas Nymphon, where isolated farmsteads, variously dated between the late fifth century and the Hellenistic period, show that the northern seaboard was an active agricultural area for centuries (Riginos, Bouligea, Spanodimos, et al. 2007: 817–26; Bonelou 2018). Cemeteries with modest graves discovered nearby—one located inland from Almyros beach and another at Aphiona—were in use by the late Archaic and Classical periods (Morgan 1998: 286; Preka-Alexandri 2010: 139–43; *Cf-el* #4070).[42] The graves indicate that this part of the *chōra* of Corcyra was settled no later than the sixth

---

39. A cemetery with mostly Hellenistic graves was excavated to the north of Kamara (*Cf-el* #3293). The dating and quantity of the ancient capitals from the published report have been revised by coauthor of this essay Philip Sapirstein after a recent visit to the churches.

40. The θεοῖ Διοσκόροι Ἰστωναῖοι appears in a Roman-era inscription, although it is listed among the "tituli falsi" (*IG* IX.1².4: pg. 342 = *IG* I.1.1057).

41. Of note is an Egyptian scarab from the lowest layer beneath the temple's altar, dated 725–640 by its excavator (Dontas 1967: 369). Although at least indicative of pre-Classical activity, an isolated find like this need not imply cult as early as the seventh century, since it might have been an heirloom at the time it was dedicated. Archaic pottery was recovered in rescue excavations carried out nearby, but most discoveries along the northern coast date between the latter half of the fifth century and the Hellenistic period (*Cf-el* #3294–96, 4070; see also Morgan 1998: n. 33).

42. Prehistoric tumulus burials from Almyros reveal a deep history of occupation (Arvanitou-Metallinou 2017: 363, with additional references).

century, when we can imagine a sanctuary at Roda, still without permanent architecture, situated in a bucolic landscape not unlike that described by Xenophon in the passage quoted in Section 4.8.2. Cassiope, the first major settlement in this part of Corfu, was not founded until late in the Hellenistic period; it was situated c. 8 km to the east of Roda, near an excellent harbor. Cassiope later became the site of an important sanctuary of Zeus (Gehrke and Wirbelauer 2004: 361; Preka-Alexandri 2010: 68–71; Bonelou 2018: 695).

Other parts of Corfu have yielded little Archaic material. On the western coast of the island, late Archaic through Hellenistic pottery was recovered among rich Early Bronze Age, Middle Bronze Age, and Late Antique material to the south of the Bay of Timoni, which is located at the southwestern tip of the Aphiona peninsula (Bulle 1934: 196–213; Preka-Alexandri 2010: 139). Most of the post–Bronze Age materials come from Classical and Hellenistic farmstead buildings, and the Archaic activity in this area was probably agricultural as well. Farther south along the western coast, a pottery workshop was established at Rekini by the fifth century, and perhaps earlier, though the finds are as yet unpublished (Metallinou 2010: 22; *Cf-el* #2610). Purple-dye production facilities have been identified in the southern part of the island as well as in the town of Corcyra itself, but again, these do not appear to have been operating until the late Classical and Hellenistic eras (Metallinou 2010: 22). Near the southern tip of the island, outside a small settlement near Lefkimme, fragments of Archaic pithoi may have originated from a rural cemetery (Kostoglou-Despini 1971: 350–1).

In sum, the excavated finds to date indicate that rural agricultural and production facilities had been established over much of central and northern Corfu by the fifth and fourth centuries. The distances involved mean that families working land in the northern or southern parts of the island could not have lived full-time in the main urban center, and at least scattered residential areas must have existed elsewhere on the island, with the earliest signs of development along the northern coast in the environs of the Roda temple. Because the entire island seems to have been united in a single *polis* since the arrival of the Greek colonists, one might speculate that Corcyra town served as the primary urban center and port, and settlement spread gradually from there toward good agricultural land in the center of the island as well as along its northern shores. As we will see (see Section 4.4.4), by the latter half of the seventh century, the Corcyraeans had also begun developing strategic mainland locations opposite the northern and southern ends of the island.

### 4.4.4. *Peraia* of Corcyra

The Corcyraeans possessed from an early period a sizable *peraia* that is referenced by Thucydides (3.85.2). The mainland between the Ksamil peninsula (across from the northern end of Corfu) and Sybota (across from the southern end of Corfu) would have been readily accessible (Carusi 2011: 103–4; Psoma 2022: 37–9). One of the more significant sites in the Corycraean *peraia* was Butrint (ancient Bouthrotos), which, in addition to its agricultural potential, enjoys an advantageous position. It has easy access to good harbors and was built on a defensible, rocky hill at the end of the small Butrint peninsula, which is itself located at the southeastern end of the much larger Ksamil peninsula (see Map 4.1). However, the extant literary sources have nothing to say about either the nature of Archaic occupation at Bouthrotos or its relationship with Archaic Corcyra. Bouthrotos was identified as a *polis* by Hecataeus of Miletus in c. 500 (*FGrH* 1 F106 = Steph. Byz. s.v. Ὡρικός), yet it is absent from any other Archaic or Classical account, which could mean that the site was controlled by Corcyra (Hammond 1967: 474, 499; Arafat and Morgan 1995: 31–3; Hernandez 2017: 212–13, 258–9).[43] Indeed, geographically, Bouthrotos occupies the most strategic position for monitoring maritime traffic between the Greek mainland, Italy, and the Adriatic coast. It would be difficult to imagine the Corcyraeans tolerating an independent *polis* situated just 6 km from the northeastern shores of their island and next to the choke point where the strait separating Corfu from the mainland narrows to little more than 2 km in breadth (Arafat and Morgan 1995: 28–9).

David R. Hernandez (2017) has recently published a detailed study of Bouthrotos in the Archaic period. He argues that it was settled by Corcyraeans and that fortifications and a monumental temple to Athena Polias were constructed on its acropolis sometime around 500. However, since those early remains were largely destroyed or concealed by urban development from the Hellenistic through Late Antique periods, this study should be understood as a maximalist view of the evidence (Greenslade, Leppard, and Logue 2013). Pottery, mostly in secondary deposition, indicates some manner of occupation beginning in the latter half of the seventh century, and the site may have been abandoned by c. 475, based on the lack of artifacts between the Archaic and Hellenistic eras (Hernandez 2017: 220–1, 229, 256–9).[44] At least one sanctuary on the acropolis is attested by a *bothros*, imported fine-ware vases, and several dedicatory inscriptions (Greenslade, Leppard, and Logue 2013: 50–1; Hernandez 2017: 247–8), while the identification of a second sanctuary to Athena Polias is conjectural (Hernandez 2017: 241–4). As for the architecture, a segment of the earliest walling on the acropolis might be Archaic, since it has a stratigraphically determined terminus post quem of c. 500

---

43. For discussion of the mythico-historical account of events in this area, provided by Apollonius Rhodius 4.537–49 (Hyllus' campaign on the mainland), see Antonetti 2006: 60.

44. However, some Attic fine wares of the fifth and fourth centuries have been reported from the acropolis (Arafat and Morgan 1995: 37; Greenslade, Leppard, and Logue 2013: 51, 73 n. 14).

(Arafat and Morgan 1995: 36; Greenslade, Leppard, and Logue 2013: 50–2, 73 n. 8; Hernandez 2017: 245–50, 260–1). A hypothetical Temple of Athena has been reconstructed from a single block bearing a late Archaic relief of a lion devouring a bull, which was reused in the late Roman Lion Gate below the acropolis (Hernandez 2017: 230–8, 262–3).[45] No domestic architecture has yet been identified at Bouthrotos, and other remains on the Ksamil peninsula are Classical or later.

Signs of Archaic activity elsewhere within the presumed extent of the Corcyraean *peraia* have been identified by a recent extensive survey in Epirus. At Mastilitsa, a late Archaic cemetery was discovered near a sanctuary that was active between the late seventh and early fifth centuries (Tzortzatou and Fatsiou 2009: 46–50; *Cf-el* #2522). Architectural remains at the sanctuary include the foundations of a 10 x 14 m building and molded roof tiles from the sixth century. To the south, Pyrgos Ragiou may have been fortified as early as the Archaic period, and a collection of figurines excavated in the area establish activity by the early sixth century (Hammond 1967: 82–3; Tzortzatou and Fatsiou 2009: 45–6). Both sites were in view of the main urban center of Corcyra and well situated for monitoring maritime activity near the southern tip of the island.

## 4.4.5. Ceramic Assemblage

A general overview of Corcyraean pottery, its stylistic development, and the techniques of its production has yet to be published for any period, let alone the Archaic. Nonetheless, the various excavations of the last century have brought to light a plethora of material. The earliest Greek pottery, consisting of Late Geometric and Early Protocorinthian material from the latter half of the eighth century, is consistent with the foundation date of c. 730 supplied by the literary sources (see Section 4.5.2). Later periods are represented through fine wares painted in the Corinthian style, both imported and of local manufacture. Smaller numbers of imports from Attica, Laconia, Ionia, southern Italy, and Etruria attest to the extensive trade connections of the island.

During the Archaic period, the Corcyraeans strongly preferred fine wares of the style of their metropolis. Some quantitative evidence is available from the

---

45. This block might alternatively have belonged to some other kind of structure, such as a gateway (Arafat and Morgan 1995: 37; Pojani 2007: 63). No other architectural fragment has been positively identified from an Archaic temple. The exiguous traces of pavement and bedrock cuttings identified by Hernandez (2017: 238–41) as the foundation of the monumental Temple of Athena could as easily date from any time before the completion of the basilica, which overlies them, in the fifth century CE (Greenslade, Leppard, and Logue 2013: 51, 56–9, 73 n. 16). Arafat and Morgan (1995: 37) report discovering roof tiles with a "Corinthian yellow fabric" whose date cannot be determined without further information.

528  THE OXFORD HISTORY OF THE ARCHAIC GREEK WORLD

main necropolis, where close to 80% of the Archaic vases are in the Corinthian style, with only a small quantity of Attic and other imports in any particular burial (Georgiadou and Tzortzatou 2009: 173–4; Spanodimos 2017: 250).[46] This does not, however, necessarily mean that Corcyra was importing most of its fine pottery. It has long been recognized that a substantial fraction of the Corinthianizing pottery from Corfu was produced either locally or by some other center outside Corinth; this is evident through idiosyncrasies in the fabric and decoration of certain vases from the island that are absent from Corinth itself (Dontas 1968: 335–7). However, more often than not, it is impossible to distinguish the local Corinthianizing fine wares from those of Corinth itself without compositional testing, which so far has been too limited in scope to assess the ratio of local to imported products (Farnsworth, Perlman, and Asaro 1977; Morgan 1998: 284–5, 300).[47] Local production of Corinthianizing pottery may have been quite substantial by the later Archaic period, since Vasilis Kallipolitis (1982) identified such "imitations" as early as the late eighth and early seventh centuries, that is, shortly after the foundation of the *apoikia*.[48] (See Section 4.8.2 for discussion of Corcyraean transport amphoras.)

### 4.4.6. Burial Customs

Recent analyses of the many hundreds of graves from the main necropolis around Soter hill (see Section 4.4.2.8) have provided valuable insight into the norms of Corcyraean burials during the Archaic period (Preka-Alexandri 2010: 135–8). We begin with the general patterns revealed by the 2000–2007 excavations in the area of the law courts and the opera house and then review the better-known but exceptional monumental tombs discovered in the 19th century.

More than 1,000 burials of various types were identified by recent excavations in the necropolis around Soter hill (see Fig. 4.2).[49] The cemetery was in

---

46. The ratio is not dissimilar for the fine and plain wares at Butrint (Hernandez 2017: 247).

47. Furthermore, it is difficult to pinpoint provenance through chemical testing and ceramic petrography, which are more effective for eliminating the centers such as Corinth that did *not* produce a particular vessel.

48. Several pieces among the c. 250 sherds from the urban excavations available to Kallipolitis were identified as local based on painted decoration. Without compositional analyses, it would be unwise to comment further, and Kallipolitis admits to being unable to distinguish the local from imported Corinthian fabrics (Kallipolitis 1982: 72).

49. At the time of writing, Spanodimos 2017 and Lazari, Riginos, Spanodimos, et al. 2018 have the most complete statistical information available for the cemeteries. Other useful summaries with references to previous reports include Georgiadou and Tzortzatou 2009; Riginos and Spanodimos 2009; cf. Calligas 1968: 313–15.

use roughly between 700 and the first century, and a majority of the burials lack datable finds. Only about 100 tombs are certain to be Archaic (Lazari, Riginos, Spanodimos, et al. 2018: 707–11), although up to hundreds of undated burials could also have come from this period. Both inhumation and cremation were practiced. Inhumations, including both adults and subadults, were usually interred inside a pot (*enchytrismos*). Roughly a third of the Archaic burials are cremations, which drops to about 5% in the Classical and later periods (Lazari, Riginos, Spanodimos, et al. 2018: 707 fig. 2).

The most striking form of *enchytrismos* was in a pithos installed upright in a pit such that its rim was at ground level (Dierichs 2004: 44–5 fig. 42; Spanodimos 2017: 250–2; Lazari, Riginos, Spanodimos, et al. 2018: 710). The pithoi are a distinctive local type with a spherical body, a small pointed toe, and relief decoration with horizontal bands and a wavy line (see Figure 4.10). The largest pithoi are more than 1.5 m in diameter and have an impressive capacity of 1,000–2,000 liters, which not only greatly exceeds the space requirement for the single body placed in such a vessel but is on par with the largest ceramic jars produced in ancient Greece (typically for wine fermentation and agricultural

**FIGURE 4.10.** Burial pithos from the Bali Plot in the necropolis in the modern suburb of Garitsa; first half of the sixth century; height: 1.42 m, maximum diameter: 1.14 m.

storage).[50] The rim could be closed with slabs and occasionally more elaborate coverings such as an upside-down basin, roof tiles, or even a capital, though most of the excavated pithoi were found open as if they had originally been sealed with earth or perishable materials. About 60%–70% of the inhumations were found in such pithoi, and most of the other inhumation burials are inside smaller jars that were presumably employed for children and adolescents (Spanodimos 2017: 247; Lazari, Riginos, Spanodimos, et al. 2018: 708 fig. 3). Cremations were also in some cases deposited within an urn, which in exceptional cases could be made of bronze (Preka-Alexandri 2010: 41–3). The recent excavations also recovered 16 stone sarcophagi, at least six of which are datable to the sixth century (Spanodimos 2017: 247–8). Burial patterns appear to have shifted dramatically with the transition to the Classical period, when *enchytrismos* was supplanted by simple pit inhumation or brick-lined cists, some with pitched roofs made from terracotta pan tiles.[51]

In contrast to the considerable investment in the pithoi and sarcophagi containing inhumed corpses, the grave goods associated with both inhumations and cremations are modest (Lazari, Riginos, Spanodimos, et al. 2018: 709). Many burials have no identifiable grave goods, and those that do were typically accompanied by just one to three and at most 15 Corinthianizing vases, and metal is rare (Spanodimos 2017: 250; Lazari, Riginos, Spanodimos, et al. 2018: 711). Sympotic vessels predominate, followed by closed forms suitable for perfumes, oils, or cosmetics. Traces of pyres and burial pottery indicate that secondary burials might cluster around a central pithos. Most of the graves do not preserve any kind of marker, although the recent excavations recovered three stone fragments from a lion, the head of a sphinx, and a shield that no doubt were once displayed above ground (Lazari, Riginos, Spanodimos, et al. 2018: 709). At least some pithos burials were installed within the perimeter of a stone enclosure.

A pithos with a storage capacity greater than 1,000 liters would have been as valuable as hundreds of smaller vases (Cahill 2002: 228–29, 332 n. 26), which suggests both that the occupant was of fairly high social status and that more and finer grave goods, above-ground markers, and the like were well within the

---

50. The reports published to date suggest but do not categorically state that these pithoi were used for single rather than multiple burials.

51. Of the dated pithoi, 90% are Archaic—i.e., 69 of 77 are Archaic, including those from Classical and Hellenistic tombs. Just one each of the 63 ceramic-lined cists and 115 pits with datable objects is Archaic. On two plots with *eschara* from the fifth and fourth centuries, see Metallinou 2010: 23–5. On a fifth-century tile grave outside of Bouthrotos, see Hernandez 2017: 254–6.

economic reach of the families who commissioned such tombs. We can hypothesize that Corcyraean social norms favored investment in huge ceramic containers whose installation would have made for a spectacle during the funeral itself but which would be largely hidden from view afterward. The limited array of grave goods also suggests some restrictions on interring lavish funeral gifts.

The tombs and associated monuments discovered in the mid-19th century CE on the east flank of Soter hill are still the most impressive known from Corcyra, and they seem to have been honorific memorials reserved for a select few (see Figure 4.2). The largest and most distinctive is the Tomb of Menecrates (see Figure 4.11), which takes the form of a cylindrical drum, 4.7 m in diameter and 1.9 m high, faced with dressed ashlar masonry and capped by a roughly hewn rectangular cornice (Riemann 1879–1880: vol. 1: 30; Schmidt 1890: 47–8; Dierichs 2004: 52).

The roofing slabs behind the cornice are set at a low slope, creating the impression of a small tumulus not unlike examples from Etruria and Latium (see Section 4.12.2). Lacking any firmly associated pottery, the structure can only be roughly dated in the first half of the sixth century on the basis of the letter forms within an inscription carved below the cornice, and encircling the drum (*IG* IX.1.867 = *IG*

**FIGURE 4.11.** Tomb of Menecrates; first half of the sixth century.

532 THE OXFORD HISTORY OF THE ARCHAIC GREEK WORLD

IX.1².4.882, see also van Effenterre and Ruzé 1994–1995: vol. 1: 146).[52] This epitaph, the text of which is presented in Section 4.5.3 due to its relevance to Corcyra's political organization, honors the deceased *proxenos* Menecrates and implies that the monument was a cenotaph. It also makes clear that Menecrates died at sea, whereupon the *damos*—an incipient political unit comprising the island's citizens—commissioned a monument for him that is without parallel in the city's necropoleis.

Although the Menecrates monument is capped by a flat slab that would be suitable for acroterial sculpture, the so-called "Lion of Menecrates" discovered about 7 m to its west must have rested on a different tomb (see Figure 4.12). The finely carved lion crouching on a 1.22 x 0.4 m plinth is generally regarded as Corcyra's earliest extant stone sculpture carved in the round; a date in the last decades of the seventh century is indicated by comparison with vase painting and later feline sculptures (Rodenwaldt 1939: 176–98; Gabelmann 1965: 44–7; Ridgway 1977: 153–4; Mertens-Horn 1986: 24; Dontas 1997: 130–4). Stylistically attributed to a local artisan, the lion has a hemispherical head with abstracted furrows encircling the muzzle, palmette-like ripples on the cheeks, knobbly brows, and back-folded ears that blend local idiosyncrasies with elements inspired by older Assyrian and Hittite models. A smaller grave lion from the same sculptural tradition was discovered nearby (Rodenwaldt 1939: 187–9; Gabelmann 1965: 46), and a fragment of a third lion was recently excavated in the grounds of the law courts (Lazari, Riginos, Spanodimos, et al. 2018: 709).

To the south of the Menecrates tomb, several private burial plots from the late seventh century were more recently discovered between densely spaced modern buildings facing Cyprus Street (Preka-Alexandri 2010: 138). Masonry walls standing about 1.5–2.0 m tall delimit rectangular platforms containing several burials, no doubt members of one family. An enclosure 5.5 x 6.1 m in plan located near the Church of the Agioi Apostoloi contained three burial pithoi.

---

52. Wallace (1970: 189–94) appeals to a similar historical contextualization for a dating to the mid-sixth century but only on the basis of a late dating of the Cypselids established by Beloch, which is rejected here (see Section 4.1). Two olpai in the British Museum in the Corinthian Transitional Style (c. 630–620/15) are reported to be "probably from the tomb of Menecrates" (Rodenwaldt 1939: 172 n. 1; see also Dontas 1968: 336–7; Jeffery 1990: 232). They are also thought to be of local manufacture, which has led some to propose a date near the end of the seventh century based on an unproven assumption that pottery produced in Corcyra would have lagged behind that of its metropolis. More importantly, there is no reason to believe that the olpai have any stratigraphic relationship with the construction of the monument, since much of the pottery and sculpture excavated in the vicinity between 1843 and 1866 clearly originated from other graves (Schmidt 1890: 47–8).

FIGURE 4.12. Limestone sculpture known as the Lion of Menecrates; last quarter of seventh century; plinth of statue is 122 cm long. Archaeological Museum of Corfu.

Before closing, two tomb inscriptions found near the Menecrates tomb deserve mention. One is carved into a limestone *stēlē* that was discovered in 1846 during the demolition of the Venetian fortifications by the British government. The *stēlē*, though broken in two parts, is largely intact, with the caveat that its bottom part is missing. In its current form, it stands 1.93 m tall (and so was probably more than 2 m high originally), 0.50 m wide, and 0.15 m thick. Some architectural fragments were excavated with the *stēlē*, and the Lion of Menecrates might have come from the same tomb as this *stēlē* (Franz 1846: 378–82; Roehl 1882: 80 #343). The inscription (*IG* IX.1.868 = *IG* IX.1$^2$.4.880), dated c. 600 on letter forms, consists of four lines of hexameter poetry written *boustrophedon* that commemorate the bravery of someone named Arniadas (see Section 4.7.5 for the text and further discussion).

The second inscription is a hexameter carved retrograde on the abacus of a Doric capital from *poros* limestone (*IG* IX.1.869 = *IG* IX.1$^2$.4.881). Hans Schleif listed this as the earliest in his seriation of Corcyraean capitals, and—even without assuming that a strict linear evolution in proportion already existed at the inception of the Doric capital in stone—it is unlikely to significantly postdate the first

534 THE OXFORD HISTORY OF THE ARCHAIC GREEK WORLD

quarter of the sixth century (Schleif, Rhomaios, and Klaffenbach 1940: 76–8; Barletta 2001: 47–8 n. 12; Dierichs 2004: 45). The letter forms support a date in the first or second quarter of the sixth century.[53] The text of the inscription reads as follows:

στάλα Ξενϝάρεος τοῦ Μhεί̄ξιός εἰμ᾽ ἐπὶ τύ|μōι.

I, the *stēlē* of Xenwares, son of Mheixis, am on his mound. (trans. D. G. Miller)

Only the capital, which was found in 1866, is extant, but it must originally have formed part of a freestanding column that stood on and marked Xenwares' tomb. Nail holes on two sides of the abacus indicate that something, perhaps a ribbon or garland, was attached to the capital (McGowan 1995: 618 with illustration at fig. 1).

Although the evidence is too limited to be certain, we might imagine that the community discouraged most of its members from erecting ostentatious grave markers but also that it specially demarcated those who had distinguished themselves through a death in service of the polity. As discussed in Section 4.12.2, these burial customs have little in common with those of Corinth, and they align with other signs that the Corcyraeans from early generations were formulating an identity independent from their metropolis.

## 4.5. Political History
### 4.5.1. Overview

There never seems to have been more than one *polis* on Corfu, which is perhaps somewhat surprising given the size of the island and its topography, which divided it into three distinct parts (see Section 4.3).[54] It is likely that the unipolar nature of the political arrangements on Corfu was a legacy of its colonization, with the initial wave of settlers concentrating themselves in and around the Kanoni peninsula (the site of what became the island's main urban center) and then gradually spreading out to the rest of the island (see Section 4.4.3). That pattern of activity may well have been a response to the presence on the island of

---

53. Jeffery (1990: 233) suggested a date in the second quarter of the sixth century.

54. The political history of Archaic Corcyra is entangled with its external relations due to its complicated relationship with Corinth. As a result, some key aspects of Corcyra's political history are discussed in conjunction with Corcyra's diplomatic history in Section 4.7. A brief overview of Corcyra's foundation and of its later political history is offered here in order to provide the requisite background for this section of the essay.

a substantial indigenous population that was only gradually subsumed (Calligas 1971: 84).

Although the *politeia* of Corcyra seems from the outset to have been modeled at least in part on that of its metropolis, Corinth, Corcyra evidently distanced itself from Corinth in the decades after its foundation. Nevertheless, Corcyra was directly governed by Corinth under Periander, whose son Lycophron ruled the island during some of Periander's tyranny (627/6–587/6). The Corcyraeans assassinated Lycophron in c. 590, whereupon Periander appointed his nephew Psammetichus as successor. Corinthian rule over Corcyra seems to have come to an end when Psammetichus left Corcyra for Corinth in order to take over its government in the wake of Periander's death in 587/6 (see Section 4.7 for details).

An inscription on the Tomb of Menecrates (see Section 4.5.3) points to the existence, in the first half of the sixth century, of a *politeia* in which a collectivity calling itself the *damos* played an important role. Although it is impossible to be certain, that *politeia* is likely to have formed after Corcyra became fully independent from Corinth in 587/6. One could plausibly assume that wealthy landowners played a key role in the *damos*, and that same group probably had a similarly important role in governing Corcyra prior to the period of Corinthian domination during Periander's tyranny.

The Corcyraeans seem to have originally been divided into the three standard Dorian tribes. At some point after the foundation of the *apoikia*, possibly during a period of Corinthian-Corcyraean entente during the reign of Cypselus in the mid-seventh century, a reform was carried out that added at least five new tribes to the preexisting three. The tribes seem to have been further subdivided, though the evidence for those subdivisions is exiguous. (See below for details on the *politeia* of Corcyra and civic subdivisions.)

## 4.5.2. Colonization of Corfu by Greeks

The etymology of the name Corcyra may suggest that the island was originally inhabited by speakers of an Illyrian language.[55] Some have also observed a possible connection between the name of the Hyllaic harbor in the main urban center of Corcyra (see Section 4.4.2.4) and the Illyrian tribe of the Hylloi, also known as the Hylleis and Hyllaioi (Jones 1987: 177 n. 1; Hallof 2001: 4). However, given the distance of that group, which inhabited the area around Split (Strauch

---

55. Bürchner (1922: 1400) points to the Albanian word "*kark*" ("curvature"). See also Meyer 1975: 305, as well as Hammond 1967: 418 n. 1.

536    THE OXFORD HISTORY OF THE ARCHAIC GREEK WORLD

1996), from Corfu, the harbor was more plausibly named after Hyllus, the son of Heracles and the eponym of one of the Dorian *phylai*, of which there is also evidence in Corcyra.[56] In any case, archaeological exploration has not produced any evidence for complex political entities on Corfu at the time of the Greek colonization. Its prehistoric sites reflect a limited exploitation of its landscape for agriculture, pastoralism, and perhaps foraging by relatively small, kin-based groups.[57]

The primary literary source for the foundation of the *apoikia* of Corcyra is Strabo:

> Archias, sailing from Corinth, founded Syracuse about the same period that Naxos and Megara [Hyblaea] were built. . . . While Archias was on his voyage to Sicily, he left Chersikrates, of the *genos* of the Heracleidae, with a part of the expedition to help colonize what is now called Corcyra, but was formerly called Scheria. Chersikrates ejected the Liburnians, who held possession of the island, and colonized it with new settlers.[58] (6.2.4; trans. H. Jones, modified)

Strabo synchronizes the foundation of a Corinthian colony on Corfu with the foundation of Syracuse, which suggests an absolute date of 734/3.[59] Timaeus (*FGrH* 566 F80) puts the founding of Corcyra 600 years after the destruction of Troy, which, by our system of reckoning, he dates to 1194/3 (*FGrH* 566 F125). That, in turn, gives a foundation in 594/3, which is clearly impossible. Timaeus' date can, however, be adjusted upward by using the date of 1334/3 for the fall of Troy given by Duris of Samos (*FGrH* 76 F41). A foundation that took place

---

56. So already Schmidt 1890: 22. On the Corcyraean *phylai*, see Section 4.5.4. The same reasoning probably explains the stories surrounding another Hyllus, who is supposed to have become the eponym of the Illyrian Hyllaeans, as the son of Heracles by the naiad Melete from the island of Scheria (Ap. Rhod. 4.522–51; on this variant, see Antonetti 2006: 60). Conclusions about the relationship between the Illyrian and Dorian Hyllaeans that have been drawn from those stories cannot be grounded in historical linguistics (Neumann 1975). Such a relationship is nothing more than mytho-historical speculation.

57. See the bibliography cited in Section 4.4.1.

58. This passage presumably draws directly on the work of Ephorus. Hammond (1967: 415–16) attributes it to Antiochus of Syracuse.

59. On the founding date of Syracuse (733, from Thuc. 6.5.3 and 6.3.2) as "*à peu près exacte,*" see Vallet and Villard 1952: 298. See also Drögemüller 1973: 818 (who calls the date "uncontested") and the discussion in De Angelis and Mignosa 2024: Section 3.4.4.1.

*Corcyra* 537

600 years after 1334/3 aligns neatly with the foundation date given by Strabo's synchronization of the foundations of Syracuse and Corcyra.[60]

Although this date coincides with the oldest Greek pottery excavated from urban Corcyra, which is placed in the final third of the eighth century, we cannot interpret this apparent agreement as a confirmation of the texts (see Section 4.4.1). To do so is a logical circularity, in that absolute chronology was assigned to the stylistic seriation of the pottery in order to fit the colonial foundation dates extracted from the ancient writers (Snodgrass 1987: 52–64; Amyx 1988: 399–434; Fletcher 2007: 9–12). In relative terms, however, the ceramic evidence from Corfu is roughly in sync with that of Syracuse, whose earliest Greek imports are likewise dated in the third and especially the fourth quarters of the eighth century (Fletcher 2007: 9, 81; Osborne 2009: 83).

Which Greeks first settled Corfu is debated. According to Plutarch, Corinthian colonists under Charikrates expelled Eretrians in order to gain control of the island. This information is supplied in response to the question "Who are the men repulsed by slings?" (Τίνες οἱ ἀποσφενδόνητοι;). Plutarch's answer is as follows:

Men from Eretria used to inhabit the island of Corcyra. But Charikrates[61] sailed thither from Corinth with an army and defeated them in war; so the Eretrians embarked in their ships and sailed back home. Their fellow-citizens, however, having learned of the matter before their arrival, barred their return to the country and prevented them from disembarking by showering upon them missiles from slings. Since the exiles were unable either to persuade or to overcome their fellow-citizens, who were numerous and inexorable, they sailed to Thrace and occupied a territory in which, according to tradition, Methon, the ancestor of Orpheus, had formerly lived. So the Eretrians named their city Methone, but they were

---

60. On these chronological and chronographic issues, see Jacoby's comments on *FGrH* 566 F80 and F125; Champion's comments on those fragments in *Brill's New Jacoby*; and Hallof 2001: 4. Another approach is to suggest that Timaeus' reckoning is related to the time of the return of the Heraclidae (Vallet and Villard 1952: 298). On that date, see also Antonelli 2000: 59–60. Antonelli (2000: 113–14) connects the year that results from an unemended application of Timaeus' chronology, 594/3, with the acquisition of power over Corcyra by the tyrant Periander, but this seems rather artificial. Finally, Jerome gives a foundation date of the fourth year of the 18th Olympiad ("condiderunt et Corinthii Corcyram," *Chronicon* pg. 91.26 Helm) and hence 705. Bernstein (2004: 56) favors this date.

61. The name of the oikist is given as Chersikrates by other relevant literary sources (Timaeus *FGrH* 566 F80; scholiast to Apollonius Rhodius 4.1212–14, 1216; Strabo 6.2.4), and a group called the Chersikratidai appear in an inscription dating to the second century (*IG* IX.1².4.1140). Plutarch thus seems to have gotten the name of the oikist slightly wrong.

538    THE OXFORD HISTORY OF THE ARCHAIC GREEK WORLD

also named by their neighbors the "men repulsed by slings."[62] (*Moralia* 293a–b; trans. F. C. Babbitt)

Based on this passage, many scholars have subscribed to the idea that Euboeans had settled Corfu prior to the arrival of the Corinthians.[63] In light of the important role that the Euboeans played in the early settlement of Italy, this tradition should not be dismissed outright. There are further indications in favor of Plutarch's claim. The place name "Euboea" on Corcyra (Strabo 10.1.15; the site remains unlocated) and the resemblance between coin motifs of Corcyra and Carystus on the island of Euboea are by no means compelling evidence,[64] but more significantly, other mytho-historical sources perhaps point to the presence of Euboean settlers in the region, especially Orikos in Epirus.[65]

The pottery, however, lends little support to the idea that Euboeans were the first Greek colonists on Corfu. Only a handful of Euboean pots have been found among the early imports, which has fueled the skepticism expressed by Catherine Morgan (1998) and others over whether Euboeans ever resided on Corfu.[66]

62. According to the scholiast to Apollonius Rhodius 4.1212, it was Colchians, not Eretrians, who were expelled. This is an explanation of the later version of the Corcyraean foundation story found in Apollonius Rhodius 4.1205–14, according to which Colchians lived on Corcyra with the Phaeacians after their fruitless pursuit of Medea and then yielded to the Bacchiads from Ephyra—i.e., the Corinthians.

63. Proponents include Calligas 1982; Malkin 1998a: 3–4; Malkin 1998b: 74–81; Antonelli 2000: 15–57; Metallinou 2010: 13–15; Psoma 2015; Psoma 2022: 43–51, with references to onomastics and more confident in the numismatic evidence. For counterarguments against a Euboean presence, see Morgan 1998 (with n. 5 for previous literature); Fauber 2002: 61–99; Hernandez 2017: 214–15. See also De Fidio 1995; Parker 1997: 55–7.

64. Gardner 1883: xlvi–iii; Busolt 1893–1904: vol. 3, part 1: 443 n. 1. See also Hammond 1967: 415, but the arguments against it (Head 1911: 325) are persuasive (despite Kraay 1976: 128; Cigaina 2015: 54–7).

65. Ps.-Scymnus 442–3, on which see Lepore 1962: 129–30. There are other places in the vicinity with mytho-historical links to Euboeans (or the synonymous Abantes): Makridia (as yet not precisely located but situated somewhere on the mainland opposite Corcyra; scholiast to Apollonius Rhodius 4.1175) and Thronion (as yet not precisely located but situated somewhere in Thesprotia; Pausanias 5.22.1–4). See also Antonelli 2000: 15–57 (discussing the role of the Abantes in Epirus, part of which is very hypothetical); Intrieri 2010: 191 n. 62; Metallinou 2010: 13–14; D'Agostino 2012: 294–95; Šašel Kos 2015: 8–9. An onomastic linkage is evident through the name Meixis, from an early sixth-century epigram from Corcyra's cemetery (*IG* IX.1².4.881; see Section 4.4.6), which is otherwise only attested in Eretria and Attica; see Psoma 2015: 145–6, n. 3. Von Wilamowitz-Moeöllendorff (1884: 170–1) observed that the original Hellenic name of the island was reportedly Drepane, or "sickle," which might imply a pre-Corinthian presence; see Section 4.3.

66. One should note, however, that Euboean pottery imports at Greek colonial sites in Sicily and southern Italy are generally outnumbered by Corinthian wares, both in the eighth-century

Furthermore, if we accept Corcyra and Syracuse as contemporary Corinthian *apoikiai*, in order to detect a potential presence of Euboean forerunners, we would expect to have found Greek imports of some kind at Corcyra that are appreciably older than those at Syracuse, but, as previously noted, the first sherds from both places are chronologically indistinguishable. A future discovery, of course, could change this picture, but, at present, it seems prudent to reject the possibility of Euboean colonization of Corfu. The arrival of Corinthian settlers c. 730 thus marked the decisive transition in Corfu's history toward becoming a Greek center.

### 4.5.3. Corcyraean *Politeia* in the Archaic Period

The evidence for Corcyra's *politeia* in the Archaic period is limited. We can assume that the most important official was called *prytanis*, a title attested from the end of the fourth century onward, which we can extrapolate back to the foundation (see Section 4.7.1). The *prytanis* was supported by a group of minor colleagues called *synarchoi* (Gschnitzer 1973: 748–9), though nothing is known about their function. They were presumably introduced after the *prytanis*, at an unknown point in time but clearly before the fourth century, when they are first attested. The *prytanis* was the eponymous magistrate and thus, with all probability, at a minimum responsible for the organization of legal proceedings, though the duties and powers of the office almost certainly evolved over the course of the Archaic period.[67] An inscribed weight (*IG* IX.1².4.1158) from the main urban center, dated to the fifth century on letter forms, demonstrates the existence of *agoranomoi* by that point in time, and those officials may well have existed before the end of the Archaic period.

More information on the Corycraean *politeia* during the Archaic period can be derived from the epigram (*IG* IX.1².4.882) on Menecrates' tomb (see Section 4.4.6):

hιοῦ Τλασίαϝο Μενεκράτεος τόδε σᾶμα:          *1*
Οἰανθέος γενεάν, τόδε δ᾽ αὐτῶι δᾶμος ἐποίει:
ἔς γὰρ πρόξενϝος δάμου φίλος· ἀλλ᾽ ἐνὶ πόντοι [:]

---

foundations associated with Euboeans and in those associated with other metropoleis (Fletcher 2007: 117). On the relevant pottery from Corcyra, see Kallipolitis 1982:73–6, figs. 7–9; Morgan 1998: 281–4; D'Agostino 2012: 296 (noting one sherd possibly of Euboean origin); Psoma 2015: 145 n. 2; Psoma 2022: 44 n. 23 (on unpublished Euboean pottery, citing personal communication with S. Avgerinou and A. Spetsieri-Choremi).

67. Since it is most likely that the Corcyraeans were or became independent from Corinth when the Corinthians abolished tyranny (see Section 4.7.5), one cannot connect the office of the *probouloi*, as attested for Corcyra from the fourth century onward (see *IG* IX.1².4 p. 364 for references) with one of the most characteristic institutions of the post-Cypselid Corinthian *politeia*, the eight *probouloi* (Nic. Dam. *FGrH* 90 F60.9).

# 540 THE OXFORD HISTORY OF THE ARCHAIC GREEK WORLD

ὄλετο, δαμόσιον δὲ καϙὸν ρο[˘ ˉ ˘ ˘ ˉ ˘]:
Πϙαξιμένες δ᾽ αὐτōι γ[αία]ς ἄπο πατρίδος ἐνθὸν:                    5
σὺν δάμοι τόδε σᾶμα κασιγνέτοιο πονέθε:

This is the tomb of Menecrates, Tlasias' son,
An Oianthean by birth. The *damos* made it for him.
For he was a revered *proxenos* of the *damos*, but in the sea
He perished, a bane for the *damos* [ ... ]
Praximenes coming here from Menecrates' fatherland,
Built this tomb of his brother together with the *damos*. (trans. J. Day,
    modified)

The six hexameter lines refer to the *damos* of Corcyra no fewer than four times. The term *damos* doubtless designates the Corcyraean people as a political unit— the whole people, not just the lower class or some other subgroup of the citizen body. Its emphatic repetition reveals a self-understanding and consequently a political order in which the people, that is, the entirety of the citizen body, had decisive influence. We need not imagine the kind of democracy that developed in Greek communities in the fifth century, but the political system seems to have been more inclusive than an aristocracy or oligarchy. We might rather assume that independent landowners, many of whom would have been quite wealthy, asserted themselves as the political representatives of the entire populace. Following this interpretation of the political system, we might also connect it with the "assembly of the people" (*halia*) attested in Hellenistic inscriptions from Corcyra (Gehrke and Wirbelauer 2004: 362).

The Menecrates inscription, which is dated to the first half of the sixth century on the basis of letter forms (Jeffery 1990: 232, 34 #9; van Effenterre and Ruzé 1994–1995: vol. i: 146), provides a terminus ante quem for the emergence of this partially democratized political system, but it remains unclear precisely when it came into being. It could possibly have been created at the time of the foundation of the *apoikia*, with the relevant institutions continuing until the period of tyranny on Corcyra in the later seventh and early sixth centuries (see Section 4.7.3). However, the distinctive emphasis on the *damos* in the Menecrates inscription may instead celebrate the recent establishment of a new political framework, as might be expected if the tomb dates to the period after the departure of Psammetichus for Corinth and the concomitant liberation from Corinthian rule in the second decade of the sixth century.

The political changes that would have taken place after the departure of Psammetichus may have led to an enlargement of the proportion of the populace that actively participated in the governance of the community. We do not, however, have to assume that those changes caused a massive or sudden change in the social order, which might have evolved gradually. It seems likely that moderate and large property owners were in control, their wealth rooted in the distribution of the land at the foundation of the colony. One can easily imagine that a ruling class with aristocratic habitus developed from these first settlers, similar to the Gamoroi in Syracuse (Hdt. 7.155; Luraghi 1994: 281–6; De Angelis and Mignosa Forthcoming: Section 3.4.5). The reputed outcasts from Corinth could hardly have imported the entire dynastic structure of the Bacchiads from their metropolis, but they may have created an equivalent hierarchy. We must not think of this upper stratum as entirely exclusive, since after all, even those owning moderate parcels of land had opportunities to increase their wealth and social position, a general characteristic of elites in Archaic Greece (Stein-Hölkeskamp 1989: 109–10).

In any case, the upper stratum among the Corcyraeans was probably relatively broad. The extant literary sources mention no major episodes of civil strife in Corcyra in the Archaic period, which may suggest that the elite governed the *polis* at least in part by means of a broad-based consensus that embraced much of the populace of the polity. Whatever the arrangement, it broke down in the fifth century under external pressures. The ancient sources supply eloquent testimony to the virulent conflict between oligarchs and democrats in Corcyra during the Peloponnesian War (Thuc. 3.70–85; Diod. *Sic.* 12.57, 13.48; Gehrke 1985: 89–93). After the *stasis*, the Corcyraean political system was democratic; a *boulē* and *boulētai* are attested by Thucydides (3.70.5–6). Civil strife re-emerged by 411/10 (Diod. *Sic.* 13.48.5–8), and oligarchs gained power in 361 (Aen. Tact. 11.15).

## 4.5.4. Subdivisions of the Citizen Body

An inscription (*IG* IX.1².4.798.3, 5) from the second century mentions the name of the *phylē* of the Hyllaeans in masculine form (Hylleus) and in feminine (Hyllis).[68] Additional names of *phylai* are attested on Corcyra, primarily on a series of eight miniature lead tablets dating to c. 500 and recording private financial transactions (*IG* IX.1².4.865–72 = *SEG* 30.519–26 and 42.489; Calligas 1971; Jones 1987: 159–61), on which appear several tribal names: Aworeis, Amphineis, Machchidai, Hynthianes (?), and Philo( . . . ). (See Section 4.8.4 for further discussion of these tablets.) It remains unclear how this system functioned and how these "new" *phylai* related to the Dorian ones. Nicholas Jones (1987: 159–61)

---

68. The text, carved on a *stēlē* that was found at an unrecorded location on the island of Corfu, records the establishment of an endowment to pay for performances at a Dionysiac festival.

542 THE OXFORD HISTORY OF THE ARCHAIC GREEK WORLD

postulates a existence between distinct old and new tribal systems in the manner of Cleisthenes' Athens, but in the aforementioned second-century inscription (*IG* IX.1².4.798), the Dorian *phylē* Hylleis is linked to a personal name, and precisely the same usage is found on the lead tablets. This suggests that both the old and the new tribes had identical purposes and that the Dorian *phylai* were simply increased by adding a particular number of others, similar to what happened in Sicyon (Gehrke 1986: 129).[69] This points to the existence of at least eight *phylai* on Corcyra: the three Dorian ones and the five epigraphically attested additions. One cannot say to what extent this reform of *phylai* was connected to a change of *politeia*. For example, it may have been caused by an increase in the number of citizens or of potential officeholders.

In this context, it is also important to observe that two of the new *phylai* have close homonyms in Corinth: the Aworeis with the Aoreis and the Machchidai with the phratry Homakchiadai. This is further emphasized by the fact that one can connect the Aworeis or the Aoreis with the Lycian hero Aor, whose daughter Aletes is said to have married one of the legendary founders of Corinth (Hadzis 1997: 8).[70] This expansion or supplementation of *phylai* beyond the old Dorian ones is thus very likely to have happened when Corcyra was under Corinthian influence. Hence Jones suggests that a tribal reform was carried out during the period when Periander was tyrant on Corcyra (Jones 1987: 160). However, given Periander's unpopularity (at least later in his rule), one wonders why *phylai* created by Periander would have been kept after the fall of the tyranny.[71] That, in turn, suggests that the tribal reform perhaps took place instead during a period of entente between Corcyra and Corinth during the reign of Cypselus (see Section 4.7.3).[72]

## 4.5.5. Corcyraean Whips and Their Social Connotations

A potential source of information about socio-political dynamics in Archaic Corcyra can be found in the comments by ancient authors on Corcyraean

---

69. Salmon (1984: 413–19) has assumed similar things for Corinth. Overall, one can understand why Hallof stated that the relations of the *phylai* to one another are "obscurum" (*IG* IX.1² 4 at pg. 54). This also applies to two Ἀμφινεῖς (*IG* IX.1².4.866.5–7), who may have been members of another type of civic subdivision.

70. This observation had been made previously by Antonetti; see *SEG* 47.603. See also Antonetti 2006: 66–8, with remarks on other *phylai* and with further evidence.

71. Hölkeskamp (1999: 157–8) is cautious with respect to a "lawgiver" Periander.

72. It is also possible that the tribal reform reflected the Corinthian *politeia* after the fall of the tyranny there, but the sparse testimonia make that quite uncertain. See Salmon 1984: 236–40; Gehrke 1985: 82; Stickler 2010: 25–34.

whips. The earliest reference to these whips is in Aristophanes' *Birds*, first produced in 414. In the following passage, Peisetairos drives off an Athenian sycophant who, having heard about the founding of Nephelokokkugia, comes seeking wings:

Sycophant: I'll not disgrace my family: informing has been our livelihood since my grandfather's day. Just rig me with the light, fast wings of a hawk or a kestrel, so I can subpoena the foreigners, get a judgment here, then fly back there again.
Peisetairos: I get it: you mean the foreigner's case will be lost by default before he gets here.
Sycophant: Quite right.
Peisetairos: And then while he's sailing here, you're flying back there to snatch his property.
Sycophant: That's the whole story. It means whizzing around just like a top.
Peisetairos: A top—I know what you mean. (*rummaging in a bag*) And by god I've actually got some wings here that'll do just perfectly; they're from Corcyra.
Sycophant: Good grief, that's a whip!
Peisetairos: No, a pair of wings; I'll use them this very day to make you whizz around like a top!
Sycophant: Good grief!
*Exit informer on the run.* (l. 1452–66; trans. J. Henderson)

The humor relies on knowing that certain kinds of tops were spun by whipping them and being familiar with the Corcyraeans' reputation for whips (Dunbar 1998: 467–8). The scholia to the *Birds* explain this passage in part by quoting two lines from Phrynichus' *Satyrs* (F45 Edmonds) that mention Corcyraean whips, which were twin-tailed, large, and ivory-handled and evidently well known in Athens in the last quarter of the fifth century. The same scholiast makes a connection between the Corcyraeans' predilection for whips and endemic *stasis*: "For there were constant disorders among the Corcyraeans, and, on account of *stasis*, the whip was in customary use among them."

A different perspective on Corcyraean whips was offered in the Aristotelian *Constitution of the Corcyraeans* (F513 Rose = 518.1–3 Gigon; see also Hose 2002: 36). Heschyius' entry for Κερκυραία μάστιξ states that Aristotle said that the Corcyraeans, on account of their wealth (εὐπραγοῦντας), became arrogant (ὑπερηφάνους). Hesychius does not explicitly explain the connection between the Corcyraeans' wealth and arrogance on one hand and their predilection for elaborate whips on the other, but the implication is surely that wealthy Corcyraeans had a habit of flogging their subordinates.

544   THE OXFORD HISTORY OF THE ARCHAIC GREEK WORLD

Strabo gives an entirely different account of Corcyraean whips:

> The proverbial phrase, "the copper vessel in Dodona"[73] originated thus: in the temple was a copper vessel with a statue of a man situated above it and holding a copper scourge, dedicated by the Corcyraeans; the scourge was three-fold and wrought in chain fashion, with bones strung from it; and these bones, striking the copper vessel continuously when they were swung by the winds, would produce tones so long that anyone who measured the time from the beginning of the tone to the end could count to 400. Whence, also, the origin of the proverbial term, "the scourge of the Corcyraeans" [Η Κερκυραίων μάστιξ]. (7.3; trans. H. Jones)[74]

Peter Calligas (1976) has described the bronze handles from votive whips from the late Classical and Hellenistic periods found at two mainland sanctuaries of Apollo. The majority (more than 15) are from Dodona, and another is from the Apollo Korynthos sanctuary at Longa in Messenia. Several handles from Dodona are bipartite, like the twin-tailed Corcyraean whips described in the ancient literary sources, and the type might have been dedicated by Corcyraeans. Calligas argues that the Corcyraeans used whips in initiation rites that bore some similarity to those that took place at the Sanctuary of Artemis Orthia in Sparta.[75]

The association between Corcyra and whips is thus difficult to explain in simple terms. If, as Calligas suggests, the whips were designed to be used in religious rituals, they would tell us little about socio-political dynamics. Indeed, the connection between *stasis* and whips made by the Aristophanic scholiasts is likely a late invention, conflating the Corcyraeans' reputation for elaborate whips in Athenian Old Comedy with the prominent role of Corcyra's *stasis* in Thucydides' account of the Peloponnesian War. However, the Aristotelian claim that the Corcyraeans habitually used whips on their subordinates testifies rather clearly to the existence of a steep status hierarchy. One might then connect the Cocyraeans' predilection for whips with the signs that wealthy Corcyraean landholders owned large numbers of slaves (see Section 4.8.2), as well as the offer of freedom made to slaves by both the oligarchs and democrats during the period of *stasis* in 427–425, when the slaves preferred the democratic faction (Thuc. 3.73). Therefore, it is at

---

73. This phrase was used in reference to especially garrulous individuals (Steph. Byz. s.v. Δωδώνη).

74. See Šašel Kos 2015: 20–2 for a discussion and hypothetical reconstruction of this dedication.

75. Cf. Ducat 1995: 364–6; Antonetti 2006: 69. Note, however, that Quantin (1999: 86–7) interprets the miniature whips in Dodona as votive offerings of shepherds.

least possible that ivory-handled whips carried by wealthy Corcyraean landowners had at some point become synonymous with slavery, although such whips, of course, may have found different uses and connotations at different times and in different contexts.

## 4.6. Legal History

Given the incomplete state of our sources, it is not possible to provide an overview of the history of the judicial development of Corcyra. What can be reconstructed of the *politeia* of the Corcyraeans was discussed in Section 4.5.3. In their speech to the Athenian Assembly as recorded by Thucydides (1.37.3), the Corinthians accuse the Corcyraeans of being judges in their own cases instead of arranging matters by treaty with other states (see Section 4.8.4). This suggests that in the second half of the fifth century, the Corcyraean legal system had provisions for trying cases involving individuals, presumably merchants, who were not citizens of Corcyra. Whether this was also true in the Archaic period is impossible to establish.

## 4.7. Diplomatic History
### 4.7.1. Relationship with Corinth at the Time of Foundation

It remains unclear whether the foundations of Syracuse and Corcyra, the temporal proximity of which is virtually undoubted, were coordinated or separate undertakings. The former view postulates a kind of colonizing program by the Corinthians or their ruling elite, the Bacchiads.[76] In addition to the synchronism of the two foundations found in the ancient literary sources, the significance of Corcyra for the control of the sea route to Italy supports the coordinated model.

In support of the latter scenario, one might note that a wide-ranging colonization plan seems anachronistic and that Corcyra's strategic significance may not have emerged until a later period, after the settlements of Sicily and southern Italy and their maritime connections to the mainland had been firmly established.

---

76. This is a common view; see, for example, D'Agostino 2012: 293. Antonelli (2000: 133–5) presents this view in an especially striking way, though with an anachronistic characterization of trade relations. The Bacchiads, who traced themselves back to Heracles, exercised a collective rule by having one among them take up the highest office (*prytanis*) each year, like a temporary king (Diod. Sic. 7 F7.6; Paus. 2.4.4; Nic. Dam. *FGrH* 90 F57; Strabo 8.6.20). Their rule was supposed to have lasted 90 years until its overthrow by Cypselus. On Bacchiad chronology, see Section 4.1.

546 THE OXFORD HISTORY OF THE ARCHAIC GREEK WORLD

Timaeus' account of the foundation of Corcyra also argues against an organized process:

> And Timaeus says that after 600 years from the Trojan War Chersikrates, descendant of the Bacchiads, colonized the island. And the Colchians crossing over to the nearest island and after this to the Ceraunian mountains, setting upon the Abantes and Nestaioi, founded Orikos. And the one of the Bacchiads leading the colony was Chersikrates, who was stripped of honors by the Corinthians.[77] (Timaeus *FGrH* 566 F80 *apud* the scholiast to Apollonius Rhodius 4.1216; trans. C. Champion)

This passage claims that the oikist Chersikrates was excluded from the elite of Corinth, which in turn suggests that the colonization venture that he led was neither instigated nor supervised by the Corinthian state.[78]

In the same vein, there is a notable lack of connections between Corinth and Corcyra in the extant mythico-historical narratives, which reflect collective identities, associations, and distinctions that were already abundant in Archaic Greece (Gehrke 2014: 1–64). In light of how frequently the relationships between Greek communities were expressed in this way, the relationship between Corinth and Corcyra does not appear to have been much emphasized (with the exception of the founding narrative featuring Chersikrates).[79] On the contrary, traditions that connected the Corcyraeans to the Phaeacians were elaborated, thereby distinguishing their origins from Corinth. Phaiax, for instance, the eponym of

---

77. See also the scholiast to Apollonius Rhodius 4.1212. The identification of Chersikrates as a Bacchiad fits with his characterization as a Heraclid in Strabo 6.2.4.

78. Bernstein (2004: 45–77, esp. 72) has argued that the same was true of Archias and the colonial venture he led to Syracuse. On the background to possible conflicts within the Bacchiads, see Will 1955: 286–98, whose basic attitude is skeptical. The claim that the Bacchiads who were driven out by Cypselus found refuge in Corcyra (Nic. Dam. *FGrH* 90 FF57–8; Jer. *Chron.* pg. 94.21 Helm) does not conflict with the idea that Chersikrates was in disfavor among the Bacchiads when he left Corinth. Decades had passed, and it is quite possible that in the meantime, positive relationships had come into being. Furthermore, one can see the animosity toward Cypselus as a connecting element (see Section 4.7.3).

79. An additional connection to the important Corinthian figure Aletes via the *phylē* of the Aoroi evidently belongs to a later time, in all probability to a phase of rapprochement between Corinth and Corcyra under Cypselus (see Section 4.7.3). The variant of the marriage of Jason and Medea on Corcyra, which presumably goes back to the Corinthian poet Eumelus (Zahrnt 2012: 85, with further evidence), creates a secondary connection between the two cities, because these mythical figures are not genuinely connected to either of them. Moreover, it remains questionable to what extent this variant, which is primarily known through Apollonius of Rhodes, was known on Corcyra and represented in a cult context (see Section 4.11.1).

the Phaeacians, is attested at least from the fifth century onward as the son of Poseidon and Corcyra, the eponymous heroine of the island who was the daughter of the mytho-historically significant river god Asopus.[80]

In the end, one cannot make a firm decision in favor of one possibility or the other. Regardless of whether Corcyra was founded as part of a larger program of colonization planned in advance by political leaders in Corinth, or whether the foundation of Corcyra was instigated and supervised by Corinth, Chersikrates seems to have modeled many rules and customs, *nomima*, of the new settlement after those of Corinth, as was usual in other *apoikiai*. We have direct indications that Corinth was officially recognized as its mother city in the following century, since, "according to the old custom," the Corcyraeans summoned a founder "from the mother city" when establishing Epidamnus in 627/6 (Thuc. 1.24.2).[81] Another fundamental congruence between Corinth and Corcyra is linguistic: their use of Doric Greek. They shared the same epichoric alphabet, which may reflect collective identification or association among different Greek communities (Luraghi 2010). In addition, there are correspondences in the calendar: all six attested names of months in Corcyra have an equivalent in the complete set of names on the Antikythera mechanism, and the terminology on that instrument has been connected to Corinth and its colonies.[82] Furthermore, there were also commonalities in cults and worship of gods (Hadzis 1995).

Corcyra and Corinth also shared common political forms. The position of the *prytanis*, a key magistracy in the Bacchiad regime, represents an especially significant adoption from Corcyra's metropolis. The *prytanis*, assisted by three or four subordinate colleagues, was the highest official in Corcyra and served as eponym from at least the fourth century onward.[83] Since the same title is attested

---

80. This story was already known to Hellanicus (*FGrH* 4 FF17, 30). See also Pausanias 5.22.6, as well as Diodorus Siculus 4.72.1 and the scholiast to Pindar *Olympian* 6.144.

81. On the date, see Antonetti 2007: 90, n. 7.

82. On month names in Corcyra; see *IG* IX.1².4 at p. 367. On the Antikythera mechanism, see Freeth, Jones, Steele, et al. 2008, with fig. 2. On the Corinthian names of months in Epirus, which are nearly identical with those inscribed on the mechanism, see Trümpy 1997: 155–64; Cabanes 2003; see also Hadzis 1995. The Antikythera mechanism dates to the Hellenistic period, but calendrical terminology tends to be quite stable over time, so there is every reason to believe that the month names found on the mechanism were in use in Corinth and Corcyra in the Archaic period.

83. *IG* IX.1².4.786.1 (end of the fourth century), as well as *IG* IX.1² 4.838–40, with Gschnitzer 1973: 737, 48–9. See now in general Crema 2010: 202–10 (also on other places; and Antonetti 2011: 54.

## 548 THE OXFORD HISTORY OF THE ARCHAIC GREEK WORLD

in other Corinthian colonies (Gschnitzer 1973: 737; Crema 2010: 202–10), it seems likely that this office was established at the time of Corcyra's foundation rather than recreated there centuries after the demise of the Bacchiad system. Another indication of convergence can be found in the Corcyraean adoption of Dorian *phylai*, even if only one of them is explicitly attested, that of the Hyllaeans (see Section 4.5.4).

### 4.7.2. Sea Battle with Corinth and Its Ramifications

Thucydides provides information about the first-known event in the diplomatic history of Corcyra after its foundation. He states that "the earliest sea fight in history was between the Corinthians and the Corcyraeans; this was about 260 years ago" (1.13.4). Without any reason to dismiss his testimony of this battle—which was both significant and recent enough to have been preserved in the collective memory of the Greeks—we should accept it as a historical fact from which we may draw additional conclusions, especially concerning the importance of Corcyra and its fleet.

Still, much about the battle remains enigmatic, first of all its dating. Without miring ourselves in the complexities of the "Thucydidean Question," we may presume that Thucydides reckons from the end of the entire Peloponnesian War, not the end of its Archidamian phase. Since Thucydides himself offers only approximate dates, it is safer to place the sea battle between Corinth and Corcyra not precisely at 664 but rather in the decade 670–60.[84]

If we attempt to situate the sea battle in a specific historical context, it is not hard to imagine tensions arising between a rapidly developing colony, founded six or seven decades previously, and a mother city determined to retain control of its many *apoikiai*. In this regard, Herodotus observed that "from the moment of colonization of Corcyra by Corinth, the two states had been at enmity with one another [ἀλλήλοισι διάφοροι] despite their kinship" (3.49.1; trans. D. Grene).[85] Following Ettore Lepore (1962: 132), a general explanation for the naval conflict would be the divergent interests of an *apoikia* focused

---

84. On the problem of the date and on Thucydides' possible sources, see Gomme, Andrewes, and Dover 1945–1981: vol. 1: 122; cf. Hornblower 1991–2008: vol. 1: 44–5, who argues that Thucydides was probably reckoning time on the basis of generations and that the resulting dates are too early in this section of his work. Hornblower is inclined to date the naval battle between Corinth and Corcyra to the late seventh or early sixth century and to attach it to hostilities between Corcyra and Corinth at the end of Periander's tyranny.

85. Cf. the accusation of the Corinthians in Thucydides 1.68.1–4. On this, see Lepore 1962: 131; Stickler 2010: 74–5; Carusi 2011: 102.

*Corcyra* 549

on its own local and regional area and a mother city operating with broader objectives.

This general claim, while a plausible speculation, is still fairly sweeping, and it invites comparison of the sea battle between the Corcyraeans and Corinthians with other attested incidents. Doing so allows us to explore more deeply the political background of that battle in particular and Corcyraean diplomatic history during the Archaic period in general. Given the limited collection of relevant source material, much must remain hypothetical, but a consideration of the surviving testimonies offers the possibility of an interpretation. The most adequate reconstruction is one that is potentially accurate, "*im Potentialis*," as it were. The following discussion relies on an early dating of the Cypselids (see Section 4.1).

### 4.7.3. Detente with Corinth under the Cypselid Tyranny

First, we might connect the sea battle mentioned by Thucydides to two contemporary events that are transmitted in the ancient tradition, namely Cypselus' seizure of power at Corinth (657/6) and the flight of the Bacchiads to Corcyra after they had been expelled by the tyrant (Nic. Dam. *FGrH* 90 F58 with Jer. *Chron.* p. 94.21 Helm [first year of the 30th Olympiad]).[86] A plausible historical scenario begins around 660, when Cypselus, who himself came from the ranks of the Bacchiads on his mother's side, seized supreme power in Corinth. At least some of the Bacchiads fled and sought refuge in Corcyra, which had been founded by a disaffected member of the Bacchiads (see Section 4.7.1) but had maintained a relationship of some kind with its metropolis. From there, the Bacchiads tried— as Greek exiles often did (Gehrke 1985: 224–32)—to damage the new regime at home. Cypselus might have thus been motivated to attack Corcyra, which had given refuge to the exiles, leading to the sea battle. Indeed, Thucydides' formulation, Κορινθίων πρὸς Κερκυραίους (1.13.4), identifies the Corinthians as aggressors.

Lacking any information about the outcome of the sea battle, we cannot say whether the dominance of Corinth over Corcyra in later times was its result. It seems more likely that Corcyra maintained its independence and even political leverage for at least a while. Later sources refer to a Corcyraean thalassocracy at this time (Appian *Civil War* 2.39),[87] and the next known event in Corcyra's diplomatic history, the foundation of Epidamnus, is also consistent with a degree of

---

86. On the connection of the battle with the events around Cypselus' seizure of power, see also Antonelli 2000: 62–3.

87. However, the passage is replete with exaggerations, so one should not take it too literally.

## 550 THE OXFORD HISTORY OF THE ARCHAIC GREEK WORLD

independence from Corinth. This foundation, which can be placed in the years 630–25,[88] is described by Thucydides (1.24.2):

> The city of Epidamnus . . . was colonized by the Corcyraeans, though the founder-colonist [οἰκιστής] was a Corinthian, Phalius the son of Eratocleides, of the Heraclid family: as was the old custom, the founder was invited from the original mother city. A number of other settlers joined from Corinth and the rest of the Dorian peoples.

We must keep two points in mind. First, the initiative was taken by Corcyra, which speaks not only for its independence but apparently also for its prosperity and a collective orientation toward the expansion of its interests. Second, relations with Corinth were apparently amicable, since they followed the old custom (Malkin 1987: 132–3) of requesting an oikist from the mother city. Phalius was a Heraclid and hence almost certainly a member of the Corinthian elite, possibly even connected with the Cypselids.[89]

Given that the foundation of Epidamnus (see Map 4.3) seems to have taken place after the sea battle between Corinth and Corcyra, some sort of rapprochement must have occurred in the intervening decades. We cannot say definitively whether this rapprochement occurred during Cypselus' reign (657/6–627/6) or immediately after his death (Antonelli 2000: 83), but there are other signs that Corinth and Corcyra had a cooperative relationship prior to the foundation of Epidamnus.

The most important indication of a cooperative relationship between Corinth and Corcyra in the mid-seventh century is the founding of Anactorium, which was located on the south side of the Ambracian Gulf (and hence c. 100 km south of the main urban center of Corcyra), during Cypselus' reign. According to Thucydides (1.55.1) it was an *apoikia* of the Corinthians and the Corcyraeans.[90]

---

88. On the foundation of Epidamnus, see also Diodorus Siculus 12.30.2. On the date, see Jerome *Chronicon* pg. 97.2; Helm (second year of the 38th Olympiad); Cabanes and Drini 1995: 24; a date of c. 625 seems reasonable. It is in this context that Appian speaks of the aforementioned thalassocracy.

89. Gomme counts Phalius among the Bacchiads because of his Heraclid descent (Gomme, Andrewes, and Dover 1945–1981: vol. 1: 159). But one can also understand the term in a wider sense. Furthermore, Cypselus through his maternal line (Nic. Dam. *FGrH* 90 F57.1), and hence also his son Periander, belonged to the Bacchiads in a wider sense and thus also to the Heraclidae. Tellingly, in Diogenes Laertius 1.94, Periander is called a descendant of Heracles (in terms similar to Thucydides' account of Phalius). See Antonelli 2000: 83 n. 56.

90. The participation of the Corcyraeans here is controversial, since other sources know nothing of it; the evidence is discussed in Gehrke and Wirbelauer 2004: 356. Thucydides' testimony, however, has more weight, *pace* Fantasia 2017: 23–4. While we assume common action here, the general account is not affected very much if one excludes Corcyra from the foundation.

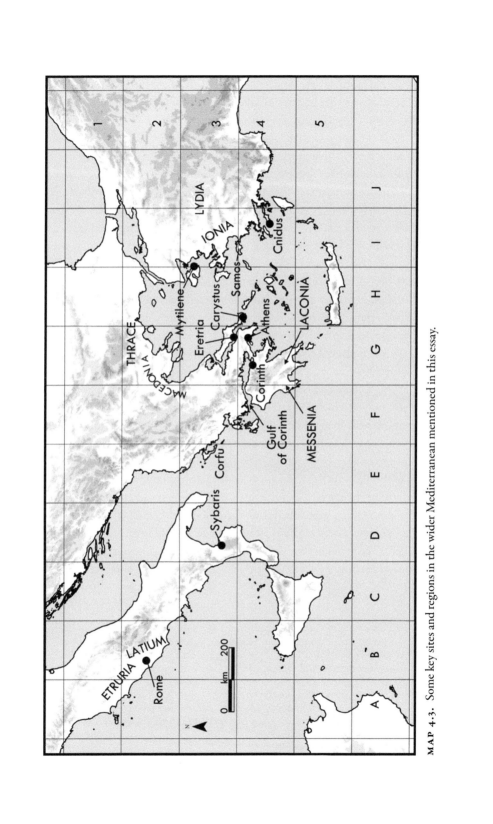

MAP 4-3. Some key sites and regions in the wider Mediterranean mentioned in this essay.

## 552    THE OXFORD HISTORY OF THE ARCHAIC GREEK WORLD

This foundation, together with that of Ambracia (situated on the Aratthos river c. 10 km north of the northern shore of the Ambracian Gulf), was part of the broader colonial policies of Cypselus, who set up outposts in these two places that were governed by his sons and hence under strong Corinthian control.[91] Evidently, the initiative was his, but Cypselus seems to have allowed the Corcyraeans to participate at least in the foundation of Anactorium.

The founding of the *apoikia* of Leucas (on the island of the same name, just to the south of the mouth of the Ambracian Gulf), might have involved a comparable collaboration between Corinth and Corcyra, although there are greater doubts here (Gehrke and Wirbelauer 2004: 365). The ancient sources indicate that Leucas was founded during Cypselus' reign (Strabo 10.2.8 with Gehrke 1990: 34), and Plutarch (*Vit. Them.* 24.1) states that Themistocles served as an arbitrator in a dispute between Corcyra and Corinth, deciding that "the Corinthians should pay an indemnity of 20 *talanta*, and administer Leucas as a common colony of both cities" (trans. B. Perrin). Plutarch claims that the Corcyraeans thus considered Themistocles to be a benefactor, which in turn led Themistocles to make Corcyra his first place of refuge when he was fleeing pursuers sent by both Athens and Sparta (Frost 1980: 200–3; Fragoulaki 2013: 71–2). However, the story about the arbitration could be a later invention to explain why Themistocles was a benefactor of Corcyra, which Thucydides (1.136.1) does not mention.[92] Evidently, participation in such foundations was registered very precisely (meaning that our sources likely had access to such information) but was also contested (whence the different versions).

All of this suggests that Corcyra extended its position independently and purposefully after the sea battle of the 660s, while temporarily improving relations with its mother city, probably during the tyranny of Cypselus, a state of affairs that seems to have lasted until the later years of Cypselus' reign or the early part of Periander's. The apparent Corinthian influence on the Corcyraean tribal reform discussed in Section 4.5.4 should be read against this background.

---

91. See Section 4.7.4. On Corinthian governance in Anactorium, see Nicolaus of Damascus *FGrH* 90 F57.7, as well as Strabo 10.2.8; Pausanius 5.23.3; Stephanus of Byzantium 92.15–16. The reference to Periander in Plutarch *Moralia* 552e is not a valid counterexample because it occurs in anything but a neutral context, and the story is exaggerated in certain ways. See also Domingo-Forasté 1988: 8–11. On the founding of Ambracia under Cypselus, see Gehrke and Wirbelauer 2004: 355 and now especially Fantasia 2017: 18–26. The attribution of this foundation to Periander by Antonelli 2000: 85–103 makes a great many assumptions, too many to be very plausible. But with respect to the reconstruction of Corcyra's history, this is, in any case, secondary.

92. Gomme characterizes the story in Plutarch as "very suspicious" (Gomme, Andrewes, and Dover 1945–1981: vol. 1: 438).

## 4.7.4. Establishment and Disintegration of Corinthian Rule

During the reign of Periander (627/6–587/6), any degree of cooperation that had existed between Corcyra and Corinth was decisively ruptured. The relevant sources, Herodotus and Nicolaus of Damascus, provide accounts that are at times contradictory, and interpretation of each author's claims raises complex historiographical issues that cannot be treated in detail here. For our purposes, Herodotus' account seems to be the more trustworthy overall, and regardless of how we assess the veracity of specific details, it is highly probable that Corcyra came under the direct rule of Periander; that Periander appointed his son, Lycophron, as tyrant of Corcyra (cf. Cypselus' placing his sons in charge of Anactorium and Ambracia); and that the Corcyraeans killed Lycophron in c. 590 (Hdt. 3.52.6, 3.53.7).[93]

To avenge the murder of Lycophron, Periander sent 300 sons of the leading families of Corcyra to King Alyattes of Lydia to be castrated. They were saved by the Samians on Samos and finally, probably after Periander's death, returned home. According to certain sources, the Cnidians also actively participated in their rescue, leading to a friendship among the Corcyraeans, Samians, and Cnidians (Hdt. 3.48.2–4, 49.2; Diog. Laert. 1.95; Plut. *Mor.* 860b [with Antenor *FGrH* 463 F61 and Dionysius Chalcidensis *FHG* IV p. 396, F13]).[94]

After the Corcyraeans killed Lycophron c. 590, Periander appointed his nephew Psammetichus, son of his brother Gorgos, as ruler of Corcyra (Nic. Dam. *FGrH* 90 F60). Psammetichus ruled Corcyra until returning to rule in Corinth in the wake of his uncle's death in 587/6, changing his name to that of his grandfather Cypselus in the process. Periander thus seems to have ruled Corcyra with considerable severity, which probably would have hindered Corcyra's own interests in expansion. One might even suspect that Periander acted in ways that constrained Corcyraean activity and influence, especially if one connects the foundation of Apollonia (located c. 130 km north of Corcyra's main urban center) in c. 600 to Periander.[95] Apollonia was a threat to Corcyra, because it opened

---

93. Herodotus integrated these two points (Periander ruling Corcyra and appointing his son Lycophron as his deputy) into a complex narrative characterizing Periander's behavior as grossly tyrannical (as he is presented in 5.92) and explaining the later behavior of the Corinthians; see Luraghi 2005: 83–5; and, with more references, Giangiulio 2005: 114 n. 68; Baragwanath 2008: 91–3; Froehlich 2013: 114–17. Nicolaus of Damascus (*FGrH* 90 F60) provides a different version of events in which the son that Periander sent to rule Corcyra is Nicolaus, with Lycophron having already died in an attempt to establish himself as tyrant elsewhere.

94. On the interpretation of these sources, see, for example, Mastrocinque 1988: 9.

95. Apollonia is represented as either a purely Corinthian (Thuc. 1.26.2; Pliny *HN* 3.145; Plut. *Mor.* 552e; cf. Steph. Byz. s.v Ἀπολλωνία) or a joint Corinthian-Corcyraean foundation (Ps.-Scymnus 439–40; Strabo 8.3.32; Paus. 5.22.3). Thucydides' account has greater weight,

554 THE OXFORD HISTORY OF THE ARCHAIC GREEK WORLD

up a land route running from Ambracia to Apollonia, on the mainland opposite Corfu, that was beyond Corcyra's control.[96]

There is little doubt that the Corcyraeans, especially their elites, would have perceived the period of direct rule from Corinth as one of oppressive domination, and it is unlikely that the Cypselids were able to maintain control over the rebellious island after Psammetichus left for Corinth in 587/6. Due to the lack of textual evidence, we cannot reconstruct precisely what happened, but it is highly probable that the Corcyraeans liberated themselves from Corinthian control at the time of Psammetichus' departure or soon afterward, even before Psammetichus died in 584/3. After the latter's death and the end of tyranny in Corinth (Nic. Dam. *FGrH* 90 F60.1; Plut. *Mor.* 859c–d),[97] the Corinthians would not have been able to preserve or re-establish a rigid dominion over Corcyra. At this time, Corcyra must have been free and would have made good use of the possibilities that came with its liberation from Corinthian control.

### 4.7.5. An Independent Corcyra

Despite the major change in the nature of Corcyra's relationship with Corinth resulting from these events, it is not generally viewed as a complete rupture. The archaeological remains from the first half of the sixth century suggest that contact with Corinth continued, at least in the importation of Corinthian pottery and other goods (see Section 4.4.5). Nonetheless, as discussed in Section 4.12.2, past assumptions that Corinthian artisans routinely worked at Corcyra during this period are not well-supported by the style and techniques witnessed on the surviving monuments and sculpture. Already by the seventh century, when the

---

especially because of the sensitivity he displays in such contexts (despite Piccirilli 1995: 175–6; cf. also Antonetti 2007: 91, n. 13). The later addition of the Corcyraeans can be explained more easily in light of their subsequent supremacy in the region;, see Section 4.7.5; see also Antonelli 2000: 126 n. 27. Periander's leadership in the foundation of Apollonia is referenced only in the problematic passage in Plutarch, but, unlike other Corinthian colonies, Apollonia is not explicitly connected with Cypselus. On the foundation date, see van Compernolle 1953.

96. See Antonelli 2000: 108–9. Even if one does not accept Antonelli's speculative interpretation of the founding of Ambracia, the possible land connection from Ambracia to Apollonia presented an additional threat to Corcyra. On the route from Ambracia to the north, see Fantasia 2017: 16. Later events (Thuc. 1.26.1–2) confirm the reality of this threat (cf. Antonelli 2000: 109–12): when the Corinthians attacked Epidamnus by land in 435, they marched from Ambracia to Apollonia (Fantasia 2017: 38–9).

97. The problems connected to this—e.g., whether Psammetichus' death should be ascribed to a popular revolt (Nicolaus) or to Spartan intervention (Plutarch)—are secondary for our purposes, since we can hardly assume, given the previous events, that Corinthian dominance over Corcyra remained intact following Periander's death and Psammetichus' departure.

political relationship should nominally have been more conducive to Corinthian influence, the Corcyraeans appear to have been stylistically oriented more within their region and to the western colonies than toward their metropolis. The lack of a tight correspondence between politics and art is hardly surprising, for we do not have to assume that abrupt political changes necessarily would have had a direct effect on local stylistic preferences, the activities of artisans in the region, or even long-term economic activity.

Moreover, one can surmise that the political relations between mother city and colony gradually normalized or, at the very least, were not shaped by permanent enmity. The aforementioned remark of Herodotus (3.49.1) about their perpetual conflict, while important, is a sweeping generalization about a long period of time that included episodes when the two communities cooperated politically. In addition to the joint colonial ventures, Syracuse was supported by joint Corinthian-Corcyraean intervention around 493/2 in its struggle against the tyrant Hippocrates of Gela (Hdt. 7.154.3; Salmon 1984: 276, 388–9; Luraghi 1994: 156–9). We should not be surprised at such cooperation in cases where both shared interests and loyalties were in play.

But overall, Corcyra was following its own course from the 580s, pursuing its own goals, and it was evidently rewarded with success. With the end of Corinthian rule and the fall of the tyranny in Corinth itself soon thereafter, and the resulting weakening of the mother city, the Corcyraeans had considerable freedom to maneuver and probably began building up their power and influence. Thucydides, in his account of the events leading to the outbreak of the Peloponnesian War, makes clear that the Corcyra of his time was wealthy, powerful, aggressive, and in possession of a formidable fleet:

> They [the Corcyraeans] looked down on the Corinthians: at that time
> the Corcyraeans' wealth compared with that of the richest Greek states;
> in military resources they were more powerful than Corinth; they could
> boast of substantial naval superiority, even basing their claim on the nautical fame of the island's original inhabitants, the Phaeacians (this did
> indeed encourage them to build up their fleet, and they were a substantial
> force: at the outbreak of the war they had 120 triremes). (1.25.4)

One may identify this era of complete independence as the florescence of Corcyra, which is reflected by its considerable investment in monumental architecture and sculpture at its sanctuaries at home and abroad (see Sections 4.4.2.7 and 4.12.2).

Corcyra was able not only to resume its past activities in the Adriatic region but also to expand them. There are signs that it was able to gain a certain level of control over Apollonia, which was represented no longer as purely Corinthian

## 556 THE OXFORD HISTORY OF THE ARCHAIC GREEK WORLD

but as a shared foundation (Antonelli 2000: 126). The foundation of Corcyra Melaina (on the island of Korčula, c. 450 km north of the main urban center of Corcyra), settled by Cnidians sometime around 600 (Ps.-Scymnus 426–30; Strabo 7.5.5; Pliny *HN* 3.152), may be regarded as a sign of a friendly relationship between Corcyra and Cnidus, which was also evident in the Cnidian support for the return of the Corcyraean boys dispatched to Lydia by Periander (Calligas 1968: 308; Mastrocinque 1988: 7–11; cf. Intrieri 2010: 196).[98]

The period of independence also may have been the context for the actions of the Corcyraean Arniadas, known through a funerary epigram (*IG* IX.1².4.880) inscribed on a limestone *stēlē* found in the necropolis near Soter hill (see Section 4.4.6):

> σᾶμα τόδε Ἀρνιάδα· χαροπὸς τόνδ᾽ ὄλε—
> σεν Ἄρες / βαρνάμενον παρὰ ναυσ—
> ὶν ἐπ᾽ Ἀράθθοιο ῥοϝαῖσι, / πολλὸ—
> ν ἀριστεύ{τ}οντα κατὰ στονόϝεσαν ἀϝυτάν.

This is the grave marker of Arniadas. This man
fierce-eyed Ares destroyed
battling by the ships beside the streams of the Aratthos
achieving great excellence amid the battle-roar that brings mourning.
(trans. E. Bowie)

The colony of Ambracia was located on the Aratthos river (Roller 2018: 390, 94), at a particularly strategic position for Corinth. Datable to c. 600 or a little later by letter forms, the inscription might belong to the period of increased Corcyraean activity after the departure of Psammetichus, though different views are tenable.[99]

One might also date to this era the tradition connecting the Corcyraeans to the Phaeacians, mentioned in the quotation from Thucydides given above. Generally speaking, people throughout Greece were at this time constructing specific connections to a heroic past situated within the world of the Homeric epics (Gehrke 2014: 9–64). Evidently, the intentional history of the Corcyraeans— that is, their history in their own view and collective identity—was refocused on the Phaeacians, relegating the Corinthians to the background. A manifestation of this process was probably the establishment of a sanctuary and cult for

---

98. On the founding of Corcyra Melaina, see Kiechle 1979: 179–80; Šašel Kos 2015: 19–20.

99. For example, Antonelli (2000: 86) places Arniadas' death in the reign of Periander.

the Homeric king of the Phaeacians, Alcinous, in the immediate vicinity of the main harbor, even if we cannot date the origin of this cult with any specificity (see Section 4.4.2.7.6). Phaiax, the eponymous hero of the Phaeacians, later also appeared as the son of Poseidon and the nymph Corcyra, who in turn was a daughter of the river god Asopus.[100] This genealogy is unknown to Homer, who names Poseidon as Alcinous' grandfather (*Od.* 7.54–9).

Corcyra's wealth was due not only to its rich and well-exploited natural resources, its wide-ranging maritime connections, and its naval power (see Section 4.8) but also to its cautious foreign policy. Given their advantages, the Corcyraeans could be sure that others would approach them carefully, even if legal claims or international conflicts were at issue. Thucydides (1.37.3) recounts the Corinthians' criticism of this self-sufficient (*autarkēs*) reserve. Indeed, the Corcyraeans were able to approach external affairs from a position of strength, confident that no one else could significantly harass them, let alone pose an existential threat. When the Greeks were threatened by the Persian armada in 480, the Corcyraeans prepared 60 ships but awaited the result of the Battle of Salamis off the Messenian coast, concocting an excuse that they had been prevented from sailing by Etesian winds at Cape Malea (Hdt. 7.168.1–4).[101] They did not really have to fear punishment from the Greek side. The Corcyraeans enjoyed this strong position until their precipitous collapse in a whirl of external and civil war in the last third of the fifth century.

## 4.8. Economic History

When the first Greeks saw Corfu, they might have grasped the potential of a place not unlike the uncultivated island offshore from the land of the Cyclopes described by Homer:

> For the island isn't bad at all and would bear all things in season. For on it, by the gray sea's banks, there are meadows, watered, soft ones. Vines would be very hardy there. On it there's smooth land for plowing. They would always reap a deep crop in season, since beneath the surface it is very fertile. The harbor in it is safe anchorage, so there's no need for moorings,

---

100. On the later common identification of Scheria as Corcyra, as well as on the cult of Alcinous, see especially Section 4.5.2. On the personification of Corcyra, see Gehrke and Wirbelauer 2004: 361.

101. According to Salmon (1984: 277), this behavior was possibly a reaction to the active participation of the Corinthians, i.e., an indicator of renewed tensions between mother city and *apoikia*.

558 THE OXFORD HISTORY OF THE ARCHAIC GREEK WORLD

neither to cast anchors nor secure stern cables; instead, those who bring a ship to shore can await the time when sailors' hearts urge them and breezes favorably blow. (*Od.* 9.130–9; trans. J. Huddleston)

## 4.8.1. Natural Resources

The waters off the coast of Corfu teemed with tuna at certain times of the year, and the Corcyraeans profited handsomely from that resource (Lytle 2006: 132–5; Intrieri 2010: 192–4; Psoma 2015: 147; Bresson 2016b: 178), as is evident from the following story recounted by Pausanias:

On entering the temenos [at Delphi] you come to a bronze bull, a votive offering of the Corcyraeans made by Theopropos of Aegina. The story is that in Corcyra a bull, leaving the cows, would go down from the pasture and bellow on the shore. As the same thing happened every day, the herdsman went down to the sea and saw a countless number of tuna fish. He reported the matter to the Corcyraeans, who, finding their labor lost in trying to catch the tuna, sent envoys to Delphi. So they sacrificed the bull to Poseidon, and straightway after the sacrifice they caught the fish, and dedicated their offerings at Olympia and at Delphi with a tithe of their catch. (10.9.3–4; cf. 5.27.9; trans. W. Jones)

Theopropos' period of activity can be dated by an inscription from Delphi (possibly but not certainly on a base that once held the Corcyraeans' bull) to the early part of the fifth century (see *SEG* 38.417).[102] The veracity of the story behind the dedication of the bull has been questioned (see, for example, Habicht 1985: 76), but it does at least show that the Corcyraeans had a reputation for catching tuna in significant quantities. Most large-scale fishing in the ancient Mediterranean took place near the shore (Marzano 2013: 66–78), and the waters between Corfu and the mainland were ideal for that purpose.[103]

The importance of maritime activity among the Corcyraeans meant that access to timber resources was a matter of considerable significance (Psoma 2015: 150–1; Psoma 2022: 80–1). The monumental temples the Corycraeans built during the Archaic period would also have required the acquisition of large

102. There has been much discussion about the inscriptions on this base; see in particular *SEG* 31.546–56 with a cautionary note about the readings proposed by Vatin.

103. See also F54 Olson-Sens of the fourth-century writer Archestratos of Gela, who praises the octopus caught in the waters around Corfu.

timbers. A lead tablet found near the Alcinous harbor and dated to the fifth century (*IG* IX.1².4.874) records the delivery of wooden beams to the dockyards from the workshop of someone named Alkimos. Angelos Choremis, who produced the *editio princeps*, argued that the mention of Alkimos' workshop suggests that the timber was sourced locally, possibly from the mountainous northern part of Corfu (Choremis 1992–1998: 354). The Corcyraeans almost certainly also had ready access to timber from outside Corfu, either in their *peraia* or in Illyria or both.

## 4.8.2. Agriculture and Animal Husbandry

As was the case throughout the Archaic Greek world (Gehrke 1986: 18–19), agricultural activity inevitably must have accounted for the majority of economic production in Corcyra. The ancient literary sources refer to Corfu as *lipare* (Dionys. Per. 492–4), *polyphoros*, and *eukarpos* (Eust. *Commentarium in Dionysii periegetae orbis descriptionem apud* Müller 1855–1861, vol. 2: 309.9–16). In fact, everything speaks in favor of thinking that the Corcyraeans made good use of their agricultural resources (Will 1955: 300–2; Lepore 1962: 130–2; Antonelli 2000: 61; Psoma 2015: 147–51; Psoma 2022: 75–82). The fertility of Corcyra's *chōra* did more than ensure harvests of staple crops such as wheat, olives, grapes, and other fruits sufficient for subsistence (Partsch 1887: 83–92, esp. 85; Schmidt 1890: 80). Any crop could become a cash crop if produced in excess of local demand for trade outside the island. The historic land usage on Corfu indicates that the intensification for export would have largely been due to olives and grapes, which were used in the making of wine (Partsch 1887: 91 n. 1, with Ovid, *Metamorphoses* 13.719). Although most of the evidence for raising cash crops comes from the Classical period, there is no reason to doubt that Corcyraeans were already doing so in the Archaic period.

The evidence for export-oriented viticulture on Corfu is particularly rich (Busolt 1893–1904: vol. 3 part 1: 445 n. 1; Bürchner 1922: 1407; Gehrke 1985: 369 n. 4; Psoma 2015: 148–9; Bresson 2016b: 127; Psoma 2022: 78–80). In the year 373, Spartans under the leadership of Mnasippos attacked Corcyra. According to Xenophon:

> [they ravaged] the land, which was most beautifully cultivated and planted and destroyed magnificent dwellings and wine-cellars with which the farms were furnished; the result was, it was said, that his soldiers became so luxurious that they would not drink any wine unless it had a fine bouquet. Furthermore, very many slaves and cattle were captured on the farms (*Hell.* 6.2.6; trans. C. Brownson, modified; cf. Ath. 33b).

560 THE OXFORD HISTORY OF THE ARCHAIC GREEK WORLD

This vivid characterization belongs to the fourth century, but a particular focus on making wine can be traced back into the fifth century and beyond. In his account of the *stasis* in 427, Thucydides (3.70.4–6) mentions that a prominent democrat named Peithias accused five of the wealthiest Corcyraeans of cutting wood in lands sacred to Zeus and Alcinous in order to make stakes used to prop up grapevines. Peithias secured a conviction, and the penalty levied—one *statēr* per stake—was cumulatively so large that the convicted men begged to be allowed to pay it in installments. This suggests that in the second half of the fifth century, wealthy Corcyraean landowners were growing grapes in large quantities, presumably with an eye to making wine. We should also mention the sanctuary dedicated to Dionysus in the southern part of the Kanoni peninsula, where the late Archaic pediment bears an unusual sculptural depiction of a symposium, including a kratēr and other vessels for wine consumption (see Section 4.4.2.7.4, esp. Figure 4.9).

As one would expect from their renown for wine, the Corcyraeans also appear to have produced amphoras. The pseudo-Aristotelian *On Marvelous Things Heard* (839b, 104; cf. Hsch. s.v. Κερκυραῖοι ἀμφορεῖς) mentions that merchants plying the Adriatic carried "Corcyraean" amphoras with them, which suggests the existence of a vase with a distinctive shape that was closely associated with Corcyra. The vases in question were in all probability what is currently known as the Corinthian "Type B" amphora, introduced c. 525 and in production through the third or second century.[104] These vases have an ovoid body, a flaring rim, vertical handles in the form of arches, and a typical capacity of 19–28 liters. Although such jars could be used to transport any number of products, wine was surely an important commodity, and examples coated with a resinous substance that prevented liquids from soaking into the porous clay, which would have been inappropriate for oil, were well-suited to wine (Koehler 1986; Whitbread 1995: 260).

Whether or not wine transport was its primary use, it is doubtful how recognizable the origin of a Type B amphora would have been to an ancient consumer. Corcyra was certainly an important manufacturer, since at least 13,000 fragments of Type B amphoras have been tallied, including some misfires, from the excavations at the Figareto pottery workshop (Preka-Alexandri 2016: 227–8; see Section 4.4.2.6). Yet multiple centers were producing nearly indistinguishable versions of these amphoras, potentially including Corinth itself. Compositional

---

104. While the Corinthian "Type A" amphora was certainly developed in Corinth in the seventh century, Type B is a separate series that has a different profile, fabric, and production technique, and it may not have been produced in Corinth at all despite its conventional name (Farnsworth, Perlman, and Asaro 1977; Whitbread 1995: 264–85).

tests and petrographic analysis of 19 jars from Gela in Sicily found that the clays of most had in fact originated in Calabria, probably Sybaris/Thurii in light of its ancient reputation for wine (Barone, Crupi, Galli, et al. 2004). In other words, if the type was indeed called "Corcyraean" in antiquity, purchasers of a freshly potted jar would have wanted other information besides the shape to confirm that its contents had actually originated from Corfu.

Due to these uncertainties, it is unclear how much of the extensive collection of Type B amphoras is attributable to Corcyra. Generally speaking, the type is found in many important Greek trading sites in the Adriatic, southern Italy, Sicily, southern France, and North Africa (Whitbread 1995: 258–61; Metallinou 2010: 17; Intrieri 2010: 195). In light of the literary references to "Corcyraean" amphoras, one could imagine that potters in Corcyra introduced a new amphora shape as a distinctive container for their valuable local product, presumably wine, but the market was eventually flooded by imitators, while the name stuck. But this is little more than speculation without significantly more study of the extant examples, and compositional testing at the various points of production and consumption is sorely needed.[105]

Even if the contents and origins of every Type B amphora remain uncertain, the Corcyraeans were certainly exporting their wine by some means. Viticulture was particularly labor-intensive (Bresson 2016b: 170–4), and the labor force on larger farms would have consisted largely of slaves (Gehrke 1985: 88–9). Note, for example, that Xenophon ends his discussion of Mnasippos' soldiers quaffing fine wine by stating that "very many slaves and cattle were captured on the farms." Thucydides emphasizes that both parties involved in the *stasis* of 427, oligarchs as well as the democrats, tried to mobilize the slaves "in the fields" by promising manumission (Thuc. 3.73; cf. Diod. *Sic.* 13.48.7). The whips for which Corcyra was known (see Section 4.5.5) may well have been regularly employed to castigate slaves.

Xenophon points to the existence of large numbers of cattle on Corfu (*Hell.* 6.2.6; Bürchner 1922: 1405–6). That was almost certainly already the case in the Archaic period, since Corfu's early coins (see Section 4.8.5) feature a suckling cow on the obverse. Also relevant is the existence of an as-yet-unlocated place called Euboea somewhere on the island (Strabo 10.1.15).

---

105. Some Type B amphoras were stamped beginning in the late sixth or early fifth century, but the significance of those stamps remains unclear. See Panagou 2016, esp. 219–21. Of the Geloan specimens thought to have been imported from Greece, a few display a good match with the clays sampled from the Kanoni peninsula (Finocchiaro, Barone, Mazzoleni, et al. 2018). Without more testing of Type B jars, it is difficult to say how many of the supposed "Corcyraean amphoras" were in fact made at Corcyra.

It is also important to bear in mind that Corcyra controlled a considerable, easily accessed *peraia* that significantly enhanced the island's already substantial agricultural potential (see Section 4.4.4). After their defeat in the *stasis* during the early years of the Peloponnesian War, the remaining oligarchs fled to the *peraia*, occupied fortifications located there, and launched raids on Corfu—leading to famine on the island (Thucydides 3.85.1–2). We learn from this account not only that the mainland properties were secured by fortifications but also that by the latter half of the fifth century, the produce from the *peraia* had become vital to nourishing the residents of the urban center. In light of the ready communication between the mainland and the island and the high quality of the land on the *peraia*, we can assume that it began to play a similar role earlier in Corcyra's history. The Corcyraeans probably took control of parts of the mainland relatively soon after the foundation of the *apoikia* and developed them economically. One generally thinks of cattle breeding and fishing as important industries, especially in the area of the lagoon of Butrint, which has been identified as likely within the northern boundary of the *peraia* (Carusi 2011: 95–104; see here Section 4.4.4).[106]

### 4.8.3. Craft Production

By the later Archaic period, we may imagine a bustling artisanal zone in the low-lying, western parts of the Kanoni peninsula, from Figareto to near the Panagia Kassopitra Monastery (see Section 4.4.2.6). The pottery workshop at Figareto is the best known to date. An important product was the Corinthian Type B amphoras discussed in Section 4.8.2. Not only does their presence in Figareto prove that they were being manufactured on Corcyra, but the amphoras appear to have been the workshop's primary output, at least by the Classical period.

Furthermore, the Figareto workshop produced a wide variety of ceramic wares besides transport jars, including Corinthianizing fine wares, kalathiskoi, lamps, loom weights, and roof tiles (Kourkoumélis and Démesticha 1997: 555; Preka-Alexandri 2010: 78–82; Preka-Alexandri 2016: 227–30). Terracotta figurines were an important second specialty, and many female figurines were discovered along with several molds of popular Archaic figurine types found at the workshop itself and elsewhere in Corcyra, notably the "small Artemis sanctuary" (see Section 4.4.2.7.5 for a broader discussion of this sanctuary, and see Figure 4.13 for examples of these figurines). The nearby production sites in the Stratia district and the Demesianou Plot are less well understood, but roof tiles and lamps were

---

106. The suggested connection with Butrint has a long scholarly history: Partsch 1887: 56, 85; Schmidt 1890: 80–1; Lepore 1962: 134–5.

FIGURE 4.13. Terracotta figurines from the "Small Artemis Sanctuary"; sixth through fifth centuries. Archaeological Museum of Corfu. Photo by Philip Sapirstein.

important products (see Section 4.4.2.6). Although their production sites would be difficult to detect, the dozens of gigantic pithoi used to hold burials in the necropolis at Soter hill (see Section 4.4.2.8) were doubtless another important Corcyraean product, and many others must have been manufactured for agricultural installations elsewhere in Corfu. The extraordinary terracotta roofs from the two earliest surviving monumental temples in Corcyra (the temple at Mon Repos and the Artemision; see Sections 4.4.2.7.2 and 4.4.2.7.1, respectively) demonstrate the considerable skills developed by Corcyraean coroplasts already in the late seventh century.

By the latter half of the seventh century, Corcyra was also an important center for metalworking.[107] A bronze mold now in the Ashmolean Museum but purchased in Corfu would have been used for hammering thin metal sheets to decorate shield bands or possibly helmet decoration (Treister 1995). Vignettes of animals and narrative scenes blend elements found on Corinthian vases and in Argive and Attic metalworking, with some parallels identified farther afield in Thrace. Datable to around the 620s, the object provides a tantalizing glimpse into the sophistication of metalworking on the island, as it appears to be the earliest surviving example of an intaglio matrix from the Greek world (Treister 1995: 98, 101–2). Sixth-century bronze figurines found on Corfu, including examples from Mon Repos and a late Archaic dedication from Rachonas, are thought to have been made locally (see Sections 4.11.2 and 4.4.3, respectively).

Finally, the considerable investment in temple architecture during the Archaic period was unrivaled at any other point in Corcyra's history. Builders familiar with stone- and woodworking must have labored alongside the island's coroplasts, and many may have traveled outside Corfu between the numerous local projects to participate in building commissions abroad (see Section 4.12.1). This skilled workforce may have honed its skills in shipbuilding as well, since the Corcyraeans had built up their own fleet not long after the *apoikia* (see Section 4.7.2).

## 4.8.4. Trade and Other Mercantile Activity

Xenophon notes that Corfu was "situated in a favorable position with respect to the Corinthian Gulf and the states that reach down to its shores, in a favorable position for doing damage to the territory of Lacedaemon, and in an extremely

---

107. Without the archaeological evidence, we would be in the dark regarding Corcyraean artists, who are not named in any surviving literary or epigraphic sources. Ptolichos of Corcyra, a bronze caster active in the early Classical period, worked in Athens (Paus. 5.9.1, 6.10.9; Kanta-Kitsou 1996: 96).

favorable position with respect to Epirus across the strait and the coastwise route from Sicily to the Peloponnese" (*Hell.* 6.2.9; trans. C. Brownson; cf. Thuc. 1.36.2, 1.44.3). The strategic location of Corfu meant that merchants found it necessary to visit the island and transact business there, as the Corinthians point out in the speech Thucydides gives to the Corinthians during the debate in the Athenian Assembly in 433 over the possibility of Athens forming an alliance with Corcyra:

> Besides, their [the Corcyraeans'] geographical situation makes them independent of others [καὶ ἡ πόλις αὐτῶν ἅμα αὐτάρκη θέσιν κειμένη], and consequently the decision in cases where they injure any lies not with judges appointed by mutual agreement, but with themselves, because while they seldom make voyages to their neighbors, they are constantly being visited by foreign vessels which are compelled to put into Corcyra. (1.37.3; trans. R. Crawley)

The Corcyraeans are portrayed by the Corinthians as possessing *autarkeia*, by which Thucydides means the capacity to import whatever the Corcyraeans might need with ease and to export whatever surpluses they might have (Bresson 2016a: 53–6). The same no doubt held true in the Archaic period.

Corcyra's role as a commercial hub created opportunities for gainful economic activity that went beyond engaging directly in trade. Think of the customs duties that they would be able to collect or other business that they could conduct, for example, in the form of maritime loans. As noted in Section 4.5.4, finds from the main urban center include eight lead plaques (*IG* IX.1².4.865–72 = *SEG* 30.519–26 and 42.489), dated to c. 500 on letter forms, that record loans in relatively substantial amounts. (The sums go all the way up to 660 units of currency, which could be either *drachmai* or *statēres*; see Del Monaco and Parise 2010.) In addition to the amount of the loan, each tablet supplies the name of the creditor, the name of the debtor, and the names of two witnesses. Calligas argued that those plaques, which were found in the vicinity of the agora of Corcyra, recorded bottomry loans (Calligas 1971: 86; Hornblower 1991–2008: vol. 1: 80–1), although this interpretation remains speculative (Millett 1991: 252 n. 43; *SEG* 42.489). In addition, the presence of many foreign seafarers on the island would have offered considerable opportunities for Corcyraeans to enrich themselves (Head 1911: 325–6; Kraay 1976: 128–9).

The Corcyraeans' mercantile activities were no doubt protected and enhanced by their fleet. The construction of a substantial fleet (see Section 4.7.2) was not motivated by commercial interests, but it nonetheless benefited the economy. For example, the suppression of piracy—surely, pirates did not first appear in the third century in these areas (Kiechle 1979: 182–6)—by a growing Corcyraean navy that controlled and secured the waters and coasts in its area also raised the chances that their commercial products would reach their intended destination (Psoma 2015: 158–62; Psoma 2022: 118–26).

## 4.8.5. Coinage

Corcyra minted coins in a silver-copper alloy starting in the late sixth or early fifth century (Carbè 1987; Nicolet-Pierre 2009; Psoma 2015: 153–8; Psoma 2016: 100–1; Psoma 2022: 89–116). The obverses typically featured a cow bending down toward a suckling calf, the reverses two incuse rectangles decorated with a vegetative motif. The Archaic coinage from Corcyra is best known from a hoard of 158 coins that was excavated in 1978 in the area of its agora. The Corcyraeans employed their own weight standard based on a *statēr* of 11.4 g, which was equal to four Corinthian *drachmai* or a reduced Aeginetan *statēr*, with divisions of half *statēres*, quarter *statēr*, and so on. The weight standard used by the Corcyraeans, which was adopted by Cephallenia, Zacynthus, Epidamnus, and Apollonia, meant that their coins could easily be exchanged for those minted on either the Corinthian or Aeginetan standard. Corcyraean coins rarely traveled significant distances from Corfu, but they are found in some numbers in southern Italy and Sicily. Tests of the coins from the aforementioned hoard indicate that the Corcyraean coins contained 70%–90% silver, with the remainder consisting of copper. It is likely that the Corcyraeans set the value of their coins as if they were made from solid silver and thereby turned a profit from minting, as was the case in other Archaic *poleis* (see, for example, Ellis-Evans 2019: 189–90 on the billon coins struck by Mytilene).

## 4.8.6. Summary

The limitations in our sources prevent a diachronic study of changes in economic activity during the Archaic period. A plausible view expressed some time ago by Lepore (1962: 132) is that the Corcyraeans would first have focused on exploiting the resources of their island and later have turned to the neighboring *peraia*.[108] They probably developed certain markets for the trade of their most valuable agricultural products, especially wine, over an expanding radius along the Adriatic coast, and they no doubt also profited from the rapidly growing connections between Greece and Italy. Evidently, the Corcyraeans had made substantial

---

108. See now also Carusi 2011: 102, as well as Antonetti 2006: 63–5, who points out the focus on the Ionian islands and the mainland, which she detects in the Corcyraean *imaginaire*.

progress developing their agricultural basis and export market within the first two generations after the *apoikia*, since by the first half of the seventh century, they already possessed a fleet that they could wield against their mother city (see Section 4.7.2). We may perhaps recognize some signs of growth connected to agricultural exports by the late sixth century in the material evidence, notably in the form of the Type B amphoras discussed in Section 4.8.2.

Although the position of Corfu was such that the Corcyraeans naturally focused much of their commercial activity in the Adriatic and southern Italy and Sicily, we can also detect significant connections to the mainland and eastern Mediterranean in their *technai*. For example, the terracotta sculptures produced in Figareto and nearby Corcyraean workshops (see Section 4.4.2.6) display a variety of influences, including Corinth itself, other parts of the northern Peloponnese, Laconia, Attica, and Ionia (Dontas 1997: 69–82; Preka-Alexandri 2016: 226, 30–2). The replication of features from Assyrian and Neo-Hittite models evident in the Lion of Menecrates (see Section 4.4.6) and on the roof of the Mon Repos temple (see Section 4.4.2.7.2), both from the late seventh century, suggest that Corcyraean artists not only had access to imported Near Eastern objects but were also carefully studying them.

## 4.9. Familial/Demographic History

When it comes to producing demographic figures for Corcyra, testimonies about the size of its fleet are especially important, since they make it possible to offer an estimate of the population of Corfu during the Archaic period.

Every population estimate must begin with Thucydides' statements (1.29.3–5, 1.47.1–2, 1.55.2) about the conflicts just prior to the Peloponnesian War, when Corcyra possessed about 120 triremes, which presumably would have been operated by about 24,000 adult males. We must also take account of the presence of a sizable number of slaves. As we have seen (see Section 4.8.2), the Corcyraeans' dedication to viticulture on a large scale was in part made possible by slave labor. Slaves also played an important role as rowers in the Corcyraean fleet in the fifth century (Thuc. 1.55.2; Gomme, Andrewes, and Dover 1945–1981: vol. 1: 196; Hunt 1998: 84).[109] One can plausibly project these circumstances back to the Archaic period, especially in light of the early importance of the Corcyraean fleet.

Julius Beloch argued that the population of Corfu in the fifth century was "not less than 10,000 free adult men," as well as around 40,000 slaves (of all

---

109. These individuals would not have been permanent galley slaves. Regarding the slaves on landed properties, also see Xenophon *Hellenica* 6.2.6.

ages and genders), while noting that, since this is a minimum to sustain a navy attested in the aforementioned sources, "the population could have been very much larger" (Beloch 1886: 91–2). Indeed, others have extrapolated a Classical population of at least 100,000 (including the enslaved), which is not far from the 141,000 residents of the island in the 19th century CE (e.g., Bürchner 1922: 1406; Hammond 1967: 417; Fauber 2002: 4–5).

Mogens Herman Hansen (2006: 94–5), using his "shotgun" method for estimating population, has argued that the walls of Corcyra's urban core enclosed an area suitable for approximately 10,000 inhabitants. Although much of the circuit wall was probably not built until the Classical period, at least the isthmus of the Kanoni peninsula seems to have been walled off by the Archaic period (see Section 4.4.2.3). The primary sanctuaries near the north and south of the peninsula had all been founded no later than the sixth century (see Section 4.4.2.7). Therefore, we may reasonably retroject Hansen's figure of 10,000 for Corcyra's urban core to the end of the Archaic period. Hansen also applied the same method to suggest that roughly another 20,000 people lived in the *chōra* of Corcyra. Comparing that to figures derived from naval forces, he arrived at a minimum total population (including slaves and metics) of 55,000 in the fifth century. This minimum figure could easily have been reached as early as the sixth century. We might also add that the island's residents should be tallied alongside those living on the *peraia*, a sizable territory potentially including fortresses at Bouthrotos and elsewhere (see Section 4.4.4).

Due to the lack of sources, it is not possible to say anything in detail about the familial structures in Corcyra. There is no evidence of any peculiarities in comparison with the practices and institutions common in Greece. The Chersikratidai, who evidently were descendants of the founder Chersikrates, attest a rather long line of familial descent. But they were apparently a hereditary family of priests (see Section 4.5.2).

## 4.10. Social Customs and Institutions

The state of our sources does not provide any information that goes beyond what has already been said, but we can surely assume that generally common practices were widespread, especially among the elite, such as the symposium and gymnastic exercises. Several Olympic victors from Corcyra are attested: Archilochus (in 544; Moretti 1957: #111) and Agatharchus (in 536; Moretti 1957: #118) in the *stadion*, Philo in the boys' *stadion* (in 504?; Moretti 1957: #155), and another (or the same?) Philo son of Glaukon, who won twice in boxing (in 500 and 496; Moretti 1957: #161, #168); a victory epigram dedicated to him is transmitted under the name of Simonides (Hallof 2001: 4–5). We have already commented (see Section 4.5.5) on the ancient references to Corcyraean whips and dedications of bronze whips, which may indicate the existence of an initiation rite involving flagellation.

## 4.11. Religious Customs and Institutions

Artemis and Hera appear to have been the most important deities early in Corcyra's history, while Apollo and Dionysus attracted offerings comparatively late in the Archaic period. The following discussion begins with Artemis and Apollo, whose cults are the most clearly attested on Corcyra, and then moves to Hera, who certainly had an important sanctuary even if its location is debatable. We conclude with Dionysus and then list other deities known to have been worshipped in Corcyra, most of which are not firmly attested until after the Archaic period.

### 4.11.1. Sanctuaries of Artemis and Apollo

The thousands of sixth- and fifth-century terracotta figurines excavated at many places in the Kanoni peninsula (see especially Preka-Alexandri 2016) are an important source for understanding Corcyraean religious practices. The most common types are enthroned and standing females (some holding a bird, a flower, or a stag), groups of dancers, and depictions of deities. Substantial assemblages of such dedications are generally consistent with cults of Hera, Aphrodite, and the Nymphs. However, by far the most popular deity seems to have been Artemis, who appears in multiple guises on molded terracottas: as a huntress or master over wild animals and in compositions emphasizing her associations with fertility and sacrifice, such as dancing, in procession, or riding a chariot (see Figure 4.13) (Preka-Alexandri 2016: 231–2). Most of these terracottas were locally made, and in fact molds from the Figareto workshop (see Section 4.4.2.6) were used to create several types encountered in sanctuary deposits elsewhere in the city. Artemis figurines were found within most of the known Archaic cult deposits on the Kanoni peninsula, which emphasizes her popularity among the Corcyraean people.

Artemis appears to have had just one major sanctuary on the Kanoni peninsula. The grand temple with the Gorgon pediment located in the northwestern part of the Kanoni peninsula (see Section 4.4.2.7.1) is widely accepted as hers, even if the association is not absolutely certain (Rignanese 2016). The strongest evidence is a third-century pillar bearing a dedication to Artemis found at a Hellenistic podium or *bēma* constructed north of the temple (*IG* IX 1².4.852; Schleif, Rhomaios, and Klaffenbach 1940: 163–4). This has been connected to another Artemis dedication on a statue base dating to the latter half of the fourth century, which was probably from the same general area (*IG* IX 1$^2$.4.37 = *IG* IX.1 706; Rhomaios 1925: 209–10). The pediment of the temple, with its monumental Gorgon flanked by panthers, has also been linked to Artemis in the guise of the *potnia therōn* (Kanta-Kitsou 1996: 105 n. 41; Antonetti 2006: 58; Sciarma 2009), though this is little more than a conjecture due to the general lack of correspondence between Archaic pedimental compositions and the deity to which the temple belonged.[110] In light of the general popularity of Artemis in Archaic Corcyra, we find no reason to doubt her conventional association with its grandest temple, even if the epigraphic evidence for her worship within the temenos is relatively late.[111]

The so-called "small Artemis sanctuary" near the southern tip of Kanoni has been hypothetically connected with Artemis Agrotera, although in fact a wide array of female figurines is represented in the thousands of finds from that site, and Artemis appears there in multiple guises (see Sections 4.4.2.7.1 and 4.4.2.7.5). The Figareto workshop that manufactured many of her figurines (see Section 4.4.2.6) installed a stone *korē* for a protective shrine that is plausibly linked to Artemis, for whom we might imagine an epithet Epiklivanios (guardian of the kilns). The late Archaic votive cache from a private shrine found nearby in the Stratia quarter (see Section 4.4.2.7.1) might have been for offerings to Artemis, Hera, and the Nymphs, and a similar range of figurine types was found during excavations at the Evelpidi Plot to the south, again probably from domestic cults (Spetsieri-Choremi 1991; Preka-Alexandri 2016: 226–7). While there is no doubt that Artemis was popular among the Corcyraean people relative to other female deities, we should also point out that her terracottas happen to be highly recognizable. The worship of deities who received gifts made from less durable materials or whose votives are more generic will inevitably be less easily discerned in the archaeological record.

In light of his epithet, Apollo Corcyraios might have been a key patron deity of the polity (Gehrke and Wirbelauer 2004: 363). The identification of the relevant cult site, which is the most certain of any sanctuary from the Archaic settlement, is based on several dedicatory inscriptions naming him (*IG* IX.1$^2$.4.822–4, 826, 829) on votives, all from the first half of the fifth century, excavated near a

---

110. For example, the nearby early temple at Mon Repos, which cannot have been dedicated to Artemis (see Section 4.11.2), is also decorated with the heads of Gorgons and lions, which demonstrates that neither motif had an exclusive connection to that goddess in Corcyra.

111. For an (unconvincing) argument that the imagery of the pediment demonstrates that the temple was dedicated to Athena, see Weber 2007. Rignanese (2016: 458), based on the same tradition of Apollonius Rhodius that was discussed in connection with the Kardaki Temple, suggests the temple was dedicated to Apollo.

*Corcyra* 571

small, open-air altar near the temple at Mon Repos (see Section 4.4.2.7.2). Yet this Apollo sanctuary does not appear to have been active until late in the sixth century and is among the smallest public cults identified anywhere in Corcyra, especially in contrast to the much larger and older temple for a female deity, presumably Hera, just to its north. The votives, which include numerous spearheads, along with miniature bronze shields, bronze bay leaves, bronze and clay sandals, stamped clay disks, relief plaques depicting roosters, and male protomes, are predominantly, though not exclusively, related to martial aspects of Apollo (Calligas 1968: 309–13; Calligas 1969: 54-5).

Apollo was worshipped in other guises elsewhere in Corcyra. A fifth-century *horos* of "Pythaios" was discovered a short distance from the Artemision, in the northwestern part of the Kanoni peninsula (*IG* IX.1².4.863 = *IG* IX.1.699; Rhomaios 1925: 211–18). Understood as the marker for a Sanctuary of Apollo Pythios, the stone's conjectural total height of 2–3 m suggests that it might also have been a baetyl, an aniconic pillar sacred to Apollo Agyieus, whose worship was closely associated with aniconic representations of the deity (Rhomaios 1925: 217; Schleif, Rhomaios, and Klaffenbach 1940: 165–6; Kanta-Kitsou 2001b: 452, nn. 77–9). It seems likely that the *horos* should be connected to a small Classical temple and altar 150 m to the northeast (Spetsieri-Choremi 1980a: 292–5; Kanta-Kitsou 1996: 106 n. 49; Kanta-Kitsou 2001b: 447, 459).

Various finds from around the Panagia Kassopitra Monastery at the southern end of the Kanoni peninsula, including an Archaic marble *kouros* and what was perhaps another baetyl,[112] may have been associated with a sanctuary of Apollo Agyieus (Kanta-Kitsou 1996: 84–5, 101–7; Kanta-Kitsou 2001b: 445–60; *SEG* 52.545). While the cult of Apollo Agyieus is well attested in other Corinthian colonies such as Ambracia and Apollonia, the case for this cult at Corcyra remains speculative.[113]

The ascription of a divinity to the Kardaki Temple must remain open (see Section 4.4.2.7.3), but the connection to Apollo Nomios proposed by Dörpfeld and Rhomaios has a certain attraction (Rhomaios 1925: 217; Kanta-Kitsou

---

112. The stone in question is the unfluted base of a small column found reused in a Hellenistic house.

113. A more careful study of the epistyle blocks found at the monastery in 1915 is long overdue, since they belonged to a small Doric building of some kind; see Kanta-Kitsou 2001b: 449 nn. 47–8 and here Section 4.4.2.7.5. One additional Archaic dedication has also been interpreted as another *agyieus* from its shape, but its find-spot within Corcyra is unknown (Six 1894; Jeffery 1990: 234 #12; Kanta-Kitsou 2001b: 451). For doubts about its form, see Rhomaios 1925: 213 n. 1; *IG* IX.1².848 = *IG* IX.1.704. The connection made by Calligas (1968: 313) between Apollo Agyieus and the dedications of sandals and clay feet from the aforementioned sanctuary of Apollo Corcyraios is entirely speculative.

572    THE OXFORD HISTORY OF THE ARCHAIC GREEK WORLD

1996: 105; Kanta-Kitsou 2001b: 450–1; Preka-Alexandri 2010: 33, 111; Andrikou 2017). Apollonius Rhodius (4.1217–19b; cf. *FGrH* 566 F87) recounts a *mythos* about the early history of Corcyra, including a story about Medea having founded altars that still received sacrifices to the Fates and the nymphs in a place sacred to Apollo Nomios. Insofar as an altar located near the Kardaki Temple could be identified with the worship of the nymphs, a cave on the shore immediately below the sanctuary could at least hypothetically have been that dedicated to Medea (Ap. Rhod. 4.1153–4). Given the fact that votive spears like those offered to Apollo Corcyraios were discovered at Kardaki, there are reasons to connect the temple at Kardaki to Apollo. But Asclepius and Poseidon Hippios are viable alternatives, and bronze horse figurines that were also excavated at Kardaki strengthen the case for the latter.[114]

### 4.11.2.  Sanctuary of Hera

The Mon Repos sanctuary (see Section 4.4.2.7.2) has been identified as a Heraion, albeit only with some reservations (Schmidt 1890: 32–46; Calligas 1969: 53–4; Fauber 2002: 145–7; Sapirstein 2012: 32 n. 5). The finds from that sanctuary include Late Geometric votive bronzes that constitute the earliest signs of cult activity in Corcyra. Thucydides (3.79.1; cf. 3.81.2) implies that a Hera temple was located somewhere inside the city (Schmidt 1890: 42–3) and also that her sanctuary was large enough to accommodate no fewer than 400 suppliants who sought refuge there during the *stasis* of the 420s (3.75.5). The cult may have been to Hera Akraia, which is attested epigraphically by a *horos* inscription (*IG* IX.1².4.862 = *IG* IX.1.698) dated to the second half of the fifth century on letter forms:

ὅρϝος hιαρὸς
τᾶς Ἀκρίας

The votives excavated at the site are consistent with a female deity. In particular, a common type of miniature kalathos is similar to offerings to Hera at Perachora (Dontas 1966b: 320; Calligas 1969: 53–4). Many of the ceramic objects appear to have been made at the nearby Figareto workshop (see Section 4.4.2.6), and there is a good deal of overlap with the types of female figurines dedicated elsewhere

---

114. Schmidt (1890: 30–1) thought of a healing god because of the adjacent spring, but worship of Asclepius probably did not begin in this area until later. The proximity to the sea, and the past identification of the structure inside the temple as supporting two statues of divinities— rather than as an *eschara*, as is supported by more recent excavation (see Section 4.4.2.7.3)— also suggests the possibility of Poseidon next to Amphitrite (Calligas 1969: 53, cf. 55–8).

Corcyra

in Corcyra (Preka-Alexandri 2016: 225–8), and so the lack of representations of Artemis at Mon Repos is significant. Since it can be ruled out as an Artemision, the siting of the Mon Repos sanctuary on a prominence above the eastern plateau, the considerable area enclosed by its temenos walls, and its obvious cultic significance—with Corcyra's oldest bronze votives and first monumental temple— all argue for its identification as the site of Thucydides' intramural Heraion.

Such an identification is nonetheless uncertain. Most of the excavated Archaic finds from Mon Repos were jumbled up together in late fifth-century destruction debris among offerings suitable for other deities, including Aphrodite and Hermes, which were plausibly interpreted by the excavators as secondary cults within the temenos (Dontas 1966b: 320). The *horos* inscription was discovered near the convent of Agia Euphemia, which is just east of the ancient agora and a good 550 m north of the sanctuary. Since it would need to have been carried there after the site's abandonment, it hardly can be treated as evidence linking Hera specifically to the Mon Repos sanctuary.[115]

Another hypothesis is that the *horos* demarcated an as-yet-unexcavated sanctuary near the convent, as proposed already by Schmidt (1890: 34–6, 40–6; see also Bürchner 1922: 1411–12; Rhomaios 1925: 214–15; Kanta-Kitsou 2001b: 450 n. 51; Fauber 2002: 146). Situating the sanctuary at the harbor would make more sense of Thucydides' statement that the suppliants were transported ἐς τὴν πρὸ τοῦ Ἡραίου νῆσον (3.75.5). The only possible location for that "island" appears to be the rocky prominence occupied by the Palaio Frourio (in Corfu Town), which at least today is separated from the rest of Corfu by a narrow channel and which is located on the north side of the Garitsa bay and hence opposite (i.e., "in front of") the Alcinous harbor. A Heraion on the harbor not only fits Thucydides' description but also resembles the siting of the Geometric-period temple of Hera Akraia at the edge of the harbor in Perachora in the Corinthia. Still, the "island" is also in view of the hilltop sanctuary at Mon Repos, and Thucydides' account is concerned more with the transport of prisoners back and forth between it and the Heraion than with the precise location of either topos.[116]

---

115. Early Archaic blocks, now embedded as *spolia* in the walls of the Church of Jason and Sosipatros, were probably taken from the Artemis or Mon Repos sanctuaries, which are no less than 600 m from the church.

116. We should also note the testimony of Diodorus Siculus (13.48.6) that the Athenian general Conon left his troops inside the *polis* and then sailed somewhere else and anchored his ships near a temenos of Hera. While this is not incompatible with the Mon Repos site, again it would make more sense if the troops had been positioned in the western part of the city near the Hyllaic harbor, and then the ships sailed around the Kanoni peninsula to anchor near a Heraion at the Alcinous harbor; see Schmidt 1890: 43–5.

## 574 THE OXFORD HISTORY OF THE ARCHAIC GREEK WORLD

In sum, the evidence at present favors the identification of a single sanctuary for Hera Akraia at Mon Repos, established with the *apoikia*, but future archaeological findings could easily change this picture. Alternatively, we could imagine from the literary and epigraphic indications that a large Hera sanctuary has been concealed by the densely spaced modern buildings near the ancient agora. In that case, the Mon Repos temple might have belonged to another female deity, such as Aphrodite or Demeter.

### 4.11.3. Other Deities at Corcyra

A plausible connection has been made between the Dionysus pediment, the statue of the same deity found nearby, and the Sanctuary of Dionysus mentioned by Thucydides (3.81.5), who indicates that that sanctuary had an enclosed temple (see Section 4.4.2.7.4). However, not only are built temples for Dionysus relatively uncommon in Archaic sanctuaries, but the depiction of a symposium and vessels for the consumption of wine on its pediment is also essentially unparalleled in Greek architectural sculpture. Both should be viewed in light of Corcyra's reputation for viticulture and export of wine (see Section 4.8.2).

Some temples or sanctuaries attested in later epigraphic or literary evidence from Corcyra could well have earlier origins. Most appear only in epigraphic sources, and the associated cult sites have not been located. These include cults of the Dioscuri (Thuc. 3.75.3),[117] Aphrodite (*IG* IX.1².4.859–60; these two inscriptions being of Roman and unknown dates, respectively), Hermes and Heracles (*IG* IX.1².4.806, 855; both of which inscriptions are Hellenistic), and Zeus Hypsistos (*IG* IX.1².4.855; that inscription being of late Hellenistic date; see also Schwabl 1927: 336; Schwabl, Simon, Schindler et al. 1978: 1477). Sacred groves are also mentioned by Thucydides (3.70.4), one to Zeus and the other to Alcinous, in which it was possible to cultivate vines. The grove to Alcinous, in which the mythical king of the Phaeacians was apparently worshipped as a hero, was located in the northern harbor near the agora (see Section 4.4.2.7.6).

We naturally should assume that additional gods and heroes were worshipped besides those named in our textual sources. For example, given the maritime significance of the island, Poseidon is a plausible attribution for the seaward-oriented Kardaki Temple, if that temple did not instead belong to Apollo Nomios (see Section 4.4.2.7.3). One should also consider the cultic honors of the *heros ktistēs*,

---

117. A tombstone from the fourth century, found near the Tomb of Menecrates, that mentions the Dioscuri could be connected to this cult, although admittedly, it could also have been moved there from a different location (*IG* IX.1².4.883: II).

Chersikrates. His special recognition is suggested by the existence of a group of his descendants, the Chersikratidai, who performed certain cult functions as attested in a second-century inscription (*IG* IX.1².4.1140).

## 4.12.  Cultural History

The earliest extant inscriptions from Corfu, dated to the second half of the seventh century, show that the Corcyraeans were using the Corinthian alphabet by that point in time, which the first wave of settlers doubtless brought with them (Jeffery 1990: 232–4). Although Corcyra is mentioned often in Greek literature, especially in relation to the Phaeacians and to Homeric Scheria, no prominent authors in poetry, historiography, and other genres are attested to have been born on the island.

Thus, in order to reconstruct a cultural and artistic profile of Corcyra, we must rely on our assessment of its surviving art and architecture, as well as what we have been able to reconstruct of its socio-political history. The prosperity and ambitions of Archaic Corcyra are apparent in the erection of significant monuments at home and abroad. It is notable that much of Corcyra's architecture and sculpture is datable to the second and third quarters of the sixth century, when the polity became independent from Corinth after a period of being ruled by Cypselid tyrants (see Section 4.7.4). However, since many other Greek centers began investing in monumental architecture and sculpture during the sixth century, we should not press this point too far. Furthermore, the Corcyraeans had already begun to develop their own distinctive material culture by the latter half of the seventh century. The discussion that follows revisits and builds upon a selection of the archaeological evidence already surveyed in Section 4.4.

### 4.12.1.  Corcyraean *Technai* and Innovation

Until recently, scholars tended to take the position that much of the sculpture and architecture found in the Corinthian colonies, including Corcyra, was the work of traveling artisans who resided in the metropolis, a view crystallized in Humfrey Payne's monumental 1931 study of Corinth's Archaic pottery and sculpture, *Necrocorinthia*. This assumption has jaundiced our view of Corcyra's place within the history of early Greek art and technology, such that its major works were characterized as Corinthian achievements.[118]

118. For example, the section on sculpture is peppered with comments such as "[t]he Corfu sculptures are, it is true, recognized as Corinthian" (Payne 1931: 232). The series of antefixes

576    THE OXFORD HISTORY OF THE ARCHAIC GREEK WORLD

Since the 1990s, however, after regional-systems models had come into vogue, many reappraisals of Corcyraean art began to appear that recognized the possibility that Corcyra was home to its own independent schools of artisans or at least recruited individuals active within the colonies around the Ionian Sea (e.g., Barletta 2001; Winter 1993: 110–12, 121–2, 299–301, 311; Bookidis 1995: 236–7; Kanta-Kitsou 1996: 94–5; Dontas 1997).[119] These craftspeople appear to have drawn from a diverse array of sources, many outside the Peloponnese, and developed their own recognizable styles. Given the literary evidence for the fractious relationship between Corcyra and its metropolis from an early date (see Section 4.7), it is perhaps unsurprising that Corinth would have had little direct impact on the material culture of its colony (Morgan 1998: 300).

We can already perceive signs of an independent and creative Corcyraean artistic school in the island's earliest surviving monumental sculpture, the Lion of Menecrates from the final quarter of the seventh century (see Section 4.4.6). The lion is now recognized as a stylistic palimpsest drawing from various Near Eastern sculptural prototypes as well as modeled and painted Greek examples in terracotta, and it shares as much in common with Ionian as with Corinthian examples (see Figure 4.12) (Gabelmann 1965: 40, 44; Ridgway 1977: 154; Dontas 1997: 134–5, 168–9). The form of the Menecrates lion is generally relatable to the sculpted felines or lion heads depicted on waterspouts and on the feet of perirrhantēria, which developed over the course of the seventh century (Gabelmann 1965: 22–38; Mertens-Horn 1988: 16–17). However, the Menecrates lion was precocious at its time within the Greek world in its employment as an apotropaic guardian of a tomb. Together with two other fragmentary sculpted lions from the Corcyra necropolis and a similar tomb marker from Apollonia dated to the middle of the sixth century, we can perceive the development of a local custom for demarcating graves (von Hesberg, Fiedler, and Toci 2018: 134–7). The long-lived tradition of grave lions would not emerge farther afield until

decorated with human heads from the decades around 600 found in Corcyra (Mon Repos), Kalydon, and Thermum, are treated without reservation as pure Corinthian works, and, after dismissing some initial doubts, all of Corcyra's pedimental sculpture from the sixth century is taken to be Corinthian (Payne 1931: 234–5, 39–44). Architectural decoration is similarly treated (Payne 1931: 250–5). Rodenwaldt (1939: 138, 153–8, 169–76, 191, 195–8) followed suit in his characterization of both the Artemis temple pediments and the Lion of Menecrates, although he allowed that the work could be from a Peloponnesian rather than just a Corinthian school.

119. Brunilde Ridgway (1977: 154, 191–2) deserves special recognition for her avant-garde characterization of Corcyra's sculpture as independent from Corinth. Likewise, locally made fine wares that are "Corinthianizing" but still distinguishable from the pottery made in Corinth itself have been recognized since the 1960s; see Section 4.4.5.

the latter half of the following century, perhaps independently, in Attic and other Greek sites (Mertens-Horn 1986: 18–28; Grossman 2013: 26–7).

The Mon Repos sanctuaries produced several notable finds, especially the head of a nearly life-size marble *kouros* from the middle of the sixth century, as well as a smaller head in limestone from late in the century, both of which exhibit affinities with Ionian and Attic sculpture (Calligas 1968: 308; Kanta-Kitsou 1996: 86–7 table 2; Dontas 1997: 55–8, 62–9, 73–4).[120] The marble *kouros* of c. 530 excavated near the Panagia Kassopitra Monastery in the southern part of the Kanoni peninsula has been identified as the work of a Corinthian sculptor under Parian influence, but that conclusion is based largely on a hypothesis that the island of Corfu, lacking access to marble, could not have developed local expertise in carving this material (Kanta-Kitsou 1996: 94–101).[121]

The architecture and sculpture adorning the temple at Mon Repos (see Section 4.4.2.7.2), which should be placed slightly later than the Menecrates lion but still within the seventh century, can be more emphatically severed from any direct dependency on Peloponnesian models. Its terracotta roof is the best-preserved example of the "Northwest Greek" roofing type (see Figure 4.8)—an Archaic system, attested in many sanctuaries in Aetolia and Illyria, that is distinguished by not only its massive plain tiles but also its elaborately molded and flamboyantly painted decoration (Schleif, Rhomaios, and Klaffenbach 1940: 145–62; Winter 1993: 110–33; Sapirstein 2016b: 54–5). At the perimeter of the roof, relief antefixes decorated with female heads or *gorgoneia* alternate with eaves geison tiles bearing lion head waterspouts, whose daring projection and modeling almost fully in the round demonstrate the virtuoso skill of Corcyraean coroplasts (Sapirstein 2012: 72–5; Sapirstein 2016b: 54–7). The 150-kg lion head waterspouts, notably, are a fusion of separately formed elements: an eaves pan tile whose outside face supports a vertical plaque, from which projects a 40-cm-tall mane and face of a lion molded almost fully in the round (Sapirstein 2012: 43–6). A complex series of struts added behind both held the pan and plaque together and funneled rainwater from the roof behind through the lion's gaping jaws. These eaves pan tiles also doubled as a terracotta geison, and their painted soffits show that the piece projected by 30 cm beyond the wall below, such that more than half its mass was unsupported.

120. Calligas connects this *kouros* with the story of the ransom and return of Corcyraean youths by the Samians (see Section 4.7.4); however, the marble is possibly Naxian (Kanta-Kitsou 1996: 86–7 n. 44).

121. As Kanta-Kitsou (1996: 100) admits, much of the island's statuary was plundered by the Romans, and in later times, most of the stone from Corcyra's sanctuaries was aggressively pillaged by stone looters.

The temple at Mon Repos is notable for a list of tangible "firsts" in the realm of Greek architecture. As far as technology, the scale of the molds for its terracottas is not attested elsewhere in the Greek world until several decades later (Sapirstein 2012: 58–60). Furthermore, the artisans employed a system of layered ceramic pastes, using coarsely tempered clay on the interior to provide strength, and lined visible surfaces with fine clay that could be precisely modeled and brightly painted—a sophisticated coroplastic technique not attested in Corinthian terracotta sculpture until decades after the Mon Repos project. The lion head waterspouts are not just by far the most ambitious molded terracottas of their era, but they are also one of the earliest, if not the earliest, extant examples of their kind. Evidently, the adaptation of a feline head to the gable as a waterspout was invented by Northwest Greek artisans, possibly Corcyraeans, under Etruscan influence.[122] This idea was soon disseminated throughout the Greek world and would continue as a mainstay through the Hellenistic period (Mertens-Horn 1988: 16–18, 28–52; Hübner 2018).

Since roofs in the northern Peloponnese had previously been hipped (Sapirstein 2016b: 47–50), the Mon Repos design also represents an important first step toward the introduction of the tympanum, through its termination at the front and back in a triangular, pediment-like space (Sapirstein 2012: 62–3, 70–1, 76).[123] At the same time, the terracotta rosettes, female and lion heads, and *gorgoneia* attached to plaques up to 60 cm tall draw attention to the borders of this space rather than its interior, indicating that a fully conceived Doric pediment had yet to emerge. A stone lower leg of a warrior might have belonged to sculpture displayed inside this triangular frame, which would make it the first surviving pedimental statuary, although other reconstructions are possible (Dontas 1976: 128–9 fig. 8; Ridgway 1977: 191). Which of the assortment of Doric capitals and other stone members from the destruction debris belong to this early temple has yet to be determined, but at least one element—a corner triglyph with

---

122. The question of where and by whom feline head waterspouts were invented cannot be resolved satisfactorily at present, since it depends on the relative sequence of at least two other early roofs from Thermum and Poggio Civitate (Murlo), both of which are typically dated a decade or two before that of Mon Repos (Winter 1993: 311; Winter 2009: 77–80, 573–4, 77 (Murlo); Sapirstein 2012: 75–6, nn. 185, 91; Sapirstein 2016b: 55). Furthermore, Hübner (2018: 39–45, with additional bibliography) has recently argued for a substantial downdating of the Thermum roof, which might then postdate the temple at Corcyra. In any case, the Mon Repos and Thermum roofs share so many decorative and technical features in common that some of the same individuals probably worked on both projects. The Murlo roof is stylistically and technically quite unlike the two Greek examples, and there is additional ambiguity about the directions of influence and innovation (Winter 2002).

123. The roof of the temple at Mon Repos cannot have been hipped, as had previously been assumed based on a misunderstanding of fragments from the eaves geison tiles.

typologically early features—is plausibly associated with the cella or altar of the temple (Schleif, Rhomaios, and Klaffenbach 1940: 75–6; Barletta 2001: 69, 178–9 n. 43; Wilson Jones 2014: 55, 82–3). While its exact date and assignment are uncertain, it must be among the first surviving stone triglyphs.

Moving into the sixth century, the Artemis temple at Corcyra (see Section 4.4.2.7.1) is best known for its sculpture. Despite some uncertainty, one of the oldest surviving relief metopes, depicting part of a warrior, is plausibly restored in the Doric frieze above the peristyle (Ridgway 1977: 228–31; Barletta 2001: 64–7 n. 127; Marconi 2007: 6, 186). But the pediments were its major accomplishment. Within at most a few decades, the Corcyraeans had moved from the experimental triangular space witnessed in the terracotta roof of the temple at Mon Repos to what would become the canonical frame in stone Doric temple architecture for the display of sculpture (see Figures 4.5–4.7). Along with Athens and Sicily, Corcyra was evidently a leader in the articulation of a pediment decorated with narrative reliefs (Ridgway 1977: 191–3; Bookidis 1995: 236–9; Marconi 2007: 10–14; Sapirstein 2012: 76), a form to which Corinth appears to have contributed relatively little despite its reputation conveyed by the ancient literary sources.[124] Attempts to attribute the style of the pediment to a particular school of sculpture have been inconclusive, because it is the earliest well-preserved Greek work at this position and scale and because its elements resonate with the arts of not only the northern Peloponnese but also farther afield.[125] We might attribute the workmanship to a foreign master recruited from the mainland, perhaps Corinth, but the arguments for local or western artisans are no less compelling.[126]

---

124. See, for example, Pindar *Olympian* 13.21; cf. Pliny *Natural History* 35.5, 35.43, on early travels of its artisans. Admittedly, these sources are quite limited in their scope, and Corinth's reputation for architecture has been amplified by the aforementioned tendency in the scholarship to attribute to its artisans the major extant works from its former colonies. In order to reconcile the literary attributions of the sculpted pediment to Corinth with the lack of material evidence from the northeastern Peloponnese itself, it has been proposed that the Bacchiads, while in exile from Corinth during the Cypselid tyranny, brought Corinthian artisans with them and commissioned several key monuments in Sicily and Rome (Mertens-Horn 1995; Winter 2002; cf. Payne 1931: 250 n. 3).

125. The first pedimental sculpture from the Athenian acropolis belongs within a generation of the Artemision, but it is not from the same school; see Dontas 1997: 102–10; Marconi 2007: 18–20, with additional references.

126. For more recent arguments in support of a Peloponnesian or Corinthian school, see Weber 2007: 17–21; Cigaina 2015: 47–8. Supporting a local or western school are Mertens-Horn 1995: 269; Dontas 1997: 97–117. Further complicating matters is that the pediment influenced later works in the region. For example, the peculiar moon-shaped head of its leopanthers appears to have been directly copied on a mid-sixth-century grave lion from Apollonia (von Hesberg, Fiedler, and Toci 2018: 134–6).

Indeed, the architecture of the Artemision exhibits many features indicating that its designers looked west for inspiration, altogether bypassing the mainland (Mertens 2006: 110, 32–3). The widely flaring Doric capitals from the peristyle and a series of early Corcyraean freestanding votive columns have a leaf molding at the transition between the shaft and the base of the echinus, a distinctive element of the "Ionian Sea Style" as characterized by Barbara Barletta (1990: 45–52; 2001: 83; also see Dontas 1997: 118; Wilson Jones 2014: 82, 117). At the eaves on both the flanking and raking cornices, the terracotta roof has a unique format combining a vertical sima with hanging geison revetment plaques, the faces of which were decorated with a wild variety of patterns modeled in low relief and brightly painted with alternating colors; along the flanks, rainwater was emitted through tubular spouts at the base of the vertical sima (see Figure 4.14) (Schleif, Rhomaios, and Klaffenbach 1940: 97–124). The profile, decorations, and spouts are all features of western, and specifically Sicilian, terracotta roofs, unparalleled anywhere in the Greek mainland (Ridgway 1977: 191; Wikander 1990; Winter

**FIGURE 4.14.** Terracotta sima and geison revetment from the Temple of Artemis; c. 580; height 80.5 cm. Archaeological Museum of Corfu. Photo by Philip Sapirstein.

1993: 299–300; Mertens 2006: 131). Yet the fusion of sima with geison revetment, the relief decoration, and the clay indicate local manufacture by artisans who were inspired by but not rigidly beholden to Sicilian precursors.[127] The framing of the Gorgon's head at the apex of the pediment also recalls the disembodied terracotta *gorgoneia* that decorated the pedimental space of many Sicilian temples or, as found more widely between the Greek northwest and Etruscan Italy, capped the terminal ridge tile and overhung the pediment (Ridgway 1977: 192–3, 220; Kästner 1990; Danner 2000; Marconi 2007: 49–50, 58, 214–18).

On the basis of these stylistic and technical criteria, the construction of the Temple of Artemis seems more likely to have begun *after* the end of direct Corinthian rule in 587/6 than before this date (see Section 4.4.2.7.1). In either case, unless the construction proceeded at exceptional speed, it was probably not completed until the time of Corcyra's independence. As a result, we might conclude that this magnificent example of Archaic architecture and sculpture is not the result of a tyrannical Corinthian construction policy but rather a paradigm of the representation of the *polis* itself, a distinctive sign of its self-consciousness and its wealth. We will return to the potential religious, societal, and political statements discernible from the pediment of the Artemision after we finish this review of Corcyraean artistic production.

The Corcyraeans commissioned at least two more smaller limestone temples late in the sixth century, those at Kardaki and the Dionysus sanctuary, and perhaps a third can be construed on the basis of recut entablature blocks from the cloister of Panagia Kassopitra (see Section 4.4.2.7.5). The unusual proportions and noncanonical Doric entablature of the Kardaki Temple suggest that it was probably the work of local builders. The architrave blocks are articulated with a taenia lacking regulae, indicating that the usual triglyph-metope frieze was omitted.[128]

---

127. The design was not entirely successful, possibly due to the tendency for local clays to lose their paint after exposure to the elements. During the last quarter of the sixth century, the terracotta simas on the Artemis temple appear to have been replaced with a new design executed in Parian marble (Schleif, Rhomaios, and Klaffenbach 1940: 38–43, 54, 126). The molding of the new sima is very close to that on the geison of the Kardaki Temple, which may suggest local workmanship (Dinsmoor Jr. 1973: 171–2). The marble sima may have been carved locally. Its moldings are very close to those carved on the geison blocks of the Kardaki Temple. But it is equally possible that the Kardaki geison was a local copy in limestone of an imported marble sima.

128. This conclusion is strengthened by the total absence of such blocks, even though the geison course is well represented at the site, and the match between the lever pries in the architrave and the length of the geison blocks (Dinsmoor Jr. 1973: 169–71). Hernandez (2017: 233–6) discusses the omission of the triglyph-metope frieze as a Corcyraean trait, although the early triglyphs from Mon Repos, the Artemis temple, and its altar show that the Corcyraeans had played an important role in the development of the normative Doric frieze not long before

## 4.12.2. Material Culture and Identity

Christos Spanodimos (2017) has recently highlighted the remarkable disparity between the funerary practices witnessed in Corcyra's main necropolis and those of its metropolis (Spanodimos 2017). While burials in Corinth during the Archaic period were almost exclusively inhumations, roughly 30% of the Corcyraean graves are cremations, which is among the highest ratios attested in the western colonies (Spanodimos 2017: 246–8, 253).[129] Roughly 90% of the Corinthian burials known from the eighth century were interred in stone sarcophagi, a practice adopted in some of its dependencies, including Ambracia (Tzortzatou and Fatsiou 2009: 49; Spanodimos 2017: 247–8). In contrast, fewer than 10% of the Archaic burials from the Soter hill necropolis were placed in sarcophagi, which are instead dominated numerically by pithos tombs (see Section 4.4.6 and Spanodimos 2017: 251–2).[130]

Also unlike Corinth, many of the tombs in Corcyra have above-ground elements, some with stone walls enclosing family plots, and the most ostentatious group of tombs, from near the Tomb of Menecrates, feature inscribed epitaphs and sculpture (Morgan 1998: 300–1; Spanodimos 2017: 248–9). The Tomb of Menecrates is unlike any other grave in Corcyra itself or in the contemporary Greek mainland (see Figure 4.10), but it does recall the Bronze Age tumulus tradition that persisted as late as the Hellenistic era in Epirus and southern Illyria (Oikonomidis, Papayiannis, and Tsonos 2011; von Hesberg, Fiedler, and

---

the time of the Kardaki Temple (Hernandez 2017: 233–6). The Kardaki architrave is comparable to the block with an Archaic relief from Bouthrotos, which is also plausibly attributed to Corcyraean artisans; see Section 4.2.7.3.

129. By comparison, the Corinthian colony of Syracuse has just 8% cremations, whereas the ratios are c. 25% and 50% at Megara Hyblaea and Gela, respectively. On the diversity of burial practices in the western colonies, see also Osborne 2009: 92.

130. Pithos burials are, of course, not unknown in the Greek world (examples are found in Archaic cemeteries in Achaea, Argos, and Macedonia), but most take the form of smaller vessels laid on their sides, not set at a vertical position into a pit such that the lip is at ground level. The immediate inspiration of the format at Corcyra might have been agricultural pithos installations.

Toci 2018: 137). However, its masonry more closely resembles the exteriors of contemporary Etruscan tumuli, especially those of Cerveteri (Prayon 1975: 14–31, 81–5; cf. Spanodimos 2017: 249 n. 27). In sum, Corcyra's necropolis has an eclectic range of grave types which may imply that its inhabitants had diverse origins, whereas its distinctive pithos burials may represent a local form developed between the late seventh and sixth centuries along with a more coherent Corcyraean identity.

In this light, we return to the iconography and potential meanings embedded in the west pediment of the Artemis temple, the most prominent and complex work of art to have survived from Corcyra (see Figures 4.5–4.7). As we have seen (see Section 4.4.2.7.1), the center of that pediment features a Gorgon flanked by her offspring Pegasus to the viewer's left and Chrysaor (or, less likely, Perseus) on the other side, followed by opposing pairs (moving out toward the edges) of leopanthers, two-person groups, and fallen warriors. The identification of the individuals represented in the two-figure groups remains a subject of discussion, though one figure, a beardless male shown wielding a thunderbolt, is almost certain to be Zeus. A juxtaposition of the destruction of Troy (left) with a Titanomachy (right) (Marconi 2007: 12–13; Cigaina 2015: 44–6) or two episodes from the Titanomachy (Antonetti 2006: 58–61) are the most likely of the proposed solutions.[131]

The majority of the composition is occupied by the enormous Gorgon and leopanthers; those three sculptures replace a direct depiction of Artemis herself with apotropaic guardians, facing out in order to engage the viewer directly and inspire awe and terror (Stucchi 1981: 47–52; Marconi 2007: 215–20; Cigaina 2015: 43). On this level, the beasts adorning the Artemis temple operate similarly to the lion heads and *gorgoneia* projecting from the terracotta roof for Hera at Mon Repos, exceeding them primarily through their even grander scale. But with the ornamental focus directed to the interior of the tympanum, the designers of the Artemision open up rich new possibilities for a sophisticated communicative program, one that allows certain themes to emerge through the assembly of narrative groups together within a unified space.

The pediment may be understood as a statement about the establishment of divine order, possibly presenting the viewer with contrasting examples of

---

131. Mertens-Horn (1995: 266–8), however, excluded the Titans because of their immortality, whereas the figures at the corners of the pediment are dying. She identifies the seated figure at the left as a female, who would then be Hera in her bedchamber under assault by the giant Porphyrion; cf. Apollodorus 1.6.2 and Weber 2007: 15. The Gigantomachy is generally rejected because Zeus has no beard, which should mean that he had not yet become king of the Olympian gods (Marconi 2007: 12; Cigaina 2015: 64–8).

584    THE OXFORD HISTORY OF THE ARCHAIC GREEK WORLD

glorious deeds against sacrilege (as in Marconi 2007: 12–13), or other equally edifying messages if we recognize different narratives from the groups at the wings (e.g., Stucchi 1981: 59–86; Sciarma 2009). Others have argued the temple was an overtly political statement, reading from its mytho-historical elements an assertion of Corinthian power at the behest of Periander (Marconi 2007: 13; Cigaina 2015), or else the patronage of the exiled Bacchiads living in Corcyra (Mertens-Horn 1995: 259–76). Such interpretations emphasize the inclusion of Pegasus, who is certainly an important early symbol of Corinth, but rest on shakier grounds, given the many indications that the temple project postdated the period of direct Corinthian rule over Corcyra.[132] Avoiding the temptation of pressing hypothetical political connotations further than the evidence can bear, another approach treats the pediment as a religious document created at an early moment during the gradual synthesis of Corcyra's narratives about its own mythical origins (as in Antonetti 2006; Antonetti 2007: 104). In this reading, the pediment's unique combination of the iconic Medusa with her off-spring, flanked by narrative episodes drawn from the Titanomachy, had been carefully selected to emphasize not so much its relationship with Corinth but rather the mythical genealogies specifically connected to the island of Corfu, Epirus, and Illyria. Corcyra's topographical pedigree would thus have resonated with contemporary epic, in particular the *Theogony*, as well as literary themes preserved in later texts.

Before closing, we should add that Corcyra also projected its image through patronage outside its immediate territory, flying its flag, as it were, in Panhellenic sanctuaries. First, a treasury at Delphi is identifiable as Corcyraean through its distinctive terracotta roof, which is essentially a miniaturized version of the terracottas from the Artemis temple (Schleif, Rhomaios, and Klaffenbach 1940: 106; Winter 1993: 300–1; Jacquemin 1999: 64, 142 A.233, 320 #123). The architectural style of this building would have struck contemporary visitors to Delphi as ostentatiously *not* Corinthian, which was the dominant roofing type in the Archaic sanctuary. Second, reportedly in gratitude to Poseidon for sending a bull which guided them to a tremendous tuna catch, the Corcyraeans dedicated a tenth of the proceeds in the form of two bronze statues of bulls, one in Delphi and the other in Olympia, as early as the beginning of the fifth

---

132. As discussed in Section 4.7.1, Corcyraean mythico-historical narratives separate their origins from Corinth in favor of the Phaeacians. If the pediment were indeed planned after the departure of the end of direct Corinthian rule, then the inclusion of Pegasus might be attributed to factions at Corcyra who were still sympathetic to Corinth or the fact that the stories of the mythoi connecting the Phaeacians and the Corcyraeans had yet to develop fully at that point in time, both of which seem likely given that the political rupture with the metropolis had just occurred. See Antonetti 2006: 57–8.

century (Paus. 5.27.9, 10.9.3–4; see Section 4.8.1 for further discussion of fishing in Corcyra).[133]

The evidence reviewed here reiterates Morgan's (1998: 301) conclusions that "far from simply echoing Corinthian styles, Archaic Corfiote architecture and sculpture shows a very individual mixture of influences which may reflect an aristocracy casting widely for ideas to express its own status and identity, individually and collectively." We may now add that the Corcyraeans did more than simply combine an eclectic array of external styles but also introduced their fair share of new decorative forms and technologies to the developing monumental arts of Greece. Corfu's geographical position between West and East, its central position in maritime trade, and its complex identity as both a free-spirited *polis* and a colony of Corinth placed it in an unparalleled position to engage with and further develop the diverse ideas and styles it encountered from its wide network of contacts.

## 4.13. Conclusion

Soon after the founding of Corcyra, we see a social and political community that spread its wings independently and effectively developed the resources of the island as well as those of the opposite coast. In the course of conflicts with the mother city, which occurred not least because of the growing importance of the *apoikia*, the Corcyraeans became dependent on Corinth as the latter built a maritime empire, especially in western Greece, under the tyrant Cypselus and his descendants, the Cypselids. But after the death of Periander, the Corcyraeans were able to free themselves and create their own sphere of influence in complete independence and with great self-confidence while they traced themselves back to the Homeric Phaeacians. They controlled and secured the sea routes between Greece and Italy so that their harbors were unavoidable, and they increased their revenues through expanded trade in all directions.

In this way, the Corcyraeans enjoyed a great degree of independence and, as a neutral power, did not let themselves be dragged into the political conflicts of the world of the Greek *poleis*. With respect to the cultural accomplishments of the Corcyraeans and their contributions to the visual arts and literature, we find several impressive testimonia, especially in the realm of architectural

---

133. The statue in Delphi, which is conventionally dated somewhere in the first half of the fifth century, stood at the beginning of the Sacred Way (Jacquemin 1999: 64–5, 320 #122; Intrieri 2010: 192–3). Pausanias (5.27.9) implies that the bull at Olympia was part of a pair dedicated jointly with Eretria, both cast by Philesios of Eretria (Cigaina 2015: 57–62).

sculpture. Selene Psoma (2015: 145) has with much justification referred to the "Corcyraean miracle"—a phenomenon that was by no means limited to the arts.

Much also has been lost. Overall, one has the impression that the strengths of the Corcyraeans were in the practical sphere of economics and politics, as their artistic innovations would not continue long after the sixth century. The wealth of Archaic material culture between the latter half of the seventh and the sixth centuries was unmatched in any later period of Corcyra's history, and other Greek centers took the lead in *technai* as elaborate dedications in Corcyra abated. Virtually no evidence of new monumental dedications has survived from after the late Classical period, when the Corcyraeans seem to have allowed their Archaic sanctuaries to fall gradually into disrepair and ruin. In any case, at the beginning of the Persians' great attack on Greece in 480, they were a strong, stable, and proud power, uncontested but also rather restrained and neutral: they armed and were present with the great fleet, not in the battle of Salamis but at a safe distance, powerful yet reserved.

## Guide to Further Reading

A "classical account," based on the written sources and the limited archaeological knowledge of the time but still valuable, is Schmidt's *Korkyraeische Studien* (1890). Psoma's monograph published in 2022 provides a more up-to-date and thorough study of Corcyra's history. General historical works representative of the current state of research include Antonelli (2000) and Antonetti and Cavalli (2015). An instructive early examination of the epigraphic and archaeological finds is Rhomaios (1925). Those seeking a comprehensive and up-to-date review of the island's history from an archaeological perspective should begin with Preka-Alexandri's guide published by the Greek Ministry of Culture (2010); a brief but very informative summary in English is Metallinou (2010). On the Corinthian background to the island, see in particular Salmon (1984) and Stickler (2010). Monumental architecture and sculpture from Corcyra are approached from diverse perspectives in Barletta (1990); Dontas (1997); Marconi (2007); and Sapirstein (2012). Kourkoumélis and Démesticha (1997) remains the most important source for the ceramic workshop at Figareto. For recent excavations and study of the extensive necropoleis, see Spanodimos (2017); for the harbors, see Baika (2013) and Finkler, Fischer, Baika, et al. 2017.

## Gazetteer

| Name | Figure/Map # | Grid Designation |
| --- | --- | --- |
| Achaea | Map 4.2 | F/G3–4 |
| Acharavi | Map 4.1 | B2 |
| Adriatic Sea | Map 4.2 | B/C/D1–2 |
| Aegina | Map 4.2 | G4 |
| Aetolia | Map 4.2 | F3 |
| Agia Euphemia Convent | Figure 4.3 | D2 |
| Agioi Apostoloi Chapel, Corfu Town | Figure 4.2 | C3 |
| Agioi Deka | Map 4.1 | C3 |
| Agioi Theodoroi Monastery, Corfu Town | Figure 4.3 | C3 |
| Agios Athanasios Church, Corfu Town | Figure 4.3 | D2 |
| Agora, Corfu Town | Figure 4.2 | C4 |
| | Figure 4.3 | C2 |
| Airport, Corfu town | Figure 4.1 | B/C5 |
| | Figure 4.2 | B/C4 |
| | Figure 4.3 | A/B2 |
| Alcinous harbor, Corfu Town | Figure 4.1 | D4 |
| | Figure 4.2 | C3 |
| | Figure 4.3 | C/D2 |
| Aleuki | Map 4.1 | C/D4 |
| Almyros beach | Map 4.1 | B2 |
| Ambracia | Map 4.2 | inset |
| Ambracian Gulf | Map 4.2 | inset |
| Anactorium | Map 4.2 | inset |
| Analipsis Chapel, Corfu Town | Figure 4.3 | D4 |
| Analipsis hill, Corfu Town | Figure 4.1 | D6/7 |
| | Figure 4.2 | C/D4–5 |
| | Figure 4.3 | D4–5 |
| Aphiona | 4.1 | inset |
| Aphiona peninsula | Map 4.1 | inset |
| Aphra | Map 4.1 | C3 |
| Apollonia | Map 4.2 | E2 |

588 THE OXFORD HISTORY OF THE ARCHAIC GREEK WORLD

| Name | Figure/Map # | Grid Designation |
|---|---|---|
| Apulia | Map 4.2 | D/E2 |
| Aratthos river | Map 4.2 | inset |
| Argos | Map 4.2 | G4 |
| Athens | Map 4.2 | G4 |
| Bay of Garitsa | Figure 4.1 | C1 |
| | Figure 4.2 | D3 |
| | Figure 4.3 | D/E1 |
| Bay of Timoni | Map 4.1 | inset |
| Bouthrotos | Map 4.1 | inset |
| Butrint | modern name for site of ancient Bouthrotos | |
| Butrint peninsula | Map 4.1 | inset |
| Calabria | Map 4.2 | D3 |
| Cape Malea | Map 4.2 | G4 |
| Carystus | Map 4.3 | H3 |
| Cassiope | Map 4.1 | C2 |
| Cephallenia | Map 4.2 | F3 |
| Ceramic workshops, Corfu Town | Figure 4.3 | B6 |
| Cerveteri | Map 4.2 | B1/2 |
| Chalikiopoulos lagoon | Figure 4.1 | C6 |
| | Figure 4.2 | B5 |
| | Figure 4.3 | A/B4 |
| Classical Sanctuary (Apollo Pythios?), Corfu Town | Figure 4.3 | C2 |
| Cnidus | Map 4.3 | I4 |
| Corcyra Melaina | Map 4.2 | D1 |
| Corfu (island) | Map 4.2 | inset |
| | Map 4.3 | E3 |
| Corfu Town | Map 4.1 | C3 |
| | Figure 4.1 | C/D2 |
| | Figure 4.2 | C2 |
| Corinth | Map 4.2 | G4 |
| Cyprus Street, Corfu Town | Figure 4.2 | C3 |

| Name | Figure/Map # | Grid Designation |
| --- | --- | --- |
| Daviou Sanctuary | Figure 4.2 | A4 |
| Delphi | Map 4.2 | C3 |
| Dionysus pediment | Figure 4.3 | C5 |
| Dodona | Map 4.2 | inset |
| Dontas site | see Shipseds 2 | |
| Epidamnus | Map 4.2 | E2 |
| Epirus | Map 4.2 | F3 |
| Eretria | Map 4.3 | G3 |
| Ermones | Map 4.1 | B3 |
| Etruria | Map 4.3 | A/B1 |
| Euboea | Map 4.2 | G3 |
| Evelpidi Plot, Corfu Town | Figure 4.3 | C4 |
| Figareto | Figure 4.1 | C6 |
| | Figure 4.2 | C4 |
| | Figure 4.3 | C4 |
| Garitsa | Figure 4.1 | C4 |
| | Figure 4.2 | C3 |
| | Figure 4.3 | C1 |
| Gela | Map 4.2 | C4 |
| Gulf of Corcyra | Map 4.4 | D3 |
| Gulf of Corinth | Map 4.3 | F3 |
| Hyllaic harbor, Corfu Town | Figure 4.1 | C6 |
| | Figure 4.2 | C4 |
| | Figure 4.3 | B/C4 |
| Illyria | Map 4.2 | F2 |
| Ionia | Map 4.3 | I3/4 |
| Ithaca | Map 4.2 | F3 |
| Jason and Sosipatros Church, Corfu Town | Figure 4.3 | D2 |
| Kalydon | Map 4.2 | F3 |
| Kamara | Map 4.1 | C3 |
| Kanalia | Figure 4.1 | A5 |
| | Figure 4.2 | A3/4 |

| Name | Figure/Map # | Grid Designation |
|---|---|---|
| Kanoni | Figure 4.1 | C7 |
| | Figure 4.2 | C5 |
| | Figure 4.3 | C7 |
| Kanoni peninsula | Figure 4.1 | inset |
| | Figure 4.2 | D5 |
| | Figure 4.3 | D5 |
| Kardaki spring, Corfu Town | Figure 4.1 | D5/6 |
| Kardaki Temple, Corfu Town | Figure 4.2 | D4 |
| | Figure 4.3 | D4 |
| Kardamatika | Map 4.1 | C3 |
| Kokotou site | see Shipsheds 1 | |
| Ksamil peninsula | Map 4.1 | inset |
| Laconia | Map 4.3 | G4 |
| Lagoon of Butrint | Map 4.1 | inset |
| Lefkimme | Map 4.1 | D4 |
| Leucas | Map 4.2 | inset |
| Longa | Map 4.2 | F4 |
| Lydia | Map 4.3 | I/J3 |
| Macedonia | Map 4.3 | F/G2–3 |
| Mastilitsa | Map 4.1 | E3 |
| Megara Hyblaea | Map 4.2 | C4 |
| Mese | Map 4.1 | B/C3 |
| Messenia | Map 4.3 | F4 |
| Modern harbor, Corfu Town | Figure 4.2 | B1 |
| Mon Repos Villa, Corfu Town | Figure 4.1 | D5 |
| | Figure 4.2 | D4 |
| | Figure 4.3 | D3 |
| Mon Repos Temple (Hera?), Corfu Town | Figure 4.2 | C4 |
| | Figure 4.3 | D4 |
| Naxos (Sicily) | Map 4.2 | C4 |
| Necropolis, Corfu Town | Figure 4.2 | C3, C4 |
| | Figure 4.3 | B2 |

| Name | Figure/Map # | Grid Designation |
| --- | --- | --- |
| Neo Frourio | Figure 4.1 | C2 |
| | Figure 4.2 | C2 |
| North wall, Corfu Town | Figure 4.2 | C3/4 |
| | Figure 4.3 | C2/B3 |
| Old City, Corfu Town | Figure 4.1 | D2 |
| | Figure 4.2 | C2 |
| Olympia | Map 4.2 | F4 |
| Orikos | Map 4.2 | E2 |
| Oros | Map 4.1 | B2 |
| Othoni | Map 4.2 | E3 |
| Palaio Frourio | Figure 4.1 | D/E2 |
| | Figure 4.2 | D2 |
| Palaiopolis | Figure 4.1 | C/D5 |
| | Figure 4.2 | C/D3 |
| | Figure 4.3 | D2 |
| Palaiopolis Basilica | Figure 4.3 | C3 |
| Panagia Blachernon Monastery islet | Figure 4.2 | C6 |
| Panagia Kassopitra Monastery, Corfu Town | Figure 4.2 | C5 |
| | Figure 4.3 | C6 |
| Panagia Narantzicha Church, Corfu town | Figure 4.3 | B3 |
| Pantokrator | Map 4.1 | C2 |
| Papakostas Plot, Corfu Town | Figure 4.3 | B3 |
| Perachora | Map 4.2 | G3 |
| Perama | Map 4.1 | C3 |
| | Figure 4.1 | B/C8 |
| | Figure 4.2 | B/C6 |
| Platonas Nymphon | Map 4.1 | B2 |
| Poggio Civitate | Map 4.2 | A1 |
| Pontikonisi | Figure 4.2 | C6 |
| Pottery workshops, Corfu Town | Figure 4.3 | C3 |
| Pyrgos Ragiou | Map 4.1 | E3 |
| Rekini | Map 4.1 | B3 |
| Roda | Map 4.1 | B2 |

| Name | Figure/Map # | Grid Designation |
|---|---|---|
| Rome | Map 4.3 | B2 |
| Sanctuary of Apollo Corcyraios, Corfu Town | Figure 4.3 | D4 |
| Shipsheds 1, Corfu Town | Figure 4.3 | D2 |
| Shipsheds 2, Corfu Town | Figure 4.3 | C2 |
| Shipsheds 3, Corfu Town | Figure 4.3 | C5 |
| Shrine (Temple of Alcinous?), Corfu Town | Figure 4.3 | C2 |
| Sicyon | Map 4.2 | G4 |
| Siris | Map 4.2 | D3 |
| Small Artemis Sanctuary, Corfu Town | Figure 4.3 | B6 |
| Soter hill, Corfu Town | Figure 4.1 | C3/4 |
|  | Figure 4.2 | C2 |
| South wall, Corfu Town | Figure 4.2 | C5 |
|  | Figure 4.3 | C/D5 |
| Sparta | Map 4.2 | G4 |
| Split | Map 4.2 | D1 |
| Stratia | Figure 4.1 | C5 |
|  | Figure 4.2 | C4 |
|  | Figure 4.3 | C3 |
| Sybaris | Map 4.3 | D3 |
| Sybota | Map 4.1 | E4 |
| Syracuse | Map 4.2 | C4 |
| Temple of Artemis, Corfu Town | Figure 4.2 | C4 |
|  | Figure 4.3 | C3 |
| Temple of Hera, Corfu Town | see Mon Repos Temple | |
| Thermum | Map 4.2 | F3 |
| Thesprotia | Map 4.2 | inset |
| Thrace | Map 4.3 | G/H2 |
| Tomb of Menecrates | Figure 4.2 | C3 |
| Zacythnus | Map 4.2 | F4 |

*Corcyra* 593

BIBLIOGRAPHY

Agallopoulou, P. 1972. "Ἀνασκαφές, Κέρκυρα. Προάστιον Φιγαρέτο." *Ἀρχαιολογικόν Δελτίον* 27 Β2: 478–9.

—. 1976. "Ἀνασκαφές, Κέρκυρα. Φιγαρέτο." *Ἀρχαιολογικόν Δελτίον* 31 Β2: 230–2.

Amyx, D. A. 1988. *Corinthian Vase-Painting of the Archaic Period*. Berkeley: University of California Press.

Andrikou, D. 2017. "Ο ναός στο Καρδάκι της Κέρκυρας." PhD diss., National and Metsovian Polytechnicum of Athens.

Antonelli, L. 2000. *Κερκυραϊκά: Ricerche su Corcira alto-arcaica tra Ionio e Adriatico*. Rome: Bretschneider.

Antonetti, C. 2006. "Die Rolle des Artemisions von Korkyra in archaischer Zeit: Lokale und überregionale Perspektiven." In *Kult–Politik–Ethnos: Überregionale Heiligtümer im Spannungsfeld von Kult und Politik, Kolloquium, Münster, 23.–24. November 2001*, edited by K. Freitag, P. Funke, and M. Haake, 55–72. *Historia* Einzelschriften 189. Stuttgart: Franz Steiner Verlag.

Antonetti, C. 2007. "Epidamno, Apollonia e il santuario olimpico: Convergenze e discontinuità nella mitologia delle origini." In *Épire, Illyrie, Macédoine: Mélanges offerts au professeur Pierre Cabanes*, edited by D. Berranger-Auserve, 89–111. Collection ERGA Recherches sur l'Antiquité 10. Clermont-Ferrand: Presses Universitaires Blaise Pascal.

Antonetti, C. 2011. "La madrepatria ritrovata: Corinto e le poleis della Grecia nord-occidentale." In *Ethne, identità e tradizioni: La "terza" Grecia a l'Occidente*, edited by L. Breglia, A. Moleti, and M. Luisa, 1: 53–71. 2 vols. Pisa: Edizioni ETS.

Antonetti, C., and E. Cavalli, eds. 2015. *Prospettive corciresi*. Diabaseis 5. Pisa: Edizioni ETS.

Arafat, K. W., and C. A. Morgan. 1995. "In the Footsteps of Aeneas: Excavations at Butrint, Albania 1991–2." *Dialogos: Hellenic Studies Review* 2: 25–40.

Arvanitou-Metallinou, G. 2007. "Η Προϊστορική έρευνα στην Κέρκυρα και η συμβολή του Αύγουστου Σορδίνα. Θεωρητικές προσεγγίσεις-προοπτικές." In *Η Προϊστορική Κέρκυρα και ο ευρύτερος περίγυρος της Προβλήματα–Προοπτικές: Πρακτικά ημερίδας τιμητικής στον Αύγουστο Σορδίνα, Κέρκυρα 17 Δεκεμβρίου 2004*, edited by G. Arvanitou-Metallinou, 35–47. Corfu: Υπουργείο Πολιτισμού.

Arvanitou-Metallinou, G. 2017. "Corfu in the Adriatic Network of Contacts in the Second Half of the Third Millennium B.C." In *Ἕσπερος: The Aegean Seen from the West, Proceedings of the 16th International Aegean Conference, University of Ioannina, 18–21 May 2016*, edited by M. Fotiadis, R. Laffineur, Y. Lolos, et al., 363–8. *Aegaeum* 41. Leuven: Peeters.

Baika, K. 2013. "Corcyra (Corfu)." In *Shipsheds of the Ancient Mediterranean*, edited by D. Blackman, 319–34. Cambridge: Cambridge University Press.

Baika, K. 2014. "Ancient Harbour Cities: New Methodological Perspectives and Recent Research in Greece." In *Harbors and Harbor Cities in the Eastern Mediterranean from*

*Antiquity to the Byzantine Period: Recent Discoveries and Current Approaches*, edited by S. Ladstätter, F. Pirson, and T. Schmidts, 445–91. Byzas 19, Sonderschriften Österreichisches Archäologisches Institut 52. Istanbul: Deutsches Archäologisches Institut.

Baragwanath, E. 2008. *Motivation and Narrative in Herodotus*. Oxford: Oxford University Press.

Barletta, B. A. 1990. "An 'Ionian Sea' Style in Archaic Doric Architecture." *American Journal of Archaeology* 94: 45–72.

Arvanitou-Metallinou, G. 2001. *The Origins of the Greek Architectural Orders*. Cambridge: Cambridge University Press.

Barone, G., V. Crupi, S. Galli, et al. 2004. "Archaeometric Analyses on 'Corinthian B' Transport Amphorae Found in Gela (Sicily, Italy)." *Archaeometry* 46: 553–68.

Beloch, J. 1886. *Die Bevölkerung der griechisch-römischen Welt*. Leipzig: Duncker & Humblot.

Bernstein, F. 2004. *Konflikt und Migration: Studien zu griechischen Fluchtbewegungen im Zeitalter der sogenannten Großen Kolonisation*. Mainzer Althistorische Studien 5. St. Katharinen, Germany: Scripta Mercaturae Verlag.

Bonelou, E. 2018. "Η οργάνωση της κατοικίας στη Βόρεια Κέρκυρα βάσει των προσφάτων ανασκαφικών ερευνών." In *Α´ Συνέδριο "Το Αρχαιολογικό Έργο στη Βορειοδυτική Ελλάδα και τα νησιά του Ιονίου," 10–13 Δεκεμβρίου 2014, Ιωάννινα. Πρακτικά*, edited by V. Theophilopoulou, 695–704. Athens: Υπουργείο Πολιτισμού. Ταμείο Αρχαιολογικών Πόρων και Απαλλοτριώσεων.

Bookidis, N. 1995. "Archaic Corinthian Sculpture: A Summary." In *Corinto e l'Occidente: Atti del Trentaquattresimo Convegno di Studi sulla Magna Grecia, Taranto 7–11 ottobre 1994*, 1: 231–56. 2 vols. Atti del Convegno di Studi sulla Magna Grecia (Taranto) 34. Taranto: Istituto per la Storia e l'Archeologia della Magna Grecia.

Bresson, A. 2016a. "Aristotle and Foreign Trade." In *The Ancient Economy: Markets, Households, and City-States*, edited by E. M. Harris, D. M. Lewis, and M. Woolmer, 41–65. Cambridge: Cambridge University Press.

Bresson, A. 2016b. *The Making of the Ancient Greek Economy: Institutions, Markets, and Growth in the City-States*. Princeton, NJ: Princeton University Press.

Bulle, H. 1934. "Ausgrabungen bei Aphiona auf Korfu." *Mitteilungen des Deutschen Archäologischen Instituts, Athenische Abteilung* 59: 147–240.

Bürchner, L. 1922. "Korkyra and Korkyraia." In *Paulys Real-encyclopädie der classischen Altertumswissenschaft*, edited by A. F. von Pauly, XI.2: 1400–16, 17. 44 vols. Stuttgart: J. B. Metzler.

Busolt, G. 1893–1904. *Griechische Geschichte bis zur Schlacht bei Chaeroneia*. 2nd ed. 3 vols. Gotha: F. A. Perthes.

Cabanes, P. 2003. "Recherches sur le calendrier corinthien en Épire et dans les régions voisines." *Revue des études anciennes* 105: 83–102.

Cabanes, P., and F. Drini. 1995. *Corpus des inscriptions grecques d'Illyrie méridionale et d'Épire 1: Inscriptions d'Épidamne-Dyrrhachion et d'Apollonia, Vol. 1, Inscriptions d'Épidamne-Dyrrhachion*. Études Épigraphiques 2. Athens: École Française d'Athènes.

Cahill, N. 2002. *Household and City Organization at Olynthus*. New Haven, CT: Yale University Press.

Calligas, P. 1968. "Ἀρχαιότητες καὶ Μνημεία Ἰονίων Νησών." *Ἀρχαιολογικὸν Δελτίον* 23 B2: 302–22.

Calligas, P. 1969. "Τὸ ἐν Κερκύρα ἱερὸν τῆς Ἀκραίας Ἥρας." *Ἀρχαιολογικὸν Δελτίον* 24 A: 51–8.

Calligas, P. 1971. "An Inscribed Lead Plaque from Korkyra." *Annual of the British School at Athens* 66: 79–94.

Calligas, P. 1976. "Κερκυραία Μάστιξ." *Athens Annals of Archaeology* 9: 61–8.

Calligas, P. 1982. "Κέρκυρα, ἀποικισμὸς καὶ ἔπος." *Annuario della Scuola Archeologica di Atene e delle Missioni Italiane in Oriente* 60: 57–68.

Carbè, A. 1987. "Il ruolo di Corcira tra Oriente ed Occidente riflesso nel documento monetale." *Rivista italiana di numismatica e scienze affini* 89: 3–14.

Carter, J. B. 1996. "Korkyra (Korfu)." In *Encyclopedia of the History of Classical Archaeology*, edited by N. T. de Grummond, 649–50. London: Routledge.

Carusi, C. 2011. "La Grecia nord-occidentale e il problema storico del rapporto fra isole e peree." In *Ethne, identità e tradizioni: La "terza" Grecia a l'Occidente*, edited by L. Breglia, A. Moleti, and M. Luisa, 1: 89–112. 2 vols. Pisa: Edizioni ETS.

Choremis, A. 1973–1974. "Ἀρχαιότητες καὶ μνημεία Ἰονίων Νήσων." *Ἀρχαιολογικὸν Δελτίον* 29 B3: 627–44.

Choremis, A. 1974. "Ἀρχαϊκόν ἀέτωμα εκ Κέρκυρας." *Athens Annals of Archaeology* 7: 183–6.

Choremis, A. 1977. "Ἐφορεία Ἀρχαιοτήτων Κέρκυρας." *Ἀρχαιολογικὸν Δελτίον* 32 B1: 181–3.

Choremis, A. 1992–1998. "Μολύβδινὸ ἐνεπίγραφο ἔλασμα ἀπὸ τὴν Κέρκυρα." *Ὅρος: Ἕνα Ἀρχαιογνωστικό Περιοδικό* 10–12: 347–54.

Cigaina, L. 2015. "Il frontone dell'Artemision di Corcira (Palaiopolis): Contenuto religioso e possibili riferimenti politici alla tirannide dei Cipselidi." *Hesperia: Studi sulla grecità di Occidente* 32: 41–98.

Crema, F. 2010. "Pritania e spazio civico." In *Lo spazio ionico e le comunità della Grecia nord-occidentale: Territorio, società, istituzioni, Atti del Convegno Internazionale Venezia, 7–9 gennaio 2010*, edited by C. Antonetti, 201–23. Diabaseis 1. Pisa: Edizioni ETS.

Cremer, M. 1981. "Zur Deutung des jüngeren Korfu-Giebels." *Archäologischer Anzeiger*: 317–28.

D'Agostino, B. 2012. "Le isole ionie sulle rotte per l'Occidente." In *Alle origini della Magna Grecia: Mobilità, migrazioni, fondazioni, Atti del Cinquantesimo Convegno di Studi sulla Magna Grecia, Taranto 1–4 ottobre 2010*, 1: 279–304. 3 vols. Atti del

Convegno di Studi sulla Magna Grecia (Taranto) 50. Taranto: Istituto per la Storia e l'Archeologia della Magna Grecia.

Danner, P. 2000. "Westgriechische Giebeldekorationen, 1: Gorgoneia." *Mitteilungen des Deutschen Archäologischen Instituts, Römische Abteilung* 42: 19–97.

De Angelis, F. and V. Mignosa. Forthcoming. "Syracuse." In *The Oxford History of the Archaic Greek World*, edited by P. Cartledge and P. Christesen, The Oxford History of the Archaic Greek World, Volume 6. New York: Oxford University Press.

De Fidio, P. 1995. "Corinto e l'Occidente tra VIII e VI sec. A.C." In *Corinto e Occidente: Atti del Trentaquattresimo Convegno di Studi sulla Magna Grecia, Taranto 7–11 ottobre 1994*, 1: 47–141. 2 vols. Atti del Convegno di Studi sulla Magna Grecia (Taranto) 34. Taranto: Istituto per la Storia e l'Archeologia della Magna Grecia.

Del Monaco, L., and N. Parise. 2010. "Unità di conto a Corcira nell'età arcaica." *Annali dell'Istituto Italiano di Numismatica* 56: 8–28.

Dierichs, A. 2004. *Korfu-Kerkyra: Grüne Insel im Ionischen Meer von Nausikaa bis Kaiser Wilhelm II.* Mainz: Philipp von Zabern.

Dinsmoor, W. B. Jr. 1973. "The Kardaki Temple Reexamined." *Mitteilungen des Deutschen Archäologischen Instituts, Athenische Abteilung* 85: 165–74.

Domingo-Forasté, D. 1988. "A History of Northern Coastal Acarnania to 167 B.C.: Alyzeia, Leukas, Anaktorion and Argos Amphilochikon." Ph.D. diss., University of California, Santa Barbara.

Dontas, G. 1965a. "Ἀνασκαφαὶ Κερκύρας." *Πρακτικὰ τῆς ἐν Ἀθήναις Ἀρχαιολογικῆς Ἑταιρείας*: 66–77.

———. 1965b. "Τοπογραφικὰ θέματα τῆς πολιορκίας τῆς Κερκύρας τοῦ ἔτους 373 π.Χ." *Ἀρχαιολογικὴ Ἐφημερίς*: 139–44.

Dontas, G. 1966a. "Ἀνασκαφαὶ Κερκύρας." *Πρακτικὰ τῆς ἐν Ἀθήναις Ἀρχαιολογικῆς Ἑταιρείας*: 85–94.

Dontas, G. 1966b. "Ἀρχαιότητες καὶ μνημεῖα Ἰονίων Νήσων." *Ἀρχαιολογικὸν Δελτίον* 21 B2: 316–30.

Dontas, G. 1967. "Ἀρχαιότητες καὶ μνημεῖα Ἰονίων Νήσων." *Ἀρχαιολογικὸν Δελτίον* 22 B2: 360–70.

Dontas, G. 1968. "Local Imitation of Corinthian Vases of the Later Seventh Century B.C. Found in Corfu." *Hesperia* 37: 331–7.

Dontas, G. 1976. "Denkmäler und Geschichte eines kerkyräischen Heiligtums." In *Neue Forschungen in griechischen Heiligtümern: Internationales Symposion in Olympia vom 10. bis 12. Oktober 1974 anlässlich der Hundertjahrfeier der Abteilung Athen und der deutschen Ausgrabungen in Olympia*, edited by U. Jantzen, 121–33. Tübingen: Wasmuth.

Dontas, G. 1977. "Ἀνασκαφὴ στὸ Καρδάκι Κερκύρας." *Πρακτικὰ τῆς ἐν Ἀθήναις Ἀρχαιολογικῆς Ἑταιρείας*: 154–8.

Dontas, G. 1978. "Ἐργασίες στὸ Καρδάκι Κερκύρας." *Πρακτικὰ τῆς ἐν Ἀθήναις Ἀρχαιολογικῆς Ἑταιρείας*: 108–10.

Dontas, G. 1997. "Σκέψεις, προβληματισμοὶ καὶ προτάσεις γιὰ τὴν γλυπτικὴ τῆς Κέρκυρας στοὺς ἀρχαϊκοὺς καὶ τοὺς πρώιμους κλασικοὺς χρόνου." In Ἔπαινος Ἰωάννου Κ. Παπαδημητρίου, edited by B. Petrakos, 53–170. Βιβλιοθήκη της εν Αθήναις Αρχαιολογικής Εταιρείας 168. Athens: Η εν Αθήναις Αρχαιολογική Εταιρεία.

Dörpfeld, W. 1914. "Ausgrabungen auf Korfu im Fruhjahr 1914." *Mitteilungen des Deutschen Archäologischen Instituts, Athenische Abteilung* 39: 161–76.

Drögemüller, H.-P. 1973. "Syrakusai." In *Paulys Real-encyclopädie der classischen Altertumswissenschaft*, edited by A. F. von Pauly, Supplementband XIII, 815–36. Munich: Druckenmüller.

Dubbini, R. 2011. *Dei nello spazio degli uomini: I culti dell'agora e la costruzione di Corinto arcaica.* Supplemente e Monografie della *Rivista Archeologia Classica* 7. Rome: Bretschneider.

Ducat, J. 1995. "Un ritual samien." *Bulletin de correspondance hellénique* 119: 339–68.

Dunbar, N., ed. 1998. *Aristophanes Birds: Edited with an Introduction and Commentary.* Oxford: Clarendon Press.

Ellis-Evans, A. 2019. *The Kingdom of Priam: Lesbos and the Troad between Anatolia and the Aegean.* Oxford: Oxford University Press.

Fantasia, U. 2017. *Ambracia dai Cipselidi ad Augusto: Contributo alla storia della Grecia nord-occidentale fino alla prima età imperiale.* Diabaseis 7. Pisa: Edizioni ETS.

Farnsworth, M., I. Perlman, and F. Asaro. 1977. "Corinth and Corfu: A Neutron Activation Study of Their Pottery." *American Journal of Archaeology* 81: 455–68.

Fauber, C. M. 2002. "Archaic Kerkyra: An Historiographical Examination of the Formation and Formulation of an Ancient Greek *Polis.*" Ph.D. diss., University of Chicago.

Finkler, C., K. Baika, D. Rigakou, et al. 2017. "The Sedimentary Record of the Alkinoos Harbour of Ancient Corcyra (Corfu Island, Greece): Geoarchaeological Evidence for Rapid Coastal Changes Induced by Co-seismic Uplift, Tsunami Inundation and Human Interventions." In *Signatures of Extreme Events Recorded in Geological Archives of the Mediterranean*, edited by K. Reicherter, A. Vött, M. Mathes-Schmidt, et al., 197–246. *Zeitschrift für Geomorphologie* Supplements Neue Folge 62.2. Stuttgart: Bornträger.

Finkler, C., K. Baika, D. Rigakou, et al. 2018. "Geoarchaeological Investigations of a Prominent Quay Wall in Ancient Corcyra: Implications for Harbour Development, Palaeoenvironmental Changes and Tectonic Geomorphology of Corfu Island (Ionian Islands, Greece)." *Quaternary International* 473: 91–111.

Finkler, C., P. Fischer, K. Baika, et al. 2017. "Tracing the Alkinoos Harbor of Ancient Kerkyra, Greece, and Reconstructing Its Paleotsunami History." *Geoarchaeology* 33: 24–42.

Finocchiaro, C., G. Barone, P. Mazzoleni, et al. 2018. "New Insights on the Archaic 'Corinthian B' Amphorae from Gela (Sicily): The Contribution of the Analyses of Corfu Raw Materials." *Mediterranean Archaeology and Archaeometry* 18: 179–89.

Fletcher, R. N. 2007. *Patterns of Imports in Iron Age Italy*. BAR International Series 1732. Oxford: Archaeopress.

Fragoulaki, M. 2013. *Kinship in Thucydides: Intercommunal Ties and Historical Narrative*. Oxford: Oxford University Press.

Franz, J. 1846. "Corcyräische Inschriften." *Archäologische Zeitung* 48: 378–86.

Freeth, T., A. Jones, J. Steele, et al. 2008. "Calendars with Olympiad Display and Eclipse Prediction on the Antikythera Mechanism." *Nature* 454: 614–17.

Froehlich, S. 2013. *Handlungsmotive bei Herodot*. Collegium Beatus Rhenanus 4. Stuttgart: Franz Steiner Verlag.

Frost, F. 1980. *Plutarch's Themistocles: A Historical Commentary*. Princeton, NJ: Princeton University Press.

Funke, P. 1999. "PERAIA: Einige Überlegungen zum Festlandbesitz griechischer Inselstaaten." In *Hellenistic Rhodes: Politics, Culture, and Society*, edited by V. Gabrielsen, 55–75. Studies in Hellenistic Civilization 9. Aarhus: Aarhus University Press.

Gabelmann, H. 1965. *Studien zum frühgriechischen Löwenbild*. Berlin: Mann Verlag.

Gardner, P. 1883. *A Catalogue of the British Museum: Thessaly to Aetolia (Catalogue of Greek Coins in the British Museum)*. London: British Museum Press.

Gehrke, H.-J. 1985. *Stasis: Untersuchungen zu den inneren Kriegen in den griechischen Staaten des 5. und 4. Jahrhunderts v. Chr.* Vestigia 35. Munich: C. H. Beck.

Gehrke, H.-J. 1986. *Jenseits von Athen und Sparta: Das Dritte Griechenland und seine Staatenwelt*. Munich: C. H. Beck.

Gehrke, H.-J. 1990. "Herodot und die Tyrannenchronologie." In *Memoria rerum veterum: Neue Beiträge zur antiken Historiographie und Alten Geschichte, Festschrift für C. J. Classen zum 60. Geburtstag*, edited by W. Ax, 33–49. Palingenesia 32. Stuttgart: Franz Steiner Verlag.

Gehrke, H.-J. 2014. *Geschichte als Element antiker Kultur: Die Griechen und ihre Geschichte(n)*. Münchner Vorlesungen zu Antiken Welten 2. Berlin: Walter de Gruyter.

Gehrke, H.-J., and E. Wirbelauer. 2004. "Akarnania and Adjacent Areas." In *An Inventory of Archaic and Classical Poleis*, edited by M. H. Hansen and T. H. Nielsen, 351–78. Oxford: Oxford University Press.

Georgiadou, G., and A. Tzortzatou. 2009. "Η Πρωτοκορινθιακή και Κορινθιακή αρχαϊκή κεραμική της Κέρκυρας: Μια συστηματική προσέγγιση των ευρημάτων από το οικόπεδο του Δικαστικού Μεγάρου Κέρκυρας." In *Η' Διεθνές Πανιόνιο Συνέδριο, Κύθηρα 21–25 Μαΐου 2006, Πρακτικά*, 1: 163–81. 2 vols. Cythera: Εταιρεία Κυθηραϊκών Μελετών.

Giangiulio, M. 2005. "Tradizione storica e strategie narrative nelle Storie di Erodoto: Il caso del discorso di Socle Corinzio." In *Erodoto e il 'modello erodoteo': Formazione e trasmissione delle tradizioni storiche in Grecia*, edited by M. Giangiulio, 91–122. Labirinti 88. Trento: Editrice Università degli Studi di Trento.

Gomme, A. W., A. Andrewes, and K. J. Dover. 1945–1981. *A Historical Commentary on Thucydides*. 5 vols. Oxford: Clarendon Press.

Greenslade, S., S. Leppard, and M. Logue. 2013. "The Acropolis of Butrint Reassessed." In *The Archaeology and Histories of an Ionian Town*, edited by S. Leppard, I. L. Hansen, and R. Hodges, 47–76. Butrint 4. Oxford: Oxbow Books.

Grossman, J. B. 2013. *Funerary Sculpture*. Athenian Agora 35. Athens: American School of Classical Studies at Athens.

Gschnitzer, F. 1973. "Prytanis." In *Paulys Real-encyclopädie der classischen Altertumswissenschaft*, edited by A. F. von Pauly, Supplementband XIII, 730–816. Munich: Druckenmüller.

Habicht, C. 1985. *Pausanias' Guide to Ancient Greece*. Berkeley: University of California Press.

Hadzis, C. D. 1995. "Fêtes et cultes à Corcyre et à Corinthe: Calendriers d'Épire, calendriers des cités coloniales de l'Ouest et calendrier de Corinthe." In *Corinto e l'Occidente: Atti del Trentaquattresimo Convegno di Studi sulla Magna Grecia, Taranto 7–11 ottobre 1994*, 1: 445–52. 2 vols. Atti del Convegno di Studi sulla Magna Grecia (Taranto) 34. Taranto: Istituto per la Storia e l'Archeologia della Magna Grecia.

Hadzis, C. D.1997. "Corinthiens, Lyciens, Doriens et Cariens: Aoreis à Corinthe, Aoroi à Corcyre, Aor fils de Chrysaor et Alétès fils d'Hippotès." *Bulletin de correspondance hellénique* 121: 1–14.

Hallof, K. 2001. "Fasti." In *Inscriptiones Graecae IX 1,4*, 4–11. Berlin: Walter de Gruyter.

Hammond, N. G. L. 1967. *A History of Greece to 322 B.C.* 2nd ed. Oxford: Clarendon Press.

Hammond, N. G. L. 1972. *A History of Macedonia, Volume I: Historical Geography and Prehistory*. Oxford: Clarendon Press.

Hansen, M. H. 2006. *The Shotgun Method: The Demography of the Ancient Greek City-State Culture*. Columbia, MO: University of Missouri Press.

Head, B. V. 1911. *Historia Numorum: A Manual of Greek Numismatics*. 2nd ed. Oxford: Clarendon Press.

Hernandez, D. R. 2017. "Bouthrotos (Butrint) in the Archaic and Classical Periods: The Acropolis and Temple of Athena Polias." *Hesperia* 86: 205–71.

Higgins, M. D., and R. A. Higgins. 1996. *A Geological Companion to Greece and the Aegean*. London: Duckworth.

Hölkeskamp, K.-J. 1999. *Schiedsrichter, Gesetzgeber und Gesetzgebung im archaischen Griechenland*. *Historia* Einzelschriften 131. Stuttgart: Franz Steiner Verlag.

Hornblower, S. 1991–2008. *A Commentary on Thucydides*. 3 vols. Oxford: Clarendon Press.

Hose, M. 2002. *Aristoteles: Die historischen Fragmente*. Aristoteles Werke in Deutscher Übersetzung 20, Fragmente Teil III. Berlin: Akademie Verlag.

Hübner, G. 2018. "Die Dächer des großen Tempels von Thermos (Ätolien): Der plastische Schmuck." In *Πήλινα γλυπτά και κεραμώσεις: Νέα ευρήματα & νέες προοπτικές, Παρασκευή 15 Μαΐου 2015, Upper House, Βρετανική Σχολή Αθηνών: Πρακτικά*, edited by A. Moustaka, 33–60. Athens: Υπουργείο Πολιτισμού. Ταμείο Αρχαιολογικών Πόρων και Απαλλοτριώσεων.

# 600 THE OXFORD HISTORY OF THE ARCHAIC GREEK WORLD

Hunt, P. 1998. *Slaves, Warfare, and Ideology in the Greek Historians*. Cambridge: Cambridge University Press.

Intrieri, M. 2010. "Autarkeia: Osservazioni sull'economia corcirese fra V e IV sec. a.C." In *Lo spazio ionico e le comunità della Grecia nord-occidentale: Territorio, società, istituzioni, Atti del Convegno Internazionale Venezia, 7–9 gennaio 2010*, edited by C. Antonetti, 181–99. Diabaseis 1. Pisa: Edizioni ETS.

Jacquemin, A. 1999. *Offrandes monumentales à Delphes*. Bibliothèque des Écoles Française d'Athènes et de Rome 304. Paris: De Boccard.

Jeffery, L. H. 1990. *The Local Scripts of Archaic Greece: A Study of the Origin of the Greek Alphabet and Its Development from the Eighth to the Fifth Centuries B.C.* Rev. ed. with a supplement by Alan Johnston. Oxford: Oxford University Press.

Johnson, F. P. 1936. "The Kardaki Temple." *American Journal of Archaeology* 40: 46–54.

Jones, N. F. 1987. *Public Organization in Ancient Greece: A Documentary Study*. Memoirs of the American Philosophical Society 176. Philadelphia: American Philosophical Society.

Kallipolitis, V. G. 1982. "Κεραμεικά εὑρήματα ἀπὸ την Κέρκυρα." *Annuario della Scuola Archeologica di Atene e delle Missioni Italiane in Oriente* 60: 68–76.

Kanta-Kitsou, K. 1996. "Der Kouros von Kerkyra." *Mitteilungen des Deutschen Archäologischen Instituts, Athenische Abteilung* 111: 79–107.

Kanta-Kitsou, K. 2001a. "Ἕνας νεώσοικος, τμῆμα των νεωρίων του Ὑλλαϊκού λιμανιού της Αρχαίας Κέρκυρας." In *Tropis VI, Proceedings of the Sixth International Symposium on Ship Construction in Antiquity, Lamia, 28, 29, 30 August 1996*, edited by H. Tzalas, 273–99. Athens: Hellenic Institute for the Preservation of Nautical Tradition.

Kanta-Kitsou, K. 2001b. "Η λατρεία του Απόλλωνα Αγυιέα στην Κέρκυρα." In *Καλλίστευμα: Μελέτες προς τιμήν της Ολγας Τζάχου-Αλεξανδρή*, edited by A. Alexandre and I. Leventi, 439–60. Athens: Ὑπουργείο Πολιτισμού.

Kästner, V. 1990. "Scheibenförmige Akrotere in Griechenland und Italien." *Hesperia* 59: 251–64.

Kiechle, F. 1979. "Korkyra und der Handelsweg durch das Adriatische Meer." *Historia* 28: 173–91.

Koehler, C. G. 1986. "Handling of Transport Amphoras." In *Recherches sur les amphores grecques: Actes du Colloque International Organisé par le Centre National de la Recherche Scientifique, l'Université de Rennes II et l'École Française d'Athènes (Athènes, 10–12 septembre 1984)*, edited by J.-Y. Empereur and Y. Garlan, 50–2. *Bulletin de correspondance hellénique* Supplément 13. Paris: De Boccard.

Kostoglou-Despini, K. 1971. "Ἀρχαιότητες και μνημεία Ιονίων Νήσων." *Ἀρχαιολογικόν Δελτίον* 26 B2: 344–55.

Kourkoumelis, D. 1995. "Χάλκινο ενεπίγραφο αγαλμάτιο από την Κέρκυρα." *Ἀρχαιολογική Εφημερίς* 134: 257–65.

Kourkoumélis, D., and S. Démesticha. 1997. "Les outils de potier de l'atelier de Figaretto à Corfou." *Bulletin de correspondance hellénique* 121: 553–71.

Kraay, C. M. 1976. *Archaic and Classical Greek Coins*. Berkeley: University of California Press.

Lane Fox, R. 2008. *Travelling Heroes: Greeks and Their Myths in the Epic Age of Homer*. London: Allen Lane.

Lang, F. 1996. *Archaische Siedlungen in Griechenland: Struktur und Entwicklung*. Berlin: Akademie Verlag.

Lapini, W. 1996. *Il POxy 664 di Eraclide Pontico e la cronologia dei Cipselidi*. Studi e Testi per il Corpus dei Papiri Filosofici Greci e Latini 7. Florence: Leo S. Olschki.

Lazari, K., G. Riginos, C. Spanodimos, et al. 2018. "Ανασκαφικές έρευνες στα οικόπεδα του Δικαστικού Μεγάρου και του 'Λυρικού Θεάτρου' στη βόρεια νεκρόπολη της αρχαίας Κέρκυρας (2000–2007)." In *Α΄ Συνέδριο "Το Αρχαιολογικό Έργο στη Βορειοδυτική Ελλάδα και τα νησιά του Ιονίου," 10–13 Δεχεμβρίου 2014, Ιωάννινα. Πρακτικά*, edited by V. Theophilopoulou, 705–16. Athens: Υπουργείο Πολιτισμού. Ταμείο Αρχαιολογικών Πόρων και Απαλλοτριώσεων.

Lechat, H. 1891. "Terres cuites de Corcyre." *Bulletin de correspondance hellénique* 15: 1–112.

Leekley, D., and R. Noyes. 1975. *Archaeological Excavations in the Greek Islands*. Park Ridge, NJ: Noyes Press.

Lepore, E. 1962. *Ricerche sull'antico Epiro: Le origini storiche e gli interessi greci*. Collana di Studi Greci 38. Naples: Libreria Scientifica Editrice.

Luraghi, N. 1994. *Tirannidi arcaiche in Sicilia e Magna Grecia: Da Panezio di Leontini alla caduta dei Dinomenidi*. Studi e Testi Fondazione Luigi Firpo, Centro di Studi sul Pensiero Politico 3. Florence: Leo S. Olschki.

Luraghi, N, ed. 2001. *The Historian's Craft in the Age of Herodotus*. Oxford: Oxford University Press.

Luraghi, N. 2005. "Le storie prima delle Storie: Prospettive di ricerca." In *Erodoto e il 'modello erodoteo': Formazione e trasmissione delle tradizioni storiche in Grecia*, edited by M. Giangiulio, 61–90. Labirinti 88. Trento: Editrice Università degli Studi di Trento.

Luraghi, N. 2010. "The Local Scripts from Nature to Culture." *Classical Antiquity* 29: 68–91.

Lytle, E. 2006. "Marine Fisheries and the Ancient Greek Economy." Ph.D. diss., Duke University.

Malkin, I. 1987. *Religion and Colonization in Ancient Greece*. Studies in Greek and Roman Religion 3. Leiden: Brill.

Malkin, I. 1998a. "Ithaka, Odysseus and the Euboeans in the Eighth Century." In *Euboica, l'Eubea e la presenza euboica in Calcidica e in Occidente: Atti del Convegno Internazionale di Napoli, 13–16 novembre 1996*, edited by M. Bats and B. D'Agostino, 1–10. Collections du Centre Jean Bérard 16. Naples: L'Arte Tipografica.

Malkin, I. 1998b. *The Returns of Odysseus: Colonization and Ethnicity*. Berkeley: University of California Press.

Manning, S. W. 2022. "Climate, Environment, and Resources." In *The Cambridge Companion to the Ancient Greek Economy*, edited by S. von Reden, 373–91. Cambridge: Cambridge University Press.

Marconi, C. 2007. *Temple Decoration and Cultural Identity in the Archaic Greek World*. Cambridge: Cambridge University Press.

Marzano, A. 2013. *Harvesting the Sea: The Exploitation of Marine Resources in the Roman Mediterranean*. Oxford: Oxford University Press.

Mastrocinque, A. 1988. *Da Cnido a Corcira Melaina: Uno studio sulle fondazioni greche in Adriatico*. Pubblicazioni del Dipartimento di Storia della Civiltà Europea 4. Trento: Università degli Studi di Trento.

Matton, R. 1960. *Corfou*. Athens: Institut Français d'Athènes.

McGowan, E. P. 1995. "Tomb Marker and Turning Post: Funerary Columns in the Archaic Period." *American Journal of Archaeology* 99: 615–32.

Mertens, D. 2006. *Städte und Bauten der Westgriechen: Von der Kolonisationszeit bis zur Krise um 400 vor Christus*. Munich: Hirmer.

Mertens-Horn, M. 1986. "Studien zu griechischen Löwenbildern." *Mitteilungen des Deutschen Archäologischen Instituts. Römische Abteilung* 93: 1–61.

Mertens-Horn, M. 1988. *Die Löwenkopf-Wasserspeier des griechischen Westens im 6. und 5. Jahrhundert v. Chr.: Im Vergleich mit den Löwen des griechischen Mutterlandes*. *Mitteilungen des Deutschen Archäologischen Instituts, Römische Abteilung*. Ergänzungsheft 28. Mainz: Philipp von Zabern.

Mertens-Horn, M. 1995. "Corinto e l'Occidente nelle immagini: La nascita di Pegaso e la nascita di Afrodite." In *Corinto e l'Occidente: Atti del Trentaquattresimo Convegno di Studi sulla Magna Grecia, Taranto 7–11 ottobre 1994*, 1: 257–89. 2 vols. Atti del Convegno di Studi sulla Magna Grecia (Taranto) 34. Taranto: Istituto per la Storia e l'Archeologia della Magna Grecia.

Metallinou, G. 2010. "Kerkyra through the Excavations of the Last Years: Myths and Realities." In *Lo spazio ionico e le comunità della Grecia nord-occidentale: Territorio, società, istituzioni, Atti del Convegno Internazionale Venezia, 7–9 gennaio 2010*, edited by C. Antonetti, 11–34. Diabaseis 1. Pisa: Edizioni ETS.

Metallinou, G., T. Provata, and M. Nakou. 2008. "Η Εφορεία Προϊστορικών και Κλασικών Αρχαιοτήτων. Ανασκαφικές έρευνες." *Αρχαιολογικόν Δελτίον* 63 Β1: 821–42.

Meyer, E. 1975. "Korkyra." In *Der Kleine Pauly*, edited by K. Ziegler and W. Sontheimer, 3: 305–7. 5 vols. Stuttgart: Druckenmüller.

Millett, P. 1991. *Lending and Borrowing in Ancient Athens*. Cambridge: Cambridge University Press.

Moretti, L. 1957. *Olympionikai: I vincitori negli antichi agoni olimpici*. Rome: Accademia Nazionale dei Lincei.

Morgan, C. A. 1998. "Euboians and Corinthians in the Area of the Corinthian Gulf?" In *Euboica, l'Eubea e la presenza euboica in Calcidica e in Occidente: Atti del Convegno*

*Internazionale di Napoli, 13–16 novembre 1996*, edited by M. Bats and B. D'Agostino, 281–302. Collections du Centre Jean Bérard 16. Naples: L'Arte Tipografica.

Müller, K., ed. 1855–1861. *Geographici Graeci Minores.* 2 vols. Paris: Didot.

Neumann, G. 1975. "Hylli.2.Sprache." In *Der Kleine Pauly*, edited by K. Ziegler and W. Sontheimer, 2: 1266. 5 vols. Stuttgart: Druckenmüller.

Nicolet-Pierre, H. 2009. "A propos du monnayage archaïque de Corcyre." *Schweizerische Numismatische Rundschau* 88: 103–16.

Oikonomidis, S., A. Papayiannis, and A. Tsonos. 2011. "The Emergence and the Architectural Development of the Tumulus Burial Custom in NW Greece (Epirus and the Ionian Islands) and Albania and Its Connections to Settlement Organization." In *Ancestral Landscapes: Burial Mounds in the Copper and Bronze Ages (Central and Eastern Europe-Balkans-Adriatic-Aegean, 4th–2nd Millennium B.C.), Proceedings of the International Conference Held in Udine, May 15th–18th 2008*, edited by E. Borgna and S. Müller Celka, 185–201. Travaux de la Maison de l'Orient et de la Méditerranée 58. Lyon: Maison de l'Orient et de la Méditerranée Jean Pouilloux.

Osborne, R. 2009. *Greece in the Making, 1200–479 BC.* 2nd ed. London: Routledge.

Panagou, T. 2016. "Patterns of Amphora Stamp Distribution: Tracking Down Export Tendencies." In *The Ancient Greek Economy: Markets, Households, and City-States*, edited by E. M. Harris, D. M. Lewis, and M. Woolmer, 207–29. Cambridge: Cambridge University Press.

Papadimitriou, I. 1939. "Ἀνασκαφαί ἐν Κερκύρα, Α. Ἀνασκαφή Δωρικού Ναού ἐν Ῥόδα." *Πρακτικά τῆς ἐν Ἀθήναις Ἀρχαιολογικῆς Ἑταιρείας*: 85–92.

Parker, V. 1997. *Untersuchungen zum Lelantischen Krieg und verwandten Problemen der frühgriechischen Geschichte. Historia* Einzelschriften 109. Stuttgart: Franz Steiner Verlag.

Partsch, J. 1887. *Die Insel Korfu, eine geographische Monographie.* Gotha: J. Perthes.

Payne, H. 1931. *Necrocorinthia: A Study of Corinthian Art in the Archaic Period.* Oxford: Clarendon Press.

Philippson, A. 1958. *Die griechischen Landschaften: Eine Landeskunde, Band II, Der Nordwesten der griechischen Halbinsel, Teil 2, Das westliche Mittelgriechenland und die westgriechischen Inseln.* Frankfurt: Klostermann.

Piccirilli, L. 1995. "Corinto e l'Occidente: Aspetti di politica internazionale fino al V secolo a.C." In *Corinto e l'Occidente: Atti del Trentaquattresimo Convegno di Studi sulla Magna Grecia, Taranto 7–11 ottobre 1994*, 1: 143–76. 2 vols. Atti del Convegno di Studi sulla Magna Grecia (Taranto) 34. Taranto: Istituto per la Storia e l'Archeologia della Magna Grecia.

Pojani, I. 2007. "The Monumental Togate Statue from Butrint." In *Roman Butrint: An Assessment*, edited by I. L. Hansen, R. Hodges, and R. A. Abdy, 62–77. Oxford: Oxbow Books.

Prayon, F. 1975. *Frühetruskische Grab- und Hausarchitektur: Mitteilungen des Deutschen Archäologischen Instituts, Römische Abteilung.* Ergänzungsheft 22. Heidelberg: F. H. Kerle.

Preka-Alexandri, K. 1991. "Ταρίτσα. Οικόπεδο Κωνστ. Μπαλή." *Αρχαιολογικόν Δελτίον* 46 Β1: 261–7.

Preka-Alexandri, K. 1992. "A Ceramic Workshop in Figareto, Corfu." In *Les ateliers de potiers dans le monde grec aux époques géométrique, archaïque et classique: Actes de la Table Ronde Organisée à l'Ecole Française d'Athènes, les 2 et 3 octobre 1987*, edited by F. Blondé and J. Y. Perreault, 41–52. *Bulletin de correspondance hellénique* Supplément 23. Paris: De Boccard.

Preka-Alexandri, K. 2010. *Οι αρχαιότητες της Κέρκυρας.* Athens: Υπουργείο Πολιτισμού. Ταμείο Αρχαιολογικών Πόρων και Απαλλοτριώσεων.

Preka-Alexandri, K. 2016. "La coroplathie de Corcyre: Atelier et sanctuaires." In *Figurines de terre cuite en Méditerranée grecque et romaine 1: Production, diffusion, étude*, edited by A. Muller, E. Lafli, and S. Huysecom-Haxhi, 223–37. *Bulletin de correspondance hellénique* Supplément 54. Paris: De Boccard.

Psoma, S. E. 2015. "Corcyra's Wealth and Power." In *Prospettive corciresi*, edited by C. Antonetti and E. Cavalli, 145–67. Diabaseis 5. Pisa: Edizioni ETS.

Psoma, S. E. 2016. "Choosing and Changing Monetary Standards in the Greek World during the Archaic and Classical Periods." In *The Ancient Greek Economy: Markets, Households, and City-States*, edited by E. M. Harris, D. M. Lewis, and M. Woolmer, 90–115. Cambridge: Cambridge University Press.

Psoma, S. E. 2022. *Corcyra: A City at the Edge of Two Greek Worlds.* Μελετήματα 83. Athens: Εθνικό Ίδρυμα Ερευνών, Ινστιτούτο Ιστορικών Ερευνών.

Quantin, F. 1999. "Aspects épirotes de la vie religieuse antique." *Revue des études grecques* 112: 61–98.

Rhomaios, K. A. 1925. "Les premières fouilles de Corfou." *Bulletin de correspondance hellénique* 49: 190–218.

Ridgway, B.S. 1977. *The Archaic Style in Greek Sculpture.* Princeton: Princeton University Press.

Riemann, O. 1879–1880. *Recherches archéologiques sur les îles ioniennes.* 3 vols. Bibliothèque des Écoles françaises d'Athènes et de Rome 8,12,18. Paris: Thorin.

Riginos, G., E. Bouligea, C. Spanodimos, et al. 2007. "Η' Εφορεία Προϊστορικών και Κλασικών Αρχαιοτήτων. Ανασκαφικές εργασίες." *Αρχαιολογικόν Δελτίον* 62 Β1: 795–826.

Riginos, G. and C. Spanodimos. 2009. "Εμπορικές σχέσεις και ανταλλαγές της αρχαίας Κέρκυρας με βάση τα πρώτα πορίσματα των αρχαιολογικών ερευνών στο οικόπεδο του Λυρικού Θεάτρου." In *Η' Διεθνές Πανιόνιο Συνέδριο, Κύθηρα 21-25 Μαΐου 2006, Πρακτικά*, 1: 372–87. 2 vols. Cythera: Εταιρεία Κυθηραϊκών Μελετών.

Rignanese, G. 2016. "L'Artemision di Corfù: Nuove considerazioni su un 'vecchio' monumento." In *ΔΡΟΜΟΙ: Studi sul mondo antico offerti a Emanuele Greco dagli allievi della Scuola Archeologica Italiana di Atene*, edited by F. Longo, R. Di Cesare, and S. Privitera, 2: 447–62. 2 vols. Athens: Pandemos.

Rodenwaldt, G. 1939. *Korkyra. Archaische Bauten und Bildwerke II. Die Bildwerke des Artemistempels von Korkyra*. Berlin: Mann Verlag.

Roehl, H. 1882. *Inscriptiones Graecae Antiquissimae Praeter Atticas in Attica Repertas*. Revised and expanded ed. Berlin: G. Reimer.

Roller, D. W. 2018. *A Historical and Topographical Guide to the Geography of Strabo*. Cambridge: Cambridge University Press.

Salmon, J. 1984. *Wealthy Corinth. A History of the City to 338 B.C.* Oxford: Clarendon Press.

Sapirstein, P. 2012. "The Monumental Archaic Roof of the Temple of Hera at Mon Repos, Corfu." *Hesperia* 81: 31–91.

Sapirstein, P. 2016a. "The Columns of the Heraion at Olympia. Dörpfeld and Early Doric Architecture." *American Journal of Archaeology* 120: 565–601.

Sapirstein, P. 2016b. "Origins and Design of Terracotta Roofs in the Seventh Century BCE." In *A Companion to Greek Architecture*, edited by M.M. Miles, 46–59. Malden, MA: Wiley-Blackwell.

Šašel Kos, M. 2015. "Corcyra in Strabo's Geography." In *Prospettive corciresi*, edited by C. Antonetti and E. Cavalli, 1–31. Diabaseis 5. Pisa: Edizioni ETS.

Schleif, H., K. A. Rhomaios, and G. Klaffenbach. 1940. *Korkyra: Archaische Bauten und Bildwerke 1, Der Artemistempel: Architektur, Dachterrakotten, Inschriften*. Berlin: Mann Verlag.

Schmidt, B. 1890. *Korkyraeische Studien: Beiträge zur Topographie Korkyras und zur Erklärung des Thukydides, Xenophon und Diodoros*. Leipzig: Teubner.

Schwabl, H. 1927. "Zeus." In *Paulys Real-encyclopädie der classischen Altertumswissenschaft*, edited by A. F. von Pauly, 10 A: 253–376. 44 vols. Stuttgart: J. B. Metzler.

Schwabl, H., E. Simon, J. Schindler, et al. 1978. "Zeus." In *Paulys Real-encyclopädie der classischen Altertumswissenschaft*, edited by A. F. von Pauly, Supplementband XV, 993–1481. Munich: Druckenmüller.

Schwandner, E.-L., and J. Riederer. 1985. *Der ältere Porostempel der Aphaia auf Aegina*. Denkmäler Antiker Architektur 16. Berlin: Walter de Gruyter.

Sciarma, A. 2009. "La 'timè' di Artemide: Alcune osservazioni sulla decorazione figurata del frontone dell' 'Artemision' di Corfù." *Ostraka: Rivista di Antichità* 18: 509–18.

Servais, J. 1969. "Hérodote et la chronologie des Cypsélides." *L'Antiquité classique* 38: 28–81.

Six, J. P. 1894. "Der Agyieus des Mys." *Mitteilungen des Deutschen Archäologischen Instituts, Athenische Abteilung* 19: 340–5.

Snodgrass, A. M. 1987. *An Archaeology of Greece: The Present State and Future Scope of a Discipline*. Berkeley: University of California Press.

Sordinas, A. 1969. "Investigations of the Prehistory of Corfu during 1964–66." *Balkan Studies* 10: 393–424.

Sordinas, A. 2007. "Ἀπολογισμός προϊστορικῆς ἔρευνας στα Ιόνια νησιά κατά τη διετία 1964-66." In *Η Προϊστορική Κέρκυρα και ο ευρύτερος περίγυρος της Προβλήματα–Προοπτικές: Πρακτικά ημερίδας τιμητικῆς στον Αύγουστο Σορδίνα, Κέρκυρα 17 Δεκεμβρίου 2004*, edited by G. Arvanitou-Metallinou, 21–33. Corfu: Ὑπουργεῖο Πολιτισμοῦ.

Souyoudzoglou-Haywood, C. 1999. *The Ionian Islands in the Bronze Age and Early Iron Age 3000–800 BC.* Liverpool: Liverpool University Press.

Spanodimos, C. 2017. "Κόρινθος-Κέρκυρα: Ανιχνεύοντας τη σχέση δύο πόλεων με οδηγό τους τάφους της Αρχαϊκῆς Περιόδου." In *Κερκυραϊκά Χρονικά, Περίοδος Β, Τόμος ΙΑ, Πρακτικά Ι ΄ Διεθνούς Πανιόνιου Συνεδρίου, Κέρκυρα, 30 Απριλίου–4 Μαΐου 2014, IV. Φιλοσοφία–Αρχαιολογία–Αρχαιογνωσία–Αρχιτεκτονική–Θέατρο*, edited by D. Konidaris, 245–55. Corfu: Εταιρεία Κερκυραϊκῶν Σπουδῶν.

Speich, R., and H. Speich. 1982. *Korfu und die Ionischen Inseln.* Stuttgart: W. Kohlhammer.

Spetsieri-Choremi, A. 1980a. "Location of an Ancient Temple in Kerkyra." *Athens Annals of Archaeology* 13: 284–96.

Spetsieri-Choremi, A. 1980b. "Εντοπισμός αρχαίου ιεροῦ στὴν Κέρκυρα." *Athens Annals of Archaeology* 13: 284–96.

Spetsieri-Choremi, A. 1991. "Un dépôt de sanctuaire archaïque à Corfou." *Bulletin de correspondance hellénique* 115: 183–211.

Stein-Hölkeskamp, E. 1989. *Adelskultur und Polisgesellschaft: Studien zum griechischen Adel in archaischer und klassischer Zeit.* Stuttgart: Franz Steiner Verlag.

Stickler, T. 2010. *Korinth und seine Kolonien: Die Stadt am Isthmus im Mächtegefüge des klassischen Griechenland. Klio* Beihefte Neue Folge 15. Berlin: Walter de Gruyter.

Strauch, D. 1996. "Hylloi." In *Der neue Pauly: Enzyklopädie der Antike*, edited by H. Cancik, H. Schneider, A. F. von Pauly, et al., 5: 782. 15 vols. Stuttgart: J. B. Metzler.

Stucchi, S. 1981. *Delle figure del grande frontone di Corfù: Di un mitreo e di un oracolo a Cirene.* Divagazioni Archeologiche 1. Rome: Bretschneider.

Treister, M. Y. 1995. "A Bronze Matrix from Corfu in the Ashmolean Museum." *Mitteilungen des Deutschen Archäologischen Instituts, Athenische Abteilung* 110: 83–102.

Trümpy, C. 1997. *Untersuchungen zu den altgriechischen Monatsnamen und Monatsfolgen.* Bibliothek der Klassischen Altertumswissenschaften. Neue Folge 2, Reihe 98. Heidelberg: Carl Winter Universitätverlag.

Tzortzatou, A., and L. Fatsiou. 2009. "New Early Iron Age and Archaic Sites in Thesprotia." In *Thesprotia Expedition I: Towards a Regional History*, edited by B. Forsén, 39–53. Papers and Monographs of the Finnish Institute at Athens 15. Helsinki: Foundation of the Finnish Institute at Athens.

Vallet, G., and F. Villard. 1952. "Les dates de la fondation de Megara Hyblaea et de Syracuse." *Bulletin de correspondance hellénique* 76: 289–346.

Van Compernolle, R. 1953. "La date de la fondation d'Apollonie d'Illyrie." *L'Antiquité classique* 22: 50–64.

Van Effenterre, H., and F. Ruzé. 1994–1995. *Nomima: Recueil d'inscriptions politiques et juridiques de l'archaïsme grec.* 2 vols. Rome: École Française de Rome.

Von Hesberg, H., M. Fiedler, and B. Toci. 2018. "Skulpturenfragmente archaischer und klassischer Zeit aus Apollonia (Albanien)." *Jahrbuch des Deutschen Archäologischen Instituts* 133: 49–185.

Von Wilamowitz-Moellendorff, U. 1884. *Homerische Untersuchungen.* Philologische Untersuchungen 7. Berlin: Weidmann.

Wallace, M. B. 1970. "Early Greek *Proxenoi.*" *Phoenix* 24: 189–208.

Weber, M. 2007. "Der Artemistempel von Korfu." *Thetis: Mannheimer Beiträge zur Klassischen Archäologie und Geschichte Griechenlands und Zyperns* 13/14: 11–22.

Whitbread, I. K. 1995. *Greek Transport Amphorae: A Petrological and Archaeological Study.* Fitch Laboratory Occasional Paper 4. Athens: British School at Athens.

Wikander, C. 1990. "The Artemision Sima and Its Possible Antecedents." *Hesperia* 59: 275–83.

Will, E. 1955. *Korinthiaka: Recherches sur l'histoire et la civilisation de Corinthe des origines aux guerres médiques.* Paris: De Boccard.

Williams, C. K. II. 1981. "The City of Corinth and Its Domestic Religion." *Hesperia* 50: 408–21.

Wilson Jones, M. 2014. *Origins of Classical Architecture: Temples, Orders and Gifts to the Gods in Ancient Greece.* New Haven, CT: Yale University Press.

Winter, N. A. 1993. *Greek Architectural Terracottas from the Prehistoric to the End of the Archaic Period.* Oxford: Clarendon Press.

Winter, N. A.2002. "Commerce in Exile: Terracotta Roofing in Etruria, Corfu and Sicily, a Bacchiad Family Enterprise." *Etruscan Studies* 9: 227–36.

Winter, N. A. 2009. *Symbols of Wealth and Power: Architectural Terracotta Decoration in Etruria and Central Italy, 640–510 B.C. Memoirs of the American Academy in Rome* Supplementary Volume 9. Ann Arbor: University of Michigan Press.

Zahrnt, M. 2012. "Was haben Apollonios' Argonauten auf dem Istros zu suchen?" *Klio* 94: 82–99.